Manufacturing Planning and Control for Supply Chain Management

The McGraw-Hill/Irwin Series Operations and Decision Sciences

OPERATIONS MANAGEMENT

Beckman and Rosenfield
Operations, Strategy: Competing in the 21st Century
First Edition

Benton
Purchasing and Supply Chain Management
Second Edition

Bowersox, Closs, and Cooper
Supply Chain Logistics Management
Third Edition

Brown and Hyer
Managing Projects: A Team-Based Approach
First Edition

Burt, Petcavage, and Pinkerton
Supply Management
Eighth Edition

Cachon and Terwiesch
Matching Supply with Demand: An Introduction to Operations Management
Second Edition

Finch
Interactive Models for Operations and Supply Chain Management
First Edition

Fitzsimmons and Fitzsimmons
Service Management: Operations, Strategy, Information Technology
Seventh Edition

Gehrlein
Operations Management Cases
First Edition

Harrison and Samson
Technology Management
First Edition

Hayen
SAP R/3 Enterprise Software: An Introduction
First Edition

Hill
Manufacturing Strategy: Text & Cases
Third Edition

Hopp
Supply Chain Science
First Edition

Hopp and Spearman
Factory Physics
Third Edition

Jacobs, Berry, Whybark and Vollmann
Manufacturing Planning & Control for Supply Chain Management
Sixth Edition

Jacobs and Chase
Operations and Supply Management: The Core
Second Edition

Jacobs and Chase
Operations and Supply Management
Thirteenth Edition

Jacobs and Whybark
Why ERP?
First Edition

Larson and Gray
Project Management: The Managerial Process
Fifth Edition

Leenders, Johnson, Flynn, and Fearon
Purchasing and Supply Management
Thirteenth Edition

Nahmias
Production and Operations Analysis
Sixth Edition

Olson
Introduction to Information Systems Project Management
Second Edition

Schroeder, Goldstein, Rungtusanatham
Operations Management: Contemporary Concepts and Cases
Fifth Edition

Seppanen, Kumar, and Chandra
Process Analysis and Improvement
First Edition

Simchi-Levi, Kaminsky, and Simchi-Levi
Designing and Managing the Supply Chain: Concepts, Strategies, Case Studies
Third Edition

Sterman
Business Dynamics: Systems Thinking and Modeling for Complex World
First Edition

Swink, Melnyk, Cooper, and Hartley
Managing Operations Across the Supply Chain
First Edition

Thomke
Managing Product and Service Development: Text and Cases
First Edition

Ulrich and Eppinger
Product Design and Development
Fourth Edition

Zipkin
Foundations of Inventory Management
First Edition

QUANTITATIVE METHODS AND MANAGEMENT SCIENCE

Hillier and Hillier
Introduction to Management Science: A Modeling and Case Studies Approach with Spreadsheets
Fourth Edition

Stevenson and Ozgur
Introduction to Management Science with Spreadsheets
First Edition

Manufacturing Planning and Control for Supply Chain Management

Sixth Edition

F. Robert Jacobs
Indiana University

William L. Berry
The Ohio State University (Emeritus)

D. Clay Whybark
University of North Carolina (Emeritus)

Thomas E. Vollmann
International Institute for Management Development

McGraw Hill Education (India) Private Limited
CHENNAI

McGraw Hill Education Offices
Chennai New York St Louis San Francisco Auckland Bogotá Caracas
Kuala Lumpur Lisbon London Madrid Mexico City Milan Montreal
San Juan Santiago Singapore Sydney Tokyo Toronto

McGraw Hill Education (India) Private Limited

MANUFACTURING PLANNING AND CONTROL FOR SUPPLY CHAIN MANAGEMENT, SIXTH EDITION

McGraw Hill Education (India) Edition 2014

Sixth reprint 2018
RLAQCRLERYYBX

Reprinted in India by arrangement with McGraw-Hill Global Education Holdings, LLC, New York

Sales territories: India, Pakistan, Nepal, Bangladesh, Sri Lanka and Bhutan

Library of Congress Cataloging-in-Publication Data

Manufacturing planning and control for supply chain management / F. Robert Jacobs . . .
[et al.]. —6th ed.
p. cm.—(The McGraw-Hill/Irwin series in operations and decision sciences)
Manufacturing planning and control for supply chain management / Thomas E. Vollmann . . .
[et al.],
5th ed., 2005
Includes bibliographical references and index.
ISBN 978-0-07-337782-7
I. Production planning. 2. Production control. I. Jacobs, F. Robert.
TS176.V63 2011
658.5—dc22 2009047862

ISBN-13: 978-93-392-0533-1
ISBN-10: 93-392-0533-2

06 07 08 09 10 RAJ 22 21 20 19 18

Published by McGraw Hill Education (India) Private Limited,
444/1, Sri Ekambara Naicker Industrial Estate, Alapakkam, Porur, Chennai 600 116, Tamil Nadu, India,
and Printed and bound in India at Rajkamal Electric Press, Kundli 131 028, Haryana

Visit us at: www.mheducation.co.in
Write to us at: info.india@mheducation.com

CIN: U22200TN1970PTC111531

We dedicate this book to Professor Thomas E. Vollmann. Tom's enthusiasm and brilliance have influenced virtually every page of this book since the first edition was published 25 years ago. Tom will be greatly missed by the author team and by the worldwide community of Operations Management colleagues of which he was a part. We are truly indebted to Professor Vollmann.

Preface

One of the more pervasive changes in the manufacturing environment is the implementation of enterprise resource planning (ERP) systems. Manufacturing planning and control (MPC) is now embedded in ERP systems in a great number of organizations. This both increases the opportunities for effective management and the complexity of integration required. No MPC activity can now ignore the pervasiveness of ERP systems.

Market requirements are critical in the competitive manufacturing environment. The capabilities of manufacturing plus the expectations of the market has led to increased pressure for both speed and variety. Customers are demanding more tailoring in the products that they order and want them faster than ever. Part of this is derived from the expectation of shortened product life cycles, while part is derived from customers wanting more individualized treatment.

A major change that has continued over all the editions of this book is that of globalization. Even small and medium-size enterprises now have manufacturing facilities in countries other than their own. In some instances, this is a complex network of facilities. In others it is a single manufacturing or manufacturing/marketing subsidiary. The implications of this are that the geographic reach and diversity of environments within which the manufacturing planning and control system must operate has increased and will continue to do so.

Partly as consequence of the internationalization of business and partly as a response to outsourcing as companies focus on their core competencies, the interconnectedness of manufacturing firms has increased substantially. The implication of this is that companies are now often integrated as customers of their suppliers and integrated with their customers whom they supply in complicated ways. This has created the need to manage some very complex supply chains or networks. In some instances, firms in these supply networks will find themselves competing with customers and suppliers while simultaneously trying to develop mutually beneficial relationships for some portion of their product line. Increasingly, firms have a mixture of industrial and consumer markets that require different channels, which also increases the complexity of the manufacturing relationships. These relationships must be incorporated in the MPC system of the firm.

Comments on the Sixth Edition

In a sense, this edition of the book is designed to recognize the maturity of much of the material in this book. Since the first edition, published in 1984, the techniques and concepts in the book have developed to where now most of the ideas are commonly available in ERP systems. So, in this edition, we have significantly streamlined the presentation of the basic ideas. Our idea is that many of the readers of this book are students just learning the material who will appreciate a concise presentation of the material with clear examples. We have, therefore, removed much of the "research"-oriented material that was included in previous editions. We have removed some of the ideas that are not in common use while adding new ideas that are now commonly used.

The first eight chapters of the book provide a thorough coverage of manufacturing planning and control. In the spirit of previous editions of the book, our coverage is extensive and complete, yet as concise as we feel is reasonable. We are careful in our use of terminology so as not to confuse the reader by minimizing the use of "lingo" while introducing the vernacular of the operations and supply chain management professional. Terminology and the organization of the topics closely follow that used by APICS—the Association for Operations Management—in the *APICS Dictionary* and in the *APICS Body of Knowledge Framework* (which was co-authored by an author of this book).

The last four chapters of the book focus on the integration of manufacturing with the supply chain. In these chapters, our emphasis is on the basic techniques and concepts, and we cover them in a manner that corresponds to how they are commonly implemented in ERP systems. Integration of MPC with the logistics and warehousing functions in the firm can no longer be an "arm's length" activity. Speed and efficiency require tight integration of these activities with minimal inventory buffering. Complicating matters is the oft-common outsourcing of the shipping and warehousing activities, which places complex supply chain–related demands on the MPC system.

It is our contention that the supply chain professional of the future needs a very strong understanding of the material in this book. Just like the professional accountant must understand the basics of assets, liabilities, the balance sheet, and the income and expense statements, together with the transactions that generate the data in the accounting systems, so too must the supply chain professional understand a set of basic techniques and concepts. The sales and operations plan, master schedule, material requirements planning, and distribution requirements planning records tie the manufacturing function to the supplier on the inbound side and the customer on the outbound side in terms of material and inventory. Logic such as regression analysis, exponential smoothing, available-to-promise, material planning, and reorder points are the decision support tools that assist the professional making rational decisions within the realm of manufacturing and supply chain planning.

This book is designed to be an essential resource for both the student of the field and the practicing professional. Mastery of the contents provides a solid foundation on which comprehensive, firm-specific implementations can be developed. It is our contention that each firm has unique requirements dependent on special supplier and market requirements. A sustainable competitive advantage comes from taking an innovative approach to how material and inventory is managed. A comprehensive understanding of the key concepts and techniques available is essential to structuring and implementing the supply chain material and inventory planning systems used by the firm. This book is designed to support this understanding.

Acknowledgments

All editions of *Manufacturing Planning and Control Systems* have benefited from the comments of reviewers. In the first edition, we had:

Gene Groff
Georgia State University

Robert Millen
Northeastern University

Richard Penlesky
Carroll College

Reviewers for the second edition were:

Jeff Miller
Boston University

William Sherrard
San Diego State University

Urban Wemmerlov
University of Wisconsin

In the third edition, we were helped by the reviews of:

Stanley Brooking
University of Southern Mississippi

Henry Crouch
Pittsburgh State University

Marilyn Helms
University of Tennessee

Robert Johnson
Pennsylvania State University

Ted Lloyd
Eastern Kentucky University

Dan Reid
University of New Hampshire

Dwight Smith-Daniels
Arizona State University

Herman Stein
Bellarmine College

Glen Wilson
Middle Tennessee State University

In the fourth edition, we enjoyed, were challenged by, and are very grateful for the thoughtful reviews by:

Paul M. Bobrowski
Syracuse University

Philip S. Chong
California State University–Long Beach

Ted Lloyd
Eastern Kentucky University

Daniel S. Marrone
SUNY Farmingdale

R. Dan Reid
University of New Hampshire

William Sherrard
San Diego State University

Herman Stein
Bellarmine College

Urban Wemmerlov
University of Wisconsin–Madison

In the fifth edition, the following reviewers provided comments that shaped our thinking for the current revisions in content and organization:

William Sherrard
San Diego State University
Victor Sower
Sam Houston State University
Robert Vokurka
Texas A&M University
Ted Lloyd
Eastern Kentucky University
Stephen Chapman
NC State University
Donna Summers
University of Dayton
Jeffrey Herrmann
University of Maryland
Harish Bahl
California State University–Chico
Kim LaScola Needy
University of Pittsburgh
Daniel Steele
University of South Carolina

In this edition of the book, we were helped by the reviews of:

Debra Bishop
Drake University
Thomas Brady
Purdue University, North Central
Cem Canel
University of North Carolina–Wilmington
Yasser Dessouky
San Jose State University
James Hill
The Ohio State University
Okenwa Okoli
Florida A&M University–Florida State University
Patrick Penfield
Syracuse University
Theresa Wells
University of Wisconsin–Eau Claire

As before, our ideas have been greatly shaped by the manufacturing practitioners and college students whom we teach and by the colleagues at our schools. The education executives who have supported us in this edition are Dean Robert Sullivan, University of North Carolina; Dean Joseph Alutto, The Ohio State University; Dean Dan Dalton, Indiana University; and President Peter Lorange, IMD. We thank all of these friends and associates for their support and help.

Bob Fetter, our consulting editor for the first and second editions, was a champion as well as a critical reviewer. Dick Hercher has exhausted his patience with us but is still there to help when we need him.

The task of revising was made much more tolerable by the support of our very understanding families. Thanks folks!

F. Robert Jacobs

William L. Berry

D. Clay Whybark

Brief Contents

Table of Contents

Chapter 3
Forecasting 53

Chapter 4
Sales and Operations Planning 88

Chapter 4A
Advanced Sales and Operations Planning 131

Chapter 5
Master Production Scheduling 152

Chapter 6
Material Requirements Planning 182

Chapter 6A
Advanced MRP 220

Chapter 7
Capacity Planning and Management 242

Chapter 1

Manufacturing Planning and Control

The manufacturing planning and control (MPC) system is concerned with planning and controlling all aspects of manufacturing, including managing materials, scheduling machines and people, and coordinating suppliers and key customers. Because these activities change over time and respond differently to different markets and company strategies, this chapter provides a model for evaluating responses to changes in the competitive environment. We believe that the development of an effective manufacturing planning and control system is key to the success of any goods producing company. Moreover, truly effective MPC systems coordinate supply chains—joint efforts across company boundaries. Finally, MPC systems design is not a one-time effort; MPC systems need to continuously adapt and respond to changes in the company environment, strategy, customer requirements, particular problems, and new supply chain opportunities. The critical question is not what one has accomplished; it is "What should the firm, together with its supply chain partners, do next?" To put these ideas in perspective, this chapter is organized around the following four managerial concerns:

- *The MPC system defined:* What are the typical tasks performed by the MPC system and how do these tasks affect company operations?
- *An MPC system framework:* What are the key MPC system components and how do they respond to a company's needs?
- *Matching the MPC system with the needs of the firm:* How do supply-chain product and process issues affect MPC system design?
- *Evolution of the MPC system:* What forces drive changes in the MPC system and how do companies respond to the forces?

The MPC System Defined

In this section we define what the MPC system does and some of the costs and benefits associated with effective MPC systems. The essential task of the MPC system is to manage efficiently the flow of material, to manage the utilization of people and equipment, and to respond to customer requirements by utilizing the capacity of our suppliers, that of our internal facilities, and (in some cases) that of our customers to meet customer demand. Important ancillary activities involve the acquisition of information from customers on product needs and providing customers with information on delivery dates and product status. An important distinction here is that the MPC system provides the information upon which managers make effective decisions. The MPC system does not make decisions nor manage the operations—managers perform those activities. The MPC system provides the support for them to do so wisely.

Typical MPC Support Activities

The support activities of the MPC system can be broken roughly into three time horizons: long term, medium term, and short term. In the long term, the system is responsible for providing information to make decisions on the appropriate amount of capacity (including equipment, buildings, suppliers, and so forth) to meet the market demands of the future. This is particularly important in that these decisions set the parameters within which the firm responds to current demands and copes with short-term shifts in customer preferences. Moreover, long-term planning is necessary for the firm to provide the appropriate mix of human resource capabilities, technology, and geographical locations to meet the firm's future needs. In the case of supply chain planning, the long term has to include the same kind of capacity planning for the key suppliers. For companies that outsource their manufacturing to outside companies, the planning of supplier capacity can be more critical than internal capacity planning. Moreover, the choice of outsourcing partners has to consider their capabilities to ramp up and adjust capacities to the actual dictates of the marketplace.

In the intermediate term, the fundamental issue addressed by the MPC system is matching supply and demand in terms of both volume and product mix. Although this is also true in the longer term, in the intermediate term, the focus is more on providing the exact material and production capacity needed to meet customer needs. This means planning for the right quantities of material to arrive at the right time and place to support product production and distribution. It also means maintaining appropriate levels of raw material, work in process, and finished goods inventories in the correct locations to meet market needs. Another aspect of the intermediate-term tasks is providing customers with information on expected delivery times and communicating to suppliers the correct quantities and delivery times for the material they supply. Planning of capacity may require determining employment levels, overtime possibilities, subcontracting needs, and support requirements. It is often in the intermediate time frame that specific coordinated plans—including corporate budgets, sales plans and quotas, and output objectives—are set. The MPC system has an important role in meeting these objectives.

In the short term, detailed scheduling of resources is required to meet production requirements. This involves time, people, material, equipment, and facilities. Key to this activity is people working on the right things. As the day-to-day activities continue, the MPC system must track the use of resources and execution results to report on material consumption, labor utilization, equipment utilization, completion of customer orders, and other important measures of manufacturing performance. Moreover, as customers change their minds, things go wrong, and other changes occur, the MPC system must provide the information to managers, customers, and suppliers on what happened, provide problem-solving support, and report on the resolution of the problems. Throughout this process, communication with customers on production status and changes in expectations must be maintained.

To effectively manage the manufacturing processes, a number of manufacturing performance indicators need to be compiled. Among these are output results; equipment utilization; and costs associated with different departments, products, labor utilization, and project completions. Also, measures of customer satisfaction such as late deliveries, product returns, quantity errors, and other mistakes are needed. The implications physically and financially of the activities on the manufacturing floor are collected, summarized, and reported through the MPC system.

The initial costs for a manufacturing planning and control system can be substantial. Moreover, the ongoing operational costs are also significant. An effective MPC system requires a large number of professionals and all their supporting resources, including computers, training, maintenance, and space. It's not uncommon to find the largest number of indirect employees at a manufacturing firm to be involved in the MPC area.

An MPC System Framework

It is most typical now to find the MPC system imbedded in an enterprise resource planning (ERP) system. Many essential activities that need to be performed in the MPC system have not changed. However, the details have evolved as changes in our knowledge, technology, and markets have occurred. The MPC activities are now carried out in more areas of the firm and differ to meet the strategic requirements of the company. In this section, we'll provide our framework for understanding the MPC system.

MPC System Activities

Figure 1.1 is a schematic of the general MPC system that would be used within a firm for planning and controlling its manufacturing operations. But linking customer and supplier firms in a supply chain requires coordinating the MPC activities between the firms. The model shown in Figure 1.1 is essentially what one will find as a key part of any packaged ERP system. The figure is divided into three parts or phases. The top third, or front end, is the set of activities and systems for overall direction setting. This phase establishes the overall company direction for manufacturing planning and control. Demand management encompasses forecasting customer/end-product demand, order entry, order promising, accommodating interplant and intercompany demand, and spare parts requirements. In essence, demand management coordinates all activities of the business that place demands on manufacturing capacity.

Sales and operations planning balances the sales/marketing plans with available production resources. The result is an agreed-on company game plan that determines the manufacturing role in meeting company strategy. Increasingly, this activity is receiving more management attention as the need for coordination is recognized in progressive firms. The master production schedule (MPS) is the disaggregated version of the sales and operations plan. That is, it states which end items or product options manufacturing will

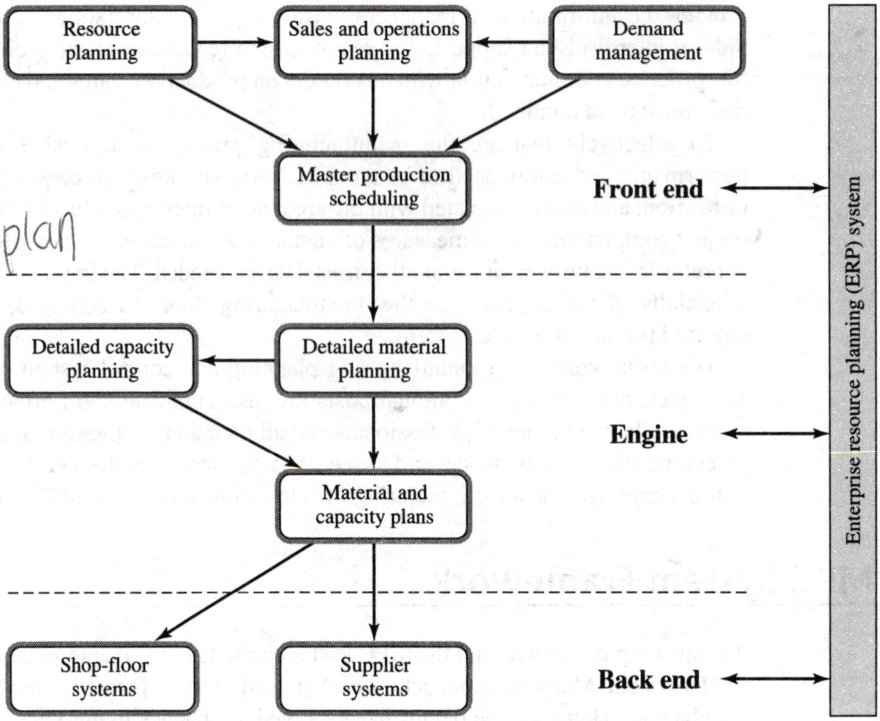

FIGURE 1.1 **Manufacturing Planning and Control System (simplified)**

build in the future. The MPS must support the sales and operations plan. Resource planning determines the capacity necessary to produce the required products now and in the future. In the long run this means bricks and mortar, while in the short run it means labor and machine hours. Resource planning provides the basis for matching manufacturing plans and capacity.

The middle third, or engine, in Figure 1.1 encompasses the set of MPC systems for detailed material and capacity planning. The master production schedule feeds directly into the detailed material planning module. Firms with a limited product range can specify rates of production for developing these plans. However, for firms producing a wide variety of products with many parts per product, detailed material planning can involve calculating requirements for thousands of parts and components, using a formal logic called material requirements planning (MRP). MRP determines (explodes) the period-by-period (time-phased) plans for all component parts and raw materials required to produce all the products in the MPS. This material plan can thereafter be utilized in the detailed capacity planning systems to compute labor or machine center capacity required to manufacture all the component parts.

The bottom third, or back end, of Figure 1.1 depicts MPC execution systems. Here, again, the system configuration depends on the products manufactured and production processes employed. For example, firms producing a large variety of products using thousands of parts often group all equipment of a similar type into a single work center. Their shop floor system establishes priorities for all shop orders at each work center so the orders can be properly scheduled. Other firms will group mixtures of equipment that produce a similar set of parts into work centers called production cells. For them, production rates and just-in-time (JIT) systems for execution are appropriate.

The supplier systems provide detailed information to the company suppliers. In the case of arm's length relationships with these suppliers, the supplier systems will produce purchase orders that will be transmitted to the suppliers. Thereafter, the company MPC systems should provide suppliers with updated priority information, based on current conditions in the company—as well as in their customers' companies. In the case of closer (partnership) relations with suppliers, information can also include future plans—to help the suppliers understand expected needs. In a general sense the receiving end of this information is the demand management module of the front end in the suppliers' MPC systems.

In firms using MRP systems, execution of the detailed material and capacity plans involves detailed scheduling of machines and other work centers. This scheduling must reflect such routine events as starting and completing orders for parts and any problem conditions, such as breakdowns or absenteeism. These schedules are often available on a real-time basis from the ERP system database. Real-time data are particularly important in factories with complex manufacturing processes and/or customers demanding responsiveness to volume, design, or delivery schedule changes.

Components and materials sourced from outside the organization require an analogous detailed schedule. In essence, purchasing is the procurement of outside work center capacity. It must be planned and scheduled well to maximize final customer satisfaction. Best-practice purchasing systems typically separate the procurement or contractual activity from routine order release and follow-up. Procurement, a highly professional job, involves contracting for vendor capacity and establishing ground rules for order release and order follow-up. These tasks take on extra dimensions as procurement involves global sourcing and multinational coordination of schedules.

An important activity that is not depicted in Figure 1.1 is the measurement, follow-up, and control of actual results. As products are manufactured, the rate of production and timing of specific completion can be compared to plans. As shipments are made to customers, measures of actual customer service can be obtained. As capacity is used, it too can be compared to plans. If actual results differ from plan, appropriate actions to bring the results back to plan or modifications of the plan must be made. These measurements and control actions are part of all three of the phases of the MPC system.

The three-phase framework for manufacturing planning and control is supported by widely available MPC systems and software, from master production scheduling to the back-end systems. This software is not only integrated to follow the framework, it is also linked to other business activities in the ERP systems of many firms. That means that the MPC systems provide inputs to the financial, distribution, marketing, and human resources systems that require the information.

Matching the MPC System with the Needs of the Firm

The specific requirements for the MPC system design depend on the nature of the production process, the degree of supply chain integration, customers' expectations, and the needs of management. As the MPC system is required to integrate with other company systems in the supply chain and/or with the ERP system of the firm, additional design parameters are introduced. Moreover, these MPC system requirements are not static. As competitive conditions, customer expectations, supplier capabilities, and internal needs change, the MPC system needs to change. In addition, the changes that are being addressed as we make one set of modifications may well be different when we move to another change that needs addressing. The result is a different emphasis on various MPC system modules over time.

MPC technology continues to change over time as well. The present trend is to more online data access and systems. MPC status is also a product of the increasing speeds, decreasing costs, and increasing storage capabilities of modern computers. Online systems provide multiple advantages, particularly between firms. Internet-based systems are becoming an important way to support intrafirm coordinated efforts. For these firms the amount of paper moving between departments of a company or between companies has been greatly reduced. Planning cycles have been speeded up. Inventories between partners in the supply chain are being replaced by speedier information. All of these changes dramatically affect the way users interact with the MPC system. As information-processing capabilities increase, MPC systems have evolved to utilize the latest technologies.

MPC systems must also reflect the physical changes taking place on the factory floor. Outsourcing, contract manufacturing, and the hollowing out of the corporation dramatically affect MPC systems design. Moves from job shops to flow processes to cellular manufacturing approaches affect the MPC systems design as well. Providing information at the level where decisions are made in appropriate time frames has greatly augmented the use of computers on the factory floor and the speed of interaction between planning and execution.

It's not, however, just on the factory floor that changes dictate the MPC system needs. As the firm shapes its manufacturing strategy, different modules of the MPC system may need to be modified to respond. As an example, firms that are increasing product variety may need to strengthen the master production scheduling and detailed material planning modules in order to more quickly phase in and phase out new products. Firms that are competing on delivery speed may need to improve shop floor execution and feedback systems to more closely monitor the progress of products through the manufacturing facility. This matching of strategic direction with MPC system design is as dynamic as any of the other elements that shape the MPC system requirements.

An MPC Classification Schema

Figure 1.2 shows the relationship between MPC system approaches, the complexity of the manufactured product as expressed in the number of subparts, and the repetitive nature of production, expressed as the time between successive units. Figure 1.2 also shows some example products that fit these time and complexity scales.

Several MPC approaches presented in Figure 1.2 are appropriate for products that fit in various points in the schema. The figure demonstrates that the MPC emphasis changes as the nature of the product, process, or both change. For example, as a product's sales volume grows over time, the MPC emphasis might shift from right to left. Regardless of where the company is on Figure 1.2, it's necessary to perform all the activities depicted in Figure 1.1. However, how they are performed can be quite different for firms at different points on Figure 1.2.

FIGURE 1.2
MPC Classification Schema

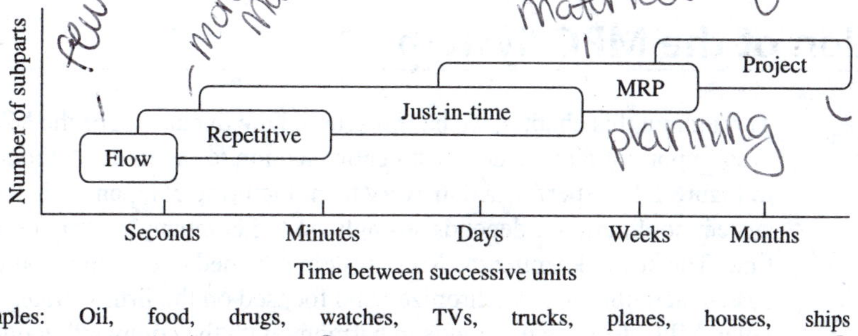

The lower left-hand corner of Figure 1.2 shows a flow-oriented manufacturing process typical of many chemical, food, petroleum, and bulk product firms. Because products are produced in streams instead of discrete batches, virtually no time elapses between successive units. With these processes, the front-end concern of the MPC system is primarily the flow rates that become the master production schedule. Typically, these products have relatively few component parts, so engine management is straightforward. Depending on how components are purchased, the back end may involve some complexity. Typically, these firms' major cost is for raw materials, although transportation costs can also be significant.

Repetitive manufacturing activities are found in many plants that assemble similar products (e.g., automobiles, watches, personal computers, pharmaceuticals, and televisions). For such products, component-part management is necessary, but everything is coordinated with the flow or assembly rate for the end items.

In the middle of the figure we show a large application area for just-in-time systems. Using lean manufacturing approaches, many firms today try to move their processes from right to left in the figure. That is, they try to make processes more repetitive as opposed to unique in order to achieve the operational advantages of repetitive manufacturing (shorter production cycles, reduced lead times, lower inventories, and the like). JIT is shown as spanning a wide variety of products and processes. This MPC approach is increasingly being integrated with more traditional MRP-based systems. The goal is to achieve better MPC system performance and to reduce costs of maintaining the MPC system.

Figure 1.2 also shows material requirements planning as spanning a wide area. MRP is often the platform for ERP applications and is key to any MPC system involving management of a complicated parts situation. The majority of manufacturing firms have this sort of complexity, and MRP-based systems continue to be widely applied. For many firms, successful use of MRP is an important step in evolving their approaches to MPC. Once routine MRP operation is achieved, portions of the product and processes that can be executed with JIT methodologies can be selected.

The last form of MPC depicted in Figure 1.2, the project type, is applied to unique long-lead-time products, such as ships and highly customized products. Here, the primary concern is usually management of the time dimension. Related to time is cost. Project management attempts to continually assess partially completed projects' status in terms of expected completion dates and costs. Some firms have successfully integrated MRP approaches with the problems of project management. This is particularly effective in planning and controlling the combined activities of engineering and manufacturing.

Evolution of the MPC System

Throughout this chapter, we have discussed the dynamism of the MPC system. This notion is so important that we devote an entire section to the topic. Although the activities shown in Figure 1.1 are performed in every manufacturing company, whether large or small, MPC system configuration depends strongly on the company's attributes at a particular point in time. The key to keeping the MPC system matched to evolving company needs is to ensure system activities are synchronized and focused on the firm's strategy. This ensures that detailed MPC decision making is in harmony with the company's game plan. But the process is not static—the need for matching is ongoing.

The Changing Competitive World

Figure 1.3 depicts some manufacturing firms' typical responses to changing marketplace dictates. New technology, products, processes, systems, and techniques permit new competitive initiatives; global competition intensifies many of these forces. Marketplace dictates drive revisions in company strategy, which in turn often call for changes in manufacturing strategy, manufacturing processes, and MPC systems.

Shorter product life cycles come about partly because consumers have access to products from all over the world. This has spawned the move to "time-based competition." Who can get to the market quickest? Similarly, today's market insists on ever-higher quality, which in turn has led to many changes in manufacturing practices. Cost pressures have translated into reductions of all manufacturing cost components from material and labor to overhead and energy.

But increasingly, cost and quality are the ante to play the game—winning requires flexibility and responsiveness in dealing with even more fickle customer demands. Clearly, these pressures and responses require changes in both the MPC system and the underlying

FIGURE 1.3
Evolutionary Responses to Forces for Change

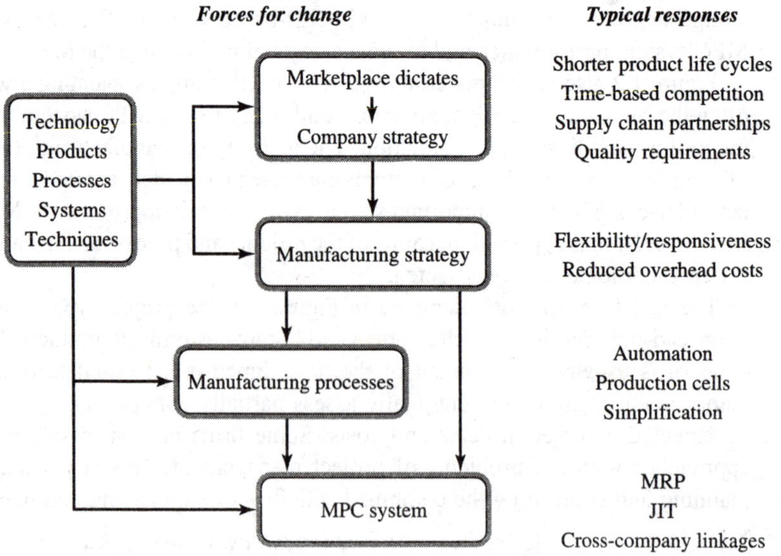

manufacturing process. As Figure 1.3 shows, typical MPC responses are MRP and JIT. Process responses include automation, simplification, and production cells for cellular manufacturing.

Reacting to the Changes

If the MPC system has remained unchanged for a significant length of time, it may no longer be appropriate to the company's needs. The system, like the strategy and processes themselves, must change to meet the dictates of the market. In many instances, this may simply imply a different set of evaluative criteria for the MPC system. In other cases, new modules or information may be required. In yet other cases, entire MPC activities may need to be eliminated. For example, JIT systems frequently move materials so quickly through the factory that MRP and shop-floor scheduling systems to track them are not needed. In supply chain management approaches, the emphasis shifts to the total costs (and values created) in the joint activities of more than one firm. The typical focus is on the dyad: two firms where time and inventories are substantially reduced.

The need for evolution in MPC systems implies the need for periodic auditing that compares system responses to the marketplace's requirements. The audit must address not only the system's focus but also the concomitant training of people and match with current objectives. Although the MPC framework in Figure 1.1 is general, its application is specific and evolving. Keeping it on track is an essential feature of MPC itself.

Concluding Principles

This chapter lays the groundwork for the rest of the book. Defining and adjusting the MPC system to support the manufacturing activity are an ongoing challenge. We hope that, as you read the rest of the book, you constantly ask how the general framework applies in specific instances, and what is happening to ensure a better match between MPC system design and marketplace dictates. From the chapter we draw the following principles:

- The framework for MPC is general, and all three phases must be performed, but specific applications necessarily reflect particular company conditions and objectives.
- In supply chain environments, the MPC system must coordinate the planning and control efforts across all companies involved.
- Manufacturing planning and control systems should support the strategy and tactics pursued by the firm in which they are implemented.
- Different manufacturing processes often dictate the need for different designs of the MPC system.
- The MPC system should evolve to meet changing requirements in the market, technology, products, and manufacturing processes.
- The manufacturing planning and control system should be comprehensive in supporting the management of all manufacturing resources.
- An effective MPC system can contribute to competitive performance by lowering costs and providing greater responsiveness to the market.
- In firms that have an integrated ERP system and database, the MPC system should integrate with and support cross-functional planning through the ERP system.

Discussion Questions

1. The discussion of the framework for manufacturing planning and control seems to imply that overall direction setting must be done before detailed material and capacity planning activities can be accomplished. The latter must be done before executing and controlling the plans is possible. Do you agree? Give an example supporting your position.
2. Apply the MPC framework to a college setting. In particular, identify the front end, engine, and back end.
3. We have suggested that as changes take place in the world, the MPC system would require modifications to adapt. What changes can you see that will require changes in the MPC system?
4. One of the local company's production managers asked you to advise her on installing an MPC system. She starts by asking you which particular software brand you prefer and if you believe in ERP systems. What questions would you ask her?

Chapter 1A

Enterprise Resource Planning (ERP)

This chapter concerns the integrated enterprise resource planning (ERP) systems that are now commonly used by large companies to support MPC decisions. Major software vendors such as SAP, Oracle, PeopleSoft, and i2 Technologies offer state-of-the art systems designed to provide real-time data to support better routine decision making, improve the efficiency of transaction processing, foster cross-functional integration, and provide improved insights into how the business should be run. This chapter is organized around five major topics:

- *What ERP is:* What is the scope of ERP implementations and how are the various modules of the software organized?
- *How ERP connects the functional units:* That is, how does ERP help integrate overall company operations?
- *How manufacturing planning and control (MPC) decisions are supported by ERP:* What are the detailed MPC issues addressed by ERP and how does an ERP package help address these issues?
- *Performance metrics to evaluate integrated system effectiveness:* Why do we need overall metrics to break out of "functional silo" thinking?
- *What the experience with ERP is:* How have some example firms gone about implementation and what have been the results?

In most companies, ERP provides the information backbone needed to manage day-to-day execution. Many of the standard production planning and control functions are supported by ERP. In particular, standard applications include demand management covered in Chapter 2, sales and operations planning in Chapter 4, master production scheduling found in Chapter 5, materials requirements planning in Chapter 6, production activity control in Chapter 8, inventory control in Chapter 11, and forecasting covered in Chapter 3. The software is often extended through either commercial software designed to work with the ERP system or through custom programmed modules built with spreadsheets and other general purpose software.

What Is ERP?

The term *enterprise resource planning* (ERP) can mean different things, depending on one's viewpoint. From the view of managers in a company, the emphasis is on the word *planning;* ERP represents a comprehensive software approach to support decisions concurrent with planning and controlling the business. On the other hand, for the information technology community, ERP is a term to describe a software system that integrates application programs in finance, manufacturing, logistics, sales and marketing, human resources, and the other functions in a firm. This integration is accomplished through a database shared by all the functions and data-processing applications in the firm. ERP systems typically are very efficient at handling the many transactions that document the activities of a company. For our purposes, we begin by describing our view of what ERP should accomplish for management, with an emphasis on planning. Following this, we describe how the ERP software programs are designed and provide points to consider in choosing an ERP system. Our special interest is in how the software supports MPC systems.

ERP systems allow for integrated planning across the functional areas in a firm. Perhaps more importantly, ERP also supports integrated *execution* across functional areas. Today the focus is moving to coordinated planning and execution across companies. In many cases this work is supported by ERP systems.

Consistent Numbers

ERP requires a company to have consistent definitions across functional areas. Consider the problem of measuring demand. How is demand measured? Is it when manufacturing completes an order? When items are picked from finished goods? When they physically leave the premises? When they are invoiced? When they arrive at the customer site? What is needed is a set of agreed-on definitions that are used by all functional units when they are processing their transactions. Consistent definitions of such measures as demand, stockouts, raw materials inventory, and finished goods inventory, for example, can then be made. This is a basic building block for ERP systems.

ERP, with the emphasis on planning, is designed to allow much tighter integration, thus eliminating the problem of local optimization. Tom Wallace and Mike Kremzar, noted manufacturing industry experts, describe ERP as:

- an enterprisewide set of management tools that helps balance demand and supply;
- containing the ability to link customers and suppliers into a complete supply chain;
- employing proven business processes for decision making; and
- providing high degrees of cross-functional integration among sales, marketing, manufacturing, operations, logistics, purchasing, finance, new product development, and human resources; thereby
- enabling people to run their business with high levels of customer service and productivity, and simultaneously lower costs and inventories, and providing the foundation for effective e-commerce.

Companies implementing ERP strive to derive benefits through much greater efficiency gained by an integrated MPC planning and control process. In addition, better responsiveness to the needs of customers is obtained through the real-time information provided by the system. To better understand how this works, we next describe features of ERP software.

Software Imperatives

There are four aspects of ERP software that determine the quality of an ERP system:

1. The software should be **multifunctional in scope** with the ability to track financial results in monetary terms, procurement activity in units of material, sales in terms of product units and services, and manufacturing or conversion processes in units of resources or people. That is, excellent ERP software produces results closely related to the needs of people for their day-to-day work.
2. The software should be **integrated.** When a transaction or piece of data representing an activity of the business is entered by one of the functions, data regarding the other related functions are changed as well. This eliminates the need for reposting data to the system. Integration also ensures a common vision—we all sing from the same sheet of music.
3. The software needs to be **modular** in structure so it can be combined into a single expansive system, narrowly focused on a single function, or connected with software from another source/application.
4. The software must **facilitate classic manufacturing planning and control activities,** including forecasting, production planning, and inventory management.

An ERP system is most appropriate for a company seeking the benefits of data and process integration supported by its information system. Benefit is gained from the elimination of redundant processes, increased accuracy in information, superior processes, and improved speed in responding to customer requirements.

An ERP software system can be built with software modules from different vendors, or it can be purchased from a single vendor. A multivendor approach can provide the opportunity to purchase "best in class" of each module. But this is usually at the expense of increased cost and greater resources needed to implement and integrate the functional modules. On the other hand, a single-vendor approach may be easier to implement, but the features and functionality may not be the best available.

Routine Decision Making

It is important to make a distinction between the transaction processing capability and the decision support capability of an ERP system. **Transaction processing** relates to the posting and tracking of the activities that document the business. When an item is purchased from a vendor, for example, a specific sequence of activities occurs. The solicitation of the offer, acceptance of the offer, delivery of goods, storage in inventory, and payment for the purchase are all activities that occur as a result of the purchase. The efficient handing of the transactions as goods move through each step of the production process is the primary goal of an ERP system.

A second objective of an ERP system is decision support. **Decision support** relates to how well the system helps the user make intelligent judgments about how to run the business. A key point here is that *people,* not software, make the decisions. The system *supports* better decision making. In the case of manufacturing planning and control, for example, decisions concerning the amount to purchase, the selection of the vendor, and how it should be delivered will need to be determined. These decisions are made by MPC professionals while ERP systems are oriented toward transaction processing. But over time, they evolve using decision logic based on parameters set in the system. For example, for items stored in inventory, the specific reorder points, order quantities, vendors, transportation vendors, and storage locations can be established when the items are initially entered in the system. At a later point, the decision logic can be revisited to improve the results. A major industry has been built around the development of **bolt-on** software packages designed to provide more intelligent decision support to ERP systems.

Choosing ERP Software

Key considerations when evaluating ERP software are:

1. The complexity of the business, degree of vertical integration, and level of international operations.
2. The size of the business.
3. The scope of functionality needed—is decision making reasonably routine, or is complex optimization required?
4. The differences in the conversion processes. Is discrete manufacturing used or process manufacturing, or both? The needs of these entities are different and perhaps difficult to accommodate with a single system.
5. The degree of sophistication and unique requirements of the firm's processes. Are there unique customer information requirements? How much of a custom solution is needed?
6. The alignment of the manufacturing planning and control modules with the needs of the firm. For example, are the mechanisms for aggregating demand for forecasting purposes adequate? Can the inventory control module accommodate the requirement to uniquely identify production batches?
7. The money available for implementing the system. Are radical process changes needed?
8. The computer hardware and telecommunications availability. Is the existing infrastructure compatible? Where does the company see the future? Where is the industry going? Do we need to be state of the art?

How ERP Connects the Functional Units

A typical ERP system is made up of functionally oriented and tightly integrated modules. All the modules of the system use a common database that is updated in real time. Each module has the same user interface, similar to that of the familiar Microsoft Office products, thus making the use of the different modules much easier for users trained on the system. ERP systems from various vendors are organized in different ways, but typically modules are focused on at least the following four major areas: finance, manufacturing and logistics, sales and marketing, and human resources.

One can see the evolution of ERP systems in much the same way as car models evolve at automobile manufacturers. Automobile manufacturers introduce new models every year or two and make many minor refinements. Major (platform) changes are made much less frequently, perhaps every five to eight years. The same is true of ERP software. ERP vendors are constantly looking for ways to improve the functionality of their software, so new features are often added. Many of these minor changes are designed to improve the usability of the software through a better screen interface or added features that correspond to the "hot" idea of the time. Major software revisions that involve changes to the structure of the database, changes to the network, and computer hardware technologies, though, are made only every three to five years. The basic ERP platform cannot be easily changed because of the

FIGURE 1A.1
The Scope of ERP Applications

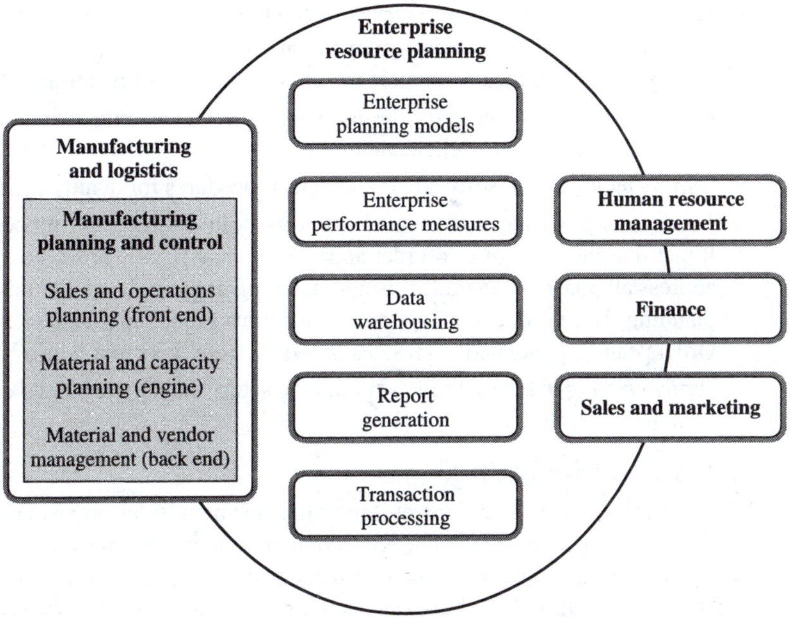

large installed base of users and support providers. But these changes do occur. As an example, SAP has moved from version R/2 to R/3, a major change in the software.

Figure 1A.1 depicts the scope of ERP applications. The diagram is meant to show how a comprehensive information system uses ERP as the core or backbone of the information system. Many other software-based functions may be integrated with the ERP system but are not necessarily included in the ERP system. The use of more specialized software such as decision support systems can often bring significant competitive advantage to a firm. The following brief descriptions of typical module functionality give an indication of how comprehensive the applications can be.

Finance

As a company grows through acquisition, and as business units make more of their own decisions, many companies find themselves with incompatible and sometimes conflicting financial data. An ERP system provides a common platform for financial data capture, a common set of numbers, and processes, facilitating rapid reconciliation of the general ledger. The real value of an ERP system is in the automatic capture of basic accounting transactions from the source of the transactions. The actual order from a customer, for example, is used not only by manufacturing to trigger production requirements, but also becomes the information for the update of accounts payable when the order is actually shipped.

Manufacturing and Logistics

This set of applications is the largest and most complex of the module categories. The MPC system components discussed in this book (front end, engine, back end) are concentrated in this area. Typical components include:

- *Sales and operations planning* coordinates the various planning efforts including marketing planning, financial planning, operations planning, and human resource planning.

- *Materials management* covers tasks within the supply chain, including purchasing, vendor evaluation, and invoice management. It also includes inventory and warehouse management functions to support the efficient control of materials.
- *Plant maintenance* supports the activities associated with planning and performing repairs and preventive maintenance.
- *Quality management* software implements procedures for quality control and assurance.
- *Production planning and control* supports both discrete and process manufacturing. Repetitive and configure-to-order approaches are typically provided. Most ERP systems address all phases of manufacturing, including capacity leveling, material requirements planning, JIT, product costing, bill of materials processing, and database maintenance. Orders can be generated from sales orders or from links to a World Wide Web site.
- *Project management* systems facilitate the setup, management, and evaluation of large, complex projects.

Sales and Marketing

This group of systems supports customer management; sales order management; forecasting, order management, credit checking configuration management; distribution, export controls, shipping, transportation management; and billing, invoicing, and rebate processing. These modules, like the others, are increasingly implemented globally, allowing firms to manage the sales process worldwide. For example, if an order is received in Hong Kong, but the products are not available locally, they may be internally procured from warehouses in other parts of the world and shipped to arrive together at the Hong Kong customer's site.

Human Resources

This set of applications supports the capabilities needed to manage, schedule, pay, hire, and train the people who make an organization run. Typical functions include payroll, benefits administration, applicant data administration, personnel development planning, workforce planning, schedule and shift planning, time management, and travel expense accounting.

Customized Software

In addition to the standard application modules, many companies utilize special add-on modules that link to the standard modules, thus tailoring applications to specific needs. These modules may be tailored to specific industries such as chemical/petrochemical, oil and gas, hospital, and banking. They may also provide special decision support functions such as optimal scheduling of critical resources.

Even though the scope of applications included in standard ERP packages is very large, it is usually the case that additional software will be required because of the unique characteristics of each company. A company generates its own unique mix of products and services that are designed to provide a significant competitive advantage to the firm. This unique mix of products and services will need to be supported by unique software capability, some of which may be purchased from vendors and others that will need to be custom designed. Customized software applications are also widely used to coordinate the activities of a firm with its supply chain customers and suppliers.

Data Integration

The software modules, as described earlier, form the core of an ERP system. This core is designed to process the business transactions to support the essential activities of an enterprise in an efficient manner. Working from a single database, transactions document each of the activities that compose the processes used by the enterprise to conduct business. A major value of the integrated database is that information is not reentered at each step of a process, thus reducing errors and reducing work.

Transactions are processed in **real time,** meaning that as soon as the transaction is entered into the system, the effect on items such as inventory status, order status, and accounts receivable is known to all users of the system. There is no delay in the processing of a transaction in a real-time system. A customer could, for example, call into an order desk to learn the exact status of an order—or determine the status independently through an Internet connection. From a decision analysis viewpoint, the amount of detail available in the system is extremely rich. If, for example, one wishes to analyze the typical lead time for a product produced to order, the analyst could process an information request that selects all of the orders for the product over the past three months, then a calculation of the time between the order date and delivery date for each order would be done, and finally the average of this time for the whole set of orders can be calculated. Analyses, such as this lead time, can be valuable for evaluating improvements designed to make the process more responsive, for example.

To facilitate queries not built into the standard ERP system software, a separate **data warehouse** is commonly employed. A data warehouse is a special program (often running on a totally separate computer) that is designed to automatically capture and process data for uses that are outside the basic ERP system applications. For example, the data warehouse could, on an ongoing basis, capture and perform the calculations needed for the average lead time question. The data warehouse software and database is set up so that users may access and analyze data without placing a burden on the operational ERP system. This is a powerful mechanism to support higher-level decision support applications.

A good example of a company making use of a data warehouse is Walmart. Walmart is now able to put two full years of retail store sales data online. The data are used by both internal Walmart buyers and outside suppliers—sales and current inventory data on products sold at Walmart and Sam's Club stores. Vendors, who are restricted to viewing products they supply, use a Web-based extranet site to collaborate with Walmart's buyers in managing inventory and making replenishment decisions. A vendor's store-by-store sales results for a given day are available to vendors by 4 a.m. the following day. The database is more than 130 terabytes in size. Each terabyte is the equivalent of 250 million pages of text. At an average of 500 pages per book, a terabyte is a half million books. For Walmart as a whole, that is about 20 major university libraries.

How Manufacturing Planning and Control (MPC) Fits within ERP

MPC is concerned with planning and controlling all aspects of manufacturing, including managing materials, scheduling machines and people, and coordinating suppliers and key customers. The coordination required for success runs across all functional units in the firm. Consider the following simple example to illustrate the degree of coordination required.

Simplified Example

The Ajax Food Services Company has one plant that makes sandwiches. These are sold in vending machines, cafeterias, and small stores. One of the sandwiches is peanut butter and jelly (PBJ). It is made from bread, butter, peanut butter, and grape jelly. When complete, it is wrapped in a standard plastic package used for all Ajax sandwiches. One loaf of bread makes 10 sandwiches, a package of butter makes 50 sandwiches, and containers of peanut butter and jelly each make 20 sandwiches.

Consider the information needed by Ajax for manufacturing planning and control. First Ajax needs to know what demand to expect for its PBJ sandwich in the future. This might be forecast by analyzing detailed sales data from each location where the sandwiches are sold. Because sales are all handled by sales representatives who travel between the various sites, data based on the actual orders and sales reports provided by the reps can be used to make this forecast. The same data are used by human resources to calculate commissions owed to the reps for payroll purposes. Marketing uses the same data to analyze each current location and evaluate the attractiveness of new locations.

Freshness is very important to Ajax, so daily demand forecasts are developed to plan manufacturing. Consider, for example, that Ajax sees that it needs to make 300 PBJ sandwiches to be delivered to the sales sites this Friday. Ajax will actually assemble the sandwiches on Thursday. According to the usage data given earlier, this requires 30 loaves of bread, six packages of butter, and 15 containers of peanut butter and jelly. Freshness is largely dictated by the age of the bread, so it is important that Ajax works closely with the local baker because the baker delivers bread each morning on the basis of the day's assembly schedule. Similarly, the delivery schedules for the butter, peanut butter, and jelly need to be coordinated with the vendors of these items.

Ajax uses college students who work on a part-time basis to assemble the sandwiches. Manufacturing knows that a student can make 60 sandwiches per hour and that sandwiches must be ready for loading into the delivery trucks by 4:00 p.m. on the day prior to delivery. Our 300 sandwiches require five hours of work, so any one student doing this work needs to start at or before 11:00 a.m. on Thursday to make the sandwiches on time.

An ERP system is designed to provide the information and decision support needed to coordinate this type of activity. Of course, with our simplified example, the coordination is trivial, but consider if our company were making hundreds of different types of sandwiches in 1,000 cities around the world, and these sandwiches were sold at hundreds of sites in each of these cities. This is exactly the scale of operations that can be handled by a modern ERP system.

Precisely how all of these calculations are made is, of course, the main focus of this book. All of the details for how material requirements are calculated, how capacity is planned, and how demand forecasts are made, for example, are explained in great detail. To illustrate the MPC features within ERP systems, the following section describes mySAP Supply Chain Management, a software package offered by SAP, a major ERP vendor.

Supply Chain Planning with mySAP SCM

In this section we see how SAP has approached the details of manufacturing planning and control. Detailed discussions of these applications are the topic of other sections of this book. Here, we are using SAP to show how one vendor organizes the functions. Other major vendors like PeopleSoft, Oracle, and BAAN each have a unique approach to packaging supply chain software.

SAP labels all MPC applications as part of its supply chain software, divided into four main functions: supply chain planning, supply chain execution, supply chain collaboration, and supply chain coordination. Current information about products is on vendors' websites, and readers are encouraged to download the white papers that describe a vendor's current thinking. These publications are informative and indicate where a vendor will move in the future. Moreover, comparing/contrasting this information can be very educational—and help in making key choices as to which business processes can be supported by standard (plain vanilla) software.

The *supply chain design module* provides a centralized overview of the entire supply chain and key performance indicators, which helps identify weak links and potential improvements. It supports strategic planning by enabling the testing of various scenarios to determine how changes in the market or customer demand can be addressed by the supply chain. Here, for our simplified example of Ajax food services, we could evaluate the relative profitability of particular market channels and locations such as vending machines versus shops in train stations.

Collaborative demand and supply planning helps match demand to supply. Demand-planning tools take into account historical demand data, causal factors, marketing events, market intelligence, and sales objectives and enable the supply chain network to work on a single forecast. Supply planning tools create an overall supply plan that covers materials management, production, distribution and transportation requirements, and constraints. Here Ajax would be able to anticipate the demands for each kind of sandwich in each location and plan replenishments accordingly.

Supply Chain Execution with mySAP SCM

Materials management shares inventory and procurement order information to ensure that the materials required for manufacturing are available in the right place and at the right time. This set of applications supports plan-driven procurement, inventory management, and invoicing, with a feedback loop between demand and supply to increase responsiveness. In this set of applications, Ajax would plan for all the sandwich components to be delivered to the right places at the right times. Inventories might be maintained on some items such as peanut butter, while others such as bread might be planned on a just-in-time basis.

Collaborative manufacturing shares information with partners to coordinate production and enable everyone to work together to increase both visibility and responsiveness. These applications support all types of production processes: engineer-to-order, configure-to-order, make-to-order, and make-to-stock. They create a continuous information flow across engineering, planning, and execution and can optimize production schedules across the supply chain, taking into account material and capacity constraints. Here Ajax might do joint planning with key suppliers and perhaps organize the planning of special promotions.

Collaborative fulfillment supports partnerships that can intelligently commit to delivery dates in real time and fulfill orders from all channels on time. This set of applications includes a global available-to-promise (ATP) feature that locates finished products, components, and machine capacities in a matter of seconds. It also manages the flow of products through sales channels, matching supply to market demand, reassigning supply and demand to meet shifts in customer demand, and managing transportation and warehousing. Clearly all these logistics activities are critical to Ajax in order to deliver fresh sandwiches in the right amounts.

Supply Chain Collaboration with mySAP SCM

The *inventory collaboration hub* uses the Internet to gain visibility to suppliers and manage the replenishment process. Suppliers can see the status of their parts at all plants, receive automatic alerts when inventory levels get low, and respond quickly via the Web. The hub can also be integrated with back-end transaction and planning systems to update them in real time. Here Ajax could provide real-time inventory views to its suppliers—not only of material suppliers, but also of down stream inventories (i.e., sandwiches).

Collaborative replenishment planning is particularly useful in the consumer products and retail industries. These applications allow manufacturers to collaborate with their strategic retail customers to increase revenue, improve service, and lower inventory levels and costs. They enable an exception-based collaborative planning, forecasting, and replenishment (CPFR) process that allows the firm to add retail partners without a proportional increase in staff. This set of applications would be particularly useful to Ajax, as it grows its global business and adds new channels of distribution.

Vendor-managed inventory (VMI) is a set of processes to enable vendor-driven replenishment and can be implemented over the Web. Now Ajax vendors would no longer receive "orders." They would replenish Ajax inventories as they like—but be paid for their materials only when consumed by Ajax.

Enterprise portal gives users personalized access to a range of information, applications, and services supported by the system. It uses role-based technology to deliver information to users according to their individual responsibilities within the supply chain network. It can also use Web-based tools to integrate third-party systems in the firm's supply chain network. Here, for example, marketing people at Ajax might like to examine the detailed sales data (and perhaps customer questionnaires) in relation to a new product introduction.

Mobile supply chain management is a set of applications so that people can plan, execute, and monitor activity using mobile and remote devices. Mobile data entry using personal data assistant devices and automated data capture using wireless "smart tags," for example, are supported. Here Ajax can have marketing and even delivery personnel report on actual store conditions—not just sales but also category management. For example, how well does the actual assortment of sandwiches match the standard?

Supply Chain Coordination with mySAP SCM

Supply chain event management monitors the execution of supply chain events, such as the issue of a pallet or the departure of a truck, and flags any problems that come up. This set of applications is particularly useful for product tracking/traceability. For Ajax, if there is a customer complaint about a sandwich, it is critical to quickly determine if this is an isolated instance or whether there might be a large group of bad quality sandwiches—and how to find them.

Supply chain performance management allows the firm to define, select, and monitor key performance indicators, such as costs and assets, and use them to gain an integrated, comprehensive view of performance across the supply chain. It provides constant surveillance of key performance measures and generates an alert if there is a deviation from plan. It can be used with mySAP Business Intelligence and SAP's data warehousing and data analysis software. Here Ajax needs to not only assess profit contribution by sandwich type and location, it also needs to determine which are the best supplier and customer partners.

Performance Metrics to Evaluate Integrated System Effectiveness

As indicated, one significant advantage that a firm gains from using an integrated ERP system is the ability to obtain current data on how the firm is performing. An ERP system can provide the data needed for a comprehensive set of performance measures to evaluate strategic alignment of the various functions with the firm's strategy. An example of the comprehensiveness of the measures is tracking the time from spending cash on purchases until the cash is received in sales.

The balance sheet and the income and expense statements contain financial measures, such as net profit, that traditionally have been used to evaluate the success of the firm. A limitation of traditional financial metrics is that they primarily tell the story of past events. They are less helpful to guide decision makers in creating future value through investments in customer infrastructure, suppliers, employees, manufacturing processes, and other innovations.

Our goal is a more holistic approach to management of the firm. Figure 1A.2 depicts three major functional areas that make up the internal supply chain of a manufacturing enterprise: purchasing, manufacturing, and sales and distribution. Tight cooperation is required between these three functions for effective manufacturing planning and control. Considered independently, purchasing is mainly concerned with minimizing materials cost, manufacturing with minimum production costs, sales that result in selling the greatest amount, and distribution with minimum distribution and warehousing costs. Let us consider how each independently operating function might seek to optimize its operation.

The "Functional Silo" Approach

The purchasing function is responsible for buying all of the material required to support manufacturing operations. When operating independently, this function wishes to know what materials and quantities are going to be needed over the long term. The purchasing group then solicits bids for the best price for each material. The main criterion is simply the cost of the material, and the purchasing function is *evaluated* on this criterion: what is latest actual cost versus standard cost? Of course, quality is always going to be important to the group, so typically some type of quality specification will need to be guaranteed by the supplier. But quality is more of a constraint than a goal; suppliers must achieve some minimal level of specification. Consideration of delivery schedules, quantities, and responsiveness are also important, but again these considerations are often secondary at best in how the purchasing function is evaluated in a traditional firm.

For manufacturing, making the product at the lowest possible cost is the classic metric. To do this requires minimum equipment downtime, with high equipment and labor utilization.

FIGURE 1A.2
Manufacturing Operating Cycle

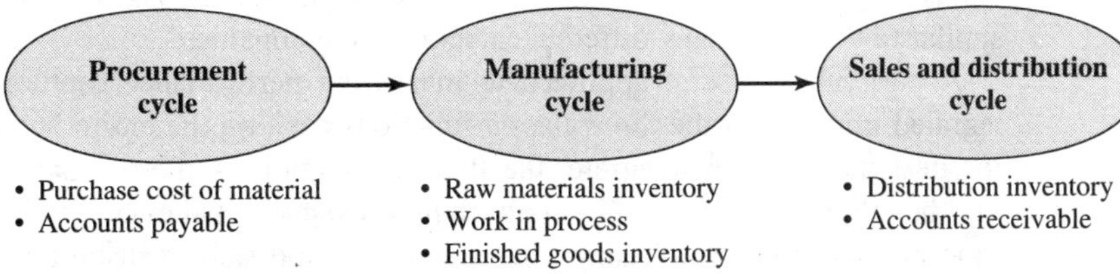

Stopping to set up equipment is not the desire of this group. This group is focused on high-volume output, with minimum changeovers. Quality is again "important"—but as in purchasing it is more of a minimum hurdle. Large batches foster better quality performance, because defects often occur during changeovers. Once production reaches some steady state, it is easier to maintain a quality standard.

Long production runs lead to lower unit costs, but they also generate larger cycle stock inventories. For sales, larger inventories appear at first to be desirable, since these should support customer service. Alas, it is not so; a one-year supply of product A is of no help when we are out of product B.

Distribution can be equally narrow-minded and suboptimal. In the classic case its job is moving the product from the manufacturing site to the customer at the lowest possible cost. Depending on the product, it may need to be stored in one or more distribution centers and be moved via one or more different modes of transportation (truck, rail, etc.). Evaluation of distribution activities tends to focus on the specific distribution activity involved. For example, many firms focus on the lowest price quotation for moving a product from one stage of the distribution chain to another, rather than on the *total* costs of moving materials *into* and *out of* the overall firm. And even here this cost focus needs to be integrated with other objectives such as lower inventories, faster response times, and customer service.

Consider the implications if all three areas are allowed to work independently. To take advantage of discounts, purchasing will buy the largest quantities possible. This results in large amounts of raw material inventory. The manufacturing group desires to maximize production volumes in order to spread the significant fixed costs of production over as many units as possible. These large lot sizes result in high amounts of work-in-process inventory, with large quantities of goods pushed into finished goods whether they are needed or not. Large lot sizes also mean that the time between batches increases; therefore, response times to unexpected demand increase. Finally, distribution will try to fully load every truck that is used to move material to minimize transportation cost. Of course, this may result in large amounts of inventory in distribution centers (perhaps the wrong ones) and might not match well with what customers really need. Given the opportunity, the sales group might even sell product that cannot possibly be delivered on time. After all, they are evaluated on sales, not deliveries. A more coordinated approach is facilitated by the use of an ERP system. The following is an example of a consistent set of metrics useful for managing supply chain functions effectively.

Integrated Supply Chain Metrics

The Supply Chain Council has developed many metrics to measure the performance of the overall supply chain. It has used these standardized measures to develop benchmarks for comparisons between companies. Figure 1A.3 contains a list of some of these measures with average and best-in-class benchmarks. The average and best-in-class measures are for typical large industrial products. The Supply Chain Council has developed sets of measures similar to these for many different categories of companies.

A particularly useful approach to measuring performance captures not only the integrated impact that the three classic functions have on the entire business supply chain; the best metrics also integrate the finance function. A metric that does so in measuring the relative efficiency of a supply chain is **cash-to-cash cycle time.** Cash-to-cash cycle time integrates the purchasing, manufacturing, and sales/distribution cycles depicted in

FIGURE 1A.3
Supply Chain Metrics

Source: Supply Chain Council.

Measure	Description	Best in Class	Average or Medium
Delivery performance	What percentage of orders is shipped according to schedule?	93%	69%
Fill rate by line item	Orders often contain multiple line items. This is the percentage of the actual line items filled.	97%	88%
Perfect order fulfillment	This measures how many complete orders were filled and shipped on time.	92.4%	65.7%
Order fulfillment lead time	The time from when an order is placed to when it is received by the customer.	135 days	225 days
Warranty cost of % of revenue	This is the actual warranty expense divided by revenue.	1.2%	2.4%
Inventory days of supply	This is how long the firm could continue to operate if all sources of supply were cut off.	55 days	84 days
Cash-to-cash cycle time	Considering accounts payable, accounts receivable, and inventory, this is the amount of time it takes to turn cash used to purchase materials into cash from a customer.	35.6 days	99.4 days
Asset turns	This is a measure of how many times the same assets can be used to generate revenue and profit.	4.7 turns	1.7 turns

Figure 1A.2. But it also relates well to the financial maxim: cash is king! Calculating the measure requires the use of data related to purchasing, accounting, manufacturing, and sales.

Actually, cash-to-cash cycle time is a measure of cash flow. Cash flow indicates where cash comes from (its source), where cash is spent (its use), and the net change in cash for the year. Understanding how cash flows through a business is critical to managing the business effectively. Accountants use the term *operating cycle* to describe the length of time that it takes a business to convert cash outflows for raw materials, labor, etc. into cash inflows. This cycle time determines, to a large extent, the amount of capital needed to start and operate a business. Conceptually, cash-to-cash cycle time is calculated as follows:

$$\text{Cash-to-cash cycle time} = \text{Inventory days of supply} + \text{Days of sales outstanding} - \text{Average payment period for material} \quad \textbf{(1A.1)}$$

The overall result is the number of days between paying for raw materials and getting paid for the product. Going through the details of calculating cash-to-cash cycle time

FIGURE 1A.4
Integrated ERP Data for Cash-to-Cash Cycle Time Calculation

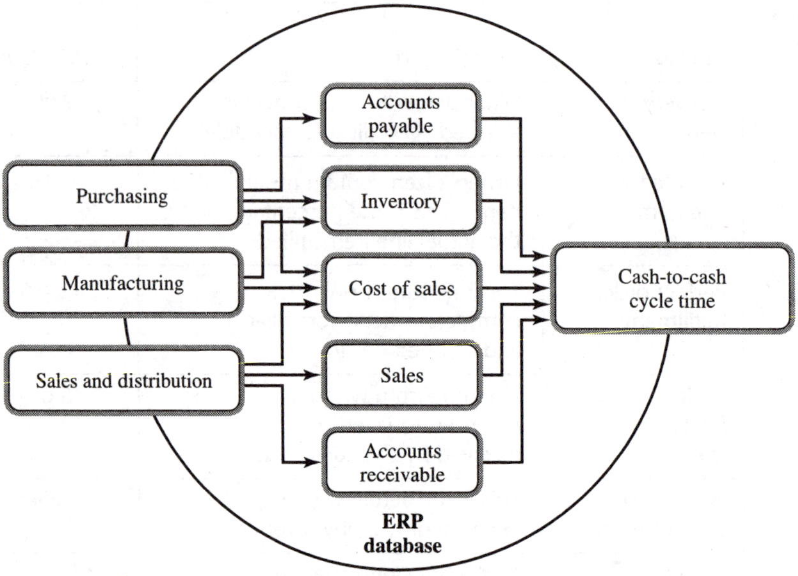

demonstrates the power of integrated information. These calculations are straightforward in an ERP system. The calculation can be divided into three parts: the accounts receivable cycle, the inventory cycle, and the accounts payable cycle.

Figure 1A.4 shows the data that are used for calculating cash-to-cash cycle time. The data are controlled by different functions within the company. The current accounts payable amount, an account that is dependent on the credit terms that purchasing negotiates with suppliers, gives the current money that that firm owes its suppliers. As will be seen in the calculation, this is a form of credit to the company.

The inventory account gives the value of the entire inventory within the company. This includes raw materials, work in process, finished goods, and distribution inventory. The value of inventory depends on the quantities stored and also the cost of the inventory to the firm. All three major functional areas affect the inventory account. Purchasing has the major influence on raw materials. Manufacturing largely determines work in process and finished goods. Sales/distribution influences location of finished goods—as well as amounts through their forecasts and orders.

Just as inventory is affected by all three functions, the cost of sales is dependent on costs that are incurred throughout the firm. For the purposes of the cash-to-cash cycle time calculation, this is expressed as a percentage of total sales. This percentage depends on such items as material cost, labor cost, and all other direct costs associated with the procurement of materials, manufacturing process, and distribution of the product.

Sales are simply the total sales revenue over a given period of time. Finally, accounts receivable is the amount owed the firm by its customers. The accounts receivable amount will depend on the firm's credit policy and its ability to deliver product in a timely manner. Figure 1A.4 shows how the three major functional areas influence the cash-to-cash cycle calculation.

Calculating the Cash-to-Cash Time

As noted, the first task in determining the cash-to-cash cycle time is to calculate accounts receivable cycle time. This measures the length of time it takes a business to convert a sale into cash. In other words, how long does it take a business to collect the money owed for goods already sold? One way is to calculate the number of days of sales invested in accounts receivable:

$$S_d = \frac{S}{d} \tag{1A.2}$$

where

S_d = average daily sales

S = sales over d days

$$\text{AR}_d = \frac{\text{AR}}{S_d} \tag{1A.3}$$

where

AR_d = average days of accounts receivable

AR = accounts receivable

The next part of the calculation is the inventory cycle time. This is the number of days of inventory measured relative to the cost of sales:

$$C_d = S_d CS \tag{1A.4}$$

where

C_d = average daily cost of sales

CS = cost of sales (percent)

$$I_d = \frac{I}{C_d} \tag{1A.5}$$

where

I_d = average days of inventory

I = current value of inventory (total)

Next, the accounts payable cycle time measures the level of accounts payable relative to the cost of sales:

$$\text{AP}_d = \frac{\text{AP}}{C_d} \tag{1A.6}$$

where

AP_d = average days of accounts payable

AP = accounts payable

Finally, the cash-to-cash cycle time is calculated from the three cycle times.

$$\text{Cash-to-cash cycle time} = \text{AR}_d + I_d - \text{AP}_d \tag{1A.7}$$

Figure 1A.5 shows an example of the cash-to-cash cycle time calculation.

The cash-to-cash cycle time is an interesting measure for evaluating the relative supply chain effectiveness of a firm. Some firms are actually able to run a negative value for the

FIGURE 1A.5
Example of Cash-to-Cash Cycle Time Calculation

Data: Sales over last 30 days = \$1,020,000
Accounts receivable at the end of the month = \$200,000
Inventory value at the end of the month = \$400,000
Cost of sales = 60% of total sales
Accounts payable at the end of the month = \$160,000

$$S_d = \frac{S}{d} = \frac{1{,}020{,}000}{30} = 34{,}000$$

$$AR_d = \frac{AR}{S_d} = \frac{200{,}000}{34{,}000} = 5.88 \text{ days}$$

$$C_d = S_d CS = 34{,}000(0.6) = 20{,}400$$

$$I_d = \frac{I}{C_d} = \frac{400{,}000}{20{,}400} = 19.6 \text{ days}$$

$$AP_d = \frac{AP}{C_d} = \frac{160{,}000}{20{,}400} = 7.84 \text{ days}$$

$$\text{Cash-to-cash cycle time} = AR_d + I_d - AP_d = 5.88 + 19.6 - 7.84 = 17.64 \text{ days}$$

measure. Dell Computer, for example, typically runs cash-to-cash cycle times of −10 to −20 days. This implies the ability to invest in the business as needed—with no requirement for additional funds! Metrics, such as cash-to-cash cycle time, can be efficiently reported using ERP data. These metrics can even be reported in real time if needed.

What Is the Experience with ERP?

In this section we examine the implementation trials and tribulations of several firms. ERP implementation is not easy, but the results can be dramatic, and there are some key lessons to be learned.

Eli Lilly and Company—Operational Standards for Manufacturing Excellence

Eli Lilly is a multinational company with 35,000 people, manufacturing plants in 16 countries, and medicine sales in more than 150 different countries. Eli Lilly uses ERP to manage the coordination of its manufacturing, sales, and research facilities around the globe as new products are developed and introduced. Developing and deploying a new product is a complex process that requires extensive research, a complex government approval process, marketing plans, and manufacturing coordination. The promise of ERP information integration was compelling for this global company managed from its corporate headquarters in Indianapolis.

Managing such a large company can be done in one of two ways. One approach is to essentially decentralize the company around autonomous units located in the United States, Europe, Japan, and other major world centers. Each entity might operate independently from a sales and manufacturing standpoint, sharing products developed by the research centers operated by the company. This is largely the way the company operated prior to standardizing processes beginning in the 1990s.

The company felt that a single-vendor ERP system would generate the following benefits:

- *Process improvements.* Significant reduction in the number of transactions processed and reconciliations needed.
- *Training.* Simplified employee training and more efficient job rotation because of the similarity of operations across different functions.
- *Information technology.* Significantly reduced support and infrastructure costs, since hundreds of legacy systems could be replaced.
- *Strategic direction.* Resources more efficiently allocated because of visibility from all operating entities.
- *Organization flexibility.* Changing more quickly with new products more quickly deployed, quicker response to changing market conditions.

The decision to move to ERP certainly seemed sound to Eli Lilly, but the details have proved to be difficult. Implementing an ERP system is only part of true enterprise integration. Reengineering processes to fully utilize the integrated information support is essential. In practice, process reengineering is more difficult to achieve than the implementation of ERP computer hardware and software. Moreover, if processes are not changed, the ERP system will usually create additional work for people rather than less.

At Eli Lilly, a set of global policies was adopted. These policies are documented (and updated) in a book entitled *Operational Standards for Manufacturing Excellence: Materials Management Policies.* The book has been extremely important to integration of manufacturing processes in the company, defining a common set of measures to guide the manufacturing management. The book contains a comprehensive set of policies, activities, measures, and goals that defines how manufacturing activities are evaluated across Eli Lilly global operations. Figure 1A.6 is an example of how customer service level is defined.

Figure 1A.6 defines precisely the manufacturing policy related to customer service satisfaction, integrated with a set of essential activities to support the policy, and a specific set of measures and goals. In a similar manner, Eli Lilly defines policies for the following:

- Independent demand management
- Dependent demand management
- Sales and operations planning/requirements and operations planning
- Master scheduling
- Material requirements planning
- Shop floor control
- Inventory control
- Capacity management
- Lead time reduction
- Data quality
- Training
- Evaluation

Deployment of this common set of policies to all manufacturing units set the stage for a unified vision of manufacturing excellence around the world. Further, processes as well as measurements and goals are also commonly based on the activities defined in the policies.

FIGURE 1A.6
Eli Lilly Definition of Customer Service Level

Rationale: *Service level* is a critical element of customer satisfaction and is defined as consistently meeting customer needs related to delivery of product.

Policy: Our *service level goal* to all customers (external and internal) is to fully satisfy valid orders 100% of the time and to position Lilly as one of the best suppliers in the industry.

Fundamental activities:

1. Develop a site program directing efforts toward attainment of the service level goal.
2. Establish a monthly measurement system to report the number of "fully satisfied" *orders* delivered "on time" versus the total number of orders delivered.
3. Report the number of *lines* delivered "on time" versus the total number of lines delivered.
4. Publish order lead times (at least annually) for make-to-order and make-to-stock products that meet the customers' needs and make economic sense.
5. Document the number of incompatible orders, determine causes, and take corrective action as necessary.

Measurements and goals:

1. For both internal and external customers, monthly measure and report the number and percentage of valid customer orders not fully satisfied. Pareto root causes for *not* fully satisfying a customer's valid order so that appropriate corrective action can be taken.
2. Compare results of the "customer service surveys" with your service level measurement to assure that your perceptions of service match those of your customers.
3. Customer inquiries should receive a response before the end of the next work day.
4. When delivery dates change, customers should be notified within two work days after the problem causing the change occurs. This must be measured and documented.
5. Incompatible orders must be routinely measured and should not exceed 10 percent of the total orders per month.

At Eli Lilly, terms were precisely defined so that the meaning of the measures and goals is understood. This was facilitated through diagrams such as Figure 1A.7, the order management process. Horizontally across the middle of the diagram is a sequential list of all the major processes associated with make-to-order and make-to-stock orders. Vertically, various lead times are defined on the basis of beginning and ending points of the required processes.

A final feature of Lilly's book is the precise definition of how measurement calculations should be done. These calculations are illustrated by examples. Consider the following calculation of days of stock (DOS). Assume 30 days per month and these data:

March ending inventory (at standard cost)	$1,000,000
Forecast demand (at standard cost)	
April	$400,000
May	$300,000
June	$500,000

To calculate DOS, consider how many full months can be covered with inventory on hand. In this case March inventory will fully cover April and May demand ($1,000,000 − $400,000 − $300,000 = $300,000), projecting that $300,000 worth of inventory will be

FIGURE 1A.7 Lilly Order Management Processes and Lead Time Definitions

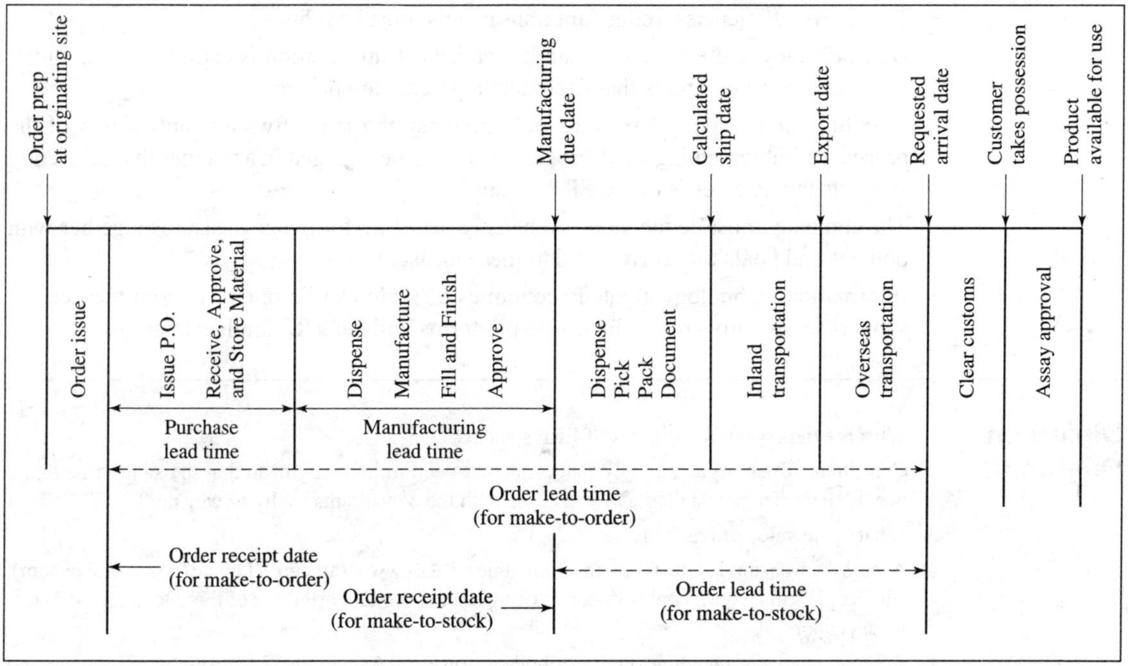

left for June. Sixty percent of June demand can be met ($300,000/$500,000 = 0.6). Sixty percent of June demand is equivalent to 18 days (0.6 × 30 = 18). The total DOS is 78 days (30 for April + 30 for May + 18 for June = 78 days).

In the mid-1990s Lilly began implementing an SAP ERP product, R/3. The ideas from the company's policy book have been embedded in the ERP system. Processes have been defined to correspond to those outlined, as have performance measures and reports. In essence, the ERP system has now replaced the policy book, since the concepts are part of the logic of the processes used by the company and supported by the ERP system. In the case of Lilly, developing these common standards began years before the actual implementation of the ERP system.

Concluding Principles

The value of ERP to a company depends to a great extent on the potential savings that can be derived from the ability to centralize information and decision making. For example, a company like Eli Lilly that makes and distributes drugs around the world can derive great benefit from an ERP system because of the similarity of manufacturing and distribution at its sites around the world. It is important to recognize that the value of the system is derived from the synergies obtained from quick access to information from multiple functions in the company. ERP is especially valuable when these functions are located at many different sites within a country or around the world.

We provide the following principles regarding implementation of an ERP system:

- To achieve efficiencies, redundant transactions must be reduced.
- Data accuracy and efficiencies can be realized if information is captured at the initial entry and the transactions that document a process are preserved.
- Installing the computer hardware and implementing the software is only a part of the process of implementing ERP. Processes need to be changed in a manner that efficiently supports the data needs of the ERP system.
- The company must define a comprehensive set of performance measures together with policies and goals that correspond to these measures.
- Information technology–related economies of scale can be obtained from the need to support fewer software and hardware platforms with an ERP implementation.

Discussion Questions

1. What are the essential attributes of ERP systems?
2. Consultants often argue strongly that processes need to be reengineered at the same time that a new ERP system is installed. Do you agree with the consultants? Why or why not?
3. What is the value of real-time data?
4. Access the websites for the following companies: SAP (www.sap.com), Oracle (www. oracle.com), and PeopleSoft (www.peoplesoft.com). Compare the product offerings of these leading ERP software vendors.
5. i2 Technologies is a leading vendor of bolt-on software. Access the i2 website (www.i2.com) and develop a list of the features of this company's offerings.

Problems

1. The following data were obtained from a recent quarterly report for Dell Computer (in millions):

Net revenue	$8,028
Cost of revenue	$6,580
Inventories:	
Production materials	$126
Work-in-process and finished goods	$224
Accounts receivable	$2,689
Accounts payable	$4,326

   Calculate the cash-to-cash cycle time for Dell.
2. Obtain from the Internet the current data needed to calculate cash-to-cash cycle time for Dell Computer, Gateway, and Cisco Systems. Calculate the measure for each company and critically evaluate the differences in how the companies operate their supply chains.
3. Evaluate the effect of the following changes that a company makes on cash-to-cash cycle time. Indicate simply the direction of movement of the measurement (i.e., up, down or no change).

   Reduction in cost-of-goods sold
   More frequent deliveries from suppliers
   Reductions in time customers are allowed to pay for goods
   Change from paying suppliers on receipt of goods to waiting 60 days to pay suppliers
   Write-off of obsolete inventory
   Reduction in labor content in a production process
   Outsourcing the production of a major product

4. Return to the Ajax sandwich example on page 17. Suppose that in addition to the 300 peanut butter and jelly sandwiches to be delivered on Friday, Ajax also needs to make 2,000 sandwiches of other varieties. Assume that the same amount of time is needed to assemble sandwiches and that each part-time student can work for five hours. How many students are needed on Thursday?
5. If the average selling price per sandwich is $2.00 and the cost of materials and labor is $1.25, what is the daily profit if Ajax sells 2,100 sandwiches (unsold sandwiches are discarded at the end of the day)? What if it is a really bad day and it only sells 1,500?
6. Supposing a new bread supplier provides bread that increases the shelf life for sandwiches from one day to two. What does this imply for the calculations in problem 5? What kind of MPC system linkages would be required from Ajax to its customers?
7. Suppose that in one college location Ajax typically sells 500 tuna and 500 roast beef sandwiches per day. Every week, the sales of roast beef are going down by 10 percent because some students are concerned about eating beef. About one-half of these students now buy tuna instead. How many of each sandwich should be made per day for the third week?
8. Continuing with the data in problems 5 and 7, how much are the profits to Ajax reduced in problem 6 by the new student behavior in the third week?
9. Suppose that the peanut butter for the 300 daily peanut butter and jelly sandwiches is delivered once per week and one delivery costs $20. A week's supply of peanut butter is valued at $100 and the cost of capital is 15 percent. Further suppose that the invoice for peanut butter is paid immediately. What would be the costs and benefits of delivering monthly, using VMI, where payment is made immediately upon use by Ajax?
10. Continuing problem 9, what information linkages might be established from the Ajax ERP systems to the peanut butter supplier to make the VMI work? What would the information links be if the payment to the supplier was paid based on sale of the sandwiches? What else would need to be included?
11. Ajax has established a new sandwich shop format for airports and train stations. Here, the sandwiches are only made from a specially made, long, individual loaf of bread. But the innovation is that the sandwiches are not made ahead in large batches. Instead, a few of each variety of sandwich are made at a time, in the shop, with the result being a better ability to exactly match supply to demand. If prior to this change the shop had roughly 5 percent leftovers of one-half of the sandwich varieties each day, but could have sold 10 percent more of the two best sellers that day, what are the potential benefits of the new format if the store sells 12 different sandwiches each with an average demand of 20 per day?
12. Continuing with problem 11, how might an ERP system help plan the replenishment orders for sandwich ingredients?
13. A leading company in the electronics industry estimates that a reduction of 10 days of supply held in inventory is the equivalent of an increase of 1 percent of sales. What would be the difference between average performance and best in class according to Figure 1A.3?
14. Returning to the ideas of problem 13 and Figure 1A.3, what might be said about the difference between two firms in the same industry with average and best in class results for asset turns?
15. In the Eli Lilly example, how much would be saved by reducing inventory by 10 days?

Chapter 2

Demand Management

This chapter covers issues concerned with how a firm integrates information from and about its customers, internal and external to the firm, into the manufacturing planning and control system. It is in this module that all potential demands on manufacturing capacity are collected and coordinated. Demand management includes activities that range from determining or estimating the demand from customers, through converting specific customer orders into promised delivery dates, to helping balance demand with supply. A well-developed demand management system within the manufacturing planning and control (MPC) system brings significant benefits to the firm. Proper planning of all externally and internally generated demands means capacity (ultimately, supply) can be better managed and controlled. Information that helps to integrate the needs of the customers with the capabilities of the firm can be developed. Timely and *honest* customer order promises are possible. Physical distribution activities can be improved significantly. This chapter shows how to achieve these benefits. The focus is a combination of management concepts necessary to perform this integrative activity. This chapter is organized around the following topics:

- *Demand management in MPC systems:* What role does demand management play in the manufacturing planning and control system?
- *Demand management and the MPC environment:* How do the different manufacturing environments shape the demand management activities?
- *Communicating with other MPC modules and customers:* What are the communication linkages between demand management, other MPC modules and customers?
- *Information use in Demand Management:* How can the information collected be used to enhance the current and future performance of the firm?
- *Managing demand:* What day-to-day management activities are required to manage demand?

Demand Management in MPC Systems

Demand management is a gateway module in manufacturing planning and control (MPC), providing the link to the marketplace, sister plants, warehouses, and other important "customers." As such, it is in demand management that we gather information from and about the market doing things like forecasting customer demand, entering orders, and determining specific product requirements. Moreover, it is through this module that we communicate with

FIGURE 2.1 Demand Management in the MPC System

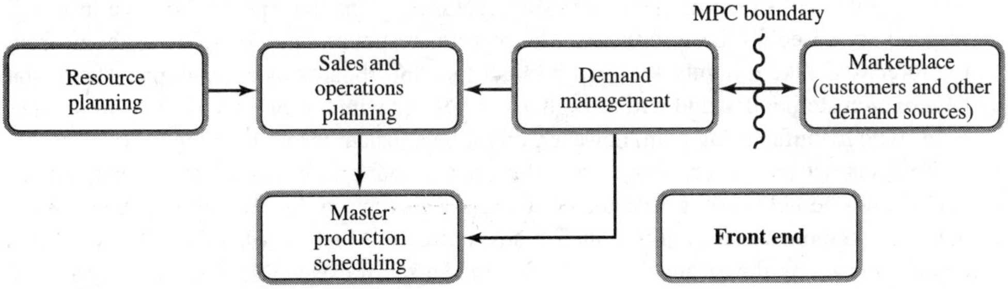

our customers by promising delivery dates, confirming order status, and communicating changes. Demand management is also concerned with identifying all sources of demand for manufacturing capacity, including service-part demands, intracompany requirements, and promotional inventory buildup or other needs for pipeline inventory stocking.

The position of demand management in the MPC system is shown in Figure 2.1. It is the key connection to the market in the front end of the MPC system. The external aspects of the demand management module are depicted as the double-ended arrow connected to the marketplace outside the MPC system. This simply underscores the need to communicate with the customers as well as to gather information from and about them. The other linkages are with the sales and operations planning (SOP) module and the master production scheduling (MPS) module. The information provided to SOP is used to develop sales and operations (including manufacturing) plans covering a year or more in duration at a fairly high level of aggregation. Both forecast and actual demand information is provided to the MPS module. It is in the MPS module that short-term, product-specific manufacturing plans are developed and controlled as actual demand becomes available and information is provided to provide delivery promises and order status to customers.

It is through these linkages that quantities and timing for all demands must be collected and coordinated with the **planning** and **control** activities of the company. The planning part of manufacturing planning and control (MPC) involves determining the capacity that will be made available to meet actual future demands for products. Much of this planning activity occurs in the sales and operations module. The control part determines how the capacity will be converted into products as the orders come in. The company **executes** the plan as actual demand information becomes available. The control function determines how the company will modify the plans in light of forecast errors and other changes in assumptions that inevitably occur. A substantial portion of the control activity is conducted in the master production scheduling module. Both the SOP and MPS modules require the information provided through the demand management module.

For many firms, planning the execution and controlling demand quantities and timings are a day-to-day interactive dialogue with customers. For other firms, particularly in the process industries, the critical coordination is in scheduling large inter- and intracompany requirements. For still others, physical distribution is critical, since the factory must support a warehouse replenishment program, which can differ significantly from the pattern of final customer demand.

The difference between the pattern of demand and the response by the company points out the important distinction between **forecasts** and **plans.** In demand management, forecasts of the quantities and timing of customer demand are developed. These are estimates of what might occur in the marketplace. Manufacturing plans that specify how the firm will respond are based on these forecasts. The plan for response can look quite different from the forecasts. Take a highly seasonal product like snowboards as an example. The actual pattern of customer demand will be high in the fall and winter months and very low at other times. The manufacturing plan, however, might be constant throughout the year.

This distinction between forecasts and plans is important for two reasons. First, a manager cannot be held responsible for not getting a forecast right. We can and should hold managers responsible for making their plans, however. Much of what the MPC system is about is providing the means for making as good a set of executable plans as possible and then providing the information to execute them. When conditions change, the control function should change the plans and the new plans should be executed faithfully. As much as we like to hold the weatherman responsible for not forecasting the rain, the forecast is only a guess, albeit an intelligent one. If the forecast is for rain, an intelligent plan would be to carry an umbrella. If you don't, it is hard to feel sorry for you when you get wet. You have control over the plan and execution, and not the demand.

This brings us to the second reason for making a distinction between the plan and the forecast. The demands of customers are **independent demands.** When (and if) a customer decides to buy our product, that decision is independent of the actions of the company. Obviously, we can influence the timing (and quantities) through advertising, pricing, promotions, and so forth, but the ultimate decision rests with the customer. On the other hand, if we have plans for building snowboards at a constant rate throughout the year, the demand for the decals that are needed can be calculated. The demand for the decals depends on our plans for producing the snowboards. It is **dependent demand.** Similarly, the "demand" from our warehouses for snowboards depends on our plans for replenishing the warehouses. When conditions change, the plans may need to change and this, in turn, could change the dependent demands that need to be coordinated in the demand management module.

It also may be necessary to reconcile different sources of demand information, provide forecasts for new products, and modify forecasts to meet the requirements of the users or otherwise adjust the information for use in the company. All these considerations are taken into account in the demand management process. Techniques for forecasting, aggregating (pooling) demand, and disaggregating demand can facilitate this process.

The linkage between demand management, sales and operations planning, and master production scheduling in the front end makes clear the importance of providing complete forecasts and providing them at the appropriate level of detail. The importance of identifying all sources of demand is obvious, but sometimes overlooked. If material and capacity resources are to be planned effectively, we must identify *all* sources of demand: spare parts, distribution, inventory changes, demonstration stock, new items, promotions, and so on. Only when we have accounted for all demand sources can we develop realistic MPC plans.

Demand Management and the MPC Environment

Demand management activities must conform to the strategy of the firm, the capabilities of manufacturing, and the needs of customers. Different strategies, capabilities, and customer needs define different MPC environments within which demand management activities are

FIGURE 2.2 Customer Order Decoupling Point in Different Environments

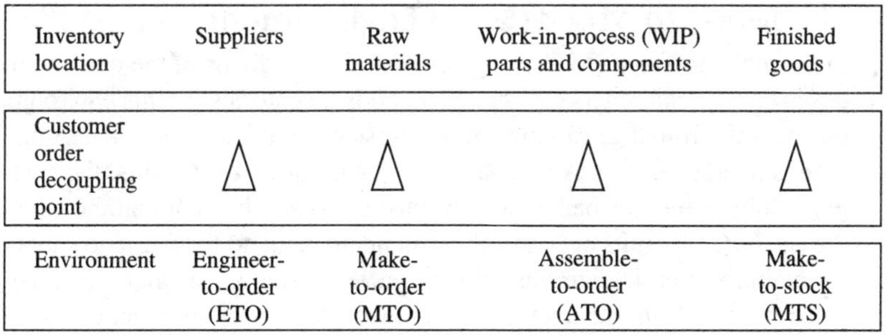

carried out. In order to understand how the activities might differ from environment to environment, we first develop a broad classification of manufacturing environments. Key to this classification is the concept of the **customer order decoupling point** or, as it is sometimes called, the **order penetration point.**

The customer order decoupling point can be looked at as the point at which demand changes from independent to dependent. It is the point at which the firm—as opposed to the customer—becomes responsible for determining the timing and quantity of material to be purchased, made, or finished. Consider for a moment a small tailor shop. If customers go into the shop and buy suits from the available stock (off the rack), the customer order decoupling point is the finished suit (the finished goods inventory). In this case, the customer decides which suit to buy and when to buy it (independent demand for the suits). The tailor decides what suits to make and when to make them (dependent demand for the fabric).

If, on the other hand, customers look over the available inventory of fabrics, make their choice, and request a specific suit design, the customer order decoupling point is the raw material inventory of fabric. Similarly, if the customer looks at catalogs of fabrics, chooses one, and requests the tailor to make a specific design, the customer order decoupling point is the supplier. In this latter case, both the customer and the supplier are included in the tailor's manufacturing decisions. In the examples of buying or making suits, the customer order decoupling point has moved deeper into the tailor's organization.

Figure 2.2 provides a means for visualizing the customer order decoupling point as it might move from finished goods inventory through the company all the way back to the supplier. The different locations of the customer order decoupling point give rise to different categories of manufacturing environments. Firms that serve their customers from finished goods inventory are known as **make-to-stock** firms. Those that combine a number of options together to meet a customer's specifications are called **assemble-to-order** firms. Those that make the customer's product from raw materials, parts, and components are **make-to-order firms.** An **engineer-to-order** firm will work with the customer to design the product, then make it from purchased materials, parts, and components. Of course, many firms will serve a combination of these environments, and a few will have all simultaneously.

For our purposes in describing the role of demand management in different situations, we will characterize the MPC environments as make-to-stock, assemble-to-order, or make-to-order (we will consider the engineer-to-order and make-to-order environment together).

The Make-to-Stock (MTS) Environment

In the make-to-stock (MTS) environment, the key focus of the demand management activities is on the maintenance of finished goods inventories. In this environment, the customers buy directly from the available inventory, so customer service is determined by whether their item is in stock or not. As we saw with the tailor that sold suits, the customer order decoupling point is the finished goods inventory. It is at this point that the independent demand of the customer for suits becomes the dependent demand for fabric to support the tailor's plans for making suits. Unlike the tailor, however, inventory of manufactured goods may be located very far from the manufacturing plant. Moreover, there may be several locations from which the customers buy their goods. This means that there is both a geographical and temporal dimension to the maintenance of finished goods inventory. Thus, tracking of demand by location throughout the supply chain is an important activity in the MTS environment.

A key aspect of the management of the finished goods inventory is the determination of when, how much, and how to replenish the stock at a specific location. This is the **physical distribution** concern in demand management. This can be an extremely broad concern, encompassing numerous locations in many countries, and involving several levels of distribution and storage. Some MTS firms employ plant warehouses, distribution centers, local warehouses, and even **vendor-managed inventory** inside their customers' locations. Management of this supply chain requires information on the status of inventory in the various locations, relationships with transportation providers, and estimates of the customers' demands by location and item. Formal methods of forecasting customer demand can help in this process.

The essential issue in satisfying customers in the make-to-stock environment is to balance the level of inventory against the level of service to the customer. If unlimited inventory were possible and costless, the task would be trivial. Unfortunately, that is not the case. Providing more inventory increases costs, so a trade-off between the costs of the inventory and the level of customer service must be made. The trade-off can be improved by better estimates (or knowledge) of customer demand, by more rapid transportation alternatives, by speedier production, and by more flexible manufacturing. Many MTS firms are investing in such **lean manufacturing** programs in order to shift the trade-off, that is, to achieve higher service levels for a given inventory investment. Regardless of how the trade-off comes out, the focus of demand management in the make-to-stock environment is on providing finished goods where and when the customers want them.

The Assemble-to-Order (ATO) Environment

Returning to our tailor for a moment, imagine that you were interested in buying an ensemble consisting of a jacket, a matching pair of slacks, a contrasting pair of slacks, and a vest. You would make your choices from the finished items of each, and the tailor would then cut and sew them to your size. This is a form of assemble-to-order (ATO) business. Many manufacturing examples exist. You may have experienced this yourself when you ordered a personal computer. You decided what components you wanted, and the company assembled the components to complete your order. Many people buy their cars this way, and some industrial products are assembled to meet the users' specifications.

In the assemble-to-order environment, the primary task of demand management is to define the customer's order in terms of alternative components and options, for example, a two-door versus four-door car, with or without antilock brakes. It is also important to assure that they can be combined into a viable product in a process known as **configuration management.** This is a critical step, because it might not be possible to assemble certain combinations. In a sports car, for example, mounting the center "boom box" of a deluxe sound system might fill the cavity in which the convertible top fits. Not only is that not desirable, it may not be physically possible to assemble that combination. In addition to combinations that can't go together, there may be combinations that must go together. For example, a heavy-duty radiator might be required for certain air conditioning units in a car. One of the capabilities required for success in the assemble-to-order environment is engineering design that enables as much flexibility in combining **components, options,** and **modules** into finished products as possible.

The assemble-to-order environment clearly illustrates the two-way nature of the communication between customers and demand management. Customers need to be informed of the allowable combinations, and the combinations should support marketplace desires, such as sports trim for cars. Moreover, customers' orders must be configured, and the customers must be informed of the delivery date of the finished product. In this environment, the independent demand for the assembled items is transformed into dependent demand for the parts required to produce the components needed. The inventory that defines customer service is the inventory of components, not the inventory of finished product.

Some ATO firms have applied lean manufacturing principles to dramatically decrease the time required to assemble finished goods. By so doing they are delivering customers' orders so quickly that they appear to be MTS firms from the perspective of the customer.

There are some significant advantages from moving the customer order decoupling point from finished goods to components. The number of finished products is usually substantially greater than the number of components that are combined to produce the finished product. Consider, for example, a computer for which there are four processor alternatives, three hard disk drive choices, four CD-DVD alternatives, two possible speaker systems, and four monitors available. If all combinations of these 17 components are valid, they can be combined into a total of 384 different final computer configurations. It is much easier to manage and forecast the demand for 17 components than for 384 computers. If N_i is the number of alternatives for component i, the total number of combinations for n components (given all are viable) is:

$$\text{Total number of combinations} = N_1 * N_2 * \cdots * N_n \tag{2.1}$$

The Make (Engineer)-to-Order (MTO) Environment

The focus of demand management in the MTS and ATO environments was largely on satisfying customers from the appropriate inventory—finished goods or components. In the make-to-order and engineer-to-order environments, there is another resource that needs to be taken into account—engineering. Moving the customer order decoupling point to raw materials or even suppliers puts independent demand information further into the firm and reduces the scope of dependent demand information. Moreover, the nature of the information needed from customers changes. We knew what the customers could buy in the MTS and ATO environments, but not if, when, or how many; in the make (engineer)-to-order environment, on the other hand, we are not sure what they are going buy. We need, therefore, to get the product specifications from the customers and translate these into manufacturing

FIGURE 2.3 **Key Demand Management Tasks for Each Environment**

Tasks	MTS	ATO	MTO
Information	Provide forecast	Configuration management	Product specifications
Planning	Project inventory levels	Determine delivery dates	Provide engineering capacity
Control	Assure customer service levels	Meet delivery dates	Adjust capacity to customer needs

terms in the company. This means that a task of demand management in this environment is to coordinate information on customers' product needs with engineering.

The need for engineering resources in the engineer-to-order case is somewhat different than in the make-to-order case. In the make-to-order environment, engineering determines what materials will be required, what steps will be required in manufacturing, and the costs involved. The materials can come from the company's inventory or be purchased from suppliers. In the engineer-to-order environment, more of this same information is needed from customers, although more of the detail design may be left to the engineers than the customer. Because of the need for engineering resources in this environment, demand management's forecasting task now includes determining how much engineering capacity will be required to meet future customer needs. This may be complicated because some orders can be in progress, even though they aren't completely specified and engineered, so material coordination is still important. Although there is certainly some overlap among them, a summary of the major tasks in demand management for each of the environments is provided in Figure 2.3.

The customer order decoupling point could actually be with the supplier in the engineer-to-order case. In all the environments, suppliers' capabilities may limit what we are able to do, so coordination with them is essential. This span of involvement from customer to supplier gives rise to the term **supply chain** (sometimes called the **demand chain**), and the coordination of activities along the supply chain is referred to as **supply chain management.** This is a concept that we will see again in our discussion of demand management.

Communicating with Other MPC Modules and Customers

Regardless of the environment, demand management has important internal and external communication tasks. Forecast information must be provided to sales and operations planning (SOP). Detailed demand information must be communicated to master production scheduling (MPS), and information on product availability must be made available to customers both for planning purposes and to manage the day-to-day customer order activities. Some of the major communication needs are shown in Figure 2.4.

Sales and Operations Planning

A key requirement for demand management communication with sales and operations planning is to provide demand forecast information. In turn, sales and operations planning

FIGURE 2.4 **Demand Management Communication Activities for Each Environment**

Connection	MTS	ATO	MTO
SOP	Demand forecasts	Demand forecasts, product family mix	Demand forecasts, engineering detail
MPS	Actual demands	Mix forecasts, actual demands	Final configuration
Customer(s)	Next inventory replenishment	Configuration issues, delivery date	Design status, delivery date

will provide coordinated sales and operations plans. In order for these plans to be comprehensive, all sources of demand must be accounted for, both in quantity and timing. It is not sufficient to simply determine the market needs for product. To get a complete picture of the requirements for manufacturing capacity, engineering resources, and material needs, we must gather demand information for spare parts, inter- and intracompany transfers, promotion requirements, pipeline buildups, quality assurance needs, exhibition or pilot project requirements, and even charitable donations. Sometimes this is more difficult than it appears. The difficulty seems to be greatest for companies with a significant number of interplant transfers. We've often heard plant managers complain that their worst customer is a sister plant or division.

Choosing the appropriate measure for determining capacity needs is important to effective communication between demand management and SOP. The measure can vary with the environment. For instance, material capacity may be most important in the make-to-stock environment, while it may be machine and/or labor hours in the make-to-order case. Engineering capacity is often most critical in the engineer-to-order environment. It is essential that the demand management communication with sales and operations planning be in the proper units for the development of their plans. Moreover, both internal and external timing issues need to be communicated. For instance, if changes in the timing of deliveries to a significant customer could affect the plans, this information must be communicated to sales and operations planning. Similarly, a major change in distribution inventory policy might influence the plan.

Sales and operations planning may develop plans by product families, geographical regions, organizational units, or even combinations of these and other categories. This means the plans may not line up completely with the market. For instance, some customers may want only some units from each of several families, while others may want several complete families. Moreover, the sales and operations plans may be stated in dollars or some other aggregate measure, while the market buys specific products. This creates the need for demand management to translate and synchronize the communication of data between market activities and SOP.

Master Production Scheduling

Interactions between demand management and master production scheduling (MPS) are frequent and detailed. As customer orders are received and entered into the MPS, the detailed order information must be provided to the master production scheduler as the orders occur. Similarly, demand management needs information on the status of orders, capacity

FIGURE 2.5
Forecasts Consumed by Orders

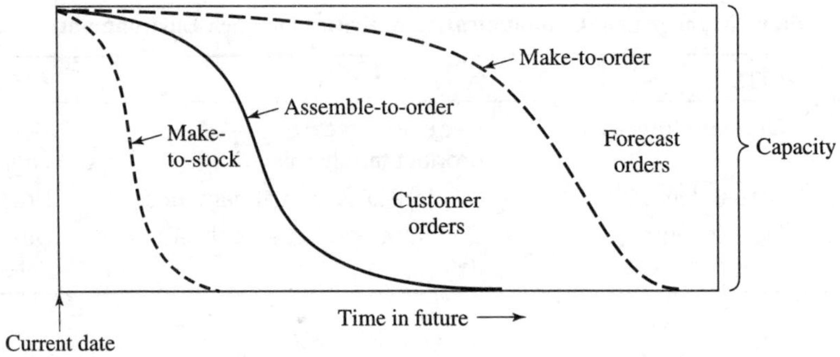

consumed, and capacity available so customers can be kept informed. Details vary significantly between make-to-stock, assemble-to-order, and make-to-order environments. In all instances, however, the underlying concept is that forecasts are consumed over time by actual customer orders, as Figure 2.5 shows. In each case, forecast future orders lie to the right and above the line, while actual customer orders are to the left and below the line.

Observe in Figure 2.5 that the lines for the three environments are quite different. For the make-to-stock environment, there are very few actual customer orders, since demand is generally satisfied from inventory. This reflects the need to manage the finished goods inventory. In the assemble-to-order environment there are customer orders already booked for several periods into the future, reflecting the need to provide accurate delivery promise dates to the customers. Still different demand management problems confront the firm with a make (engineer)-to-order environment, even though there's a larger backlog of customer orders. Communication between the firm and the customer first involves engineering, as orders become completely specified, and then project management status and delivery date promising.

The types of uncertainty also differ between these environments. In the make-to-stock case, uncertainty is largely in the demand variations around the forecast at each of the inventory locations. In this case, additional levels of inventory **(safety stock)** are held in order to provide the service levels required. In the assemble-to-order case, the uncertainty involves not only the quantity and timing of customer orders but product mix as well. For the make-to-order environment, the uncertainty is often not the timing or quantity of the customer order but, rather, what level of company resources will be required to complete the engineering and produce the product once the exact requirements are determined. One aspect of the communications between master production scheduling and demand management is to facilitate buffering against the uncertainties that exist.

Dealing with Customers on a Day-to-Day Basis

A primary function of the demand management module is converting specific day-to-day customer orders into detailed MPC actions. Through the demand management function, actual demands consume the planned materials and capacities. Actual customer demands must be converted into production actions regardless of whether the firm manufactures make-to-stock, assemble-to-order, or make-to-order products. Details may vary, depending on the nature of the company's manufacturing environment.

In make-to-order environments, the primary activity is controlling the progress of customer orders in order to meet the promised delivery dates. Any engineering or manufacturing changes must be related to the master production scheduler to determine their impact on the final delivery to the customer. While firms often perform this function the same way for assemble-to-order products, only limited communication with engineering would be needed to determine promise dates. In both these environments, there's communication from the customer (a request for a product) and to the customer (a delivery date) through the demand management module. Later there may be additional communication with the customer to respond to order status requests. These aspects of demand management have such names as **order entry, order booking,** and **customer order service.**

In a make-to-stock environment, demand management doesn't ordinarily provide customer promise dates. Because finished goods are stocked, the customer is most often served from inventory. If there's insufficient inventory for a specific request, the customer must be told when more will be available or, if there's allocation, told what portion of the request can be satisfied. Conversion of customer orders to MPC actions in the make-to-stock environment triggers resupply of the inventory from which sales are made. This conversion is largely through forecasting, since the resupply decision is in anticipation of customer orders.

In all these environments, extraordinary demands often must be accommodated. Examples include replacement of items after a disaster, advance orders in the make-to-stock environment, unexpected interplant needs, large spare-part orders, provision of demonstration units, and increased channel inventories. These all represent "real" demands on the material system.

Some clear principles emerge from this consideration of the relationship between demand management and the other modules in the front end of the MPC system. It is essential that all sources of demand be identified and incorporated in the planning and control activities of the firm. Demand management is responsible, as well, for communicating with the customers. Keeping the customer honestly informed of the status of an order is important to customer satisfaction, even if it is bad news that must be communicated.

Information Use in Demand Management

The information gathered in demand management can be used to enhance current and future performance of the firm. Some ways in which this is done are discussed below.

Make-to-Knowledge

As shown in Figure 2.5, a basic concept of demand management is that there is a "pipe" of capacity, which is filled in the short run with customer orders and the long run with forecasts; order entry is a process of consuming the forecast with actual orders. Performance has improved for many state-of-the-art situations, where supply chain partnerships are created. Between these suppliers and customers the goal is to improve the competitiveness of the entire chain, not just that of each of the companies independently. In some cases this allows the two firms to operate with **knowledge** of the other firm's needs. Figure 2.6 depicts this situation where a supplier has a forecast of demand, a set of actual orders, and also knowledge of the situation in some key customers. Examples of such knowledge would include the customer's inventory position (when using vender managed inventories, for example) and/or production schedule. This information allows one to know as closely as the customer when an order will be needed. This reduces the dependency on forecasts.

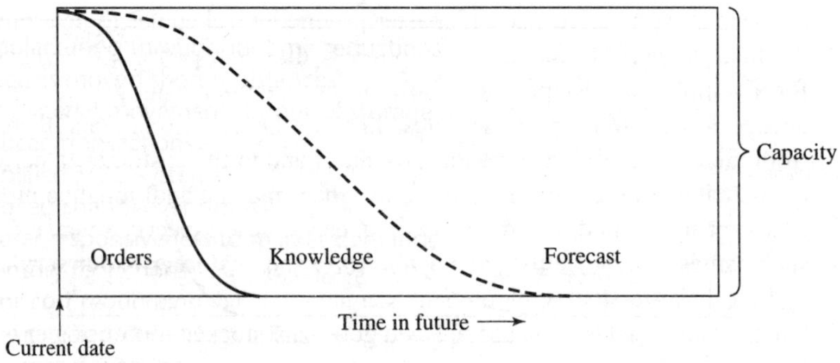

FIGURE 2.6
Replacing Forecasts with Knowledge

The knowledge comes from a natural evolution in the use of **electronic data interchange (EDI)** and **Internet**-based systems. The first interfirm applications of these communication means tends to consist of electronically processing transactions, such as orders, invoices, and payments. But a logical next step is to use the information channels to enhance knowledge. This requires determining the key data in the customers' and suppliers' companies that could be accessed by the partnership for better overall effectiveness. There are important potential implications from using knowledge. One example is the decreasing number of order transactions. If the goal is to maximize effectiveness of the overall supply chain, many of these types of transactions can be eliminated.

Data Capture and Monitoring

Data capture and monitoring activities of demand management fall into two broad categories: the overall market and the detailed product mix. The data most appropriate for sales and operations planning is overall market trends and patterns for the product familes. The intent is to determine on an ongoing basis any changes in the general levels of actual business for input to the sales and operations planning process. The second activity concerns monitoring the product mix for master production scheduling and customer order promising. The intent is to quickly determine changes in customer preferences for adjusting manufacturing and providing delivery information.

For both the overall market and the detailed product mix, it's important to capture actual demand data where possible. Many companies use sales instead of demand for purposes of making demand projections. Unless all demands have been satisfied, sales can understate actual demand. In other instances we know of firms that use shipments as the basis for projecting demands. In one such instance, the company concluded its demand was increasing since its shipments were increasing. Not until they had committed to increased raw-material purchases did they realize the increased shipments were replacement orders for two successive overseas shipments lost at sea.

It's in demand management that we explicitly define service levels and resultant safety stocks. The requisite degree of production flexibility for responding to mix or engineering design changes is set here as well. Then, through conversion of day-to-day customer orders into product shipments, we realize the company's actual service levels. Careful capture and management of actual demands can provide the stability needed for efficient production, and that stability provides the basis for realistic customer promises and service. Booking actual orders also serves to monitor demand against forecasts. As changes occur in the marketplace, demand management can and should routinely pick them up, indicating when managerial attention is required.

Customer Relationship Management

An important tool for gathering information on customers is **customer relationship management (CRM).** This is a very broad topic in its own right, so we discuss only a few of the demand management uses of the tool. In many consumer product companies, particularly those establishing supply chain relationships over the Internet, individual customer data is being captured and monitored by using CRM software. Because the data comes from requests by individual customers, it reflects more closely actual customer demand. In addition, it can provide closer insights on the real current needs of customers than historical data or projected trends. For MTS firms, capturing information at this level of detail can help to discern early demand and mix trends, provide the basis for new products and services, and lead to the development of knowledge-gaining activities that improve efficiency along the supply chain.

In the make- or assemble-to-order environments, CRM can be a useful means for developing similar insights into the customers. Data from CRM can be used to develop make-to-knowledge plans on an individual customer basis. Gathering current information on the customers' preferences can provide early warnings of shifts in design and mix preferences. This can be a big advantage to engineering and also provide information that could be useful in the development of raw material purchasing and manufacturing scheduling. Although not as explicit as the knowledge available with vendor-managed inventories, it can be useful in managing mix and service levels.

Outbound Product Flow

Physical distribution (outbound product flow) activities are planned on the basis of the information developed in the demand management function. Customer delivery promise dates, inventory resupply shipments, interplant shipments, and other such information from demand management are used to develop short-term transportation schedules. Information on the specific timing for resupply shipments can be integrated with distribution planning as well. For example, the information can be used to schedule resources at the warehouse and provide for the delivery capacity needed.

The distribution equivalent of the SOP and MPS function is the determination of the overall plans for moving the product to the customer and scheduling the shipments through the distribution system. This means determining the transportation and warehouse capacity, scheduling the movement of product and accounting for product availability so customers can be kept informed. The management of product distribution requires the same comprehensiveness of demand determination that the other functions need, since it is within this capacity derived from that demand that the day-to-day distribution function operates. Adequate planning of the capacity needs greatly facilitates day-to-day distribution operations.

Managing Demand

As we said at the start of this chapter, demand management is the gateway module between the company and marketplace. As such, it is where market intelligence is gathered, forecasts of demand are developed, and status information on customer orders is maintained. Much of what is required in managing demand is the discipline to be honest with both the internal and external customers. This is partly political, partly organizational, and partly a systems issue. In this section we look at some of the internal demand management activities that are required to effectively manage demand, including organization and systems monitoring. We'll also look at demand management's role in balancing supply and demand.

Organizing for Demand Management

Most companies already perform many, if not all, the activities associated with demand management. In many instances, organizational responsibility for these activities is widely scattered throughout the firm. The finance or credit department performs credit checks and order screening associated with customer orders. Sales, customer service, or supply chain management departments handle order entry or booking. Outbound product activities are associated with the distribution, traffic, or logistics departments of firms.

Organizational responsibility for demand management tends to be a function of the organization's history and nature. In marketing-oriented firms (where success requires close contact with demand trends and good customer relations), demand management might well be performed by the marketing or sales organization. In firms where product development requires close interaction between engineering and customers, a technical services department might manage demand. Some companies establish a materials or supply chain management function to coordinate demand management activities. These tend to be firms that feel it important to manage the flow of materials from purchasing raw materials through the production process to the customer. In all instances, we must clearly assign responsibilities to make sure nothing is left to chance.

If flexibility is a key objective, then management must carefully design and enforce rules for interacting with the system and customers so the system can provide this flexibility. By this we mean customer order processing must be established and enforced through the communication to the master production scheduling module. It involves carefully establishing rules for serving particular special customers. For example, if an extraordinarily large order is received at a field warehouse, procedures need to be established for determining whether that order will be allowed to consume a large portion of the local inventory or be passed back to the factory. We must define and enforce limits within which changes can be made. If a manager violates any of these procedures—for example, by saying, "I don't care how you do it, but customer X must get the order by time Y"—demand management is seriously undercut.

A useful technique for defining and managing these areas of responsibility is to require higher and higher levels of approval the nearer to the current date that a change is requested. This procedure doesn't preclude a change but does force a higher level of review for schedule changes to be made near term. The underlying concept is to take the informal bargaining out of the system. By establishing and enforcing such procedures for order entry, customer delivery date promising, changes to the material system, and responses to mix changes in the product line, everyone plays by the same rules. Clearly this is more a matter of management discipline than technique. The ability to respond "What don't you want?" to the statement "I have to have it right away" for a particular customer request helps establish this discipline.

Monitoring the Demand Management Systems

If demand management is to perform its role in the MPC system well, the data that are produced must be accurate, timely, and appropriate. This goes not only for the information that is consumed internally, but also for information that is provided to customers. Obviously this means that the data (both input and output) must be monitored, and it also means that the systems themselves must be monitored. If forecasts for a particular product line suddenly increase fourfold, there had better be a way that someone can find this out and start tracking down why. To do this requires data monitoring capability, not only of the input data but the calculated data as well. The last thing you want is to be communicating patently wrong information to your customers. Think of the implications of either a too short or a too long delivery date promise, for example.

Monitoring the input and output of the configuration management system can disclose product opportunities and provide insights for managing the priorities for producing product modules and options. If customers are increasingly requesting product combinations that can't be built, it might be a signal to engineering to work on making the products feasible. These combinations could represent new product offerings. If the combinations that are being correctly configured are changing, it might mean that the demand for specific components is changing and manufacturing priorities should be adjusted. When manufacturing and/or engineering starts complaining that too many "bad" combinations are getting through configuration, it could mean that something has gone awry in the configuration management system.

Similar opportunities and concerns can arise in the order entry system. At order entry time there is an opportunity to pick up market intelligence through CRM, cross-sell complementary products, and further customer relationships. The essence of the complaints from customers, incorrect orders, missing information, and other such tips may signal the need for more training. Complaints from manufacturing about insufficient information from the customer may also mean more training is needed or could disclose a problem in the system itself. Consistent late or early delivery could signal a problem in the MPS–demand management communication link or some other aspect of delivery date promising.

The common theme in all of these examples is that data must be captured and evaluated to keep the system honest. As a key communication link to the market, it is particularly important to monitor the systems in demand management. An effective demand management module will gather marketing information, generate forecast information, screen and monitor performance information, and provide detailed action instructions to the material planning and control system. Only by careful monitoring of the system can we be assured that this is done effectively.

Balancing Supply and Demand

A key element of the demand management module is providing the information to help balance the supply of products with the demand. Gathering intelligence on actual conditions in the marketplace provides the basis for deciding whether to change the company's plans. We saw, in the forecasting section, the use of pyramid forecasting to harmonize various forecasts, other sources of information on the market, and company goals. At times this process will leave some potential demand unfulfilled. There are a myriad of legitimate reasons for this. Investments in capacity may not be warranted, some product lines may not be sufficiently profitable, key materials may be in short supply, and so forth.

At this time real management discipline is required. Purposely leaving some demand on the table is extremely difficult. A pleading customer is hard to turn away. Perhaps the most important activity in demand management is to be honest with customers. In our experience, customers prefer honest answers (even if they're unpleasant) to inaccurate information. A demand management module with discipline in the management and effective systems provides the basis for honest communication with customers. They can be told when to expect delivery or when inventory will be replenished—and they can count on it. Providing the basis for honest communication with customers can pay handsome dividends in terms of customer loyalty.

Collaborative Planning, Forecasting, and Replenishment (CPFR)

CPFR represents a major enhancement of the principles of demand management presented earlier in this chapter. This approach is a recent innovation for dramatically improving communications between customers and suppliers in forecasting product demand. It was developed by the Voluntary Interindustry Commerce Standards Association to help retailers in fast-paced demand situations improve their competitiveness in both cost and delivery performance. CPFR focuses on reducing the variance between supply and demand for individual products. It is based on making organizational changes in both customer and supplier companies to improve communication and collaboration, developing new business processes for creating forecast information, and introducing daily communication between companies of a shared forecast. CPFR can benefit both the customer and the supplier by helping increase sales and fill rates while, at the same time, reducing inventories. This approach is especially powerful when one or a few customers represent a large portion of a supplier's business.

The concept of CPFR is to enable customers and suppliers to work together in a close, collaborative way to improve the understanding and communication of product forecast information. The mutual objective is to improve business results for each individual company and for the combined supply chain. Successful adoption of CPFR was reported by Sears and Michelin in their joint initiation of collaboration involving 220 Michelin stock-keeping units (SKUs) at all of Sears's Auto Center and National Tire and Battery locations.[1] In this case, Sears reduced in-store stock levels by 4.3 percent, increased distribution centers-to-store fill rates by 10.7 percent, and generated additional margin dollars. The combined Michelin and Sears inventory levels were reduced by 25 percent.

In another case, CPFR was initiated by a manufacturer to improve its competitiveness. Motorola reports the implementation of CPFR in its Mobile Device Division, where sales were both highly variable and not synchronized with actual customer demand.[2] Motorola lacked visibility into its retailer's distribution centers, and as a result, forecast error was very high, resulting in excessive stockouts. After implementing CPFR Motorola reports that there were dramatic improvements in forecast accuracy, inventory reserved for retailers decreased by 30 percent, transportation costs were cut in half, cell phone promotions improved, and new product launches were better executed. Motorola's retailers reported

[1]Hank Steermann, The "Sears-Michelin Experience," *Supply Chain Management Review,* July/August 2003.

[2]Jerold P. Cederlund, Rajiv Kohli, Susan A. Sherer, and Yuliang Yao, "How Motorola Put CPFR into Action," *Supply Chain Management Review,* October 2007.

FIGURE 2.7
The Nine-Step CPFR Process Model

Step 1
Establish collaborative relationship
Step 2
Create joint business plan
Step 3
Create sales forecast
Step 4
Identify exceptions to the sales forecast
Step 5
Resolve/collaborate on exception items
Step 6
Create order forecast
Step 7
Identify exceptions to order forecast
Step 8
Resolve/collaborate on exception items
Step 9
Generate order

Source: Voluntary Interindustry Commerce Standards Association.

quick reductions in inventory at their distribution centers because of less need for buffer stock. Stockouts were reduced by one-third.

Nine-Step CPFR Process Model

The Voluntary Interindustry Commerce Standards Association developed a nine-step CPFR process model to provide a general framework for companies interested in implementing CPFR (see Figure 2.7). This framework provides retailers and suppliers with general guidelines for sharing key supply chain information and coordinating their plans. Under CPFR, supply chain partners develop one consensus forecast. This forecast can be developed collaboratively, or one of the partners can provide an initial forecast that is then used as the basis for developing a collaborative forecast. Once the collaborative forecast is developed, then the supply chain partners can go about optimizing the activities of their companies. As a result, production schedules can then be developed by the supplier based on the actual demand at the retailer.

Steps 1 and 2 of the CPFR Model

The first two steps in the model, establishing a collaborative relationship and creating a joint business plan, are critical in ensuring a successful CPFR implementation. In many companies, this means moving away from a culture of arm's length transactional relationships with customers or suppliers. Changing a company's culture can take many months to accomplish. CPFR projects can fail because of a lack of executive support, lack of collaboration rigor, or unclear objectives at the outset.

It is important to change the firm's business strategy to one that supports close collaboration between companies and to share sensitive demand information. Key activities at both the supplier and the customer include coming to agreement on common business objectives and strategy, changing the organization structure to facilitate close collaboration, and redesigning the planning processes so that effective problem identification and resolution can actually occur. Data sharing and the choice of data-sharing technology represent critical management issues in developing a solid business partnership. Deciding what information will be shared with the customers or suppliers, sharing the business strategy, and getting customers' or suppliers' agreement to it are major issues. If these changes are made, the close collaborative in supply chain relationships emphasized under CPFR can be achieved, leading to a better forecasting of demand and product requirements.

Motorola reports that an early step was to convince retailers that a long-term collaborative relationship would be in the retailer's best interest and that Motorola's organization would support such close collaborative efforts with customers.[3] For the first six weeks, the Motorola team focused on existing delivery problems by holding daily meetings to review every purchase order, demonstrating improved on-time delivery in order to gain trust. Motorola also pre-built products in anticipation of a stock shortage well before the customer placed the order. This enabled Motorola to frequently surprise the customer by calling for the order at the same time that the customer was preparing to place the order. Motorola changed its organization to form a core business team and the related customer-focused operations teams. These teams worked with the selected retailers to agree upon appropriate service levels, metrics, and a plan for continuous improvement. They focused on common business goals and performance plans that represented both Motorola and customer metrics, such as inventory and sell-through.

Process Redesign

Process changes are essential in implementing a collaborative relationship and business strategy. Further, changes in information technology are often required to support the new process design and to provide more effective information sharing. The Sears-Michelin implementation experience illustrates the way process redesign and information technology improvements can be made in implementing CPFR.[4]

Figure 2.8 shows the Sears-Michelin project teams that were created to implement the project plan and achieve the activity timetables. These teams were created by the two companies to be responsible for the individual project activities. They included both business and technical personnel, working on a part-time basis. The teams took between 1 and 4 weeks to complete their assigned task, depending on the complexity of the task.

The initial team's task was to document the current supply chain business process, starting with the planning and forecasting activities and culminating with the product reaching the customer. This task involved understanding how the people in the Sears-Michelin supply chain interfaced. Individual activities were identified, noting who was involved, when the activities took place, and what systems were involved. People in both firms were asked to contribute information on sales forecasting, demand planning, production, store replenishment, and logistics. Once the process document was complete, a second team identified and evaluated opportunities for improvement by following the nine-step CPFR model. This

[3]Ibid.

[4]Steermann. "The Sears-Michelin Experience."

FIGURE 2.8
Project Teams

Business	Technical
Current business process	GNX Access/ setup
Evaluate opportunities	Software setup
Front-end arrangement	System testing/ quality assurance
Future business process	Evaluation and assessment

Source: Hank Steermann, "The Sears-Michelin Experience," *Supply Chain Management Review*, July/August 2003.

team focused on obtaining improvement in the areas of inventory reduction and increasing information visibility at the two companies.

Based on the areas of opportunity, a third team began to map the future business processes, documenting the improvement decisions and goals in a front-end arrangement. This work identified the items/SKUs involved, the data to be considered, program participants, business rules, and project accountability. Three of the teams shown in Figure 2.8 were involved in the process analysis and redesign. Four other teams were concerned with the Internet software aspects of this process. These teams are also shown in Figure 2.8.

Early in the project, Sears and Michelin decided they would share all supply chain information necessary under CPFR, using the Internet software provided by GNX (GlobalNetXchange) that provided a business-to-business exchange for the retail industry. GNX had previously reached an agreement with Manugistics Inc. to make its NetWORKS Collaboration software available online, enabling collaboration via the Internet. This system enables Sears and Michelin users to access CPFR information through a browser with a user ID and password. The software is flexible and allows views of the data to be tailored to users' specific needs. For example, a user can view information at the item level or aggregate to the desired level of the merchandise or location hierarchy. It allows the software to meet the needs of users who have different responsibilities while still allowing for meaningful analysis to be conducted.

The redesigned business process at Sears-Michelin has several important characteristics. First, *all of the CPFR data have been consolidated at a centralized location that is accessible to both the customer and the supplier.* Through the use of the hosted CPFR software, both companies can send files with the agreed-upon data components to GNX each week. Such data includes sales forecasts for regular and promotional products, inventory at both the Sears and Michelin locations, inventory on order for Sears, Michelin production plans, Sears future inventory demand, and actual sales for both regular and promotional products.

Although both companies may have had all of the required supply chain information previously, each company may have had only a portion of the data held by the other company. Consequently, decisions were often based on incomplete information.

Centralized data to support close collaboration has two advantages. The data are meaningful and consistent. The data are meaningful because they contain the key information required to develop good plans and forecasts. The data are consistent because the user is assured that the same data elements are updated at the same time each week. Also, because all of the supply chain data are available at a centralized location, it is easy to develop the key performance metrics into the software. For example, sales forecast accuracy can be routinely calculated for the two companies.

Second, *the centralized data can be used with disciplined business rules to create meaningful exception reports* that are e-mailed weekly to alert Sears and Michelin personnel to problems that are occurring within the supply chain. Such reports enable Sears and Michelin personnel to anticipate inventory and ordering problems and to take action to resolve problems/issues early enough to prevent such problems from affecting supply chain performance. The automated exception reports provide valuable information that allows issues to be discussed by users in regularly scheduled conference calls.

Finally, the *CPFR process has made meetings between the two companies much more productive.* Instead of having to expend substantial manual effort to create reports for these meetings, this work has been replaced by the information directly available from the CPFR software. The centralized information has created a new tool to view information such as an item's current inventory or the aggregated inventory for an item at different levels in the supply chain. For example, information enables users to track actual monthly performance versus planned performance.

Steps 3 through 9 in the CPFR Model

The organizational changes, adjustments to business strategy, and business process redesign efforts undertaken jointly by a customer and its supplier (as described in steps 1 and 2 of the model) are essential in achieving a close collaborative relationship. Once these steps have been taken, improvements in the daily communication of forecast, inventory, and order information can be made to improve organizational performance.

The daily communication of supply chain information is normally organized as a part of a regular monthly cycle and includes conference call meetings. Replenishment activities during the prior and current week as well as the sell-through position at the retailer are discussed with Motorola and its retailer in these meetings. This cycle represents an important part of the demand planning activity that occurs within the sales and operations planning cycle at the supplier firm. (See Chapter 4 of this text for a discussion of the sales and operations planning cycle.)

The CPFR process at Motorola provides a good example of the individual weekly activities in this cycle.[5] The communication process includes regular weekly meetings involving multiple points along the supply chain. As shown in Figure 2.9, the meeting in week 1 involves an operations review of the past month's performance. Early in the meeting, the teams review the positive and negative events of the past four weeks. The rest of the meeting is concerned with the strategic implications of what has occurred and the implications for the future forecast.

Forecasting is the focus of the meeting during week 2 of the cycle. Here, the teams develop the collaborative forecasts. On Monday the retailer loads its forecast for the next month. On Tuesday Motorola loads its forecast. On Wednesday, during the weekly call, the two teams

[5]Cederlund, Kohli, Sherer, and Yao, "How Motorola Put CPFR into Action."

FIGURE 2.9 **Monthly Meeting Communication Process**

Week	Objective	Motorola Participants	Retailer Participants	Topic for Review
1	Operations review	Replenishment analyst Sales manager Operations manager	Purchasing Sales operations Logistics and inventory management	Replenishment review Prior/current week sell-through Inventory position Open order review
2	Forecasting	Replenishment analyst Sales manager Business operations manager Marketing analyst	Purchasing Sales operations Logistics and inventory management Product marketing	Above plus the promotional schedule
3	Process improvement	Replenishment analyst Sales manager Business operations manager	Purchasing Sales operations Logistics and inventory management Product operations	Above plus 6-month forecast Forecast accuracy metrics Promotional schedule
4	Financial implications	Replenishment analyst Sales manager Business operations manager Financial analyst	Purchasing Sales operations Logistics and inventory management Finance	Above plus product performance review next 6 months Pricing Rebates Competitive information

Source: Jerold P. Cederlund, Rajiv Kohli, Susan A. Sherer, and Yuliang Yao, "How Motorola Put CPFR into Action," *Supply Chain Management Review,* October 2008.

jointly resolve differences line-by-line in the forecasts. The presence of the marketing analyst ensures that the teams can immediately resolve issues related to the discrepancies.

Process improvement is the primary concern of the meeting during week 3 of the cycle. The teams examine the issues brought up during the operational review and assign specific actions. They review what is working correctly in the business process and what is not working properly. They then focus on improving the forecasting and ordering process.

The financial implications of the process are the subject of the week 4 meeting. The effect that CPFR can have on a company's period-end goals is often overlooked. Having the financial planners attend the meeting with the customer account team helps in assessing the financial implications of the CPFR process. The participants can carefully plan the fiscal period ends for more accurate predictions of profit-and-loss and balance sheet items.

Concluding Principles

In this chapter we have reviewed the pivotal role of demand management in communicating with the market. Through the demand management module, information on the market is gathered, orders are entered, products are configured, manufacturing specifications are developed, and customers are informed of product availability and delivery times. The following principles will help managers to effectively carry out these tasks.

- Demand management systems and procedures must be aligned with the market environment of the firm.
- All demands on product resources must be identified and accounted for in providing forecast information to sales and operations planning and master production scheduling.
- Data capture must not be limited to sales (demand) but should include knowledge, trends, systems performance, and demand management performance.
- Implementing CPFR can lead to important organizational and business process improvements for the customer and the supplier.
- The CPFR process can improve customer service, sales, inventory, and margin performance for customers and suppliers in a supply chain.

Discussion Questions

1. The customer order decoupling point was described as the point at which the demand changed from independent to dependent. Describe what this means and why it is important to managers.
2. Provide examples of make-to-stock, assemble-to-order, and make-to-order products available in your area. What advantages do you see in moving from make-to-stock to assemble or make-to-order?

Problem

1. When a firm is able to move to an assemble-to-order capability from a make-to-stock approach, there can be a substantial reduction in the number of things that must be tracked and stored. For example, the Northland Computer Shop had decided to stop stocking assembled computers and moved to an assemble-to-order approach. Northland even invited customers to the work area to see their computer being assembled, a great customer relations ploy. The company estimated that there were seven hard disk choices, six mother boards (including the processor), five CD/DVD alternatives, three operating systems, and four other options.
   a. What was the total number of potential finished products?
   b. If it cost $10 per item to make a forecast each week, what is the weekly savings from forecasting just the components and options as compared to the potential number of finished products?

Chapter 3

Forecasting

In this chapter, we deal primarily with preparing forecast information for the MPC linkages within the MPC front end (e.g., those between SOP and MPS and demand management). Forecasting information can come from a variety of sources, have different levels of aggregation, incorporate different assumptions about the market, and manifest other differences that need reconciliation before it can be used for planning and control. Here we look at some of the bases upon which forecasting methods are determined, some of the reasoning behind aggregating forecasts, and some of the means by which forecasts are reconciled for planning purposes.

This chapter is organized around the following topics:

- *Providing appropriate forecast information:* What are the needs for forecast information within the firm?
- *Regression Analysis and Cyclic Decomposition Techniques:* What are the most used techniques for intermediate-term forecasts? How is seasonality considered in the forecasting model?
- *Short-term forecasting techniques:* What techniques are useful for short-term individual item forecasts and what are the metrics of forecast quality?
- *Using the forecasts:* What techniques are useful in keeping the detailed forecasts and aggregate management plans synchronized?

Providing Appropriate Forecast Information

Managers need forecasts for a variety of decisions. Among these are strategic decisions involving such things as constructing a new plant, developing more supplier capacity, expanding internationally, and other long-run companywide considerations. Forecasts for this type of decision are highly aggregated estimates of general business trends over the long term. These broadly based forecasts are much too general for sales and operations planning, even though some aggregation is necessary for SOP. The forecast needs for both these applications (strategic considerations and sales and operations planning) are different, as well, from the forecasts that are needed for short-term scheduling and execution decision making in master production scheduling. Not only is the basis of the forecast different for each of these applications, but the investment in forecasting, the nature of the techniques used, and the frequency varies as well. A framework for some of the differences is provided in Figure 3.1.

FIGURE 3.1 **A Framework for Forecasting**

Nature of the Decision	Strategic Business Planning	Sales and Operations Planning	Master Production Scheduling and Control
Level of aggregation	Total sales or output volume	Product family units	Individual finished goods or components
Top management involvement	Intensive	When reconciling functional plans	Very little
Forecast frequency	Annual or less	Monthly or quarterly	Constantly
Length of forecast	Years by years or quarters	Several months to a year by months	A few days to weeks
Management investment in the forecast(s)	Very large	Moderate	Very little
Cost of data processing and acquisition	High	Moderate	Minimal
Useful techniques	Management judgment, economic growth models, regression	Aggregation of detailed forecasts, customer plans, regression	Projection techniques (moving averages, exponential smoothing)

The general principle indicated here is that the nature of the forecast must be matched with the nature of the decision. The level of aggregation, the amount of management review, the cost, and the time frame of the forecast needed really depends on the nature of the decision being made. Moreover, the source of the forecast can vary by need as well, as indicated by the useful techniques line in Figure 3.1. The frequency and number of forecasts needed for most short-term operating decisions don't warrant extensive management involvement, so computer-generated forecasts are utilized. Strategic decisions, on the other hand, are less frequent and involve more risk, thus justifying use of more expensive procedures and management involvement.

Forecasting for Strategic Business Planning

Among the decisions that require long-term, broadly based forecasts are those involving capital expansion projects, proposals to develop a new product line, and merger or acquisition opportunities. The forecasts are usually stated in very general terms such as total sales dollars or some output measure such as total tons, board feet, or engineering hours. This level of aggregation can be related to economic and business indicators such as the gross national product, net disposable income, or market share of a particular industry. In turn, it is related to measures of capacity that may be required to meet the future demands. Substantial managerial judgment is required in preparing and reviewing these forecasts since the risk from making (or not making) an investment can be very large.

Causal models and the statistical tools of regression and correlation analysis can be used to augment the managerial insight and judgment needed for making these forecasts. Such models relate the firm's business to indicators that are more easily forecast or are available as general information. For example, household fixtures and furniture sales are closely related to housing starts. Housing starts and building permits in an area are usually public information, readily available to the firm. The relationship between housing starts and furniture sales may be statistically modeled to provide another forecast of demand. In addition, there are accuracy measures available with the statistical techniques to help determine the usefulness of the forecast. Moreover, using these models can lead to improved forecasting results and can help neutralize any emotion involved in the decision.

Forecasting for Sales and Operations Planning

The forecasts needed for sales and operations planning ultimately provide the basis for plans that are usually stated in terms of planned sales and output of product families in dollars or some other aggregate measure. The plans extend for a few months up to a year into the future for each of the product lines they cover. The forecasts, then, must also be aggregated to the product family level and cover the same (or a greater) number of periods.

One important input into the forecasts for SOP is information on customer plans and current demand information. Insights into the customers' future plans are gained through discussions with marketing and communication with customers through demand management. This information can be augmented with current data on inventory balances, demand levels, and product mix preferences through programs like CRM and vendor-managed inventory (VMI). These are important sources of information for the development of the sales and operations plans.

A common means for producing an aggregated forecast for SOP is to sum the forecasts for the individual products in each product line. These totals can then be adjusted by incorporating knowledge of customers' plans, current trends, and any marketing plans that would influence demand. However the forecasts are developed, managerial insight and judgment are important in using them to develop the plans. Developing the forecast is not the same as developing the plan.

Forecasting for Master Production Scheduling and Control

Demand management supports the decisions made in the master production scheduling module by providing detailed forecasts on a nearly continuous basis. The result of the MPS decisions is a statement of how many of a finished product or component to make and when to do so. These decisions occur constantly as conditions change in the market and in manufacturing. Consequently, the flow of forecast information to the MPS is frequent and detailed.

Also occurring constantly are control decisions that change priorities for production, allocation of inventory, and destinations of shipments. As products move from purchasing of raw material to distribution of finished goods, changes that require adjustments occur in all areas of the process. To compensate for these changes, control decisions must be made quickly and efficiently to keep the product moving to the customer. If the demand for the product is dependent, then the timing and quantities can be calculated from the plans for their **parents** (the products that they are used on); if the demand is independent, then it must be forecast. Forecasting to support these day-to-day control decisions must be frequent, detailed, and timely.

To produce these detailed forecasts, it is most common to use mechanical procedures, procedures that can be incorporated into the demand management software. Most often, these are models for "casting forward" historical information to make the "fore cast." Implicit in this process is a belief that the past conditions that produced the historical demand won't change. However, we shouldn't draw from this the impression that managers can always rely on past information to estimate future activity. In the first place, in certain instances, we simply have no past data. This occurs, for example, when a new product is introduced, a future sales promotion is planned, a new competitor appears, or new legislation affects our business. These circumstances all illustrate the need for managerial review and modification of the forecast where special knowledge should be taken into account.

These different approaches simply underscore the variety of sources, aggregation, and purposes of forecasts. In the next two sections, we illustrate techniques that are appropriate for two different forecasting purposes. In the first, we address the issue of forecasting demand for the next 6 to 18 months in the future. This would be appropriate for making plans that relate to staffing sales teams, production capacity planning, estimating aggregate inventory levels, and cash flow analysis. Here, we introduce linear regression analysis and show how to augment the approach with adjustments for seasonal and other cyclical factors. After this, we discuss techniques appropriate for forecasts that extend out for 2 to 8 weeks in the future. These short-term forecasting techniques are commonly used in inventory control systems to trigger replenishment orders for items that are being actively controlled (we discuss these types of systems in Chapter 11).

Regression Analysis and Cyclic Decomposition Techniques

Regression can be defined as a functional relationship berween two or more correlated variables. It is used to predict one variable given the other. The relationship is usually developed from observed data. The data should be plotted first to see if they appear linear or if at least parts of the data are linear. *Linear regression* refers to the special class of regression where the relationship between variables forms a straight line.

The linear regression line is of the form $Y = a + bX$, where Y is the value of the dependent variable that we are solving for, a is the Y-intercept, b is the slope, and X is the independent variable. (In time series analysis, X is units of time.)

Linear regression is useful for long-term forecasting of major occurrences and aggregate planning. For example, linear regression would be very useful to forecast demands for product families. Even though demand for individual products within a family may vary widely during a time period, demand for the total product family is surprisingly smooth.

The major restriction in using **linear regression forecasting** is, as the name implies, that past data and future projections are assumed to fall about a straight line. Although this does limit its application, sometimes, if we use a shorter period of time, linear regression analysis can still be used. For example, there may be short segments of the longer period that are approximately linear.

Linear regression is used both for time series forecasting and for causal relationship forecasting. When the dependent variable (usually the vertical axis on a graph) changes as a result of time (plotted as the horizontal axis), it is time series analysis. If one variable changes because of the change in another variable, this is a causal relationship (such as the number of deaths from lung cancer increasing with the number of people who smoke).

We use the following example to demonstrate linear least squares regression analysis.

Example

Least Squares Method

A firm's sales for a product line during the 12 quarters of the past three years were as follows:

Quarter	Sales
1	600
2	1,550
3	1,500
4	1,500
5	2,400
6	3,100

Quarter	Sales
7	2,600
8	2,900
9	3,800
10	4,500
11	4,000
12	4,900

The firm wants to forecast each quarter of the fourth year—that is, quarters 13, 14, 15, and 16.

Solution

The least squares equation for linear regression is

$$Y = a + bx \tag{3.1}$$

where

Y = dependent variable computed by the equation

y = the actual dependent variable data point (used below)

a = Y-intercept

b = slope of the line

x = time period

The least squares method tries to fit the line to the data *that minimizes the sum of the squares of the vertical distance* between each data point and its corresponding point on the line. If a straight line is drawn through the general area of the points, the difference between the point and the line is $y - Y$. Figure 3.2 shows these differences. The sum of the squares of the differences between the plotted data points and the line points is

$$(y_1 - Y_1)^2 + (y_2 - Y_2)^2 + \cdots + (y_{12} - Y_{12})^2$$

The best line to use is the one that minimizes this total.

As before, the straight line equation is

$$Y = a + bx$$

FIGURE 3.2
Least Squares Regression Line

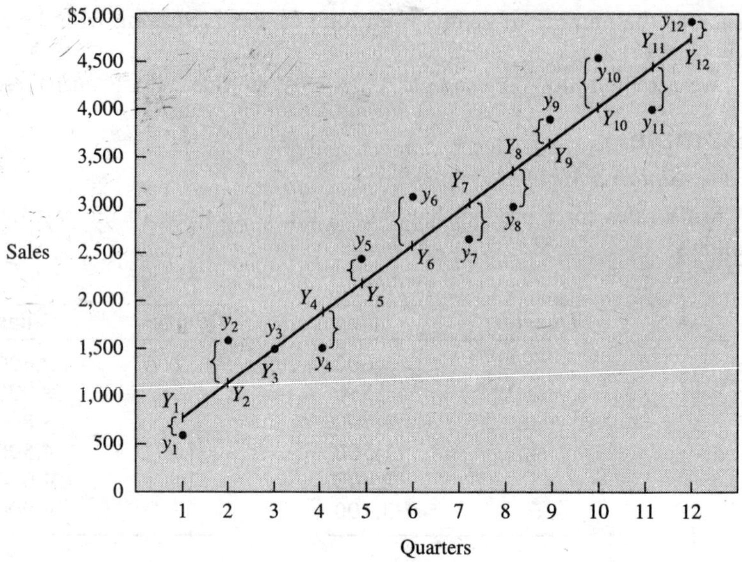

Previously we determined *a* and *b* from the graph. In the least squares method, the equations for *a* and *b* are

$$a = \bar{y} - b\bar{x} \quad \textbf{(3.2)}$$

$$b = \frac{\sum xy - n\bar{x} . \bar{y}}{\sum x^2 - n\bar{x}^2} \quad \textbf{(3.3)}$$

where

a = Y intercept

b = slope of the line

$\bar{y}$ = average of all y's

$\bar{x}$ = average of all x's

x = x value at each data point

y = y value at each data point

n = number of data points

Y = value of the dependent variable computed with the regression equation

Figure 3.3 shows these computations carried out for the 12 data points in the problem. Note that the final equation for Y shows an intercept of 441.6 and a slope of 359.6. The slope shows that for every unit change in X, Y changes by 359.6.

FIGURE 3.3
Least Squares Regression Analysis

(1) x	(2) y	(3) xy	(4) x^2	(5) y^2	(6) Y
1	600	600	1	360,000	801.3
2	1,550	3,100	4	2,402,500	1,160.9
3	1,500	4,500	9	2,250,000	1,520.5
4	1,500	6,000	16	2,250,000	1,880.1
5	2,400	12,000	25	5,760,000	2,239.7
6	3,100	18,600	36	9,610,000	2,599.4
7	2,600	18,200	49	6,760,000	2,959.0
8	2,900	23,200	64	8,410,000	3,318.6
9	3,800	34,200	81	14,440,000	3,678.2
10	4,500	45,000	100	20,250,000	4,037.8
11	4,000	44,000	121	16,000,000	4,397.4
12	4,900	58,800	144	24,010,000	4,757.1
78	33,350	268,200	650	112,502,500	

$\bar{x} = 6.5$ $b = 359.6153$

$\bar{y} = 2{,}779.17$ $a = 441.6666$

Therefore, $Y = 441.66 + 359.6x$

$S_{yx} = 363.9$

Strictly based on the equation, forecasts for periods 13 through 16 would be

$$Y_{13} = 441.6 + 359.6(13) = 5{,}116.4$$

$$Y_{14} = 441.6 + 359.6(14) = 5{,}476.0$$

$$Y_{15} = 441.6 + 359.6(15) = 5{,}835.6$$

$$Y_{16} = 441.6 + 359.6(16) = 6{,}195.2$$

The standard error of estimate, or how well the line fits the data, is

$$S_{yx} = \sqrt{\frac{\sum_{i=1}^{n}(y_i - Y_i)^2}{n-2}} \tag{3.4}$$

The standard error of estimate is computed from the second and last columns of Figure 3.3:

$$S_{yx} = \sqrt{\frac{(600 - 801.3)^2 + (1{,}550 - 1{,}160.9)^2 + (1{,}500 - 1{,}520.5)^2 + \cdots + (4{,}900 - 4{,}757.1)^2}{10}}$$

$$= 363.9$$

Microsoft® Excel has a very powerful regression tool designed to perform these calculations. To use the tool, a table is needed that contains data relevant to the problem (see Figure 3.4). The tool is part of the Data Analysis ToolPak that is accessed from the Tools menu

FIGURE 3.4
Excel Regression Tool

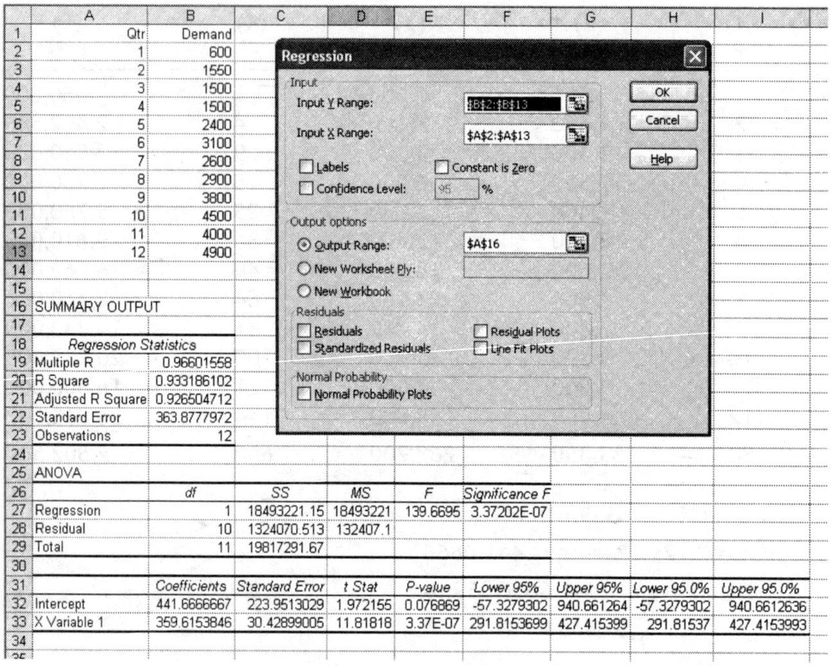

(or Data tab in Excel 2007). You may need to add this by using the Add-In option under Tools.

To use the tool, first input the data in two columns in your spreadsheet, then access the Regression option from the Tools → Data Analysis menu. Next, specify the Y Range, which is B2:B13, and the X-Range, which is A2:A13 in our example. Finally, an Output Range is specified. This is where you would like the results of the regression analysis placed in your spreadsheet. In the example, A16 is entered. There is some information provided that goes beyond what we have covered, but what you are looking for is the Intercept and X Variable coefficients that correspond to the intercept and slope values in the linear equation. These are in rows 32 and 33 in Figure 3.4.

We discuss the possible existence of seasonal components in the next section on decomposition of a time series.

Decomposition of a Time Series

A *time series* can be defined as chronologically ordered data that may contain one or more components of demand: trend, seasonal, cyclical, autocorrelation, and random. *Decomposition* of a time series means identifying and separating the time series data into these components. In practice, it is relatively easy to identify the trend (even without mathematical analysis, it is usually easy to plot and see the direction of movement) and the seasonal component (by comparing the same period year to year). It is considerably more difficult to identify the cycles (these may be many months or years long), autocorrelation, and random components. (The forecaster usually calls random anything left over that cannot be identified as another component.)

FIGURE 3.5 **Additive and Multiplicative Seasonal Variation Superimposed on Changing Trend**

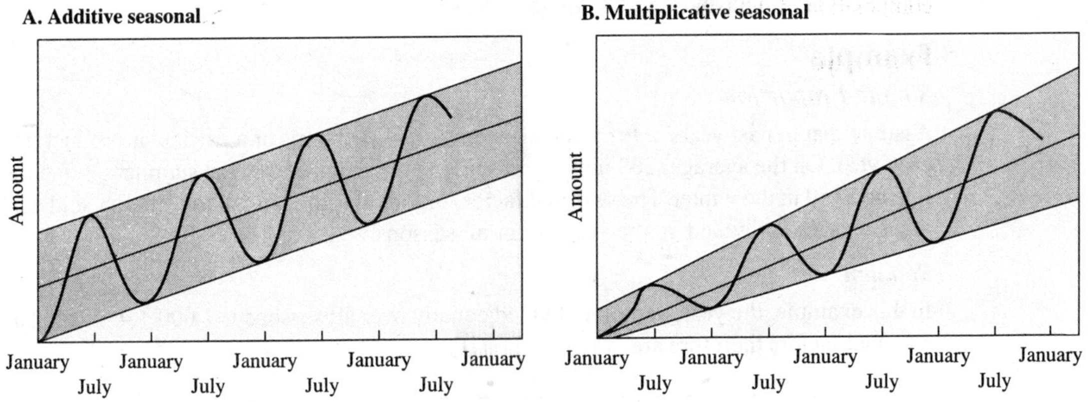

When demand contains both seasonal and trend effects at the same time, the question is how they relate to each other. In this description, we examine two types of seasonal variation: *additive* and *multiplicative.*

Additive Seasonal Variation

Additive seasonal variation simply assumes that the seasonal amount is a constant no matter what the trend or average amount is.

$$\text{Forecast including trend and seasonal} = \text{Trend} + \text{Seasonal}$$

Figure 3.5A shows an example of increasing trend with constant seasonal amounts.

Multiplicative Seasonal Variation

In multiplicative seasonal variation, the trend is multiplied by the seasonal factors.

$$\text{Forecast including trend and seasonal} = \text{Trend} \times \text{Seasonal factor}$$

Figure 3.5B shows the seasonal variation increasing as the trend increases because its size depends on the trend.

The multiplicative seasonal variation is the usual experience. Essentially, this says that the larger the basic amount projected, the larger the variation around this that we can expect.

Seasonal Factor (or Index)

A seasonal factor is the amount of correction needed in a time series to adjust for the season of the year.

We usually associate *seasonal* with a period of the year characterized by some particular activity. We use the word *cyclical* to indicate other than annual recurrent periods of repetitive activity.

The following examples show how seasonal indexes are determined and used to forecast (1) a simple calculation based on past seasonal data and (2) the trend and seasonal index from a hand-fit regression line. We follow this with a more formal procedure for the decomposition of data and forecasting using least squares regression.

Example

Simple Proportion

Assume that in past years, a firm sold an average of 1,000 units of a particular product line each year. On the average, 200 units were sold in the spring, 350 in the summer, 300 in the fall, and 150 in the winter. The seasonal factor (or index) is the ratio of the amount sold during each season divided by the average for all seasons.

Solution

In this example, the yearly amount divided equally over all seasons is 1,000 ÷ 4 = 250. The seasonal factors therefore are

	Past Sales	Average Sales for Each Season (1,000/4)	Seasonal Factor
Spring	200	250	200/250 = 0.8
Summer	350	250	350/250 = 1.4
Fall	300	250	300/250 = 1.2
Winter	150	250	150/250 = 0.6
Total	1,000		

Using these factors, if we expected demand for next year to be 1,100 units, we would forecast the demand to occur as

	Expected Demand for Next Year	Average Sales for Each Season (1,100/4)		Seasonal Factor		Next Year's Seasonal Forecast
Spring		275	×	0.8	=	220
Summer		275	×	1.4	=	385
Fall		275	×	1.2	=	330
Winter		275	×	0.6	=	165
Total	1,100					

The seasonal factor may be periodically updated as new data are available. The following example shows the seasonal factor and multiplicative seasonal variation.

Example

Computing Trend and Seasonal Factor from a Hand-Fit Straight Line

Here we must compute the trend as well as the seasonal factors.

Solution

We solve this problem by simply hand fitting a straight line through the data points and measuring the trend and intercept from the graph. Assume the history of data is

Quarter	Amount
I—2008	300
II—2008	200
III—2008	220
IV—2008	530

Quarter	Amount
I—2009	520
II—2009	420
III—2009	400
IV—2009	700

First, we plot as in Figure 3.6 and then visually fit a straight line through the data. (Naturally, this line and the resulting equation are subject to variation.) The equation for the line is

$$\text{Trend}_t = 170 + 55t$$

Our equation was derived from the intercept 170 plus a rise of $(610 - 170) \div 8$ periods. Next we can derive a seasonal index by comparing the actual data with the trend line as in Figure 3.7. The seasonal factor was developed by averaging the same quarters in each year.

FIGURE 3.6
Computing a Seasonal Factor from the Actual Data and Trend Line

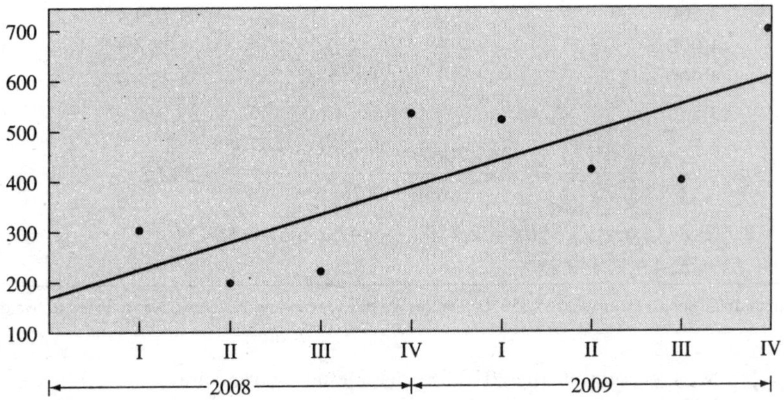

Quarter	Actual Amount	From Trend Equation $T_t = 170 + 55t$	Ratio of Actual ÷ Trend	Seasonal Factor (Average of Same Quarters in Both Years)
2008				
I	300	225	1.33	
II	200	280	.71	
III	220	335	.66	I—1.25
IV	530	390	1.36	II—0.78
2009				III—0.69
I	520	445	1.17	IV—1.25
II	420	500	.84	
III	400	555	.72	
IV	700	610	1.15	

FIGURE 3.7 Deseasonalized Demand

(1) Period (x)	(2) Quarter	(3) Actual Demand (y)	(4) Average of the Same Quarters of Each Year	(5) Seasonal Factor	(6) Deseasonalized Demand (y_d) Col. (3) ÷ Col. (5)	(7) x^2 (Col. 1)^2	(8) $x \times y_d$ Col. (1) × Col. (6)
1	I	600	(600 + 2,400 + 3,800)/3 = 2,266.7	0.82	735.7	1	735.7
2	II	1,550	(1,550 + 3,100 + 4,500)/3 = 3,050	1.10	1,412.4	4	2,824.7
3	III	1,500	(1,500 + 2,600 + 4,000)/3 = 2,700	0.97	1,544.0	9	4,631.9
4	IV	1,500	(1,500 + 2,900 + 4,900)/3 = 3,100	1.12	1,344.8	16	5,379.0
5	I	2,400		0.82	2,942.6	25	14,713.2
6	II	3,100		1.10	2,824.7	36	16,948.4
7	III	2,600		0.97	2,676.2	49	18,733.6
8	IV	2,900		1.12	2,599.9	64	20,798.9
9	I	3,800		0.82	4,659.2	81	41,932.7
10	II	4,500		1.10	4,100.4	100	41,004.1
11	III	4,000		0.97	4,117.3	121	45,290.1
12	IV	4,900		1.12	4,392.9	144	52,714.5
78		33,350		12.03	33,350.1*	650	265,706.9

$$\bar{x} = \frac{78}{12} = 6.5 \qquad b = \frac{\Sigma x y_d - n\bar{x}\bar{y}_d}{\Sigma x^2 - n\bar{x}^2} = \frac{265{,}706.9 - 12(6.5)2{,}779.2}{650 - 12(6.5)^2} = 342.2$$

$\bar{y}_d = 33{,}350/12 = 2{,}779.2 \qquad a = \bar{y}_d - b\bar{x} = 2{,}779.2 - 342.2(6.5) = 554.9$

Therefore, $Y = a + bx = 554.9 + 342.2x$

*Column 3 and column 6 totals should be equal at 33,350. Differences are due to rounding. Column 5 was rounded to two decimal places.

We can compute the 2010 forecast including trend and seasonal factors (FITS) as follows:

$$\text{FITS}_t = \text{Trend} \times \text{Seasonal}$$

$$\text{I—2008 FITS}_9 = [170 + 55(9)]1.25 = 831$$

$$\text{II—2008 FITS}_{10} = [170 + 55(10)]0.78 = 562$$

$$\text{III—2008 FITS}_{11} = [170 + 55(11)]0.69 = 535$$

$$\text{IV—2008 FITS}_{12} = [170 + 55(12)]1.25 = 1{,}038$$

Decomposition Using Least Squares Regression

Decomposition of a time series means finding the series' basic components of trend, seasonal, and cyclical. Indexes are calculated for seasons and cycles. The forecasting procedure then reverses the process by projecting the trend and adjusting it by the seasonal and cyclical indexes, which were determined in the decomposition process. More formally, the process is

1. Decompose the time series into its components.
   a. Find seasonal component.

   b. Deseasonalize the demand.
   c. Find trend component.
2. Forecast future values of each component.
   a. Project trend component into the future.
   b. Multiply trend component by seasonal component.

Note that the random component is not included in this list. We implicitly remove the random component from the time series when we average as in step 1. It is pointless to attempt a projection of the random component in step 2 unless we have information about some unusual event, such as a major labor dispute, that could adversely affect product demand (and this would not really be random).

Figure 3.7 shows the decomposition of a time series using least squares regression and the same basic data we used in our earlier examples. Each data point corresponds to using a single three-month quarter of the three-year (12-quarter) period. Our objective is to forecast demand for the four quarters of the fourth year.

Step 1. Determine the seasonal factor (or index). Figure 3.7 summarizes the calculations needed. Column 4 develops an average for the same quarters in the three-year period. For example, the first quarters of the three years are added together and divided by three. A seasonal factor is then derived by dividing that average by the general average for all 12 quarters $\left(\frac{33{,}350}{12}, \text{ or } 2{,}779\right)$. These are entered in column 5. Note that the seasonal factors are identical for similar quarters in each year.

Step 2. Deseasonalize the original data. To remove the seasonal effect on the data, we divide the original data by the seasonal factor. This step is called the deseasonalization of demand and is shown in column 6 of Figure 3.7.

Step 3. Develop a least squares regression line for the deseasonalized data. The purpose here is to develop an equation for the trend line Y, which we then modify with the seasonal factor. The procedure is the same as we used before:

$$Y = a + bx$$

where

y_d = deseasonalized demand (see Figure 3.8)

x = quarter

Y = demand computed using the regression equation $Y = a + bx$

a = Y intercept

b = slope of the line

The least squares calculations using columns 1, 7, and 8 of Figure 3.7 are shown in the lower section of the exhibit. The final deseasonalized equation for our data is $Y = 554.9 + 342.2x$. This straight line is shown in Figure 3.8.

Step 4. Project the regression line through the period to be forecast. Our purpose is to forecast periods 13 through 16. We start by solving the equation for Y at each of these periods (shown in step 5, column 3).

FIGURE 3.8
Straight Line Graph of Deseasonalized Equation

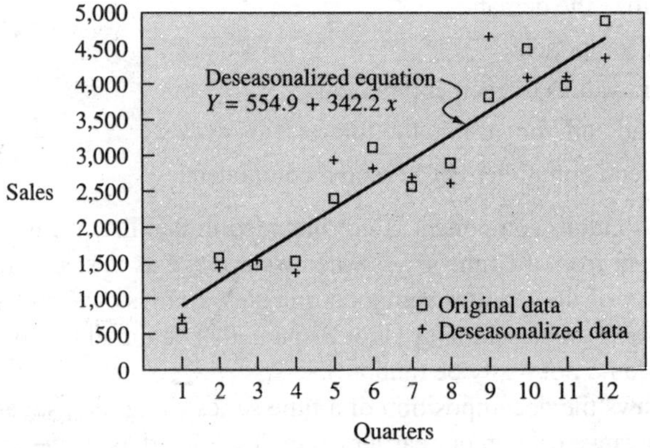

Step 5. Create the final forecast by adjusting the regression line by the seasonal factor. Recall that the *Y* equation has been deseasonalized. We now reverse the procedure by multiplying the quarterly data we derived by the seasonal factor for that quarter:

Period	Quarter	*Y* from Regression Line	Seasonal Factor	Forecast (*Y* × Seasonal Factor)
13	1	5,003.5	0.82	4,102.87
14	2	5,345.7	1.10	5,880.27
15	3	5,687.9	0.97	5,517.26
16	4	6,030.1	1.12	6,753.71

Our forecast is now complete. The procedure is generally the same as what we did in the hand-fit previous example. In the present example, however, we followed a more formal procedure and computed the least squares regression line as well.

Error Range

When a straight line is fitted through data points and then used for forecasting, errors can come from two sources. First, there are the usual errors similar to the standard deviation of any set of data. Second, there are errors that arise because the line is wrong. Figure 3.9 shows this error range. We develop the statistic later in the chapter; here, we will briefly show why the range broadens. First, visualize that one line is drawn that has some error such that it slants too steeply upward. Standard errors are then calculated for this line. Now visualize another line that slants too steeply downward. It also has a standard error. The total error range, for this analysis, consists of errors resulting from both lines as well as all other possible lines. We included this exhibit to show how the error range widens as we go further into the future.

FIGURE 3.9
Prediction Intervals for Linear Trend

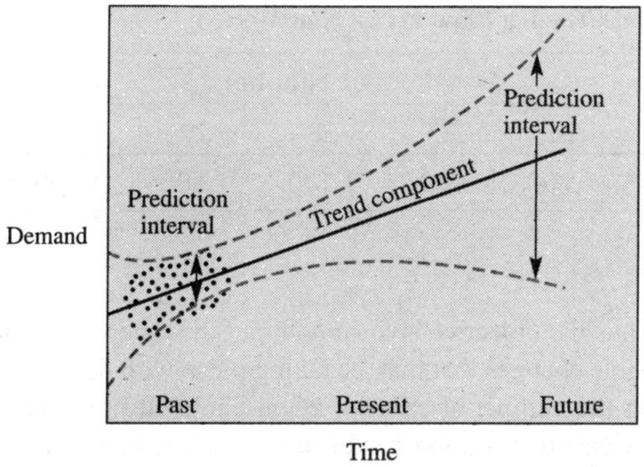

Short-Term Forecasting Techniques

In this section, we'll introduce two very common short-term forecasting techniques: **moving averages** and **exponential smoothing.** We choose these procedures since they are commonly available in commercial software and meet the criteria of low cost and little management involvement. The techniques are simple mathematical means for converting past information into forecasts. The procedures, often called *statistical forecasting models,* can easily be automated and incorporated into demand management activities.

There are a number of more complicated forecasting procedures that have been developed and we contemplated including some of them in this book, but research has shown the simple procedures to be at least as effective, especially for detailed, frequent forecasts. For example, Bernard Smith developed a novel approach to short-term forecasting called *focus forecasting*. It involves evaluating several simple forecasting models and choosing the one that performed best in the past to make the current forecast. Flores and Whybark compared focus forecasting and an average of all the forecasts produced with simple exponential smoothing. Simple exponential smoothing performed the best.

In another study, Spyros Makridakis and his colleagues challenged experts to a forecasting competition. A total of 21 forecasting models were tested on 1,001 actual data sets. Forecasting accuracy was determined with five different measures. There was no one model that consistently outperformed all the others for all series, but one conclusion was very clear. Simple methods do better than the more sophisticated models for detailed forecasts, especially over short periods. Another conclusion was that any special knowledge about demand patterns should be used to develop the forecast. If you ignore the seasonal sales pattern of swimsuits, you do so at your peril.

Moving-Average Forecasting

Moving-average and exponential smoothing forecasting are both concerned with averaging past demand to project a forecast for future demand. This implies that the underlying demand pattern, at least for the next few days or weeks, is constant with random fluctuations

FIGURE 3.10 **Demand for Household Cleaning Liquid (Past Nine Weeks)**

	Week Number								
	24	25	26	27	28	29	30	31	32
Cases shipped	1,600	1,500	1,700	900	1,100	1,500	1,400	1,700	1,200

about the average. Thus the objective is to smooth out the random fluctuations while being sensitive to any possible changes that may be taking place with the underlying average.

Figure 3.10 shows the number of cases of a household cleaning liquid shipped to retail stores from an East Coast distribution center in each of the last nine weeks. If there were requests for shipments that couldn't be fulfilled, it would be desirable to capture that information to get better estimates of the actual demand. For our examples, though, we will consider the shipments to represent the demand. The past demand is plotted in Figure 3.11.

A tempting procedure would be to simply draw a line through the data points and use that line as our estimate for week 33 and subsequent weeks. This would require constant management involvement in making the forecasts, however. Rather than draw a line through the points in Figure 3.11 to find the average, we could simply calculate the arithmetic average of the nine historical observations. Since we're interested in averaged past data to project into the future, we could even use an average of all past demand data available for forecasting purposes. There are several reasons, however, why this may not be a desirable way of smoothing. In the first place, there may be so many periods of past data that storing them all is an issue. Second, often the most recent history is most relevant in forecasting short-term demand in the near future. Recent data may reveal current conditions better than data several months or years old. For these reasons, the moving average procedure uses only a few of the most recent demand observations.

FIGURE 3.11
Plot of the Past Demand for Household Cleaning Liquid

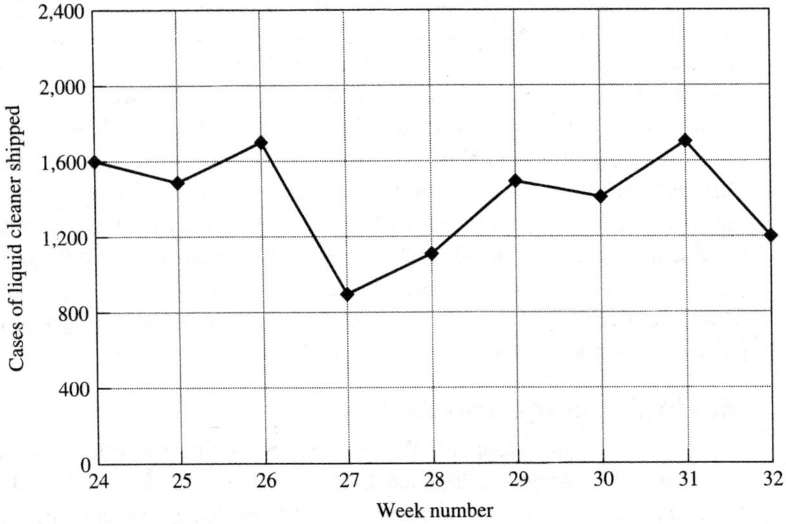

FIGURE 3.12 **Example Moving-Average Calculations**

	Period					
	27	28	29	30	31	32
Actual demand	900	1,100	1,500	1,400	1,700	1,200

6-period MAF made at the end of period 32 $= \sum_{27}^{32}$ actual demand/6

$= (900 + 1{,}100 + 1{,}500 + 1{,}400 + 1{,}700 + 1{,}200)/6 = 1{,}300$

3-period MAF made at the end of period 32 $= \sum_{30}^{32}$ actual demand/3

$= (1{,}400 + 1{,}700 + 1{,}200)/3 = 1{,}433$

The moving-average model for smoothing historical demand proceeds, as the name implies, by averaging a selected number of past periods of data. The average moves because a new average can be calculated whenever a new period's demand is determined. Whenever a forecast is needed, the most recent past history of demand is used to do the averaging.

Equation (3.5) shows the model for finding the moving average. The equation shows the moving average forecast always uses the most recent n periods of historical information available for developing the forecast. Notice the moving average is the forecast of demand for the next and subsequent periods. This timing convention needs to be clearly understood. We are at the end of period t; we know the demand in period t and forecasts are made for periods $t + 1$, or $t + X$ periods into the future. Forecasts are not made for period t since that period's demand is known. Figure 3.12 shows sample calculations for the number of cases shipped.

$$\text{Moving average forecast (MAF) at the end of period } t\text{: } \text{MAF}_t = \sum_{i=t-n+1}^{t} \text{Actual demand}_i/n \quad \textbf{(3.5)}$$

where:

i = period number

t = current period (the period for which the most recent actual demand is known)

n = number of periods in the moving average

You'll note the moving-average model does smooth the historical data, but it does so with an equal weight on each piece of historical information. We could adjust this, of course, by incorporating different weights on past periods. In fact the *weighted-moving-average* model does exactly that, but at the cost of complexity and more data storage. In addition, some data play no part in making a moving average forecast. For example, the demand of 900 in week 27 has no weight in the three-period moving average forecast for period 33. Exponential smoothing addresses both of these considerations in making forecasts.

Exponential Smoothing Forecasting

The exponential smoothing model for forecasting doesn't eliminate *any* past information, but so adjusts the weights given to past data that older data get increasingly less weight (hence the name exponential smoothing). The basic idea is a fairly simple one and has a great deal of intuitive appeal. Each new forecast is based on an average that's adjusted each time there's a new forecast error. For example, if we forecast 90 units of demand for an item in a particular period and that item's actual demand turns out to be 100 units, an appealing idea would be to increase our forecast by some portion of the 10-unit error in making the next period's forecast. In this way, if the error indicated demand was changing, we would begin to change the forecast. We may not want to incorporate the entire error (i.e., add 10 units), since the error may have just been due to random variations around the mean.

The proportion of the error that will be incorporated into the forecast is called the **exponential smoothing constant** and is identified as α. The model for computing the new average appears in Equation (3.6) as we've just described it. Equation (3.7) gives the most common computational form of the exponentially smoothed average. The new exponentially smoothed average is again the forecast for the next and subsequent periods. The same timing convention is used; that is, the forecast is made at the end of period t for period $t + X$ in the future. Figure 3.13 shows example calculations for the number of cases shipped.

Exponential smoothing forecast (ESF) at the end of period t:

$$\text{ESF}_t = \text{ESF}_{t-1} + \alpha(\text{Actual demand}_t - \text{ESF}_{t-1}) \quad \textbf{(3.6)}$$

$$= \alpha(\text{Actual demand}_t) + (1 - \alpha)\text{ESF}_{t-1} \quad \textbf{(3.7)}$$

where:

α = the smoothing constant ($0 \le \alpha \le 1$)

t = current period (the period for which the most recent actual demand is known)

ESF_{t-1} = exponential smoothing forecast made one period previously (at the end of period $t - 1$)

FIGURE 3.13
Example Exponential Smoothing Calculations

	Period	
	27	28
Actual demand	900	1,100

Assume:

ESF_{26} = exponential smoothing forecast made at the end of period 26 = 1,000, $\alpha = 0.1$

ESF_{27} (made at the end of period 27 when actual demand for period 27 is known but actual demand in period 28 is not known) =

$1{,}000 + 0.1(900 - 1{,}000) = 990$

$0.1(900) + (1 - 0.1)1{,}000 = 990$

$\text{ESF}_{28} = 0.1(1{,}100) + (1 - 0.1)990 = 1001$

FIGURE 3.14 **Relative Weights Given to Past Demand by a Moving Average and Exponential Smoothing Model**

	Period								
	20	21	22	23	24	25	26	27*	28
5-period MAF weights	0%	0%	0%	20%	20%	20%	20%	20%	—
ESF weights (α = 0.3)	2%	4%	5%	7%	10%	15%	21%	30%	—

*Forecast made at the end of period 27.

Let's compare exponential smoothing and moving average forecasting procedures. Figure 3.14 compares a five-period MAF with an ESF using $\alpha = 0.3$. In preparing the forecast for period 28, the five-period MAF would apply a 20 percent weight to each of the five most recent actual demands. The ESF model (with $\alpha = 0.3$) would apply a 30 percent weight to the actual demand in period 27 as seen here:

$$ESF_{27} = \text{Period 28 forecast} = 0.3\ (\text{Period 27 actual demand}) + 0.7\ (ESF_{26})$$

By looking at the ESF for period 27, made at the end of period 26 (i.e., ESF_{26}), we see it was determined as

$$ESF_{26} = 0.3\ (\text{Period 26 actual demand}) + 0.7\ (ESF_{25})$$

By substitution, ESF_{27} can be shown to be

$$ESF_{27} = 0.3\ (\text{Period 27 actual demand}) + 0.7\ [0.3\ (\text{Period 26 actual demand}) + 0.7\ (ESF_{25})]$$

The result of this calculation is a weight of 0.21 (0.7 × 0.3) being applied to the actual demand in period 26 when the forecast for periods 28 and beyond is made at the end of period 27. By similar substitution, we can derive the entire line for the ESF weights in Figure 3.14.

Figure 3.14 shows, for the forecast made at the end of period 27, 30 percent of the weight is attached to the actual demand in period 27, 21 percent for period 26, and 15 percent for period 25. The sum of these weights, 66 percent, is the weight placed on the last three periods of demand. The sum of all the weights given for the ESF model in Figure 3.14 is 94 percent. If we continue to find the weights for periods 19, 18, and so on, the sum for all weights is 1.0, as intuition would tell us. If the smoothing constant were 0.1 instead of 0.3, a table like Figure 3.14 would have values of 0.1, 0.09, and 0.081 for the weights of periods 27, 26, and 25, respectively. The sum of these three (27 percent) is the weight placed on the last three periods. Moreover, (1 − 27% = 73%) is the weight given to all actual data *more than* three periods old.

This result shows larger values of α give more weight to recent demands and utilize older demand data less than is the case for smaller values of α; that is, larger values of α provide more responsive forecasts, and smaller values produce more stable forecasts. The same argument can be made for the number of periods in an MAF model. This is the basic trade-off in determining what smoothing constant (or length of moving average) to use in a forecasting procedure. The higher the smoothing constant or the shorter the moving average, the more responsive forecasts are to changes in underlying demand, but the more "nervous" they are in the presence of randomness. Similarly, smaller smoothing constants or longer moving averages provide stability in the face of randomness but slower reactions to changes

FIGURE 3.15
Example Bias Calculation

	Period (i)			
	1	2	3	4
(1) Actual demand	1,500	1,400	1,700	1,200
(2) Forecast demand	1,600	1,600	1,400	1,300
Error (1) − (2)	−100	−200	300	−100

$$\text{Bias} = \sum_{i=1}^{4} \text{error}_i/4 = (-100 - 200 + 300 - 100)/4$$
$$= -100/4 = -25$$

in the underlying demand. Ultimately, however, the trade-off between stability and responsiveness is reflected in the quality of the forecasts, a subject to which we now turn.

Evaluating Forecasts

Ultimately, of course, the quality of any forecast is reflected in the quality of the decisions based on the forecast. This leads to suggesting the ideal comparison of forecasting procedures would be based on the costs of producing the forecast and the value of the forecast for the decision. From these data, the appropriate trade-off between the cost of developing and the cost of making decisions with forecasts of varying quality could be made. Unfortunately, neither cost is easily measured. In addition, such a scheme suggests that a different forecasting procedure might be required for each decision, an undesirably complex possibility. As a result of these complications, we rely on some direct measures of forecast quality.

For any forecasting procedure we develop, an important criterion is honesty, or lack of bias; that is, the procedure should produce forecasts that are neither consistently high nor consistently low. Forecasts shouldn't be overly optimistic or pessimistic, but rather should "tell it like it is." Because we're dealing with projecting past data, lack of **bias** means smoothing out past data's randomness so that forecasts that are too high are offset by forecasts that are too low. To measure bias, we'll use the **mean error** as defined by Equation (3.8). In this equation, the **forecast error** in each period is actual demand in each period minus forecast demand for that period. Figure 3.15 shows an example calculation of bias.

$$\text{Mean error (bias)} = \frac{\sum_{i=1}^{n}(\text{Actual demand}_i - \text{Forecast demand}_i)}{n} \quad \textbf{(3.8)}$$

where:

i = period number

n = number of periods of data

As Figure 3.15 shows, when forecast errors tend to cancel one another out, the measure of bias tends to be low. Positive errors in some periods are offset by negative errors in others, which tends to produce an average error, or bias near zero. In Figure 3.15, there's a bias and the demand was over forecast by an average of 25 units per period for the four periods.

FIGURE 3.16
Sample MAD Calculations

	Period (i)			
	1	2	3	4
(1) Actual demand	1,500	1,400	1,700	1,200
(2) Forecast demand	1,600	1,600	1,400	1,300
Error (1) − (2)	−100	−200	300	−100

$$\text{MAD} = \sum_{i=1} |\text{error}_i|/4$$

$$= (|-100| + |-200| + |300| + |-100|)/4 = 175$$

	Period (i)			
	1	2	3	4
(1) Actual demand	100	100	5,500	100
(2) Forecast demand	1,600	1,600	1,400	1,300
Error (1) − (2)	−1,500	−1,500	4,100	−1,200

$$\text{Bias} = \sum_{i=1}^{4} |\text{error}_i|/4 = (-1{,}500 - 1{,}500 + 4{,}100 - 1{,}200)/4$$

$$= -100/4 = -25$$

$$\text{MAD} = \sum_{i=1}^{4} |\text{error}_i|/4$$

$$= (|-1{,}500| + |-1{,}500| + |4{,}100| + |-1{,}200|)/4$$

$$= 8{,}300/4 = 2{,}075$$

Having an unbiased forecast is important in manufacturing planning and control, since the unbiased estimates, on average, are about right. But that's not enough. We still need to be concerned with the errors' magnitude. Note, for the example in Figure 3.15, we obtain the identical measure of bias if actual demand for the four periods had been 100, 100, 5,500, and 100, respectively. (This is shown as part of the calculations in Figure 3.16.) However, the individual errors are much larger, and this difference would have to be reflected in extra inventory if we were to maintain a consistent level of customer service. Let's now turn to a widely used measure of forecast error magnitude, the **mean absolute deviation (MAD).** The equation for calculating MAD is provided in Equation (3.9), while Figure 3.16 shows example calculations.

$$\text{Mean absolute deviation (MAD)} = \frac{\sum_{i=1}^{n} |\text{Actual demand}_i - \text{Forecast demand}_i|}{n} \quad \textbf{(3.9)}$$

The mean absolute deviation expresses the size of the average error irrespective of whether it's positive or negative. It's the combination of bias and MAD that allows us to evaluate forecasting results. Bias is perhaps the most critical, since we can compensate for forecast errors through inventory, expediting, faster delivery means, and other kinds of responses. MAD indicates the expected compensation's size (e.g., required speed). However, if a forecast is consistently lower than demand, the entire material-flow pipeline will run dry; it will be necessary to start over again with raw materials. Inventory buildups can arise with a consistently high forecast.

Before turning to some managerial issues concerning forecasting, we would like to provide one other relationship that is quite useful. The most widely used measure of deviation or dispersion in statistics is the **standard deviation.** MAD also measures deviation (error) from an expected result (the forecast). When the forecast errors are distributed normally, there is a direct relationship between the two measures that can be used to develop statistical insights and conclusions. The standard deviation of the errors is arithmetically related to MAD by Equation (3.10):

$$\text{Standard deviation of forecast errors} = 1.25\ \text{MAD} \qquad \textbf{(3.10)}$$

In the demand management module we are interested in providing the appropriate level of detail and frequency of the forecast to the other modules in the front end of the MPC system. This may require modification of the forecasts or reconciliation with other forecast sources before they can be used for decision making.

Using the Forecasts

Using the forecasts requires a heavy dose of common sense, as well as application of techniques. In this section, we'll look at some technical reasons for aggregating forecasts and some of the methods for readying the forecasts for use in sales and operations planning. We'll also review some means for incorporating management information into the forecasts.

Considerations for Aggregating Forecasts

In Figure 3.1 we pointed out different means of developing forecasts for different uses in the company. For sales and operations planning, one source of forecast might be the aggregation by product family of the detailed forecasts for individual products. Other inputs might come from marketing and our knowledge of customers. The result of reconciling all these sources is an aggregate demand forecast that is used for developing the sales and operations plans.

There are several reasons for aggregating product items in both time and level of detail for forecasting purposes. We must do it with caution, however. Aggregating individual products into product lines, geographical areas, or customer types, for example, must be done in ways that are compatible with the planning systems. Product groupings must also be developed, so that the forecast unit is sensible to forecasters. Provided we follow these guidelines, we can use product groupings to facilitate the forecasting task.

It's a well-known phenomenon that long-term or product-line forecasts *are more accurate than short-term and/or detailed forecasts.* This merely verbalizes a statistical verity. Consider the example in Figure 3.17. Monthly sales average 20 units but vary randomly with a standard deviation of two units. This means 95 percent of the monthly demands lie between 16 and 24 units when demand is normally distributed. This corresponds to a forecast error of plus or minus 20 percent around the forecast of 20 units per month.

FIGURE 3.17
Effect of Aggregating on Forecast Accuracy

Now suppose, instead of forecasting demand on a monthly basis, we prepare an annual forecast of demand—in this case, 240 (12 months × 20 units/month) units for the year. If monthly sales are independent, the resulting standard deviation is 6.9 units. This is found by noting that the variance of the monthly distribution is 4 units (2^2). The variance of the yearly distribution is 48 (12 months × 4), so the standard deviation is 6.9 ($\sqrt{48}$). This corresponds to a 95 percent range of 226 to 254 units or a ±5.8 percent deviation. The reduction from ±20 percent to ±5.8 percent is due to using a much longer time period. The same effect can be seen in forecasting demand for product lines instead of for individual items.

In the assemble-to-order environment, Equation (2.1) shows the number of items that need to be forecast when finished products are used instead of the components. This is often a substantial increase in the number and, because of the detail, often results in very poor forecasting performance. For example, what is the forecast for red, two-door, small engine, antilock-brake cars with sport stripes. It is much easier to forecast demand for the components than the detailed component combinations. Many of the same advantages of error reduction that accrue to aggregating are possible here as well.

An issue arises whenever aggregations of products, regions, or time periods are used to develop strategic or sales and operations plans. The total forecast must be consistent with the individual product forecasts. The whole must be equal to the sum of the parts. Very often an individual product's share of the aggregate product line totals remains fairly constant. That is, there is more uncertainty in the day-to-day demand for the item than for its share in the demand for the total line. We can use this knowledge to disaggregate the aggregate forecasts and thereby maintain the consistency between the detail and the totals. We may even be able to show improvements in the accuracy of the detail forecasts by doing it this way. One formal method for achieving consistency is described next.

Pyramid Forecasting

When the basis of the aggregated forecast for sales and operations planning is the sum of product level forecasts produced by, say, exponential smoothing, it is unlikely that this sum would match the aggregate forecasts developed by other sources. Yet, for example, knowledge of customers' and marketing plans need to be taken into account at the individual item level. In addition, there may be budget restrictions, income goals, or other company considerations that shape the aggregate forecasts that need to be taken into account in developing the final forecasts at the item level. One procedure for doing this is **pyramid forecasting.** It provides a means of coordinating, integrating, and assuring consistency between the various sources of forecasts and any company constraints or goals.

FIGURE 3.18
Pyramid Forecasting Example

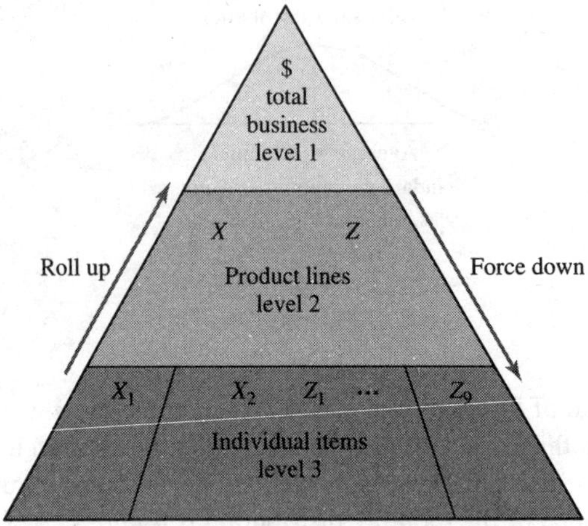

FIGURE 3.19
Initial and Roll-Up Forecasts

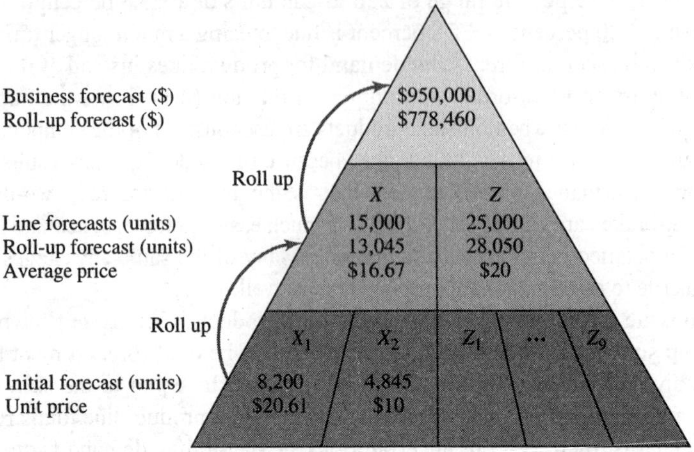

Figure 3.18 provides the basic framework for pyramid forecasting. The procedure used in implementing the approach often begins with individual product item forecasts at level 3, which are rolled up into forecasts for product lines shown as level 2. We then aggregate forecasts for product lines into a total business forecast (in dollars) at level 1 in Figure 3.18. Once the individual item and product line forecasts have been rolled up and considered in finalizing the top management forecast (plan), the next step is to force down (constrain) the product line and individual item forecasts, so they're consistent with the plan.

In the example shown in Figure 3.19, the 11 individual product items are divided into two product lines. Two of these items, X_1 and X_2, form product line X (which we'll study in detail), while the remaining products, Z_1 through Z_9, are included in product line Z. These two product lines, X and Z, represent the firm's entire range of products. Figure 3.19 shows unit prices and initial forecasts for each level.

The roll-up process starts by summing the individual item forecasts (level 3) to provide a total for each line (level 2). For the X line, the roll-up forecast is 13,045 units (8,200 + 4,845).

FIGURE 3.20
Forcing down the Management Forecast of Total Sales

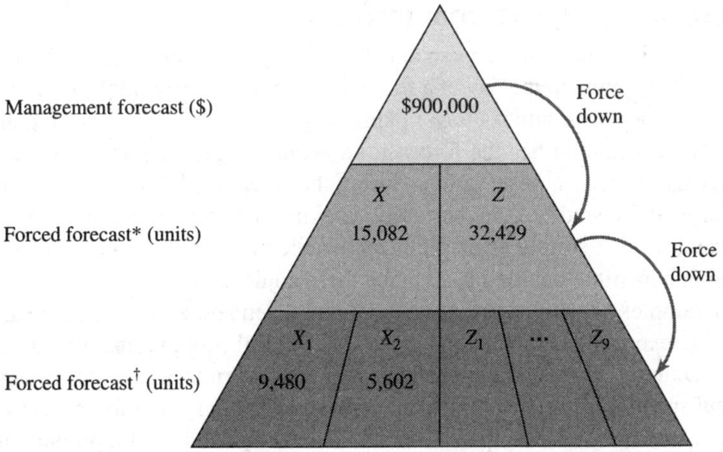

$$\text{*Forced forecast } (X) = \frac{\$900{,}000}{\$778{,}460} \times (13{,}045) = 15{,}082 \text{ units}$$

$$\text{*Forced forecast } (Z) = \frac{\$900{,}000}{\$778{,}460} \times (28{,}050) = 32{,}429 \text{ units}$$

$$^{\dagger}\text{Forced forecast } (X_1) = \frac{15{,}082}{13{,}045} \times (8{,}200) = 9{,}480 \text{ units}$$

$$^{\dagger}\text{Forced forecast } (X_2) = \frac{15{,}082}{13{,}045} \times (4{,}845) = 5{,}602 \text{ units}$$

The sum of the individual Z line items gives a forecast of 28,050 units. Note that the X line roll-up doesn't correspond to the forecast of 15,000 units for the line. If there's substantial disagreement at this stage, reconciliation could occur or an error might be discovered. If there's to be no reconciliation at this level, we needn't prepare independent forecasts for the lines. If dollar forecasts are required at level 2, prices at level 3 can be used to calculate an average price.

To roll up to the level 1 dollar forecasts, the average prices at the line level are combined with the line roll-up forecasts. The total of $778,460:

$$\$778{,}460 = (13{,}045 \times 16.67) + (28{,}050 \times 20.00)$$

is less than the independent business forecast of $950,000. For illustrative purposes, we'll assume management has evaluated the business forecast and the roll-up forecast and has decided to use $900,000 as the forecast at level 1. The next task is to make the line and individual item forecasts consistent with this amount. To bring about the consistencies, we use the forcing-down process. The ratio between the roll-up forecast at level 1 ($778,460) and the management total ($900,000) is used to make the adjustment.

The forecasts at all levels appear in Figure 3.20. The results are consistent forecasts throughout the organization, and the sum of the parts is forced to equal the whole. Note, however, the process of forcing the consistency needs to be approached with caution. In the example, forecasts at the lower level are now higher than they were originally and incorporate the plans at the higher levels. Even though the sum of the parts equals the whole, it's possible the people responsible for the forecast won't "own" the number. They mustn't be made to feel they're simply being given an allocation of someone else's wish list.

Incorporating External Information

Many kinds of information can and should be used to make good forecasts. For example, in a college town on the day of a football game, traffic around the stadium is a mess. An intelligent forecaster adjusts travel plans on game days to avoid the stadium traffic, if possible. He or she modifies the forecast, knowing the game's impact on traffic. A mechanical procedure based on observations during the week would probably forecast very little traffic around the stadium. We certainly wouldn't use such a forecast without adjusting it for game day. That simple principle is applicable to business forecasting as well, but it's surprising how often people fail to make these adjustments.

Examples of activities that will influence demand and perhaps invalidate the use of a routine exponential forecasting model are special promotions, product changes, competitors' actions, and economic changes. One of the primary ways to incorporate information about such future activities into the forecast is to change the forecast directly. We might do this if we knew, for example, there was to be a promotion of a product in the future, or we were going to open more retail outlets, or we were going to introduce a new product that would cannibalize the sales of an existing product. In these instances, we could adjust the forecast directly to account for the activities, just as we do for the game day. By recognizing explicitly that future conditions won't reflect past conditions, we can modify the forecast directly to reflect our assessment of the future.

We may need to change the forecasting method as well. If technology has prolonged the life of our products, we may need to change the parameters in the model that relates replacement sales to the average life of our products in the field. If, for example, we know one of our competitors is going to introduce a new product, we suspect the market will change, but we may not be sure of the change's direction or magnitude. In this case, we may want to do frequent forecasting and model testing to assess the effect of the new product. We could also make the smoothing constant larger in an exponential smoothing model and be more responsive to any changes. There may be circumstances where our knowledge would lead us to change both the forecast and the forecasting parameters.

Key in all of these adjustments is that intelligence must be included in the forecasts, and the forecasts must be readied for use in preparing and controlling the plans of the firm. Determining the appropriate level of aggregation and reconciling various forecasting approaches (perhaps with pyramid forecasting) are important steps in making the modifications.

Concluding Principles

In this chapter, we have reviewed a few of the most basic forecasting techniques. We have also covered the reasoning behind aggregating forecasts and how forecasts are reconciled for planning purposes.

- The forecasting models should not be any more complicated than necessary. Simple models often work better than more complicated ones.
- Input data and output forecasts should be routinely monitored for quality and appropriateness.
- Information on the sources of variation in sales, such as seasonality, market trends, and company policies, should be incorporated into the forecasting system.
- Forecasts from different sources must be reconciled and made consistent with company plans and constraints.

Discussion Questions

1. In the lower levels of the pyramid forecasting system, how would you prevent abdication of the responsibility for forecasting?
2. Can a grocery store capture true demand data? How might a warehouse capture demand data?
3. Some experts have argued it's more important to have low bias (mean error) than to have a low MAD. Why would they argue this way?

Problems

1. Demand for stereo headphones and MP3 players for joggers has caused Nina Industries to grow almost 50 percent over the past year. The number of joggers continues to expand, so Nina expects demand for headsets to also expand, because, as yet, no safety laws have been passed to prevent joggers from wearing them. Demand for the stereo units for last year was as follows:

Month	Demand (Units)	Month	Demand (Units)
January	4,200	July	5,300
February	4,300	August	4,900
March	4,000	September	5,400
April	4,400	October	5,700
May	5,000	November	6,300
June	4,700	December	6,000

   a. Using least squares regression analysis, what would you estimate demand to be for each month next year? Using a spreadsheet, follow the general format in Figure 3.3. Compare your results to those obtained by using the forecast spreadsheet function.

   b. To be reasonably confident of meeting demand, Nina decides to use three standard errors of estimate for safety. How many additional units should be held to meet this level of confidence?

2. Historical demand for a product is

	Demand
January	12
February	11
March	15
April	12
May	16
June	15

   a. Using a weighted moving average with weights of 0.60, 0.30, and 0.10, find the July forecast.

   b. Using a simple three-month moving average, find the July forecast.

   c. Using single exponential smoothing with $\alpha = 0.2$ and a June forecast ≈ 13, find the July forecast. Make whatever assumptions you wish.

   d. Using simple linear regression analysis, calculate the regression equation for the preceding demand data.

   e. Using the regression equation in *d*, calculate the forecast for July.

3. The following tabulations are actual sales of units for six months and a starting forecast in January.
   a. Calculate forecasts for the remaining five months using simple exponential smoothing with $\alpha = 0.2$.
   b. Calculate MAD for the forecasts.

	Actual	Forecast
January	100	80
February	94	
March	106	
April	80	
May	68	
June	94	

4. Zeus Computer Chips Inc. used to have major contracts to produce the Centrino-type chips. The market has been declining during the past three years because of the dual-core chips, which it cannot produce, so Zeus has the unpleasant task of forecasting next year. The task is unpleasant because the firm has not been able to find replacement chips for its product lines. Here is demand over the past 12 quarters:

2007		2008		2009	
I	4,800	I	3,500	I	3,200
II	3,500	II	2,700	II	2,100
III	4,300	III	3,500	III	2,700
IV	3,000	IV	2,400	IV	1,700

Use the decomposition technique to forecast the four quarters of 2010.

5. Sales data for two years are as follows. Data are aggregated with two months of sales in each "period."

Months	Sales	Months	Sales
January–February	109	January–February	115
March–April	104	March–April	112
May–June	150	May–June	159
July–August	170	July–August	182
September–October	120	September–October	126
November–December	100	November–December	106

   a. Plot the data.
   b. Fit a simple linear regression model to the sales data.
   c. In addition to the regression model, determine multiplicative seasonal index factors. A full cycle is assumed to be a full year.
   d. Using the results from parts *b* and *c*, prepare a forecast for the next year.

6. The demand manager of Maverick Jeans is responsible for ensuring sufficient warehouse space for the finished jeans that come from the production plants. It has occasionally been necessary to rent public warehouse space, something that Maverick would like to avoid. In order to estimate the space requirements the demand manager is evaluating moving-average forecasts. The demand (in 1,000 case units) for the last fiscal year is shown below.

Month	1	2	3	4	5	6	7	8	9	10	11	12
Demand	20	18	21	25	24	27	22	30	23	20	29	22

a. Use a three-month moving average to estimate the month-in-advance forecast of demand for months 4–12 and generate a forecast for the first month of next year. Calculate the average forecast error and mean absolute error.

b. Use a three-month weighted moving average with weights of 0.6, 0.3, 0.1 (most recent to last recent, respectively) to calculate month-in-advance forecasts for months 4–12 and forecast for the first month of next year. Calculate the average forecast error and mean absolute error.

c. Compare the average forecast error and MAD for the forecasting methods in parts *a* and *b*. Based on these error calculations, which of the two forecast methods would you recommend? Why?

7. Maverick Jeans' demand manager decided to evaluate exponential smoothing. To maintain comparability, she used the data from problem 6.

a. Use a starting forecast of 20 for month 4 to develop forecasts for months 5–12 and the first month of next year. Use smoothing constants (α) of 0.2, 0.5, and 0.8. Calculate the average forecast error and mean absolute error.

b. What observations do you have? How does exponential smoothing compare to the results for moving averages from problem 6?

8. Talbot Publishing Company's production planning manager has provided the following historical sales data for its leading textbook on forecasting:

Year	4	5	6	7
Sales (in 1,000 units)	21	18	20	17

The firm is considering using a basic exponential smoothing model with $\alpha = 0.2$ to forecast this item's sales.

a. Use the sales average of 20,000 units through year 3 as the forecast for period 4. Prepare forecasts for years 5 through 7 as of the end of year 4.

b. Calculate the average error and MAD value for the three forecasts using the actual sales data provided. Estimate the standard deviation of the forecast errors using the calculated MAD.

c. Redo the forecasts and MAD calculations, updating the forecasts for years 6 and 7 at the end of years 5 and 6, respectively. What do you observe?

9. Use a spreadsheet program to compare a three-period moving average forecasting model with a basic exponential smoothing model (ESF). Ten periods of past actual demand data are available (27, 26, 32, 41, 28, 35, 43, 47, 28, and 38). Use the first five periods data to seed the model (as described next) and the last 5 periods to test the model.

a. Use the average of the first five periods to seed the ESF model (i.e., the "past forecast") and a smoothing model with $\alpha = 0.3$. Compare this ESF model with a 3-period moving average model using the last 5 periods of data. Use MAD as the criterion for comparing the techniques.

b. Does your comparison change if you use the past three periods data to seed the ESF model? What is the best alpha (smoothing) value to use for this model?

10. The following two demand sets are to be used to test two different basic exponential smoothing models. The first model uses $\alpha = 0.1$, and the second uses $\alpha = 0.5$. In both cases, the model should be initialized with a beginning forecast value of 50; that is, the ESF forecast for period 1 made at the end of period 0 is 50 units. In each of the four cases (two models on two demand sets), compute the average forecast error and MAD. What do the results mean?

Demand Set I		Demand Set II	
Period	**Demand**	**Period**	**Demand**
1	51	1	77
2	46	2	83
3	49	3	90
4	55	4	22
5	52	5	10
6	47	6	80
7	51	7	16
8	48	8	19
9	56	9	27
10	51	10	79
11	45	11	73
12	52	12	88
13	49	13	15
14	48	14	21
15	43	15	85
16	46	16	22
17	55	17	88
18	53	18	75
19	54	19	14
20	49	20	16

11. In an effort to improve customer service and reduce the cost of inventory, the Thanskavel Company invested in a number of lean manufacturing initiatives. One result of these investments was a reduction of the manufacturing lead time for the company's specialty product, Eggsbar, from six weeks to four weeks. A study of Eggsbar disclosed that the demand averages 200 units per week, with a standard deviation of 22 units. The demand from one week to the next week was found to be independent.

a. What was the mean and standard deviation of the demand during manufacturing lead time for this product before and after the initiatives?

b. Thanskavel has a policy of holding safety stock of finished goods inventory in the amount of 2.5 times the standard deviation of demand during manufacturing lead time. In the past, this amounted to $10,000 of safety stock inventory for this product. What reduction in safety stock for this product resulted from the reduction of the manufacturing lead time?

12. Five individual products in a product family of the Cumberland Company have identical sales patterns. Each averages 100 units per month, with a standard deviation of 10 units. Assuming normal distributions and independent demands:

a. What is the expected yearly sales distribution of each product?

b. What is the expected monthly aggregate sales distribution for all products together?

c. What is the expected yearly aggregate sales distribution for all products together?

13. Using ±3 standard deviations for the values obtained in parts *a*, *b*, and *c* of problem 12, compare your results to the results of a Cumberland Company survey of its managers concerning the accuracy of the company's forecasts (shown below).

	Expected Forecast Error for a Period of:		
Level of Detail	**1 Month**	**1 Quarter**	**1 Year**
Total Volume			
Family	12*	8	8
Type in Family	15	10	8
Grade in Type	15	NF†	12
SKU‡	30	NF	NF

*±12%.

†NF = no forecast.

‡Stockkeeping unit.

14. MacRonald's Restaurant uses a monthly exponential smoothing forecast for demand of each of its products. MacRonald's has four product families: burgers, chicken, hoagies, and pizza. MacRonald's also asks the shift managers to come up with a forecast for each product family. The exponential forecast for each product and the family forecast are given below.

Family	Product	Forecast	$/Unit
Burgers	Regular	1,200	1.00
	Super	2,700	1.50
	Super-Duper	2,100	1.80
Chicken	Regular	1,800	2.50
	Cajun	2,700	2.75
Hoagies	Italian	2,250	3.50
	French	1,650	3.00
	American	1,350	3.25
Pizza	Cheese	750	1.75
	Pepperoni	1,200	2.25

Family	$ Sales
Burgers	10,000.00
Chicken	15,000.00
Hoagies	20,000.00
Pizza	5,000.00

a. Calculate a roll-up of the individual forecasts and compare it to the product family forecast.

b. Roll up the individual product forecast to the top level and compare it to an overall corporate forecast of $65,000. Roll the forecast back down to families and individual forecast (dollars and units).

15. The general sales manager at Knox Products Corporation has just received next year's sales forecast (in units) for two of the firm's major products (Less Knox and More Knox) from sales managers of the Eastern and Western sales regions:

Eastern Region Forecast		Western Region Forecast	
Less Knox	More Knox	Less Knox	More Knox
150	300	300	450

Less Knox sells for $4.50 per unit and More Knox sells for $8.50 per unit.

a. The corporate economist has forecast a total corporation-wide sales volume for these two products of $11,000 for next year. What's the disparity between the two forecasts at the item level?

b. If top management agrees to a total corporation-wide sales forecast volume of $9,000, what's the sales forecast at the item level?

16. The Gonzales Electric Company's 12 products are further grouped into four product families. Products A, B, and C compose family l; D, E, and F compose family 2; G, H, and I compose family 3; and products J, K, and L make up family 4. Dick Gonzales has the following exponential smoothing forecasts of monthly demand for each product.

Family	Product	Forecast	$/Unit
1	A	10	1,000
	B	15	1,200
	C	20	900
2	D	5	5,000
	E	3	7,000
	F	2	9,000

Family	Product	Forecast	$/Unit
3	G	100	250
	H	180	100
	I	220	100
4	J	2	10,000
	K	4	9,000
	L	3	8,000

Gonzales's sales force has also come up with the monthly forecasts of sales for each product family.

Family	$ Sales
1	50,000
2	50,000
3	75,000
4	75,000

a. Roll up the individual product forecasts and compare them to the forecast provided by the sales force. Using a spreadsheet, roll down the forecast to make the individual item forecast agree with the sales force forecast. Calculate dollar value and number of units in the individual item forecast.

b. Top management has independently decided to set a $300,000 overall monthly sales goal for the company. Adjust the sales force forecast to reflect this new goal; then roll down the forecast to the individual item level. Calculate dollar value and number of units in the individual item forecast.

17. The analysts at Gonzales were kept busy performing "what-if" analyses of the data in problem 16.

a. Suppose a top-management meeting produces a decision that the family forecast for product family 3 (products G, H, and I) in problem 16 can't be increased. At the same meeting, the company's overall forecast ($300,000) is maintained. Roll the forecasts up and down to determine the dollar and unit forecasts.

b. Suppose the family forecast data in problem 16 are assumed to be correct, except in any case where the sum of the exponential smoothing forecast data for items exceeds the family forecast. In these cases, the sum of the item forecasts will be used instead of the family forecast. Roll up the resultant overall forecast and roll down the resultant item forecasts.

c. Suppose a major customer order has just been received for 10 units of product J. This order wasn't expected and is in addition to any other forecasts for product J. The company still wants to plan a total monthly sales volume of $300,000. Use the family forecasts (revised) to roll the forecasts up and down to get revised individual product forecasts.

Case

Forecasting at Ross Products

Ross Products Division of Abbott Laboratories is headquartered in Columbus, Ohio. The company produces a variety of nutritional products, including adult medical nutrition supplements and pediatric infant formulas, as well as ancillary equipment. An example of this equipment is a pump that supplies nutritional liquids to the stomach and that can also monitor the rate of flow. There are four manufacturing facilities in the United States, and Ross markets its products in the United States and overseas. Managers use a program entitled Log*Plus to perform demand management activities.

The firm uses a comprehensive approach to assure that all demands on capacity are included in the forecast. Figure 3.21 illustrates the system's key features. The demand management aspects of Log*Plus produces forecasts from national inputs and monitors actual demand against these forecasts. The process of producing the forecast used for planning starts with forecasts from marketing and sales

FIGURE 3.21
Forecasting Procedure for Ross Products Division, Abbott Laboratories

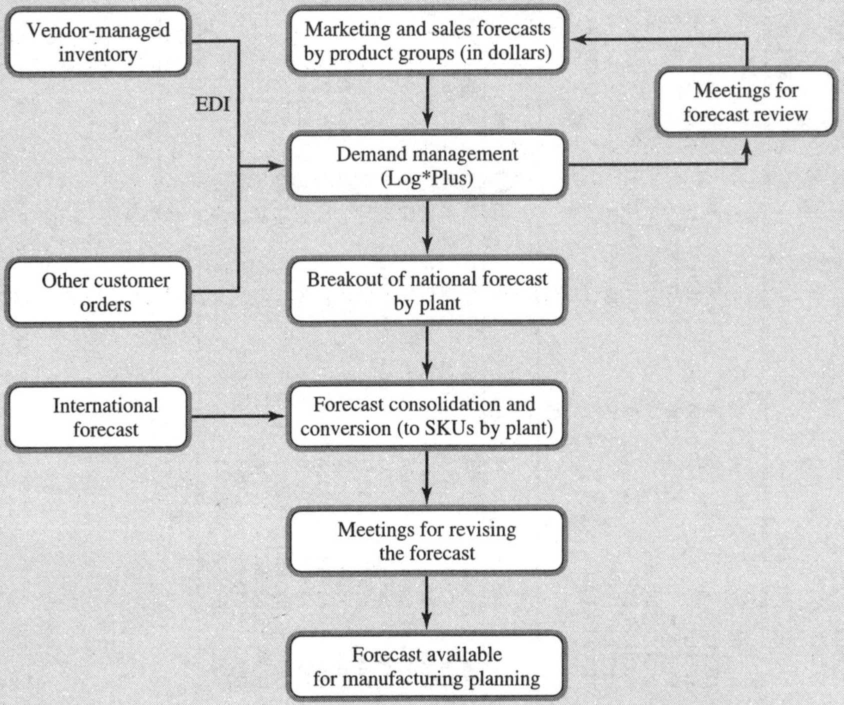

FIGURE 3.22 Example Forecast for Ross Products Division, Abbott Laboratories

FCST: 8/31
PLAN: 9/20
STOCK: 9/20

ROSS LABORATORIES
PLOT DEMAND REPORT

PAGE: 1
RUN: 9/27 13:04

MPS OPERATIONS DATA BASE

INDEX = 150

LEVEL	0	HIST LENGTH	104	REPLN DB FRC	FORCE PLT	LEAD TIME	0.00
TREND	0.0000	HIST USED	0	DATE TO MPS	61396	STK ON HAND	19313
MSE	0.00	0UTLRS FND	0	PLANNER	67 KNO/BE	INTRANSIT	430
MODEL TERMS	1	OUTLIER THR	0.00	SRC NAME	DEFAULT	SCHEDULED IN	8100
MODLFT EXPT	1	SMOOTH CONST	0.0000	LEADTIME	DEFAULT	CURR PR FCST	58,971
MODLFT DATE	6/19	PER FAST SMT	0	PWD LBS CONV	1.6552	EST. MONTH	53,491
TRND DISCNT	0.00	MAX SS/LT	409681	UNITS/CASE	24	MTD USAGE	48,142

DEMAND

	year −3	year −2	year −1	year 0	year +1	year +2
JAN	43344	63774	69839	64317	58507	54903
FEB	43492	61651	70819	60291	55323	57160
MAR	57933	56175	75732	57044	55528	54626
APR	54347	57004	61323	56381	55863	52434
MAY	50963	69295	72861	58564	57226	56359
JUN	59525	75039	81655	51098	60778	61925
JUL	58633	65850	70063	66546	61189	62623
AUG	61982	89558	81310	60501	60610	60790
SEP	63433	69850	69198	*58971	61638	60834
OCT	57188	62077	73592	66375	62563	59988
NOV	62559	58514	62432	59910	58150	55395
DEC	71563	67954	55607	63417	55834	
TOT	684962	796741	844431	723415	703209	637037

DEMAND DETAIL

PERIOD ENDING	STAT MODEL	MKT INTEL	PROMO	SCHED BACKLOG	DEP DEMAND	DIST DEMAND	TOTAL
9/30		58971					58971
10/31		66375					66375
11/30		59910					59910
12/31		63417					63417
1/31		58507					58507
2/27		55323					55323
3/31		55528					55528
4/30		55863					55863
5/31		57226					57226
6/30		60778					60778
7/31		61189					61189
8/31		60610					60610
TOTAL		713697					713697

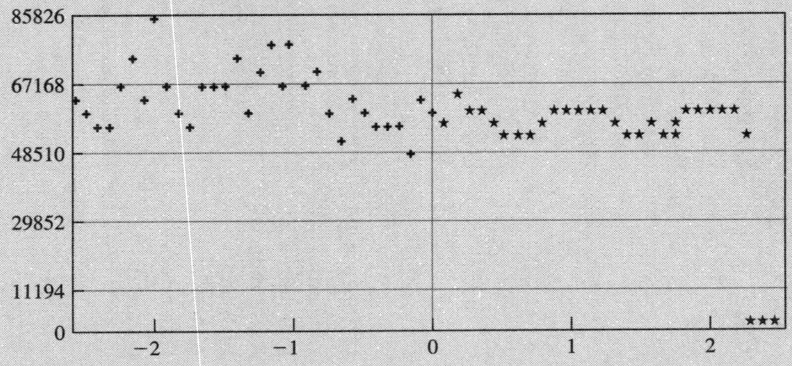

in dollars by product groups. These are broken out by region in Log*Plus to provide plant-level forecasts of national demand. These data are consolidated with the forecast for international sales and the total is converted to an item level forecast by plant. The process is not finished, however, until marketing, the product manager, and the production and inventory manager review the forecasts. Three times a year, meetings are held to review forecasts for all products in conjunction with budget meetings. These meetings can be held monthly for products that are experiencing changes, promotions, or other factors that could change demand.

To provide a service to customers and directly capture information on the market, Ross manages product inventory in some of its customers' facilities using VMI. Information on the use of these products is transmitted to Ross by electronic data interchange (EDI). These data are combined with the forecasts to produce reports such as the one shown in Figure 3.22 for SKU XYZ, a medical nutrition product in 8-ounce cans. The top of the figure shows several years' actual sales with two years and three months of forecast sales. (The current month is shown with an asterisk in year 0.) To facilitate any review of the forecasts, the data are plotted in the bottom half of the report. Here the seasonality is quite evident as is a sales peak about a year and a half ago (because of a promotion). These forecasts are a basic input to the master production scheduling module of the firm.

Assignment

1. Using the historic data given in Figure 3.22 (through August of year 0), develop your own forecast for the next two years. Use the regression techniques described in the chapter.
2. How do your forecasts compare to those shown in the Ross report?

Chapter 4

Sales and Operations Planning

Sales and operations planning (SOP) is probably the least understood aspect of manufacturing planning and control. However, the payoffs from a well-designed and -executed sales and operations plan are large. Here we discuss the process for determining aggregate levels of production. The managerial objective is to develop an overall business plan, which integrates the various functional planning efforts in a company whose manufacturing portion is embodied in the operations plan. The sales and operations plan links strategic goals to production and coordinates the various planning efforts in a business, including marketing planning, financial planning, operations planning, human resource planning, etc. If the sales and operations plan does not represent an integrated, cross-functional plan, the business can fail to succeed in its markets.

Our discussion of sales and operations planning is organized around four topics:

- *Sales and operations planning in the firm:* What is sales and operations planning? How does it link with strategic planning and other MPC functions?
- *The sales and operations planning process:* What are the fundamental activities in sales and operations planning and what techniques can be used?
- *The new management obligations:* What are the critical issues in developing an effective sales and operations planning function?
- *Operating with sales and operations planning:* What is the state of the art in practice?

Sales and Operations Planning in the Firm

Sales and operations planning provides the key communication links for top management to coordinate the various planning activities in a business. These linkages are shown in Figure 4.1. For example, marketing initiatives dealing with the entry of a new product in the market can be coordinated with an increase in manufacturing capacity to support the marketing promotional plans at the same time financial resources are coordinated to support the working capital for the buildup of pipeline inventories.

FIGURE 4.1
Key Linkages in Sales and Operations Planning

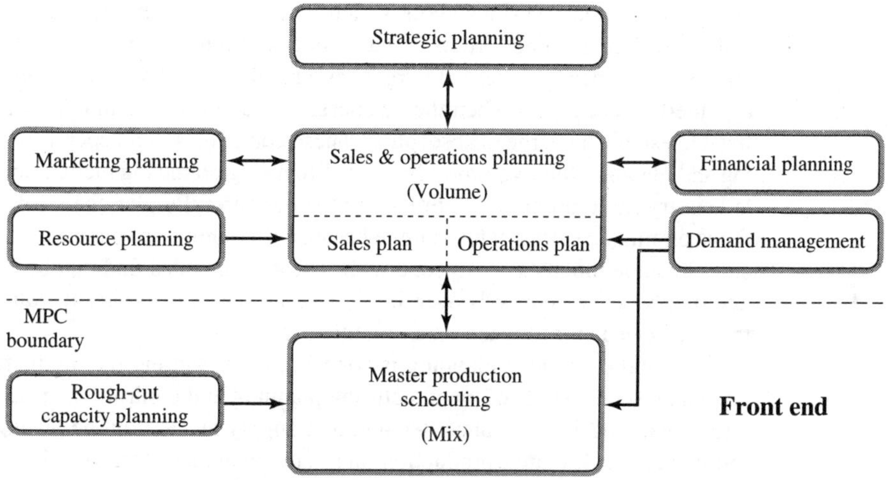

From a manufacturing perspective, sales and operations planning provides the basis to focus the detailed production resources to achieve the firm's strategic objectives. The sales and operations plans provide the framework within which the master production schedule is developed, subsequent MPS decisions can be planned and controlled, and material resources and plant capacities can be coordinated in ways that are consistent with strategic business objectives. We now describe the sales and operations planning function in terms of its role in top management, necessary conditions for effective planning, linkages to other MPC system functions, and the payoffs from effective sales and operations planning.

Sales and Operations Planning Fundamentals

There are four fundamentals in sales and operations planning: demand, supply, volume, and mix. First, let's consider the **balance between demand and supply.** When demand exceeds supply, customer service suffers because manufacturing cannot provide the volume of products required by the customer. Costs increase because of overtime and premium freight rates, and quality suffers because of the rush to ship products, all of which are unfavorable to the business. Likewise, when supply exceeds demand, the effect on the business is unfavorable. Inventories increase because of the imbalance between demand and manufacturing capacity; layoffs result from production rate cuts, causing plant efficiency and morale to decline; and profit margins are squeezed because of price cuts and discounting. Therefore, the key to good business performance is to maintain a proper balance between demand and supply. It is important to have business processes in place to maintain a proper balance between demand and supply, and to provide early warning signals when they are becoming unbalanced. This is the role of sales and operations planning, and it can be accomplished through the effective coordination of the plans of the different functional areas in a business with the active involvement of top management.

Two other fundamentals are **volume and mix.** These need to be treated separately in managing the manufacturing planning and control function. Volume concerns big-picture decisions about how much to make and the production rates for product families, while mix concerns detailed decisions about which individual products to make, in what sequence, and for which customer orders. What happens in many companies is that the focus is on mix decisions because these are urgent as a result of customer pressures. Volumes are only considered once a year when the business plan is developed and production rates must be fixed to establish overhead absorption. These companies don't spend enough time forecasting and planning their volumes. Instead of focusing on the big picture, they focus on the details in trying to predict mix. Smart companies carefully plan their volumes first and then focus on mix decisions. This is done because if volumes are planned effectively, mix decisions become much easier to cope with. These companies find that imbalances in demand and supply occur frequently over the course of a year, and as a result volume decisions need to be reviewed and adjusted on a monthly basis.

Sales and operations planning is concerned with getting the big picture right and then attending to the details of manufacturing planning and control. The role of sales and operations planning is to balance demand and supply at the volume level. Volume concerns rates: overall sales rates, production rates, aggregate inventories, and order backlogs. Once volume (rates and levels) is effectively planned, the problems of mix (individual products and orders) become easier to cope with. Understanding the fundamentals of sales and operations planning makes this function easier to understand as a part of a company's manufacturing planning and control system.

Sales and Operations Planning and Management

Sales and operations planning provides a direct and consistent dialogue between manufacturing and top management as well as between manufacturing and the other business functions. As Figure 4.1 shows, many key linkages of sales and operations planning are *outside* the manufacturing planning and control (MPC) system. Therefore the plan necessarily must be in terms that are meaningful to the firm's nonmanufacturing executives. Only in this way can the sales and operations planning function noted in Figure 4.1 become consistent for each basic functional area in the business. Likewise, the operations portion of the overall plan must be stated in terms that the MPC functions can use, so detailed manufacturing decisions are kept in concert with the overall strategic objectives reflected in the sales and operations plan.

The basis for consistency of the functional plans in a business is the resolution of broad trade-offs at the top management level. Suppose, for example, there's an opportunity to expand into a new market, and marketing requests additional production to do so. When a given operations plan has been authorized, this could be accomplished only by decreasing the currently authorized production for some other product group. If this is seen as undesirable—that is, the new market is to be a direct add-on—by definition a new sales and operations plan is required, with an updated and consistent set of plans in marketing, finance, and production. The feasibility of the added volume must be determined and agreed on before detailed execution steps are taken. This debate is of the type typically discussed in regular sales and operations planning meetings, and illustrates why top management involvement in sales and operations planning is critical.

The operations portion of the sales and operations plan states the mission manufacturing must accomplish if the firm's strategic objectives are to be met. How to accomplish the operations plan in terms of detailed manufacturing and procurement decisions is a problem for manufacturing management. Within an agreed-on operations plan, the job in manufacturing is to "hit the operations plan." Similar job definitions hold for sales, marketing, and finance.

Figure 4.1 also indicates that the planning in other MPC system functions is necessarily detailed, and the language is quite different from that required for the operations plan. The operations plan is normally stated in terms of aggregate units of output per month, while the master production schedule (MPS) is stated in terms of end product units per week. The MPS might be stated in units that use special bills of materials to manage complicated options and do not correspond to the units used to communicate with top management.

To perform the necessary communication role, the operations plan must be stated in commonly understood, aggregated terms. In many companies the operations plan is stated in total units for each product line (or major product family groupings). In other companies the operations plan is stated as the dollar value of total monthly output. Still other firms need to break the total output down by individual factories. Some firms also use measures that relate to capacity, such as direct labor hours and tons of product. The key requirement is that the operations plan be stated in some commonly understood homogenous unit that thereafter can be kept in concert with other functional plans.

The operations plan needs to be expressed in meaningful units, but it also needs to be expressed in a manageable number of units. Experience indicates that 6 to 12 family groups seem to be about right for a top management group to handle. Each family grouping has to be considered in terms of expectations on sales, manufacturing, and the resultant inventories and backlogs. The cumulative result, expressed in monetary units, also has to be examined and weighed against overarching business plans.

The operations plan is *not* a forecast of demand! It's the planned production, stated on an aggregate basis, for which manufacturing management is to be held responsible. The operations plan is not necessarily equal to a forecast of aggregate demand. For example, it may not be profitable to satisfy all of the demand in a peak monthly period, but the production would be leveled over the course of a seasonal cycle. Likewise, a strategic objective of improved customer service could result in aggregate production in excess of aggregate demand. These are important management trade-offs to be debated in the context of the sales and operations plan.

The operations plan is a result of the sales and operations planning process. Inputs to the process include sales forecasts, but these need to be stated on the basis of shipments (not bookings) so that the inventory projections match physical inventories and so that manufacturing goals are expressed correctly with respect to time.

Operations Planning and MPC Systems

So far we have emphasized sales and operations planning linkages to activities outside MPC system boundaries. Because of these linkages, the sales and operations plan is often called "top management's handle on the business." To provide execution support for the operations plan, we need linkages to the MPC systems. The most fundamental linkage is that to the master production schedule, which is a disaggregation of the operations plan. The result drives the detailed scheduling through detailed material planning and other MPC functions.

The MPS must be kept in concert with the operations plan. As the individual daily scheduling decisions to produce specific mixes of actual end items and/or options are made, we must maintain parity between the sum of the MPS quantities and the operations plan. If the relationship is maintained, then "hitting the schedule" (MPS) means the agreed-on operations plan will be met as well.

Another critical linkage shown in Figure 4.1 is the link with demand management. Demand management encompasses order entry, order promising, and physical distribution coordination as well as forecasting. This function must capture every source of demand against manufacturing capacity, such as interplant transfers, international requirements, and service parts. In some form, one or more of these demand sources may be of more consequence than others. For the firm with distribution warehouses, for example, replenishing those warehouses may create quite a different set of demands on manufacturing than is true for other firms. The contribution of demand management, insofar as operations planning is concerned, is to ensure that the influence of all aspects of demand is included and properly coordinated.

As a tangential activity, the match between actual and forecast demand is monitored in the demand management function. As actual demand conditions depart from forecast, the necessity for revising the operations plan increases. Thus, the assessment of changes' impact on the operations plan and the desirability of making a change depend on this linkage. It's critical for top management to change the plans, rather than to let the forecast errors in themselves change the aggregate production output level.

The other direct MPC linkage to sales and operations planning shown in Figure 4.1 is that with resource planning. This activity encompasses long-range planning of facilities. Involved is the translation of extended operations plans into capacity requirements, usually on a gross or aggregate basis. In some firms the unit of measure might be constant dollar output rates; in others, it might be labor-hours, head counts, machine-hours, key-facility–hours, tons of output, or some other output measure. The need is to plan capacity, at least in aggregate terms, for a horizon at least as long as it takes to make major changes.

Resource planning is directly related to operations planning, since, in the short term, the resources available provide a set of constraints to operations planning. In the longer run, to the extent that operations plans call for more resources than available, financial appropriations are indicated. A key goal of the linkage between operations planning and resource planning is to answer what-if questions. Maintaining current resource planning factors related to the product groupings used for planning is the basis for performing this analysis.

Much of the very near term operations plan is constrained by available material supplies. Current levels of raw material, parts, and subassemblies limit what can be produced in the short run, even if other resources are available. This is often hard to assess unless information links from the detailed material planning and shop status databases are effective.

Links through the MPS to material planning and other MPC functions provide the basic data to perform what-if simulations of alternative plans. Being able to quickly evaluate alternatives can facilitate the sales and operations planning process. This is not an argument to always change the operations plan. On the contrary, having the ability to demonstrate the impact of proposed changes may reduce the number of instances in which production "loses" in these negotiations.

The value of the sales and operations planning function is certainly questionable if there's no monitoring of performance. This requires linkages to the data on shipment/sales, aggregated into the sales and operations planning groupings. Measuring performance is an important input to the planning process itself. Insofar as deviations in output are occurring, they must be taken into account. If the plan can't be realized, the entire value of the sales and operations planning process is called into question.

One final performance aspect where effort must be expended is in the reconciliation of the MPS with the operations plan. As day-to-day MPS decisions are made, it's possible to move away from the operations plan unless constant vigilance is applied. Like other performance monitoring, it requires a frequent evaluation of status and comparison to plan.

Payoffs

Sales and operations planning is top management's handle on the business. It provides important visibility of the critical interactions between sales, marketing, production, and finance. If sales and marketing wants higher inventories, but top management decides there's not sufficient capital to support the inventories, the operations plan will be so designed. Once such critical trade-off decisions are made, the operations plan provides the basis for monitoring and controlling manufacturing performance in a way that provides a much more clear division of responsibilities than is true under conventional budgetary controls.

Under sales and operations planning, manufacturing's job is to hit the schedule. This can eliminate the battle over "ownership" of finished-goods inventory. If actual inventory levels don't agree with planned inventory levels, it's basically not a manufacturing problem, if they hit the schedule. It's either a sales and marketing problem (the products didn't sell according to plan) or a problem of product mix management in the demand management activity (the wrong individual items were made).

The operations plan provides the basis for day-to-day, tough-minded trade-off decisions as well. If sales and marketing want more of some items, it must be asked, "Of what do you want less?" There's no other response, because additional production without a corresponding reduction would violate the agreed-on operations plan. In the absence of a new, expanded operations plan, manufacturing, sales, and marketing must work to allocate the scarce capacity of the completing needs (via the master production schedule).

The reverse situation is also true. If the operations plan calls for more than sales and marketing currently needs, detailed decisions should be reached about which items will go into inventory. Manufacturing commits people, capacities, and materials to reach company objectives. The issue is only how best to convert these resources into particular end products.

Better integration between functional areas in a business is one of the major payoffs from sales and operations planning. Once a consistent sales and operations plan between top levels of the functional areas is developed, it can be translated into detailed plans that are in concert with top-level agreements. This results in a set of common goals, improved communication, and transparent systems.

Without a sales and operations plan, the expectation is that somehow the job will get done—and in fact, it does get done, but at a price. The price is organizational slack: extra inventories, poor customer service, excess capacity, long lead times, panic operations, and poor response to new opportunities. Informal systems will, of necessity, come into being. Detailed decisions will be made by clerical-level personnel with no guiding policy except "get it out the door as best we can." The annual budget cycle won't be tied in with the detailed plans and will probably be inconsistent and out of date before it's one month old. Sales and marketing requests for products won't be made so as to keep the sum of the detailed end products in line with the budget. In many cases detailed requests for the first month are double the average monthly volume. Only at the end of the year does the reconciliation between requests and budget take place, but in the meantime it has been up to manufacturing to decide what's really needed.

We've seen many companies with these symptoms. Where are these costs reflected? There's no special place in the chart of accounts for them, but they affect the bottom-line profit results. More and more firms are finding that a well-structured monthly sales and operations planning meeting allows the various functional areas to operate in a more coordinated fashion and to better respond to the marketplace. The result is a dynamic overall plan for the company, one that changes as needed and fosters the necessary adaptation in each function.

The Sales and Operations Planning Process

This section views aids to managing the sales and operations planning process. Specifically, we'll be concerned with the monthly sales and operations planning process, the tabular spreadsheet display, and the basic operations planning trade-offs. We will examine these techniques with an example.

The Monthly Sales and Operations Planning Process

Sales and operations planning involves making decisions on each product family concerning changes to the sales plan, the operations plan, and the inventory/backlog. These decisions are made on the basis of recent history, forecasts, and the recommendations of middle management and top management's knowledge of business conditions. A formal process for accomplishing sales and operations planning developed by Tom Wallace is shown in Figure 4.2 (see Wallace reference for additional details). This process begins

FIGURE 4.2
The Monthly Sales and Operations Planning Process

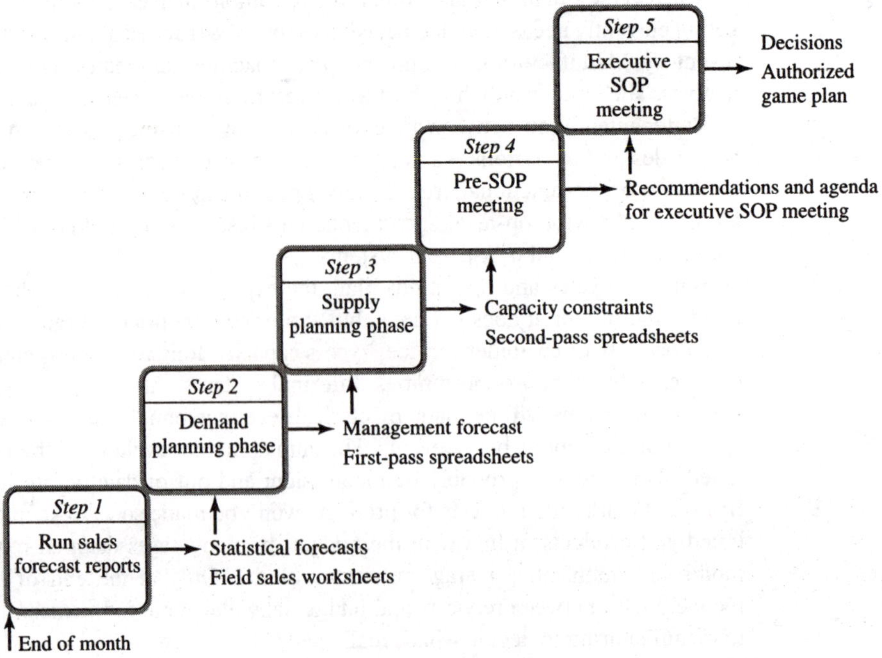

shortly after a month's end and continues for some days. These steps involve middle management and others throughout the company as well as top management, and include:

- Updating the sales forecast.
- Reviewing the impact of changes to the operations plan and determining whether adequate capacity and material will be available to support them.
- Identifying alternatives where problems exist.
- Formulating agreed-on recommendations for top management regarding overall changes to the plans and identifying areas of disagreement where consensus is not possible.
- Communicating this information to top management with sufficient time for them to review it prior to the executive SOP meeting.

Having accomplished this work with the appropriate staff personnel during the month means that a productive two-hour Executive SOP meeting can be held each month to make the appropriate decisions regarding changes to the sales and operations plan.

Five steps form the basis for the monthly planning cycle:

1. *Run the sales forecasting reports.* This step occurs shortly after the month end and involves the information systems department updating the files with data from the month just ended—actual sales, production, inventories, etc. This information is disseminated to the appropriate people, and forms the basis for sales and marketing people to use in developing sales analysis reports, and changes to sales forecasts.
2. *The demand planning phase.* The information received in step 1 for new and existing products is reviewed by sales and marketing and discussed with the view of generating a new management forecast covering the next 12 or more months. For example, in the case of consumer make-to-stock products, price changes, competitive activity, economic conditions, and field sales input regarding large customers are considered in revising the sales forecast. The task here is to override the statistical forecasts when appropriate, and to bring senior marketing and sales management into the loop. It is also necessary to consider the new forecast along with the actual sales, production, and inventory data from the past month. Once the new forecast has been authorized by sales and marketing, it is applied to last month's operations plan. Once this is done it is easy for the operations people to see where the operations plan needs to be changed, and where it is acceptable. The necessary changes are then made that produce the new operations plan.
3. *The supply (capacity) planning phase.* Here is where the capacity planning activity (resource planning) takes place. The new operations plan for each product family grouping is compared with any changes made in the sales forecast or changes that have occurred in inventory or customer order backlog levels. It may be necessary to modify the operations plan if, for example, demand exceeds supply by a margin that is too large to reach with the current plant, or vendor, capacity. In cases where a change in the operations plan is necessary, spending authorization by top management may be required. These are the types of issues that are carried into the pre-SOP meeting.
4. *The pre-SOP meeting.* The purpose of this meeting involving representatives from the various business functions is to (a) make decisions regarding the balance of demand and supply, (b) resolve problems where differences in recommendations exist,

(c) identify areas that cannot be resolved to be discussed in the executive SOP meeting, (d) develop alternative courses of action, and (e) set the agenda for the executive SOP Meeting. This meeting includes a review of the plans for each product family grouping, the development of an updated financial view of the business, recommendations for each product family grouping, recommendations for changes in resource requirements, and recommendations regarding alternatives to be discussed in the Executive SOP Meeting.

5. *The Executive SOP Meeting.* The culminating meeting each month is one that includes the senior executives in the business. Its purpose is to (a) make decisions on the sales and operations plans for each product family, (b) authorize spending for changes in production/procurement rate changes, (c) relate the collective impact of the dollarized version of the product grouping sales and operations plans to the overall business plan, (d) break ties in areas where the pre-SOP team was unable to reach consensus, and (e) to review customer service and business performance.

The discipline required in routinizing the sales and operations planning process is to replan when conditions indicate it's necessary. If information from the demand management function indicates differences between the forecast and actual have exceeded reasonable error limits, replanning may be necessary. Similarly, if conditions change in manufacturing, a new market opportunity arises, or the capital market shifts, replanning may be needed.

Since the purpose of the planning process is to arrive at a coordinated set of plans for each function, mechanisms for getting support for the plans are important. Clearly, a minimum step here is to involve the senior executive team in the business in the process. This does more than legitimize the plan; it involves the people who can resolve issues in the trade-off stage. A second step used by some firms is to virtually write contracts between functions on what the agreements are. The contracts serve to underscore the importance of each function performing to plan, rather than return to informal practices.

To illustrate the nature of the sales and operations planning decisions, we now turn to an example based on a firm with a seasonal sales pattern on its make-to-stock products. We raise the issues in the context of a single product family produced in a dedicated production facility. In this context, there are two issues for discussion:

1. The sales and operations plan must be adjusted frequently to bring sales and production into a proper balance.
2. It is important to find a low cost operations plan when the cost of inventories, overtime, changes in the work force levels, and other capacity variations that meet the company's sales and operations requirements are considered.

This example presents both a cumulative charting and a tabular representation of alternative strategies to resolve these issues.

Sales and Operations Planning Displays

Figure 4.3 shows the aggregate sales forecasts for our example, the AA product family at our mythical XYZ Company, for the year. Monthly totals vary from a high of $15.8 million to a low of $7 million. Figure 4.4 shows these monthly sales data in the form of a **cumulative chart display** (see the solid line). In addition, the dashed straight line represents the

FIGURE 4.3
XYZ Company AA Product Family Monthly Sales Forecast

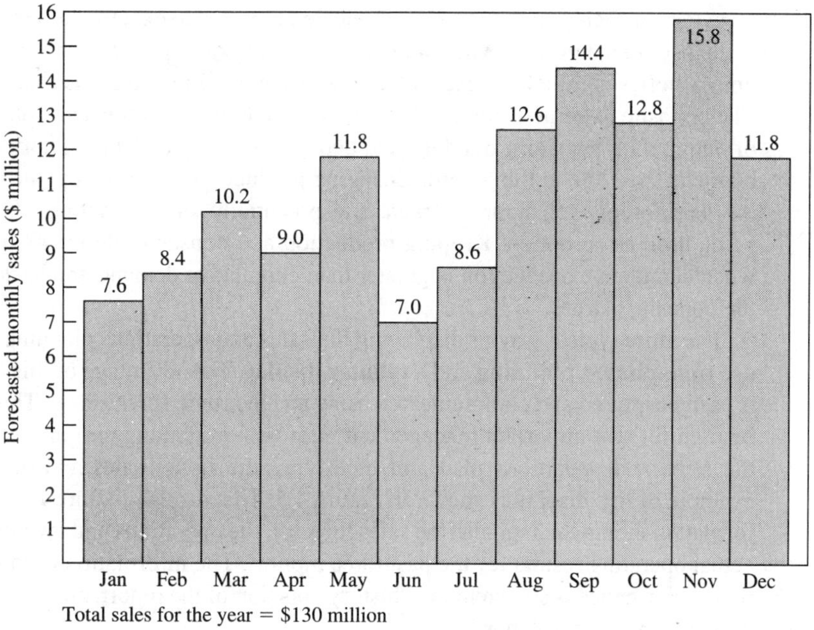

FIGURE 4.4
XYZ Company Cumulative Chart

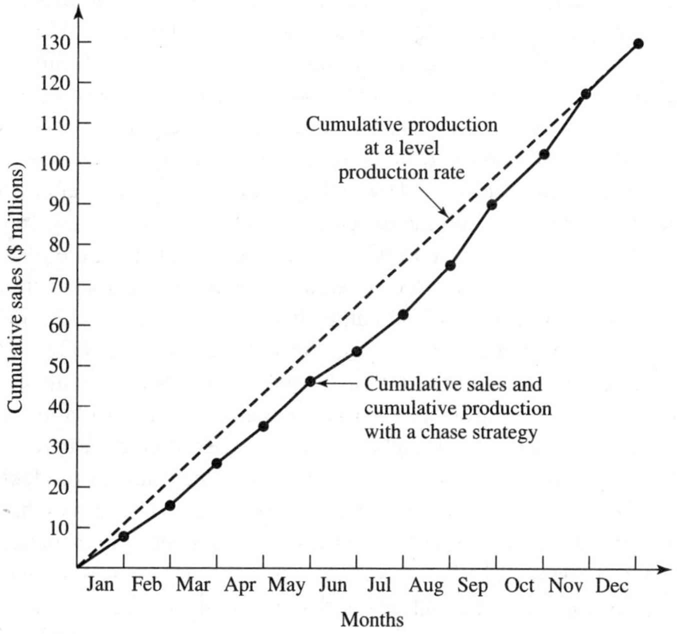

cumulative production if we chose to produce a constant amount each month and that amount was calculated so that we would produce exactly what we needed over the next year.

The cumulative chart shows clearly the implications of alternative plans. For example, the vertical distance between the dashed line and the solid line represents the expected inventory at each point in time. If we elected to produce exactly the same amount as what we expect demand to be each month, we would not expect to carry any inventory. This unique policy is called a **chase strategy,** where production output is changed to chase sales. The opposite extreme is the **level strategy,** where production is at a constant uniform rate of output with inventory buildups and depletions over the planning horizon (and as shown by the dashed line in the graph). Changing production output incurs the costs of changing the workforce level, hours worked, and potentially subcontracting, if subcontracting is being used as an option. Keeping production at a constant rate incurs inventory holding, when cumulative production is greater than cumulative demand and backorder costs when the opposite is true.

The more typical way of displaying the sales and operations planning information is to use **time-phased planning** and a **tabular display.** The advantage of this approach is that it is easily captured and communicated using an electronic spreadsheet. This information can be used for two important management purposes: evaluating current performance against the sales and operations plan and modifying the future sales and operations plan. An example of this display is shown in Figure 4.5. This display requires several important information inputs each month: the sales forecast, the operations and inventory plans, and the actual operating results for the past three months. The information used for assessing current performance is shown in the "history" portion of the report, and the plan for the future is shown in the "plan" portion.

In the *Sales* section of the report shown in Figure 4.5, a planning factor of $30 per unit is used to convert sales dollar to units of sales. This statistic would be obtained from accounting records and represents the average value of a unit sold. Similarly, in the *Operations* portion of the report, an employee productivity factor is used to estimate the required number of employees needed to produce planned production. In our example it is assumed that eight units can be produced by each employee. In the *Inventory* section, we see a days of supply figure. This is calculated by finding the expected sales per day for the next period and dividing that number into the expected end of month inventory. In the *history* part of the report actual sales and inventory level are used, whereas in the *plan* portion expected values are used. In the case of December, actual ending inventory is used (215,000 units), and planned sales are used (253,000 units divided by 20 days = 12,650 units/day). So the days of supply at the end of December is 215,000/12,650 = 16.99 days. Note that we have rounded the numbers in our report. Finally, the customer service numbers shown in the *history* portion are reported from an external source and not a calculation from report data.

The actual plan shown in Figure 4.5 depicts a chase strategy, where we plan to make the forecast demand for each month. Note how much the planned production changes each month and how the number of needed employees varies. The reason that there are only 10 working days in July is due to a planned two-week summer shutdown that occurs every year at our example plant. Whether this plan is feasible or not would depend greatly on the availability of workers that could be shuttled in and out to meet the widely varying production requirements. We discuss this plan relative to cost later in the section, but note how hires and layoffs are calculated based on the changing number of workers from one month to the next.

In revising a plan from month to month, the recent history shown in the report can be quite valuable. Figure 4.5 shows the recent history covering the last three months of sales, production, and inventory levels for this product line. Note that in this case, the

FIGURE 4.5 Chase Demand Operating Plan

	History			Plan												Future
	October	November	December	January	February	March	April	May	June	July	August	September	October	November	December	January
Sales																
Forecast (in million $)	10	13.1	6.9	7.6	8.4	10.2	9	11.8	7	8.6	12.6	14.4	12.8	15.8	11.8	8
(in 1,000 units)	333	437	230	253	280	340	300	393	233	287	420	480	427	527	393	267
Actual (in 1,000 units)	300	400	200													
Difference month	−33	−37	−30													
Difference cumulative		−70	−100													
Operations																
Plan (in 1,000 units)	333	437	230	253	280	340	300	393	233	287	420	480	427	527	393	
(in employees)	1,892	2,731	1,437	1,581	1,667	1,848	1,875	2,235	1,326	3,583	2,283	3,000	2,424	3,292	2,458	
Number working days/month	22	20	20	20	21	23	20	22	22	10	23	20	22	20	20	20
Actual (in 1,000 units)	360	455	300													
Difference month	27	18	70													
Difference cumulative		45	115													
Inventory																
Plan (in 1,000 units)	100	100	100	215	215	215	215	215	215	215	215	215	215	215	215	
(in 1,000 $)	3,000	3,000	3,000	6,440	6,440	6,440	6,440	6,440	6,440	6,440	6,440	6,440	6,440	6,440	6,440	
Actual (in 1,000 units)	60	115	215													
Days of supply	3.0	11.5	17.0	16.1	14.5	14.3	12.0	20.2	7.5	11.8	8.9	11.1	8.2	10.9	16.1	
Customer service (%)	98	100	100													

Employee productivity	8 units/day													
Hiring cost	$200 per employee	Hires	144.3	85.4	181.2	27.2	359.8	0.0	2257.6	0.0	717.4	0.0	867.4	0.0
Layoff cost	$500 per employee	Layoffs	0.0	0.0	0.0	0.0	0	909.1	0.0	1300.7	0.0	575.8	0.0	833.3
Inventory carrying cost	2% per month (applied to the monthly ending inventory)													
Minimum inventory level	5 days of supply													
Beginning labor force	1,437 employees													

Cost of:	January	February	March	April	May	June	July	August	September	October	November	December	Totals
Hiring	$28,850	$17,083	$36,232	$5,435	$71,970	$0	$451,515	$0	$143,478	$0	$173,485	$0	$928,048
Layoffs	$0	$0	$0	$0	$0	$454,545	$0	$650,362	$0	$287,879	$0	$416,667	$1,809,453
Inventory	$128,800	$128,800	$128,800	$128,800	$128,800	$128,800	$128,800	$128,800	$128,800	$128,800	$128,800	$128,800	$1,545,600
												Total cost	$4,283,101

actual sales have fallen short of the forecast sales each month during the past quarter. This is indicated as a negative difference in the fourth and fifth row of Figure 4.5 (difference month and difference cumulative) and amounts to a cumulative difference of −100,000 units (or about 40 percent of the January sales forecast) as of the end of the last quarter as shown in the table. This trend in sales indicates the need to focus on re-forecasting to better estimate sales during the demand planning phase of the sales and operations planning cycle.

Furthermore, the actual production has exceeded the operations plan every month during the past quarter, and the cumulative difference equals +115,000 units. The fact that actual sales are less than the sales plan, and that production has exceeded the operations plan in each month, has produced a major increase in finished goods inventory. As shown in Figure 4.5, the number of days of supply has increased from 3 to 17 over this period.

These results signal a need to adjust the operations plan to bring sales and production into balance. There are many ways in which this could be accomplished. One way would be to reduce the January production plan in order to bring the inventory level back to a reasonable level. It does not appear that our current plan does this. In the next section, we consider the basic trade-offs involved in developing the sales and operations plan and evaluate these trade-offs based on cost.

The Basic Trade-Offs

The trick to a good sales and operations plan is to find a low-cost operations plan. Later in the section, we show a plan that has been "optimized." An optimized plan is interesting, but it may not be valuable because so many of the nonquantitative issues associated with a plan are not captured in the costs. In this section, we again look at the two most basic strategies, a chase strategy and a level strategy. In the chase strategy, just as the name implies we just chase demand. In the level strategy, we keep a constant production rate each month. These are usually good starting points for developing a practical strategy.

In Figure 4.6 we depict a *chase strategy* that is a little more intelligent than the one shown in Figure 4.5. Here, rather than just producing expected demand each period, we produce at a level that allows us to maintain a target days of supply inventory level at the end of each month. This can be useful because the days of supply inventory level target can ensure that we have enough to cope with uncertainty in demand, but not produce an excessive amount. How these targets can be set using statistics is covered in Chapter 11, but for our purposes here, assume that we would like to target five days of supply at the end of each month.

In Figure 4.6, we show a plan that maintains five days of supply at the end of each month. The trick to calculating this plan is to first calculate the required ending inventory balances for each month that represent five days of future supply. For example, in February we expect demand to be 280,000 units or 13,333 units per day (280,000/21). Five-days supply would be 66,666.67 units, which is our inventory target for the end of January. The operations plan for January is then calculated by taking the expected demand, subtracting beginning inventory (actual in this case), and then adding the needed ending inventory (253,000 − 216,000 + 67,000 = 105,000). Doing this for each month allows us to find a "chase" type operating plan that results in a five-week supply of inventory at the end of each month.

FIGURE 4.6 Chase Demand Operating Plan—Target Days of Supply = 5 days

	History			Plan												Future
	October	November	December	January	February	March	April	May	June	July	August	September	October	November	December	January
Sales																
Forecast (in million $)	10	13.1	6.9	7.6	8.4	10.2	9	11.8	7	8.6	12.6	14.4	12.8	15.8	11.8	8.0
(in 1,000 units)	333	437	230	253	280	340	300	393	233	287	420	480	427	527	393	267
Actual (in 1,000 units)	300	400	200													
Difference month	−33	−37	−30													
Difference cumulative		−70	−100													
Operations																
Plan (in 1,000 units)	333	437	230	105	287	341	314	357	324	235	449	457	461	493	362	
(in employees)	1,892	2,731	1,437	656	1,710	1,854	1,965	2,028	1,839	2,933	2,439	2,856	2,621	3,083	2,260	
Number working days/month	22	20	20	20	21	23	20	22	22	10	23	20	22	20	20	20
Actual (in 1,000 units)	360	455	300													
Difference month	27	18	70													
Difference cumulative		45	115													
Inventory																
Plan (in 1,000 units)	100	100	100	67	74	75	89	53	143	91	120	97	132	98	67	
(in 1,000 $)	3,000	3,000	3,000	2,000	2,217	2,250	2,682	1,591	4,300	2,739	3,600	2,909	3,950	2,950	2,000	
Actual (in 1,000 units)	60	115	215													
Days of supply	4.4	5.8	17.0	5.0	5.0	5.0	5.0	5.0	5.0	5.0	5.0	5.0	5.0	5.0	5.0	
Customer service (%)	98	100	100													

Emplyee productivity	8	units/day												
Hiring cost	$200	per employee	Hires	0.0	1053.5	143.9	111.2	63.3	0.0	1094.1	0.0	417.5	0.0	461.9	0.0
Layoff cost	$500	per employee	Layoffs	780.8	0.0	0.0	0.0	0	189.4	0.0	494.4	0.0	234.7	0.0	822.9
Inventory carrying cost	2%	per month (applied to the monthly ending inventory)												
Minimum inventory level	5	days of supply												
Beginning labor force	1,437	employees												

Cost of:	January	February	March	April	May	June	July	August	September	October	November	December	Totals
Hiring	$0	$210,710	$28,787	$22,246	$12,655	$0	$218,826	$0	$83,499	$0	$92,390	$0	$669,112
Layoffs	$390,375	$0	$0	$0	$0	$94,697	$0	$247,204	$0	$117,338	$0	$411,458	$1,261,072
Inventory	$40,000	$44,348	$45,000	$53,636	$31,818	$86,000	$54,783	$72,000	$58,182	$79,000	$59,000	$40,000	$663,767
												Total cost	$2,593,951

Summarizing, **a chase strategy with a five weeks of supply target can be found as follows:**

Step 1. Calculate end of month inventory target values.

$$\text{Inventory}_t = \text{Target days} \times \text{Expected demand}_{t+1}/\text{Working days}_{t+1} \qquad \textbf{(4.1)}$$

Step 2. Calculate the operations plan in units.

$$\text{Planned production}_t = \text{Forecast sales}_t - \text{Inventory}_{t-1} + \text{Inventory}_t \qquad \textbf{(4.2)}$$

Step 3. Calculate the number of employees required.

$$\text{Employees}_t = \text{Planned production}_t/\text{Employee productivity} \qquad \textbf{(4.3)}$$

Step 4. Calculate hires and fires each period.

$$\text{If Employees}_t > \text{Employees}_{t-1} \text{ then Hires} = \text{Employees}_t - \text{Employees}_{t-1}$$

$$\text{else Fires}_t = \text{Employees}_{t-1} - \text{Employees}_t \qquad \textbf{(4.4)}$$

Note that a spreadsheet with these calculations can be found at http://www.pom.edu/mpc6e.

The next basic strategy that we will develop is the *level strategy*. Here, we are looking at the exact opposite extreme, where we keep a constant workforce for the entire planning horizon. The plan shown in Figure 4.7 shows this type of plan. In this case, the labor force is kept at a constant 2,153 employees. Of course, the trick in this case is to figure out where the 2,153 employees came from. We do this by figuring out exactly how much we expect to need to produce over the planning horizon and then divide this by how much one employee can produce over that same period of time. For our example, forecast demand over the 12 months is 4,333,333 units. We can subtract out our beginning inventory of 215,000 units, but we need to add back the inventory needed for our days of supply target at the end of the planning horizon (we refer to this as period T in the equations below). From our analysis in Figure 4.6, we know we need 66,667 units at the end of December. So in total we need to produce $4{,}333{,}333 - 215{,}000 + 66{,}667 = 4{,}185{,}000$ units. An employee can produce eight units/day and will work for 243 days over the 12 months (this is the sum of the working days from January through December), and an employee can produce $8 \times 243 = 1{,}944$ units. From this we can calculate that we need $4{,}185{,}000/1{,}944 = 2{,}152.8$ employees. We could round this to 2,153 employees if we like, but for our calculations in Figure 4.7 we used the fraction.

After calculating the number of employees needed, we can then fill in the rest of our table by calculating planned production, planned end of month inventory, and planned days of supply. Summarizing, a **level strategy with a constant number of employees and an end of the horizon days of supply target level can be found as follows:**

Step 1. Calculate the number of employees needed.

$$\text{Inventory}_T = \text{Expected demand}_{T+1}/\text{Working days}_{T+1} \qquad \textbf{(4.1)}$$

Total production required =

$$\text{Total forecast demand} - \text{Beginning inventory} + \text{Ending inventory}_T \qquad \textbf{(4.5)}$$

Planned production each period =

$$\text{Total production required}/\text{Number of periods} \qquad \textbf{(4.6)}$$

FIGURE 4.7 Level Operating Plan—Constant Number of Employees

Number of employees required 2,152.8

	History			Plan												Future
	October	November	December	January	February	March	April	May	June	July	August	September	October	November	December	January
Sales																
Forecast (in million $)	10	13.1	6.9	7.6	8.4	10.2	9	11.8	7	8.6	12.6	14.4	12.8	15.8	11.8	8.0
(in 1,000 units)	333	437	230	253	280	340	300	393	233	287	420	480	427	527	393	267
Actual (in 1,000 units)	300	400	200													
Difference month	−33	−37	−30													
Difference cumulative		−70	−100													
Operations																
Plan (in 1,000 units)	333	437	230	344	362	396	344	379	379	172	396	344	379	344	344	
(in employees)	1,892	2,731	1,437	2,153	2,153	2,153	2,153	2,153	2,153	2,153	2,153	2,153	2,153	2,153	2,153	
Number working days/month	22	20	20	20	21	23	20	22	22	10	23	20	22	20	20	20
Actual (in 1,000 units)	360	455	300													
Difference month	27	18	70													
Difference cumulative		45	115													
Inventory																
Plan (in 1,000 units)	100	100	100	306	388	444	488	474	619	505	481	346	298	116	67	
(in 1,000 $)	3,000	3,000	3,000	9,183	11,633	13,317	14,650	14,217	18,583	15,150	14,433	10,367	8,933	3,467	2,000	
Actual (in 1,000 units)	60	115	215													
Days of supply	4.4	5.8	17.0	23.0	26.2	29.6	27.3	44.7	21.6	27.7	20.0	17.8	11.3	5.9	5.0	
Customer service (%)	98	100	100													

			January	February	March	April	May	June	July	August	September	October	November	December
Emplyee productivity	8 units/day													
Hiring cost	$200 per employee	Hires	715.8	0.0	0.0	0.0	0.0	0.0	0.0	0.0	0.0	0.0	0.0	0.0
Layoff cost	$500 per employee	Layoffs	0.0	0.0	0.0	0.0	0	0.0	0.0	0.0	0.0	0.0	0.0	0.0
Inventory carrying cost	2% per month (applied to the monthly ending inventory)													
Minimum inventory level	5 days of supply													
Beginning labor force	1,437 employees													

Cost of:	January	February	March	April	May	June	July	August	September	October	November	December	Totals
Hiring	$143,156	$0	$0	$0	$0	$0	$0	$0	$0	$0	$0	$0	$143,156
Layoffs	$0	$0	$0	$0	$0	$0	$0	$0	$0	$0	$0	$0	$0
Inventory	$183,667	$232,667	$266,333	$293,000	$284,333	$371,667	$303,000	$288,667	$207,333	$178,667	$69,333	$40,000	$2,718,667
												Total cost	$2,861,823

Employees required each period =

$$\text{Planned production each period/Employee productivity/Day} \quad \textbf{(4.7)}$$

Step 2. Calculate ending inventory levels and days of supply.

$$\text{Inventory}_t = \text{Inventory}_{t-1} + \text{Planned production}_t - \text{Forecast demand}_t \quad \textbf{(4.8)}$$

$$\text{Days of supply}_t = \text{Inventory}_t/(\text{Expected demand}_{t+1}/\text{Working days}_{t+1}) \quad \textbf{(4.9)}$$

The example shows the basic trade-offs in operations planning. In our example we focused on two alternatives, where the first required hiring and laying off workers based on meeting required demand, and the second required inventory accumulation to allow a constant compliment of workers. Other alternatives that may be considered are undertime and overtime options and alternative capacity forms such as outside contracting. Evaluating these trade-offs is very firm-specific. In the following we look at how to evaluate alternative plans based on economic analysis.

Economic Evaluation of Alternative Plans

To illustrate the analysis when cost data are available, we assume Figure 4.8 cost data were provided for our sample company. The cost to hire an employee is estimated to be $200, whereas the cost to lay off is $500. The final cost element, inventory carrying cost, is estimated to be 2 percent per month, on the basis of monthly ending inventory value.

We must establish the starting conditions before beginning the operations planning analysis. Here, we assume the current actual employment status with 1,437 employees and January inventory of 215,000 units. In Figure 4.9 we have captured the costs associated with the chase strategy shown in Figure 4.6 and the level strategy in Figure 4.7. With these plans we are assuming that the total amount produced is the same with both plans because we start and end with the same amount of inventory and produce to meet the forecast

FIGURE 4.8
XYZ Company Operations Planning Data

Hiring cost	$200 per employee
Firing cost	$500 per employee
Inventory carrying cost	2% per month (applied to the monthly ending inventory)
Beginning and ending inventory	215,000 product units
Beginning labor force	1,437 persons

FIGURE 4.9
Costs of Alternative Operations Plans

Cost of:	Chase Sales Plan*	Level Production Plan	Mixed Plan
Hiring	$669,112	$ 143,156	$ 259,765
Layoff	1,261,072	0	237,705
Carrying inventory	663,767	2,718,667	895,073
Total	$2,593,951	$2,861,823	$1,392,543

*Note: The chase sales plan costs have been adjusted to reflect the −100,000 unit adjustment made in January.

demand. Given this, we have not considered the actual cost of production and only calculated the incremental cost of hiring, layoffs, and carrying inventory. From this analysis the chase plan looks like the winner, at least from the cost analysis data.

The last alternative, evaluated in Figure 4.9 and shown in Figure 4.10, is a mixed strategy calling for adding employees in April, July, and August, and laying off employees in December. In this strategy, we plan to carry the five days of supply at the end of December, as was done in the other two plans. In this plan we have some periods when inventory is being drawn down (January, February, and March) and other periods when inventory is being built in anticipation of future demand (August and October). As can be seen, this strategy looks attractive due to its low cost.

Developing a mixed strategy is probably best done using a trial-and-error approach based on the actual situation and options that are available. If labor flexibility is needed, it may be possible to have a temporary labor pool that is available during certain times each year. For example, during the summer college students may be available, and it may be possible to take advantage of this talent at fairly reasonable cost. Many companies use temporary labor pools during certain peak demand times of the year as part of the operations strategy.

Setting up a spreadsheet that allows trial-and-error testing of ideas can be done with equations similar to those used for the chase and level strategies. A key decision that must be made is deciding what will be the decision variables. Decision variables are those cells in the spreadsheet that can be varied as part of the trial-and-error process. In the case of the mixed strategy spreadsheet shown in Figure 4.10, the decision variables are the hiring and layoff decisions in January through December. The spreadsheet is designed so that changes in these cells are tied directly to the number of employees row in the operations part of the plan. So, for example, if we hire 554 employees in April, this is reflected in the number of employees in April being 554 higher than the March compliment. Planned production is then tied to the number of employees by multiplying by employee productivity and number of working days in the period. Inventory is then calculated by taking the inventory from the previous period plus planned production and then subtracting forecast sales.

The solution shown in Figure 4.10 was actually found by using the Solver optimizer that comes with Microsoft Excel. Details for how to actually set this up are found in Chapter 4A, Advanced Sales and Operations Planning. In the next section, we turn our attention to how to actually implement a sales and operations planning process, including the role of management and the various functions in the firm.

The New Management Obligations

Implementing sales and operations planning requires major changes in management, particularly in top management coordination of functional activities in the business. If the sales and operations plan is to be the game plan for running a manufacturing company, it follows that top management needs to provide the necessary direction.

Top Management Role

Top management's first obligation is to commit to the sales and operations planning process. This means a major change in many firms. The change involves establishing the framework for sales and operations planning: getting the right team together, setting meetings,

FIGURE 4.10 Mixed Operating Plan—Optimized

	History			Plan												Future
	October	November	December	January	February	March	April	May	June	July	August	September	October	November	December	January
Sales																
Forecast (in million $)	10	13.1	6.9	7.6	8.4	10.2	9	11.8	7	8.6	12.6	14.4	12.8	15.8	11.8	8.0
(in 1,000 units)	333	437	230	253	280	340	300	393	233	287	420	480	427	527	393	267
Actual (in 1,000 units)	300	400	200													
Difference month	−33	−37	−30													
Difference cumulative		−70	−100													
Operations																
Plan (in 1,000 units)	333	437	230	230	241	264	319	350	350	208	503	438	482	438	362	
(in employees)	1,892	2,731	1,437	1,437	1,437	1,437	1,991	1,991	1,991	2,598	2,736	2,736	2,736	2,736	2,260	
Number working days/month	22	20	20	20	21	23	20	22	22	10	23	20	22	20	20	20
Actual (in 1,000 units)	360	455	300													
Difference month	27	18	70													
Difference cumulative		45	115													
Inventory																
Plan (in 1,000 units)	100	100	100	192	153	77	96	53	170	91	175	132	187	98	67	
(in 1,000 $)	3,000	3,000	3,000	5,748	4,590	2,322	2,879	1,591	5,103	2,739	5,241	3,973	5,618	2,950	2,000	
Actual (in 1,000 units)	60	115	215													
Days of supply	4.4	5.8	17.0	14.4	10.4	5.2	5.4	5.0	5.9	5.0	7.3	6.8	7.1	5.0	5.0	
Customer service (%)	98	100	100													

			January	February	March	April	May	June	July	August	September	October	November	December
Emplyee productivity	8 units/day													
Hiring cost	$200 per employee	Hires	0.0	0.0	0.0	553.9	0.0	0.0	607.4	137.5	0.0	0.0	0.0	0.0
Layoff cost	$500 per employee	Layoffs	0.0	0.0	0.0	0.0	0	0.0	0.0	0.0	0.0	0.0	0.0	475.4
Inventory carrying cost	2% per month (applied to the monthly ending inventory)													
Minimum inventory level	5 days of supply													
Beginning labor force	1,437 employees													

Cost of:	January	February	March	April	May	June	July	August	September	October	November	December	Totals
Hiring	$0	$0	$0	$110,786	$0	$0	$121,489	$27,490	$0	$0	$0	$0	$259,765
Layoffs	$0	$0	$0	$0	$0	$0	$0	$0	$0	$0	$0	$237,705	$237,705
Inventory	$114,952	$91,802	$46,446	$57,576	$31,818	$102,061	$54,783	$104,818	$79,457	$112,361	$59,000	$40,000	$895,073
												Total cost	$1,392,543

participating in the process, and so on. The change may also imply modifications of performance measurement and reward structures to align them with the plan. We should expect at the outset that many existing goals and performance measures will be in conflict with the integration provided by the sales and operations planning activity. These should be rooted out and explicitly changed. Enforcing changes implies a need to abide by and provide an example of the discipline required to manage with the planning system. This implies even top management must act within the planned flexibility range for individual actions and must evaluate possible changes that lie outside the limits.

As part of the commitment to the planning process, top management *must force* the resolution of trade-offs between functions prior to approving plans. The sales and operations plan provides a transparent basis for resolving these conflicts. It should provide basic implications of alternative choices even if it doesn't make decisions any easier. If trade-offs aren't made at this level they'll be forced into the mix of day-to-day activities of operating people who'll have to resolve them—perhaps unfavorably. If, for example, manufacturing continues long runs of products in the face of declining demand, the mismatch between production and the market will lead to increased inventories.

One of the benefits of sales and operations planning is to be able to run the business with one set of numbers. Top management should lead the cultural change to make that happen. Sales and operations activities must encompass all formal plans in an integrated fashion. If budgeting is a separate activity, it won't relate to the sales and operations plan and operating managers will need to make a choice. Similarly, if the profit forecast is based solely on the sales forecast (revenue) and accounting data (standard costs) and doesn't take into account implications for production, its value is doubtful. The sales and operations planning process intention is to produce complete and integrated plans, budgets, objectives, and goals that are used by managers to make decisions and provide the basis for evaluating performance. If other planning activities or evaluation documents are in place, the end result will be poor execution. An unfortunate but frequent approach is to invest management time in the sales and operations planning activity, but thereafter allow the company to be run by a separate performance measurement system or budget.

Functional Roles

The primary obligation under sales and operations planning is to "hit the plan" for all functions involved: manufacturing, sales, engineering, finance, and so on. A secondary obligation is the need to communicate when something will prevent hitting the plan. The sooner a problem can be evaluated in terms of other functional plans, the better. The obligation for communication provides the basis for keeping all groups' plans consistent when changes are necessary.

The purpose of the monthly planning cycle shown in Figure 4.2 is to facilitate cross-functional communication. This cycle ensures that critical demand and supply issues and important business trade-offs are considered on a routine basis. Further, the pre-SOP and executive SOP meetings are structured to ensure that decisions are made to resolve important demand and supply issues. In managing this process, it is important to have a cross-functional team with the appropriate skills to implement and execute sales and operations planning. There are six areas to be addressed in terms of roles and responsibilities.

1. *Executive champion/sponsor.* This role needs to be filled by a senior executive in the business who can keep top management focused on the process, clear major obstacles,

and acquire the necessary resources. Either the president or a senior executive who has a solid working relationship with the president is a good candidate.

2. *SOP process owner.* This needs to be a person who can lead the implementation effort and can provide the leadership for the sales and operations planning process, normally as a part of other responsibilities. A well-organized person who has good people skills and can run meetings is a good choice. This person might come from any of the following jobs: director of sales administration, demand manager, materials manager, production control manager, controller, or sales manager.
3. *Demand planning team.* This team typically includes people with the following job titles: demand manager, product manager, forecast analyst, sales manager, salesperson, customer service manager, sales administration manager, new products coordinator, and SOP process owner.
4. *Supply planning team.* This team is made up of the following group: plant manager, materials manager, purchasing manager, master scheduler, distribution manager, production control manager, new products coordinator, and SOP process owner.
5. *Pre-SOP team.* This team needs to provide effective cross-functional skills within the business and could include the demand manager, materials manager, customer service manager, forecast analyst, product manager, master scheduler, plant manager, purchasing manager, controller, new products coordinator, and SOP process owner.
6. *Executive SOP team.* This group should include the president (general manager, chief operating officer), vice presidents of sales, marketing, operations, product development, finance, logistics, and human resources, and the SOP process owner.

In addition, information technology support is needed to support the sales and operations planning team because the planning process is most often carried out with electronic spreadsheets. This role might be filled by a spreadsheet developer or by having an appropriate level of spreadsheet skills in the team. An example of the software used for SOP is shown by Roger Brooks (see references).

Other cross-functional issues involve defining product families and determining how many of them to consider in developing the sales and operations plan. Experience suggests that if more that a dozen are used, that is too many. Six to twelve appears to be the best number. A larger number involves getting into too much detail and losing top management's attention during the monthly planning meetings. Figure 4.11, from Tom Wallace's book *Sales and Operations Planning,* shows a range of possibilities to consider in defining the product family groupings. It is difficult to do sales and operations planning at the top of the pyramid because there is not enough granularity at that level on which to base the demand/supply decisions. Likewise, at the bottom of the pyramid there is too much detail, and it will be difficult to see an overall picture of volume in aggregate planning.

The other problem in defining the product families is how to structure these families in a way that is convenient for the different functions in the business. Some of the possibilities include structuring the product family groupings by product type, product characteristics, product size, brand, market segment, or customer. The fundamental question is simply "How do you go to market?" Since products are what a company provides to customers, the product family groupings should be set up on that basis. Setting up the product family groupings in a way that is consistent with how the sales and marketing people think about

FIGURE 4.11
Product Family Grouping

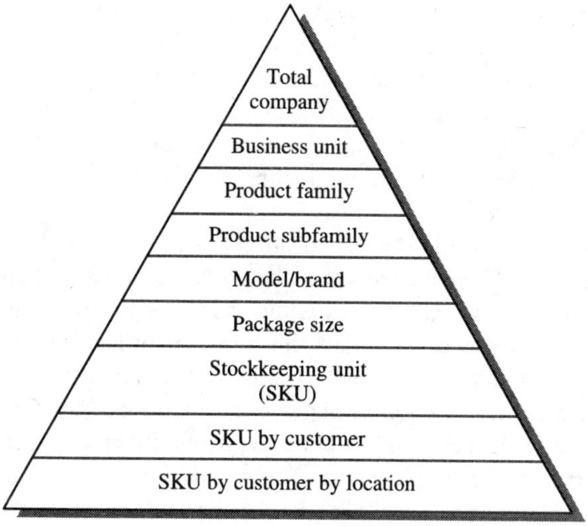

the market is best. However, when the product groupings line up with the market segments or customer groups, they often do not line up with the resources—plants, departments, and processes. This can, however, be handled by identifying the production resources and reviewing their status separately.

A final problem in structuring the product families is to choose the appropriate unit of measure for each family. Choices include: units, pounds, gallons, cases, etc. Here the best approach is to select a measure that is based on how the company goes to market. If the plants need to use a different measure, this can be handled in capacity planning through conversion routines.

Still another cross-functional issue is that the process of budgeting usually needs to change and to be integrated with sales and operations planning and subsequent departmental plans. In many firms, budgeting is done on an annual basis, using data that aren't part of the manufacturing planning and control system. Manufacturing budgets are often based on historical cost relationships and a separation of fixed and variable expenses. These data aren't as precise as data obtained by utilizing the MPC system database. By using the database, we can evaluate tentative master production schedules in terms of component part needs, capacities, and expected costs. We can then analyze the resultant budgets for the effect of product mix changes as well as for performance against standards.

Another important aspect of relating budgeting to the sales and operations planning activity and underlying MPC systems and database is that the cycle can be done more frequently. We won't need to collect data—they always exist in up-to-date form. Moreover, inconsistencies are substantially cut. The budget should always agree with the sales and operations plan, which, in turn, is in concert with the disaggregated end-item and component plans that support the operations plan. As a result, an operating manager should have to choose between a budget and satisfying the operations plan far less often.

With budgeting and sales and operations planning done on the same basis with the same underlying dynamic database, it's natural to incorporate cost accounting. This enables us to perform detailed variance accounting as well as cross-check transaction accuracy.

The most obvious need for integrated planning and control is between sales, marketing, and production. Yet it's often the most difficult to accomplish. Firms must ensure product availability for special promotions, match customer orders with specific production lots, coordinate distribution activities with production, and deal with a host of other cross-functional problems.

The sales and marketing job under integrated sales and operations planning is to sell what's in the sales plan. We must instill the feeling that overselling is just as bad as underselling. In either case, there will be a mismatch with manufacturing output, financial requirements, and inventory/backlog levels. If an opportunity arises to sell more than the plan, it needs to be formally evaluated via a change in the sales and operations plan. By going through this process, we can time this increase so it can be properly supported by both manufacturing and finance. And once the formal plan has been changed, it's again each function's job to achieve its specified objectives—no more and no less.

Similarly, it's manufacturing's job to achieve the plan—exactly. Overproduction may well mean that too much capacity and resources is being utilized. Underproduction possibly means the reverse (not enough resources) or means poor performance. In either case, performance against the plan is poor. This can be the fault of either the standard-setting process or inadequate performance. Both problems require corrective action.

When manufacturing is hitting the schedule, it's a straightforward job for sales and marketing to provide good customer order promises and other forms of customer service. It's also a straightforward job for finance to plan cash flows and anticipate financial performance.

If the sales and operations planning results can't be achieved, whatever component can't meet its plan must be clearly responsible for reporting this condition promptly. If, for example, a major supplier can't meet its commitments, the impact on the detailed sales, marketing, and operations plans must be quickly ascertained.

Integrating Strategic Planning

An important direction-setting activity, strategic planning can be done in different ways. Some companies approach it primarily as an extension of budgeting. Typically, these firms use a bottom-up process, which is largely an extrapolation of the departmental budgets based on growth assumptions and cost-volume analysis. One key aspect of these firms' strategic plans is to integrate these bottom-up extrapolations into a coherent whole. Another is to critically evaluate the overall outcome from a corporate point of view.

A more recent approach to strategic planning is to base the plan more on products and markets, and less on organizational units. The company's products/markets are typically grouped into strategic business units (SBUs), with each SBU evaluated in terms of its strength and weakness vis-à-vis competitors' similar business units. The budgetary process in this case is done on an SBU basis rather than an organizational unit basis. Business units are evaluated in terms of their competitive strengths, relative advantages, life cycles, and cash flow patterns (e.g., when does an SBU need cash and when is it a cash provider?). From a strategic point of view, the objective is to carefully manage a portfolio of SBUs to the firm's overall advantage.

Sales and operations planning and departmental plans to support these strategic planning efforts can be important. In the case of the operations plan, the overall database and systems must ensure that the sales and operations plans will be in concert with disaggregated decision making. In other words, the MPS and related functions ensure that strategic planning decisions are executed!

All the advantages of integrating sales and operations planning with budgeting also apply when the SBU focus is taken. It makes sense to state the sales and operations plan in the same SBU units; that is, rather than use dollar outputs per time unit, the sales and operations plan should be stated in SBU terminology.

Controlling the Operations Plan

A special responsibility in sales and operations planning involves control of performance against the plan. As a prerequisite to control, the sales and operations planning process should be widely understood in the firm. The seriousness with which it's regarded should be communicated as well as the exact planned results that pertain to each of the organization's functional units. In other words, the planning process must be transparent, with clear communication of expectations, to control actual results. For the operations plan, this means wide dissemination of the plan and its implications for managers.

Key issues in sales and operations planning are when and how to change the plan, and how stable to keep the operations portion of the plan from period to period. No doubt a stable operations plan results in far fewer execution problems by the detailed master production scheduling, material planning, and other execution functions. Stability also fosters achievement of some steady-state operations where capacity can be more effectively utilized.

Increasingly, companies are using lean manufacturing concepts, with many aspects of the system based on manual controls. One key to making lean manufacturing work is a stable operations plan. The output rate is held constant for long time periods and is modified only after extensive analysis. This means the production rate at each step of the manufacturing process can be held to very constant levels, providing stability and predictability.

Concluding Principles

Sales and operations planning provide key inputs to MPC systems. It represents management's handle on the business. This chapter emphasizes the key relationships of top management and functional management in developing and maintaining an effective sales and operations plan. The following important principles summarize our discussion.

- The operations plan is not a forecast; it must be a managerial statement of desired production output.
- The operations plan should be a part of the sales and operations planning process so it will be in complete agreement with the other functional plans (sales plan, budget, and so on) that make up the business plan.
- The trade-offs required to frame the operations plan must be made *prior* to final approval of the plan.
- There must be top-management involvement in the sales and operations planning process, which should be directly related to strategic planning.
- The MPC system should be used to perform routine activities and provide routine data, so management time can be devoted to important tasks.
- The MPC system should be used to facilitate what-if analyses at the sales and operations planning level.
- Reviews of performance against sales and operations plans are needed to prompt replanning when necessary.

References

Brooks, Roger. *JDA Executive Workbench for S&OP.* www.jda.com.

Wallace, T. F. *Sales and Operations Planning: The How To Handbook.* Cincinnati: Tom Wallace Publications, 1999.

Discussion Questions

1. The sales and operations plan is sometimes called "management's handle on manufacturing." Discuss.
2. What would you guess would be the aggregate terms used in managing a university as a whole? The computer center? Buildings and grounds? An individual major?
3. What are the differences between sales and operations planning and budgeting?
4. Some experts argue the sales and operations planning process ought to be done only on exception, that is, only when conditions have changed enough to warrant replanning. Others argue it should be done on a periodic basis and when required by exception. What's your view?
5. Discuss the relative merits of cumulative charts (e.g., Figure 4.4) and tabular plans (e.g., Figure 4.5) for sales and operations planning.
6. What are some implications of not making the trade-offs explicit in the sales and operations planning process?
7. In incorporating the firm's strategic objectives into the sales and operations planning process, what differences exist between such firms as coal mines or cardboard manufacturers versus fashion or manufacturers of machine tools?

Problems

1. Complete the history portion of the Elm Co. sales and operations planning spreadsheet given below. Inventory is valued at $700 per unit. The actual inventory at the end of September was 150 units.

Elm Co. Sales and Operations Planning Spreadsheet

		History		
		October	November	December
Sales				
Forecast	(in million $)	0.80	0.85	0.90
	(in units)	800	850	900
Actual	(in units)	826	851	949
Diff. month				
Diff. cumulative				
Operations				
Plan	(in units)	800	800	800
	(in employees)	6	8	8
Number working days/mo.		23	19	19
Actual	(in units)	798	802	800
Diff. month				
Diff. cumulative				
Inventory				
Plan	(in units)			
	(in 1,000 $)			
Actual	(in units)	122	73	−76
Days of supply				

2. The Trapper Lawn Equipment Company manufactures a line of riding mowers. The company currently uses a chase strategy in its sales and operations planning. Management attempts to maintain a line fill rate of at least 99 percent and hold inventory of five days. Employees can produce three units a day on average. The historical records for the last three months and the plan for the next six months are given as follows:

Trapper Lawn Equipment Company Sales and Operations Planning Spreadsheet: Riding Mowers Product Group (Make-to-Stock)

		History			Plan					
		Oct	Nov	Dec	Jan	Feb	Mar	Apr	May	Jun
Sales										
Forecast	(in million $)	12.50	10.00	16.25	5.00	5.00	7.50	10.00	12.50	17.50
	(in units)	5,000	4,000	6,500	2,000	2,000	3,000	4,000	5,000	7,000
Actual	(in units)	4,384	3,626	6,065						
Diff. month		−616	−374	−435						
Diff. cumulative			−990	−1,425						
Operations										
Plan	(in units)	5,000	4,000	6,500	2,000	2,000	3,000	4,000	5,000	7,000
	(in employees)	72	70	114	33	32	43	67	76	106
Number working days/mo.		23	19	19	20	21	23	20	22	22
Actual	(in units)	5,649	4,091	7,279						
Diff. month		649	91	779						
Diff. cumulative			740	1,519						
Inventory										
Plan	(in units)	1,270	1,270	1,270	3,944	3,944	3,944	3,944	3,944	3,944
	(in 1,000 $)	2,223	2,223	2,223	6,902	6,902	6,902	6,902	6,902	6,902
Actual	(in units)	2,265	2,730	3,944						
Days of supply		12	12	12	39	41	30	20	17	12

a. Given this information, suggest a revised production plan for the next three months (January, February, March) that will hit the five days of inventory supply target if you accept the sales forecast.

b. What are the implications of this plan, considering the qualitative factors?

3. As production manager for the Trapper Lawn Equipment Company, you are concerned about the impact of marketing's forecast accuracy on inventory performance. If the future actual sales for January through June are off by the same average historical error percentage as the last three months (see table in problem 2):

a. What is the historical forecast error?

b. What would your estimate of actual sales be for January through June?

c. What would the days of supply and inventory level be assuming the production plan is executed according to the current plan and your estimate in part b is correct?

d. What options would you consider to address this problem?

4. On December 20 (the end of the fourth quarter), Ivar Jorgenson, head operations planner for Ski & Sea, Inc., is in charge of developing a sales and operations plan for the coming year. Ski & Sea assembles jet skis and snowmobiles from subassemblies and component parts provided by reliable vendors. Both products (end items) utilize the same small engines and many of the same parts. They require the same assembly time and employee labor skills. The available planning information is as follows:

Demand Forecasts

Quarter	Jet Skis	Snowmobiles
1	10,000	9,000
2	15,000	7,000
3	16,000	19,000
4	3,000	10,000

Anticipated Quarter 1 Beginning inventory	600 skis	400 Snowmobiles

Production and costs

Regular time	$15.00 per unit
Overtime	$22.50 per unit
Subcontract	$30.00 per unit
Part-time	$36.00 per unit
Inventory	$3.00 per unit per quarter, based on average inventory during each quarter
Back order	$24.00 per unit per quarter (based on back orders at end of quarter)
Hiring	$300.00 per full-time employee (no cost if part-time)
Layoff	$1,500.00 per full-time employee (no cost if part-time)

Production rates

Regular	500 units per full-time employee per quarter (of either unit)
Overtime (max.)	200 units per full-time employee per quarter (of either unit)
Part-time	400 units per part-time employee per quarter (of either unit)
Initial workforce size	44 full-time employees (beginning of quarter 1)

Additional assumptions

1. Part-time employees may not work overtime.
2. Assume 100% utilization of employees on regular time (i.e., all employees on the payroll during a period produce at least 500 units). If overtime is used, up to another 200 units can be produced per employee.

a. Develop an operations plan that utilizes a level, or constant, rate of output each quarter using full-time regular employees only. Ending inventory and back orders for quarter 4 must be equal to zero. Summarize the plan, its costs, and its consequences.

b. Prepare a cumulative chart for your plan in part a of this problem.

c. If each shipping container for completed jet skis and snowmobiles requires 20 cu. ft. of space, what is the maximum finished-goods warehouse space you will need next year if the plan in part b of this problem is adopted.

d. If the cost of each completed end item is $600, what is the maximum amount of capital that will be tied up in finished-goods inventory during the year?

5. Suppose that Ivar Jorgenson finds out on December 21 that the long-range weather forecast was revised by the weather service and now more snow than normal is predicted. As a result, the marketing department at Sea & Ski raises its forecast for quarter 1 sales of snowmobiles from 9,000 to 11,000 units. He will now have to develop and analyze several alternative level plans for next year. Keep in mind that each of these plans must consider:
   - Beginning inventory of 600 skis and 400 snowmobiles.
   - Ending inventory and back orders for quarter 4 must be zero.
   - Each plan must have the same level total-output rate each quarter.

   a. Develop a level plan that uses overtime by regular, full-time employees to meet the new demand conditions (with no additional hiring). Calculate the total annual cost of this plan.

   b. Develop a second plan that will use regular employees (no overtime) plus subcontracting to meet the new demand conditions (with no additional hiring). Calculate the total annual costs.

   c. Another possibility would be to hire an additional full-time employee on January 2 and employ him/her for the full year. Calculate the total annual cost.

6. Susie Svensen, the VP of marketing at Ski & Sea, is not happy with having back orders in any sales and operations plan for the future. She asks Ivar to develop a plan that requires no back orders at any time during the year. The VP of manufacturing, Josef Jaeger, says he will insist that any such plan specify the same output each quarter and use full-time employees on a regular time only. The VP of finance, Thor Ledger, states that quarter 4 ending inventory need not be zero, but it should be as low as possible.

   a. Use the original forecasts, beginning inventory, and other data from problem 4. Develop a plan that will meet the requirement of all three VPs. (*Hint:* Examine the graphs you prepared for problem 4b. What slope is required for the output line to eliminate backlogs?)

   b. What will the ending inventory for quarter 4 be?

7. On December 22, Thor Ledger informs Ivar that the cost of capital will be extremely high next year. As a consequence he asks him to develop a radically different type of sales and operations plan based on a chase strategy and the data from problem 4. Ending inventory is to be *zero* at the end of each quarter. The VP of manufacturing says he realizes this type of strategy will require him to adandon his beloved "level" strategy and asks Ivar to vary the total output rate from one quarter to the next. When necessary to do so, the following options and priorities should be used in developing the required output each period.

Priority	Option	Limit (maximum)
1	Full-time employees (FTE)	500 units/quarter/worker
2	Overtime (FTE)	Up to 200 units/worker
3	Subcontract	Up to 5,000 units/quarter
4	Part-time employees	Up to 25 workers/quarter

Finally, the personnel manager reports that because of end-of-year retirements, only 36 (not 44) full-time employees will be on the payroll as of January 2.

a. Develop a chase plan that varies the number of full-time workers per quarter to meet demand without using overtime, subcontracting, or part-time employees.

b. Develop a chase plan following the guidelines noted above. Summarize your plan on the worksheet (you may not hire any additional regular-time workers, but you can lay them off).

c. What hiring/layoff actions will the personnel department need to take each quarter in parts a and b, above?

8. An operations planner, Lovell Bradley, is developing a sales and operations plan that involves back orders. The company's demand and production rates for the next four periods are as follows:

Period	Demand	Production
1	8,200	8,000
2	10,000	8,000
3	7,000	8,000
4	6,600	7,600

Beginning inventory at the start of period 1 is 400 units. Calculate beginning inventory, ending inventory, average inventory, and the back order amount, if any, for each of the next four periods.

9. The VP of manufacturing for the N. L. Hyer Company is ready to decide on her sales and operations plan for next year. The firm's single product (known throughout the adult puzzle trade as "Hyer's Hexagon") is "red hot," according to the VP of marketing, so she insists that backorders are not acceptable next year. Since the United Puzzlemakers Union is trying to organize the plant, the manufacturing VP decided the number of employees must remain constant (i.e., level) throughout all four quarters. Pertinent information is as follows:

Quarter	Production Days	Demand Forecast
1	60	12,000
2	58	13,000
3	61	13,590
4	70	9,000

Beginning inventory = 1,000 units
Regular time output rate = 10 units/day employee

a. What daily production rate and number of employees will be required?

b. How many units will be in inventory at the end of quarter 4?

10. Below is the plotted cumulative demand for Joan's Joyous Nature Food (in pounds) for the next four months. Beginning inventory is 10 pounds.

Month	Demand
1	120
2	160
3	20
4	70

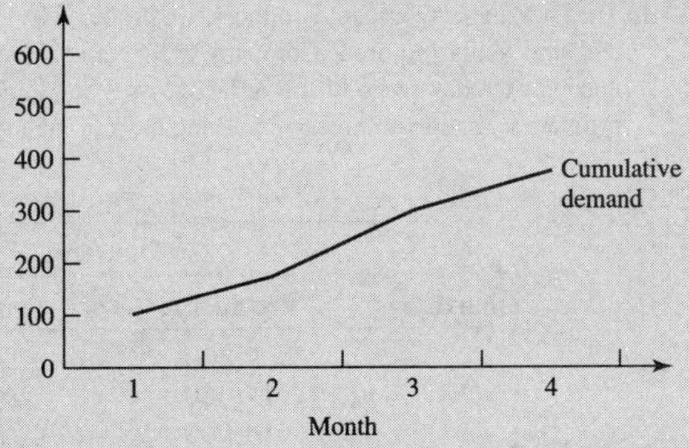

a. How much should Joan produce each month if she wishes to have a level operations plan with no back orders or stockouts? Plot your cumulative production on the preceding graph.
b. What is ending inventory for month 4 under this plan?
c. Joan decides to have a level-production, level-employment sales and operations plan with no ending inventory at the end of the planning horizon. How much should she make each month? What are the monthly back orders?
d. Given inventory carrying costs of $5/pound/month (based on the average inventory) and back orders of $8/pound/month (based on month-end back orders), calculate the cost of back orders and inventory for the plan in part c.

11. The Oro del Mar Company's forecast (in 1,000 pounds) for the first three months of next year is: January—100. February—0, March—300. Beginning inventory is 100,000 pounds.
a. Plot cumulative demand and a level operations plan that meets demand with no back orders and no ending inventory in March.
b. What production each month is needed to meet part a's conditions?

12. Crazy Tubb Thumpers uses a level plan to produce its snowshoe covers. Beginning inventory for January is zero. Demand for covers in January, February, and March is as follows:

Month	Demand
January	5,000
February	0
March	20,000

a. Graph cumulative production for a level operations plan of 10,000 units per month. Show cumulative demand for the months January through March and indicate the ending inventory for March.
b. Consider the following additional data for Crazy Tubb Thumpers:
Employment = 9 people.
Production = 1,000 units/month/employee (regular time).
Standard hours/months = 166 hours (regular time).
Regular-time labor rate = $1,200/month.
Overtime rate = 1.5 times regular-time rate.
Assuming a production rate of 10,000 units per month, what's the labor cost of one month's production at Crazy Tubb Thumpers?

13. The Bi-Product Company produces two products (A and B) that are similar in terms of labor content and skills required. Company management wishes to "level" the number of employees needed each day so no hiring or layoffs will be required during the year. A complication to this problem is that the number of working days in each quarter varies.

	Demand		
Quarter	**Product A**	**Product B**	**Working Days**
1	9,800	14,500	68
2	12,000	30,000	56
3	14,000	19,500	62
4	31,000	25,000	58

Beginning inventory: 2,400 units of Product A
900 units of Product B
Inventory holding cost: $10 per unit per quarter (either product)
No back orders allowed
No variations in size of workforce allowed
Output rate = 25 units of either product per day per employee

a. What daily production rate will be required to meet the demand forecast and yield zero inventory at the end of quarter 4?

b. How many employees will be required each day? What are the inventory levels each quarter?

14. Cubby Compressors has had relatively steady sales volume for years. The introduction of a new high-end "biscuit" model for the professional contractor market has added the potential for additional sales. The operations manager is also concerned about losing sales if product is not readily available. The current sales and operations plan is given below. Assume all days-of-supply calculations are based on a 20-day month and that back orders are to be filled from current production.

a. Propose a revised production plan that brings the days of supply to the target of five days for the next six months.

b. What would the plan look like if you had a hiring freeze at 45 employees maximum and still want to achieve the target five days of supply?

c. What other options are available to not exceed the 45-employee limit and still not experience inventory shortages and related customer service problems?

Cubby Compressors Sales and Operations Planning Spreadsheet

		History			Plan					
		Oct	**Nov**	**Dec**	**Jan**	**Feb**	**Mar**	**Apr**	**May**	**Jun**
Sales										
Forecast	(in million $)	0.56	0.60	0.63	0.63	0.63	0.63	0.63	0.63	0.63
	(in units)	800	850	900	900	900	900	900	900	900
Actual	(in units)	826	851	949						
Diff. month		26	1	49						
Diff. cumulative			27	76						

		History			Plan					
		Oct	Nov	Dec	Jan	Feb	Mar	Apr	May	Jun
Operations										
Plan	(in units)	800	800	800	900	900	900	900	900	900
	(in employees)	34	42	42	45	43	39	45	41	41
Number working days/mo.		23	19	19	20	21	23	20	22	22
Actual	(in units)	758	842	824						
Diff. month		−42	42	24						
Diff. cumulative			0	24						
Inventory										
Plan	(in units)	150	100	0	−52	−52	−52	−52	−52	−52
	(in 1,000 $)	74	49	0	0	0	0	0	0	0
Actual	(in units)	82	73	−52						
Days of supply		2.3	1.6	−1.0						

15. The ABC Consumer Electronics Company has a hard time forecasting demand on its current mix of products. In order to be sure to not run out during periods of unforecast high demand, the management team has decided to raise the inventory target from 5 to 10 days of supply. They currently use a chase production strategy. Their five-day target plan follows. Propose a level build plan that gradually brings the days of supply to the 10-day level over the next three months. Use 30 days per month for all days of supply calculations. Employees can build an average of 1,000 units per workday. Note that July is a short work month due to a two-week vacation shutdown.

ABC Sales and Operations Planning Spreadsheet

		History			Plan		
		Apr	May	Jun	Jul	Aug	Sep
Sales							
Forecast	(in million $)	$22.50	$25.50	$28.50	$31.50	$34.50	$37.50
	(in million units)	1.50	1.70	1.90	2.10	2.30	2.50
Actual	(in million units)	0.78	1.95	1.63			
Diff. month		−0.72	0.25	−0.27			
Diff. cumulative			−0.47	−0.74			
Operations							
Plan	(in million units)	1.50	1.70	1.90	2.10	2.30	2.50
	(in employees)	75	77	86	210	110	109
Number working days/mo.		20	22	22	10	21	23
Actual	(in million units)	1.51	1.70	1.88			
Diff. month		0.01	0.00	−0.02			
Diff. cumulative			0.01	−0.01			
Inventory							
Plan	(in units)	250,000	250,000	250,000	250,001	250,001	250,001
	(in 1,000 $)	$2,625	$2,625	$2,625	$2,625	$2,625	$2,625
Actual	(in units)	250,001	250,000	250,001			
Days of supply		7.4	2.4	2.9	3.6	3.3	3.0

16. Mike Blanford, master scheduler at General Avionics, has the following demand forecast for one line in his factory:

Quarter	Unit Sales
1	5,000
2	10,000
3	8,000
4	2,000

At the beginning of quarter 1, there are 1,000 units in inventory. The firm has prepared the following data:

Hiring cost per employee = \$200

Firing cost per employee = \$400

Beginning workforce = 60 employees

Inventory carrying cost = \$2 per unit per quarter of ending inventory

Stockout cost = \$5 per unit

Regular payroll = \$1,200 per employee per quarter

Overtime cost = \$2 per unit

Each employee can produce 100 units per quarter. Demand not satisfied in any quarter is lost and incurs a stockout penalty. If Mike produces exactly enough to meet demand each quarter, with no inventories at the end of quarters and no overtime, how much will he produce each quarter, and what is the overall cost? (Use a spreadsheet model for the calculations.)

17. Use the data in problem 16 to calculate production amounts and costs for a level rate of output with no ending inventory. In this case, allow items to be backordered. When this occurs, a \$5 penalty is incurred.

18. For the data in problem 16, at the end of the first quarter, inventory is 2,000 units. Marketing has revised the forecasts for quarters 2, 3, and 4 with a 20 percent reduction (i.e., remaining sales = 16,000). Develop a level and chase plan for the revised forecast that provides for an inventory of at least 1,000 units at the end of each quarter. (Assume 50 people were in the workforce in the first quarter.)

Case

Delta Manufacturing Company's Integrated Sales and Operations Planning Process

The sales and operations planning process is a top-down process that begins with a senior management commitment to orchestrating the process. It is focused on positioning the business enterprise to support expected future sales requirements. The end results of this activity are (1) a financial projection of the future sales and operations plans and (2) a road map for the company activities so the individual areas in the business arrive at the same destination at the same time.

Delta's management believes that the following criteria are necessary for the successful implementation of sales and operations planning:

1. The development of a company unit of measure that all of the business functions agree can be used for the process of sales and operations planning.
2. An understanding of the capacity of the producing entity that is stated in the company's standard unit of measure.
3. Agreement on the product level that will be used in the process, e.g., end items or some agreed-on grouping of end items.
4. Establishment of the business requirement for each product item. This involves determining whether the product will be built to stock or built to order and determining the appropriate level of inventory or back orders to be maintained.

Delta Manufacturing Company's Operations

Delta manufactures plastic components for products that are sold to major retailers and to the health care industry. The company has two major business units, and annual sales are approximately $200 million. Delta produces 750 end products that are grouped into 150 product groupings for planning purposes. The 150 product groupings can be further aggregated into 12 market segments that relate to the two business units. The 150 product groupings were developed so that each category is defined in terms of similar manufacturing capabilities. The company's products are produced in two plants that include a total of 14 manufacturing work centers. Approximately 70 percent of the production volume is shipped directly from inventory. For sales and operations planning purposes, the company uses pounds of extruded plastic as the sales and operations planning measure. The total annual production output exceeds 100 million pounds of product.

Delta's Sales and Operations Monthly Planning Cycle

Each month the sales and operations planning process develops a full sales and operations plan covering the next 12 months. Figure 4.12 provides an example of an SOP calendar that shows the timing for each step during the monthly SOP cycle. This calendar is prepared and sent one quarter in advance to all of the SOP participants. During one of the SOP monthly cycles each year, a five-year SOP is completed as a part of the annual budgeting process.

The sales forecast is a key input to the monthly SOP process. The sales forecast is the result of an interactive process involving the manufacturing planning group and the sales representatives for each of the 750 end items forecast. This forecasting activity begins with a statistical forecast that utilizes several moving-average and exponential smoothing techniques and that identifies the forecasting technique that provides the "best fit" to the actual sales history data. Figure 4.13 provides an example of the one-year sales forecast for one of the product groupings, "Market 005 Patient Care." This product grouping includes five individual products.

A statistical sales forecast is sent electronically to each of the sales representatives that covers their individual products and accounts. The sales representatives update the statistical forecast with additional information received from customers. The statistical forecast for each of the 750 items is then updated and aggregated into product categories. These product categories represent the product level used in the SOP process. The final updated forecast with all the customer modifications included is sent to the business unit directors for their review and approval.

At midnight on the last day of the month, the finished goods inventory status (organized by product category and net of any past due orders) is updated for use in the SOP process. At this point all of the information needed in the SOP monthly cycle is available. This information includes the currently available capacity, the sales forecasts, and the inventory status.

Figure 4.14 shows the sales and operations plan spreadsheet for the Market 005 Patient Care product grouping. These plans can be displayed for various levels of aggregation in Delta's planning process, including the company level, the business unit level, and at a product grouping level. In the case of Figure 4.14 the inventory goal is a 20-day supply. At the end of July the actual inventory was at a 16-day supply. This means that the production plan for some of the items in Market 005 Patient Care product grouping will have to be increased beyond the forecast in order to increase the inventory to the required level. For example, the planned production in September is 403,000 pounds and the forecast sales are 369,000 pounds.

Once the production plan for each product grouping has been determined, the detailed planning for individual production facilities is developed. For example, the product category 05C RP embossed pad (which is a part of the Market 005 Patient Care product grouping) is planned for production on extrusion line 2. This is shown in Figure 4.15. This particular product category did not require

FIGURE 4.12 **Sales and Operations Planning Calendar, August Year 1**

Monday	Tuesday	Wednesday	Thursday	Friday
			1 **12:00 p.m.** Sales closing complete **12:00 p.m.** Scheduled trials due to master scheduler **12:00 p.m.** Inventory reports due to demand manager from plants	2 **12:00 p.m.** Send on-time shipments reports (e-mail)
5 **12:00 p.m.** Production plan to operations	6 **2:00 p.m.** On-time shipments	7 **2:00 p.m.** Supply planning meeting	8 **9:00 a.m.** Final forecast due to operations analysis	9 **12:00 p.m.** Send on-time shipments reports (e-mail)
12	13 **2:00 p.m.** On-time shipments	14 **2:00 p.m.** Capacity call	15 **12:00 p.m.** Send SOP agenda/spreadsheets (e-mail)	16 **12:00 p.m.** Send on-time shipments reports (e-mail)
19	20 **1:00 p.m.** Operations & engineering meeting **2:00 p.m.** On-time shipments **5:00 p.m.** Forecast feedback to sales	21 **8:00 a.m.** Operations & engineering meeting **1:00 p.m.** SOP meeting	22	23 **12:00 p.m.** Send on-time shipments reports (e-mail) **4:00 p.m.** Send SOP meeting notes (e-mail)
26 **9:00 a.m.** Sales forecast due to demand manager **5:00 p.m.** Sales forecast due to business unit directors (BUDs)	27 **2:00 p.m.** On-time shipments	28 **1:00 p.m.** Final forecast due to demand manager from BUDs **2:00 p.m.** Capacity call	29 **8:30 a.m.** Production planning **1:00 p.m.** Forecast due to master scheduler	30 **12:00 p.m.** Send on-time shipments reports (e-mail)

FIGURE 4.13 **Final Sales Forecast, August Year 1**

Market 005 Patient Care	Historical Demand			Forecast												
	May Y1	Jun Y1	Jul Y1	Aug Y1	Sept Y1	Oct Y1	Nov Y1	Dec Y1	Jan Y2	Feb Y2	Mar Y2	Apr Y2	May Y2	Jun Y2	Jul Y2	Total
Product Code:																
05A PP Patient Care Embossed Pad	48,158	70,051	60,887	65,000	78,000	65,000	65,000	50,000	65,000	65,000	65,000	65,000	65,000	65,000	65,000	**778,000**
05B PP Patient Care Nonembossed	0	0	0	0	0	0	0	0	0	0	0	0	0	0	0	**0**
05C RP Patient Care Embossed Pad	0	0	0	120,000	200,000	200,000	200,000	200,000	200,000	200,000	200,000	200,000	200,000	200,000	200,000	**2,320,000**
05D BP Patient Care Nonembossed Pad	39,632	68,535	54,584	55,002	55,000	55,000	55,002	45,001	55,000	55,000	55,000	55,000	55,002	54,998	55,001	**650,006**
05E SP Patient Care Embossed Pad	28,475	29,148	27,689	30,000	35,999	29,999	30,001	25,000	30,000	30,000	30,000	30,000	30,000	30,000	35,999	**366,998**
Total for Patient Care	116,356	167,734	143,160	270,002	358,999	349,999	350,003	320,001	350,000	350,000	350,000	350,000	350,002	349,998	356,000	**4,115,004**

FIGURE 4.14 Sales and Operations Plan

Business: Unit A   Market: Patient Care   Segment: Pads   August Y1
Unit of measure: 1,000 pounds

Budget Dollars X $1,588

	Target On-Time to Promise 95%				Inventory Goal—20 Days' Supply										
	May	Jun	Jul	FYTD	Aug	Sep	Oct	Nov	Dec	Jan	3rd 3 mos.	4th 3 mos.	Next 12 months	Latest Call	Budget Plan
Sales															
Old forecast	150	150	155	1562	150	169	150	150	120	150	450	450	1,789	1,817	1,800
New forecast					270	369	350	350	320	350	1,050	1,056	4,115	2,117	
New vs. old fcst.					120	200	200	200	200	200	600	606	2,326	320	
Open orders					20	0	0	0	0	0	0	0	20		
Excess deficit					250	369	350	350	320	350	1,050	1,056	4,095		
Actual sales	116	168	143	1,498											
Diff. month	−34	18	−12	−64											
Cum.	−34	−16	−28												
Operations															
Old plan	113	115	102	1,096	170	149	154	122	148	150	448	450	1,791		
New plan					270	403	380	370	330	348	1,043	1,054	4,198		
New vs. old plan					100	254	226	248	182	198	595	604	2,407		
Actual	154	193	103	1,561											
Diff. month	41	78	1	465											
Cum.	41	119	120												
Inventory															
Plan FGI					8	22	32	32	32	32	32	32			
Plan cons.					134	154	174	194	204	202	195	193			
Finished	41	37	35												
Consignment	115	144	106												
Master rolls	0	−7	0												
Doctor	0	0	0												
Actual	156	174	142												
Days' supply	24	53	16		12	16	18	22	21	20	20	20			
On time—request date	100	99	100												
On time—promise date	100	99	100												

FIGURE 4.15 Production Plan, August Y1

		Daily Capacity	Aug Y1	Sep Y1	Oct Y1	Nov Y1	Dec Y1	Jan Y2	Feb Y2	Mar Y2	Apr Y2	May Y2	Jun Y2	Jul Y2
Extrusion line 2														
05A	PP embossed pad	12,031	65,000	0	0	22,800	34,872	42,273	7,182	42,273	31,000	42,816	30,336	36,075
05D	BP nonembossed pad	11,812	55,002	69,000	65,000	55,002	45,001	55,000	55,000	55,000	55,000	55,002	54,998	55,001
05C	RP embossed pad	11,812	120,000	200,000	200,000	200,000	200,000	200,000	200,000	200,000	200,000	200,000	200,000	200,000
17R	PP label	14,074	80,000	32,000	29,000	0	0	0	0	0	0	0	0	0
22Y	SP cover	12,426	21,260	21,260	21,260	21,260	25,000	25,000	25,000	25,000	25,000	25,000	25,000	25,000
05E	SP embossed pad	10,567	30,000	22,172	39,999	40,001	25,000	30,000	30,000	30,000	30,000	30,000	30,000	35,999
	Forecast pounds		371,262	344,432	355,259	339,063	329,873	352,273	317,182	352,273	341,000	352,818	340,334	352,075
	Estimated capacity		365,745	346,147	355,359	339,298	329,661	352,828	316,758	352,828	340,814	352,840	340,799	352,011
	Excess/(deficit)		–5,517	1,716	100	235	–212	555	–424	555	–186	22	465	–64
Required production days			30.5	28.9	30.0	29.0	28.0	30.0	27.0	30.0	29.0	30.0	29.0	30.0
Scheduled production days			30.0	29.0	30.0	29.0	28.0	30.0	27.0	30.0	29.0	30.0	29.0	30.0
Excess/(deficit)			–0.5	0.1	0.0	0.0	0.0	0.0	0.0	0.0	0.0	0.0	0.0	0.0
Cumulative excess/(deficit)			–0.5	–0.3	–0.3	–0.3	–0.3	–0.3	–0.3	–02	–0.3	–0.3	–0.2	–0.2

FIGURE 4.16 Agenda, Executive Sales and Operations Planning Meeting

August 23, Y1
2:00 p.m.

1. On-time shipments review
   a. Review of July and August-to-date performance
2. Capacity issues
   a. Planned downturns
   b. Production line graphs and summary
3. Inventory review
   a. Inventory turns
   b. Total inventory value graphs
   c. Finished goods DOH (days on hand) graphs
   d. Raw materials DOH graphs

15-minute break

4. SOP follow-ups and spreadsheet review
   a. Process of review
   b. Follow-ups from prior meeting
   c. Spreadsheet review and decisions
5. Critique of meeting

any inventory adjustments to increase the number of days' supply, and the planned production will equal the forecast sales amount. Since the product category 05A PP embossed pad requires more production than is available on extrusion line 2, this will result in a portion of the requirements being planned on an alternative line.

The resulting plan for extrusion line 2 shows that the required production days will equal the scheduled production days (available capacity) for the next 12 months. (Rounding the numbers shows a slight difference.) After the planning is complete for each extrusion line, the plans are reviewed with the plants for their agreement. This step is indicated on the SOP calendar in Figure 4.12. These plans may be further modified as necessary during this plant review. This review is completed approximately one week before the monthly SOP meeting in order to allow time for the needed changes to be incorporated into the plan.

SOP Monthly Meeting

The formal agenda shown in Figure 4.16 is sent to the SOP meeting attendees prior to each meeting. The senior operating officer of the company chairs this meeting, and attendance is mandatory.

The first item on the agenda is a review of customer satisfaction performance as shown by the example in Figure 4.17. The percentage of time that shipments met both the company's promise of shipment and the customer's request for shipment is charted and reviewed. For each area where the company failed to meet either of these criteria, a discussion is held and corrective action plans are assigned.

The second agenda item is a review of plant capacity. The graphs in Figure 4.18 show the planned downtime and capacity by line, the actual sales, and the production over the past three months. Actual

FIGURE 4.17 Current 12 Months' versus Previous 12 Months' Performance to Promise and Request Dates

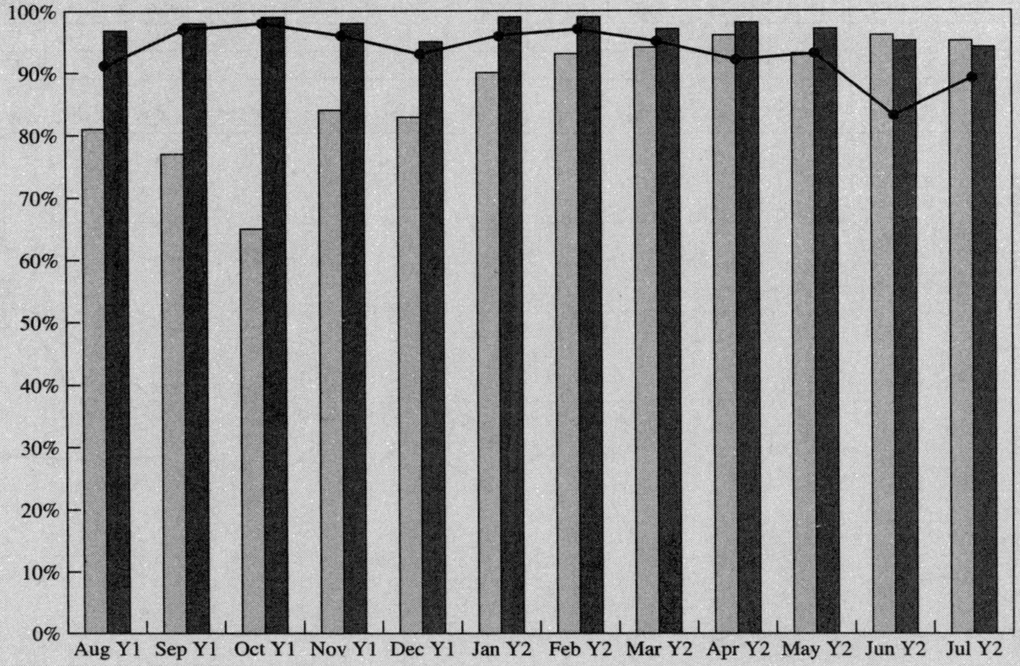

	Aug Y1	Sep Y1	Oct Y1	Nov Y1	Dec Y1	Jan Y2	Feb Y2	Mar Y2	Apr Y2	May Y2	Jun Y2	Jul Y2
Prev. 12 mo. on time (prom.)	81%	77%	65%	84%	83%	90%	93%	94%	96%	93%	96%	95%
Cur. 12 mo. on time (prom.)	97%	98%	99%	98%	95%	99%	99%	97%	98%	97%	95%	94%
Cur. 12 mo. on time (req.)	91%	97%	98%	96%	93%	96%	97%	95%	92%	93%	87%	89%

FIGURE 4.18 **Company Total Pounds versus Estimated Capacity, Including Actual Sales and Production (Unit of Measure: Million Pounds)**

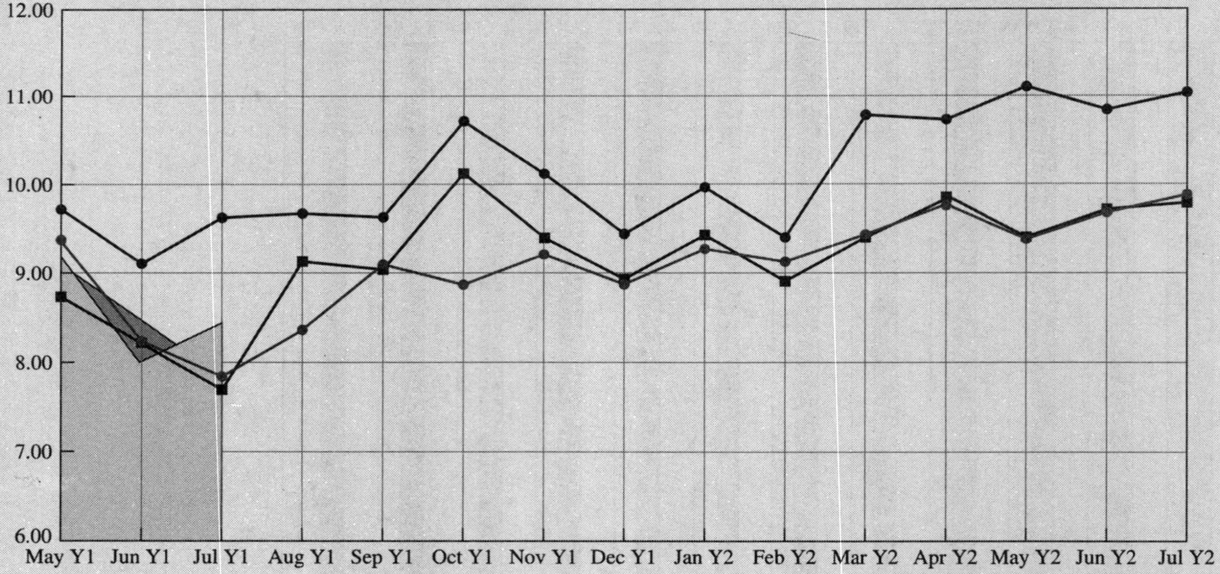

	May Y1	Jun Y1	Jul Y1	Aug Y1	Sep Y1	Oct Y1	Nov Y1	Dec Y1	Jan Y2	Feb Y2	Mar Y2	Apr Y2	May Y2	Jun Y2	Jul Y2
Actual sales	9.10	8.56	7.82												
Actual production	9.14	8.04	8.51												
Production plan	8.74	8.31	7.64	9.15	9.09	10.14	9.50	8.93	9.53	8.85	9.41	9.84	9.41	9.67	9.82
Sales forecast	9.37	8.32	7.84	8.43	9.17	8.87	9.27	8.86	9.36	9.15	9.45	9.77	9.40	9.63	9.88
Staffed capacity	9.83	9.12	9.60	9.68	9.62	10.73	10.20	9.41	9.93	9.41	10.78	10.74	11.06	10.84	11.05

FIGURE 4.19 **Plant 2 Total Raw Materials Inventory**

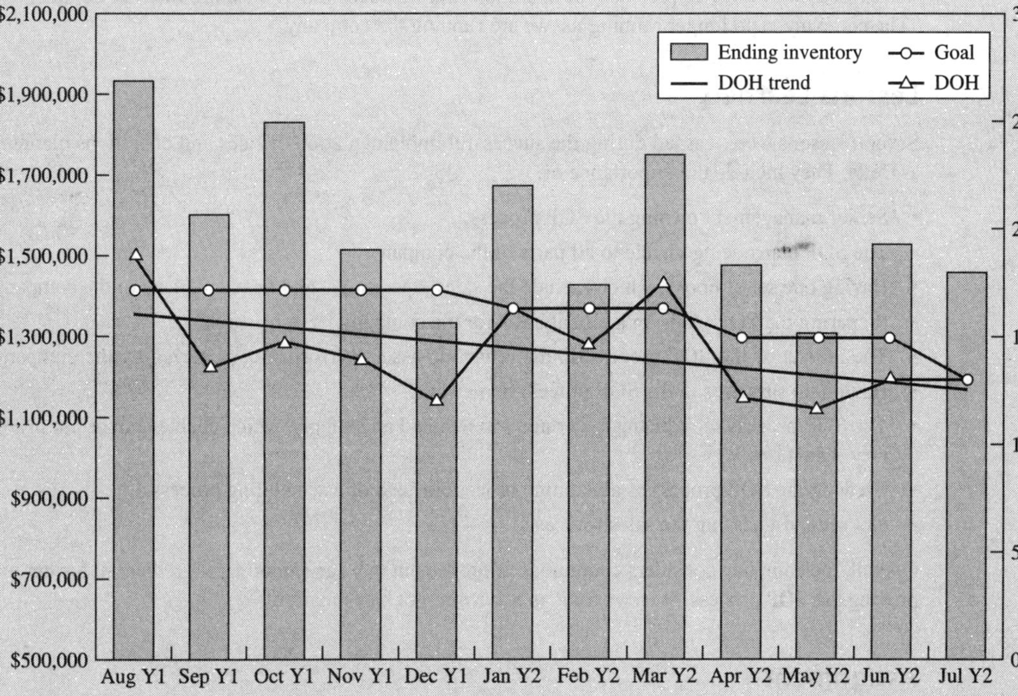

performance is compared to plan. In addition, the sales and production planned for the next 12 months is compared to the planned capacity. This review begins with the overall company performance and continues through each production line. For example, the data shown in Figure 4.18 indicate that actual sales exceeded the forecast in June, and was less than forecasted in May and July. This has resulted in adjustments in planned production in order to achieve targeted inventory levels.

The third area of discussion is a review of inventory performance. Here the past 12-month actual statistics are charted and trends developed. The example shown in Figure 4.19 is the raw materials inventory. This review also begins with overall company totals, and continues with each plant's performance. The on-hand dollar amount and the number of days' supply are compared with the goals. If the goals are not being met, specific problem areas are discussed and corrective action is assigned.

The fourth part of the meeting is a review of the sales and operations plans that were developed during the SOP process. Figure 4.14 provides an example of these plans. The majority of the meeting is spent in this area. During this discussion, the business unit directors discuss these plans for each market, the performance during the past three months, and the plans during the next 12 months for sales, production, and inventory. The final part of the meeting is a critique of the process and suggested improvements.

Results

From the beginning of the implementation of the SOP process two years ago, Delta has improved its delivery reliability by raising the on-time shipment to promise performance from 65 percent to the current level of more than 95 percent. During this same period of time the company also reduced the investment in finished goods inventories by more than $2,000,000, and the raw materials inventory by $2,500,000.

While these improvements are impressive in and of themselves, the most important improvement was expressed by the vice president of operations during a recent SOP meeting when he commented, "The company is no longer running us, we are running the company."

Lessons Learned

Several lessons were learned during the successful implementation of sales and operations planning at Delta. They include the importance of:

- Senior management owning the SOP process.
- The SOP plans being visible to all parts of the company.
- Having one set of books, which include the sales, operations, and financial plans of the company.
- Preparing the SOP plans on a global basis for the company.
- The impact of the SOP process on the return-on-assets performance achieved by the company.
- Having no surprises in the SOP process homework.
- The SOP process in reducing uncertainty in demand and supply, which enables important inventory reductions.
- Viewing the SOP process as a planning process instead of a scheduling process.
- Not second-guessing the sales forecasts.

Overall, the company considers continuous improvement to be an important ingredient in further improving the SOP process. It views SOP as a journey, not a destination!

Assignment

1. Please review the SOP process at Delta. What are your conclusions regarding the SOP process at Delta?
2. What recommendations do you have for changing the process?

Chapter 4A

Advanced Sales and Operations Planning

This chapter deals with modeling procedures for establishing the overall, or aggregate, production and inventory portion of the sales and operations plan. Given a set of product demands stated in some common denominator, the basic issue is what levels of resources should be provided in each period. Resources include items such as production capacity, employment levels, and inventory investment. Today, powerful and easily accessible tools are available for solving these models. This is important because as firms implement MPC systems, there's a natural evolution toward questions of overall production planning that provide direction to the other MPC system modules. This chapter provides a basic understanding of these models together with an introduction to how problems formulated with these models can be solved using a spreadsheet. This chapter is organized around two topics:

- *Mathematical programming approaches:* How can aggregate production planning problems be solved using mathematical programming techniques?
- *Company example: Lawn King Inc.:* How can mathematical programming approaches be used to develop an actual production plan, and what information does it provide for the company?

Mathematical Programming Approaches

In this section, we present an overview of some mathematical programming models that have been suggested for the aggregate production planning problem. We start by formulating the problem as a linear programming model. This approach is relatively straightforward but is necessarily limited to cases where there are linear relationships in the input data. Thereafter, we describe a mixed integer programming approach for preparing aggregate production plans on a product line basis.

These approaches are already substantially more sophisticated than the practice found in most firms. More common are spreadsheet programs used to explore alternative production plans. Using forecasts of demand and factors relating to employment, productivity, overtime, and inventory levels, a series of what-if analyses helps to formulate production plans and evaluate alternative scenarios. Level and chase strategies are developed to bracket the options, and alternatives are evaluated against the resultant benchmarks. Although spreadsheet programs do not provide the optimal solutions reached by the models discussed in this chapter, they do help firms better understand the inherent trade-offs and provide a focal point for important dialogue among the functional areas of the firm.

Linear Programming

There are many linear programming formulations for the aggregate production planning problem. The objective is typically to find the lowest-cost plan, considering when to hire and fire, how much inventory to hold, when to use overtime and undertime, and so on, while always meeting the sales forecast. One formulation, based on measuring aggregate sales and inventories in terms of direct labor hours, follows:

Minimize:

$$\sum_{t=1}^{m}(C_H H_t + C_F F_t + C_R X_t + C_O O_t + C_I I_t + C_U U_t)$$

subject to:

1. Inventory constraint:

$$I_{t-1} + X_t + O_t - I_t = D_t$$

$$I_t \geq B_t$$

2. Regular time production constraint:

$$X_t - A_{1t} W_t + U_t = 0$$

3. Overtime production constraint:

$$O_t - A_{2t} W_t + S_t = 0$$

4. Workforce level change constraints:

$$W_t - W_{t-1} - H_t + F_t = 0$$

5. Initializing constraints:

$$W_O = A_3$$
$$I_O = A_4$$
$$W_m = A_5$$

where:

C_H = The cost of hiring an employee.

C_F = The cost of firing an employee.

C_R = The cost per labor-hour of regular time production.

C_O = The cost per labor-hour of overtime production.

C_I = The cost per month of carrying one labor-hour of work.

C_U = The cost per labor-hour of idle regular time production.

H_t = The number of employees hired in month t.

F_t = The number of employees fired in month t.

X_t = The regular time production hours scheduled in month t.

O_t = The overtime production hours scheduled in month t.

I_t = The hours stored in inventory at the end of month t.

U_t = The number of idle time regular production hours in month t.

D_t = The hours of production to be sold in month t.

B_t = The minimum number of hours to be stored in inventory in month t.

A_{1t} = The maximum number of regular time hours to be worked per employee per month.

W_t = The number of people employed in month t.

A_{2t} = The maximum number of overtime hours to be worked per employee per month.

S_t = The number of unused overtime hours per month per employee.

A_3 = The initial employment level.

A_4 = The initial inventory level.

A_5 = The desired number of employees in month m (the last month in the planning horizon).

m = The number of months in the planning horizon.

Similar models have been successfully formulated for several variations of the production planning problem. In general, however, few real-world aggregate production planning decisions appear to be compatible with the linear assumptions. Some plans require discrete steps such as adding a second shift. For many companies, the unit cost of hiring or firing large numbers of employees is much larger than that associated with small labor force changes. Moreover, economies of scale aren't taken into account by linear programming formulations. Let's now turn to another approach, which partially overcomes the linear assumption limitations.

Mixed Integer Programming

The linear programming model provides a means of preparing low-cost aggregate plans for overall workforce, production, and inventory levels. However, in some firms, aggregate plans are prepared on a product family basis. Product families are defined as groupings of products that share common manufacturing facilities and setup times. In this case, overall production, workforce, and inventory plans for the company are essentially the summation of the plans for individual product lines. Mixed integer programming provides one method for determining the number of units to be produced in each product family.

Minimize:

$$\sum_{i=1}^{n}\sum_{t=1}^{m}(C_{si}\sigma(X_{it}) + C_{mi}X_{it} + C_{Ii}I_{it}) + \sum_{t=1}^{m}(C_H H_t + C_F F_t + C_O O_t + A_{1t}C_R W_t)$$

subject to:

1. Inventory constraint:

$$I_{i,t-1} - I_{it} + X_{it} = D_{it} \quad (\text{for } I = 1, \ldots, n \text{ and } T = 1, \ldots, m)$$

2. Production and setup time constraint:

$$A_{it}W_t + O_t - \sum_{i=1}^{n} X_{it} - \sum_{i=1}^{n} \beta_i\sigma(X_{it}) \geq 0 \quad (\text{for } t = 1, \ldots, m)$$

3. Workforce level change constraint:

$$W_t - W_{t-1} - H_t + F_t = 0 \quad (\text{for } t = 1, \ldots, m)$$

4. Overtime constraint:

$$Q_t - A_{2t}W_t \leq 0 \quad (\text{for } t = 1, \ldots, m)$$

5. Setup constraint:

$$-Q_i\sigma(X_{it}) + X_{it} \leq 0 \quad (\text{for } t = 1, \ldots, m \text{ and } I = 1, \ldots, n)$$

6. Binary constraint for setups:

$$\sum(X_{it}) = \begin{cases} 1 & \text{if } X_{it} > 0 \\ 0 & \text{if } X_{it} = 0 \end{cases}$$

7. Nonnegativity constraints:

$$X_{it}, I_{it}, H_t, F_t, O_t, W_t \geq 0$$

where:

X_{it} = Production in hours of product family i scheduled in month t.

I_{it} = The hours of product family i stored in inventory in month t.

D_{it} = The hours of product family i demanded in month t.

H_t = The number of employees hired in month t.

F_t = The number of employees fired in month t.

O_t = Overtime production hours in month t.

W_t = Number of people employed on regular time in month t.

$\sigma(X_{it})$ = Binary setup variable for product family i in month t.

C_{si} = Setup cost of product family i.

C_{Ii} = Inventory carrying cost per month of one labor-hour of work for product family i.

C_{mi} = Materials cost per hour of production of family i.

C_H = Hiring cost per employee.

C_F = Firing cost per employee.

C_O = Overtime cost per employee hour.

C_R = Regular time workforce cost per employee hour.

A_{1t} = The maximum number of regular-time hours to be worked per employee in month t.

β_i = Setup time for product family i.

A_{2t} = Maximum number of overtime hours per employee in month t.

Q_i = A large number used to ensure the effects of binary setup variables; that is,

$$Q_i \geq \sum_{t=1}^{m} D_{it}$$

n = Number of product families.

m = Number of months in the planning horizon.

The objective function and constraints in this model are similar to those in the linear programming model. The main difference is in the addition of product family setups in constraints 5 and 6. This model assumes all the setups for a product family occur in the month in which the end product is to be completed. Constraint 5 is a surrogate constraint for the binary variables used in constraint 6. This constraint forces $\sigma(X_{it})$ to be nonzero when $X_{it} > 0$ because Q_i is defined as at least the total demand for a product family over the planning horizon.

Additional constraints should be added to the model to specify the initial conditions at the start of the planning horizon; that is, constraints specifying beginning inventory for the product family, I_{io}, and workforce level in the previous month, W_o, are required. Likewise, constraints specifying workforce level at the end of the planning horizon, and minimum required closing inventory balance at the end of each month in the planning horizon, may be added.

Company Example: Lawn King Inc.

In this section we present an application of advanced production planning models. The case, Lawn King Inc., has been developed to demonstrate the role of production planning models in the sales and operations planning process. Included are the ways a company might estimate the necessary parameters, the additional information that might be generated in a sales and operations planning meeting, and the construction and use of the model. We start with a description of the company and its products, then turn to the development of the planning model, and close with how the model might be used in a sales and operations planning meeting.

FIGURE 4A.1 Profit and Loss Statement ($000)

Year	Last Year	This Year
Sales	$11,611	$14,462
Cost of goods sold		
Material	6,430	8,005
Direct labor	2,100	2,595
Depreciation	743	962
Overhead	256	431
Total CGS	9,439	11,993
G&A expense	270	314
Selling expense	140	197
Total expenses	9,849	12,504
Pretax profit	1,762	1,958

Company Background

Lawn King Inc. (disguised name) is a medium-sized producer of lawn mower equipment. The company makes four lines of gas-powered lawn mowers: an 18-inch push mower, a 20-inch push mower, a 20-inch self-propelled mower, and a 22-inch deluxe self-propelled mower. Lawn care products in general, of course, face a seasonal demand and have historically been sensitive to overall economic conditions. Lawn King Inc. enjoys a positive reputation for product quality and customer service in the industry, so, despite the recent economic downturn, it has been able to show sales growth and profitability in the last few years. Moreover, the sales team expects a significant recovery in the economy and is very optimistic about sales for the next year. Sales, costs, and profits for the last two years are shown in Figure 4A.1.

The only cloud over the rosy expectations for sales growth next year was the occurrence of some product shortages last year. These shortages occurred even though manufacturing used overtime to try to keep up with demand. It was the first time that the firm had ever needed to put any of its products on backorder, and even though the backorders were filled quickly, there was still some concern that its reputation for good customer service could be negatively impacted. This concern persuaded Lawn King's management to consider more formal planning processes to help meet the increased demand.

Deciding on a Planning Model

Up to this year, Lawn King's annual planning had been quite informal. The process consisted of gathering forecast information and establishing budgets for the fiscal year (from September 1 to August 31). Once the budgets were established, external events (big customer order or a cancellation or adverse weather pattern) would trigger informal meetings where plans would be adjusted, reduced time or overtime would be authorized, and other adjustments would be made. In discussions about preparing for next year's selling season, there was general agreement that backorders should be avoided if possible, and that more formalized meetings during the year might be helpful. Management also agreed that it would be worthwhile to evaluate a formal planning model as part of the budgeting process and as the basis for the subsequent meetings.

Though there was general agreement to proceed with the development of a planning model, there was little agreement on what approach to take, whether to hire a consultant, how extensive the model should be, and other details of the approach. During one meeting, the marketing manager, plant manager, and the managing director agreed to start simply, use internal resources (not a consultant), and not use unfamiliar technology. With this in mind, all members of management were charged to consult with their colleagues in trade associations, their classmates from school, people in their departments, and professors who they felt might be useful.

The results of these discussions turned up remarkably similar results. Most of the advice the managers received reinforced their decision to start simply. Many of their contacts recommended an aggregate production-planning model formulated as a linear program. Several of the managers were familiar with linear programming, and if the time increments were monthly, it could tie in with the more formal meetings the company was planning. Another advantage was that the model could be formulated using spreadsheet technology (such as Excel), which all of the management team currently used for some of their own management tasks. Moreover, there were several people in the company who were familiar with Excel's advanced capabilities.

The managing director and plant manager had already used Excel to estimate the results of different staffing levels and inventory policies, so they had some experience with simple production planning models. Some of the managers had studied linear programming in college and others were familiar with the use of such models to find solutions to complex problems and provide what-if capability. The end result was an agreement to focus on aggregate production planning, to determine staffing levels, to provide sufficient inventory to avoid backorders, to develop an in-house linear programming model of the process, and to assign a young engineer to assist in the model development and subsequent analysis.

The Linear Programming Model

The linear programming model the managers developed can determine aggregate inventory levels, direct labor staffing levels, and production rates for each month of the year. The objective function minimizes direct payroll, overtime, hiring and layoff, and relevant inventory costs. The model also incorporated the desired inventory level for each month and direct labor force at the end of the year. The model is shown below:

Minimize:

$$\sum_{t} \quad (C_H H_t + C_F F_t + C_R W_t + C_O O_t + C_I I_t)$$

subject to:

1. Inventory constraint:

$$I_{t-1} + P_t + O_t - D_t = I_t$$

2. Regular time production constraint:

$$P_t \leq A_1 W_t$$

3. Overtime production constraint:

$$O_t \leq A_2 W_t$$

4. Workforce level change constraint:

$$W_{t-1} + H_t - F_t = W_t$$

5. Initializing constraints:

$$W_0 = A3$$
$$I_0 = A4$$
$$W_m = A5$$
$$I_t = A6$$

where:

C_H = The cost of hiring an employee.

C_F = The cost of firing an employee.

C_R = The cost per month of an employee on regular time.

C_O = The cost per unit of production on overtime.

C_I = The cost per month of carrying one unit of inventory.

H_t = The number of employees hired in month t.

F_t = The number of employees fired in month t.

P_t = The number of units produced on regular time in month t.

O_t = The number of units produced on overtime in month t.

W_t = The number of people employed in month t.

I_t = The number of units stored in inventory at the end of month t.

D_t = The number of units of demand in month t.

A_1 = The number of units that one employee can produce in one month on regular time.

A_2 = The maximum number of units that one employee can produce in one month on overtime.

A_3 = The initial inventory level.

A_4 = The initial workforce level.

A_5 = The desired workforce level at the end of the planning horizon.

A_6 = The desired inventory level at the end of each month.

m = The number of months in the planning horizon.

Developing the Planning Parameters

In the early stages of the development of the model, management decided to use the actual sales data for the current year. This would give them a known base and might also provide some insights into what they might have done differently to avoid the shortages they incurred during the last year. In addition to the sales data, they needed estimates of the other parameters for the linear programming planning model.

Lawn King fabricates metal frames and other metal parts for its lawn mowers in its own machine shop. Much of the parts fabrication is coordinated with the assembly schedule, but some inventory is kept in order to support schedule changes, overtime, and other unanticipated events. In addition to fabrication, it purchases parts and components including engines, bolts, paint, wheels, and sheet steel directly from vendors. In the current year, approximately $8 million in parts and supplies were purchased and an inventory of $1 million in purchased parts was held to supply the machine shop and the assembly line. When a particular mower is running on the assembly line, the purchased and fabricated parts for that model are moved to the assembly line.

The workforce strategy of Lawn King might be described as a one-shift level-workforce strategy with overtime used as needed. At the time the model was being developed in the current year, a total of 93 employees worked at the plant. These employees included 52 workers on the assembly line, 6 floaters, 20 workers in the machine shop, 10 maintenance workers, and 5 office staff. Even though the employment level of the direct workforce (assembly and machine shop workers) may be varied over the course of a year, the company tried to keep it as level as possible. The company is not able to do this exactly due to turnover and short-run production requirements. There is, however, very little turnover for the office staff and the maintenance group. Overtime is used when regular time cannot meet production requirements (as was the case in the current year).

The plant is unionized, and relations between the union and the company have always been good. The company had access to good direct labor skills and provided a comprehensive training program. It estimated the total training cost in the current year was $42,000. Using this and other factors (overhead, personnel, screening, and so forth) the personnel officer estimated it cost $800 to hire a new employee. The company relied mostly on turnover to reduce the direct labor but did have some experience with layoffs. The personnel officer estimated that the cost to lay off an employee was $1,500, including the severance costs and supplemental unemployment benefits that are required.

The six floaters are kept on the workforce to fill in for people who are absent, especially on Mondays and Fridays. They also help train the new employees when they are not needed for direct production work and often perform some administrative tasks. There was some discussion about how to treat the floaters in the planning model. To be conservative, the decision was to not consider them as producing employees. This would compensate for absences, new employee training, and the time they spent in administrative tasks. This meant that, even though there are 78 direct employees, only 72 would be considered as production employees.

Since the model was an aggregate planning model, an "average" aggregate product was to be used, so an average cost of direct labor and labor productivity were needed as parameters in the model. A beginning assembly-line worker was paid $7.15 per hour plus $2.90 an hour in benefits. The maintenance and machine-shop employees earned an average of $12 per hour (including benefits). To simplify the model, the machine-shop and assembly activities were combined and the average labor cost per direct worker was calculated to be $1,828 per month, using a 12-month planning horizon. The actual production data for the current year is shown in Figure 4A.2. The average productivity for the assembly and machine shop workers combined was 83 end-product units per month per employee on regular time. Due to union restrictions, a maximum of 17 units could be produced per month per employee (on four 8-hour Saturdays) at this productivity rate. Based on this information, the labor cost per unit on regular time for the combined assembly and machine shop units was $22.03, and the overtime labor cost per unit was $33.04.

FIGURE 4A.2
Monthly Production During the Current Year (units)

	18″	20″	20″ SP	22″ SP	Total Units	Overtime Units*
September	3,000	3,100	—	—	6,100	—
October	—	—	3,400	3,500	6,900	—
November	3,000	3,800	—	—	6,800	—
December	—	—	4,400	3,750	8,150	1,000
January	4,000	4,100	—	—	8,100	1,500
February	—	—	4,400	3,500	7,900	1,620
March	3,000	3,000	2,000	—	8,000	1,240
April	—	—	2,000	4,500	6,500	—
May	3,000	2,000	2,000	—	7,000	—
June	1,000	—	2,000	3,000	6,000	—
July	2,000	3,000	2,000	—	7,000	—
August	2,000	2,000	—	2,000	6,000	—
Total	21,000	21,000	22,200	20,250	84,450	

*Number of units produced on overtime (included in the total units).

FIGURE 4A.3
Beginning Inventory, Monthly Sales, and Ending Inventory in the Current Year

	18″	20″	20″ SP	22″ SP
Beginning Inventory	4,120	3,140	6,250	3,100
September	210	400	180	110
October	600	510	500	300
November	1,010	970	860	785
December	1,200	1,420	1,030	930
January	1,430	1,680	1,120	1,120
February	2,140	2,210	2,180	1,850
March	4,870	5,100	4,560	3,210
April	5,120	4,850	5,130	3,875
May	3,210	3,310	2,980	2,650
June	1,400	1,500	1,320	800
July	710	950	680	1,010
August	400	600	660	960
Total	22,300	23,500	21,200	17,600
End inventory	2,820	640	7,250	5,750

The beginning inventory, monthly sales and closing inventory for the current year are shown in Figure 4A.3. The sales vary considerably from month to month with the strong sales season occurring from February through May. Not only are the sales highly seasonal, but total sales are dependent on a number of other factors, such as the weather and the economy. Thus, there is considerable uncertainty in addition to the seasonal variation. This can result in overall changes in volume and variations in the mix of models sold. An indication of the variation between expectations and actual sales can be seen in Figure 4A.4, which provides the forecast and actual values for the last two years and next year's forecast.

Finished goods inventory was used to buffer against the uncertainties, to decouple production and sales, and to accommodate the cycle between models on the assembly line. When Lawn King was out of stock, any sales were backordered and filled from the next available

FIGURE 4A.4
Annual Sales Data in Units

	Last Year Forecast	Last Year Actual	This Year Forecast	This Year Actual	Next Year Forecast
18″	30,000	25,300	23,000	22,300	24,000
20″	11,900	15,680	20,300	23,500	35,500
20″ SP	15,600	14,200	20,400	21,200	31,500
22″ SP	10,500	14,320	21,300	17,600	19,000
Total	68,000	69,500	85,000	84,600	110,000

FIGURE 4A.5
Actual Total Sales, Production, Employment, Inventory, and Overtime for the Current Year

Month	Actual Sales	Total Actual Production	Ending Inventory	Workforce	Overtime Production*
August			16,610	84	
September	900	6,100	21,810	73	
October	1,910	6,900	26,800	83	
November	3,625	6,800	29,975	82	
December	4,580	8,150	33,545	92	1,000
January	5,350	8,100	36,295	88	1,500
February	8,380	7,900	35,815	85	1,620
March	17,740	8,000	26,075	88	1,240
April	18,975	6,500	13,600	78	
May	12,150	7,000	8,450	84	
June	5,020	6,000	9,430	72	
July	3,350	7,000	13,080	84	
August	2,620	6,000	16,460	72	
Total	84,600	84,450			

*Included in the total actual production figures.

production run. In an effort to avoid the backorders that were incurred last year, management decided to establish a planned minimum inventory of 2,000 units for each month.

The determination of the cost of carrying inventory required estimates from nearly all of the management. The controller said that the cost of capital was on the order of 10 percent. The direct cost of storage (space, light, wages, etc.) was estimated to be about 4 percent of the amount invested, and design changes meant that there was some obsolescence which was estimated to be about 3 percent of the inventory investment. Thus, a total of 17 percent of inventory value was to be used for the carrying cost per year for inventory. The average unit produced in the current year had \$94.62 in material costs. The current year mix of regular and overtime resulted in \$30.67 in direct labor costs. Thus, the average inventory carrying cost was estimated at \$1.77/unit/month [(\$94.62 + \$30.67) × (0.17/12) = \$1.77].

The actual sales, starting conditions, and ending conditions were the only other data needed for the planning model. The actual monthly sales for the individual product has been totaled to provide the total aggregate sales for the company during the current year selling season, which is shown in Figure 4A.5. Also shown are the beginning aggregate inventory level and the beginning employment level of 84 direct workers. In addition, Figure 4A.5 provides the closing aggregate inventory level and the actual direct workforce of 72 people. Using these data, the planning model could be run to determine the improvement in operating costs that could be obtained with the linear programming (LP) model. Once this was accomplished, additional work could be initiated to apply the model to the forecasts for next year's selling season so that these improvements could be obtained in the coming year.

Figure 4A.5 also provides the data to determine a cost base against which to compare the results of the planning model. This figure shows the aggregate sales, production, inventory, workforce, and overtime production actually achieved in the current year. By applying the planning cost parameters to these data, a cost basis can be developed for comparison with the LP model results. When the planning costs are applied to the actual current year's results, the total annual cost is $2,562,925. This includes regular-time costs of $1,793,268, inventory carrying costs of $480,263, overtime costs of $177,094, firing costs of $79,500, and hiring costs of $32,800.

Solving the Linear Programming Model and Understanding the Results

The LP model was used to evaluate the actual operating performance for the current year's season. A summary of the planning assumptions and the cost parameters used in developing the model are provided in Figure 4A.6. These parameters were used along with the actual sales figures to produce the LP results shown in Figure 4A.7 for the current year's selling season. Overall, the LP model produced savings of $207,432, or 8.1% of the production planning related costs for actual operations.

In reviewing the differences between the LP model result in Figure 4A.7 and the actual operating results shown in Figure 4A.5 several conclusions can be drawn. First, substantial overtime was incurred by the plant to meet the actual sales demand. Overall, the employment-related costs of regular time and overtime totaled $1,970,362 for actual operations. Using the LP model, the total employment-related costs equaled $1,863,108, saving $107,254. The main difference is that while substantial overtime was used in actual operations ($177,094), the LP model used regular-time production capacity instead of overtime to produce nearly all of the product units.

Second, the employment level was adjusted each month, hiring and firing employees as required to meet the actual sales demand. This resulted in $112,300 in hiring and firing costs. In contrast, the LP model made small adjustments in the employment level in February and August, maintaining a relatively constant workforce throughout the year because of the magnitude of the hiring and firing costs. Thus, $87,400 was saved in hiring and firing costs.

FIGURE 4A.6
LP Model Planning Assumptions and Cost Parameters

Regular-time cost/employee/month	$1,828
Overtime cost/unit	$33.04
Inventory carrying cost/unit/month	$1.77
Hiring cost/employee	$800
Firing cost/employee	$1,500
Regular-time productivity (units/month/employee)	83
Maximum overtime units/month	17
Ending inventory must be at least 2,000 units	
The August (current year) inventory is equal to 16,460 units	
The August (current year) employment level is 72	

FIGURE 4A.7 **LP Model Optimal Results for the Current Year's Selling Season**

Month	Sales	Regular Production	Overtime Production	Workforce	Ending Inventory	Number Hired	Number Fired
September	900	6,972	—	84	22,682	—	—
October	1,910	6,972	—	84	27,744	—	—
November	3,625	6,972	—	84	31,091	—	—
December	4,580	6,972	—	84	33,483	—	—
January	5,350	6,972	—	84	35,105	—	—
February	8,380	7,221	—	87	33,946	3	—
March	17,740	7,221	—	87	23,427	—	—
April	18,975	7,221	—	87	11,673	—	—
May	12,150	7,221	—	87	6,744	—	—
June	5,020	7,221	—	87	8,945	—	—
July	3,350	7,221	—	87	12,816	—	—
August	2,620	5,976	—	72	16,460	—	15

Third, the LP model was also able to provide a small reduction in finished goods inventory and still meet the inventory goals of the company. This amounted to a reduction of $12,778 in total.

Many of the cost improvements are related to implementing an overall sales and operations plan as opposed to reacting to monthly variations in sales and customer backorders. Reducing the level of system nervousness produces a better balance of costs in managing operations. Clearly, the overall cost of operations is affected by the planning assumptions regarding the employment level and the ending inventory targets at the end of the seasonal cycle (in this case ending figures for August of the current year). Different assumptions regarding the appropriate level for employment and inventory can change the overall cost of operations. These assumptions are heavily influenced by executive judgments regarding the sales forecast for the next year and the level of safety stock inventory needed to achieve the level of customer service required by the market. Such judgments are discussed and agreed on by senior executives in the company's sales and operations meetings.

Sales and Operations Planning Issues

After the results of the LP model and the comparisons to actual operating performance were available, a formal meeting of the senior managers of Lawn King was scheduled in a planning retreat. The purpose was to look at what adjustments should be made to the parameters as the basis for starting next year's planning. Although not called a sales and operations planning meeting, that is precisely what the company was doing. Here are some of the key points and perspectives brought out during the meeting.

1. *Marketing manager:* The company's best customers are complaining about back orders during the peak selling season. A few have threatened to drop the Lawn King product line if they don't get better service next year. It is important to produce not only enough product, but also to produce the right models to service the customer demand. We need to determine the right amount of inventory to avoid shortages on individual products when we have peaks in demand.

2. *Plant manager:* Three months ago the marketing and sales group predicted sales of 98,000 units for the next year. Now the forecast has been raised by 12 percent to 110,000 units. It is difficult to do a reasonable job of production planning when the target is always moving. The plant is already operating at full capacity, and the additional units in the new forecast can't be made with one shift. A new shift might have to be added to accommodate the higher forecast. It is important to be sure these sales forecasts are realistic before hiring an entire second shift.

3. *General manager:* We have to be responsive to changing market conditions. We cannot permit the same stockout situation we experienced last year.

4. *Controller:* We must find a way to reduce costs. Last year we carried too much inventory, which required a great deal of capital. At 17 percent carrying cost, we cannot afford to build up as much inventory again next year.

5. *Personnel officer:* If we reduce our inventories by more nearly chasing demand, the labor force will fluctuate from month to month and our hiring and layoff costs will increase. These include the severance costs and supplemental unemployment benefits that are paid.

The sales and operations planning issues raised by the executives at Lawn King can be resolved using a planning model, such as a spreadsheet model or an LP model, and planning meetings can be focused on decision making by senior executives regarding the important trade-off issues between the various functions in the company. The development of the sales and operations plan can help in stimulating discussion between the executives in a company so that a consensus can be reached regarding the operating plans to be pursued by the company. It is critical to note that the sales and operations plan serves as the basis for other detailed plans and schedules in manufacturing, and provides the capacity available for responding to sales throughout the year. Business issues such as the amount of inventory investment necessary to ensure that customer demand is met, the timing and amount of investment in manufacturing capacity that is appropriate, and the acceptable level of employment costs that must be provided for in the sales and operations plan need to be resolved in order to be competitive in the market place.

Using Microsoft Excel Solver

The sales and operations planning problem at Lawn King can be addressed using the "Solver" tool in Microsoft Excel. Figure 4A.8 shows a spreadsheet design to solve the problem. The table, starting on row 9, is the aggregate plan. The decision variables are in cells D10:D21 (regular production), E10:E21 (overtime production), H10:H21 (workers hired), and I10:I21 (workers fired). As given in the first constraint set of the model, ending inventory in each month is calculated as:

Beginning inventory + Regular production + Overtime − Forecast demand

The ending inventory for a month is the beginning inventory for the next month. Similarly, the workforce level for a month is:

Previous month workforce level + Hires − Fires

These are often called *balance equations* by those familiar with setting up linear programming models.

Maximum regular time production is calculated by taking the workforce level (C10:C21) and multiplying by the number of units produced by a regular-time employee

FIGURE 4A.8 Excel Lawn King Spreadsheet

Microsoft Excel - lawnking optimal.xls

File Edit View Insert Format Tools Data Window Help

G10 =B10+D10+E10-F10

	A	B	C	D	E	F	G
1	Lawn - Optimal Solution				Costs:		
2					Cost/Employee/Month		$1,828
3					Inventory Cost/Unit/Mor		$1.77
4	Beginning Workforce =		84		OT Cost/Unit		$33.04
5	August Workforce =		72		Hire Cost/Employee		$800
6	Beginning Inventory =		16,610		Fire Cost/Employee		$1,500
7	Ending Inventory Minimum =		2,000		Reg.Time Unit/Mo/Emp		83
8	August Ending Inventory =		16,460		OT Max Units/Month		17

9	Month	Beginning Inventory	Workforce	Reg. Production	Overtime	Sales	Ending Invent.	#Hired	#Fired	Max Reg Production	Max OT Production	Total Production
10	September	16,610	84	6,972	0	900	22,682	0	0	6,972	1,428	6,972
11	October	22,682	84	6,972	0	1,910	27,744	0	0	6,972	1,428	6,972
12	November	27,744	84	6,972	0	3,625	31,091	0	0	6,972	1,428	6,972
13	December	31,091	84	6,972	0	4,580	33,483	0	0	6,972	1,428	6,972
14	January	33,483	84	6,972	0	5,350	35,105	0	0	6,972	1,428	6,972
15	February	35,105	87	7,221	0	8,380	33,946	3	0	7,221	1,479	7,221
16	March	33,946	87	7,221	0	17,740	23,427	0	0	7,221	1,479	7,221
17	April	23,427	87	7,221	0	18,975	11,673	0	0	7,221	1,479	7,221
18	May	11,673	87	7,221	0	12,150	6,744	0	0	7,221	1,479	7,221
19	June	6,744	87	7,221	0	5,020	8,945	0	0	7,221	1,479	7,221
20	July	8,945	87	7,221	0	3,350	12,816	0	0	7,221	1,479	7,221
21	August	12,816	72	5,976	288	2,620	16,460	0	15	5,976	1,224	6,264

23	Total Cost Model					
24		Hiring Cost	Firing Cost	Workf. Cost-RT	Overtime Cost	Invent. Cost	Total Cost
25		$2,400	$22,500	$1,853,592	$9,516	$467,485	$2,355,493

Lawn King

Ready NUM

per month (cell G7, 83 units). Overtime production is calculated in the same way, using the overtime maximum units per employee (G8, 17 units). These maximum levels are needed for setting up constraints that limit regular and overtime production.

Solutions are evaluated by calculating the total cost of the solution. Hiring cost is the sum of the number of employees hired during the year [SUM(H10:H21)] multiplied by $800 (G5). Firing cost is the number of employees fired during the year [SUM(I10:I21)] multiplied by $1,500 (G6). Workforce regular time cost is the number of regular time employees over the year [SUM(C10:C21)] multiplied by $1,828 (G2). Overtime cost is the number of units produced during overtime [SUM(E10:E21)] multiplied by overtime cost per unit (G4, $33.04). Inventory cost is the sum of the ending inventory levels [SUM(G10:G21)] multiplied by inventory cost per unit per month (G3, $1.77). The total cost is calculated by summing these individual costs [G25, SUM(B25:F25)].

Constraints and other parameters needed to solve this problem with Excel are specified in the Excel Parameters form (see Figure 4A.9). This form is accessed through Tools then Solver menu options. First, the target cell is set to G25 and Equal To: is set to Min. This tells Solver to minimize the value calculated in cell G25 (i.e., total cost).

Next, By Changing Cells specifies the decision variables in the model. The Solver can change the values in two blocks of cells, D10:E21 and H10:I21. D10:E21 is where regular and overtime production is put into the model. H10:I21 is the block of cells for hiring and firing numbers. By specifying these cells in By Changing Cells, we are telling the program to determine the minimum cost solution by varying the values in these cells.

FIGURE 4A.9
Solver Parameters

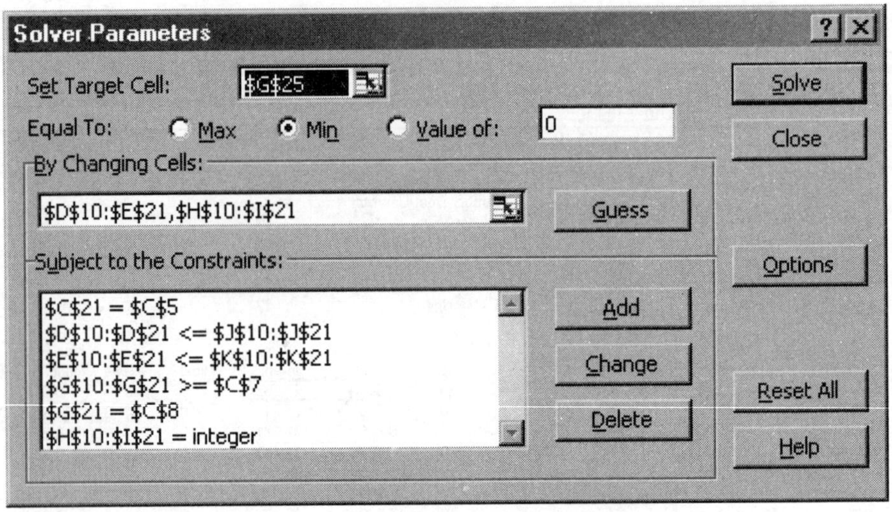

FIGURE 4A.10
Solver Options

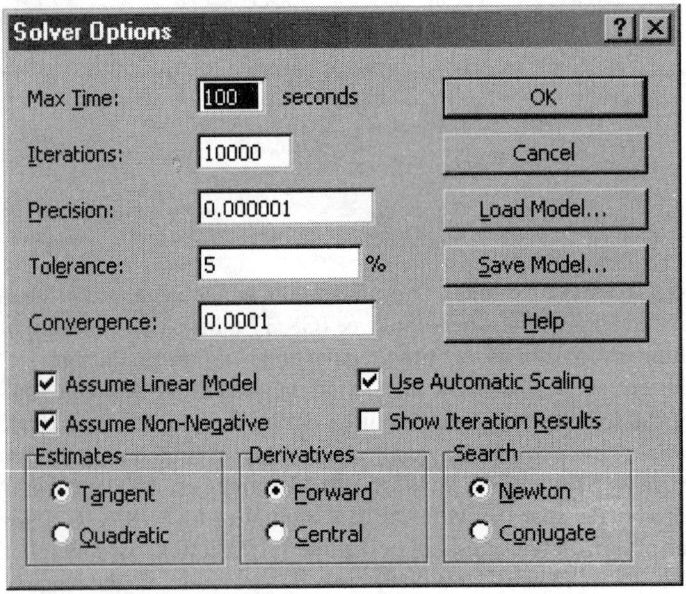

Next the remaining constraints need to be specified. Six constraints need to be specified. The first constraint forces the August workforce level to 72 employees (C21 = C5). The second requires regular-time production to be less than the maximum regular-time production (D10:D21 ≤ J10:J21). The third states that overtime production must be less than maximum overtime production (E10:E21 ≤ K10:K21). Next, we need monthly ending inventory levels to always be equal to or greater than 2,000 units (G10:G21 ≥ 2000). The fifth constraint forces ending inventory equal to 16,460 units (G21 = C8). Finally, the last constraint requires an integer number of employees.

Additional options need to be set through the Options button. Figure 4A.10 shows this form. It is important that Assume Linear Model and Assume Non-Negative be checked on this form. Clicking OK returns to the Solver Parameters form. The problem can now be solved optimally by clicking on the Solve button. The optimal solution is given in Figure 4A.8.

Concluding Principles

This chapter has introduced linear programming approaches to sales and operations planning. We stress the following principles:

- The match between the real world and the model should be as close as possible to make it easier to build the credibility necessary to use the model.
- Relatively homogeneous product lines or portions of lines allow for a closer match between model and reality.
- Investing in training, enhancing data, improving basic MPC practices, and determining clear objectives must all be done before the full potential for using advanced techniques can be realized.
- Management must realize that significant efforts in model formulation, understanding, testing, and explanation are all important to successful applications.
- Advanced techniques must be built on a foundation of good basic practice. Modeling a mess doesn't make it better.
- Spreadsheet-based models offer a better choice for use by current executives.

Discussion Questions

1. What is the least certain of the data inputs to sales and operations planning models? What can be done about this uncertainty?
2. What does a mixed integer programming formulation add over a linear programming approach?
3. What concerns should managers have about using sales and operations planning models?
4. Why must we have effective MPC systems in place before we can anticipate adoption of advanced sales and operations planning concepts?

Problems

1. The Seymore Bicycle Manufacturing Company of Boise, Idaho, has developed the following demand forecast for next year's bicycle:

Quarter	Sales
1	5,000
2	10,000
3	8,000
4	2,000

On January 1, there are 1,000 units in inventory. The firm has prepared the following data:

Hiring cost per employee = \$200.
Firing cost per employee = \$400.
Beginning workforce = 60 employees.
Inventory carrying cost = \$2 per unit per quarter of ending inventory.

Stockout cost = $50 per unit.
Regular payroll = $1,200 per employee per quarter.
Overtime cost = $2 per unit, limited to 40 units per employee per quarter.
Each employee can produce 100 units per quarter on regular time.
Demand not satisfied in any quarter is lost.

Using linear programming:

a. How much will Seymore produce during each quarter?

b. What's the total budget Seymore's plan will require for the next year?

2. Kosar Manufacturing has collected the following information on one of its major products. (Use a spreadsheet to model (a) and (b) below.)

Most efficient production rate = 2,100 units per period.
Production change costs = $15 per unit of change (from 2,100 units/period).
Inventory costs = $5 per unit per period (on closing inventory balance).
Backorder costs = $10 per unit to carry demand into next period.
Beginning inventory = 350 units.

Period	Demand (Units)
I	3,000
II	2,250
III	2,000
IV	2,700

a. Using the preceding demand schedule, calculate a level production schedule that yields zero inventory at the end of period IV.

b. Calculate the total costs associated with the production schedule in part a.

3. The Kew Toy Company's production manager wonders whether to produce at a level production rate or a rate that matches sales each quarter. His analysis of company operations yields the following information:

Beginning employment level = 10 employees.
Beginning inventory = 0
Hiring cost = $10 per employee.
Firing cost = $5 per employee.
Production per employee = 10 units per quarter.
Inventory carrying costs = $1 per unit per quarter (on ending inventory).
Target inventory at the end of the fourth quarter = 0.
Target employment level at the end of the fourth quarter equals the planned.

Employment level specified by the plan under consideration.

Quarter	Sales Forecast (Units)
1	50
2	80
3	120
4	150

a. Which of the two policies would result in the lowest annual cost?

b. What's the total annual cost of the policy adopted in part 1?

c. What production rate should he use each quarter?

d. Formulate this problem so it can be solved using linear programming.

4. Mischief Company had been experimenting with various sales and operations plans. As the firm started to lay out plans for next year, management decided to use a four-month planning horizon to reduce computation cost. The firm's basic data were:

   Employment level for this December = 20 people.
   Demand forecast for January of next year = 200.
   Demand forecast for February of next year = 220.
   Demand forecast for March of next year = 200.
   Demand forecast for April of next year = 220.
   Inventory level planned for the end of this December = 0.
   Back orders aren't allowed in the plan.
   Desired April ending inventory = 0.
   Regular time per month = $2,000 per worker-month.
   Production = 10 units/person/month.
   Overtime premium = 50 percent of regular time.
   Overtime limit = 25 percent of regular time per person per month.
   Inventory carrying cost = $150/month/unit (on the average per month).
   Hiring (or firing) cost = $2,000 per person.

   Use a spreadsheet model to compare the cost of a fixed employment production plan (i.e., 20 people) that uses overtime to meet demand to a level production plan that uses no overtime to meet production.

5. Consider the following information for the Fairmount Company:

   Production change cost = $20/unit of change (from a base of 4,000 units).
   Most efficient production rate = 4,000 units per period.
   Maximum amount of production capacity = 4,600 units per period.
   Inventory costs = $4/unit per period on the ending inventory.
   Shortage costs = $15/unit per period.
   Subcontracting costs = $18/unit (maximum of 1,000 units per period).
   Beginning inventory = 1,200 units.

Period	Demand (Units)
1	6,000
2	4,500
3	6,000
4	5,100

   a. As production manager of Fairmount, you're in charge of meeting the preceding demand schedule for periods 1 through 4. President Shea specifies that you keep your production plan level for all four months. In addition, Shea limits the total amount of production per month to 4,600 units. Also, since the market Fairmount competes in is very competitive, planned stockouts are not allowed. Therefore, you must decide if and when to subcontract. Maximum amount of subcontracting available in any one period is 1,000 units. Ending inventory at the end of period 4 should be zero. Use a spreadsheet to determine your plan's cost.

b. Assuming the same facts as in part a, except that no subcontracting is allowed, could you follow a pure chase strategy and still meet demand? Why or why not?

6. On December 31, the ABC Company forecast its next year's sales to be:

Quarter	Sales Forecast
1	9,000 units
2	12,000
3	16,000
4	12,000
	49,000

Currently, the firm has 12 employees, each producing up to 1,000 units per quarter and earning \$2,000 per quarter. The firm estimates its inventory carrying cost to be \$2 per unit of ending inventory per quarter and its hiring or layoff costs to be \$1,600 per employee. The firm could increase production by working overtime, but overtime work is limited to 25 percent of the regular production rate (or 250 units per employee per quarter). Overtime work is paid at the rate of 1.5 times the regular pay rate. Unused regular time costs the firm \$4.16 per hour. (Assume there are 60 eight-hour days per quarter.) The company currently has an inventory of 1,000 units and wishes to have an ending inventory of 1,000 units at the end of the year. The company does not plan to incur inventory shortages.

a. Develop the total incremental cost expression of this problem.
b. Formulate this problem for solution, using linear programming.
c. What's the total incremental cost of a production plan that assumes a constant production rate (include both regular and overtime production) and level workforce (assume 12 workers) each quarter?
d. Compare the cost of the production plan in c to one based on a production rate equal to sales in each quarter. Which has the lowest cost?

7. The production manager at the Boston Paint Company is preparing production and inventory plans for next year. The production manager has the following data concerning the firm:

Quarter	Sales Forecast
1	3,000 units
2	1,800
3	2,400
4	3,500

Current inventory level = 300 units.
Current employment level = 600 people.
Production rate last quarter = 2,400 units (4 units/employee/quarter).
Inventory carrying cost = \$20/unit/quarter (on ending inventory).
Hiring cost = \$200/employee hired.
Layoff cost = \$200/employee laid off.
Regular time production cost per unit = \$320/unit.
Cost of overtime = \$60/unit.
Desired closing inventory level = 100 units (minimum).

The production manager sees no equipment capacity limitations during the next two years. Employees are hired or laid off only at the beginning of each quarter.

Formulate a linear programming production planning model for this company, in sufficient detail so the production manager can solve it to determine the production plan.

8. The Pickwick Company's production director and marketing director are currently negotiating next year's production and sales plans. The marketing director confidently forecasts a major sales increase as follows:

	Quarter			
	1	2	3	4
Sales forecast (in units)	950	1,200	1,420	1,630

a. Assume that the beginning inventory is 200 units and the target ending inventory for the fourth quarter is 200 units. What production each quarter will provide a level production plan?

b. If average variable cost per unit for items produced by Pickwick is \$500, what will be the monetary value of the finished-goods inventory at the end of the second quarter if it uses a level production plan?

c. If average variable labor cost per unit for the items produced by Pickwick is \$200 and average wage rate is \$5 per hour, what's the quarterly labor budget in hours and in dollars for a level production plan?

Chapter 5

Master Production Scheduling

In this chapter, we discuss constructing and managing a master production schedule (MPS), a central module in the manufacturing planning and control system. An effective master production schedule provides the basis for making good use of manufacturing resources, making customer delivery promises, resolving trade-offs between sales and manufacturing, and attaining the firm's strategic objectives as reflected in the sales and operations plan. The prerequisites to master production scheduling are to define the MPS unit (and associated bill of materials) and to provide the master production scheduler with the supporting concepts and techniques described in this chapter.

This chapter is organized around the following eight topics:

- *The master production scheduling (MPS) activity:* What is the role of master production scheduling in manufacturing planning and control?
- *Master production scheduling techniques:* What are the basic MPS tasks and what techniques are available to aid this process?
- *Bill of materials structuring for the MPS:* How can nonengineering uses of the bill of materials assist the master production scheduling function?
- *The final assembly schedule:* How is the MPS converted into a final build schedule?
- *The master production scheduler:* What does a master production scheduler do and what are the key organizational relationships for this position?
- *Company examples:* How do actual MPS systems work in practice?
- *Master production schedule stability:* How can a stable MPS be developed and maintained?
- *Managing the MPS:* How can MPS performance be monitored and controlled?

The Master Production Scheduling (MPS) Activity

We begin with a brief overview of the role of master production scheduling (MPS) in the manufacturing planning and control (MPC) system. We look at the fundamental role of the MPS in converting the disaggregated sales and operations plan into a specific manufacturing schedule. Next we consider how the environment in which the MPS activity takes place shapes the MPS task. Finally, we discuss the linkages between the MPS, other MPC modules, and other company activities.

At the conceptual level, the master production schedule translates the sales and operations plan of the company into a plan for producing specific products in the future. Where the sales and operations plan provides an aggregate statement of the manufacturing output required to reach company objectives, the MPS is a statement of the specific products that make up that output. The MPS is the translation of the sales and operations plan into producible products with their quantities and timing determined.

On a day-to-day basis, the MPS provides the information by which sales and manufacturing are coordinated. The MPS shows when products will be available in the future, thereby providing the basis for sales to promise delivery to customers. These promises will be valid as long as manufacturing executes the MPS according to plan. When conditions arise that create customer promise dates that are unacceptable from a marketing or manufacturing perspective, the MPS provides the basis for making the required trade-offs.

At the operational level, the most basic concern is with the construction of the MPS record and updating it over time. The MPS record is developed to be compatible with the material requirements planning (MRP) system and to provide the information for coordinating with sales. Over time, as production is completed and products are used to meet customer requirements, the MPS record must be kept up to date. Doing this means implementing a periodic review and update cycle that we term "rolling through time." Updating the record involves processing MPS transactions, maintaining the MPS record, responding to exception conditions, and measuring MPS effectiveness on a routine basis. Performing these tasks effectively will keep manufacturing resources and output aligned with the sales and operations plan.

The MPS Is a Statement of Future Output

The master production schedule is a statement of planned future output. It specifies the products (or product options) that will be completed, the time of completion, and the quantities to be completed. It is the anticipated build schedule for the company. As such, it is a statement of production, not a statement of demand. The MPS specifies how product will be supplied to meet future demand. We stress the fact that the MPS is *not* a forecast, since manufacturing is held responsible for meeting the MPS requirements.

The forecast is an important input into the planning process that determines the master production schedule, but the MPS differs from the forecast in significant ways. The MPS takes into account capacity limitations, the costs of production, other resource considerations, and the sales and operations plan. As a consequence, the MPS may specify large batches of product when the demand is for single units. Or production may take place in advance of market demand in order to better utilize production capacity. It is even possible that product for which there is forecast demand may not even be made.

As the statement of output, the master production schedule forms the basic communication link between the market and manufacturing. The MPS is stated in product specifications—in part numbers for which there are **bills of materials (BOM),** the language of product manufacturing. Because the MPS is a build schedule, it must be stated in terms used to determine component-part needs and other requirements. It can't, therefore, be stated in overall dollars or some other global unit of measure. It must be in terms that relate to a producible product.

The MPS can be stated in specific end-item product designations, but this is not always the case. The MPS units might be options or modules from which a variety of end products could be assembled. Alternatively, the MPS might be stated in a number of units of an "average" final product. Doing this requires a special **planning bill of materials** designed to produce the parts and components necessary to build that "average" configuration. Converting the options, parts, and components into specific end products would be controlled by a separate **final assembly schedule (FAS),** which isn't ascertained until the last possible moment. The choice of MPS unit is largely dictated by the environment in which the MPS is implemented, a topic to which we now turn our attention.

The Business Environment for the MPS

The business environment, as it relates to master production scheduling, encompasses the production approach used, the variety of products produced, and the markets served by the company. Three basic production environments have been identified: make-to-stock, make-to-order, and assemble-to-order. Each of these environments affects the design of the MPS system, primarily through the choice of the unit used for stating the MPS—that is whether the MPS is stated in end-item terms, some average end item, product modules or options, or specific customer orders.

The **make-to-stock** company carries finished goods inventories for most, if not all, of its end items. The MPS is the production statement of how much of and when each end item is to be produced. Firms that make to stock are often producing consumer products as opposed to industrial goods, but many industrial goods, such as supply items, are also made to stock.

The choice of MPS unit for the make-to-stock company is fairly straightforward. All use end-item catalogue numbers, but many tend to group these end items into model groupings until the latest possible time in the final assembly schedule. Thus, the Ethan Allen Furniture Company uses a **consolidated item number** for items identical except for the finish color, running a separate system to allocate a lot size in the MPS to specific finishes at the last possible moment. Similarly, the Black & Decker tool manufacturing firm groups models in a series, such as sanders, which are similar, except for horsepower, attachments, and private-brand labels. All products so grouped are run together in batches to achieve economical runs for component parts and to exploit the learning curve in the final assembly areas.

The **make-to-order** (or **engineer-to-order**) company, in general, carries no finished-goods inventory and builds each customer order as needed. This form of production is often used when there's a very large number of possible production configurations, and, thus, a small probability of anticipating a customer's exact needs. In this business environment, customers expect to wait for a large portion of the entire design and manufacturing lead time.

In the make-to-order company, the MPS unit is typically defined as the particular end item or set of items composing a customer order. The definition is difficult since part of the job is to define the product; that is, design takes place as construction takes place. Production often starts before a complete product definition and bill of materials have been determined.

The **assemble-to-order** firm is typified by an almost limitless number of possible end item configurations, all made from combinations of basic components and subassemblies. Customer delivery time requirements are often shorter than total manufacturing lead times, so production must be started in anticipation of customer orders. The large number of end-item possibilities makes forecasting exact end-item configurations extremely difficult and stocking end items very risky. As a result, the assemble-to-order firm tries to maintain flexibility, starting basic components and subassemblies into production, but, in general, not starting final assembly until a customer order is received.

Examples of assemble-to-order firms include Dell with their endless variety of computer end-item combinations; the Hyster Company, which makes forklift trucks with such options as engine type, lift height, cab design, speed, type of lift mechanism, and safety equipment; and Mack Trucks, which produces trucks with many driver/owner-specified options. None of these firms know until the last minute the specific choices their customers will make.

The assemble-to-order firm typically doesn't develop a master production schedule for end items. The MPS unit is stated in planning bills of materials, such as an average Hyster forklift truck of some model series or an average Mack highway truck. The MPS unit has as its components a set of common part and options. The option usages are based on percentage estimates, and their planning in the MPS incorporates **buffering** or **hedging** techniques to maximize response flexibility to actual customer orders.

We've said here that the primary difference between make-to-stock, make-to-order, and assemble-to-order firms is in the definition of the MPS unit. However, most master production scheduling techniques are useful for any kind of MPS unit definition. Moreover, the choice of the MPS unit is somewhat open to definition by the firm. Thus, some firms may produce end items that are held in inventory, yet still use assemble-to-order approaches. Also, some firms use more than one of these approaches at the same time, so common systems across all approaches are important.

Linkages to Other Company Activities

Figure 5.1 presents a partial schematic for the overall manufacturing planning and control system showing the linkages to master production scheduling. The detailed schedule produced by the MPS drives all the engine and, subsequently, the back-end systems, as well as the rough-cut capacity planning activities. All the feedback linkages aren't shown in the figure, however. For example, as execution problems are discovered, there are many mechanisms for their resolution, with feedback to the MPS and to the other MPC modules.

FIGURE 5.1
Master Production Scheduling in the MPC System

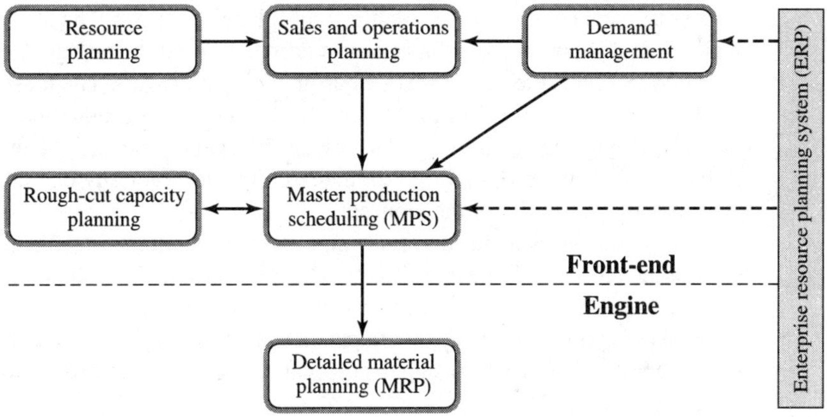

The linkages to the enterprise resource planning (ERP) system of the firm are shown as indirect, but they are important. All of the major ERP vendors have a master production scheduling module. The role of the MPS in an ERP system is the same as we have described here: disaggregating the sales and operations plan, creating a statement of the output from the factory, and providing the information for coordinating sales and manufacturing. The records for a particular ERP system may look different from the version that we use here, but all of the functions will be included.

The demand management block in Figure 5.1 represents a company's forecasting, order entry, order promising, and physical distribution activities. Demand management collects data on all sources of demand for manufacturing capacity: customer orders, forecasts of future customer orders, warehouse replenishments, interplant transfers, spare parts requirements, and so forth. These forecasts are summarized and provided to sales and operations planning. Moreover, demand management books customer orders (enters the order, determines a delivery date with the customer and provides product details to manufacturing). These booked orders are also provided to master production scheduling to coordinate product availability with customer requirements.

In sales and operations planning, the forecasts from demand management will be consolidated and incorporated into the sales and operations plan. This is sometimes referred to as the *company game plan*. The operations plan is a statement of the aggregate output that will meet the objectives of the firm, both quantitatively and qualitatively. In some firms this plan is stated in terms of the sales dollars generated for the company as a whole or for individual plants or regions. In other firms it is stated as the number of units of output to be produced in the next year. The aggregate operations plan constrains the MPS, because the sum of the detailed MPS quantities must always equal the whole as defined by the operations plan.

Rough-cut capacity planning involves an analysis of the master production schedule to discover the existence of any manufacturing resources that represent potential bottlenecks in the production flow. This is the linkage that provides a rough evaluation of potential capacity problems with a particular MPS. If any problems are disclosed, they must be resolved before attempting to execute the MPS.

The disaggregation of the operations plan into production plans for specific products defines the product mix that will be produced. These plans also provide the basic demand "forecast" for each MPS production unit. It is on the basis of these forecast data that the master production schedule is developed. The MPS, in turn, provides the input (gross requirement) data to the material requirements planning system. The MPS, then, is the driver of all the detailed manufacturing activities needed to meet the output objectives of the firm.

The MPS also is the basis for key interfunctional trade-offs. The most profound of these is between production and sales. The specification of exact production output, in terms of products, dates, and quantities, provides the basis for promising delivery to customers. Moreover, when there is a request to increase the output for any one item, the MPS helps determine the feasibility of the request.

Because the MPS is an important input to the manufacturing budget, it follows that financial budgets should be integrated with master production scheduling activities. When the MPS is extended over a time horizon sufficient to make capital equipment purchases, a better basis is provided for capital budgets. On a day-to-day basis, both cash flow and profits can be better forecast by basing the estimates on the planned production output specified in the MPS.

Master Production Scheduling Techniques

This section presents the basic logic for master production scheduling. We start with the time-phased record to show relationships between production output, the "forecast" (derived from the sales and operations plan), and expected inventory balance. We then show how plans are revised as you roll through time during a review cycle. Finally, we present the process for promising delivery to customers. This process illustrates how the actual customer orders "consume" the forecast.

The Time-Phased Record

Figure 5.2 shows an example of an MPS involving an item with a beginning on-hand inventory of 20 units, a sales forecast that is increasing each period (typically weekly), and master a production schedule of 10 units per period. The master production schedule row states the timing for *completion* of units available to meet demand. As with the sales and operations plan, the projected available balance is governed by the following relationship:

Projected available balance = Beginning balance + Master production schedule − Forecast

Data in this record show the expected condition as of the current period. The record covers a five-period planning horizon for which the total sales forecast is 43 and the total master production schedule (planned production) is 50 units.

Many different approaches can be used to meet demand. The strategy shown in Figure 5.2 is a **level strategy** where production is held constant. A **chase strategy** or some other type of mixed strategy might be appropriate. The exact strategy chosen depends on characteristics of the process employed for making the item and the constraints within the company. The goal is to find the plan that best balances costs and benefits.

Often the same production process is used to make different items. In this case, production must switch from one item to the next, and this switching usually involves some changeover time. To minimize the impact of the loss of production due to the changeover, parts are made in batches rather than one at a time. The number of units made in a batch is referred to as the **lot size.**

In Figure 5.3 we show an MPS where the lot size has been set to 30 units. In addition, in this example we have set a safety stock of five units. The safety stock provides a cushion to protect the schedule against uncertainty in demand. Safety stock, in the context of master production scheduling, is the additional inventory and capacity planned as protection

FIGURE 5.2
MPS Example

		Period				
	On hand	1	2	3	4	5
Forecast		5	5	8	10	15
Projected available balance	20	25	30	32	32	27
Master production schedule		10	10	10	10	10

FIGURE 5.3
Lot Sizing in the MPS

	On hand	Period 1	2	3	4	5
Forecast		5	5	8	10	15
Projected available balance	20	15	10	32	22	7
Master production schedule				30		
Lot size = 30						
Safety stock = 5 units						

FIGURE 5.4
Lot Sizing in the MPS

	On hand	Period 2	3	4	5	6
Forecast		20	20	20	15	20
Projected available balance	10	−10	0	−20	−35	−55
Master production schedule			30			
Lot size = 30						
Safety stock = 5 units						

against forecast errors and short-term changes in the backlog. Logically one can think of the five units as a trigger level, when projected available balance falls below five units, a new batch of parts are scheduled for production. In Figure 5.3, if we did not produce another batch in period 3, inventory would drop to two units and would be below our safety stock level. We therefore schedule a lot of 30 units to be produced in period 3 to replenish inventory. Manufacturing using a lot size procedure produces inventories that last between production runs. This inventory, called **cycle stock,** is part of the projected available inventory row in the schedule. The larger the lot size, the greater the average cycle stock carried in the schedule.

Rolling through Time

The MPS is a rolling schedule that requires updating the record to so the MPS reflects actual current conditions. The updating captures the impact of actual transactions that have occurred from one period to the next on the MPS. Figure 5.4 show the situation at the start of the second period (now for periods 2 through 6), using the original MPS for the five-week period given in Figure 5.3.

No material was received during the first week, because none was planned by the MPS. But actual sales were 10 units instead of 5 units, so now we see that on-hand inventory at the beginning of period 2 is 10 units rather than the 15 we expected last period. The projected available balance reflects these changes and assumes the master schedule planned during period 1. Our forecast has also been updated, reflecting an anticipated surge in demand in periods 2, 3, and period 4. Note that we have added a forecast for period 6 as part of rolling our plan forward one period.

FIGURE 5.5
Lot Sizing in the MPS

	On hand	2	3	4	5	6
		Period				
Forecast		20	20	20	15	20
Projected available balance	10	20	30	10	25	5
Master production schedule		30	30		30	
Lot size = 30 Safety stock = 5 units						

The increase in demand has created some problems that we need to deal with in the master schedule. If possible, we would like to move up the batch currently scheduled for production in period 3 to period 2. This would keep us from stocking out in period 2. In addition, we need to schedule batches in periods 3 and 5. These changes were made using the same triggering logic used before where we maintain a safety stock level of five units.

The revision shown in Figure 5.5 solves the problem of projected negative available inventory but puts in clear focus the question of feasibility. Does the company have the capacity to immediately produce a batch that was originally scheduled for period 3? Can the company produce batches in two consecutive periods in the future? Is material available to meet the requirements of this schedule? Furthermore, high costs are typically associated with making production changes. The master production schedule should be buffered from overreaction, with changes made only when essential.

Order Promising and Available-to-Promise (ATP)

For many products, customers do not expect immediate delivery, but place orders for future delivery. The delivery date (promise date) is negotiated through a cycle of order promising, where the customer either asks when the order can be shipped or specifies a desired shipment date. If the company has a backlog of orders for future shipments, the order promising task is to determine when the shipment can be made. Order promising can be coordinated with production schedules by using a concept known as **available-to-promise** (ATP).

Figure 5.6 builds on the lot-sized MPS depicted in Figure 5.3. The original sales forecast and MPS as of the beginning of week 1 are shown. In addition, we now consider an "Orders" row that reflects shipments that are tied to actual customer orders. That is, we now have data on expected shipments and consider these when planning the master schedule. Of course, this information could also be shared with the sales group so that they understand the precise implication of promising orders to customers on a particular date.

The row labeled "Orders" in Figure 5.6 represents the company's backlog of orders at the start of the first period. Five units are promised for shipment in the first period, three more in period 2, and an additional two units promised for delivery in period 3. Thus, the cumulative order backlog is 10 units over the three periods.

The logic for calculating available-to-promise will be explained next, but before doing this, consider the issues associated with the calculation. When we consider the situation as of the beginning of period 1, we have 20 units in inventory, and between now and when we expect to replenish our supply in period 3, we have orders for 8 units. So between now and the beginning of period 3, we could deliver an additional 12 units. We can ignore the issue

FIGURE 5.6
Available-to Promsie Order Promising Example: Week 1—Discrete ATP Logic

	On hand	Period 1	2	3	4	5
Forecast		5	5	8	10	15
Orders		5	3	2	0	0
Projected available balance	20	15	10	32	22	7
Available-to-promise		12		28		
Master production schedule				30		
Lot size = 30 Safety stock = 5						

FIGURE 5.7
Available-to-Promsie Order Promising Example: Week 1—Cumulative ATP Logic

	On hand	Period 1	2	3	4	5
Forecast		5	5	8	10	15
Orders		5	3	2	0	0
Projected available balance	20	15	10	32	22	7
Available-to-promise (cumulative)		12		40		
Master production schedule				30		
Lot size = 30 Safety stock = 5						

of safety stock in this analysis, because those units are available and could be sold if we can find customers for them. When we get to period 3, the whole cycle starts again. So far we only have orders for 2 units, so out of that second batch we could promise another 28 units for delivery in period 3 and out into the future.

The logic that we have just described is usually referred to as **discrete ATP** logic, where the first period, and every order after it, are considered independent from a planning view. We could take a **cumulative ATP** view and carry the units that we can promise from one batch forward to the next. In Figure 5.7 the cumulative ATP calculations are show.

The following is a step-by-step process for calculating the MPS including ATP calculations:

1. *Calculate projected available inventory.* Projected available inventory = Previous available inventory + Master production schedule − MAX (Forecast, Actual orders). Calculate for every period in the planning horizon.

2A. *ATP calculations (discrete logic).* For the first period, ATP = On-hand + MPS − Sum of the orders until the next MPS. For each period when a subsequent MPS occurs, ATP = MPS − Sum of the orders until the next MPS.

2B. *ATP calculations (cumulative logic).* For the first period, ATP = On-hand + MPS − Sum of the orders until the next MPS. For each period when a subsequent MPS occurs, ATP = Previous ATP + MPS − Sum of the order until the next MPS.

One nuance that we see in step 1 of our process is the calculation for projected available inventory. When calculating what we expect to have available in a period, we use the maximum of forecast and actual orders. This reflects a conservative approach to the demand side of the equation. Our hope is that during a period we will eventually sell up to the forecast, and, if this proves to be true, we want to reflect the additional sales in projecting our inventory balance. Some experts refer to this as **consuming the forecast.** Using our example in period 1 we see all five units of the forecast have been consumed.

To illustrate this idea further, let's roll our plan to period 2, assuming that we delivered the five units scheduled in period 1. Let's consider a set of new orders that come in during period 2 and see if we can accept them, assuming they are received in the following sequence:

Order Number	Amount	Desired Week
1	5	2
2	15	3
3	35	6
4	10	5

In Figure 5.8 we show how things look prior to making any changes to our master schedule. Here, the projected available balance reflects demand as the maximum of orders or forecast. As we can see, another batch needs to be scheduled in period 5 because sales were higher than expected and we would expect to stock out six periods from now.

Figure 5.9 reflects the status of our master schedule after entering a new batch in period 5 and a second batch in period 6. Using the discrete ATP logic, it is a little difficult to understand how sound the schedule is given the positive ATP values in periods 2, 3, and 5 and the negative value in period 6. Cumulative ATP values, shown in Figure 5.10, show that the

FIGURE 5.8
Availabl-to Promise Order Promising Example: Week 2—Discrete ATP Logic

		Period				
		2	3	4	5	6
Forecast		5	8	10	15	20
Orders		3 + 5 (new)	2 + 15	0	10	35
Projected available balance	15	7	20	10	−5	−40
Available-to-promise		7	−32			
Master production schedule			30			
Lot size = 30 Safety stock = 5						

FIGURE 5.9
ATP Order Promising Example: Week 2 after Update—Discrete ATP Logic

		Period				
		2	3	4	5	6
Forecast		5	8	10	15	20
Orders		3 + 5 (new)	2 + 15	0	10	35
Projected available balance	15	7	20	10	25	20
Available-to-promise		7	13		20	−5
Master production schedule			30		30	30
Lot size = 30 Safety stock = 5						

FIGURE 5.10
ATP Order Promising Example: Week 2 after Update—Cumulative ATP Logic

		Period				
		2	3	4	5	6
Forecast		5	8	10	15	20
Orders		3 + 5 (new)	2 + 15	0	10	35
Projected available balance	15	7	20	10	25	20
Available-to-promise (cumulative)		7	20		40	35
Master production schedule			30		30	30
Lot size = 30 Safety stock = 5						

schedule looks fine. What works better in practice, discrete or cumulative ATP calculations, depends on the actual situation with the company. Even though the cumulative approach looks attractive with this example, in practice it might overstate the real availability in the future due to the timing of how orders are booked. Within software packages, there are often options for how these calculations are performed and for the format of the schedules.

The use of both the projected available balance and the available-to-promise row is the key to effective master production scheduling. Using ATP to book orders means that it is unlikely that a customer promise will be made that cannot be kept. Note, this may mean some orders must be booked at the end of a planning horizon concurrent with creating an additional MPS order. As actual orders are booked (and reflected in the order row), or anticipated (in the forecast row), or shipped (as reflected in the projected available balance), the available-to-promise row provides a signal for the creation of new MPS orders.

Planning in an Assemble-to-Order Environment

The assemble-to-order firm is typified by an almost limitless number of end-item possibilities due to the myriad combinations of basic components and subassemblies. For example, the number of unique Ford automobiles runs into the billions when one considers all the

FIGURE 5.11
The MPS Hourglass

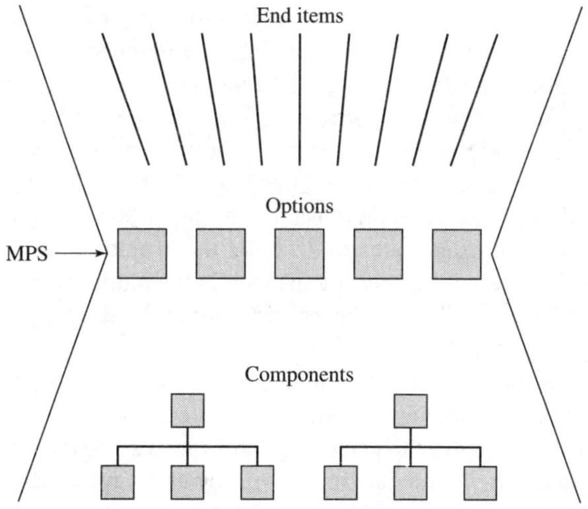

options available to the customer. Moreover, each new product option tends to double the number of end-item possibilities. This means that the MPS unit in the assemble-to-order environment cannot feasibly be based on end items. In this section, we present how this problem is addressed relative to planning the master production schedule.

The *bill of materials* specifies the ingredients required to make each part number or assembly in our system. It is a listing of all the subassemblies, intermediates, parts, and raw materials that go into a parent assembly, showing the quantity of each required to make an assembly. The bill of material may also be called the formula, recipe, or ingredients list in certain process industries. We discuss the details of what the bill of material is and how they are processed in Chapter 6. In this chapter, we discuss a special type of bill of materials, one useful for MPS management, called the *planning bill of materials.*

Figure 5.11 is a diagram that depicts how components and options come together in an assemble-to-order company. The assembly-to-order firm is unique in that a relatively few number of modular options can be combined to make a unique end item wanted by a customer. One approach that we could take to building the unique item that a customer wants would be to simply take the order and then construct the item totally from scratch, first building the components, then assembling the components into the option modules, and finally assembling the options into the final product. Of course, this could take a considerable amount of time, and our customers may not be willing to wait this long. Another approach—one that would make customer response much quicker—would be to synchronize two parallel production systems. The first system is designed to efficiently produce the components and options that are needed in the final product. The second system is a final assembly process that is designed to put together a product from the options selected by each customer. For this approach to be successful, these two systems must be tightly integrated so that the desired options are available when the customer orders the product. The **two-level MPS,** which we discuss next, is designed to support this type of integration.

A special type of planning bill is one known as the **super bill.** The super bill describes the related options or modules that make up the *average* end item. For example, a maker of notebook computers may know from past experience that the average computer has 2GB of memory, 0.5 web cameras (half the notebooks are configured with a camera), 0.3 cell phone interface modems (30 percent are configured to access a cell phone carrier), and 0.8 extra-high-contrast displays (80 percent have the optional high-contrast display). This end item is impossible to build, but it's very useful information for planning and master scheduling. Our super bill will show all the possible options as components, with their average decimal usage. The super bill combines the modules, or options, with the decimal usage rates to describe the average notebook computer. The bill of material logic forces arithmetic consistency in the mutually exclusive options; for example, the sum of two possible display screen options needs to equal the total number of notebook computers made.

The super bill is as much a marketing tool as a manufacturing tool. With it, instead of forecasting and controlling individual modules, the forecast is now stated in terms of total average units, with attention given to percentage breakdowns—to the single-level super bill of materials—and to *managing* module inventories by using available-to-promise logic on a day-to-day basis as actual customer orders are booked.

Let's consider an artificially small example. The Garden Till Company makes rototillers in the following options:

Horsepower: 3 HP, 4 HP, 5 HP

Drive train: Chain, Gear

Brand name: Taylor, Garden Till, Original Equipment Manufacturer (OEM)

The total number of end item buildable units is 18 ($3 \times 2 \times 3$). Management and master scheduling at the end-item level would mean each of these would have to be forecast. Figure 5.12 shows a super bill for 4-horsepower tillers. Using this artificial end item for an average 4-horsepower tiller, only one forecast is needed from marketing. More important,

FIGURE 5.12
The 4-Horsepower Super Bill

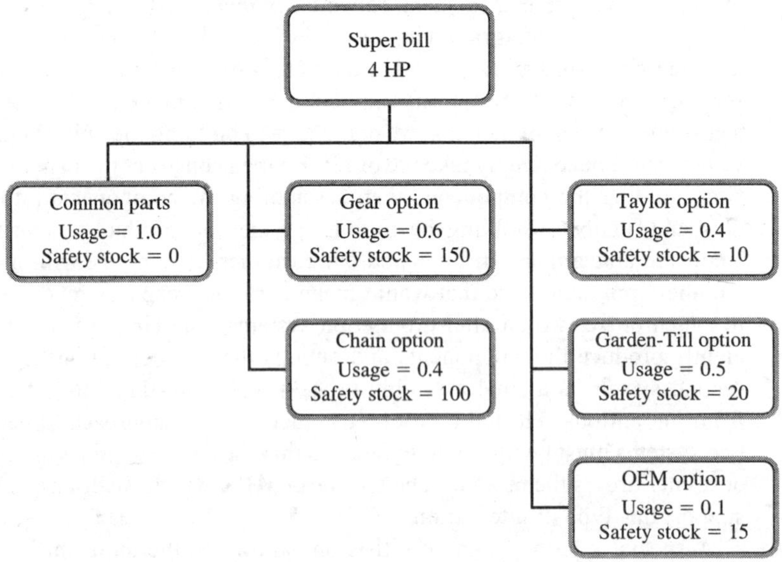

the MPS unit can be the super bill. The entry of 1,000 four-horsepower super bill units into the MPS would plan the appropriate quantities of each of the options to build 1,000 four-horsepower units in the average option proportions. Actual orders may not reflect the average in the short run.

Figure 5.12 shows the use of safety stocks for the options to absorb variations in the mix. No safety stock is shown for the common parts. This means protection is provided for product mix variances but not for variances in the overall MPS quantity of 4-horsepower tillers. A commitment to an MPS quantity for the super bill means exactly that number of common parts will be needed. In Figure 5.12's example, if 1,000 four-horsepower super bills were entered, the bill of materials would call for 1,000 common-parts modules, 600 gear options, 400 chain options, 400 Taylor options, 500 Garden Till options, and 100 OEM options. The safety stocks allow shipments to customers to vary from the usages specified by the bill of materials percentage.

Although 600 of the 1,000 four-horsepower tillers are expected to be finished with the gear drive option, as many as 750 can be promised because of the safety stock. Similar flexibility exists for all other options. Safety stocks are maintained with MRP logic, so appropriate quantities are maintained as orders arrive. Moreover, the safety stock will exist in matched sets because of the modular bill of materials structure. Matched sets occur because when one unit of the module is specified for safety stock, *all* parts required for that unit will be planned. Furthermore, costs of all safety stocks are readily visible. Marketing has the responsibility to optimize the mix and review safety stock levels.

Order entry using planning bill of materials concepts tends to be more complex than when the structure is end-item based. To accept a customer order, the available-to-promise logic must be applied to each option in the order, meaning it's necessary to check each of the affected modules. Figure 5.13 shows the flow for a particular customer order, in this case for 25 Taylor 4-horsepower units in the gear option (T4G). The safety stocks are available for promising and will be maintained by MRP as additional MPS quantities are planned. We can provide the information needed to implement the logic shown in Figure 5.13 using a concept often referred to as a *two-level MPS,* which we describe next.

FIGURE 5.13 Available-to-Promise Logic with Modular Bill Architecture (order for 25 T4Gs)

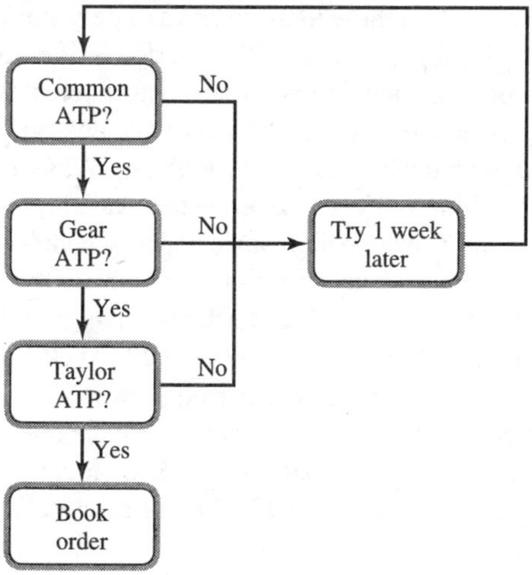

Managing Using a Two-Level MPS

When a planning bill is used, the **final assembly schedule** (FAS) is often used to state the exact set of end products to be built over some time period. It is the schedule that serves to plan and control final assembly and test operations, including the launching of final assembly orders, picking of component parts, subassembly, painting, or other finishing. In short, the FAS controls that portion of the business from fabricated components to completed products ready for shipment (for a good example, see the Hill-Rom FAS case at the end of the chapter).

Many firms have found it useful to coordinate the final assembly schedule and component production by using a concept known as **two-level master production schedules.** This technique is most useful for an assemble-to-order firm, where it is critical that before an order is promised, key components are guaranteed to be available. The technique allows the use of available-to-promise logic at both the component level and at the final assembly level in the bill of materials. The typical situation has the firm using a super bill such as that shown in Figure 5.12.

To illustrate the idea, let's consider our Garden Till Company and focus on two models of our 4-horsepower tillers, the branded Taylor product and the OEM product. Assume that we plan to sell 100 units per week and that these will be assembled to order. We expect 40 percent of the demand to be the Taylor brand and 10 percent will be OEM. The other 50 percent are sold as options in other bundled products. Figure 5.14 shows the calculations for our two-level master schedule.

The top portion of the table, 4-Horsepower Tillers, is the assembly plan for making our tillers. Here, we see that we plan to make 100 tillers each period and that they will be assembled based on actual customer orders. We have already received 100 orders to be made in period 1, 72 in period 2, and 54 in period 3. As can be seen, sales can take orders for 28 additional tillers in period 2, 46 in period 3, and 100 per period after that, using discrete ATP calculations.

The middle portion of the table is the master schedule for our Taylor Brand tiller. We expect demand to be 40 percent of 4-horsepower tiller demand. Our plan is to make to demand, but just to be safe we want to carry 10 of these in inventory as safety stock. We have firm orders for 42 of these in period 1, 37 in period 2, and 23 in period 3. We would like to assemble these in lot sizes of 80 at a time. In calculating projected available inventory, we use our rule that demand is the greater of actual orders and forecast demand, so the projected available balance for period 1 is 10 (on hand balance) + 80 (MPS) − 42 (actual demand, which is greater than the forecast) = 48 units. Period 2 projected available balance is 48 + 80 (MPS) − 40 (the forecast) = 88 units. Note here that we had to schedule another 80 units in period 2 to keep our projected inventory level above the eight-unit safety stock level.

Available-to-promise is calculated using discrete logic in Figure 5.13. For the first period, the calculation is 10 (units on hand) + 80 (MPS) − 42 (week 1 orders) = 48 units. For period 2, 80 (MPS) − (37 + 23) = 20. For period 4, when our next MPS is due, available-to-promise is calculated 80 (MPS) − 0 (no order in the planning horizon) = 80 units. Figure 5.15 calculates available-to-promise using cumulative logic. For the cumulative logic, unsold units are carried forward and included with our next MPS.

FIGURE 5.14 **Two-Level Bill of Material Example—Discrete Calculations**

4-Horsepower Tillers

	On hand	Period 1	2	3	4	5
Production plan		100	100	100	100	100
Orders		100	72	54	0	0
Projected available balance	0	0	0	0	0	0
Available-to-promise		0	28	46	100	100
Master production schedule		100	100	100	100	100
Safety stock = 0						

Taylor Brand 4-Horsepower Tillers—40% of Demand

	On hand	1	2	3	4	5
Forecast for model		40	40	40	40	40
Orders		42	37	23	0	0
Projected available balance	10	48	88	48	88	48
Available-to-promise		48	20		80	
Master production schedule		80	80		80	
Safety stock = 10						

OEM Brand 4-Horsepower Tillers—10% of Demand

	On hand	1	2	3	4	5
Forecast for model		10	10	10	10	10
Orders		10	12	3		
Projected available balance	15	15	13	13	13	13
Available-to-promise		15	−2	7	10	10
Master production schedule		10	10	10	10	10
Safety stock = 15						

The logic for calculating available-to-promise is exactly the same as used previously; by doing this at these two levels, we are able to coordinate the sales of the various models with our actual assembly schedule. Overall, the two-level MPS approach helps us align the MPC process closely to market forces. Products are planned and controlled in the way they are sold as opposed to the way they are designed or manufactured.

FIGURE 5.15 Two-Level Bill of Material Example—Cumulative Calculations

4-Horsepower Tillers

	On hand	1	2	3	4	5
Production plan		100	100	100	100	100
Orders		100	72	54	0	0
Projected available balance	0	0	28	46	100	100
Available-to-promise		0	28	74	174	274
Master production schedule		100	100	100	100	100
Safety stock = 0						

Taylor Brand 4-Horsepower Tillers—40% of Demand

	On hand	1	2	3	4	5
Forecast for model		40	40	40	40	40
Orders		42	37	23	0	0
Projected available balance	10	48	88	48	88	48
Available-to-promise		48	68		148	
Master production schedule		80	80		80	
Safety stock = 10						

OEM Brand 4-Horsepower Tillers—10% of Demand

	On hand	1	2	3	4	5
Forecast for model		10	10	10	10	10
Orders		10	12	3		
Projected available balance	15	15	13	13	13	13
Available-to-promise		15	13	20	30	40
Master production schedule		10	10	10	10	10
Safety stock = 15						

Master Production Schedule Stability

A stable master production schedule translates into stable component schedules, which mean improved performance in plant operations. Too many changes in the MPS are costly in terms of reduced productivity. However, too few changes can lead to poor customer service levels and increased inventory. The objective is to strike a balance where stability is monitored and managed.

FIGURE 5.16
Freezing and Time Fencing

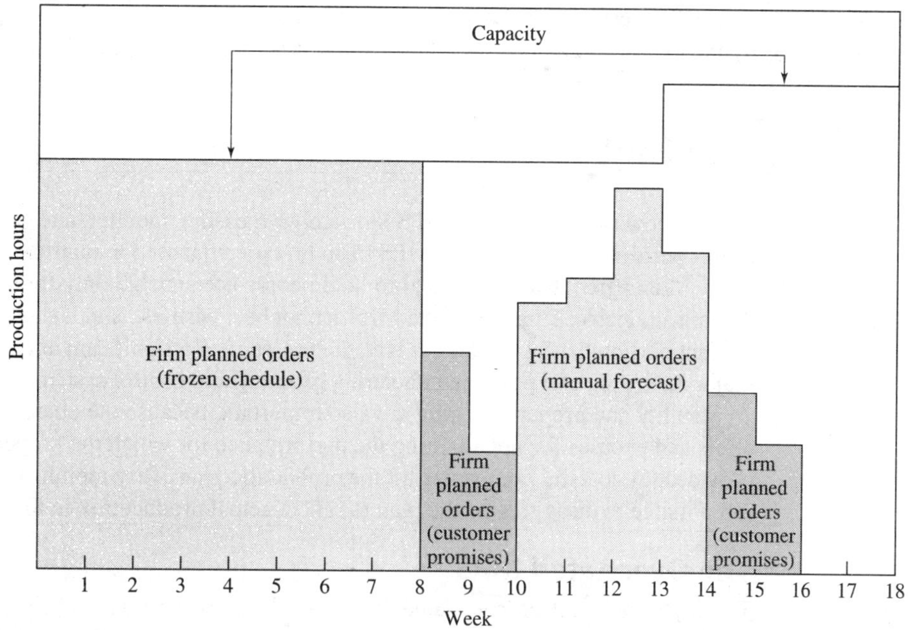

Freezing and Time Fencing

Figure 5.16 shows the first eight weeks in the MPS as **frozen.** This means *no* changes inside of eight weeks are possible. In reality, "no" may be a bit extreme. If the president dictates a change, it will probably happen, but such occurrences should be rare.

Many firms do not like to use the term *frozen,* saying that anything is negotiable—but negotiations get tougher as we approach the present time. However, a frozen period provides a stable target for manufacturing to hit. It also removes most alibis for missing the schedule!

Time fencing is an extension of the freeze concept. Many firms set time fences that specify periods in which various types of change can be handled. A common practice, for example, is to have three time fences, say 8, 16, and 24 weeks. The marketing/logistics people could make any changes that they wanted beyond the 24-week fence as long as the sum of all MPS records is synchronized with the production plan. From weeks 16 to 24, substitutions of one end item for another would be permitted, provided required parts would be available and the production plan was not violated. From weeks 8 to 16, the MPS is quite rigid; but minor changes within the model series can be made if component parts are available. The period before 8 weeks is basically a freeze period, but occasional changes are made even within this period. To achieve the productivity necessary to remain competitive, stability in short-range manufacturing plans is essential.

Two common fences are the **demand fence** and the **planning fence.** The demand fence is the shorter of the two. Inside the demand fence, the forecast is ignored in calculating the projected available balance. The theory is that customer orders—not the forecast—matter in the near term. The planning fence indicates the time at which the master production scheduler should be planning more MPS quantities. Within the demand fence it is very difficult to change the MPS. Between the demand fence and the planning fence, management trade-offs must be made to make changes; outside the planning fence, changes can be made by the master production scheduler. Some firms refer to these as the ice, slush, and water zones.

Managing the MPS

We turn now to managing the MPS: how do we measure, monitor, and control detailed day-to-day performance against the MPS? The first prerequisite for control is to have a realistic MPS. Most agree that it is critical to hold people accountable only for performance levels that are attainable. This means the MPS cannot be a wish list, and it shouldn't have any significant portion that's past due. In fact, the presence of a significant amount of past due is a major indication of a poor manufacturing planning and control system.

Stability and proper buffering are also important, because the objective is to remove all alibis and excuses for not attaining the performance for which the proper budget has been provided. Successful companies hit the production plan every month, and they do the best job possible to disaggregate the plan to reflect actual product mix in the MPS.

The Overstated MPS

The MPS must not be overstated. To do so destroys the relative priorities developed by MRP and shop-floor control; more important, the overstated MPS erodes belief in the formal system, thereby reinstituting the informal system of hot lists and black books. A key to not overstating the MPS is to always force the sum of the MPS to equal the production plan.

There should be an overall output budget for manufacturing. Capacity should be in place and should match (not be more or less than) the budget. Manufacturing and marketing should work diligently to respond to product mix changes, but within the overall budgetary constraint.

Concluding Principles

The master production schedule plays a key role in manufacturing planning and control systems. In this chapter, we've addressed what the MPS is, how it's done, and who does it. The following general principles emerge from this discussion:

- The MPS unit should reflect the company's approach to the business environment in which it operates.
- The MPS function should use the common ERP database if such a system is implemented in the firm.
- Common systems, time-phased processing, and MPS techniques facilitate effective scheduling regardless of the firm's environment.
- Customer order promising should be closely linked to the MPS.
- Available-to-promise information should be derived from the MPS and provided to the sales department.
- A final assembly schedule should be used to convert the anticipated build schedule into the final build schedule.
- The master production scheduler must keep the sum of the parts (the MPS) equal to the whole (the operations plan).

Discussion Questions

1. Why does the text stress that the master production schedule is *not* a forecast?
2. Some companies try to increase output simply by increasing the MPS. Discuss this approach.
3. What do you feel would be the key functions of the MPS in each of the following three environments: make-to-stock, make-to-order, and assemble-to-order?
4. Much of the order-promising logic is directed at telling customers when they can honestly expect delivery. Several firms, on the other hand, simply promise their customers delivery within *X* weeks (often an unrealistic claim) and then deliver when they can. Contrast these two approaches.
5. One characterization of the available-to-promise record is that the "Projected available balance" row is for the master scheduler and the "Available-to-promise" row is for customers. What's meant by this contention?
6. Explain how determining the "Projected available balance" row with the "greater of forecast or orders" logic can overstate required production.
7. Many companies have come to view their master production schedulers as key people in profitably meeting the firm's strategic goals. Would you agree? What qualities would you look for in a master production scheduler?
8. Discuss the relationship between stability and firm planned orders.

Problems

1. Excelsior Springs Ltd. schedules production of one end product, Hi-Sulphur, in batches of 80 units whenever the projected ending inventory balance in a quarter falls below 10 units. It takes one quarter to make a batch of 80 units. Excelsior currently has 30 units on hand. The sales forecast for the next four quarters is:

	Quarter			
	1	2	3	4
Forecast	20	70	70	20

   a. Prepare a time-phased MPS record showing the sales forecast and MPS for Hi-Sulphur.
   b. What are the inventory balances at the end of each quarter?
   c. During the first quarter, no units were sold. The revised forecast for the rest of the year is:

	Quarter		
	2	3	4
Forecast	30	50	70

   How does the MPS change?

2. Neptune Manufacturing Company's production manager wants a master production schedule covering next year's business. The company produces a complete line of small fishing boats for both saltwater and freshwater use and manufactures most of the component parts used in assembling the products. The firm uses MRP to coordinate production schedules of the component part manufacturing and assembly operations. The production manager has just received the following sales forecast for next year from the marketing division:

	Sales Forecast (Standard Boats for Each Series)			
Product Lines	**1st Quarter**	**2nd Quarter**	**3rd Quarter**	**4th Quarter**
FunRay series	8,000	9,000	6,000	6,000
SunRay series	4,000	5,000	2,000	2,000
StingRay series	9,000	10,000	6,000	7,000
Total	21,000	24,000	14,000	15,000

The sales forecast is stated in terms of "standard boats," reflecting total sales volume for each of the firm's three major product lines.

Another item of information supplied by the marketing department is the target ending inventory position for each product line. The marketing department would like the production manager to plan on having the following number of standard boats on hand at the end of each quarter of next year:

Product Line	Quarterly Target Ending Inventory (in Standard Boats)
FunRay series	3,000 boats
SunRay series	1,000 boats
StingRay series	3,000 boats

The inventory position for each product is:

Product Line	Current Inventory Level (in Standard Boats)
FunRay series	15,000 boats
SunRay series	3,000 boats
StingRay series	5,000 boats

The master production schedule is to specify the number of boats (in standard units) to be produced for each product line in each quarter of next year on the firm's single assembly line. The assembly line can produce up to 15,000 standard boats per quarter (250 boats per day during the 60 days in a quarter).

Two additional factors are taken into account by the production manager in preparing the master production schedule: the assembly line changeover cost and the inventory carrying cost for the finished goods inventory. Each assembly line changeover costs $5,000, reflecting material handling costs of changing the stocking of component parts on the line, adjusting the layout, and so on. After some discussion with the company comptroller, the production manager concluded that the firm's inventory carrying cost is 10 percent of standard boat cost per year. The item value for each of the product line standard units is:

Product Line	Standard Boat Cost
FunRay series	$100
SunRay series	150
StingRay series	200

The master production scheduler has calculated the production lot sizes as 5,000, 3,000, and 4,000 units, respectively.

a. Develop a master production schedule for next year, by quarter, for each of Neptune's fishing boat lines. Identify any problems.

b. Verify the lot size calculations using the EOQ formula.

3. The MPS planner at Murphy Motors uses MPS time-phased records for planning end-item production. The planner is currently working on a schedule for the P24, one of Murphy's top-selling motors. The planner uses a production lot size of 70 and a safety stock of 5 for the P24 motor.

Item: P24	On hand	Week 1	2	3	4	5	6	7	8
Forecast		30	30	30	40	40	40	45	45
Orders		13	8	4					
Projected available balance	20								
Available-to-promise									
MPS									

a. Complete the MPS time-phased record for product P24.

b. Can Murphy accept the following orders? Update the MPS time-phased record for accepted orders.

Order	Amount	Desired Week
1	40	4
2	30	6
3	30	2
4	25	3

4. The Spencer Optics Company produces an inexpensive line of sunglasses. The manufacturing process consists of assembling two plastic lenses (produced by the firm's plastic molding department) into a finished frame (purchased from an outside supplier). The company is interested in using material requirements planning to schedule its operations and has asked you to prepare an example to illustrate the technique.

The firm's sales manager has prepared a 10-week sales forecast for one of the more popular sunglasses (the Classic model) for your example. The forecast is 100 units per week. Spencer has customer orders of 110 units, 80 units, 50 units, and 20 units in weeks 1, 2, 3, and 4, respectively. The sunglasses are assembled in batches of 300 units. Presently, three such batches are scheduled: one in week 2, one in week 5, and one in week 8.

Complete the following time-phased record:

Classic Model MPS Record	On hand	Week 1	2	3	4	5	6	7	8	9	10
Forecast											
Orders											
Projected available balance	140										
Available-to-promise											
MPS											

5. Nino Spirelli has constructed the following (partial) time-phased MPS record:

	On hand	Week 1	2	3	4	5	6
Forecast		20	30	20	30	20	30
Orders		14	8	6			
Projected available balance	5						
Available-to-promise							
MPS		50		50		50	50

a. Complete the record.
b. Are there any problems?
c. What's the earliest Nino can promise an order for 44 units?
d. Assume that an order for 15 is booked for week 4. Assume the order for 44 units in part c is not booked; recompute the record.

6. Georgia Clay and Gravel was updating the MPS record for one of its products, Smell Fresh Cat Litter.

a. Complete the following MPS time-phased record.

Item: Smell Fresh	On hand	Week 1	2	3	4	5	6	7	8
Forecast		20	20	20	30	30	30	30	30
Orders		5	3	2					
Projected available balance	20	50	30	10	30	50	20	40	10
Available-to-promise									
MPS		50			50	50		50	

MPS Lot Size = 50.

The following events occurred during week 1:

- Actual demand during week 1 was 25 units.
- Marketing forecasted that 40 units would be needed for week 9.
- An order for 10 in week 2 was accepted.
- An order for 20 in week 4 was accepted.
- An order for 6 in week 3 was accepted.
- The MPS in week 1 was produced as planned.

b. Update the record below after rolling through time.

Item: Smell Fresh	On hand	Week 2	3	4	5	6	7	8	9
Forecast									
Orders									
Projected available balance	45								
Available-to-promise									
MPS									

MPS Lot Size = 50.

7. Falcon Sports Inc. makes a line of Jet Skis. There are eight different end items (catalog numbers) in the Jet Ski product line. The skis vary according to horsepower, seating capacity, and starting mechanism. The company expects to sell one-half of the Jet Skis in the 12-horsepower model and one-half in the 10-horsepower model. The seating capacity breaks down to 60 percent for dual seating and 40 percent for single seating. The breakdown for starters is 25 percent manual and 75 percent automatic.

Catalog number	2100	2101	1100	1101	2120	2121	1120	1121
Horsepower	10	10	10	10	12	12	12	12
Seating style	Dual	Dual	Single	Single	Dual	Dual	Single	Single
Starter	Manual	Auto	Manual	Auto	Manual	Auto	Manual	Auto
Component parts	602 350 400 235 320 600 250 410	602 350 400 230 320 600 254 410	602 360 400 235 315 600 250 410	602 360 400 230 315 600 254 410	601 350 400 235 320 600 250 610	601 350 400 230 320 600 254 610	601 360 400 235 315 600 250 610	601 360 400 230 315 600 254 610

a. Group the component parts. Which are common? Which are associated with horsepower? Seating style? Starter?

b. Create a super bill for Jet Skis matching the appropriate components with each option (include the usage percentages).

c. What are the advantages and disadvantages of the super bill approach to planning?

8. The Ace Electronics Company produces printed circuit boards on a make-to-order basis.

a. Prepare an MPS record for one of its items (catalogue #2400), including the available-to-promise information, using the following data:

Final assembly production lead time = 2 weeks.
Weekly forecast = 100 units.
Current on-hand quantity = 0.

Booked customer orders (already confirmed):
- 95 units in week 1.
- 105 units in week 2.
- 70 units in week 3.
- 10 units in week 5.

Master production schedule:
- 200 units to be completed at the start of week 1.
- 200 units to be completed at the start of week 3.
- 200 units to be completed at the start of week 5.
- 200 units to be completed at the start of week 7.

b. Suppose the cumulative lead time for the item (catalogue #2400) is eight weeks. What decision must the master scheduler make this week?

9. Brandy Boards produces circuit boards on a make-to-order basis. The company is currently planning production for one of its boards, the Sound Xapper. It has a weekly forecast of 50 boards, current inventory of 70 boards, and uses an MPS quantity of 150. MPS and order information for the next seven weeks are given below:

Current Booked Orders		Master Production Schedule	
Week	**Quantity**	**Week**	**Quantity**
1	60	2	150
2	70	5	150
3	20		
4	70		
5	40		
6	30		

a. Prepare an MPS record for the Sound Xapper for the next seven weeks, including available-to-promise information.

b. Suppose the planning time fence is six weeks; what decision should the master scheduler make this week?

c. Sales received the following customer requests at the start of week 1. Using the information in the MPS record completed in part a, indicate to Sales which delivery commitments can be made to the customers.

Possible New Orders	
Week	**Quantity**
1	5
3	10
6	20

10. The Parker Corporation produces and sells a machine for tending golf course greens. The patented device trims the grass, aerates the turf, and injects a metered amount of nitrogen into the soil. Machines are marketed through the Taylor Golf Course Supply Company, under the Parker Company's own original equipment brand, and, recently, through a lawn and garden supply house (Brown Thumb), which serves both commercial and consumer accounts. Addition of the lawn

EXHIBIT A
Last Year's Sales by Catalog Number

Catalog Number			Sales	Key
Body	Horsepower*	Drive	Total = 100	
T	4	C	1	
T	4	G	4	Body:
T	5	C	18	T = Taylor Supply O = OEM Parker's own
T	5	G	17	
O	4	C	13	B = Brown Thumb
O	4	G	9	
O	5	C	10	
O	5	G	8	
B	4	C	6	Drive
B	4	G	7	C = Chain G = Gear
B	5	C	2	
B	5	G	5	

*Note: The 3-HP machine would be offered in all three body styles and both drives.

and garden outlet and requests to add a 3-HP version have called into question the production planning and control process for the machines.

Forecasting the products to be produced is difficult. There are now two drive mechanisms (chain and gear), three different body styles (one for each outlet), and two sizes of engine (4- and 5-HP). This gives a total of 12 end items, all of which had some demand. (See Exhibit A.) The 3-HP motor would add six more end items. Forecasting demand for these new items would add to the difficulty of forecasting demand.

Lead times for some of the castings and for 5-HP motors have increased to the extent that it's not possible to wait until firm orders are received for the end items before the castings and motors have to be ordered. In addition, the firm's business is growing; it anticipates selling about 120 units next year. Consequently, the production manager has arranged to purchase enough material for 10 units per month. There's plenty of capacity for the small amount of parts fabrication required, but assembly capacity must be carefully planned. The current plan calls for assembly capacity of 10 units per month.

With regard to the specific issue of forecasting, the marketing manager summarized the data on the sales of each end item over the past year. (See Exhibit A.) He felt that a 20 percent growth in total volume was about right and that 3-HP machines will perhaps account for half that growth. Of course, once the forecasts were made, the production manager had to determine which motors and castings (gear or chain) to order. Each machine was made up of many common parts, but the motors, chain or gear drive subassemblies, and bodies were different (though interchangeable).

a. Suggest an improved method of forecasting demand for the firm's products.

b. As the production manager contemplated the difficulty of forecasting demand for the firm's products and determining exactly what to schedule into final assembly, two customers called. The first, from Taylor, wanted to know when the company could deliver a model T3G; the second wanted as early delivery as possible of one of Parker's own machines, an O4C. The Taylor representative said he felt that the three-horsepower models might "really take off."

EXHIBIT B
Inventories and On-Order

Item	Inventory	On Order in:	Due Date	Lot size
Common "kit"	0	5 each in:	weeks 1,3,5,7,9	5
5-HP motor	10	5 in:	week 5	5
4-HP motor	3	5 in:	weeks 3, 8	5
3-HP motor	0	5 in:	week 1	5
Chain drive	14	—	—	10
Gear drive	6	10 in:	week 3	10

	Delivery Week					
	1	2	3	4	5	6
Models	2T4G*	1B3G	1T5C	1O5G	1T5G	1O4G
	1O5C	1T4C	1B4C			
		1O4G				
Total	3	3	2	1	1	1

*2 units of T4G.

Before making any commitment at all, it was necessary to check the material availability and get back to the two customers. It was the firm's practice not to promise immediate delivery, since units scheduled for final assembly were usually already promised. The planned assembly schedule called for assembly of three units next week, two units the following week, and alternating three and two thereafter. As a matter of practice, all parts for assembly and delivery in any week would need to be ready at the start of that week.

Exhibit B shows current inventory and on-order positions for the common part "kit," the motors, and the drives. (The production manager didn't concern himself with the body styles since all three styles can be obtained in a week.) Booked orders promised for delivery over the next few weeks are also listed. Organize this information to respond to the delivery promise requests. (Assume that no safety stocks are held.) What should the delivery promises be?

Case — Customer Order Promising at Kirk Motors Ltd.

Kirk Motors Ltd. is a licensed motor vehicle dealer for Mitsubishi cars and trucks. Headquartered just outside of Wellington, New Zealand, Kirk has outlets in several cities in New Zealand. The company is a full-service distributor offering a complete range of Mitsubishi cars and trucks, with full maintenance and used-vehicle facilities. The company sells products that are assembled in New Zealand, Australia, and Japan. The wide variety of production/option combinations means that keeping a complete inventory is impossible. Moreover, because of the multiple geographical sources of product, customer order promising is complicated. To facilitate customer order promising and provide customers with information on the specific models they are interested in, the company uses an availability record. This record provides inventory and final assembly schedule information. Consequently, the firm can provide very reliable product and delivery information to its customers.

The information to produce a response to a customer request is stored centrally, and individual requests for a specific model and options are run when a customer wants the information. Figure 5.17 is an example of part of the record for the Wellington, New Zealand, location. The header information gives the name of the dealer (Kirk, Wellington), and the salesperson specifies the vehicle model number (KS6P41, containing information on engine, doors, etc.), special packages, other options, and any paint (PT) specifications. Specifying the options does limit the search but doesn't provide any

FIGURE 5.17 **Kirk Motors Available to Promise from Stock**

Vehicle Search

Dealer	**Kirkwe**
Model	KS6P41
Package	
Options	
PT	

Dealer	**Order**	**PT**	**TM**	**BS**	**RS**	**AM**	**Locn**	**Due**
KIRKWE	631194	DF	A5	BABS	RSTD	AIM	KIRKWE	STOCK
		JX	A5	BABS	RSTD	AIM	TODDPK	STOCK
		JX	A5	BABS	RSTD	AIM	TODDPK	STOCK
		WP	A5	BABS	RSTD	AIM	TODDPK	STOCK
		WP	A5	BABS	RSTD	AIM	TODDPK	STOCK
		AE	A5	BABS	RSTD	AIM	TODDPK	STOCK
KIRKLH	631426	AE	A5	BABS	RSTD	AIM	KIRKLH	STOCK
MCVEMA	631294	DF	A5	BABS	RSTD	AIM	MCVEMA	STOCK
TOUR	626477	LR	A5	BABS	RSTD		TOUR	STOCK

information for the customer to use for trading off, say, color for availability. For each vehicle listed, the paint (PT), trim (TM), brakes (BS), air bags (RS), alarm system (AM), location (Locn), and availability (Due) codes are provided. The vehicles in stock are listed first, starting with those at the Wellington dealership (KIRKWE), continuing with those in stock at the New Zealand assembly plant (Todd Park, located near Wellington), and then those at other dealers at ever-increasing distances from Wellington. If the customer finds the desired vehicle in stock, then arrangements are made for delivery at the Wellington location.

The salesperson can use the system to look at the automobile assembly schedule to determine availability if the vehicle is not in stock (or is too far away for delivery). An example is shown in Figure 5.18 on the next page, again for the Wellington dealership. The information is the same except that now the assembly dates are provided in the Due column. Vehicles that are not already promised to a dealer are available to promise to customers. In addition, for vehicles to be assembled in the future there is some flexibility for the customer to change the options that are specified for the schedule. The sales people are satisfied with their ability to provide reliable information to their customers and to close sales that might not have been possible before. The system has been such an effective device that the company is now using it in its advertising, inviting customers to come in and configure their own vehicle.

Assignment

1. A customer has called with an interest in purchasing an automobile with the following options: PT = WP, TM = A5, BS = BABS, RS = RSTD, HM = AIM. How should Kirk Motors respond to this inquiry?

Hill-Rom's Use of Planning Bills of Materials

The use of planning bill of materials concepts can be very helpful in the sales and operations planning process. An example is the application developed at Hill-Rom, a manufacturer of hospital beds, related equipment, and accessories for hospitals and nursing homes.

FIGURE 5.18 Kirk Motors Available to Promise from Assembly

Vehicle Search

Dealer	**Kirkwe**
Model	KS6P41
Package	
Options	
PT	

Dealer	Order	PT	TM	BS	RS	AM	Locn	Due
DONNDN	630606	LQ	A5	BSTD	RSTD	AIM	TODDPK	01MAR
KIRKNM	630675	DF	A5	BSTD	RSTD	AIM	TODDPK	01MAR
DALLHA	630678	DA	A5	BSTD	RSTD	AIM	TODDPK	01MAR
KIRKMA	630761	WP	A5	BSTD	RSTD	AIM	TODDPK	01MAR
		DA	A5	BABS	RSTD	AIM	TODDPK	01MAR
		DF	A5	BABS	RBDR	AIM	TODDPK	01MAR
KIRKLH	631426	DA	A5	BSTD	RSTD	AIM	TODDPK	28MAR
DALLHA	631461	LQ	A5	BSTD	RSTD	AIM	TODDPK	28MAR
WRPH	631463	LQ	A5	BABS	RSTD	AIM	TODDPK	28MAR
		DF	A5	BSTD	RSTD	AIM	TODDPK	28MAR
		DF	A5	BSTD	RSTD	AIM	TODDPK	28MAR
		WP	A5	BSTD	RSTD	AIM	TODDPK	29MAR
		WP	A5	BSTD	RSTD	AIM	TODDPK	29MAR
		DF	A5	BABS	RSTD	AIM	TODDPK	29MAR

FIGURE 5.19 Hill-Rom's "Super-Duper" Bill

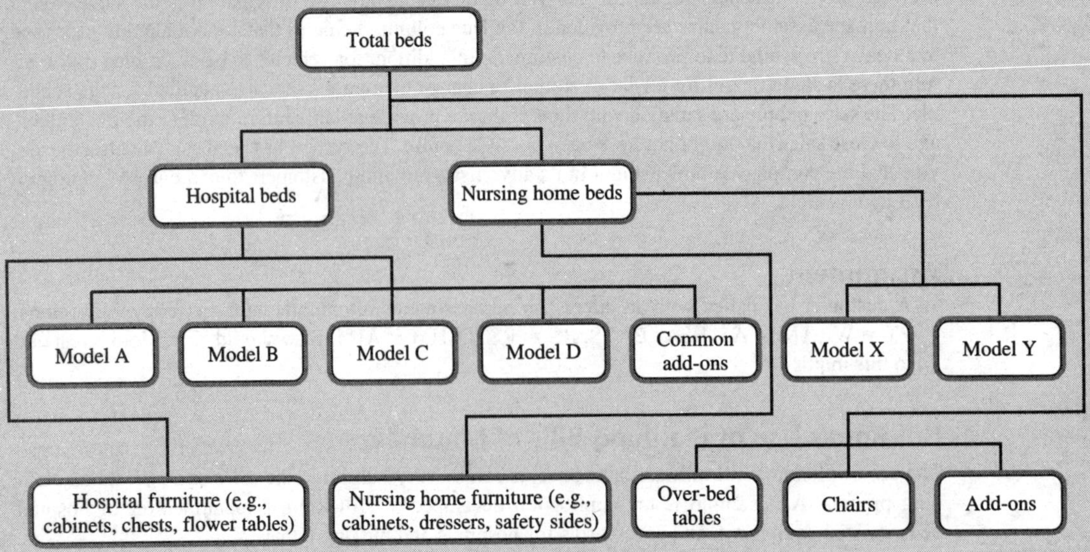

Hill-Rom has expanded the planning bill concept to what it calls the "super-duper" bill. Figure 5.19 shows an abbreviated example. In this approach, only one item is forecast: total bed sales. All other forecasts are treated as bill of materials relationships. For example, the forecast for over-bed tables is a percentage of overall bed sales.

One marketing person at Hill-Rom found the super-duper bill concept ideal for implementing an idea he'd been thinking about for some time. He believed the company makes trigger products and trailer products. Beds are trigger products, whereas over-bed tables, chairs, and add-ons (such as trapezes or intravenous fluid rods) are trailer products. Purchase of trailer products is dependent on purchase of trigger products in somewhat the same relationship as component sales depend on end-item sales. This relationship means that rather than forecast demand for over-bed tables, Hill-Rom tracks and maintains the percentage relationship between sales of beds and over-bed tables.

This bill of materials relationship will probably be a better estimate than a direct forecast of over-bed tables. If we expect bed sales to go up or down, by treating over-bed tables as a trailer product with a bill of materials linkage, we have an automatic adjustment in over-bed table forecasts, as in all trailer products.

Using bill of materials approaches to forecasting also forces a logical consistency. At one time the forecast for 84-inch mattresses at Hill-Rom exceeded combined forecasts for beds using 84-inch mattresses. Treating these relationships with bill of materials approaches reduces these inconsistencies, which always result from independent estimating.

The sales and operations planning unit for these products at Hill-Rom is total beds. Furthermore, the percentage split into hospital beds and nursing home beds is not only estimated, it's managed. Sales personnel are held to specified tolerance limits on this split because the capacity and net profit implications of the percentage split are important.

Below each of these two super-duper bills are "super" bills for the various model series. Finally, there's another trigger-trailer relationship between total hospital bed sales and sales of hospital furniture such as cabinets and flower tables. The same kind of bill of materials relationship is used to forecast nursing home furniture sales. These various bill of materials relationships pass the planning information down through the MPC system in a logically consistent way.

Finally, this entire approach is consistent with the way the firm does its strategic planning, which is in terms of strategic business units (SBUs). SBUs are established as super bills. The result is a very close integration of MPC and strategic planning.

Assignment

1. Suppose the production plan for total beds is 1,000 units per week and the percentage split for the over-bed table is 10%. How many over-bed tables will be planned for production each week?

Chapter 6

Material Requirements Planning

This chapter deals with material requirements planning (MRP), a basic tool for performing the detailed material planning function in the manufacture of component parts and their assembly into finished items. MRP is used by many companies that have invested in batch production processes. MRP's managerial objective is to provide "the right part at the right time" to meet the schedules for completed products. To do this, MRP provides *formal* plans for each part number, whether raw material, component, or finished good. Accomplishing these plans without excess inventory, overtime, labor, or other resources is also important.

Chapter 6 is organized around the following five topics:

- *Material requirements planning in manufacturing planning and control:* Where does MRP fit in the overall MPC system framework, and how is it related to other MPC modules?
- *Record processing:* What is the basic MRP record, and how is it produced?
- *Technical issues:* What additional technical details and supporting systems should you recognize?
- *Using the MRP system:* Who uses the system, how is it used, and how is the exact match between MRP records and physical reality maintained?
- *System dynamics:* How does MRP reflect changing conditions, and why must transactions be processed properly?

Material Requirements Planning in Manufacturing Planning and Control

For companies assembling end items from components produced in batch manufacturing processes, MRP is central to the development of detailed plans for part needs. It is often where companies start in developing their MPC systems. Facility with time-phased planning and the associated time-phased records is basic to understanding many other aspects of the MPC system. Finally, although the introduction of JIT and investments in lean manufacturing processes have brought about fundamental changes in detailed material planning for some firms, companies continue to adapt the MRP approach or enhance their existing systems.

For firms using MRP, the general MPC framework depicted in Figure 6.1 shows that detailed requirements planning is characterized by the use of time-phased (period-by-period) requirement records. Several other supporting activities are shown in the front end, engine, and back end of the system as well. The front end of the MPC system produces the master production schedule (MPS). The back end, or execution system, deals with production scheduling and control of the factory and with managing materials coming from vendor plants.

The detailed material planning function represents a central system in the engine portion of Figure 6.1. For firms preparing detailed material plans using MRP, this means taking a time-phased set of master production schedule requirements and producing a resultant time-phased set of component parts and raw material requirements.

In addition to master production schedule inputs, MRP requires two other basic inputs. A bill of material shows, for each part number, what other part numbers are

FIGURE 6.1
Manufacturing Planning and Control System

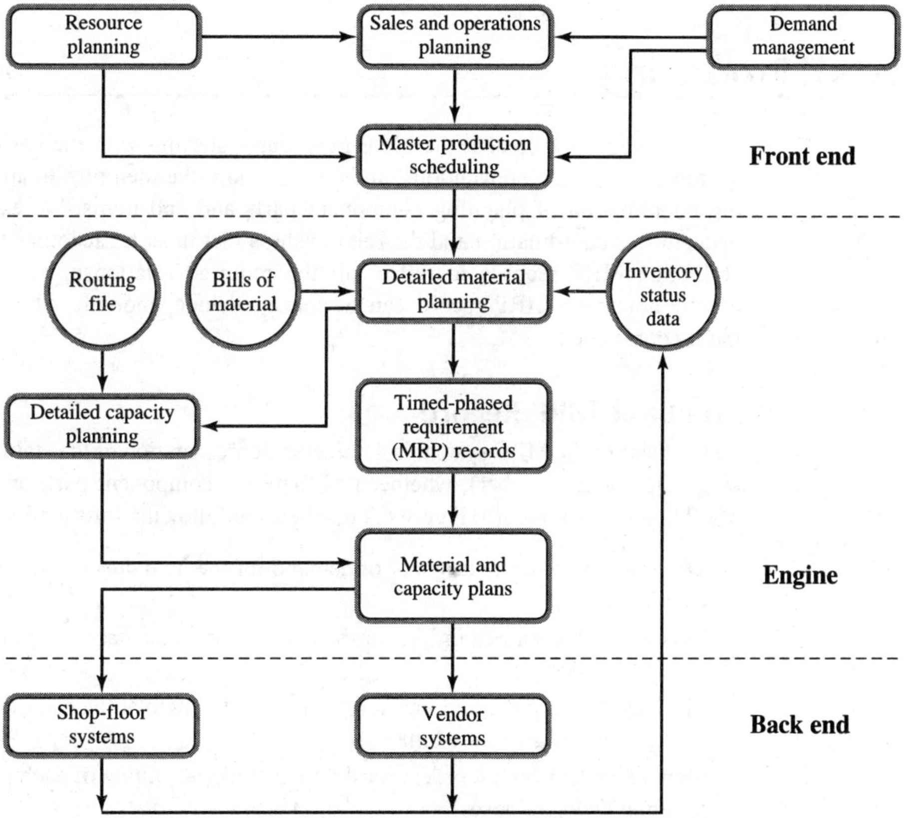

required as direct components. For example, for a car, it could show five wheels required (four plus the spare). For each wheel, the bill of materials could be a hub, tire, valve stem, and so on. The second basic input to MRP is inventory status. To know how many wheels to make for a given number of cars, we must know how many are on hand, how many of those are already allocated to existing needs, and how many have already been ordered.

The MRP data make it possible to construct a time-phased requirement record for any part number. The data can also be used as input to the detailed capacity planning models. Developing material and capacity plans is an iterative process where the planning is carried out level by level. For example, planning for a car would determine requirements for wheels, which in turn determines requirements for tires, and so on. But planning for tires has to be done *after* the planning for wheels; if the company wants to build 10 cars (50 wheels) and has 15 complete wheels on hand, it only needs 35 more—and 35 tires. If 20 wheels have already been ordered, only 15 more must be made to complete the 10 cars.

An MRP system serves a central role in material planning and control. It translates the overall plans for production into the detailed individual steps necessary to accomplish those plans. It provides information for developing capacity plans, and it links to the systems that actually get the production accomplished.

Record Processing

In this section, we present the MRP procedures starting with the basic MRP record, its terminology, timing conventions, and construction. We then turn to an example illustrating coordination of planning component parts and end items. We examine several aspects of this coordination and the relationships that must be accounted for. We then look at linking MRP records to reflect all the required relationships. We intend to show clearly how each MRP record can be managed independently while the *system* keeps them coordinated.

The Basic MRP Record

At the heart of the MPC system is a universal representation of the status and plans for any single item (part number), whether raw material, component part, or finished good: the MRP time-phased record. Figure 6.2 displays the following information:

The anticipated future usage of or demand for the item *during* each period (i.e., **gross requirements**).

Existing replenishment orders for the item due in at the *beginning* of each period (i.e., **scheduled receipts**).

The current and projected inventory status for the item at the *end* of each period (i.e., **projected available balance**).

Planned replenishment orders for the item at the *beginning* of each period (i.e., **planned order releases**).

FIGURE 6.2
The Basic MRP Record

		Period				
		1	**2**	**3**	**4**	**5**
Gross requirements			10		40	10
Scheduled receipts		50				
Projected available balance	4	54	44	44	4	44
Planned order releases					50	
Lead time = one period Lot size = 50						

The top row in Figure 6.2 indicates periods that can vary in length from a day to a quarter or even longer. The period is also called a **time bucket.** A widely used time bucket or period is one week. A timing convention is that the current time is the beginning of the first period. The initial available balance of four units is shown prior to period 1. The number of periods in the record is called the **planning horizon.** In this simplified example, the planning horizon is five periods. The planning horizon indicates the number of future periods for which plans are made.

The second row, "Gross requirements," is the anticipated future usage of (or demand for) the item. The gross requirements are **time phased,** which means they're stated on a unique period-by-period basis, rather than aggregated or averaged; that is, gross requirements are stated as 10 in period 2, 40 in period 4, and 10 in period 5, rather than as a total requirement of 60 or as an average requirement of 12 per period. This method of presentation allows for special orders, seasonality, and periods of no anticipated usage to be explicitly taken into account. A gross requirement in a particular period will be unsatisfied unless the item is **available** during that period. Availability is achieved by having the item in inventory or by receiving either a scheduled receipt or a planned replenishment order in time to satisfy the gross requirement.

Another timing convention comes from the question of availability. The item must be available at the *beginning* of the time bucket in which it's required. This means plans must be so made that any replenishment order will be in inventory at the beginning of the period in which the gross requirement for that order occurs.

The "Scheduled receipts" row describes the status of all open orders (work in process or existing replenishment orders) for the item. This row shows the quantities ordered and when we expect these orders to be completed. Scheduled receipts result from previously made ordering decisions and represent a source of the item to meet gross requirements. For example, the gross requirements of 10 in period 2 cannot be satisfied by the 4 units presently available. The scheduled receipts of 50, due in period 1, will satisfy the gross requirement in period 2 if things go according to plan. Scheduled receipts represent a commitment. For an order in the factory, necessary materials have been committed to the order, and capacity at work centers will be required to complete it. For a purchased item, similar commitments have been made to a vendor. The timing convention used for showing scheduled receipts is also at the *beginning* of the period; that is, the order is shown in the period during which the item will be available to satisfy a gross requirement.

The next row in Figure 6.2 is "Projected available balance." The timing convention in this row is the *end* of the period; that is, the row is the projected balance *after* replenishment orders have been received and gross requirements have been satisfied. For this reason, the "Projected available balance" row has an extra time bucket shown at the beginning. The bucket shows the balance *at the present time;* that is, in Figure 6.2, the beginning available balance is 4 units. The quantity shown in period 1 is the projected balance at the *end* of period 1. The projected available balance shown at the end of a period is available to meet gross requirements in the next (and succeeding) periods. For example, the 54 units shown as the projected available balance at the end of period 1 result from adding the 50 units scheduled to be received to the beginning balance of 4 units. The gross requirement of 10 units in period 2 reduces the projected balance to 44 units at the end of period 2. The term projected *available* balance is used, instead of projected *on-hand* balance, for a very specific reason. Units of the item might be on hand physically but not available to meet gross requirements because they are already promised or allocated for some other purpose.

The "Planned order releases" row is determined directly from the "Projected available balance" row. Whenever the projected available balance shows a quantity insufficient to satisfy gross requirements (a negative quantity), additional material must be planned for. This is done by creating a planned order release in time to keep the projected available balance from becoming negative. For example, in Figure 6.2, the projected available balance at the end of period 4 is 4 units. This is not sufficient to meet the gross requirement of 10 units in period 5. Because the lead time is one week, the MRP system creates a planned order at the beginning of week 4 providing a **lead time offset** of one week. As we have used a lot size of 50 units, the projected available balance at the end of week 5 is 44 units. Another way that this logic is explained is to note that the balance for the end of period 4 (4 units) is the beginning inventory for period 5, during which there's a gross requirement of 10 units. The difference between the available inventory of 4 and the gross requirement of 10 is a **net requirement** of 6 units in period 5. Thus, an order for at least 6 units must be planned for period 4 to avoid a shortage in period 5.

The MRP system produces the planned order release data in response to the gross requirement, scheduled receipt, and projected available data. When a planned order is created for the most immediate or current period, it is in the **action bucket.** A quantity in the action bucket means some action is needed now to avoid a future problem. The action is to release the order, which converts it to a scheduled receipt.

The planned order releases are *not* shown in the scheduled receipt row because they haven't yet been released for production or purchasing. No material has been committed to their manufacture. The planned order is analogous to an entry on a Christmas list, since the list comprises plans. A scheduled receipt is like an order mailed to a catalog firm for a particular Christmas gift, since a commitment has been made. Like Christmas lists versus mailed orders, planned orders are much easier to change than scheduled receipts. Not converting planned orders into scheduled receipts any earlier than necessary has many advantages.

The basic MRP record just described provides the correct information on each part in the system. Linking these single part records together is essential in managing all the parts needed for a complex product or customer order. Key elements for linking the records are the bill of materials, the explosion process (using inventory and scheduled receipt information), and lead time offsetting. We consider each of these before turning to how the records are linked into a system.

An Example Bill of Materials

Figure 6.3 shows a snow shovel, and item part number 1605. The complete snow shovel is assembled (using four rivets and two nails) from the top handle assembly, scoop assembly, scoop-shaft connector, and shaft. The top handle assembly, in turn, is created by combining the welded top handle bracket assembly with the wooden handle using two nails. The welded top handle bracket assembly is created by welding the top handle coupling to the top handle bracket. In a similar way, the scoop assembly combines the aluminum scoop with the steel blade using six rivets.

FIGURE 6.3
The 1605 Snow Shovel Shown with Component Parts and Assemblies

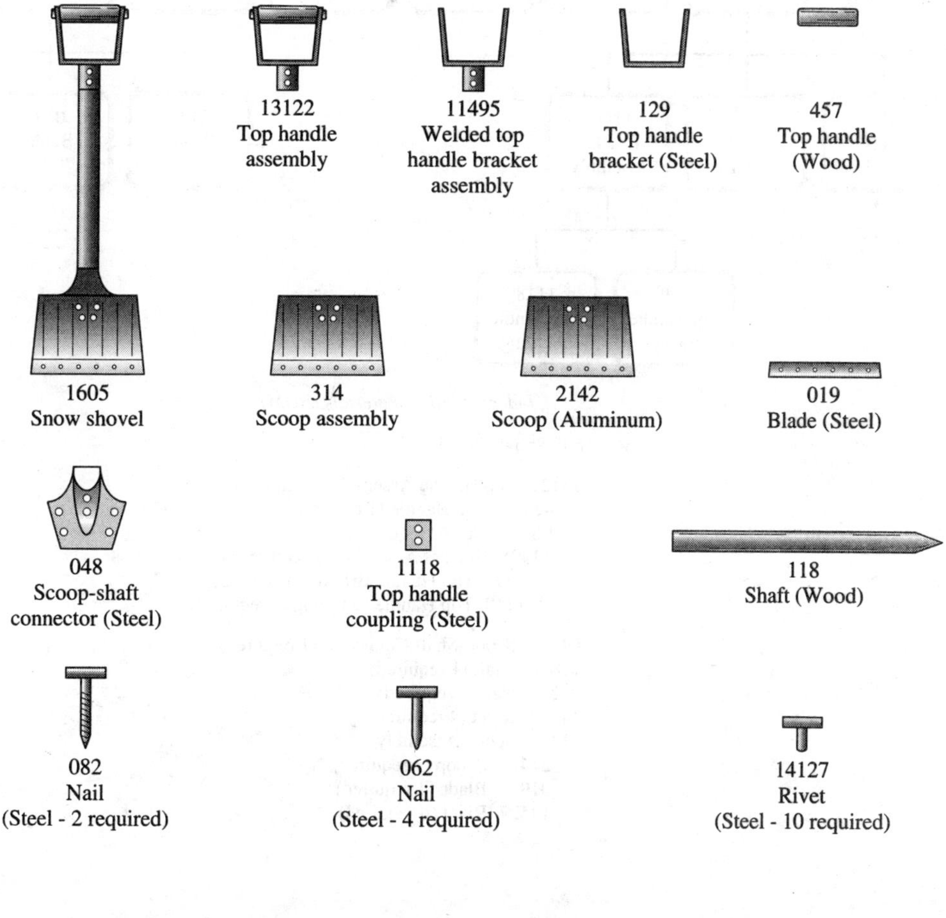

Explaining even this simple assembly process is a cumbersome task. Moreover, such diagrams as Figure 6.3 get more complicated as the number of subassemblies, components, and parts used increases, or as they are used in increasingly more places (e.g., rivets and nails). Two techniques that get at this problem nicely are the **product structure diagram** and the **indented bill of materials (BOM)** shown in Figure 6.4. Both provide the detailed information of Figure 6.3, but the indented BOM has the added advantage of being easily printed by a computer.

FIGURE 6.4 Parts for Snow Shovel

Product structure diagram

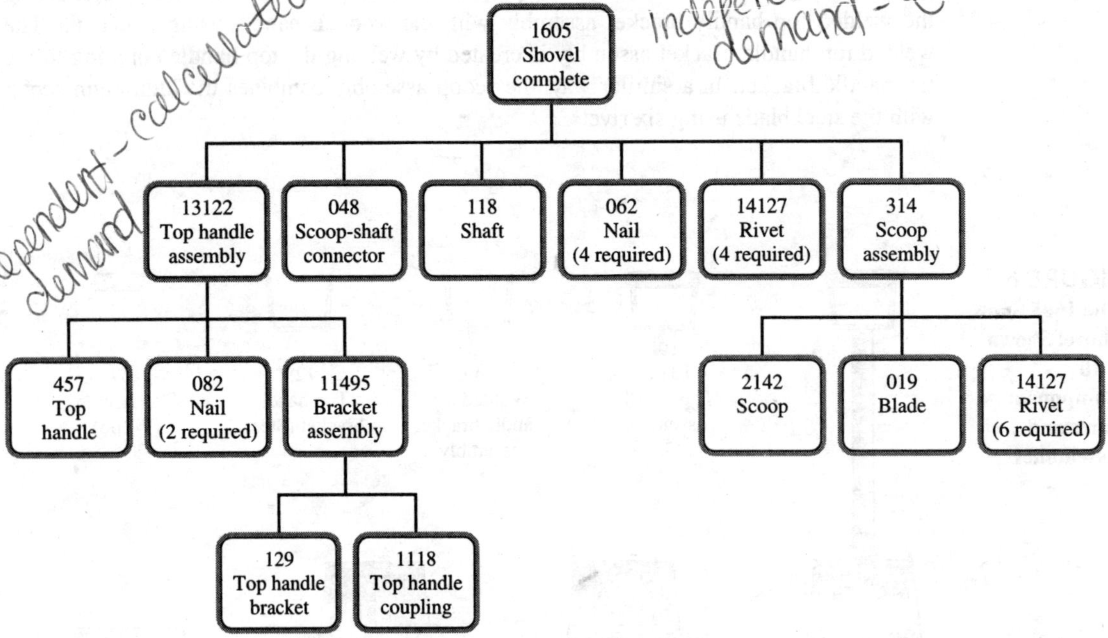

Indented bill of materials (BOM)

1605 Snow Shovel

- 13122 Top Handle Assembly (1 required)
  - 457 Top Handle (1 required)
  - 082 Nail (2 required)
  - 11495 Bracket Assembly (1 required)
    - 129 Top Handle Bracket (1 required)
    - 1118 Top Handle Coupling (1 required)
- 048 Scoop-Shaft Connector (1 required)
- 118 Shaft (1 required)
- 062 Nail (4 required)
- 14127 Rivet (4 required)
- 314 Scoop Assembly
  - 2142 Scoop (1 required)
  - 019 Blade (1 required)
  - 14127 Rivet (6 required)

Note that both the product structure diagram and the indented BOM show exactly what goes into what instead of being just a parts list. For example, to make one 13122 top handle assembly, we see by the product structure diagram that one 457 top handle, two 082 nails, and one 11495 bracket assembly are needed. The same information is shown in the indented BOM; the three required parts are indented and shown, one level beneath the 13122. Note also that we *don't* need a top handle bracket (129) or a top handle coupling (1118) to produce a top handle assembly (13122). These are only needed to produce a bracket assembly (11495). In essence, the top handle assembly does not care *how* a bracket assembly is made, only that it *is* made. Making the bracket assembly is a separate problem.

Before leaving our brief discussion of bills of material, it is important to stress that the bill of material used to support MRP may differ from other company perceptions of a bill of materials. The BOM to support MRP must be consistent with the way the product is manufactured. For example, if we're making red cars, the part numbers should be for red doors. If green cars are desired, the part numbers must be for green doors. Also, if we change to a different set of subassemblies, indentations on the BOM should change as well. Engineering and accounting may well not care what color the parts are or what the manufacturing sequence is.

Gross to Net Explosion

Explosion is the process of translating product requirements into component part requirements, taking existing inventories and scheduled receipts into account. Thus, explosion may be viewed as the process of determining, for *any* part number, the quantities of *all* components needed to satisfy its requirements, and continuing this process for *every* part number until all purchased and/or raw material requirements are exactly calculated.

As explosion takes place, only the component part requirements net of any inventory or scheduled receipts are considered. In this way, only the *necessary* requirements are linked through the system. Although this may seem like an obvious goal, the product structure can make a determination of net requirements more difficult than it seems. To illustrate, let's return to the snow shovel example.

Suppose the company wanted to produce 100 snow shovels, and we were responsible for making the 13122 top handle assembly. We are given current inventory and scheduled receipt information from which the gross requirements and net requirements for each component of the top handle can be calculated, as shown in Figure 6.5.

FIGURE 6.5 **Gross and Net Requirement Calculations for the Snow Shovel**

Part Description	Part Number	Inventory	Scheduled Receipts	Gross Requirements	Net Requirements
Top handle assembly	13122	25	—	100	75
Top handle	457	22	25	75	28
Nail (2 required)	082	4	50	150	96
Bracket assembly	11495	27	—	75	48
Top handle bracket	129	15	—	48	33
Top handle coupling	1118	39	15	48	—

The gross and net requirements in Figure 6.5 may not correspond to what we feel they should be. It might at the outset seem that since one top handle coupling (1118) is used per shovel, the gross requirements should be 100 and the net requirement 46, instead of the 48 and zero shown. To produce 100 shovels means we need (have a demand for) 100 top handle assemblies (part 13122). Twenty-five of these 100 can come from inventory, resulting in a net requirement of 75. As we need to make only 75 top handle assemblies, we need 75 top handles and bracket assemblies. This 75 is the *gross* requirement for parts 457 and 11495 (as indicated by the circled numbers in Figure 6.5). Because 2 nails (part 082) are used per top handle assembly, the gross requirement for 082 is 150. The 25 units of top handle assembly inventory contain some implicit inventories of handles, brackets, and nails, which the gross to net process takes into account. Looking on down, we see that there are 27 units of the bracket assembly in inventory, so the net requirement is for 48. This becomes the gross requirement for the bracket and coupling. Since there are 39 top handle couplings in inventory and 15 scheduled for receipt, there is *no* net requirement for part 1118.

Gross to net explosion is a key element of MRP systems. It not only provides the basis for calculating the appropriate quantities but also serves as the communication link between part numbers. It's the basis for the concept of **dependent demand;** that is, the "demand" (gross requirements) for top handles depends on the net requirements for top handle assemblies. To correctly do the calculations, the bill of material, inventory, and scheduled receipt data are all necessary. With these data, the dependent demand can be exactly calculated. It need not be forecast. On the other hand, some **independent demand** items, such as the snow shovel, are subject to demand from outside the firm. The need for snow shovels will have to be forecast. The concept of dependent demand is often called the fundamental principle of MRP. It provides the way to remove uncertainty from the requirement calculations.

Lead Time Offsetting

Gross to net explosion tells us how many of each subassembly and component part are needed to support a desired finished product quantity. What it does not do, however, is tell us *when* each component and subassembly is needed. Referring back to Figures 6.3 and 6.4, clearly the top handle bracket and top handle coupling need to be welded together before the wooden top handle is attached. These relationships are known as **precedent relationships.** They indicate the order in which things must be done.

In addition to precedent relationships, determining when to schedule each component part also depends on how long it takes to produce the part (that is, the lead time). Perhaps the top handle bracket (129) can be fabricated in one day, while the top handle coupling (1118) takes two weeks. If so, it would be advantageous to start making the coupling before the bracket, since they are both needed at the same time to make a bracket assembly.

Despite the need to take lead time differences into account, many systems for component part manufacturing ignore them. For example, most furniture manufacturers base production on what is called a **cutting.** In the cutting approach, if a lot of 100 chairs were to be assembled, then 100 of each part (with appropriate multiples) are started at the same time. Figure 6.6 is a Gantt chart (time-oriented bar chart) showing how this cutting approach would be applied to the snow shovel example. (Note that processing times are shown on the chart.)

Figure 6.6 shows clearly that the cutting approach, which starts all parts as soon as possible, will lead to unnecessary work-in-process inventories. For example, the top handle bracket (129) doesn't need to be started until the end of day 9, since it must wait for the

Starting all production of component parts at the same time

FIGURE 6.6
Gantt Chart for Cutting Approach to Snow Shovel Problem (front or earliest start schedule)

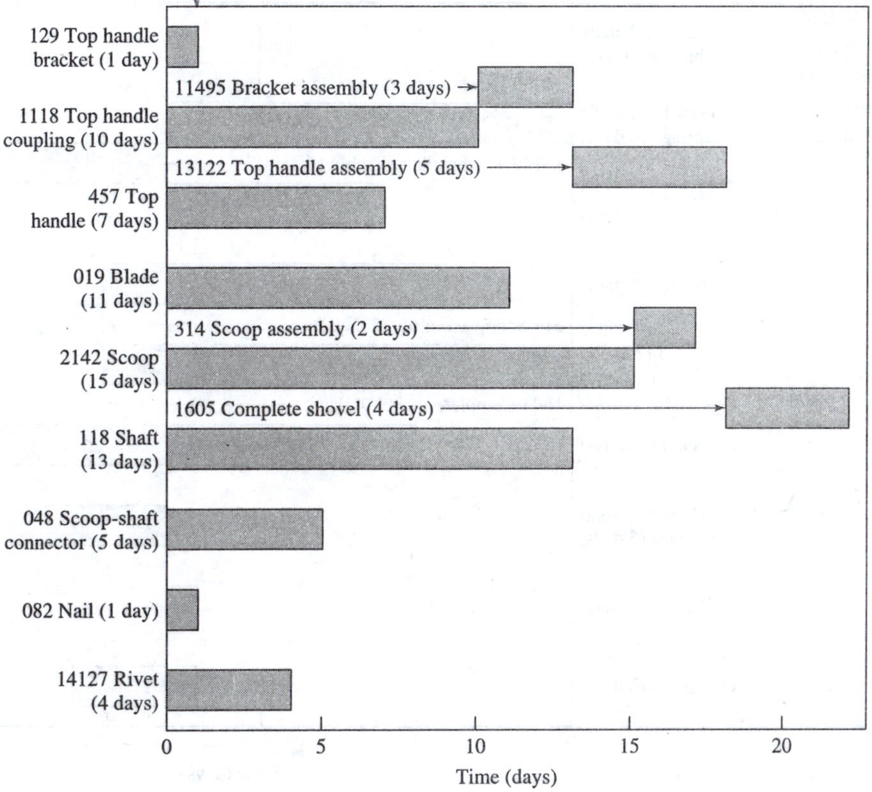

coupling (1118) before it can be put into its assembly (11495), and part 1118 takes 10 days. In the cutting approach, parts are scheduled earlier than need be. This results from using **front schedule** logic (that is, scheduling as early as possible).

What should be done is to **back schedule**—start each item as late as possible. Figure 6.7 provides a back schedule for the snow shovel example. The schedules for parts 1118, 11495, 13122, and 1605 don't change, since they form a critical path. All of the other parts, however, are scheduled later in this approach than in the front scheduling approach. A substantial savings in work-in-process inventory is obtained by this shift of dates.

Back scheduling has several obvious advantages. It will reduce work-in-process, postpone the commitment of raw materials to specific products, and minimize storage time of completed components. Implementing the back schedule approach, however, requires a system. The system must have accurate BOM data and lead time estimates, some way to ensure all component parts are started at the right times, and some means of tracking components and subassemblies to make sure they are all completed according to plans. The cutting approach is much simpler, since all component parts are started at the same time and left in the pipeline until needed.

MRP achieves the benefits of the back scheduling approach *and* performs the gross to net explosion. In fact, the combination of back schedules and gross to net explosion is the heart of MRP.

How long each component takes to produce plus assembly

FIGURE 6.7
Gantt Chart Based on Back Schedule (latest start)

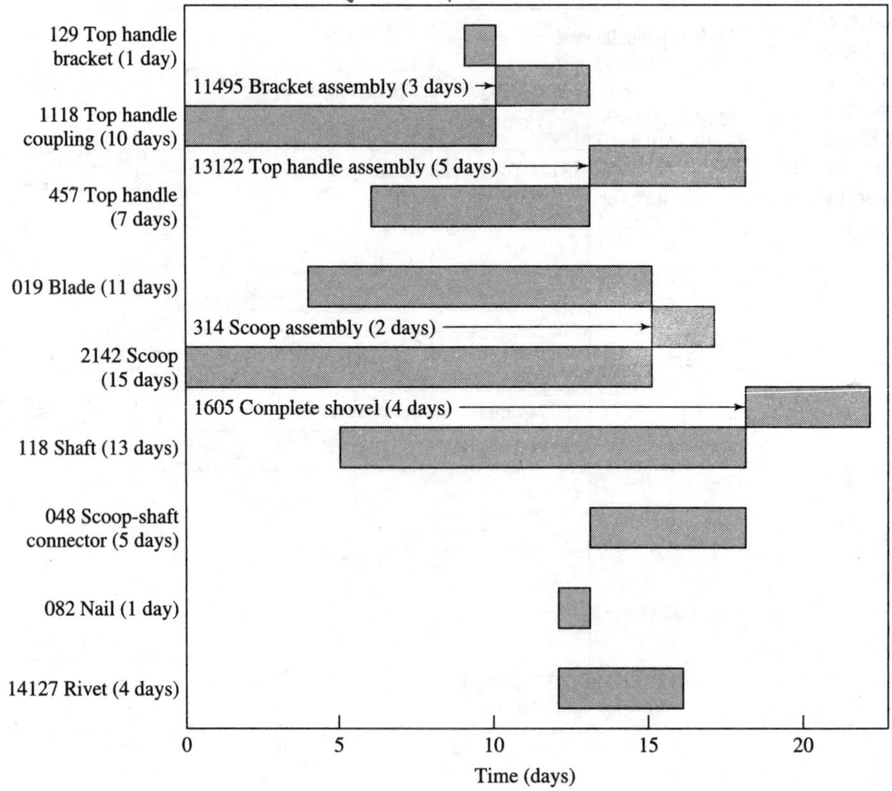

Linking the MRP Records

Figure 6.8 shows the linked set of individual time-phased MRP records for the top handle assembly of the snow shovel. We have already used the first five periods of the 082 nail record shown in Figure 6.8 as the record in Figure 6.2. To see how that record fits into the whole, we start with the snow shovels themselves. We said 100 snow shovels were going to be made, and now we see the timing. That is, the "Gross requirements" row in the MRP record for part number 13122 in Figure 6.8 shows the total need of 100 time phased as 20 in week 2, 10 in week 4, 20 in week 6, 5 in week 7, 35 in week 9, and 10 in week 10. Because each snow shovel takes a top handle assembly, the "Gross requirements" row for the top handle shows when shovel assembly is to begin. Note the total planned orders for the top handle assembly is the net requirement of 75 that we calculated before in the gross to net calculations of Figure 6.5.

The lead time for the top handle assembly is two weeks, calculated as the five days processing time shown in Figure 6.6 plus five days for paperwork. The lead time for each of the other records is similarly calculated; one week (five days) of paperwork time is added to the processing time and the total rounded to the nearest five-day week. The current inventories and scheduled receipts for each part are those shown in Figure 6.5. The scheduled receipts are shown in the appropriate periods. Using the two-week lead time and recognizing a net requirement of five units in week 4 for the top handle assembly, we see the need to plan an order for week 2 of five units.

FIGURE 6.8 MRP Records for the Snow Shovel Top Handle Assembly

Item			Week 1	2	3	4	5	6	7	8	9	10
13122 Top handle assembly Lead time = 2	Gross requirements			20		10		20	5		35	10
	Scheduled receipts											
	Projected available balance	25	25	5	5	0	0	0	0	0	0	0
	Planned order releases			5		20	5		35	10		
457 Top handle Lead time = 2	Gross requirements			5		20	5		35	10		
	Scheduled receipts				25							
	Projected available balance	22	22	17	42	22	17	17	0	0	0	0
	Planned order releases						18	10				
082 Nail (2 required) Lead time = 1 Lot size = 50	Gross requirements			10		40	10		70	20		
	Scheduled receipts		50									
	Projected available balance	4	54	44	44	4	44	44	24	4	4	4
	Planned order releases					50		50				
11495 Bracket assembly Lead time = 2	Gross requirements			5		20	5		35	10		
	Scheduled receipts											
	Projected available balance	27	27	22	22	2	0	0	0	0	0	0
	Planned order releases				3		35	10				
129 Top handle bracket Lead time = 1	Gross requirements				3		35	10				
	Scheduled receipts											
	Projected available balance	15	15	15	12	12	0	0	0	0	0	0
	Planned order releases					23	10					
1118 Top handle coupling Lead time = 3 Safety stock = 20	Gross requirements				3		35	10				
	Scheduled receipts			15								
	Projected available balance	39	39	54	51	51	20	20	20	20	20	20
	Planned order releases			4	10							

This planned order release of five units in week 2 becomes a gross requirement in week 2 for the top handles as shown by the circles in Figure 6.8. Note also the gross requirements for the nails and brackets in period 2 derive from this same planned order release (with two nails per top handle assembly). Thus, the communication between records is the dependent demand that we saw illustrated before in the gross to net calculations of Figure 6.5.

The remaining planned order releases for the top handle assembly exactly meet the net requirements in the remaining periods, offset for the lead time. The ordering policy used for these items is called **lot-for-lot** (i.e., as required) sizing. An exception to the lot-for-lot procedure is the ordering of nails, which is done in lots of 50. In the case of the nails, the total planned orders will not necessarily add up to the net requirements.

Another part for which there is a discrepancy between the planned orders and the net requirements calculated in Figure 6.5 is the top handle coupling. For this part, a safety stock of 20 units is desired. This means the planned order logic will schedule a planned order release to prevent the projected available balance from going below the safety stock level of 20 units. For the top handle couplings, this means a total of 4 units must be planned for period 2 and 10 for period 3 to maintain the 20-unit safety stock.

The one element we have yet to clearly show is the back scheduling effect. We saw in Figure 6.7 that it would be desirable to delay the start of the top handle bracket (part 129) so that this item is completed at the same time as the top handle coupling (part 1118). The MRP records show that the start of the first planned order for part 129 isn't until week 4, two weeks after the first planned order for part 1118. Both of these planned orders are to satisfy a gross requirement of 35 derived from the planned order for the bracket assembly in week 5. We see then that the orders are back scheduled. This relationship can be more complicated than our example, because the planned order release timing depends on the safety stock and inventory levels, as well as the lead times. The MRP system, however, coordinates all of that information and determines the appropriate planned order release dates, based on back scheduling.

At this point, we see fully the linking of the MRP time-phased records. The "Planned order releases" row for the top handle assembly (13122) becomes (with the appropriate multiplier) the "Gross requirements" row for each of its components (parts 457, 082, and 11495), and they are linked together. Once all the gross requirements data are available for a particular record, the individual record processing logic is applied and the planned order releases for the part are passed down as gross requirements to its components, following the product structure (BOM) on a level-by-level basis. In some cases, parts will receive their requirements from more than one source (common parts), as is true for the nails and rivets in the snow shovel. In these cases, gross requirements will reflect needs from more than one planned order release source. Again, the system accounts for this and incorporates it into the gross to net logic.

The MRP records take proper account of gross to netting. They also incorporate back scheduling and allow for explicit timings, desired lot sizing procedures, safety stocks, and part commonality. Even more important, however, is independence of the part number planning. With the MRP approach, the person planning snow shovels need not explicitly coordinate his planning with planning of the component parts. The MRP system accomplishes the coordination. Whatever is done to the MRP record for the snow shovels will result in a set of planned orders that the system will correctly pass down as gross requirements to its components. This means plans for each part number can be developed independently of the product structures, and the plans at each level will be communicated correctly to the other levels.

Technical Issues

In this section, we briefly introduce some technical issues to consider in designing MRP systems.

Processing Frequency

Thus far we've looked only at the static construction of the MRP records and how they're linked together. Since conditions change and new information is received, the MRP records must be brought up to date so plans can be adjusted. This means processing the MRP records anew, incorporating current information. Two issues are involved in the processing decision: how frequently the records should be processed and whether all the records should be processed at the same time.

Processing all of the records in one computer run is called **regeneration.** This signifies that *all* part number records are completely reconstructed each time the records are processed. When a regeneration run is conducted, all current planned orders are removed. Then, starting with the end items, each item is completely rescheduled. This can generate very large processing demands on the system. When initiated on line, the data-intensive run can negatively affect overall system performance and cause inconvenience to other users. To avoid this common problem, it is possible to conduct regeneration runs as background jobs. In addition to operating in the background, these jobs can be scheduled to take place automatically during periods of low system demand, such as late evenings or weekends.

The problem with processing less frequently is that the portrayal of component status and needs expressed in the records becomes increasingly out of date and inaccurate. This decrease in accuracy has both anticipated and unanticipated causes. As the anticipated scheduled receipts are received and requirements satisfied, the inventory balances change. As unanticipated scrap, requirement changes, stock corrections, or other such transactions occur, they cause inaccuracies if not reflected in all the time-phased records influenced by the transactions. Changes in one record are linked to other time-phased records as planned order releases become gross requirements for lower-level components. Thus, some change transactions may cascade throughout the product structure. If these transactions are not reflected in the time-phased records early enough, the result can be poor planning.

More frequent processing of the MRP records increases computer costs but results in fewer unpleasant surprises. When the records reflecting the changes are produced, appropriate actions will be indicated to compensate for the changes.

A logical response to the pressure for more frequent processing is to reduce the required amount of calculation by processing only the records affected by the changes. An alternative to regeneration is the **net change** approach. With net change, only those items that are affected by the new or changed information are reprocessed.

The argument for the net change approach is that it can reduce computer time enough to make daily or even real-time processing possible. Because only some of the records are reviewed at each processing, there's a need for very accurate computer records and transaction processing procedures. Some net change users do an occasional regeneration to clean up all records.

The most challenging aspect of net change is its hypersensitivity, or nervousness. The frequent replanning may result in continual revision of recommended user actions through the revision of planned order releases. Users may be frustrated with these frequent revisions to the plan.

Bucketless Systems

To some extent, the problems of timing are tied to the use of time buckets. When the buckets are small enough, the problems are reduced significantly. However, smaller buckets mean more buckets, which increases review, storage, and computation costs. A bucketless MRP system specifies the exact release and due dates for each requirement, scheduled receipt, and planned order. The managerial reports are printed out on whatever basis is required, including by exact dates.

Bucketless MRP systems are a better way to use the computer. Above and beyond that, the approach allows better maintenance of lead time offsets and provides more precise time-phased information. The approach is consistent with state-of-the-art software, and many firms now use bucketless systems. The major addition is that the planning cycle itself is bucketless. That is, plans are revised as necessary, not on a periodic schedule, and the entire execution cycle is also shortened.

Lot Sizing

In the snow shovel example of Figure 6.8, we use a fixed lot size (50 units for the nails) and the lot-for-lot procedure. The lot size of 50 for the nails could have been someone's estimate of a good lot size or the result of calculation. The time-phased information can be used in combination with other data to develop lot sizes conforming to organizational needs. We might reach the conclusion, for the top handle (1118) in Figure 6.8, that it's undesirable to set up the equipment for 4 parts in week 2, and again for 10 parts in week 3, so we'd combine the two orders. The time-phased record permits us to develop such **discrete lot sizes** that will exactly satisfy the net requirements for one or more periods.

Several formal procedures have been developed for lot sizing the time-phased requirements. The basic trade-off usually involves elimination of one or more setups at the expense of carrying inventory longer. In many cases, discrete lot sizes possible with MRP are more appealing than fixed lot sizes. Compare the residual inventory of nails in week 10, with that of the bracket assemblies in Figure 6.8, for example.

At first glance the lot-for-lot technique seems a bit too simple-minded since it does not consider any of the economic trade-offs or physical factors. However, batching planned orders at one level will increase gross requirements at the next level in the product structure. So larger lot sizing near the end-item level of the bill of materials cascades down through all levels. Thus, it turns out that lot-for-lot is better than we might expect in actual practice, particularly at the intermediate levels in the bill of materials. This is especially the case when a product structure has many levels, and the cascading effect becomes greatly magnified. This cascading effect can be mitigated to some extent for components and raw materials that are very common. When this is the case, again lot sizing may be appropriate.

Forecast more major end items than subcomponents

As a consequence, many firms employ lot sizing primarily at the end-item and basic component levels, while intermediate subassemblies are planned on a lot-for-lot basis.

Safety Stock and Safety Lead Time

Carrying out detailed component plans is sometimes facilitated by including **safety stocks** and/or **safety lead times** in the MRP records. Safety stock is a buffer of stock above and beyond that needed to satisfy the gross requirements. Figure 6.8 illustrates this by incorporating safety stock for the top handle coupling. Safety lead time is a procedure whereby shop orders or purchase orders are released and scheduled to arrive one or more periods before necessary to satisfy the gross requirements.

Safety stocks can be incorporated into MRP time-phased records. The result is that the projected available balance doesn't fall below the safety stock level instead of reaching zero. To incorporate safety lead time, orders are issued (planned) earlier and are scheduled (planned) to be received into inventory before the time that the MRP logic would indicate as necessary. Figure 6.9 shows the top handle bracket from Figure 6.8 being planned with a one-week safety lead time. Notice that both the planned release and planned receipt dates are changed. Safety lead time is not just inflated lead time.

Both safety stock and safety lead time are used in practice and can be used simultaneously. However, both are hedges indicating that orders should be released (launched) or that they need to be received when, in fact, this is not strictly true. To use safety stocks and safety lead times effectively, we must understand the techniques' influence on plans. If they are not well understood, wrong orders can be sent to the factory, meaning workers will try to get out part A because of safety lead time or safety stock when, in fact, part B will be required to meet a customer order.

Safety stock tends to be used in MRP systems where uncertainty about quantities is the problem (e.g., where some small amount of scrap, spare part demand, or other unplanned usage is a frequent occurrence). Safety lead time, on the other hand, tends to be used when the major uncertainty is the timing rather than the quantity. For example, if a firm buys from a vendor who often misses delivery dates, safety lead time may provide better results than safety stock.

FIGURE 6.9 **MRP Record with Safety Lead Time**

			1	2	3	4	5	6	7	8	9	10
Part 129	Gross requirements				3		35	10				
Top handle bracket lead time = 1	Scheduled receipts											
Lot-for-lot	Projected available balance	15	15	15	12	35	10	0	0	0	0	0
Safety lead time = 1	Planned order releases				23	10						

lead time 1 wk, if 2 wk 23 would shift to 4 period

Low-Level Coding

If we refer once again to Figure 6.4, we see that the rivet (part 14127) is a common part. The "Planned order" row for completed shovels will be passed down as gross requirements to the rivet. But there are additional requirements for the rivets (14127) from the scoop assembly (314). If we process the time-phased record for this common part before all of its gross requirements have been accumulated, the computations must be redone.

The way this problem is handled is to assign **low-level code numbers** to each part in the product structure or the indented BOM. By convention, the top final assembly level is denoted as level 0. In our example, the snow shovel would have a low-level code of 0. All immediate component part numbers of this part (13122, 048, 118, 062, 14127, and 314 in Figure 6.4) are given the low-level code number 1. The next level down (part numbers 457, 082, 11495, 2142, 019, and 14127) are low-level coded 2. Note the common part (rivet) has just been recoded as level 2, indicating it is used lower in the product structure. The higher the level codes, the lower in the product structure the part is used. Consequently, the last level code assigned to a part indicates the lowest level of usage and is the level code retained for that part. We finish the example when part numbers 129 and 1118 are coded level 3. The level code assigned to any part number is based on the part's usage in all products manufactured by the organization.

Once low-level codes are established, MRP record processing proceeds from one level code to the next, starting at level code 0. This ensures all gross requirements have been passed down to a part before its MRP record is processed. The result is planning of component parts coordinated with the needs of all higher-level part numbers. Within a level, the MRP record processing is typically done in part number sequence.

Pegging

Pegging relates all the gross requirements for a part to all the planned order releases or other sources of demand that created the requirements. The pegging records contain the specific part number or numbers of the sources of all gross requirements. At level 0, for example, pegging records might contain the specific customer orders to be satisfied by the gross requirements in the end-item, time-phased records. For lower-level part numbers, the gross requirements are most often pegged to planned orders of higher-level items, but might also be pegged to customer orders if the part is sold as a service part.

Pegging information can be used to go up through the MRP records from a raw material gross requirement to some future customer order. In this sense, it's the reverse of the explosion process. Pegging is sometimes compared to **where-used data.** Where-used data, however, indicate for each part number, the part numbers of all items on which the part is used. Pegging, on the other hand, is a *selective* where-used file. Pegging shows only the specific part numbers that produce the specific gross requirements in each time period. Thus, pegging information can trace the impact of a material problem all the way up to the order it would affect.

Firm Planned Orders

The logic used to illustrate the construction of an MRP record for an individual part number is automatically applied for every processed part number. The result is a series of planned order releases for each part number. If changes have taken place since the last time

Control release order changes / Command approval

the record was processed, planned order releases can be very different from one record-processing cycle to the next. Because planned orders are passed down as gross requirements to the next level, the differences can cascade throughout the product structure.

One device for preventing this cascading down through the product structure is to create a **firm planned order (FPO).** FPO, as the name implies, is a planned order that the MRP system *does not* automatically change when conditions change. To change either the quantity or timing of a firm planned order, managerial action is required. This means the trade-offs in making the change can be evaluated before authorization.

The FPO provides a means for temporarily overriding the system to provide stability or to solve problems. For example, if changes are coming about because of scrap losses on open orders, the possibility of absorbing those variations with safety stock can be evaluated. If more rapid delivery of raw material than usual is requested (say by using air freight) to meet a special need, lead time can be reduced for that one order. An FPO means the system will not use the normal lead time offset from the net requirement for that order.

Service Parts

Service part demand must be included in the MRP record if the material requirements are not to be understated. The service part demand is typically based on a forecast and is added directly into the gross requirements for the part. From the MRP system point of view, the service part demand is simply another source of gross requirements for a part, and the sources of all gross requirements are maintained through pegging records. The low-level code for a part used exclusively for service would be zero. If it's used as a component part as well, the low-level code would be determined the same way as for any other part.

As actual service part needs occur, it's to be expected that demand variations will arise. These can be partially buffered with safety stocks (inventories specifically allocated to service part usage) or by creative use of the MRP system. By careful examination of pegging records, expected shortage conditions for manufacturing part requirements can sometimes be satisfied from available service parts. Conversely, critical service part requirements can perhaps be met with orders destined for higher-level items. Only one safety stock inventory is needed to buffer uncertainties from both sources, however.

Planning Horizon

In Figure 6.8, the first planned order for top handle assemblies occurs in week 2 to meet period 4's gross requirement of 10 units. This planned order of 5 units in week 2 results in a corresponding gross requirement in that week for the bracket assembly (part 11495). This gross requirement is satisfied from the existing inventory of part 11495. But a different circumstance occurs if we trace the gross requirements for 35 top handle assemblies in week 9.

The net requirement for 35 units in week 9 becomes a planned order release in week 7. This, in turn, becomes a gross requirement for 35 bracket assemblies (part 11495) in week 7 and a planned order release in week 5. This passes down to the top handle coupling (part 1118), which creates a planned order release for 4 units in week 2. This means the **cumulative lead time** for the top handle assembly is 7 weeks (from release of the coupling order in week 2 to receipt of the top handle assemblies in week 9).

Scheduled Receipts versus Planned Order Releases

A true understanding of MRP requires knowledge of certain key differences between a scheduled receipt and a planned order. We noted one such difference before: the scheduled receipt represents a commitment, whereas the planned order is only a plan—the former is much more difficult to change than the latter. A scheduled receipt for a purchased item means a purchase order, which is a formal commitment, has been prepared. Similarly, a scheduled receipt for a manufactured item means there's an open shop order. Raw materials and component parts have *already* been specifically committed to that order and are no longer available for other needs. One major result of this distinction, which can be seen in Figure 6.8, is that planned order releases explode to gross requirements for components, but scheduled receipts (the open orders) do not.

A related issue is seen from the following question: Where would a scheduled receipt for the top handle assembly (13122) in Figure 6.8 of, say, 20 units in week 2 be reflected in the records for the component parts (457, 082, and 11495)? The answer is nowhere! Scheduled receipts are not reflected in the current records for component parts. For that scheduled receipt to exist, the component parts would have already been assigned to the shop order representing the scheduled receipt for part 13122 and removed from the available balances of the components. As far as MRP is concerned, the 20 part 457s, 40 part 082s, and 20 part 11495s don't exist! They're on their way to becoming 20 part 13122s. The 13122 record controls this process, not the component records.

Using the MRP System

In this section, we discuss critical aspects of using the MRP system to ensure that MRP system records are exactly synchronized with physical flows of material.

The MRP Planner

The persons most directly involved with the MRP system outputs are planners. They are typically in the production planning, inventory control, and purchasing departments. Planners have the responsibility for making detailed decisions that keep the material moving through the plant. Their range of discretion is carefully limited (e.g., without higher authorization, they cannot change plans for end items destined for customers). Their actions, however, are reflected in the MRP records. Well-trained MRP planners are essential to effective use of the MRP system.

Computerized MRP systems often encompass tens of thousands of part numbers. To handle this volume, planners are generally organized around logical groupings of parts (such as metal parts, wood parts, purchased electronic parts, or West Coast distribution center). Even so, reviewing each record every time the records are processed would not be an effective use of the planners' time. At any time, many records require no action, so the planner only wants to review and interpret those that do require action.

The primary actions taken by an MRP planner are:

1. Release orders (i.e., launch purchase or shop orders when indicated by the system).
2. Reschedule due dates of existing open orders when desirable.

3. Analyze and update system planning factors for the part numbers under her control. This would involve such things as changing lot sizes, lead times, scrap allowances, or safety stocks.
4. Reconcile errors or inconsistencies and try to eliminate root causes of these errors.
5. Find key problem areas requiring action now to prevent future crises.
6. Use the system to solve critical material shortage problems so actions can be captured in the records for the next processing. This means the planner works *within* formal MRP rules, *not* by informal methods.
7. Indicate where further system enhancements (outputs, diagnostics, etc.) would make the planner's job easier.

Order Launching

Order launching is the process of releasing orders to the shop or to vendors (purchase orders). This process is prompted by MRP when a planned order release is in the current time period, the **action bucket.** Order launching converts the planned order into a scheduled receipt reflecting the lead time offset. Order launching is the opening of shop and purchase orders; closing these orders occurs when scheduled receipts are received into stockrooms. At that time, a transaction must be processed—to increase the on-hand inventory and eliminate the scheduled receipt. Procedures for opening and closing shop orders have to be carefully defined so all transactions are properly processed.

The orders indicated by MRP as ready for launching are a function of lot sizing procedures and safety stock as well as timing. We saw this in Figure 6.8 where we worked with lot-for-lot approaches and fixed lot sizes. A key responsibility of the planner is managing with awareness of the implications of these effects. For example, not *all* of a fixed lot may be necessary to cover a requirement, or a planned order that's solely for replenishment of safety stock may be in the action bucket.

When an order is launched, it's sometimes necessary to include a shrinkage allowance for scrap and other process yield situations. The typical approach allows some percentage for yield losses that will increase the shop order quantity above the net amount required. To effect good control over open orders, the *total* amount, including the allowance, should be shown on the shop order, and the scheduled receipt should be reduced as actual yield losses occur during production.

Allocation and Availability Checking

A concept closely related to order launching is **allocation**—a step prior to order launching that involves an availability check for the necessary component or components. From the snow shovel example, if we want to assemble 20 of the top handle assembly (13122) in period 4, the availability check would be whether sufficient components (20 of part 457, 40 of part 082, and 20 of part 11495) are available. If not, the shop order for 20 top handle assemblies (13122) should not be launched, because it cannot be executed without component parts. The planner role is key here, as well. The best course of action might be to release a partial order. The planner should evaluate that possibility.

Most MRP systems first check component availability for any order that a planner desires to launch. If sufficient quantities of each component are available, the shop order can be created. If the order is created, then the system allocates the necessary quantities to the particular shop order. (Shop orders are assigned by the computer, in numerical sequence.) The allocation means this amount of a component part is mortgaged to the particular shop order and is, therefore, not available for any other shop order. Thus, the amounts shown in Figure 6.8 as projected available balances may not be the same as the physical inventory balances. The physical inventory balances could be larger, with the differences representing allocations to specific shop orders that have been released, but whose component parts have not been removed from inventory.

After availability checking and allocation, **picking tickets** are typically created and sent to the stockroom. The picking ticket calls for a specified amount of some part number to be removed from some inventory location, on some shop order, to be delivered to a particular department or location. When the picking ticket has been satisfied (inventory moved), the allocation is removed and the on-hand balance is reduced accordingly.

Availability checking, allocation, and physical stock picking are a type of double-entry bookkeeping. The result is that the quantity physically on hand should match what the records indicate is available plus what is allocated. If they don't match, corrective action must be taken. The resulting accuracy facilitates inventory counting and other procedures for maintaining date integrity.

Exception Codes

Exception codes in MRP systems are used "to separate the vital few from the trivial many." If the manufacturing process is under control and the MRP system is functioning correctly, exception coding typically means only 10 to 20 percent of the part numbers will require planner review at each processing cycle. Exception codes are in two general categories. The first, checking the input data accuracy, includes checks for dates beyond the planning horizon, quantities larger or smaller than check figures, nonvalid part numbers, or any other desired check for incongruity. The second category of exception codes directly supports the MRP planning activity. Included are the following kinds of exception (action) messages or diagnostics:

1. Part numbers for which a planned order is now in the most immediate time period (the action bucket). It's also possible to report any planned orders two to three periods out to check lead times, on-hand balances, and other factors while there's some time to respond, if necessary.
2. Open order diagnostics when the present timing and/or amount for a scheduled receipt is not satisfactory. Such a message might indicate that an open order exists that's not necessary to cover any of the requirements in the planning horizon. This message might suggest order cancellation caused by an engineering change that substituted some new part for the one in question. The most common type of open order diagnostic shows scheduled receipts that are timed to arrive either too late or too early and should, therefore, have their due dates revised to reflect proper factory priorities. An example of this is seen with each of the three scheduled receipts in Figure 6.8. The 457 top handle open order of 25 could be delayed one week. A one-week delay is also indicated for the 082 nail scheduled receipt. For part 1118 (the top handle coupling), scheduled receipt of 15 could be delayed from week 2 until week 5. Another open order exception code is to flag any past-due scheduled receipt (scheduled to have been received in previous periods, but

for which no receipt transaction has been processed). MRP systems assume a past-due scheduled receipt will be received in the immediate time bucket.

3. A third general type of exception message indicates problem areas for management; in essence, situations where level 0 quantities can't be satisfied unless the present planning factors used in MRP are changed. One such exception code indicates a requirement has been offset into the past period and subsequently added to any requirement in the first or most immediate time bucket. This condition means an order should have been placed in the past. Since it wasn't, lead times through the various production item levels must be compressed to meet the end-item schedule. A similar diagnostic indicates the allocations exceed the on-hand inventory—a condition directly analogous to overdrawing a checking account. Unless more inventory is received soon, the firm will not be able to honor all pick tickets issued, and there will be a material shortage in the factory.

Bottom-up Replanning

Bottom-up replanning—using pegging data to solve material shortage problems—is best seen through an example. Let's return again to Figure 6.8, concentrating on the top handle assembly and the nails (parts 13122 and 082). Let's suppose the scheduled receipt of 50 nails arrives on Wednesday of week 1. On Thursday, quality control checks them and finds the vendor sent the wrong size. This means only 4 of the 10 gross requirement in week 2 can be satisfied. By pegging this gross requirement up to its parent planned order (5 units of 13122 in week 2), we see that only 7 of the gross requirement for 10 units in week 4 can be satisfied (the 5 on hand plus 2 made from 4 nails). This, in turn, means only 7 snow shovels can be assembled in week 4.

The pegging analysis shows that 3 of the 10 top handle assemblies can't be available without taking some special actions. If none are taken, the planned assembly dates for the snow shovels should reflect only 7 units in week 4, with the additional 3 scheduled for week 5. This should be done if we cannot overcome the shortfall in nails. The change is necessary because the 10 snow shovels now scheduled for assembly in week 4 also explode to other parts—parts that won't be needed if only 7 snow shovels are to be assembled.

There may, however, be a critical customer requirement for 10 snow shovels to be assembled during week 4. Solving the problem with bottom-up replanning might involve one of the following alternatives (staying *within* the MRP system, as planners must do):

1. Issue an immediate order to the vendor for six nails (the minimum requirement), securing a promised lead time of two days instead of the usual one week. This will create a scheduled receipt for six in week 2.
2. Order more nails for the beginning of week 3, and negotiate a one-week reduction in lead time (from two weeks to one week) for fabricating this one batch of part 13122. The planned order release for five would be placed in week 3 and converted to a firm planned order, so it would not change when the record is processed again. The negotiation for a one-week lead time might involve letting the people concerned start work earlier than week 3 on the two part 13122s, for which material already exists, and a reduction in the one-week paperwork time included in the lead times.
3. Negotiate a one-week lead time reduction for assembling the snow shovels; place a firm planned order for 10 in week 5, which will result in a gross requirement for 10 top handle assemblies in period 5 instead of period 4.

FIGURE 6.10 Example MRP Record

```
    DATE-01/21
********PART NUMBER********
NONJEK OPTY SSV LAM PP UPHL           MATERIAL STATUS-PRODUCTION SCHEDULE
                                                           PLNR    BYR            REJECT    SAFETY    SHRINKG    LEAD    FAMILY
                                         DESCRIPTION       CODE    COE    U/M    QUANTITY    STOCK    ALLOWNE    TIME     DATA
USTR040                           3/16 x 7/8 MR P & C STL STRAP   01      9      LFT                   497        1        08
         ******USAGE******             ********************************ORDER POLICY AND LOT SIZE DATA*********************************
 YTD       LAST YR       YTD              POLICY          STANDARD        PERIODS       MINIMUM        MAXIMUM        MULTIPLE    MIN ORD
SCRAP                                      CODE           QUANTITY       TO COMB.         QTY            QTY            QTY        POINT
                                            3                              04
-------------------------------------------------------------------------------------------------------------------------------------------
                           PAST DUE    563     564     565      566      567      568      569      570      571      572      573
                                      01/22   01/29   02/05    02/12    02/19    02/26    03/05    03/12    03/19    03/28    04/02
REQUIREMENTS                 495                       483                                  516
SCHEDULED RECEIPTS
PLANNED RECEIPTS                                                                   491                                          337
AVAILABLE ON-HAND          1,500       508     508      25       25       25       516                                          337
PLANNED ORDERS               491                       337                                  334
-------------------------------------------------------------------------------------------------------------------------------------------
                             574       575     576     577      578      579      580      581      582      583      584      585
                            04/09     04/16   04/23   04/30    05/07    05/14    05/21    05/28    06/04    06/11    06/18    06/25
REQUIREMENTS                 337                                334
SCHEDULED RECEIPTS
PLANNED RECEIPTS                                       334
AVAILABLE ON-HAND                                      334
PLANNED ORDERS
-------------------------------------------------------------------------------------------------------------------------------------------
                           VACATION    586     587     588    589-592  593-596  597-600  601-604  605-608  609-612
                                      07/16   07/23   07/30    08/06    09/03    10/01    10/29    11/26    12/24
REQUIREMENTS
SCHEDULED RECEIPTS
PLANNED RECEIPTS
AVAILABLE
PLANNED ORDERS
**********EXCEPTION MESSAGES*********
PLANNED ORDER OF   491 FOR M-WK   568    OFFSET INTO A PAST PERIOD BY 03 PERIODS
********PEGGING DATA (ALLOC)*********
790116 455 JN25220
*********PEGGING DATA (REQMT)********
790205  483 F 17144                                790305   516 F 19938                790409   337 F 17144
790507  334 F 19938
```

Thus, we see the solution to a material shortage problem might be made by compressing lead times throughout the product structure using the system and bottom-up replanning. Planners work within the system using firm planned orders and net requirements to develop workable (but not standard) production schedules. The creativity they use in solving problems will be reflected in the part records at the next MRP processing cycle. All implications of planner actions will be correctly coordinated throughout the product structure.

It's important to note that the resolution of problems cannot *always* involve reduced lead time and/or partial lots. Further, none of these actions are free. In some cases, customer needs will have to be delayed or partial shipments made. Pegging and bottom-up replanning will provide advance warning of these problems so customers can take appropriate actions.

An MRP System Output

Figure 6.10 is an MRP time-phased record for one part number out of a total of 13,000 at the Batesville, Indiana, facility of the Hill-Rom Company. The header information includes the date the report was run, part number and description, planner code number, buyer code number (for purchased parts), unit of measure for this part number (pieces, pounds, etc.), rejected parts that have yet to receive disposition by quality control, safety stocks, shrinkage allowance for anticipated scrap loss, lead time, family data (what other parts are similar to this one), year-to-date scrap, usage last year, year-to-date usage, and order policy/lot size data. The policy code of 3 for this part means the order policy is a **periodic order quantity (POQ).** In this case, "periods to comb. = 04" means each order should combine four periods of net requirements.

The first time bucket is "past due." After that, weekly time buckets are presented for the first 28 weeks of data; thereafter, 24 weeks of data are lumped into 4-week buckets. In the computer itself, a bucketless system is used with all data kept in exact days, with printouts prepared in summary format for one- and four-week buckets. The company maintains a manufacturing calendar; in this example, the first week is 563 (also shown as 1/22), and the last week is 612.

In this report, safety stock is subtracted from the on-hand balance (except in the past-due bucket). Thus, the exception message indicating that a planned order for 491 should have been issued three periods ago creates no major problem, since the planner noted that this amount is less than the safety stock. This report also shows the use of safety lead time. *Planned* receipts are given a specific row in the report and are scheduled one week ahead of the actual need date. For example, the 337-unit planned order of week 565 is a planned receipt in week 573, although it's not needed until week 574.

The final data in the report is the pegging data section tying specific requirements to the part numbers from which those requirements came. For example, in week 565 (shop order no. 790205), the requirement for 483 derives from part number F17144. MRP records are printed at this company only for those part numbers for which exception messages exist.

System Dynamics

Murphy's law states that if anything can go wrong, it will. Things are constantly going wrong, so it's essential that the MRP system mirror actual shop conditions; that is, both the physical system and the information system have to cope with scrap, incorrect counts,

FIGURE 6.11
MRP Record for Part 1234 as of Week 1

Lead time = 2
Lot size = 50

		1	2	3	4	5
Gross requirements		30	20	20	0	45
Scheduled receipts		50				
Projected available balance	10	30	10	40	40	45
Planned order releases		50		50		

changes in customer needs, incorrect bills of material, engineering design changes, poor vendor performance, and a myriad of other mishaps.

In this section, we look at the need for quick and accurate transaction processing and review the MRP planner's replanning activities in coping with change. We discuss sources of problems occurring as a result of database changes plus actions to ensure the system is telling the truth, even if the truth hurts.

Transactions during a Period

To illustrate transaction processing issues, we use a simple example for one part. Figure 6.11 shows an MRP record (for part 1234) produced over the weekend preceding week 1. The planner for part 1234 would receive this MRP record on Monday of week 1.

The planner's first action would be to try to launch the planned order for 50 units in period 1; that is, the MPC system would first check availability of the raw materials for this part and then issue an order to the shop to make 50, if sufficient raw material is available. Launching would require allocating the necessary raw materials to the shop order, removing the 50 from the "Planned order release" row for part 1234, and creating a scheduled receipt for 50 in week 3, when they're needed. Thereafter, a pick ticket would be sent to the raw material area and work could begin.

Let's assume during week 1 the following changes occurred, and the transactions were processed:

- Actual disbursements from stock for item 1234 during week 1 were only 20 instead of the planned 30.
- The scheduled receipt for 50 due in week 1 was received on Tuesday, but 10 units were rejected, so only 40 were actually received into inventory.
- The inventory was counted on Thursday and 20 additional pieces were found.
- The requirement date for the 45 pieces in week 5 was changed to week 4.
- Marketing requested an additional five pieces for samples in week 2.
- The requirement for week 6 has been set at 25.

The resultant MRP record produced over the weekend preceding week 2 is presented as Figure 6.12.

FIGURE 6.12
MRP Record for Part 1234 as of Week 2

Lead time = 2
Lot size = 50

		2	3	4	5	6
Gross requirements		25	20	45	0	25
Scheduled receipts			50			
Projected available balance	50	25	55	10	10	35
Planned order release				50		

Rescheduling

The MRP record shown in Figure 6.12 illustrates two important activities for MRP planners: (1) indicating the sources of problems that will occur as a result of database changes and (2) suggesting actions to ensure the system is telling the truth. Note the scheduled receipt presently due in week 3 is not needed until week 4. The net result of all the changes to the database means it's now scheduled with the wrong due date, and the due date should be changed to week 4. If this change is not made, this job may be worked on ahead of some other job that is really needed earlier, thereby causing problems. The condition shown in Figure 6.12 would be highlighted by an MRP exception message, such as "reschedule the receipt currently due in week 3 to week 4."

Complex Transaction Processing

So far, we've illustrated system dynamics by using a single MRP record. However, an action required on the part of an MRP planner may have been caused by a very complex set of database transactions involving several levels in the bill of materials. As an example, consider the MRP records shown in Figure 6.13, which include three levels in the product structure. Part C is used as a component in both parts A and B as well as being sold as a service part. Part C, in turn, is made from parts X and Y. The arrows in Figure 6.13 depict the pegging data.

The part C MRP record is correctly stated at the beginning of week 1. That is, no exception messages would be produced at this time. In particular, the two scheduled receipts of 95 and 91, respectively, are scheduled correctly, since delaying either by one week would cause a shortage, and neither has to be expedited to cover any projected shortage.

While the two scheduled receipts for part C are currently scheduled correctly, transactions involving parts A and B can have an impact on the proper due dates for these open orders. For example, suppose an inventory count adjustment for part A resulted in a change in the 30-unit planned order release from week 1 to week 3. In this case, the 95 units of part C would not be needed until week 3, necessitating a reschedule. Similarly, any change in timing for the planned order release of 25 units of part A in week 4 would call for a reschedule of the due date for 91 units of part C. Finally, suppose a transaction requiring 75 additional units of part B in week 5 were processed. This would result in an immediate release of an order for 100 units of part C. This might necessitate rescheduling for parts X and Y.

FIGURE 6.13
MRP Record Relationships for Several Parts

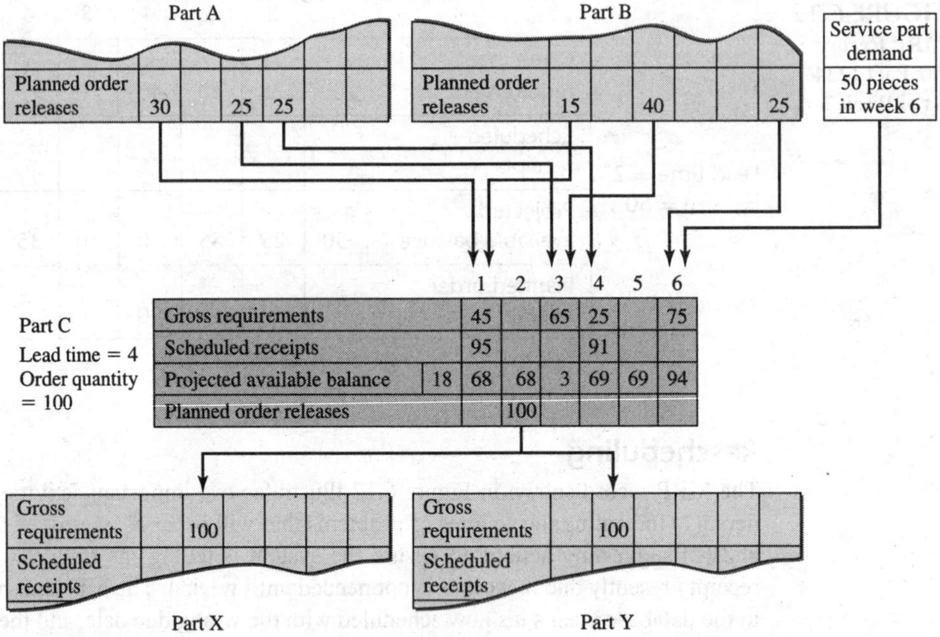

Note: This example is based on one originally developed by Joseph Orlicky. *Orlicky's Material Requirements Planning*, 2nd ed. New York: McGraw-Hill, 1994, chap. 4, pp. 69–99.

The point here is that actions required on the part of an MRP planner can occur because of a complex set of database transactions involving many different parts. They may not necessarily directly involve the particular part being given attention by the MRP planner.

Procedural Inadequacies

MRP replanning and transaction processing activities are two essential aspects of ensuring the MPC database remains accurate. However, while these activities are necessary, they aren't sufficient to maintain accurate records. Some of the procedures used to process transactions simply may be inadequate to the task.

To illustrate inadequate transaction procedures, let's return to the example in Figure 6.13. Note that, if 4 or more pieces are scrapped on the shop order for 95, there will be a shortage in week 3, necessitating rescheduling of the order for 91 one week earlier.

It's even more interesting to see what would happen if 4 pieces were scrapped on the order for 95, and this scrap transaction weren't processed. If the scrap isn't reported, MRP records would appear as shown in Figure 6.13, indicating no required rescheduling—when, in fact, that's not true. *If* the shortage were discovered by the person in charge of the stockroom when he or she puts away this order, then only one week would be lost before the next MRP report shows the problem. If, however, the stockroom person doesn't count, or if the person who made the scrap puts the defective parts at the bottom of the box where they go undetected by quality control, then the problem will be discovered only when the assembly lines are trying to build As and Bs in week 3. Such a discovery comes under the category of unpleasant surprises. An interesting sidelight to this problem is that the cure will be to rush down to the shop to get at least 1 piece from the batch of 91. The very person who failed to report the earlier scrap may well now be screaming, "Why don't those idiots know what they need!"

Still another aspect of the scrap reporting issue can be seen by noting the 95 and 91 were originally issued as lot sizes of 100. This probably means 5 and 9 pieces of scrap have occurred already, and the appropriate adjustments have been made in the scheduled receipt data. Note that, if these adjustments had *not* been made, the two scheduled receipts would show as 100 each. The resultant 14 (or 5 + 9) pieces (that don't, in fact, exist) would be reflected in the MRP arithmetic. Thus, the projected available balance at the end of period 5 would be 83 (or 69 + 14); this is more than enough to cover the gross requirement of 75 in period 6, so the planned order release for 100 in period 2 would not exist and the error would cascade throughout the product structure. Further, even if shop orders are carefully counted as they are put into storage, the five-piece shortage in period 1 is not enough to cause the MRP arithmetic to plan an order. Only after period 4 (the beginning of period 5) will the additional nine pieces of scrap be incorporated in the MRP record showing a projected shortage in period 6. This will result in an immediate order, to be completed in one week instead of four! What may be obvious is that, if accurate counting isn't done, then the shortage is discovered in week 6, when the assembly line goes down. This means procedures for issuing scrap tickets when scrap occurs and procedures for ensuring good parts are accurately counted into inventory must be in place. If not, all the MPC systems will suffer.

The long and the short of all this is that we have to believe the numbers, and an error of as little as *one* piece can cause severe problems. We have to know the truth. We have to tightly control transactions. Moreover, we have to develop iron-clad procedures for processing MPC database transactions.

Concluding Principles

Chapter 6 provides an understanding of the MRP approach to detailed material planning. It describes basic techniques, some technical issues, and how MRP systems are used in practice. MRP, with its time-phased approach to planning, is a basic building-block concept for materials planning and control systems. Moreover, there are many other applications of the time-phased record. We see the most important concepts or principles of this chapter as follows:

- Effective use of an MRP system allows development of a forward-looking (planning) approach to managing material flows.
- The MRP system provides a coordinated set of linked product relationships, thereby permitting decentralized decision making on individual part numbers.
- All decisions made to solve problems must be done within the system, and transactions must be processed to reflect the resultant changes.
- Effective use of exception messages allows focusing attention on the "vital few," not on the "trivial many."

- System records must be accurate and reflect the factory's physical reality if they're to be useful.
- Procedural inadequacies in processing MRP transactions need to be identified and corrected to ensure material plans are accurate.

Discussion Questions

1. Why is the MRP activity in the "engine" part of the MPC system shown in Figure 6.1?
2. What additional information would be helpful to you in using or following the basic MRP record?
3. Compare a bill of materials (BOM) and a cookbook recipe.
4. How does the *system* coordinate the individual item records and provide back schedule information?
5. Provide examples of potential differences between the information system and the physical reality for university activities. What are the consequences of some of these mismatches?
6. What are some of the reasons for wanting to process the records in an MRP system frequently? Provide examples and consequences of delaying the processing of the information.
7. The chapter uses a Christmas list and Christmas gift order analogy for planned order releases and scheduled receipts. What are other analogies of these two concepts? Why is it important to keep them separate in the MRP records?
8. What are the implications of *not* allocating material to a shop order after availability checking?
9. Give some examples of transaction processing for individual students at a university. What happens if they are not done well?

Problems

1. Joe's Burgers sells three kinds of hamburgers—Big, Giant, and The Football. The bills of materials are:

Big Burger		Giant Burger		Football Burger	
$\frac{1}{4}$ lb. patty	1.0	$\frac{1}{2}$ lb. patty	1.0	1 lb. patty	2.0
Regular bun	1.0	Sesame bun	1.0	Sesame bun	1.0
Pickle slice	1.0	Pickle slices	2.0	Pickle slices	4.0
Catsup	0.1 oz.	Catsup	0.2 oz.	Lettuce	0.3 oz.
		Onion	0.2 oz.	Catsup	0.2 oz.
				Cheese	0.5 oz.
				Onion	0.2 oz.

   a. If the product mix is 20 percent Big, 45 percent Giant, and 35 percent Footballs, and Joe sells 200 burgers a day, how much hamburger meat is used per day?
   b. How many pickle slices are needed per day?
   c. Suppose buns are delivered every second day. Joe is ready to order. His on-hand balance of regular buns is 25, and his on-hand balance of sesame buns is 20. How many buns should be ordered?
   d. Reconsider question c if Joe has 10 Big hamburgers, 5 Giant, and 15 Footballs all made.

2. The following illustration shows how to assemble your own computer.

Memory board (M)

Assemble 4 RAM chips (C) and 1 switch (S) onto a board type (X).

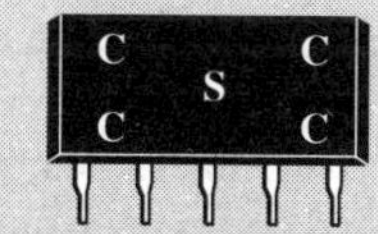

Arithmetic board (A)

Assemble 1 integrated microprocessor (Z) with 2 ROM chips (R) and 1 switch (S) onto a board type (Y).

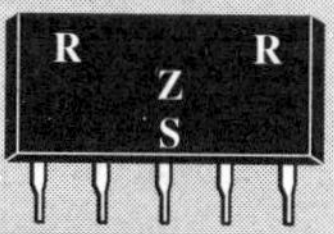

Processor unit (P)

Working from back to front of the box casing (B), assemble one switch (S) to the inside of each of the 4 plug connections at the back of the box. Then fit 3 memory boards (M) into the 3 identical rows of connectors. Finally, fit 2 arithmetic boards (A) into the front connector rows.

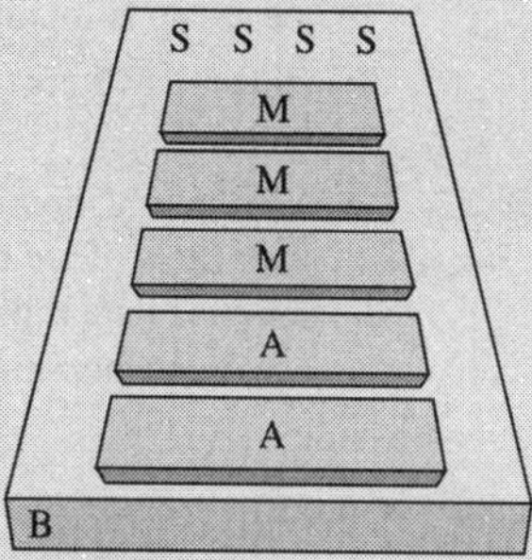

Final assembly

The video unit (V) and the keyboard unit (K) have been preassembled (with connecting cables). Simply connect the sockets on the end of their cables to the corresponding plugs at the rear of the processor unit (P). Your computer is now ready to use.

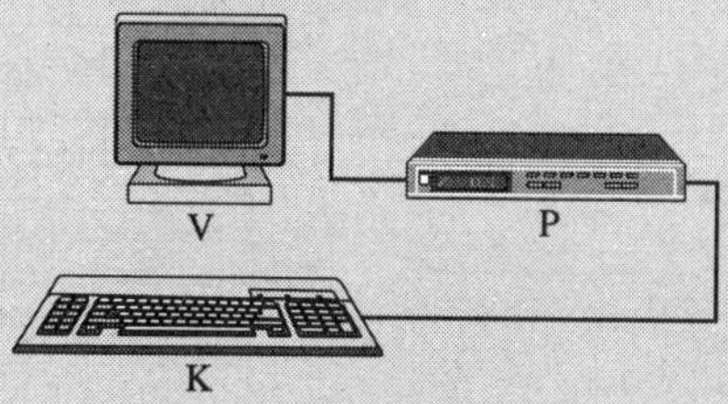

a. Draw the product structure tree corresponding to the assembly instructions.

b. Determine low-level codes for the following items: (1) A—arithmetic board, (2) B—box casing, (3) C—RAM chip, (4) K—keyboard unit, (5) M—memory board, (6) P—Processor unit, (7) R—ROM chip, (8) S—switch, (9) V—video unit, (10) X—board type X, (11) Y—board type Y, and (12) Z—integrated microprocessor.

c. Assume no inventory of any item. How many of each part should be available to assemble one completed unit?

3. Power Tools (PT) has just received an order for 70 PT band saws, to be shipped at the beginning of week 9. Information concerning the saw assembly is given here:

PT Band Saw

Item	Lead Time (weeks)	Components
Saw	2	A(2*), B, C(3)
A	1	E(3), D
B	2	D(2), F(3)
C	2	E(2), D(2)
D	1	
E	1	
F	3	

*Number of parts required to make one parent.

a. Draw the product structure tree.

b. Construct a Gantt chart for the new order using front schedule logic.

c. Construct a Gantt chart for the new order using back schedule logic.

4. The recipe for 6 servings of Martha's Triple Chocolate Smoothie calls for 4 dashes of cinnamon, 1.5 liters of vanilla ice cream, 2 liters of chocolate ice cream, 0.5 liter of chocolate milk, and 1 bag of chocolate chips.

a. Martha is planning an ice cream social for 12 people and wants to make Triple Chocolate Smoothies. How much chocolate ice cream does she need for 12 servings if her chocolate ice cream is totally gone?

b. How many liters of vanilla ice cream must be bought if Martha already has one liter of vanilla on hand?

c. Martha is planning her party for November 15. It's now November 11. The local dairy will deliver liters of ice cream and milk if given a one-day notice. Fill in the following MRP record for chocolate milk if Martha has 0.5 liter on hand and wants the rest delivered. Assume she can make the Smoothies on the day of the social.

		November				
		11	12	13	14	15
Gross requirements						
Scheduled receipts						
Projected available balance						
Planned order release						

5. Develop an MRP spreadsheet record for six periods using the following parameters for the item:

Period	1	2	3	4	5	6
Gross requirements	20	20	40	30	30	30

Lead time	1 period
Lot size	50 units
Safety stock	0 units
Inventory	2 units
Scheduled receipt	50 units in period 1

a. In what periods are there planned order releases?

b. What happens to the timing, number of planned order releases, and average inventory (for periods 1 through 6) if 15 units of safety stock are required?

c. What happens to the timing, number of planned order releases, and average inventory (for periods 1 through 6) if a one-week safety lead time is used instead of the safety stock?

6. Given the following product structure diagram, complete the MRP records for parts A, B, and C.

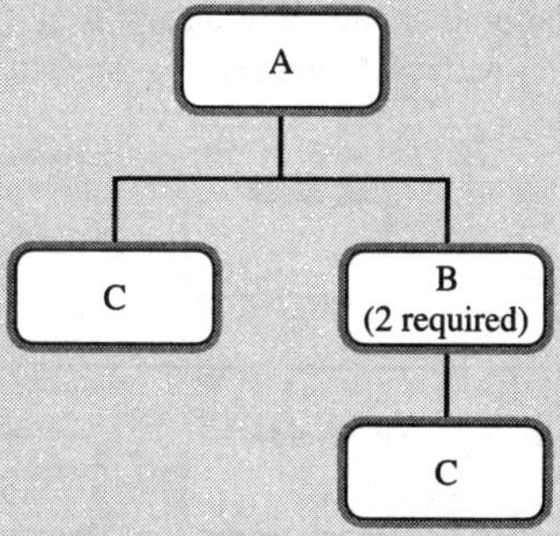

Part A		1	2	3	4	5	6
Gross requirements		5	15	18	8	12	22
Scheduled receipts							
Projected available balance	21						
Planned order release							

Q = 20; LT = 1; SS = 0.

Part B		1	2	3	4	5	6
Gross requirements							
Scheduled receipts		32					
Projected available balance	20						
Planned order release							

Q = 40; LT = 2; SS = 0.

Part C		1	2	3	4	5	6
Gross requirements							
Scheduled receipts							
Projected available balance	70						
Planned order release							

Q = LFL; LT = 1; SS = 10.

7. Given the product structure diagrams at Traci's Tomahawk shown below, complete the MRP records for parts A, F, and G using the data provided for each.

Product Structures

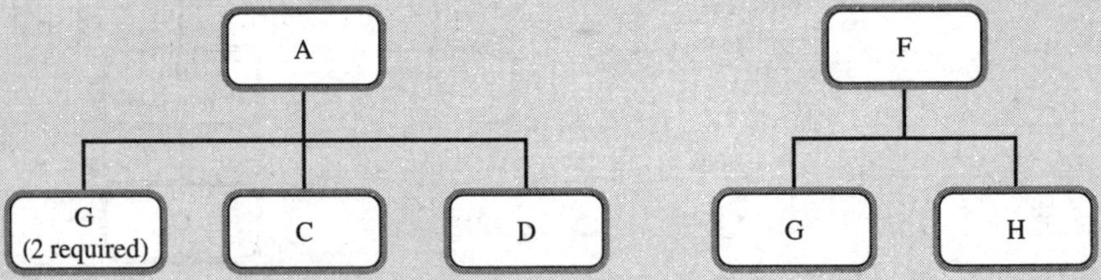

Part A		Week 1	2	3	4	5
Gross requirement		5	3	10	15	15
Scheduled receipt		5				
Projected available balance	10					
Planned order release						

Lead time = 1; Q = L4L; SS = 0.

Part F		Week 1	2	3	4	5
Gross requirement		10	20	25	15	5
Scheduled receipt			15			
Projected available balance	15					
Planned order release						

Lead time = 2; Q = L4L; SS = 0.

Part G		Week 1	2	3	4	5
Gross requirement						
Scheduled receipt		20				
Projected available balance	30					
Planned order releases						

Lead time = 1; Q = multiples of 20; SS = 10.

8. Ajax produces two basic products called A and B. Each week, Paul, the owner, plans to assemble 20 product As and 8 product Bs.

a. Given this information and the following product structure diagrams for A and B, fill out the MRP records (inventory status files) for component parts G and Y for the next seven weeks.

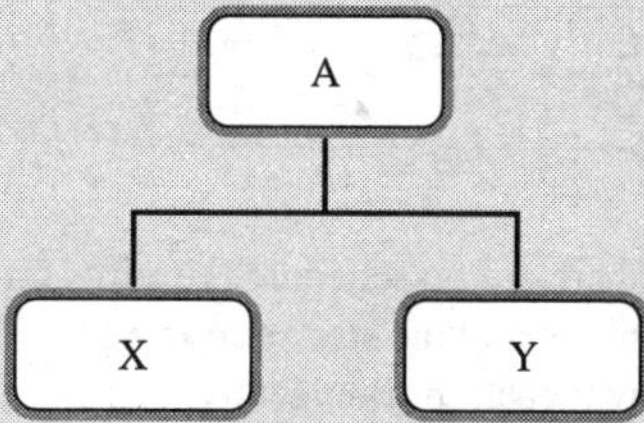

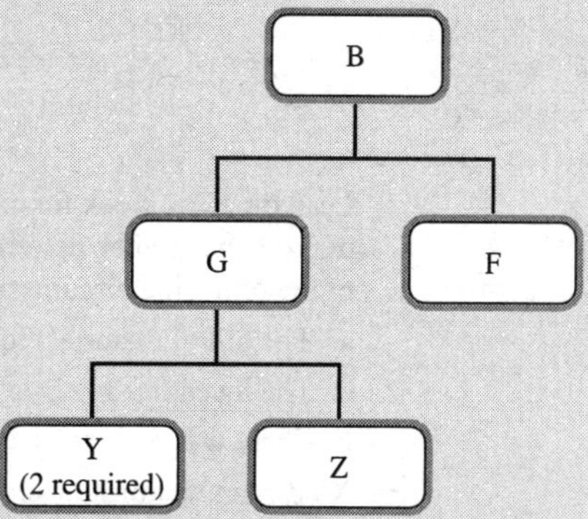

Part G		Week 1	2	3	4	5	6	7
Gross requirements								
Scheduled receipts		10						
Projected available balance	0							
Planned order release								

Q = lot for lot; LT = 1; SS = 0.

Part Y		Week 1	2	3	4	5	6	7
Gross requirements								
Scheduled receipts		10						
Projected available balance	67							
Planned order release								

Q = lot-for-lot; LT = 2; SS = 0.

b. Suppose 10 units of safety stock are required for part Y. What changes would result in the records? Would the MRP system produce any exception messages?

9. Consider the following product structure and inventory information:

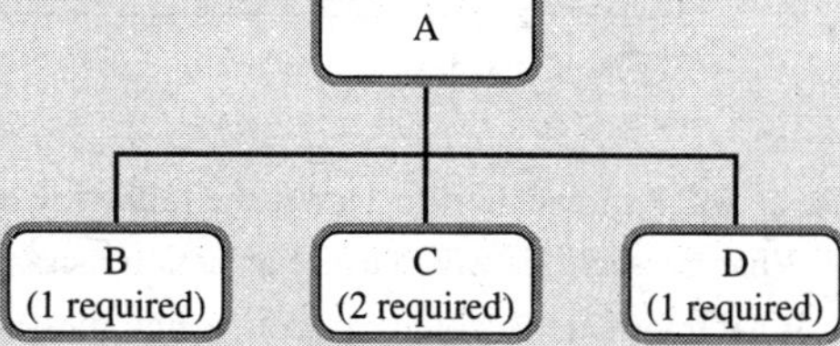

Item	Inventory
A	10
B	40
C	60
D	60

Lead time = 1 week for all items. There are no scheduled receipts for any item. How many units of product A can be delivered to customers at the start of next week (i.e., in one week) under each of the following circumstances? (Treat each independently; that is, only a, only b, or only c.)

a. The bill of materials for B is wrong. It actually takes 2 units of B to make an A.

b. The inventory for D is only 30 units.

c. There was need to scrap 5 units of the inventory for item C.

10. XYZ Manufacturing Company has collected 10 periods of data for two of its products, A and B. Using the two data sets as gross requirements data, construct MRP time-phased records. Using a spreadsheet program, create four time-phased records, two for each data set. For one case, use a lot size of 150 units, and for the other use an order quantity equal to the total net requirements for the next three periods. In all four records, start with a beginning inventory of 150 units and compute the average inventory level held over the 10 periods. What do the results mean?

	Period									
Demand	1	2	3	4	5	6	7	8	9	10
A	71	46	49	55	52	47	51	48	56	51
B	77	83	90	22	10	10	16	19	27	79

11. Consider the information contained in the planned order row of the following MRP record. The planned order releases in weeks 2 and 4 are firm planned orders and cannot be changed without managerial approval.

		Period				
		1	2	3	4	5
Gross requirements		10	30	20	15	20
Scheduled receipts		40				
Projected available balance	10	40	10	30	15	35
Planned order release (firm)			40		40	

Q = 40; LT = 1; SS = 5.

Use an MRP spreadsheet to answer the following questions:

a. What transactions would cause an action message on the firm planned order in week 2?

b. What transactions would cause an action message on the firm planned order in week 4?

12. Consider the following MRP record:

		Week 1	2	3	4	5	6
Gross requirements		25	30	5	15	5	10
Scheduled receipts			50			15	
Projected available balance	35	10	30	25	10	20	10
Planned order releases							

Q = lot-for-lot; LT = 5; SS = 0.

Suppose 15 units of the scheduled receipt for 50 units due on Monday of week 2 are scrapped during week 1, and no scrap ticket is issued. Furthermore, assume this lot isn't counted before it's put away in the stockroom on Monday of week 2, but is recorded as a receipt of 50 units. What impact will these actions have on factory operations?

13. Complete the following MRP time-phased record:

Item: Toaster		Week 1	2	3	4	5	6	7	8
Gross requirements		20	20	35	25	35	35	35	35
Scheduled receipts		50							
Projected available balance	10								
Planned order release									

Q = 50; LT = 2; SS = 5.

The following events occurred during week 1:

1. Actual demand during week 1 was only 5 units.
2. A scheduled receipt of 45 was received during week 1.
3. A cycle count of on-hand units showed 17 units at the start of week 1.
4. Marketing forecasted that 40 toasters would be required in week 9.

Update the record below after rolling through time.

Item: Toaster		Week 2	3	4	5	6	7	8	9
Gross requirements		20	25	25	35	35	35	35	
Scheduled receipts			50						
Projected available balance									
Planned order release									

Q = 50; LT = 2; SS = 5.

14. The MPC system at ABC Manufacturing Company is run weekly to update the master production schedule (MPS) and MRP records. At the start of week 1, the MPS for end products X and Y is:

Master Production Schedule

Week Number	1	2	3	4	5	6
Product X	10	—	25	5	10	—
Product Y	5	30	—	20	—	20

One unit of component C is required to manufacture one unit of either end product X or Y. Purchasing lead time for component C is two weeks, an order quantity of 40 units is used, and no (zero) safety stock is maintained for this item. Inventory balance for component C is 5 units at the start of week 1, and there's an open order (scheduled receipt) for 40 units due to be delivered at the beginning of week 1.

a. Complete the MRP record for component C as it would appear at the beginning of week 1:

		Week 1	2	3	4	5	6
Gross requirements							
Scheduled receipts							
Projected available balance							
Planned order releases							

b. During week 1, the following transactions occurred for component C:

1. The open order for 40 units due to be received at the start of week 1 was received on Monday of week 1 with a quantity of 30 (10 units of component C were scrapped on this order).
2. An inventory cycle count during week 1 revealed that five units of component C were missing. Thus, an inventory adjustment of –5 was processed.
3. Ten units of component C were actually disbursed (instead of the 15 units planned for disbursement to produce end products X and Y). (The MPS quantity of 5 in week 1 for product B was canceled as a result of a customer order cancellation.)
4. The MPS quantities for week 7 include 15 units for product X and 0 units for product Y.
5. Because of a change in customer order requirements, marketing has requested that the MPS quantity of 25 units for product X scheduled in week 3 be moved to week 2.
6. An order for 40 units was released.

Given this information, complete the MRP record for component C as it would appear at the beginning of week 2:

		Week 2	3	4	5	6	7
Gross requirements							
Scheduled receipts							
Projected available balance							
Planned order releases							

What action(s) are required by the inventory planner at the start of week 2 as a result of transactions occurring during week 1?

15. Use a spreadsheet program to develop the MRP records for parts A and B from the following product structure. Use the data from the following table:

Part	A	B
Requirements	50/period	—
Initial inventory balance	63	8
Lead time	1	1
Lot size	lot-for-lot	250
Safety stock	10	—
Scheduled receipt	—	250 in period 1

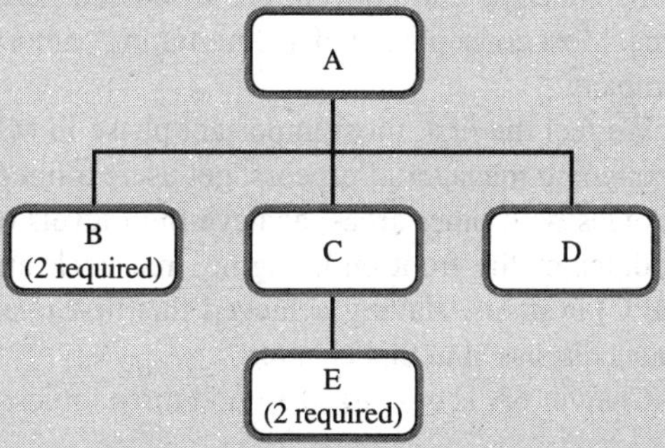

a. What are the planned orders for item B?
b. On an unlucky day (it must have been the 13th), the planner for part A found that the inventory was wrong by 13 units. Instead of 63, there were only 55 on hand. What happens to the planned orders for part B?
c. Use the spreadsheet model to generate a 10-period material plan for parts A and B. Assume that the 63 units of inventory for A were correct. Suppose that in period 1, actual demand for part A was 60 units instead of 50. Regenerate the spreadsheet for periods 2 through 11. What changes occur in the material plans for parts A and B?

Chapter 6A

Advanced MRP

This chapter concerns some advanced issues in material requirements planning (MRP). Some concepts and conventions discussed here can improve well-functioning basic systems. Most concepts are of a "fine-tuning" nature and can provide additional benefits to the company.

We feel the first, most important phase in MRP is to install the system, make it part of an ongoing managerial process, get users trained in the use of MRP, understand the critical linkages with other areas, achieve high levels of data integrity, and link MRP with other modules of the front end, engine, and back end of manufacturing planning and control (MPC) systems. Having achieved this first phase, many firms then turn to the advanced issues discussed in this chapter.

Chapter 6A is organized around three topics:

- *Determining manufacturing order quantities:* What are the basic trade-offs in lot sizing in the MRP environment, and what techniques are useful?
- *Buffering concepts:* What are the types of uncertainties in MRP, and how can we buffer against these uncertainties?
- *Nervousness:* Why are MRP systems subject to nervousness, and how do firms deal with system nervousness?

Determining Manufacturing Order Quantities

The MRP system converts the master production schedule into a time-phased schedule for all intermediate assemblies and component parts. Detailed schedules consist of two parts: scheduled receipts (open orders) and planned orders. Each scheduled receipt's quantity and timing (due date) have been determined prior to release to the shop. We determine quantities and timings for planned orders via MRP logic using the inventory position, the gross requirements data, and specific procedures for making the decisions.

A number of quantity-determination (lot-sizing) procedures have been developed for determining order quantities in MRP systems, ranging from **ordering as required (lot-for-lot),** to simple decision rules, and finally to extensive optimizing procedures. This section describes four such lot-sizing procedures using a common problem.

The primary consideration in the development of lot-sizing procedures for MRP is the nature of the net requirements data. The demand dependency relationship from the product structures and the time-phased gross requirements mean the net requirements for an item might appear as illustrated in Figure 6A.1. First, it's important to note that the requirements do *not* reflect the key independent demand assumption of a constant uniform demand. Second, the requirements are *discrete,* since they're stated on a period-by-period basis (time-phased), rather than as a rate (e.g., an average of so much per month or year). Finally, the requirements can be *lumpy;* that is, they can vary substantially from period to period and even have periods with no requirements.

MRP lot-sizing procedures are designed specifically for the discrete demand case. One problem in selecting a procedure is that reductions in inventory-related costs can generally be achieved only by using increasingly complex procedures. Such procedures require more computations in making lot-sizing determinations. A second problem concerns local optimization. The lot-sizing procedure used for one part in an MRP system has a direct impact on the gross requirements data passed to its component parts. The use of procedures other than lot-for-lot tends to increase gross requirements data lumpiness further down in the product structure.

The manufacturing lot-size problem is basically one of converting requirements into a series of replenishment orders. If we consider this problem on a local level—that is, only in terms of the one part and not its components—the problem involves determining how to group time-phased requirements data into a schedule of replenishment orders that minimizes the combined costs of placing manufacturing orders and carrying inventory.

Because MRP systems normally replan on a daily or weekly basis, timing affects the assumptions commonly made in using MRP lot-sizing procedures. These assumptions are as follows. First, since we aggregate component requirements by time period for planning purposes, we assume all requirements for each period must be available at the beginning of the period. Second, we assume all requirements for future periods must be met and can't be back ordered. Third, since the system is operated on a periodic basis, we assume ordering decisions occur at regular time intervals (e.g., daily or weekly). Fourth, we assume the requirements are properly offset for manufacturing lead times. Finally, we assume component requirements are satisfied at a uniform rate during each period. Therefore, we use average inventory level in computing inventory carrying costs.

In the following sections, we'll illustrate the results from applying four different ordering procedures to the example data in Figure 6A.1. This example will illustrate how these

FIGURE 6A.1 **Example Problem: Weekly Net Requirements Schedule**

Week number	1	2	3	4	5	6	7	8	9	10	11	12
Requirements	10	10	15	20	70	180	250	270	230	40	0	10

Ordering cost = C_P = \$300 per order
Inventory carrying cost = C_H = \$2 per unit per week
Average requirements = $\overline{D}$ = 92.1

procedures vary in their assumptions and how much they utilize available data in making lot-sizing decisions.

Economic Order Quantities (EOQ)

Because of its simplicity, people often use the **economic order quantity (EOQ)** formula as a decision rule for placing orders in a requirements planning system. As the following example shows, however, the EOQ model frequently must be modified in requirements planning system applications. Because we base the EOQ on the assumption of constant uniform demand, the resulting total cost expression won't necessarily be valid for requirements planning applications.

Figure 6A.2 shows the results of ordering material in economic lot sizes for the example data. In this example the EOQ formula used average weekly demand of 92.1 units for the entire requirements schedule to compute the economic lot size. Note, too, order quantities are shown when received, and average inventory for each period was used in computing the inventory carrying cost.

This example illustrates several problems with using economic lot sizes. When the requirements aren't equal from period to period, as is often the case in MRP, fixed EOQ lot sizes result in a mismatch between order quantities and requirements values. This can mean excess inventory must be carried forward from week to week. As an example, 41 units are carried over into week 6 when a new order is received.

In addition, we must increase the order quantity in those periods where the requirements exceed the economic lot size plus the amount of inventory carried over into the period. An example occurs in week 7. This modification is clearly preferable to the alternative of placing orders earlier to meet demand in such periods, since this would only increase inventory carrying costs. Likewise, the alternative of placing multiple orders in a given period would needlessly increase the ordering cost.

Finally, use of the average weekly requirements figure in computing economic lot size ignores much of the other information in the requirements schedule. This information concerns magnitude of demand. For instance, there appear to be two levels of component demand in this example. The first covers weeks 1 to 4 and 10 to 12; the second covers weeks 5 to 9. We could compute an economic lot size for each of these time intervals and place

FIGURE 6A.2 Economic Order Quantity Example

Week number	1	2	3	4	5	6	7	8	9	10	11	12
Requirements	10	10	15	20	70	180	250	270	230	40	0	10
Order quantity	166					166	223	270	230	166		
Beginning inventory	166	156	146	131	111	207	250	270	230	166	126	126
Ending inventory	156	146	131	111	41	27	0	0	0	126	126	116

Ordering cost	$1,800
Inventory carrying cost	3,065
Total cost	$4,865

(Economic lot size $= \sqrt{2C_P\bar{D}/C_H} = \sqrt{2(300)(92.1)/2} = 166$)

FIGURE 6A.3 Periodic Order Quantity Example

Week number	1	2	3	4	5	6	7	8	9	10	11	12
Requirements	10	10	15	20	70	180	250	270	230	40	0	10
Order quantity	20		35		250		520		270			10
Beginning inventory	20	10	35	20	250	180	520	270	270	40	0	10
Ending inventory	10	0	20	0	180	0	270	0	40	0	0	0

Ordering cost	$1,800
Inventory carrying cost	2,145
Total cost	$3,945

orders accordingly. This proposal, however, would be difficult to implement because determining different demand levels requires a very complex decision rule.

Periodic Order Quantities (POQ)

One way to reduce the high inventory carrying cost associated with fixed lot sizes is to use the EOQ formula to compute an economic **time between orders (TBO).** We do this by dividing the EOQ by the mean demand rate. In the preceding example, the economic time interval is approximately two weeks ($166/92.1 = 1.8$). The procedure then calls for ordering *exactly* the requirements for a two-week interval. This is termed the **periodic order quantity (POQ).** Applying this procedure to the data in our example (Figure 6A.1) produces Figure 6A.3. The result is the same number of orders as the EOQ produces, but with lot sizes ranging from 20 to 520 units. Consequently, inventory carrying cost has been reduced by 30 percent, thereby improving the total cost of the 12-week requirements schedule by 19 percent in comparison with the preceding EOQ result.

Although the POQ procedure improves inventory cost performance by allowing lot sizes to vary, like the EOQ procedure it too ignores much of the information in the requirements schedule. Replenishment orders are constrained to occur at fixed time intervals, thereby ruling out the possibility of combining orders during periods of light product demand (e.g., during weeks 1 through 4 in the example). If, for example, orders placed in weeks 1 and 3 were combined and a single order were placed in week 1 for 55 units, combined costs can be further reduced by $160, or 4 percent.

Part Period Balancing (PPB)

The **part period balancing (PPB)** procedure uses all the information provided by the requirements schedule. In determining an order's lot size, this procedure tries to equate the total costs of placing orders and carrying inventory. We illustrate this point by considering the alternative lot-size choices available at the beginning of week 1. These include placing an order covering the requirements for:

1. Week 1 only.
2. Weeks 1 and 2.
3. Weeks 1, 2, and 3.
4. Weeks 1, 2, 3, and 4.
5. Weeks 1, 2, 3, 4, and 5, etc.

Inventory carrying costs for these five alternatives are shown below. We base these calculations on average inventory per period, hence the 1/2 (average for one week), 3/2 (one week plus the average for the second week), and so on.

1. $(\$2) \cdot [(1/2) \cdot 10] = \$10.$
2. $(\$2) \cdot [(1/2) \cdot 10] + [(3/2) \cdot 10] = 40.$
3. $(\$2) \cdot [(1/2) \cdot 10] + [(3/2) \cdot 10] + [(5/2) \cdot 15] = \$115.$
4. $(\$2) \cdot [(1/2) \cdot 10] + [(3/2) \cdot 10] + [(5/2) \cdot 15] + [(7/2) \cdot 20] = \$255.$
5. $(\$2) \cdot [(1/2) \cdot 10] + [(3/2) \cdot 10] + [(5/2) \cdot 15] + [(7/2) \cdot 20] + [(9/2) \cdot 70] = \$885.$

In this case, the inventory carrying cost for alternative 4 (ordering 55 units to cover demand for the first four weeks) most nearly approximates the $300 ordering cost; that is, alternative 4 "balances" the cost of carrying inventory with the ordering cost. Therefore, we should place an order at the beginning of the first week and the next ordering decision need not be made until the beginning of week 5.

When we apply this procedure to all the example data, we get the result in Figure 6A.4. As seen, total inventory cost falls almost $500—it's 13 percent lower than the cost obtained with the periodic order quantity procedure. The PPB procedure permits both lot size and time between orders to vary. Thus, for example, in periods of low requirements, it yields smaller lot sizes and longer time intervals between orders than occur in high demand periods. This results in lower inventory-related costs.

Despite the fact that PPB utilizes all available information, it won't always yield the minimum-cost ordering plan. Although this procedure can produce low-cost plans, it may miss the minimum cost, since it doesn't evaluate all possibilities for ordering material to satisfy demand in each week of the requirements schedule.

Wagner-Whitin Algorithm

One optimizing procedure for determining the minimum-cost ordering plan for a time-phased requirements schedule is the **Wagner-Whitin (WW)** algorithm. Basically, this procedure evaluates all possible ways of ordering material to meet demand in each week of the requirements schedule, using dynamic programming. We won't attempt to describe the computational aspects of the Wagner-Whitin algorithm in the space available here. Rather, we'll note the difference in performance between this procedure and the part period balancing procedure.

FIGURE 6A.4 Part Period Balancing Example

Week number	1	2	3	4	5	6	7	8	9	10	11	12
Requirements	10	10	15	20	70	180	250	270	230	40	0	10
Order quantity	55				70	180	250	270	270			10
Beginning inventory	55	45	35	20	70	180	250	270	270	40	0	10
Ending inventory	45	35	20	0	0	0	0	0	40	0	0	0

Ordering cost	$2,100
Inventory carrying cost	1,385
Total cost	$3,485

FIGURE 6A.5 Wagner-Whitin Example

Week number	1	2	3	4	5	6	7	8	9	10	11	12
Requirements	10	10	15	20	70	180	250	270	230	40	0	10
Order quantity	55				70	180	250	270	280			
Beginning inventory	55	45	35	20	70	180	250	270	280	50	10	10
Ending inventory	45	35	20	0	0	0	0	0	50	10	10	0

Ordering cost	$1,800
Inventory carrying cost	1,445
Total cost	$3,245

Figure 6A.5 shows the results of applying the Wagner-Whitin algorithm to the example. Total inventory cost is reduced by $240, or 7 percent, compared with the ordering plan produced by the part period balancing procedure in Figure 6A.4. The difference between these two plans occurs in the lot size ordered in week 9. The part period balancing procedure didn't consider the combined cost of placing orders in both weeks 9 and 12. By spending an additional $60 to carry 10 units of inventory forward from week 9 to 12, we avoid the $300 ordering cost in week 12. In this case, we can save $240 in total cost. The increased number of ordering alternatives considered, however, clearly increases the computations needed in making ordering decisions.

Simulation Experiments

The example problem we've used to illustrate these procedures is for only one product item, without regard for *its* components, with no rolling through time, and with only a fixed number of weeks of requirements. To better understand lot-sizing procedures' performance, we should compare them in circumstances more closely related to company dynamics. Many simulation experiments do exactly that.

Figure 6A.6 presents summary experimental results. The first experiment in this figure is for a single level (i.e., one MRP record) with no uncertainty. PPB, POQ, and EOQ are compared to Wagner-Whitin. PPB produces results about 6 percent more costly, POQ about 11 percent, and EOQ over 30 percent greater than Wagner-Whitin. These differences may be more important than the magnitudes indicate. Total cost savings of 6 percent may not be trivial.

Moving down to the third experiment,[1] we see results for a multilevel situation, again with no uncertainty. In this case, the comparison isn't against Wagner-Whitin, but against a dynamic programming procedure that produces close to optimal results in a multilevel environment. The key finding in this experiment is that the results are roughly the same as in the first comparisons, although POQ does a little worse and PPB a little better than in the first experiment.

Perhaps the most interesting result in Figure 6A.6 comes from comparing the first and third experiments to the *second* experiment. The second experiment is for a single-level procedure, but *with* uncertainty expressed in the gross requirements data. The results here are quite

[1]B. J. McLaren, "A Study of Multiple Level Hot Sizing Techniques for Material Requirements Planning Systems," Ph.D. Dissertation, Purdue University, 1977.

FIGURE 6A.6
Summary Experimental Results

	Procedure			
	Wagner-Whitin	PPB	POQ	EOQ
Experiment 1: Percent over Wagner-Whitin cost; Single level, no uncertainty	0	5.74	10.72	33.87
Experiment 2: Percent over Wagner-Whitin cost; Single level, uncertainty	0	0.67	2.58	0.19
Experiment 3: Percent over nearly optimal procedure; Multilevel, no uncertainty	0.77	6.92	16.91	—
Computing time	0.30	0.10	0.08	—

mixed. Note PPB does *better* than Wagner-Whitin, and both POQ and EOQ are within 3 percent of Wagner-Whitin.

The conditions modeled in the second experiment replicate conditions likely to be found in actual industrial situations. Moreover, other studies show as uncertainty grows increasingly larger, it becomes very hard to distinguish between lot-sizing procedures' performance. What's more, while there were statistically significant differences among procedures in the first experiment, there were none in the second.

The message is clear. Lot-sizing enhancements to an MRP system should only be done *after* major uncertainties have been removed from the system: that is, *after* data integrity is in place, other MPC system modules are working, stability is present at the MPS level, and so on. If the MPC isn't performing effectively, that's the place to start, *not* with lot-sizing procedures.

Buffering Concepts

In this section we deal with another advanced concept in MRP, the use of buffering mechanisms to protect against uncertainties. We, however, make the same proviso as for lot sizing: Buffering is not the way to make up for a poorly operating MRP system. First things must come first.

Categories of Uncertainty

Two basic sources of uncertainty affect an MRP system: demand and supply uncertainty. These are further separated into two types: quantity uncertainty and timing uncertainty. The combination of sources and types provides the four categories of uncertainty illustrated in Figures 6A.7 and 6A.8.

Demand timing uncertainty is illustrated in Figure 6A.8 by timing changes in the requirements from period to period. For example, the projected requirements for 372 units in period 7 actually occurred in period 4. This shift might result from a change in the promise date to a customer or from a change in a planned order for a higher-level item on which this item is used.

Supply timing uncertainty can arise from variations in vendor lead times or shop flow times. Thus, once an order is released, the exact timing of its arrival is uncertain. In Figure 6A.8, for example, a receipt scheduled for period 3 actually arrived in period 1. Note in this case the uncertainty isn't over the order's amount but over its timing. The entire order may be late or early.

FIGURE 6A.7 Categories of Uncertainty in MRP Systems

Types	Sources: Demand	Sources: Supply
Timing	Requirements shift from one period to another	Orders not received when due
Quantity	Requirements for more or less than planned	Orders received for more or less than planned

FIGURE 6A.8 Examples of the Four Categories of Uncertainty

	Periods 1	2	3	4	5	6	7	8	9	10
Demand timing:										
Projected requirements	0	0	0	0	0	0	372	130	0	255
Actual requirements	0	0	0	372	130	0	146	255	143	0
Supply timing:										
Planned receipts	0	0	502	0	0	403	0	0	144	0
Actual receipts	502	0	0	0	0	403	0	0	144	0
Demand quantity:										
Projected requirements	85	122	42	190	83	48	41	46	108	207
Actual requirements	103	77	0	101	124	15	0	100	80	226
Supply quantity:										
Planned receipts	0	161	0	271	51	0	81	109	0	327
Actual receipts	0	158	0	277	50	0	77	113	0	321

Demand quantity uncertainty is manifest when the amount of a requirement varies, perhaps randomly, about some mean value. This might occur when the master production schedule is increased or decreased to reflect changes in customer orders or the demand forecast. It can also occur when there are changes on higher-level items on which this item is used, or when there are variations in inventory levels. In Figure 6A.8, period 1's projected requirements of 85 actually turned out to be 103 units of usage.

Supply quantity uncertainty typically arises when there are shortages of lower-level material, when production lots incur scrap losses, or when production overruns occur. Figure 6A.8 illustrates this category of uncertainty, where actual quantity received varied around planned receipts.

Safety Stock and Safety Lead Time

There are two basic ways to buffer uncertainty in an MRP system. One is to specify a quantity of safety stock in much the same manner as with statistical inventory control techniques. The second method, safety lead time, plans order releases earlier than indicated by the requirements plan and schedules their receipt earlier than the required due date. Both approaches produce an increase in inventory levels to provide a buffer against uncertainty, but the techniques operate quite differently, as Figure 6A.9 shows.

FIGURE 6A.9 Safety Stock and Safety Lead Time Buffering

Order quantity = 50 units
Lead time = 2 periods

No Buffering Used

Period		1	2	3	4	5
Gross requirements		20	40	20	0	30
Scheduled receipts			50			
Projected available balance	40	20	30	10	10	30
Planned order released				50		

Safety Stock = 20 Units

		1	2	3	4	5
Gross requirements		20	40	20	0	30
Scheduled receipts			50			
Projected available balance	40	20	30	60	60	30
Planned order releases		50				

Safety Lead Time = 1 Period

		1	2	3	4	5
Gross requirements		20	40	20	0	30
Scheduled receipts			50			
Projected available balance	40	20	30	10	60	30
Planned order releases			50			

The first case in Figure 6A.9 uses no buffering. A net requirement occurs in period 5, and a planned order is created in period 3 to cover it. The second case specifies a safety stock of 20 units. This means the safety stock level will be broken in period 3 unless an order arrives. The MRP logic thus creates a planned order in period 1 to prevent this condition. The final case in Figure 6A.9 illustrates use of safety lead time. This example includes a safety lead time of one period. The net result is the planned order being created in period 2 with a due date of period 4.

Most MRP software packages can easily accommodate safety stock, since we can determine planned orders simply by subtracting the safety stock from the initial inventory balance when determining the projected available balance. Safety lead time is a bit more difficult. We can't achieve it by simply inflating the lead time by the amount of the safety lead time. In our example, this approach wouldn't produce the result shown as the last case in Figure 6A.9. The due date for the order would be period 5, instead of period 4. Thus, we must change the planned due date as well as the planned release date.

Both safety stock and safety lead time illustrate the fundamental problem with all MRP buffering techniques: They lie to the system. The *real* need date for the planned order shown in Figure 6A.9 is period 5. If the *real* lead time is two periods, the *real* launch date should be period 3. Putting in buffers can lead to behavioral problems in the shop, since the resulting schedules don't tell the truth. An informal system may be created to tell people what's really needed. This, in turn, might lead to larger buffers. There's a critical need to communicate the reasoning behind the use of safety stock and safety lead times, and to create a working MPC system that minimizes the need for buffers.

Safety Stock and Safety Lead Time Performance Comparisons

Simulation experiments reveal a preference for using either safety stock or safety lead time, depending on the category of uncertainty to be buffered. These results show a distinct preference for using safety lead time in all cases where demand or supply *timing* uncertainty exists. Likewise, the experiments show a strong preference for using safety stock in all cases where there's uncertainty in either the demand or supply *quantity*.

Figures 6A.10 and 6A.11 show typical results from these experiments. Figure 6A.10 compares safety stock and safety lead time for simulated situations similar to Figure 6A.8's top two examples. The horizontal axis shows the average inventory held, and the vertical axis depicts the service level in percentage terms; that is, the horizontal axis is based on the period-by-period actual inventory values in the simulation, and the vertical axis is based on the frequency with which actual requirements were met from inventory.

FIGURE 6A.10
Experimental Results: Average Inventory versus Service Level with Timing Uncertainty

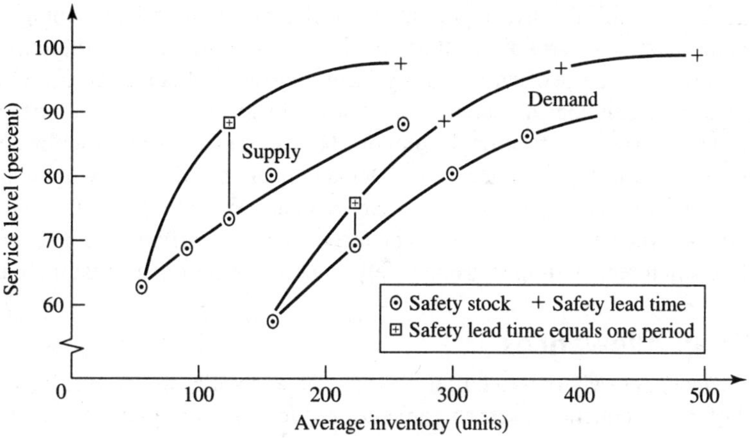

FIGURE 6A.11
Experimental Results: Average Inventory versus Service Level with Quantity Uncertainty

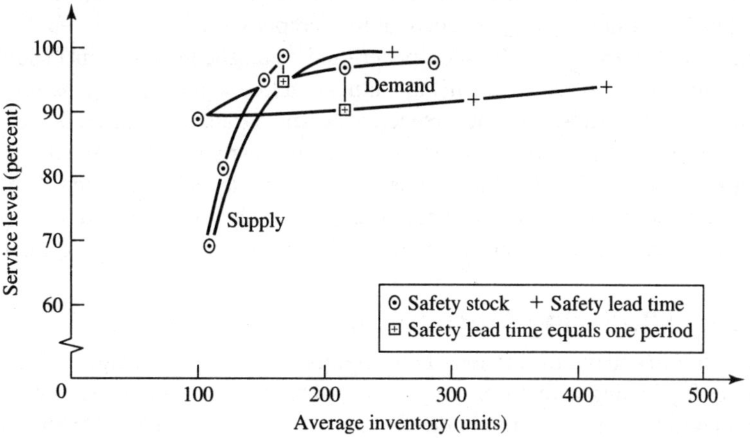

For both the supply and the demand timing uncertainty cases, Figure 6A.10 shows a strong preference for safety lead time buffering. For any given level of inventory, a higher service level can be achieved with safety lead time than with safety stock. For any given level of service, safety lead time can provide the level with a smaller inventory investment.

Figure 6A.11 shows the comparison for uncertainty in quantities. This simulated situation is similar to Figure 6A.8's bottom two examples. The results are a bit more difficult to see, since the graphs for supply and demand uncertainty overlap. Nevertheless, the results are again clear. For any given level of inventory investment, higher service levels are achieved by use of safety stocks than by use of safety lead times. This result is true for situations involving quantity uncertainty in both demand and supply.

The results of the experiments provide general guidelines for choosing between the two buffering techniques. Under conditions of uncertainty in timing, safety lead time is the preferred technique, while safety stock is preferred under conditions of quantity uncertainty. The experimental conclusions didn't change with the source of the uncertainty (demand or supply), lot-sizing technique, lead time, average demand level, uncertainty level, or lumpiness in the gross requirements data. The experiments also indicate that, as lumpiness and uncertainty levels increase, so does the importance of making the correct choice between safety stock and safety lead time.

These guidelines have important practical implications. Supply timing uncertainty and demand quantity uncertainty are the two categories with the largest differences in service levels. An obvious instance of supply timing uncertainty is in vendor lead times. Orders from vendors are subject to timing uncertainty due to variability in both production and transportation times.

These experiments strongly support the use of safety lead time for purchased parts experiencing this type of uncertainty. Demand quantity uncertainty often appears in an MRP system for parts subject to service part demand. Another cause of demand quantity uncertainty is when an end product can be made from very different options or features. The experimental results support using safety stock for buffering against these uncertainties.

Scrap Allowances

A concept closely tied to buffering is use of scrap allowances in calculating the lot size to start into production to reach some desired lot size going into the stockroom. It's a fairly straightforward procedure to use any lot-sizing procedure to determine the lot size and then adjust the result to take into account the scrap allowance. One issue that arises is whether the quantity shown on the shop paper (and as a scheduled receipt) should be the *starting* quantity or the *expected finished* quantity. Practice suggests using the former. This requires, however, that each actual occurrence of scrap be transacted and reflected in updated plans.

The overall issue of the scrap allowance is clearly related to the use of safety stocks for quantity uncertainty buffering. One or both of these techniques could be used in a particular situation. The point is, if scrap losses occur, they must be planned for and buffered. It also means this may be an area where tight control can lead to performance improvements.

Other Buffering Mechanisms

Before we end our discussion of uncertainty, it's useful to consider some additional alternatives for dealing with uncertainty. First, rather than live with uncertainty, an alternative is to reduce it to an absolute minimum. In fact, that's one of the major objectives of MPC systems.

For example, increasing demand forecasts' accuracy and developing effective procedures for translating demand for products into master schedules reduces the uncertainty transmitted to the MRP system. Freezing the master schedule for some time period achieves the same result. Developing an effective priority system for moving parts and components through the shop reduces the uncertainty in lead times. Responsive shop-floor control systems can achieve better due date performance, thereby reducing uncertainty. Procedures that improve the accuracy of the data in the MRP system reduce uncertainty regarding on-hand inventory levels. Aspects of JIT manufacturing reduce lead time, improve quality, and decrease uncertainty, providing the same benefits. Other activities could be mentioned, but all focus on the reduction of the amount of uncertainty that needs to be accommodated in an MRP system.

Another way to deal with uncertainty in an MRP system is to provide for slack in the production system in one way or another. Production slack is created by having additional time, labor, machine capacity, and so on over what's specifically needed to produce the planned amount of product. This extra production capacity could be used to produce an oversized lot to allow for that lot's shrinkages through the process. We also could use slack to allow for production of unplanned lots or for additional activities to speed production through the shop. Thus, providing additional capacity in the shop allows us to accommodate greater quantities than planned in a given time period or to expedite jobs through the shop. We must understand, however, that slack costs money, but if the people can be put to good use when production is not needed, the "costs" can become investments.

Nervousness

This chapter so far has described several enhancements to MRP systems. However, we should recognize some lot-sizing procedures can contribute to the problem of "nervousness" (i.e., instability) in the MRP plans. In this section, we discuss the problem of nervousness in MRP systems and guidelines for reducing its magnitude.

Sources of MRP System Nervousness

MRP system nervousness[2] is defined as significant changes in MRP plans, which occur even with only minor changes in higher-level MRP records or the master production schedule. Changes can involve the quantity or timing of planned orders or scheduled receipts. Figure 6A.12 illustrates just such a case. Here, a reduction of one unit in the master schedule in week 2 produced a significant change in the planned orders for item A. This change had an even more profound impact on component part B. It's hard to imagine a *reduction* at the MPS level could create a past-due condition, but that's precisely what Figure 6A.12 shows—how the change caused by a relatively minor shift in the master schedule is amplified by use of the periodic order quantity (POQ) lot-sizing procedure.

There are a number of ways relatively minor changes in the MRP system can create nervousness and instability in the MRP plans. These include planned orders released prematurely or in an unplanned quantity, unplanned demand (as for spare parts or engineering requirements), and shifts in MRP parameter values, such as safety stock, safety

[2] Daniel C. Steele, "The Nervous MRP System: How to Do Battle," *Production and Inventory Management* (4th quarter 1975), pp. 83–89.

FIGURE 6A.12
MRP System Nervousness Example

Before reducing second-week requirements by one unit:

Item A
POQ = 5 weeks
Lead time = 2 weeks

Week		1	2	3	4	5	6	7	8
Gross requirements		2	24	3	5	1	3	4	50
Scheduled receipts									
Projected available balance	28	26	2	13	8	7	4	0	0
Planned order releases		14					50		

Component B
POQ = 5 weeks
Lead time = 4 weeks

Week		1	2	3	4	5	6	7	8
Gross requirements		14					50		
Scheduled receipts		14							
Projected available balance	2	2	2	2	2	2	0	0	0
Planned order releases			48						

After second-week requirement change:

Item A
POQ = 5 weeks
Lead time = 2 weeks

Week		1	2	3	4	5	6	7	8
Gross requirements		2	(23)	3	5	1	3	4	50
Scheduled receipts									
Projected available balance	28	26	3	0	58	57	54	50	0
Planned order releases			63						

Component B
POQ = 5 weeks
Lead time = 4 weeks

Week		1	2	3	4	5	6	7	8
Gross requirements			63						
Scheduled receipts		14							
Projected available balance	2	16	−47						
Planned order releases	(47)								

Past due

lead time, or planned lead-time values. Nervousness created by such changes is most damaging in MRP systems with many levels in the product structure. Furthermore, use of some lot-sizing techniques, such as POQ, can amplify system nervousness at lower levels in the product structure, as Figure 6A.12 shows.

Reducing MRP System Nervousness

There are several ways to reduce nervousness in MRP systems. First, it's important to reduce causes of changes to the MRP plan. It's important to introduce stability into the master schedule through such devices as freezing and time fences. Similarly, it's important to reduce the incidence of unplanned demands by incorporating spare parts forecasts into MRP record gross requirements. Furthermore, it's necessary to follow the MRP plan with regard to the timing and quantity of planned order releases. Finally, it's important to control the introduction of parameter changes, such as changes in safety stock levels or planned lead times. All of these actions help dampen the small adjustments that can trigger MRP system nervousness.

A second guideline for reducing MRP system nervousness involves selective use of lot-sizing procedures; that is, if nervousness still exists after reducing the preceding causes, we might use different lot-sizing procedures at different product structure levels. One approach is to use fixed order quantities at the top level, using either fixed order quantities or lot-for-lot at intermediate levels, and using period order quantities at the bottom level. Since the fixed order quantity procedure passes along only order timing changes (and not changes in order quantity), this procedure tends to dampen lot-size–induced nervousness. Clearly, fixed order quantity values need to be monitored, since changes in the level of requirements may tend to make such quantities uneconomical over time.

A third guideline for reducing nervousness involves using firm planned orders in MRP (or in MPS) records. Firm planned orders tend to stabilize requirements for lower-level items. The offsetting cost, however, is the necessary maintenance of firm planned orders by MRP planners.

These guidelines provide methods for reducing nervousness in MRP plans. There's a distinction, however, between nervousness in the MRP *plans* and nervousness in the *execution* of MRP system plans. Nervousness in the execution of the plans can also influence behavior. If system users see the plans changing, they may make arbitrary or defensive decisions. This can further aggravate changes in plans.

One way to deal with the execution issue is simply to pass updated information to system users less often. This suggestion argues against the use of net change MRP systems, or at least against publishing every change. An alternative is simply to have more intelligent users. A well-trained user responding to the problem in Figure 6A.12 might, through bottom-up replanning, change the lot sizes to eliminate the problem. However, Figure 6A.12 does indicate this isn't an easy problem to detect. Many aspects are counterintuitive. The fact still is, more intelligent users will make more intelligent execution decisions. User education may still be the best investment!

Concluding Principles

Chapter 6A describes several advanced concepts and conventions in MRP systems. Many ideas are of research interest, but all have practical implications too. Certain kinds of enhancements can be made in a well-operating MRP system, if made by knowledgeable professionals and if implemented with knowledgeable users. The following principles are critical to successful implementation:

- MRP enhancements should be done *after* a basic MPC system is in place.
- Discrete lot-sizing procedures for manufacturing can reduce inventory-associated costs. The complexity should not outweigh the savings, however.
- Safety stocks should be used when the uncertainty is of the quantity category.
- Safety lead times should be used when uncertainty is of the timing category.
- MRP system nervousness can result from lot-sizing rules, parameter changes, and other causes. The MPC professional should take appropriate precautions to dampen the amplitude and impact.
- Uncertainty needs to be reduced (flawless execution) before implementing complex procedures.
- MRP system enhancements should follow the development of ever more intelligent users.

Discussion Questions

1. Some practitioners complain discrete lot-sizing procedures (e.g., POQ, PPB) aggravate system nervousness because of changing lot quantities. What do they mean?
2. Reviewing Figure 6A.6 and using your own powers of intuition, what do you think would happen to the difference in costs between lot-sizing procedures as uncertainty gets larger and larger? What about the absolute cost values?
3. How could the lot-sizing procedures be modified to consider quantity discounts that might occur in a purchasing situation?
4. Why is it necessary to change both the release date and the due date for safety lead time?
5. What are some of the difficulties with introducing "organizational slack" as a method of buffering against uncertainty?
6. One suggestion for reducing execution nervousness is to give the status information only at the time of need. Thus, the only time a foreman would need to determine job priorities would be when he or she was choosing the next job to put on a machine. Give pros and cons of this suggestion.

Problems

1. Consider the following information about an end-product item:

   Ordering cost = \$45/order.

   Average usage = 12 units/week.

   Inventory carrying cost = \$1/unit/week.

   a. How many orders should we place per year (52 weeks) to replenish inventory of the item based on average weekly demand?

   b. Given the following time-phased net requirements from an MRP record for this item, determine the sequence of planned orders using economic order quantity and periodic order quantity procedures. Assume lead time equals zero and current on-hand inventory equals zero. Calculate the inventory carrying cost on the basis of weekly ending inventory values. Which procedure produces the lowest total cost for the eight-week period?

	Week							
	1	2	3	4	5	6	7	8
Requirements	15	2	10	12	6	0	14	9

2. A final assembly (A) requires one week to assemble and has a component part (B) requiring two weeks to fabricate. Three units of final assembly A and four units of part B are currently on hand. The gross requirements for assembly A for the next 10 weeks are as follows (one part B is used on each A):

	Week									
	1	2	3	4	5	6	7	8	9	10
Requirements	1	4	2	8	1	0	6	2	1	3

   a. What are the planned order releases for part B using lot-for-lot lot sizing for both parts A and B?
   b. What are the planned order releases for part B using POQ = 2 for both parts A and B?

3. A company has estimated net requirements for a particular part as follows:

	Month											
	1	2	3	4	5	6	7	8	9	10	11	12
Requirements	100	10	15	20	70	250	250	250	250	40	0	100

Ordering cost associated with this part is $300. Estimated inventory carrying cost is $2 per unit per month calculated on average inventory. Currently no parts are available in inventory. The company wishes to know when and how much to order over the next 12 months.

   a. Apply the economic order quantity and the part period balancing procedures to solve this problem.
   b. What important assumptions are involved in each of the approaches used in part a?

4. The Thrifty Computer Company is trying to decide which of several lot-sizing procedures to use for its MRP system. The following information pertains to one of the typical component parts:

   Setup cost = $100/order.
   Inventory cost = $1.50/unit/week.
   Current inventory balance = 0 units.

	Week							
	1	2	3	4	5	6	7	8
Demand forecast	65	45	35	10	115	25	85	20

   a. Apply the EOQ, (only integer multiples of the EOQ can be ordered), POQ, and PPB lot-sizing procedures and show the total cost resulting from each procedure. Calculate inventory carrying cost based on the average inventory on hand at the end of each period. Assume orders are received into the beginning inventory.

b. Indicate advantages and disadvantages of using each procedure suggested in part a.

5. Apply the part period balancing (PPB) lot-sizing procedure to the following 12 periods of requirements data, indicating order receipts' size and period. Assume order costs are $100/order placed and inventory carrying cost is $1/unit/period. Calculate the inventory carrying costs on the basis of *ending* inventory values.

	Period											
	1	2	3	4	5	6	7	8	9	10	11	12
Requirements	70	30	35	60	60	25	35	70	45	70	80	55

6. The Fisher Products Company produces a line of children's parlor games. The production process includes two departments: fabrication and assembly. The fabrication shop produces game parts, such as plastic pieces, game markers, and special indicators. The company maintains inventories both of the raw material needed to produce the game parts and of finished game parts themselves. The assembly department consists of a single assembly line that collates and packages all parlor games in Fisher's product line to meet incoming customer orders. The company maintains no inventory of finished products (games) but produces only to customer order.

Each week the assembly foreman schedules the assembly line and supervises withdrawal of game parts from the stockroom that are needed on the assembly line to meet the production

EXHIBIT A
Material Requirements Planning Worksheet

		Week Number							
End Products		1	2	3	4	5	6	7	8
Game A master schedule		21	0	0	21	20	0	15	0
Game B master schedule		2	2	9	0	6	3	0	9

Toy Cup		1	2	3	4	5	6	7	8
Gross requirements									
Scheduled receipts*									
Projected available balance	44								
Planned order release									

Plastic Molding Material		1	2	3	4	5	6	7	8
Gross requirements									
Scheduled receipts*		90							
Projected available balance	20								
Planned order release									

*Received at the beginning of each week.

EXHIBIT B
Material Requirements Planning Worksheet

End Products	1	2	3	4	5	6	7	8
Game A master schedule		22		21	15			
Game B master schedule	9	1	7	7	3	10	1	2

Toy Cup		1	2	3	4	5	6	7	8
Gross requirements (2 units/game A) (1 unit/game B)									
Scheduled receipts*									
Projected available balance	55								
Planned order release (Lead time = 2 weeks)									

Plastic Molding Material		1	2	3	4	5	6	7	8
Gross requirements (2 oz./toy cup)									
Scheduled receipts*			166						
Projected available balance	10								
Planned order release (Lead time = 2 weeks)									

*Received at the beginning of each week.

schedule. Sometimes several games are assembled during a single week. Since the company uses MRP to plan and control production of games and game parts, the assembly foreman prepares a master production schedule for a period covering eight weeks into the future. Exhibit A shows his master schedule with two end products (games A and B).

a. A component (game part) called the toy cup is used in producing the two parlor games (A and B). Two units of the toy cup are needed to produce one unit of game A, and one unit of the toy cup is required to produce one unit of game B. Assuming the toy cup planned lead time is one week, current on-hand inventory is 44 units, and there are no scheduled receipts, complete the MRP record for the toy cup in Exhibit A. Use the periodic order quantity ordering policy for lot sizing. Ordering cost for the toy cup is $9/order; inventory carrying cost is $0.10/unit/week.

b. After completing the toy cup's MRP record in part a, complete the MRP record in Exhibit A for the plastic molding material needed to produce the toy cup. Two ounces of the plastic molding material are needed to produce one toy cup, planned lead time for the plastic material is one week, 20 ounces of plastic material are currently on hand, a scheduled receipt for 90 ounces of plastic material is due in week 1 from the supplier, and the periodic ordering policy is used for this item. Ordering cost is $5/order; inventory carrying cost is $0.04 per ounce per week.

c. Fisher's assembly foreman has just handed you the MRP records for the toy cup and plastic molding material in Exhibit B. These MRP records contain a different master schedule, changed on-hand inventory values, and a new scheduled receipt value. Also, planned lead time for both items is now two weeks. Complete the new MRP records for both items, assuming the part period balancing ordering policy is used for the toy cup and plastic material.

d. What problem(s), if any, are apparent after you've completed the MRP records in Exhibit B? What are the MRP planner's alternative courses of action in resolving the problem(s)? What specific course of action should be taken? Why?

7. Chambers Inc. is considering using the PBB lot-sizing approach, but first they want to compare it to their current lot-sizing method (EOQ). They have selected a sample component for the comparison, and its requirements are given below. Ordering cost is $27 per order, and carrying cost is $0.25 per unit per period. (Use average inventory.)

	Period							
	1	2	3	4	5	6	7	8
Requirements	51	14	59	93	44	12	67	60

8. The Silver brothers (Ed, Quick, and Hiho) had their very own factory. Ed was the general manager, and Quick produced the finished product from a part Hiho made. Selected data for the finished product and part are given next. Requirements for the finished product for the next few periods appear as well.

	Quick	Hiho
Order quantity (EOQ)	40	100
Safety stock	5	0
Lead time	1	1
Current inventory	7	12
Scheduled receipt in period 1	40	0

	Period							
	1	2	3	4	5	6	7	8
Requirements	23	13	36	12	21	8	34	23

a. Using a spreadsheet, develop MRP records for Quick and Hiho. What are the planned order releases for Hiho's part?

b. Devise a different ordering plan for Quick and Hiho that has the same number of orders as the solution in part a but reduces inventory levels *and* has the same amount of closing inventory (period 8) as the original plan.

9. The XYZ Company's production manager is investigating causes of nervousness in the firm's MRP system. His study has produced MRP schedules for item A as of the start of weeks 1, 2, 3, and 4.

LT = 0.

SS = 0.

Q calculated using the Wagner-Whitin algorithm.

Ordering cost = $400/order.

Inventory carrying cost = $1/unit/week.

Item A		Week 1	2	3	4
Gross requirements		177	261	207	309
Scheduled receipts					
Projected available balance	0	261	0	309	0
Planned order release		438		516	

Item A		Week 2	3	4	5
Gross requirements		261	207	309	64
Scheduled receipts					
Projected available balance	261	0	373	64	0
Planned order release			580		

Item A		Week 3	4	5	6
Gross requirements		207	309	64	182
Scheduled receipts					
Projected available balance	0	0	246	182	0
Planned order release		207	555		

Item A		Week 4	5	6	7
Gross requirements		309	64	182	0
Scheduled receipts					
Projected available balance	0	246	182	0	0
Planned order release		555			

a. Assume we need one unit of raw material item B to produce one unit of product item A. Calculate gross requirements for item B covering a four-week planning horizon as of the start of weeks 1, 2, 3, and 4. Compare gross requirements for item B for each week as they're calculated at the start of weeks 1, 2, 3, and 4. What differences do you observe in item B's gross requirements from week to week?

b. If there are no changes to either item A's gross requirements or beginning inventory over the four-week interval, how do you explain changes in the gross requirements for item B observed in part a? How do you explain this situation to the production manager? What impact would such changes in gross requirements for item B have on supplier relations if B is a purchased part?

10. The following MRP record is for an item purchased from the K. C. Jones company, a supplier to Ajax Diesel. The purchase quantity is 45 units. The history on K. C. Jones's delivery lead time shows an average lead time of three weeks. Sometimes orders from K. C. Jones show up a week late. Complete the following MRP record so that shortages do not occur even if K. C. Jones is late by one week.

		Week 1	2	3	4	5	6	7	8
Gross requirements		33	12	23	37	26	3	8	31
Scheduled receipts		45							
Projected available balance	60								
Planned order release									

11. The following MRP record is for an item purchased from Cannonball Adderly, another supplier for Ajax Diesel. This sample part requires a two-week lead time. The percent defective for purchased lots of this item averages 17 percent and has been as large as 27 percent. Defective items are removed and returned to the vendor when found. Construct an MRP record to protect against inventory shortages using a fixed order quantity. An economic order quantity of 30 units has been calculated for this item.

		Week 1	2	3	4	5	6	7	8
Gross requirements		12	0	27	8	34	3	23	29
Scheduled receipts									
Projected available balance	21								
Planned order release									

12. Atlas Wrench Company was having problems with the sensitivity of its MRP system. The following records are typical of its planning system. The two records are for the Z Wrench and for one of its components, the Z Shaft. There is one Z Shaft used in each Z Wrench.

Z Wrench		Week 1	2	3	4	5	6
Gross requirements		2	20	5	1	3	45
Scheduled receipts							
Projected available balance	26	24	4	4	3	0	0
Planned order release		5			45		

POQ = 3 weeks; LT = 2 weeks; SS = 0.

Z Shaft		Week 1	2	3	4	5	6
Gross requirements		5			45		
Scheduled receipts		5					
Projected available balance	3	3	3	3	0	0	0
Planned order release		45					

POQ = 3 weeks; LT = 3 weeks; SS = 0.

a. What happens if the gross requirement for the Z Wrench in week 2 drops to 19? Are there any problems?

b. How can Atlas Wrench deal with situations like the one that occurs here?

Chapter 7

Capacity Planning and Management

In this chapter we discuss the role of capacity planning and management in MPC systems. We focus primarily on techniques for determining the capacity requirements implied by a production plan, master production schedule, or detailed material plans. One managerial problem is to match the capacity with the plans: either to provide sufficient capacity to execute plans, or to adjust plans to match capacity constraints. A second managerial problem with regard to capacity is to consciously consider the marketplace implications of faster throughput times for making products, at the expense of reduced capacity utilization. For example, JIT production results in very fast throughput times for manufacturing products, but typically some capacities are underutilized. Similarly, by scheduling the highest-priority jobs through all work centers—taking explicit account of available capacity—it is possible to complete these jobs in much shorter times than under more conventional MPC approaches. But this gain in speed for high priority jobs comes at the expense of lower priority job throughput times and some underutilization of capacity.

This chapter is organized around five topics:

- *The role of capacity planning in MPC systems:* How does it fit, and how is capacity managed in various manufacturing environments?
- *Capacity planning and control techniques:* How can capacity requirements be estimated and capacity utilization controlled?
- *Scheduling capacity and materials simultaneously:* How can finite scheduling techniques be applied, and what are the costs/benefits of these techniques?
- *Management and capacity planning/utilization:* What are the critical managerial decisions required to plan/utilize capacity most effectively?
- *Example applications:* How are techniques for capacity planning applied, and what are some best practices?

Buildings, classrooms
Staffing, Admin

The Role of Capacity Planning in MPC Systems

MPC is often seen as encompassing two major activities: planning/control of materials and planning/control of capacities. The two need to be coordinated for maximum benefits, on the basis of managerial perceptions of what is required in the marketplace. Capacity planning techniques have as their primary objective the estimation of capacity requirements, sufficiently far enough into the future to be able to meet those requirements. A second objective is execution: the capacity plans need to be executed flawlessly, with unpleasant surprises avoided. Insufficient capacity quickly leads to deteriorating delivery performance, escalating work-in-process inventories, and frustrated manufacturing personnel. On the other hand, excess capacity might be a needless expense that can be reduced. Even firms with advanced MPC systems have found times when their inability to provide adequate work center capacities has been a significant problem. On the other hand, there are firms that continually manage to increase output from what seems to be a fixed set of capacities. The bottom line difference can be substantial.

Hierarchy of Capacity Planning Decisions

Figure 7.1 relates capacity planning decisions to other MPC system modules. It depicts a scope of capacity planning starting from an overall plan of resource needs, and then moves to planning procedures to estimate the capacity implications of a particular master production schedule. Thereafter the hierarchy depicts middle-range capacity planning, which evaluates the

FIGURE 7.1
Capacity Planning in the MPC System

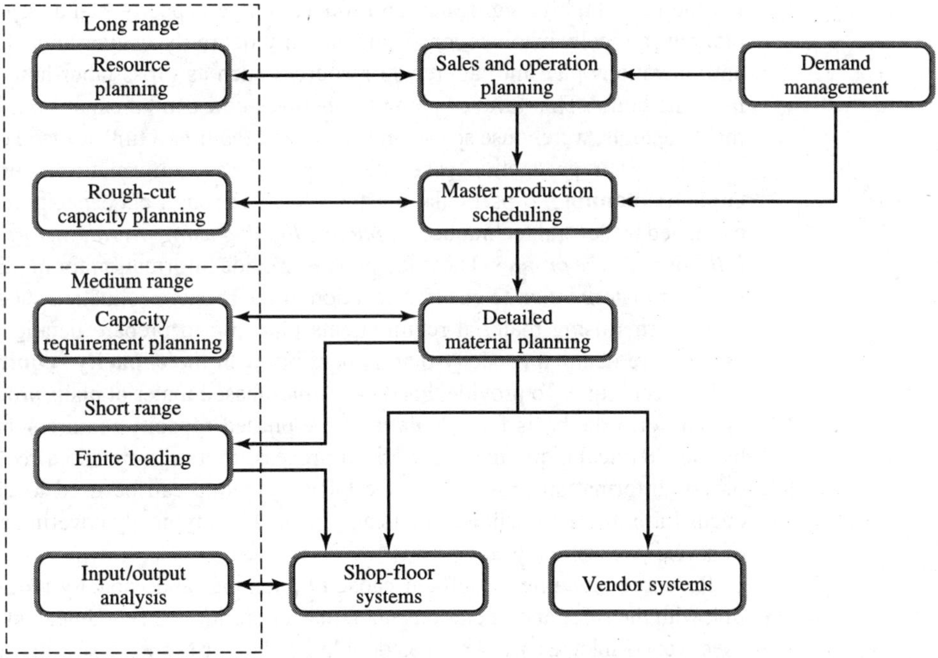

capacity implications of the detailed material plans, then to the short-range actual scheduling/capacity trade-offs, and finally to the evaluation of particular capacity plans.

These five levels of capacity planning range from large aggregate plans for long time periods to the detailed scheduling decisions as to which job to run next on a particular machine. In this chapter the focus is first on the several rough-cut capacity planning procedures. With this background, one can see how capacity requirements planning (CRP) systems are a logical extension, with a more detailed view of capacity needs. Understanding these systems allows one to appreciate the different approaches, with each providing a more exact estimate of capacity needs, but with a corresponding need for more information and system complexity. Thereafter, we can see how advanced production scheduling (APS) based on finite loading provide still another approach to the planning/management of capacity. Finally, Figure 7.1 shows input/output analysis as the last of the five levels of capacity planning. Here, the focus is on capacity management, in which capacity plans are continually compared with actual results.

Many authorities distinguish between long-, medium-, and short-range capacity planning horizons as indicated in Figure 7.1. This is a useful distinction, but the time dimension varies substantially from company to company. Moreover, in the last several years, the focus has shifted more to the short term, as firms operate with lower inventory levels and faster response times to customer needs. In this chapter, we will examine capacity planning/utilization decisions ranging from one day to a year or more in the future.

Links to Other MPC System Modules

System linkages for the capacity planning modules follow the basic hierarchy shown in Figure 7.1. **Resource planning** is directly linked to the sales and operations planning module. It's the most highly aggregated and longest-range capacity planning decision. Resource planning typically involves converting monthly, quarterly, or even annual data from the sales and operations plan into aggregate resources such as gross labor-hours, floor space, and machine-hours. This level of planning involves new capital expansion, bricks and mortar, machine tools, warehouse space, and so on, and requires a time horizon of months or years.

The master production schedule is the primary information source for **rough-cut capacity planning.** A particular master schedule's rough-cut capacity requirements can be estimated by several techniques: *capacity planning using overall factors (CPOF), capacity bills,* or *resource profiles.* These techniques provide information for modifying the resource levels or material plan to ensure execution of the master production schedule.

For firms using material requirements planning to prepare detailed material plans, a much more detailed capacity plan is possible with the **capacity requirements planning (CRP)** technique. To provide this detail, time-phased material plans produced by the MRP system form the basis for calculating time-phased capacity requirements. Data files used by the CRP technique include work in process, routing, scheduled receipts, and planned orders. Information provided by the CRP technique can be used to determine capacity needs for both key machine centers and labor skills, typically covering a planning horizon of several weeks to a year.

Resource planning, rough-cut capacity planning, and capacity requirements planning link with the sales and operations plan, master production schedule, and MRP systems, respectively. Linkages are shown as double-headed arrows for a specific reason. There must be a correspondence between capacity required to execute a given material plan and capacity made available to execute the plan. Without this correspondence, the plan will be either impossible to execute or inefficiently executed. We don't claim capacity must always be changed to meet material plans. In fact, whether this is worthwhile or whether plans should be changed to meet capacity is a managerial judgment. Capacity planning systems provide basic information to make that a *reasoned* judgment.

Finite loading in some ways is better seen as a shop scheduling process, and therefore part of production activity control (PAC), but it is also a capacity planning procedure. There are an increasing number of software systems provided by vendors, usually called **advanced production scheduling (APS)** techniques to do finite loading. The fundamental difference between the other capacity planning approaches and finite loading is that the former set does not consider any adjustment to plans because of planned capacity utilization. The latter starts with a specified capacity and schedules work through work centers only to the extent that capacity is available to do so. Moreover, by scheduling within exact capacity constraints, the APS systems allow work to flow through the necessary set of work centers more quickly. The jobs are scheduled with exact timing on all work centers—not merely in some general way, such as during a particular week.

Input/output analysis provides a method for monitoring the actual consumption of capacity during the execution of detailed material planning. It is necessarily linked to the shop floor execution systems, and supported by the database for production activity control (PAC). Input/output analysis can indicate the need to update capacity plans as actual shop performance deviates from plans, as well as the need to modify the planning factors used in the capacity planning systems.

This overview of capacity planning's scope sets the stage for the techniques the chapter discusses. The primary interaction among these techniques is hierarchical: long-range planning sets constraints on medium-range capacity planning, which in turn constrains detailed scheduling and execution on the shop floor.

Capacity Planning and Control Techniques

Here we describe four procedures for capacity planning. The first technique is *capacity planning using overall factors (CPOF)*. The simplest of the four techniques, CPOF is based only on accounting data. The second, *capacity bills,* requires more detailed product information. The third, *resource profiles,* adds a further dimension—specific timing of capacity requirements. The first three procedures are rough-cut approaches and are applicable to firms with or without MRP systems. The fourth, *capacity requirements planning,* is used in conjunction with time-phased MRP records and shop-floor system records to calculate capacity required to produce both open shop orders (scheduled receipts) and planned orders. To describe the four planning techniques, we use a simple example. The example allows us to clearly see differences in approach, complexity, level of aggregation, data requirements, timing, and accuracy among the techniques.

Capacity Planning Using Overall Factors (CPOF)

Capacity planning using overall factors (CPOF), a relatively simple approach to rough-cut capacity planning, is typically done on a manual basis. Data inputs come from the master production schedule (MPS), rather than from detailed material plans. This procedure is how long a product takes to make X = total labor components

FIGURE 7.2
Example Problem Data

Master production schedule (in units):

End Product	Period 1	2	3	4	5	6	7	8	9	10	11	12	13	Total
A	33	33	33	40	40	40	30	30	30	37	37	37	37	457
B	17	17	17	13	13	13	25	25	25	27	27	27	27	273

Direct labor time per end product unit:

End Product	Total Direct Labor in Standard Hours/Unit
A	0.95 hour
B	1.85

FIGURE 7.3 **Estimated Capacity Requirements Using Overall Factors (in standard direct labor-hours)**

Work Center	Historical Percentage	Period 1	2	3	4	5	6	7	8	9	10	11	12	13	Total Hours
100	60.3	37.87	37.87	37.87	37.41	37.41	37.41	45.07	45.07	45.07	51.32	51.32	51.32	51.32	566.33
200	30.4	19.09	19.09	19.09	18.86	18.86	18.86	22.72	22.72	22.72	25.87	25.87	25.87	25.87	285.49
300	9.3	5.84	5.84	5.84	5.78	5.78	5.78	6.96	6.96	6.96	7.91	7.91	7.91	7.91	87.38
Total required capacity		62.80*	62.80	62.80	62.05	62.05	62.05	74.75	74.75	74.75	85.10	85.10	85.10	85.10	939.20

*62.80 = (0.95 × 33) + (1.85 × 17) for the standards in Figure 7.2.

labor per product + labor per product

usually based on planning factors derived from standards or historical data for end products. When these planning factors are applied to the MPS data, overall labor or machine-hour capacity requirements can be estimated. This overall estimate is thereafter allocated to individual work centers on the basis of historical data on shop workloads. CPOF plans are usually stated in terms of weekly or monthly time periods and are revised as the firm changes the MPS.

The top portion of Figure 7.2 shows the MPS that will serve as the basis for our example. This schedule specifies the quantities of two end products to be assembled during each time period. The first step of the CPOF procedure involves calculating capacity requirements of this schedule for the overall plant. The lower portion of Figure 7.2 shows direct labor standards, indicating the total direct labor-hours required for each end product. Assuming labor productivity of 100 percent of standard, the total direct labor-hour requirement for the first period is 62.80 hours, as shown in Figure 7.3.

The procedure's second step involves using historical ratios to allocate the total capacity required each period to individual work centers. Historical percentages of the total direct labor-hours worked in each of the three work centers the prior year were used to determine allocation ratios. These data could be derived from the company's accounting records. In the example, 60.3 percent, 30.4 percent, and 9.3 percent of the total direct labor-hours were worked in work centers 100, 200, and 300, respectively. These percentages are used to estimate anticipated direct labor requirements for each work center. The resulting work center capacity requirements are shown in Figure 7.3 for each period in the MPS.

The CPOF procedure, or variants of it, is found in a number of manufacturing firms. Data requirements are minimal (primarily accounting system data) and calculations are straightforward. As a result, CPOF approximations of capacity requirements at individual work centers are valid only to the extent that product mixes or historical divisions of work between work centers remain constant. This procedure's main advantages are ease of calculation and minimal data requirements. In many firms, data are readily available and computations can be done manually.

The CPOF procedure will work reasonably well for many manufacturing environments. For example, in a just-in-time (JIT) manufacturing company, the CPOF approach would allow the firm to make fairly good estimates of capacity needs under different planning scenarios. The inherent inaccuracies of CPOF will present fewer problems in a JIT environment where execution is fast, with virtually no work-in-process inventories to confound the analysis. This might be particularly useful for estimating the capacity needs for firms that supply a JIT manufacturing company.

Capacity Bills

The **capacity bill procedure** is a rough-cut method providing more-direct linkage between individual end products in the MPS and the capacity required for individual work centers. It takes into account any shifts in product mix. Consequently, it requires more data than the CPOF procedure. A bill of materials and routing data are required, and direct labor-hour or machine-hour data must be available for each operation.

To develop a bill of capacity for the example problem, we use the product structure data for A and B shown in Figure 7.4. We also need the routing and operation time standard data in the top portion of Figure 7.5 for assembling products A and B, as well as for manufacturing component items C, D, E, and F. The bill of capacity indicates total standard time required to produce one end product in each work center required in its manufacture. Calculations involve multiplying total-time-per-unit values by the usages indicated in the bill of materials. Summarizing the usage-adjusted unit time data by work center produces the bill of capacity for each of the two products in the lower portion of Figure 7.5. The bill of capacity can be constructed from engineering data, as we've done here; similar data might be available in a standard cost system. Some firms' alternative approach is to prepare the bill of capacity only for those work centers regarded as critical.

Once the bill of capacity for each end product is prepared, we can use the master production schedule to estimate capacity requirements at individual work centers. Figure 7.6 shows the determination of capacity requirements for our example. The resultant work center estimates differ substantially from the CPOF estimates in Figure 7.3. The differences reflect the period-to-period changes in product mix between the projected MPS and historical average figures. Estimates obtained from CPOF are based on an overall historical ratio of work between machine centers, whereas capacity bill estimates reflect the actual product mix planned for each period.

It's important to note that the total hours shown for the MPS (939.20) are the same in Figure 7.3 and Figure 7.6; the differences are in work center estimates for each time period.

FIGURE 7.4
Product Structure Data

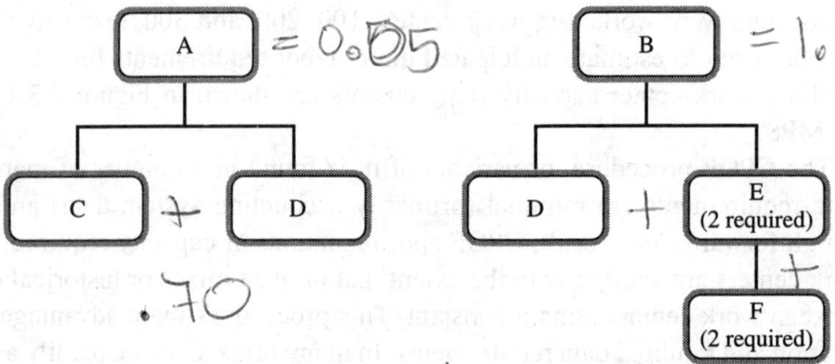

FIGURE 7.5 Routing and Standard Time Data

	Lot Sizes	Operation	Work Center	Standard Setup Hours	Standard Setup Hours per Unit	Standard Run Time Hours per Unit	Total Hours per Unit
End Products							
A	40	1 of 1	100	1.0	0.025*	0.025	0.05†
B	20	1 of 1	100	1.0	0.050	1.250	1.30
Components							
C	40	1 of 2	200	1.0	0.025	0.575	0.60
		2 of 2	300	1.0	0.025	0.175	0.20
D	60	1 of 1	200	2.0	0.033	0.067	0.10
E	100	1 of 1	200	2.0	0.020	0.080	0.10
F	100	1 of 1	200	2.0	0.020	0.0425	0.0625

Bill of Capacity: End Product

Work Center	A Total Time/Unit	B Total Time/Unit
100	0.05	1.30
200	0.70‡	0.55§
300	0.20	0.00
Total time/unit	0.95	1.85

*0.025 = Setup time ÷ Lot size = 1.0/40.
†0.05 = Standard setup time per unit + Standard run time per unit = 0.025 + 0.025.
‡0.70 = 0.60 + 0.10 for one C and one D from Figure 7.4.
§0.55 = 0.10 + 2(0.10) + 4(0.0625) for one D, two E's, and four F's.

FIGURE 7.6 Capacity Requirements Using Capacity Bills

Work Center	Period 1	2	3	4	5	6	7	8	9	10	11	12	13	Total Hours	Projected Work Center Percentage
100	23.75*	23.75	23.75	18.90	18.90	18.90	34.00	34.00	34.00	36.95	36.95	36.95	36.95	377.75	40%
200	32.45	32.45	32.45	35.15	35.15	35.15	34.75	34.75	34.75	40.75	40.75	40.75	40.75	470.05	50
300	6.60	6.60	6.60	8.00	8.00	8.00	6.00	6.00	6.00	7.40	7.40	7.40	7.40	91.40	10
Total	62.80	62.80	62.80	62.05	62.05	62.05	74.75	74.75	74.75	85.10	85.10	85.10	85.10	939.20	100%

*23.75 = (33 × 0.05) + (17 × 1.30) from Figures 7.2 and 7.5.

These differences are far more important in firms that experience significant period-to-period mix variations than in those that have a relatively constant pattern of work.

Resource Profiles

Neither the CPOF nor the capacity bill procedure takes into account the specific timing of the projected workloads at individual work centers. In developing **resource profiles,** production lead time data are taken into account to provide time-phased projections of the capacity requirements for individual production facilities. Thus, resource profiles provide a somewhat more sophisticated approach to rough-cut capacity planning.

In any capacity planning technique, time periods for the capacity plan can be varied (e.g., weeks, months, quarters). However, when time periods are long relative to lead times, much of the time-phased information's value may be lost in aggregating the data. In many firms, this means time periods longer than one week will mask important changes in capacity requirements.

To apply the resource profile procedure to our example, we use the bills of material, routing, and time standard information in Figures 7.4 and 7.5. We must also add the production lead time for each end product and component part to our database. In this simplified example, we use a one-period lead time for assembling each end product and one period for each operation required to produce component parts. Because only one operation is required for producing components D, E, and F, lead time for producing these components is one time period each. For component C, however, lead time is two time periods: one for the operation in work center 200 and another for work center 300.

To use the resource profile procedure, we prepare a time-phased profile of the capacity requirements for each end item. Figure 7.7's operations setback charts show this time phasing for end products A and B. The chart for end product A indicates that the final assembly operation is to be completed during period 5. Production of components C and D must be completed in period 4 prior to the start of the final assembly. Because component C requires two time periods (one for each operation), it must be started one time period before component D (i.e., at the start of period 3). Other conventions are used to define time phasing, but in this example we assume the master production schedule specifies the number of units of each end product that must be completed by *the end* of the time period indicated. This implies *all* components must be completed by the end of the preceding period.

For convenience, we've shown the standard hours required for each operation for each product in Figure 7.7. This information is summarized by work center and time period in Figure 7.8, which also shows the capacity requirements the MPS quantities generated in time period 5 from Figure 7.2 (40 of end product A and 13 of end product B). The capacity requirements in Figure 7.8 are only for MPS quantities in period 5. MPS quantities for other periods can increase the capacity needed in each period. For example, Figure 7.8 shows that 7.9 hours of capacity are needed in period 4 at work center 200 to support the MPS for period 5. The MPS for period 6 requires another 27.25 hours from work center 200 in period 4. This results in the total of 35.15 hours shown in Figure 7.9 for workstation 200 in period 4, which provides the overall capacity plan for the current MPS using the resource profile procedure.

Comparing the capacity plans produced by the capacity bills and the resource profile procedures (Figures 7.6 and 7.9), we see the impact of the time-phased capacity information. Total workload created by the master production schedule (939.2 hours) remains the same, as do the work center percentage allocations. But the period requirements for work centers 200 and 300 projected by the two techniques vary somewhat. A capacity

FIGURE 7.7 Operation Setback Charts for End Products A and B

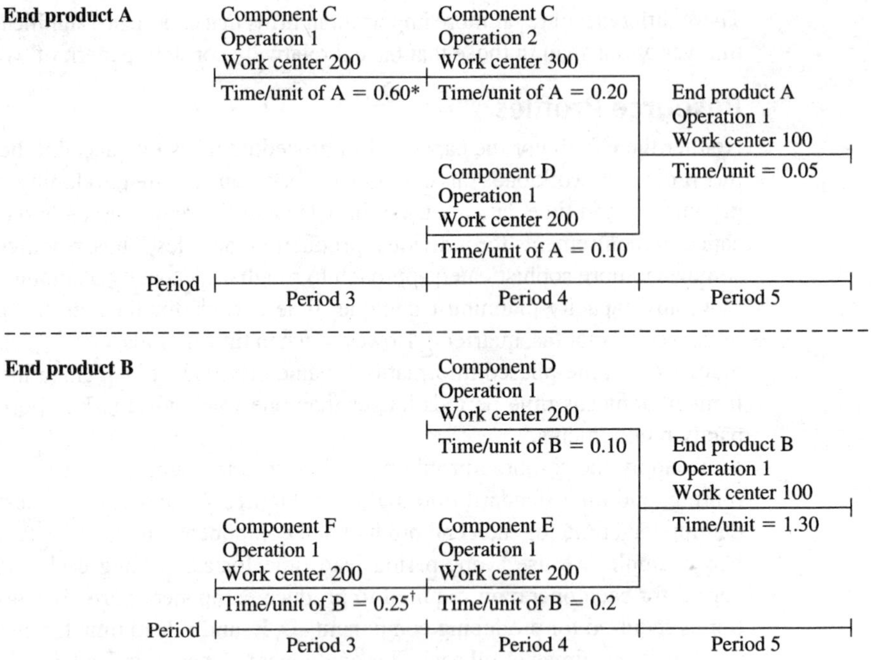

Period: *0.60 = standard time per unit of C × number of C's per unit of A = 0.60 × 1 = 0.60.
†0.25 = standard time per unit of component F × number of F's per unit of B = 0.0625 × 4 = 0.25.

requirement of eight hours was projected for work center 300 in time period 6 using capacity bills versus six hours using resource profiles, a difference of more than 30 percent. This change reflects the difference in the timing of resources required to produce the component parts, which is taken into account by the resource bill procedure.

Capacity Requirements Planning (CRP)

Capacity requirements planning (CRP) differs from the rough-cut planning procedures in four respects. First, CRP utilizes the time-phased material plan information produced by an MRP system. This includes consideration of all actual lot sizes, as well as lead times for both open shop orders (scheduled receipts) and orders planned for future release (planned orders). Second, the MRP system's gross-to-net feature takes into account production capacity already stored in the form of inventories of both components and assembled products. Third, the shop-floor control system accounts for the current status of all work-in-process in the shop, so only the capacity needed to *complete the remaining work* on open shop orders is considered in calculating required work center capacities. Fourth, CRP takes into account demand for service parts, other demands that may not be accounted for in the MPS, and any additional capacity that might be required by MRP planners reacting to scrap, item record errors, and so on. To accomplish this, the CRP procedure requires the same input information as the resource profile procedure (bills of material, routing, time standards, lead times) plus information on MRP-planned orders and the current status of open shop orders (MRP-scheduled receipts) at individual work centers.

FIGURE 7.8 **Resource Profiles by Work Center**

Time required during preceding periods for one end product assembled in period 5:

	Time Period		
	3	4	5
End product A			
Work center 100	0	0	0.05
Work center 200	0.60	0.10	0
Work center 300	0	0.20	0
End product B			
Work center 100	0	0	1.30
Work center 200	0.25	0.30	0

Time-phased capacity requirements generated from MPS for 40 As and 13 Bs in time period 5:

	Time Period		
	3	4	5
40 As			
Work center 100	0	0	2
Work center 200	24	4	0
Work center 300	0	8	0
13 Bs			
Work center 100	0	0	16.9
Work center 200	3.25	3.9	0
Work center 300	0	0	0
Total from period 5 MPS			
Work center 100	0	0	18.9
Work center 200	27.25	7.9	0
Work center 300	0	8.0	0

FIGURE 7.9 **Capacity Requirements Using Resource Profiles**

Work Center	Past Due*	Period 1	2	3	4	5	6	7	8	9	10	11	12	13	Work Total Hours	Center Percentage
100	0.00	23.75*	23.75	23.75	18.90	18.90	18.90	34.00	34.00	34.00	36.95	36.95	36.95	36.95	377.75	40%
200	56.50	32.45	35.65	35.15	35.15	32.15	34.75	34.75	39.45	40.75	40.75	40.75	11.80		470.05	50
300	6.60	6.60	6.60	8.00	8.00	8.00	6.00	6.00	6.00	7.40	7.40	7.40	7.40		91.40	10
Total	63.10	62.80	66.00	66.90	62.05	59.05	59.65	74.75	79.45	82.15	85.10	85.10	56.15	36.95	939.20	100%

*This work should be completed already for products to meet the master production schedule in periods 1 and 2. (If not, it's past due and will add to the capacity required in the upcoming periods.)

As a medium-range capacity planning procedure, CRP exploits MRP information so as to calculate only the capacity required to complete the MPS. By calculating capacity requirements for actual open shop orders and planned orders in the MRP database, CRP accounts for the capacity already stored in the form of finished and work-in-process inventories. Because MRP data include timing of both these open and planned orders, the potential for improved accuracy in timing capacity requirements is realized. This accuracy is most important in the most immediate time periods. Rough-cut techniques can overstate required capacity by the amount of capacity represented in inventories. In Figure 7.9, for example, the past-due or already completed portion of the capacity requirements is 63.1 hours—about a full time period's capacity. This work should already have been completed if we expect to meet the MPS in periods 1 and 2. CRP's potential benefits aren't without cost. A larger database is required, as well as a much larger computational effort.

The process of preparing a CRP projection is similar to that used for resource profiles. The major difference is that detailed MRP data establish exact order quantities and timing for calculating capacity required. The resultant capacity needs are summarized by time period and work center in a format similar to Figure 7.9. The CRP results would differ from those of the other techniques, primarily in the early periods, but would be a more accurate projection of work center capacity needs. Because calculations are based on all component parts and end products from the present time period through all periods included in the MRP records (the planning horizon), we can see the enormity of the CRP calculation requirements. Some firms have mitigated this cost by collecting data as the MRP explosion process is performed.

Figure 7.10 presents one of the MRP records that drive the CRP procedure for our example. To simplify the presentation, we show the MPS only for end product A and the MRP record for one of its components, component C. We've used these data to calculate capacity requirements for work center 300. These capacity requirements incorporate the influence of lot sizes, inventories, and scheduled receipts for component C. Because item C is processed at work center 300 during the second period of the two-period lead time, the planned order for 40 units due to be released in period 1 requires capacity in period 2 at work center 300.

FIGURE 7.10
CRP Example: Detailed Calculations

	Period												
	1	2	3	4	5	6	7	8	9	10	11	12	13
Product A *MPS*	33	33	33	40	40	40	30	30	30	37	37	37	37

Component C
Lot size = 40
Lead time = 2

		Period												
		1	2	3	4	5	6	7	8	9	10	11	12	13
Gross requirements		33	33	33	40	40	40	30	30	30	37	37	37	37
Scheduled receipts			40											
Projected available balance	37	4	11	18	18	18	18	28	38	8	11	14	17	20
Planned order releases		40	40	40	40	40	40		40	40	40	40		

Work center 300 Capacity Requirements Using CRP

	Period												
	1	2	3	4	5	6	7	8	9	10	11	12	13
Hours of capacity* Total = 88	8	8	8	8	8	8	8	0	8	8	8	8	

*The eight hours of capacity required is derived from the scheduled receipt and planned order quantities of 40 units multiplied by the time to fabricate a unit of component C in machine center 300, 0.20 hour (see Figure 7.7).

Required capacity is calculated using the setup and run time data from Figure 7.5 for component C.

For a lot size of 40 units, total setup and run time in work center 300 is eight hours [1.0 + (40 × 0.175)]. Each planned order for component C in Figure 7.10 requires eight hours of capacity at work center 300, one period later. Similarly, the scheduled receipt of 40 units due in period 2 requires eight hours of capacity in week 1. Note the eight hours of capacity required for the scheduled receipt may not, in fact, be required if this job has already been processed at work center 300 before the beginning of period 1. The shop order's actual status is required to make the analysis.

In comparing CRP to the other capacity planning procedures, we shouldn't expect total capacity requirements for the 13 periods or the period-by-period requirements to be the same. Comparing capacity requirements for work center 300 developed by the resource profile procedure (Figure 7.9) and CRP (Figure 7.10) indicates estimated total capacity requirements for the 13 periods are less using CRP than resource profiles (88 versus 91.4 hours) and vary considerably on a period-by-period basis. Differences are explained by the initial inventory and use of lot sizing. Any partially completed work-in-process would reduce the capacity requirements further.

Scheduling Capacity and Materials Simultaneously

Thus far in the chapter we have taken what has been the traditional view of capacity in MPC systems: one first plans the materials, and thereafter examines the capacity implications of those plans. The underlying assumption in all of this is that if one knows of capacity requirements in sufficient time, adjustments to capacity can be effected. The capacity planning techniques we have examined thus far all make this assumption: their major difference is only in sophistication of the plans produced.

Moreover, the material plans produced by classic MRP systems are based on batches of materials traveling between work centers for subsequent operations, then flowing through inventories in order to be subsequently processed/integrated into higher-level part numbers. The overall lead times associated with producing end products on this basis tend to be quite long as a multiple of actual manufacturing times, particularly when the products have many levels in the bill of materials. For many firms today this just will not do: they must respond to actual customer demands faster, without holding large inventories. This implies "smarter" scheduling, which must simultaneously reflect actual capacity conditions. Furthermore, those "capacity conditions" are tighter and tighter: in order to be profitable one must utilize capacities more effectively, and satisfy end customer demands faster with lower inventories. The bottom line is a need to simultaneously schedule both capacity and materials.

Finite Capacity Scheduling

Finite scheduling systems can first be seen as an extension of the approach used by capacity requirements planning (CRP) systems, with one major difference: CRP calculates only capacity needs—it makes no adjustments for infeasibility. If, for example, we take the capacity requirements data for work center 300 coming from Product A, as shown in Figure 7.10, these would be depicted in either a CRP or finite workload capacity profile as the top part of Figure 7.11. If similar capacity requirements were collected from *all* the MRP

FIGURE 7.11 Infinite versus Finite Loading (CRP Profile for Work Center 300)

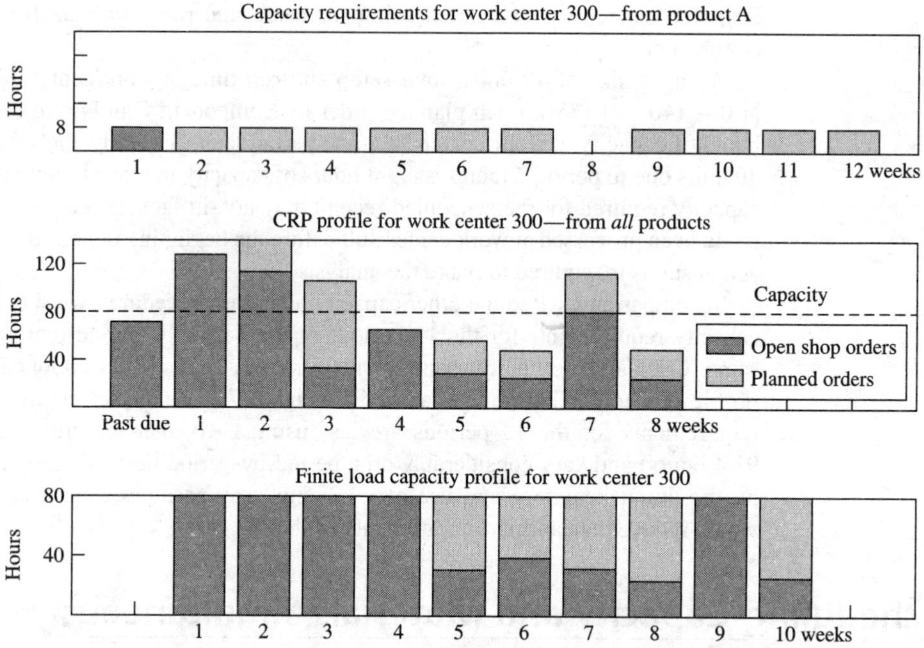

records, for all the jobs passing through work center 300, the CRP record might look like the middle portion of Figure 7.11 (where we have expanded the example to realistically include more products).

The bottom portion of Figure 7.11 shows the difference in the approach using finite scheduling. Here the capacity is scheduled only up to the 80-hour capacity limit. Thus, the 75 hours of work shown as past due in the middle of Figure 7.11 would be scheduled in week 1 in the finite scheduling approach. Finite scheduling does not solve the undercapacity problem shown here. If capacity is not increased, only 80 hours of work can be completed in any week, regardless of the scheduling procedure. Finite scheduling will determine *which* jobs will be completed, according to how the jobs are scheduled—and there are various methods used to prioritize these decisions.

Finite scheduling systems simulate actual job order starting and stopping times to produce a detailed schedule for each shop order and each machine center; that is, finite scheduling *loads* all jobs in all necessary work centers for the length of the planning horizon. For this reason, the terms *finite scheduling* and *finite loading* tend to be used interchangeably. The result of finite loading is a set of start and finish dates for each operation at each work center. Finite scheduling explicitly establishes a detailed schedule for each job through each work center based on work center capacities and the other scheduled jobs. Figure 7.1 depicts finite loading as a short-term capacity planning technique. Because it produces a detailed schedule of each work center, it tends to be most correct in the short term. That is, predictions of exact job schedules will be less valid in the longer term.

One output of finite scheduling is a simulation of how each machine center is to operate on a minute-by-minute basis for whatever time horizon is planned. For example, suppose we begin with work center 300 on Monday morning of week 1. A job is already in process and 150 pieces remain with a standard time of one minute per piece. This order consumes the first 150 minutes of capacity; if work starts at 8 a.m., the machine is loaded until 10:30 a.m. The finite scheduling system would pick the next job to schedule on this machine, and load it, taking account of setup time and run times. The process is repeated to simulate the entire day, then the next day, and so on.

Selection of the next job to schedule is not based just on those jobs physically waiting at the work center. Most finite scheduling systems look at jobs coming to the work center, when they will be completed at the prior work centers, and these jobs' priorities to decide whether to leave the work center idle and immediately available for the arrival of a particular job. Also, some systems allow for overlap operations, where a job can start at a downstream work center before all of it is complete at the upstream work center.

The approach we have just described, where a work center is scheduled, job by job, is called **vertical loading.** Its orientation is on planning/utilizing the capacity of a work center—independently. This is consistent with how most job shop scheduling research is conducted where the focus is on establishing relative job order priorities for deciding which job to schedule next in a work center. A different approach used in finite scheduling is **horizontal loading.** In this case the orientation is on entire shop orders. Here, the highest-priority shop order or job is scheduled in *all* of its work centers, then the job with the next highest priority, and so on. The horizontal loading approach is often in conflict with using the work centers to their highest capacity, since it will have more "holes" in the schedule than the vertical loading approach.

There is a temptation to see vertical loading as better than horizontal because of the capacity utilization. This is not the case. Horizontal loading will complete whole jobs faster than vertical loading. And it is whole jobs that are sold to the customers, not partial jobs, and it is harder to sell jobs that take long times to complete. It is far better to have 50 percent of the jobs completed than 90 percent that are not quite completed!

In addition to the horizontal-vertical distinction, there is also the issue of **front scheduling** versus **back scheduling.** The back-scheduling approach starts with scheduling jobs backward from their due dates, whereas front scheduling starts with the current date scheduling into the future, where each job is completed as early as possible. If a back scheduling approach produces a past due start date for a shop order, this indicates infeasibility; similarly, if a front schedule does not produce jobs by the dates needed, it is also infeasible.

Because any plan produced by any finite scheduling model is indeed a simulation, it is to be expected that errors will result. That is, the times used for the schedule are only estimates, and randomness will occur. This means that many times a job is expected to be at a work center and it is not complete at the prior center, raising the question as to whether to wait or choose another job. Furthermore, the further out the simulation model is extended, the greater the uncertainty in the expected results. If the finite schedule is prepared on Sunday night, schedules for Monday might be fairly good, while those for Tuesday will have to deal with the actual results achieved on Monday. The validity of the schedule will decay as the time horizon for scheduling is extended. One way to improve the scheduling is to reschedule more often. Even though today's computers are fast, redoing an entire finite schedule every time a job is completed is still too expensive for most firms.

Finite Scheduling with Product Structures: Using APS Systems

The complexity of scheduling increases if one wishes to schedule not only *component parts* but also *products* with part structures. Thus, if we return to Figure 7.4, the real problem is in scheduling products A and B, not just in scheduling the components C, D, E, and F. Again if all the components are 90 percent completed, we cannot ship anything! The approach used by classic MRP systems is to take a long time to complete these jobs or else to have plenty of capacity available. With present imperatives on deliveries, inventories, and capacity investments, many firms are turning to finite loading systems that schedule the entire product as an entity. These systems are called **advanced production scheduling (APS)** systems, and several leading edge software companies provide them.

Essentially, APS systems use horizontal loading and either front or back scheduling depending on whether the product is desired as soon as possible (front scheduling). But now the entire product structure is scheduled. Thus, for product A (see Figure 7.4), it is necessary to schedule A, C, and D. Let us illustrate the methodology, with back scheduling, for the 30-unit master schedule quantity shown for week 8 in Figure 7.2, the lot sizes for C and D (40 and 60) shown in Figure 7.5, and the assumptions that the MRP records are run without safety stock and that there would be no projected available balances to offset the calculations by the time week 8 is planned.

Figure 7.12 shows how the master production schedule and component MRP records would be depicted for this example. Note that the records show *only* the requirements for this particular MPS quantity (e.g., not including any requirements for component D to support end product B). Figure 7.13 shows the capacity requirements for the MPS (work center 100) as well as for work centers 300 and 200 that would be produced by the resultant APS back schedule. This figure is based on the two-shift capacity (80 hours per week) assumption used

FIGURE 7.12
Data for APS Approach to End Product A

Master production schedule

End product	Week 8
A	30
B	25

MRP records for components C and D

Component C — Lot size = 40, Lead time = 2

	5	6	7	8
Gross requirements				30
Scheduled receipts				
Projected available balance				
Planned order releases		40		

Component D — Lot size = 60, Lead time = 1

	5	6	7	8
Gross requirements				30
Scheduled receipts				
Projected available balance				
Planned order releases			60	

FIGURE 7.13
Back Schedules for the MPS and Work Centers 100, 200 and 300.

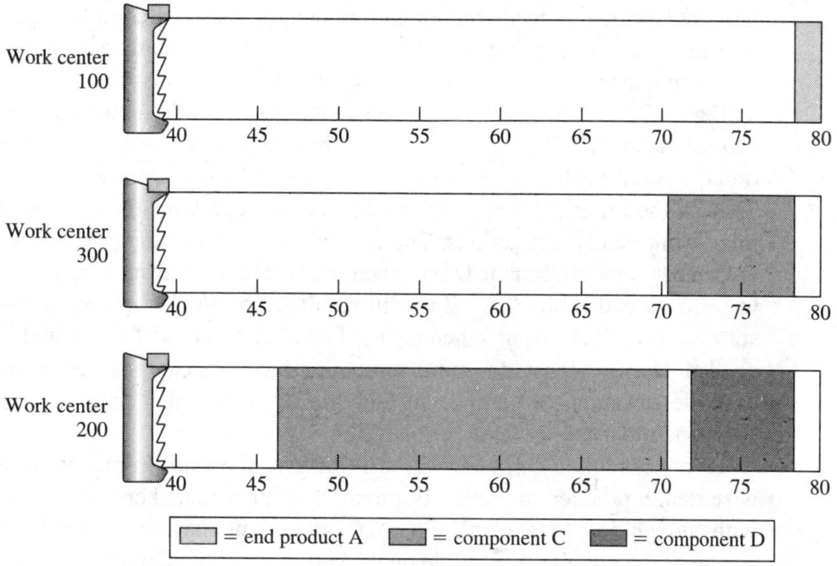

in the other calculations for this example. For work center 100, the capacity requirement is 1.5 hours, based on the data in Figure 7.7 (0.05 hour per unit × 30). Component C requires 24 hours of capacity in work center 200 (0.6 hour per unit × 40), followed by 8 hours of capacity in work center 300 (0.2 hour per unit × 40). Also shown in Figure 7.13 is a capacity requirement of 6 hours for work center 200 (0.1 hour per unit × 60) in order to fabricate the batch of component D needed to support the MPS for end product A.

Figure 7.13 allows us to discuss some of the key issues raised by using APS systems. First, let us be clear on the major benefit: The entire schedule for the MPS quantity has been fulfilled in less than 0.5 week (total elapsed time = 33.5 hours/80 = 0.41 week). This can be contrasted with an expected time of 3 weeks for standard MRP based approaches (86 percent lead time reduction). This implies a corresponding reduction in work-in-process inventories as well as a faster response to market conditions.

Executing the schedule planned in Figure 7.13 may make some people nervous. But it has been shown that this problem will absolutely not be made better by overstating the times used for the APS scheduling. Doing so puts in a *consistent* bias that degrades the planning process. The better approach is to focus on improving time estimates as much as possible (unbiased) and thereafter focus on flawless execution and recovery from any problems (work to the plan). More frequent rescheduling by the APS system allows errors to be reflected and compensated for in updated plans.

Figure 7.13 is simplified to show only the capacity requirements for one MPS quantity and its supporting components. In reality, the APS will schedule all MPS quantities, producing an overall capacity profile and detailed schedules for each work center. The *next* MPS quantity that is scheduled has to deal with the realities established by the prior schedules. That is, for example, if end product B is scheduled next in week 8, it will be back-scheduled to complete at hour 78.5 in work center 100, and its needs for capacity in work center 200 can end only at hour 46.5. One might therefore ask if the scheduling of end product B should precede that of end product A. This is a complex issue. Sequential processing of MPS quantities in APS means that one needs to determine the priorities for scheduling these end products. We will come back to this issue.

Figure 7.13 shows a "hole" in the schedule for work center 200 between hours 70.5 and 72.5. An APS system would allow this capacity to be used for another job or work order, but only if the work order had a capacity requirement equal or less than 2 hours. That is, the criterion here is to respect the schedules for the *end products,* not to optimize work center utilizations. The hole also illustrates another choice: the capacity requirement for Component D has been back-scheduled from the time when it is needed to produce end product A. This will result in the lowest inventory levels. But it could start at time 70.5 (front-schedule it), but then it would be completed 2 hours before needed. Doing so provides more surety that the MPS can proceed as planned, since now only the schedule for component C might upset it, rather than the schedules for either component part.

Front-scheduling component D will increase the work-in-process inventory, because it is started in production earlier. But there is another issue here, similar to when you arrive with enough time to take an earlier plane though not having a ticket for that flight. For the airline, if there is a seat available on the earlier flight, it is in their interest to put you on the earlier flight—regardless of what the payment/ticket conditions are—because the seat is empty, and the one you will occupy on the subsequent flight might be sold to someone else. The same issue comes up in Figure 7.13. The front schedule allows the "hole" to be shifted later, when it has a much better chance to be used, since there is not presently any work scheduled beyond hour 80 in work center 200. Front scheduling of component D allows work on another shop order to begin at hour 78.5 instead of hour 80.

What all of this illustrates is that there are "many ways to skin the cat." APS systems typically provide the ability to look at the schedules visibly to allow manual intervention and thereafter to see the resultant effects throughout the company (work centers, shop orders, MPS, customer orders). The outputs from APS are often displayed as schedule boards (bar charts showing each shop order being processed over time in each work center). APS systems are also usually linked to spread sheet models to allow users to examine the implications of various choices/schedule changes.

Management and Capacity Planning/Utilization

Capacity planning is one side of the coin; capacity management is the other. Plans need to be executed, and this needs to be done effectively; moreover, well-developed demand management can provide conditions that are much more favorable to routine execution. For example, Toyota and several other Japanese auto manufacturers develop production plans with a stable rate of output (cars per day). Product mix variations are substantially less than those for other auto companies because they carefully manage the number and timing of option combinations. The result is execution systems that are simple, effective, and easy to operate with minimal inventories and fast throughput times. Capacity planning is straightforward and execution is more easily achieved, not only for the company itself but for its suppliers as well. That is, well-managed front-end planning can rationalize the entire supply chain.

Capacity Monitoring with Input/Output Control

One key capacity management issue concerns the match between planning and execution. This implies monitoring on a timely basis to see whether a workable capacity plan has been created and whether some form of corrective action is needed. The best-known approach to this issue is **input/output control,** where the work flowing through a work center is monitored: the planned work input and planned output are compared to the work actual input and output.

Input/Output Control

The capacity planning technique used delineates the planned input. Planned output results from managerial decision making to specify the capacity level; that is, planned output is based on staffing levels, hours of work, and so forth. In capacity-constrained work centers, planned output is based on the rate of capacity established by management. In non-capacity-constrained work centers, planned output is equal to planned input (allowing for some lead-time offset).

Capacity data in input/output control are usually expressed in hours. Input data are based on jobs' expected arrivals at a work center. For example, a CRP procedure would examine the status of all open shop orders (scheduled receipts), estimate how long they'll take (setup, run, wait, and move) at particular work centers, and thereby derive when they'll arrive at subsequent work centers. A finite loading system would do the same, albeit with better results. The approach would be repeated for all planned orders from the MRP database. The resultant set of expected arrivals of exact quantities would be multiplied by run time per unit from the routing file. This product would be added to setup time, also from the routing file. The sum is a planned input expressed in standard hours.

Actual input would use the same routing data, but for the *actual* arrivals of jobs in each time period as reported by the shop-floor control system. Actual output would again use the shop-floor control data for exact quantities completed in each time period, converted to standard hours with routing time data.

The only time-data not based on the routing file are those for planned output. In this case, management has to plan the labor-hours to be expended in the work center. For example, if two people work nine hours per day for five days, the result is 90 labor-hours per week. This value has to be reduced or inflated by an estimate of the relation of actual hours to standard hours. In our example, if people in this work center typically worked at 80 percent efficiency, then planned output is 72 hours.

A work center's actual output will deviate from planned output. Often deviations can be attributed to conditions at the work center itself, such as lower-than-expected productivity, breakdowns, absences, random variations, or poor product quality. But less-than-expected output can occur for reasons outside the work center's control, such as insufficient output from a preceding work center or improper releasing of planned orders. Either problem can lead to insufficient input or a "starved" work center. Another reason for a variation between actual input and planned input was shown by our capacity planning model comparisons—some models don't produce realistic plans!

Input/output analysis also monitors backlog. Backlog represents the cushion between input and output. Backlog decouples input from output, allowing work center operations to be less affected by variations in requirements. Arithmetically, it equals prior backlog plus or minus the difference between input and output. The planned backlog calculation is based

FIGURE 7.14 Sample Input/Output for Work Center 500* (as of the end of period 5)

		Week				
		1	2	3	4	5
Planned input		15	15	0	10	10
Actual input		14	13	5	9	17
Cumulative deviation		−1	−3	+2	+1	+8
Planned output		11	11	11	11	11
Actual output		8	10	9	11	9
Cumulative deviation		−3	−4	−6	−6	−8
Actual backlog	20	26	29	25	23	31

Desired backlog: 10 hours

*In standard labor-hours.

on planned input and planned output. Actual backlog uses actual input and output. The difference between planned backlog and actual backlog represents one measure of the total, or net, input/output deviations. Monitoring input, output, and backlog typically involves keeping track of cumulative deviations and comparing them with preset limits.

The input/output report in Figure 7.14 is for work center 500 shown in weekly time buckets with input and output measured in standard labor-hours. The report was prepared at the end of period 5, so the actual values are current week-by-week variations in planned input. These could result from actual planned orders and scheduled receipts; that is, for example, if the input were planned by CRP, planned inputs would be based on timings for planned orders, the status of scheduled receipts, and routing data. The *actual* input that arrives at work center 500 can vary for any of the causes just discussed.

Work center 500's planned output has been smoothed; that is, management decided to staff this work center to achieve a constant output of 11 hours per week. The results should be to absorb input variations with changes in the backlog level. Cumulative planned output for the five weeks (55 hours) is 5 hours more than cumulative planned input. This reflects a management decision to reduce backlog from the original level of 20 hours. The process of increasing capacity to reduce backlog recognizes explicitly that flows must be controlled to change backlog; backlog can't be changed in or of itself.

Figure 7.14 summarized the results after five weeks of actual operation. At the end of week 5, the situation requires managerial attention. The cumulative input deviation (+8 hours), cumulative output deviation (−8 hours), current backlog (31 hours), or all three could have exceeded the desired limits of control. In this example, the increased backlog is a combination of more-than-expected input and less-than-expected output.

One other aspect of monitoring backlog is important. In general, there's little point in releasing orders to a work center that already has an excessive backlog, except when the order to be released is of higher priority than any in the backlog. The idea is to not release work that can't be done, but to wait and release what's really needed. Oliver Wight summed this up as one of the principles of input/output control: "Never put into a manufacturing facility or to a vendor's facility more than you believe can be produced. Hold backlogs in production and inventory control." With today's APS system, a similar dictate results: concentrate on executing the most immediate schedule—exactly. The APS system will take care of the future schedules.

FIGURE 7.15
The Capacity Bathtub

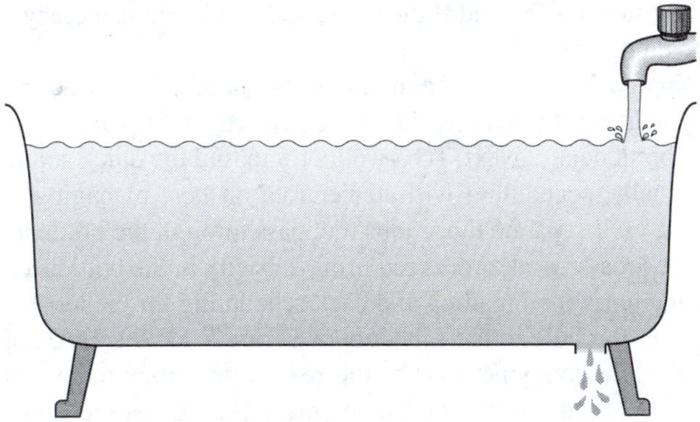

Figure 7.15 depicts a work center "bathtub" showing capacity in hydraulic terms. The input pipe's diameter represents the maximum flow (of work) into the tub. The valve represents MPC systems like MPS, MRP, and JIT, which determine **planned input** (flow of work) into the tub. Actual input could vary because of problems (like a corroded valve or problem at the water department) and can be monitored with input/output analysis. We can determine **required capacity** to accomplish the planned input to the work center with any of the capacity planning techniques. The output drain pipe takes completed work from the work center. Its diameter represents the work center's planned or **rated capacity,** which limits planned output. As with actual input, actual output may vary from the plan as well. It too can be monitored with input/output analysis. Sometimes planned output can't be achieved over time even when it's less than maximum capacity and there's a backlog to work on. When that occurs, realized output is called **demonstrated capacity.** The "water" in the tub is the **backlog** or **load,** which can also be monitored with input/output analysis.

Managing Bottleneck Capacity

Eliyahu Goldratt developed a key capacity management idea that he popularized more than 25 years ago in *The Goal.* Fundamentally, one needs to find the bottlenecks in any factory, and thereafter manage their capacities most effectively. Goldratt's maxim is that an hour of capacity lost in a bottleneck work center is an hour of capacity lost to the entire company—worth a fortune. But an hour of capacity gained in a nonbottleneck work center will only increase work-in-process inventory and confusion. Eli Goldratt has gone on to other things, but this fundamental concept remains at the base of his work. Today, he and his colleagues have generalized the ideas into what they refer to as "theory of constraints" (TOC). For the purposes of capacity planning and management, TOC teaches that the capacities of bottleneck work centers need to be planned and managed much more carefully than those of nonbottlenecks. In fact, Goldratt points out that for nonbottlenecks it may not be important to even have decent data. If sufficient capacity exists, execution of capacity plans is easy. Spend the time and energy on execution of what at first seems impossible.

Goldratt has many suggestions for how to execute the impossible. For example, why shouldn't bottleneck work centers run through lunch hours and coffee breaks—others can run these work centers while the primary personnel eat lunch and drink coffee. Alternative routing is another solution, and this is a good idea even when it "costs" much more. Usually the costs are calculated with unrealistic assumptions. Extra work done in an underutilized work center has no real cost, and if the bottleneck workload is thereby reduced, it is an excellent idea to do it.

The TOC approach to capacity planning is essentially to first determine the bottleneck work centers. This can be done with a rough-cut capacity planning model or with CRP. Where are the bottlenecks? Next, TOC would try to find the quick solutions for eliminating bottlenecks. Finally, scheduling will concentrate on best managing bottleneck capacity. Essentially, TOC will separate those jobs that pass through the bottlenecks from those that do not. Only the jobs or work orders requiring capacity in the bottleneck resource are finite scheduled, using horizontal loading and back scheduling for the most critical jobs.

If we return to the hole in the schedule of Figure 7.13, the TOC approach would definitely front-schedule component D for the reason described there: it is the schedule for component C that constrains the start of end product A. Do not let component D become a constraint to this overall product schedule. TOC treats this early schedule (front-loaded) as a buffer in order to reduce the possibility of missing the overall goal: ship the end product!

TOC uses APS systems, but concentrates their attention on what is truly critical. For nonbottleneck work centers it is more than unimportant to utilize their capacity—it is fundamentally *wrong*. Increasing utilization of nonbottlenecks will result in more work being in the factory than necessary, yielding higher inventories and confusion. Nonbottleneck work will be done easily because there is basically no constraint to it. Restricting the use of APS systems to focus on the bottlenecks allows smart users to examine the best ways to "skin the cat."

The most critical capacity requirements need to be identified and thereafter utilized to maximum effectiveness. Capacity planning techniques can help with the former, but effective management is needed for the latter. Moreover, managerial policies can also create environments that are easier to execute—environments where capacities are utilized in a predictable and stable fashion.

Capacity Planning in the MPC System

To illustrate the importance of the interrelationships in designing and using the capacity planning system, let's consider the impact of production planning and resource planning decisions on shorter-term capacity planning decisions. To the extent that production planning and resource planning are done well, problems faced in capacity planning can be reduced, since appropriate resources have been provided. If, for example, the production plan specifies a very stable rate of output, then changes in the master production schedule (MPS) requiring capacity changes are minimal. If the material planning module functions effectively, the MPS will be converted into detailed component production plans with relatively few unexpected execution problems.

A quite different but equally important linkage that can affect capacity planning system design is the linkage with shop-floor execution systems. A key relationship exists in scheduling effective use of capacity. With sufficient capacity and efficient use of that capacity ensured by good shop-floor systems, we'll see few unpleasant surprises requiring capacity analysis and change. Effective shop-floor procedures utilize available capacity to process orders according to MRP system priorities, provide insight into potential capacity problems in the short range (a few hours to days), and respond to changes in material plans. Thus, effective systems reduce the necessary degree of detail and intensity of use of the capacity planning system. The result is a better match between actual input/output and planned input/output. Again, we see attention to the material planning side of the MPC system, in this case the shop-floor module, having an effect on the capacity planning side.

Choosing the Measure of Capacity

The choice of capacity measures is an important management issue. Alternatives run from machine-hours or labor-hours to physical or monetary units. The choice depends on the constraining resource and the firm's needs. In any manufacturing company, the "bundle of goods and services" provided to customers increasingly includes software, other knowledge work, after-sales service, and other customer services. In every case, providing these goods and services requires resources—"capacities" that must be planned, managed, and developed. Appropriate measures of capacity must be established and changed as evolution in the bundle of goods and services occurs.

Several current trends in manufacturing have a significant bearing on the choice of capacity measures. Each can have a major impact on what's important to measure in capacity. One important trend is considerable change in the concept of direct labor. Direct labor has been shrinking as a portion of overall manufacturing employment. Distinctions between direct and indirect labor are becoming less important. The ability to change labor capacity by hiring and firing (or even using overtime) has been reduced; notions of "lifetime employment" have further constrained this form of capacity adjustment.

One objective in JIT systems is continual improvement, so the basis for labor capacity is constantly changing. This mandates control procedures for identifying and changing the planning factors as improvements take place.

Another important trend is decreased internal fabrication and increased emphasis on outside purchasing, i.e., outsourcing. This trend can alter the conception of what capacity requirements are important. Procurement analysis, incoming inspection, and engineering liaison may become the critical capacities to be managed, as well as planning and scheduling the capacities in vendor firms. In fact, one of the major benefits ascribed to major outsourcing companies is their ability to more flexibly respond to changing capacity needs.

For many firms engaged in fabrication, machine technology is changing rapidly. Flexible automation has greatly increased the range of parts that can be processed in a machine center. Future product mixes are likely to be much more variable than in the past, with a marked effect on the equipment capacity required. Moreover, as equipment becomes more expensive, it may be necessary to plan and control the capacity of key pieces of equipment at a detailed level.

To the extent that cellular technologies are adopted as part of JIT manufacturing, the unit of capacity may need to change. Usually the entire cell is coupled and has only as much capacity as its limiting resource. Often, the cell is labor limited, so the unit of capacity is labor-hours (continually adjusted for learning). Sometimes, however, the capacity measure needs to be solely associated with a single aspect of the cell. Also, when dissimilar items are added to the cell for manufacture, it's necessary to estimate each new item's capacity requirements in terms of individual processing steps.

The first task in choosing a capacity measure is to creatively identify resources that are critical and in short supply. Capacity control is too complicated to apply to all resources. The next step is to define the unit of measure. If the key resource is people, then labor-hours may be appropriate. In other instances, such measures as tons, gallons, number of molds, number of ovens, hours of machine time, square yards, linear feet, lines of code, customer calls, and cell hours have been used. In some cases, these are converted to some "equivalent" measure to accommodate a wider variety of products or resources.

After the resources and unit of measure have been determined, the next concern is to estimate available capacity. The primary issue here is theory versus practice. The engineer can provide theoretical capacity from the design specifications for a machine or from time studies of people. A subissue is whether to use "full" capacity or some fraction thereof (often 75 to 85 percent). A further issue is "plasticity" in capacity. For almost *any* resource, if it's *really* important, more output can be achieved. We've seen many performances that fall short of or exceed capacity calculations.

Choice of capacity measure follows directly from the objective of providing capacity to meet production plans. The appropriate measure of capacity that most directly affects meeting these plans. The measure, therefore, should be appropriate to the critical limited resources and be based on what's achievable, with allowances for maintenance and other necessary activities. It must be possible to convert the bundle of products and services into capacity measurement terms. The results must be understood by those responsible, and they should be monitored.

Choice of a Specific Technique

In this chapter's discussion, the capacity planning techniques for converting a material plan into capacity requirements include three different methods for rough-cut capacity planning (CPOF, capacity bills, and resource profiles). We also examined capacity requirements planning, CRP, which is particularly useful for medium range planning. For the detailed day-to-day capacity planning APS systems can be valuable under some circumstances. The choice of method depends heavily on characteristics of the manufacturing environment.

The three rough-cut methods are most general, being applicable even in companies using just-in-time methods for shop-floor control. Rough-cut approaches can be useful in JIT operations to estimate the impact of changes in requirements called for by revisions to the master production schedule. For example, under level scheduling conditions, a change from a production rate of 480 units per day (one unit per minute) to 528 units per day (1.1 units per minute) might be needed. A rough-cut procedure could be used to examine the impact on each work center or manufacturing cell through which this volume would pass (including those of suppliers). Any indicated problems or bottleneck conditions could be addressed *before* the crisis hits. Similarly, a planned reduction in MPS could be evaluated to determine resources that might be freed to work on other tasks.

Rough-cut approaches do vary in accuracy, aggregation level, and ease of preparation. There's a general relationship between the amount of data and computational time required, and the quality and detail of the capacity requirements estimated. The issue is whether additional costs of supporting more complex procedures are justified by improved decision making and subsequent plant operations.

The capacity bills procedure has an advantage over capacity planning using overall factors (CPOF) because it explicitly recognizes product mix changes. This can be important in JIT operations, particularly where the level schedule is based on assumptions of product mix and where different products have different capacity requirements. On the other hand, if changes in mix are easily accommodated, and there are minimal differences in capacity requirements for different products, then CPOF's simplicity can be exploited. Under JIT operations, however, there's often little need to incorporate the added sophistication of the resource profile procedure. There simply won't be any added advantage to making lead time offsets in the planning process. Work is completed at virtually the same time as it's started.

Capacity requirements planning is only applicable in companies using time-phased MRP records for detailed material planning and shop-order-based shop scheduling systems. CRP is unnecessary under JIT operations anyway because minimal work-in-process levels mean there's no need to estimate the impact in capacity requirements of partially processed work. All orders start from "raw material" with virtually no amount of "capacity" stored in component inventories. Also, under JIT, there's no formal PAC procedure. There are no work orders. Thus, there are no status data on work orders.

Input/output control isn't usually an issue under JIT operations because attention has been shifted from planning to execution. As a result, actual input should equal actual output. Actual input becomes actual output with an insignificant delay. The backlog is effectively a constant zero. However, planned input can indeed vary from actual input and so can planned output vary from actual output. These variations should be achievable without violating the equality between actual input and actual output–with backlog remaining at zero. To the extent that plan-to-actual variations are possible, the result reflects the flexibility, or bandwidth, of the JIT unit.

Using the Capacity Plan

All the techniques we've described provide data on which a manager can base a decision. The broad choices are clear—if there's a mismatch between available capacity and required capacity, either the capacity or the material plan should be changed. If capacity is to be changed, the choices include overtime/undertime authorization, hiring/layoff, and increasing/ decreasing the number of machine tools or times in use. Capacity requirements can be changed by alternate routing, make-or-buy decisions, subcontracting, raw material substitutions, inventory changes, or revised customer promise dates.

Choice of capacity planning units can lead to more effective use of the system. Capacity units need not be work centers as defined for manufacturing, engineering, or routing purposes. They can be groupings of the key resources (human or capital) important in defining the factory's output levels. Many firms plan capacity solely for key machines (work centers) and gateway operations. These key areas can be managed in detail, while other areas fall under resource planning and the shop-floor control system.

Capacity planning choices dictate the diameter of the manufacturing pipeline. Only as much material can be produced as there's capacity for its production, *regardless of the material plan*. Not understanding the critical nature of managing capacity can lead a firm into production chaos and serious customer service problems. In the same vein, the relationship between flexibility and capacity must be discussed. You can't have perfectly balanced material and capacity plans *and* be able to easily produce emergency orders! We know one general manager who depicts his capacity as a pie. He has one slice for recurring business, one for spare parts production, one for downtime and maintenance, and a final specific slice for opportunity business. He manages to pay for this excess capacity by winning lucrative contracts that require rapid responses. He *does not add* that opportunity business to a capacity plan fully committed to the other aspects of his business.

Concluding Principles

Clear principles for design and use of the capacity planning system emerge from this chapter:

- Capacity plans must be developed concurrently with material plans if the material plans are to be realized.
- The particular capacity planning technique(s) chosen must match the level of detail and actual company circumstances to permit making effective management decisions.
- Capacity planning can be simplified in a JIT environment.
- The better the resource and production planning process, the less difficult the capacity planning process.
- The better the shop-floor system, the less short-term capacity planning is required.
- The more detail in the capacity planning system, the more data and database maintenance are required.
- It's not always capacity that should change when capacity availability doesn't equal need.
- Capacity not only must be planned, but use of that capacity must also be monitored and controlled.
- Capacity planning techniques can be applied to selected key resources (which need not correspond to production work centers).
- The capacity measure should reflect realizable output from the key resources.

Discussion Questions

1. Figure 7.1 shows a hierarchy of capacity planning and material planning processes. How does a better job of long-range planning affect the medium-range planning? Is the issue similar between production planning and master production scheduling?
2. Why does JIT execution require a less-intensive capacity planning approach?
3. What are the advantages and disadvantages of using CRP over rough-cut capacity planning?
4. What are the relative advantages of horizontal versus vertical loading?
5. How does input-output analysis provide a reality check on material and capacity planning processes?
6. Why is an hour of capacity lost in a bottleneck work center so valuable?
7. How might the Montell capacity plan (Figure 7.16) allow the company to determine if its revenue projections are on target? (See the Cases at the end of the chapter.)
8. What is the thinking behind Applicon's three different capacity values for its work centers? (See the Cases at the end of the chapter.)
9. In the Manugistics APS system, what would it mean if the days of supply were negative whenever a new batch of the products was scheduled? What would it mean if each time a new batch was scheduled, the days of supply was at 5D? (See the Cases at the end of the chapter.)
10. What are some examples of capacity planning in a university? What are good and poor practices?

Problems

1. A firm makes car seats for an automaker in two varieties: leather and fabric. The standard labor hours for these are 1.2 and 1.0 hours, respectively. The seats are made in two work centers, sewing and assembly, where the average percentage of work has been 55 percent for sewing and

45 percent for assembly. Given the following schedule for the next six weeks, calculate the labor hours needed in each of the two work centers:

Week	1	2	3	4	5	6
Leather	15	20	18	21	15	13
Fabric	65	60	62	59	65	67

2. Returning to problem 1, what are the average labor-hours needed over the six-week period, and how might the company handle deviations from the average? How might they staff their departments?
3. Returning again to problem 1, the leather requires incoming inspection for each car seat in order to be sure the colors match. The time required for this is five minutes per seat. What are the expected capacity requirements for the inspection department over the next six weeks? Is there any way that this problem can usefully be combined with problem 1?
4. Returning to problem 3, what if inspection is done by the seat manufacturer in combination with assembly? How does this influence analysis of problem 1?
5. A metal fabricating company has the following master production schedule for one of its items (a frame), as well as the accompanying product structure.

	Week 1	Week 2	Week 3	Week 4
MPS	20	30	35	20

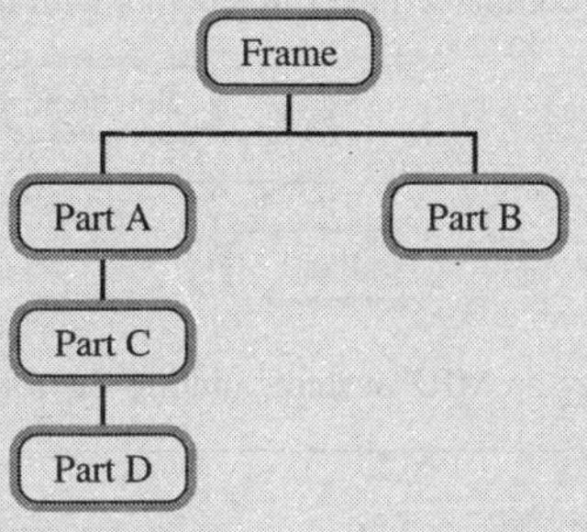

The resource profile for the frame is as follows:

Item	Work Center	Setup Hours	Run Hours/Unit	Lead Time
Frame	200	4	1.5	0 weeks
Part A	300	3	1.0	1 week
Part B	300	3	.8	1 week
Part C	400	2	1.2	2 weeks
Part D	500	2	1.0	1 week

Determine the capacity requirements for all work centers, assuming all usages are one, and that a new setup is required in each week at each work center.

6. A furniture manufacturer makes a bookcase from two end panels, four shelves, fasteners, and hangers. The end panels and shelves have the following data:

	End Panel		
Operation	Machine	Run Time	Setup Time
1	Saw	5 minutes	0.6 hour
2	Planer	3 minutes	0.3 hour
3	Router	4 minutes	0.8 hour

	Shelf		
Operation	Machine	Run Time	Setup Time
1	Saw	4 minutes	0.5 hour
2	Molder	5 minutes	1.3 hours
3	Router	5 minutes	0.7 hour
4	Sander	1 minute	0.1 hour

The master schedule for the next three weeks is 35, 50, and 40 bookcases, respectively. Each MPS quantity requires a setup.

a. What is the total number of hours required on each of the five machine centers for each week?

b. If each of the two parts is started into production one week (five days) before needed in assembly, and it takes one day per operation, generate the week-by-week load on the routing machine.

c. If, in part b, the two parts arrive at the router on the same day, which would you process first? Why?

7. An office supply company makes notebooks with the following product structure:

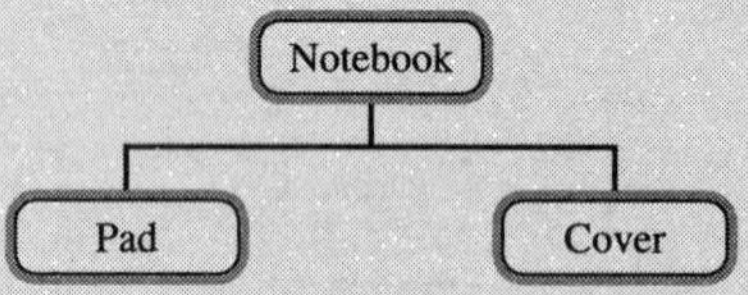

The company uses an MRP system, and has the following records for these three items.

		Week					
Notebook		1	2	3	4	5	6
Gross requirements		25	25	25	25	25	25
Scheduled receipts							
Projected available balance	30	5	0	0	0	0	0
Planned order releases		20	25	25	25	25	0

Q = L4L, LT = 1, SS = 0.

Pad		1	2	3	4	5	6
Gross requirements		20	25	25	25	25	0
Scheduled receipts		15					
Projected available balance	10	5	10	15	20	25	25
Planned order releases		30	30	30	30	0	0

Q = 30, LT = 1, SS = 0.

Cover		1	2	3	4	5	6
Gross requirements		20	25	25	25	25	0
Scheduled receipts		50					
Projected available balance	10	40	15	40	15	40	40
Planned order releases		50	0	50	0	0	0

Q = 50, LT = 2, SS = 0.

The notebooks are fabricated in the following work centers, listed with accompanying time requirements.

Operation	Work Center	Setup Time	Run Time
Notebook assembly	100	2 hours	10 minutes
Pad production	200	3 hours	5 minutes
Cover production	300	2 hours	9 minutes

Determine the weekly capacity requirements in each of the work centers. For the two scheduled receipts, assume that the setup is complete, and that in each case they are half complete.

8. The following input-output data were gathered at the end of week 8 for a work center:

	Week							
	1	2	3	4	5	6	7	8
Planned input	60	60	60	60	60	60	60	60
Actual input	68	70	75	70	68	60	55	55
Planned output	65	65	65	65	65	65	65	65
Actual output	60	62	63	63	64	65	63	60

Beginning backlog = 50 hours.

a. Complete the input/output document.

b. What was the planned objective?

c. Was it met?

d. What recommendations would you make?

9. A company with three product lines has estimated its weekly capacity requirements for three work centers as follows.

	Product Line		
Work Center	A	B	C
100	35 hours	28 hours	12 hours
200	25 hours	37 hours	56 hours
300	46 hours	35 hours	33 hours

a. How many workers (and duplicate machines) are needed in each work center if they are to work 40 hours per week?

b. What is the difference if the firm decides to work two shifts (80 hours per week)?

10. Suppose in the Montell example (Figure 7.16) a customer wanted to place the maximum order possible for the B1 line. (See the Cases at the end of the chapter.) What is the total quantity that could be provided in the next months (12, 01, and 02) with the current capacity? What might be done to improve the response?
11. Applicon has the following capacity bills for its popular items A and B.

A		B	
Work Center	Hours/Unit	Work Center	Hours/Unit
ALF-A	1.0	ALF-T	0.4
HLT-A	0.5	HLT-T	0.7
MIS-A	0.7	MIS-T	0.5
MVX-A	0.7	MVX-T	1.0
PCB-A	0.4	PCB-P	0.8
PCB-P	1.2	PCB-W	1.6

It is now June 15, and an important customer wishes to have 100 units of both A and B during the next month (20 working days). Analyze the effect of accepting this order. Assume there are adequate materials, and work center MVX-T has had its capacity increased to one full person (capacity now = 160). This was accomplished by reducing MVX-A to 6.5 persons, and no other orders have been booked since June 12. Use the capacity data and conditions of Figure 7.18 as the basis for your analysis. (See the Cases in the next section for these data.)

Case

Capacity Planning at Montell USA Inc.

Montell USA Inc. manufactures plastic pellets used in injection molding machines. The pellets are made up of combinations of plastic material, coloring agents, and other chemicals. The company's primary customers use injection molding machines to make plastic components for the automotive industry. Montell currently utilizes a combination of two software packages in its manufacturing planning and control system. Front-end activities, like master production scheduling and demand management, are done with a system termed Picaso. MRP and back-end activities, like shop-floor control and vendor scheduling, are accomplished with an enterprise resource planning system provided by SAP. The Picaso system is used to produce the capacity planning reports for the company.

Montell prepares a rough-cut capacity plan from the master production schedule. It is a rolling plan, revised each month for the coming six months. It is prepared for each of the company's production lines, using a capacity measure of thousands of pounds of output. An example of part of a plan is given in Figure 7.16. For each of the next six months, two figures are shown for each production line: FINL and PLAN. The first of these, FINL, shows the booked customer orders for the month.

The second column for each month is the PLAN column. This gives the master production schedule quantity for each of the production lines. There are a few instances where booked orders exceed the planned capacity (e.g., months 12 and 01 for line B1). In some of these cases, management action (like overtime or a partial extra shift) may be needed to meet the requirements; in others, no action is needed because of the specific products being produced. To help determine where action should be taken, the rough-cut capacity plan is also detailed by specific product. An example showing part of the capacity plan detailed by product is provided in Figure 7.17. In this report the planners can see, for instance, the breakdown of specific products that sum up the quantities of 616 FINL and 561 PLAN for line G2 in month 12. The planners at Montell use this data to determine if changes need to be made in the MPS and/or in the commitments to customers.

FIGURE 7.16 **Part of Montell's Capacity Plan by Production Line**

Line	FINL 12*	PLAN 12	FINL 01	PLAN 01	FINL 02	PLAN 02	FINL 03	PLAN 03	FINL 04	PLAN 04	FINL 05	PLAN 05
B 1	2,327	1,685	2,610	2,598	2,758	2,530	2,818	2,862	2,763	2,621	508	2,842
BW-8	887	649	792	892	713	752	686	810	615	837	76	997
C 1	264	330	426	247	672	225	262	254	42	313	42	311
CK	180	162	190	159	180	116	52	201	132	134	0	159
CT-1	0	88	0	0	0	0	0	0	0	0	0	0
E 1	0	0	0	0	0	0	0	0	0	0	0	0
E 2	0	0	0	0	0	0	0	0	0	0	0	0
E 4	0	0	0	0	0	0	0	0	0	0	0	0
E 7	0	0	0	0	0	0	0	0	0	0	0	0
G 1	910	532	1,076	1,180	887	1,230	752	1,255	440	1,265	160	1,297
G 2	616	561	645	719	637	634	509	639	600	661	16	665
G 3	582	431	716	438	600	411	458	414	219	514	62	416
G 4	1,347	791	1,494	1,391	1,182	1,222	1,074	1,292	1,102	1,471	82	1,409
G 5	1,802	1,698	2,430	1,571	2,211	1,631	2,127	1,708	1,669	1,424	320	1,449

*Month 12.

FIGURE 7.17 **Part of Montell's Capacity Plan by Product and Line**

Line	Name	FINL 12	PLAN 12	FINL 01	PLAN 01	FINL 02	PLAN 02	FINL 03	PLAN 03	FINL 04	PLAN 04	FINL 05	PLAN 05
G 2	722-44-06 BB73F KZE	30	10	25	35	33	45	35	35	35	35	0	35
	722-44-07 BB73F DC4A	60	95	70	80	99	90	100	90	90	80	0	90
	722-44-08 BB73F YCD	90	100	10	110	10	110	10	110	0	110	0	110
	722-44-09 BB73F MDD	0	0	90	0	90	0	90	0	100	0	0	0
	722-46-01 BB73F DCC	15	20	10	50	15	20	15	25	15	50	0	25
	722-46-04 BB73F YCC	10	20	15	25	10	20	10	25	10	20	0	25
	840-43-05 EXP149628	0	0	0	0	0	0	0	0	0	0	0	0
	840-43-06 EXP149629	0	0	0	0	0	0	0	0	0	0	0	0
		616	561	645	719	637	634	509	639	600	661	16	665
G 3	102-64-08 RTA3184 6P	0	0	0	0	0	0	0	0	0	0	0	0
	102-64-13 RTA3184 JA	0	0	0	0	0	0	0	0	0	0	0	0
	105-02-01 RTA3363E B	0	0	0	0	0	0	0	0	0	0	0	0
	109-03-05 CL37BC BLA	0	0	0	0	0	0	0	0	0	0	0	0
	120-05-17 CA45GC PA7	0	0	0	0	0	0	0	0	0	0	0	0
	120-05-52 CA45GC SPN	17	36	25	0	25	0	25	0	25	0	0	0

Case Capacity Planning at Applicon

Applicon, a division of Schlumberger, designs and manufactures computer-aided engineering (CAE), computer-aided design (CAD), and computer-aided manufacturing (CAM) systems. Applicon implemented numerous JIT concepts and replaced some of its MRP system modules. Its dramatic results included a reduction in lead time (20 weeks to 4 days), an inventory reduction of over 75 percent, virtual elimination of obsolescence costs, little or no inspection, and a decline in MPC personnel (86 to 14).

Figure 7.18 shows an Applicon "Capacity Status Report." Applicon divided the factory into 17 capacity groupings (work centers) for planning purposes. It used actual customer orders as a monthly MPS to drive capacity planning. Capacity bills were used to convert the MPS into the present "load" over the next month (20 working days) in standard hours (the second column in Figure 7.18). The capacities in column 3 are based on a total workforce of 48 people (e.g., ALF-A had three workers who

FIGURE 7.18
Applicon Capacity Status Report

Work Center	Load (Std. Hours)	Capacity (Standard)	Capacity (Adj. Std.)	Capacity (Maximum)
ALF-A	70	480	336	528
ALF-T	5	80	56	88
HLT-A	438	800	560	880
HLT-T	85	160	112	176
MIS-A	270	800	560	880
MIS-T	14	80	56	88
MVX-A	399	1,120	784	1,232
MVX-T	79	80	56	88
OLD-P	81	0	0	0
PCB-A	52	160	112	176
PCB-H	44	160	112	176
PCB-I	124	320	224	352
PCB-M	441	480	336	520
PCB-P	408	960	672	1,056
PCB-T	918	1,680	1,176	1,848
PCB-V	123	160	112	176
PCB-W	56	160	112	176
Totals	3,634	7,680	5,376	8,440

20 total workdays included.

worked 8 hours per day for 20 days in the month = 480 standard hours). Work center OLD-P's zero capacity indicates no worker is presently assigned to this activity.

The fourth column reduces the capacity amounts by 30 percent (the desired rate of direct production activity for Applicon workers). The remaining time was used for "whole person" activities. That is, the company operated with the direct workers taking on many other tasks, such as design of work methods, new drawings, and database maintenance. On the average, Applicon expected that 30 percent of the time would be spent on this indirect work. This was *instead* of having a larger number of indirect workers. The last column provides a "maximum" capacity value based on 10 percent overtime. Applicon felt that it had the flexibility to operate easily between these two capacity levels. Where the volume was much higher or lower, they needed to make adjustments.

This report was run on June 12 for the next 20 days. Differences between "load" and the three capacities represented Applicon's ability to take on additional work in the next month. Large orders could be included into a trial run of the MPS to examine the orders' impact in terms of existing capacity availabilities. Total load (3,634 hours) represented 47 percent of standard capacity, 68 percent of adjusted capacity, and 43 percent of maximum capacity. Management reviewed these numbers carefully—particularly if possible large orders were under negotiation. It was relatively easy to make trial runs with those orders included to examine the impact of accepting the orders.

Of all the work centers in Figure 7.18, MVX-T appeared to be in the most trouble. However, this could easily be fixed. MVX-T only had one-half person allocated to it (80 hours/month). Reducing MVX-A (or some other work center) by one-half person and increasing MVX-T's capacity to one person for the month solved the problem. OLD-P similarly needed to have a person allocated to it.

This rough-cut capacity planning system serves Applicon well. Problems can be anticipated. JIT operations mean results are very current, with little or no bias because of work-in-process inventories. Results of the capacity planning are given to shop personnel, who make their own adjustments as they see fit, making allowances for absenteeism, particular workers' relative strengths, and other local conditions.

Case

Capacity Planning with APS at a Consumer Products Company

A large European based consumer products company uses APS extensively in one of its factories. The APS software package is provided by Manugistics, and is called NetWORKS Scheduling. It is essentially a horizontal loading, back-scheduling system operating like the one illustrated in this chapter. It produces schedules for each work center that are similar to that of Figure 7.14. Figure 7.19 is a portion of a sample output report as generated by the APS software. Here we see a work center (packing line 250-ml sauce), and the 10 pasta sauces that are scheduled for production over the next seven days. Each of the items shown is a 250-ml bottle of a particular end product. For each item there are two values shown: the planned production in each day, and the expected inventory in days of supply. By using days of supply, the system makes comparisons of inventory positions more transparent. To accomplish this, there is a linkage to a demand management system that allows the calculations for days of supply to reflect forecasts, actual orders, and provisions for special promotions.

Figure 7.19 seems to reflect ample capacity to meet demands at this company. There do not appear to be any shortages predicted in this plan, except perhaps for the third item (103), which might run out on 15/9. The match of production with capacity seems fairly close, with most production quantities scheduled to occur just when the days of supply approach zero. Thus, items 102, 105, and 107 are all scheduled the day after the days of supply is one day. It is only items 108 and 109 that seem to be scheduled earlier than necessary.

FIGURE 7.19 **Sample APS Output—Pasta Sauce Line**

Res: 250-ml Sauce

Item	Description	10/9	11/9	12/9	13/9	14/9	15/9	16/9
101	250 ml			6,600				
				5D	4D	3D	2D	1D
102	250 ml						5,400	
		5D	4D	3D	2D	1D	8D	7D
103	250 ml							5,100
		5D	4D	3D	2D	1D		3D
104	250 ml	2,700						
		9D	8D	7D	6D	5D	4D	3D
105	250 ml			7,200				
		2D	1D	12D	11D	10D	9D	8D
106	250 ml	10,800						7,200
		6D	5D	4D	3D	2D	1D	3D
107	250 ml						3,100	
		5D	4D	3D	2D	1D	4D	3D
108	250 ml						1,800	
		12D	11D	10D	9D	8D	14D	13D
109	250 ml						3,600	3,900
		6D	5D	4D	3D	2D	5D	9D
110	250 ml				5,000			

Chapter 8

Production Activity Control

This chapter concerns the execution of detailed material plans. It describes the planning and release of individual orders to both factory and outside vendors. Production activity control (PAC) also concerns, when necessary, detailed scheduling and control of individual jobs at work centers on the shop floor, as well as vendor scheduling. An effective production activity control system can ensure meeting the company's customer service goals. A PAC system can reduce work-in-process inventories and lead times as well as improve vendor performance. A key element of an effective PAC system is feedback on shop and suppliers' performance against plans. This loop-closing aspect provides signals for revising plans if necessary.

This chapter is organized around three topics:

- *A framework for production activity control:* How does PAC relate to other aspects of material planning and control, and how do just-in-time production of individual firm decisions affect PAC system design?
- *Production activity control techniques:* What basic concepts and models are used for shop-floor and vendor scheduling and control?
- *Production activity control examples:* How have PAC systems been designed and implemented in several different kinds of companies?

A Framework for Production Activity Control

Production activity control (PAC) concerns execution of material plans. It encompasses activities within the shaded areas of Figure 8.1. The box entitled "Shop-floor scheduling and control," which we refer to as shop-floor control, falls completely within PAC. Vendor scheduling and follow-up is depicted as largely being part of production activity control, but not completely. Many firms, particularly those with JIT material control approaches, assign most vendor scheduling to PAC. Order release (which authorizes release of individual orders to the factory and provides accompanying documentation) is similarly becoming more a part of PAC. In purchasing, **procurement** is seen as a professional activity where information networks, relationships, terms, and conditions are established with vendor companies outside of PAC, while release of individual orders and follow-up activities are a part of PAC.

FIGURE 8.1
Production Activity Control in the MPC System

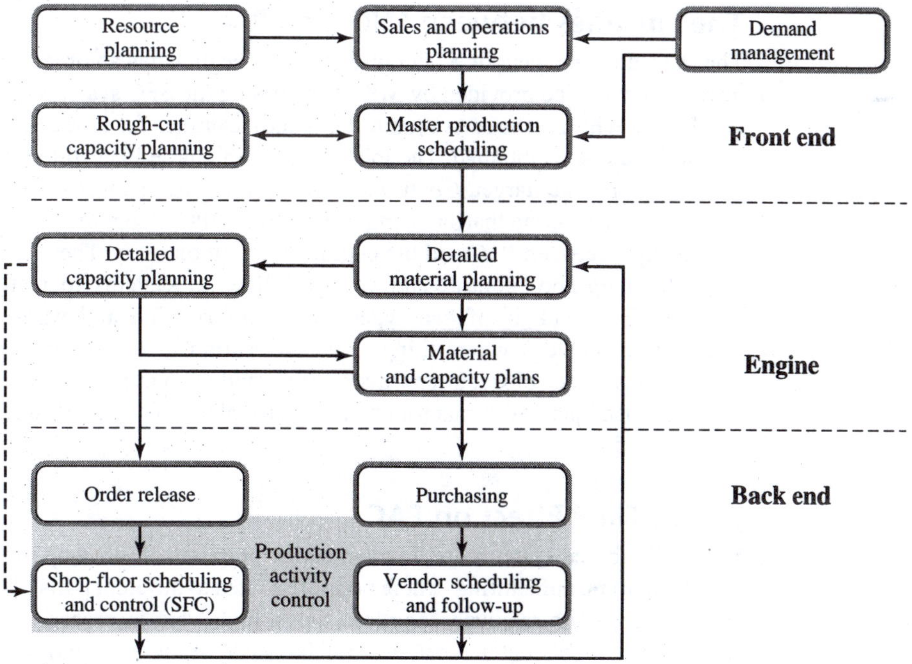

MPC System Linkages

The primary connection between PAC and the rest of the MPC systems shown in Figure 8.1 comes from the box marked "Material and capacity plans." The capacity plan is especially critical to managing the detailed shop-floor flow of materials. In essence, the capacity provided represents resource availabilities for meeting material plans.

Capacity's importance for shop-floor control (SFC) is illustrated by considering two extremes. If insufficient capacity is provided, no SFC system will be able to decrease backlogs, improve delivery performance, or improve output. On the other hand, if more than enough capacity exists to meet peak loads, almost *any* SFC system will achieve material flow objectives. It's in cases with bottleneck areas and where effective utilization of capacity is important that we see the utility of good SFC systems.

A related issue is the extent to which good capacity planning is done. If the detailed capacity planning activity in Figure 8.1 provides sufficient capacity, with relatively level loading, shop-floor control is straightforward. On the other hand, if peaks and valleys in capacity requirements are passed down to the back end, execution becomes more complex and difficult. The same general issues apply to vendor follow-up systems: vendor capacity must be carefully planned to ensure effective execution. If one does not help vendors utilize capacity effectively, total system costs increase, which in the end must be borne by the end customers.

The material plan provides information to the SFC and vendor follow-up systems and sets performance objectives. The essential objective of both execution systems is to achieve the material plan—to provide the right part at the right time. This will result in being able to hit the master production schedule and to satisfy customer service objectives.

The Linkages between MRP and PAC

The shop-floor and vendor scheduling activities begin when an order is released. A critical information service provided by MRP is apprising the SFC systems of all changes in material plans. This means revising due dates and quantities for scheduled receipts so correct priorities can be maintained. The job thereafter might be likened to that of a duck hunter following a moving target. Control and follow-up systems must keep each order lined up with its due date—one that's moving—so overall MPC is supported.

Linkages between PAC and the engine aren't all one-way. There's important feedback from the shop-floor control and vendor follow-up systems to material and capacity planning. Feedback is of two types: status information and warning signals. Status information includes where things are, notification of operational completions, count verifications, order closeout and disposition, and accounting data. The warning signals help flag inadequacies in material and capacity plans: that is, will we be able to do what was planned?

Just-in-Time Effect on PAC

Shop-order-based systems are founded on the premises of job shop (now more frequently called *batch*) manufacturing, where parts are routed to different parts of the factory for processing steps, with relatively long lead times, high work-in-process inventories, and high utilization of work center capacities. JIT has none of these. Manufacturing takes place in facilities, often in cells, where jobs are easily kept track of; work is completed quickly; work-in-process inventory levels are insignificant; and work centers have surge capacity or else are level loaded. In either case, capacity utilization is not a key issue.

Formal systems for shop-floor control are largely unnecessary under JIT. Release of orders is still part of PAC, but the typical "shop order" with associated paperwork isn't maintained. Therefore, the PAC functions in Figure 8.1 are greatly simplified. Order release can be accomplished with kanbans or other pull system methodologies, and work-in-process inventories in the factory are severely limited. Detailed scheduling is also unnecessary since orders flow through cells in predictable ways so that workers know the sequence of conversion operations. Work is completed fast enough that "order scheduling" isn't required. Detailed scheduling of workers and equipment is similarly not an issue, because design of the JIT system itself determines schedules. There's no need for data collection or monitoring since JIT basically assumes only two kinds of inventories: raw materials and finished goods. Receipt of finished goods is used to "backflush" required raw materials from inventory. The JIT-based systems dramatically reduce the number of transactions to be processed, as well as the associated inventories and lead times.

Vendor scheduling under JIT can be a bit more complex than shop-floor control, but if the relationship with the vendors is good, differences are very small. Many firms use some form of electronic kanban to authorize work at the vendor factories, and excellent vendors don't build inventories in anticipation of orders from their customers. Well-run auto companies, for example, transmit an exact build schedule to their seat vendors several times a day, as actual cars are started. By the time these cars are ready for seats to be installed, seats will be delivered by the vendor in the exact sequence required. The seats are not pulled from inventory. They are built to order and delivered in the exact sequence to match the build schedule at the assembly plant. There is no need for transactions such as shipping or receiving documents. The seat manufacturer is paid on the basis of the build schedule; one just assumes that each car has the requisite seats!

The Company Environment

The primary PAC objective is managing the materials flow to meet MPC plans. In some firms, other objectives relate to efficient use of capacity, labor, machine tools, time, or materials. Under JIT and time-based competition, the objective is material velocity. A firm's particular set of objectives is critical to PAC design.

The choice of objectives for PAC reflects the firm's position vis-à-vis its competitors, customers, and vendors. It also reflects the company's fundamental goals and the constraints under which it operates. In many countries firms find changing capacity to be more difficult than in the United States. This viewpoint colors the view of PAC. Similarly, some firms have more complex products and/or process technologies than others. The result can be a difficult shop-floor management problem and a resultant difference in the appropriate PAC system. As a result PAC system design must be tailored to the particular firm's needs.

Production Activity Control Techniques

This section begins by describing basic concepts for production activity control under batch manufacturing with an MRP system. It covers basic shop floor concepts, including the elements of lead time, operation setback charts, and lead-time management. It then examines three approaches to shop-floor control. The first, **Gantt charts,** provides graphic understanding of the shop-floor control problem; moreover, Gantt chart models can be used in manual shop-floor control systems. The second approach is based on **priority sequencing rules** for jobs at a work center under MRP. The third approach to shop-floor control, **theory of constraints scheduling,** involves the preparation of an exact schedule of jobs for bottleneck work centers, and sequencing the nonbottleneck work centers by a priority sequencing rule. We then look at vendor scheduling where the concepts are applied to supplier operations.

Basic Shop-Floor Control Concepts

Figure 8.2, an example product structure for end item A, demonstrates basic concepts underlying shop-floor control techniques. One essential input to the SFC system is the routing and lead-time data for each product item. Figure 8.3 presents this for parts D and E of

FIGURE 8.2
Example Product Structure Diagram

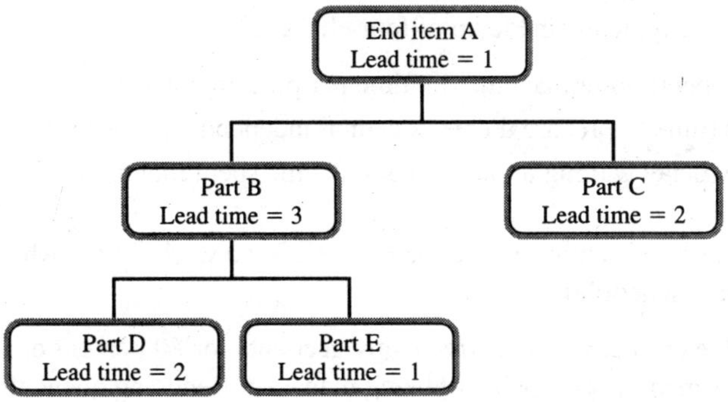

FIGURE 8.3
Routing Data and Operation Setback Chart

Operation	Work Center	Run Time	Setup Time	Move Time	Queue Time	Total Time	Rounded Time
Part D routing							
1	101	1.4	0.4	0.3	2.0	4.1	4.0
2	109	1.5	0.5	0.3	2.5	4.8	5.0
3	103	0.1	0.1	0.2	0.5	0.9	1.0
Total lead time (days) 10.0							
Part E routing							
1	101	0.3	0.1	0.2	0.5	1.1	1.0
2	107	0.2	0.1	0.3	0.5	1.1	1.0
3	103	0.3	0.2	0.1	1.5	2.1	2.0
4	109	0.1	0.1	0.1	0.5	0.9	1.0
Total lead time (days) 5.0							

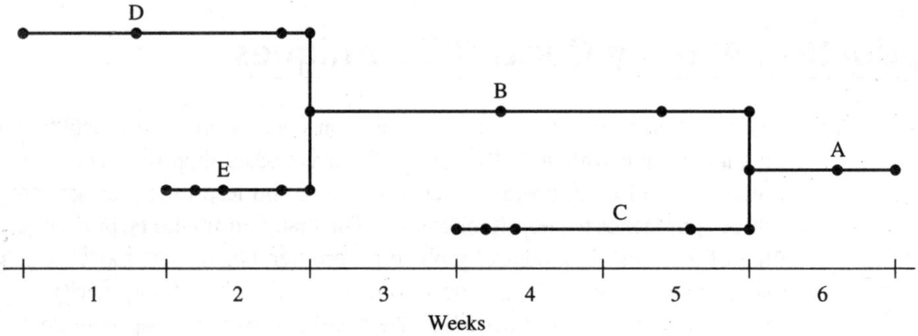

the example. The routing specifies each operation to be performed to make the part and which work center will perform the operation.

Production of part D, for example, requires three operations of 4, 5, and 1 days, respectively, for a total of 10 days, or two weeks. Part E requires four operations of 1, 1, 2, and 1 days, respectively, for a total of 5 days, or one week. The remaining lead times in Figure 8.2 are all derived the same way. Lead times used for MRP should match those in the routing file. If the MRP time for part E was set at two weeks instead of one week, orders would constantly be released one week early.

Lead times are typically made up of four elements:

Run time (operation or machine run time per piece × lot size).

Setup time (time to prepare the work center, independent of lot size).

Move time (delay waiting to be moved plus time spent moving from one work center to the next).

Queue time (time spent waiting to be processed at a work center, which depends on workload *and* schedule).

Queue time (the critical element) frequently accounts for 80 percent or more of total lead time; it's the element most capable of being managed. Reducing queue time means shorter

FIGURE 8.4
Work Center 101 Schedules

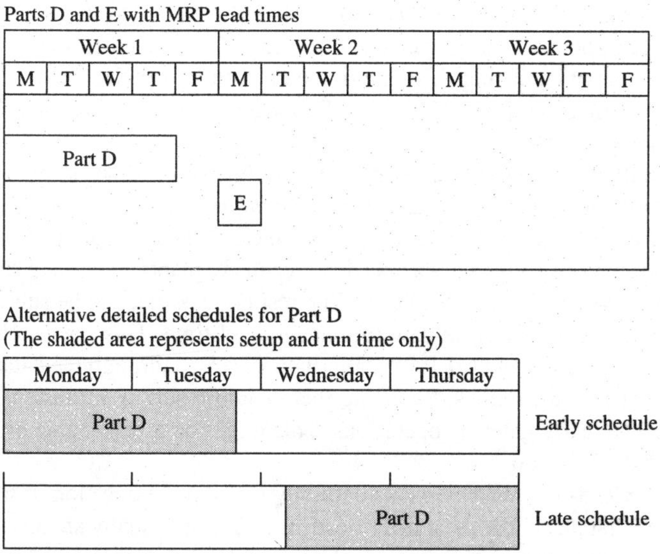

lead time and, therefore, reduced work-in-process inventory. This reduction requires better scheduling.

The bottom of Figure 8.3 shows an **operation setback chart** based on each part's lead times. Here we clearly see the implications of incorrect MRP lead time. If the MRP lead time for part E isn't the one week calculated from the routing data, the part will be released either early or late to the shop. Neither of these is a desirable outcome. Note that Figure 8.3 shows that both parts D and E go through work center 101 for their first operation. The top of Figure 8.4 shows the partial schedule for work center 101, with parts D and E scheduled according to the timing in Figure 8.3.

The bottom of Figure 8.4 shows two alternative detailed schedules for part D in week 1 at work center 101. The shaded portion represents the 1.8 days of lead time required for setup and run time. The early schedule has part D loaded as soon as possible in the four days. The late schedule loads part D into the latest possible time at work center 101. The key differences between the top and bottom of Figure 8.4 are the timing of the setup and run times. The blank area in both schedules includes queue time. Queue time represents slack that permits the choice of alternative schedules—a form of flexibility. This slack can be removed by good SFC practice; that is, this schedule allows 4 full days to complete part D, when actual time on the machine is only 1.8 days. For the remaining 2.2 days, the part waits in a queue or is moving between work centers.

The shaded portion of the schedules shown at the bottom of Figure 8.4 contains no queue time. These schedules represent loading a particular job onto a particular work center for a particular time period. The two alternatives in the bottom of Figure 8.4 are different loadings; one typically chooses between alternative loadings to utilize the machine center effectively.

Lead-Time Management

Many people think of **lead time** as a constant, such as π. In fact, it's not a value to be measured as much as a parameter to be managed. Of the four elements of lead time (run, setup, move, and queue), the last two can be compressed with good PAC design and practice.

Lead time and work-in-process (WIP) are directly related. Moreover, some critical feedback linkages operate. The longer the lead time is perceived to be, the longer the time between the order launching date and due date. The longer this time, the more orders in the shop. The more orders in the shop, the longer the queue time (and WIP); we have a self-fulfilling prophecy.

Some WIP is needed at work centers where high utilization is important. However, a basic principle of MPC systems is to *substitute information for inventory.* The firm doesn't need to have jobs physically in front of machines. Orders can be held in a computer and converted to physical units only as needed. For many plants, setup and run time constitute only 10 to 20 percent of total lead time. The rest is slack that can be substantially cut.

One interesting question is how to manage lead time. This means changing database elements for both SFC and MRP. One alternative is to go through the database and systematically change all lead times. Reducing them could result in a transient condition of dry work centers at early gateway operations. This might be a reasonable price to pay for the resulting WIP reduction.

Changing lead-time data elements naturally leads to the question of how they're established in the first place. For most firms, lead-time data are usually an input from some functional area, such as production control. An alternative is to *calculate* lead time. When we think about changing lead times as part of a management process, and when we remember that SFC lead time must be in tune with MRP lead-time offset data, this approach has increasing appeal. One firm calculated lead times as follows:

1. Nonqueue time for each operation was set equal to setup plus run (time per piece × lot size) plus move times.
2. Nonqueue time was converted to days by dividing total hours by number of shifts per day, assuming seven productive hours per day.
3. Queue time was set equal to two days if the next work center routing was in another department, one day if it was in the department but a different work center, and zero days if it was on the same machine.
4. Lead time for the total order was the sum of the queue and nonqueue times. This time was calculated with an average order quantity, rounded to a weekly lead time, and used for MRP lead-time offsetting.

Selecting queue time is the critical element in this formula. Values were chosen by taking a sample of 50 parts and using different queue time estimates to yield lead times consistent with production control personnel opinions. The initial estimates were padded, but the company was not very concerned. Once the system was in operation, estimates for queue times were systematically reduced a bit at a time. The result was a managed approach to shorter lead times and reduced work in process.

Gantt Charts

Gantt or **bar charts,** like those in Figure 8.4, show a schedule. The operation setback chart in Figure 8.4 is very similar. It too is a schedule for when to make each of the five parts based on lead times that include move and queue times.

One form of shop-floor control is to prepare operation setback charts similar to Figure 8.3 for each job, and use them with the kind of data in Figure 8.3 to prepare Gantt charts, such as those in Figure 8.4. The objective is to prepare a schedule for each machine center. This schedule can be based on the assumptions in either the top or bottom of Figure 8.4; that is, the schedule may or may not use lead times that include queue and move times.

The more usual practice is to prepare the detailed work center schedule *without* move and queue times. Many firms' systems do this. The typical approach is a **schedule board** with racks to hold pieces of paper. Each paper is a job and its length represents the setup plus run time required.

The primary problem with this kind of system is updating. Actual data must be captured and integrated into an ongoing replanning cycle. Moreover, a means to communicate with the shop floor is usually required since schedule boards typically reside in planning offices. Many companies now use large flat screen monitors positioned for easy viewing on the shop floor to display current job schedules.

Priority Sequencing Rules

Priority sequencing rules determine which job to run next at a work center. To some extent, these rules can be seen as producing a loading of jobs onto individual machines, but usually only one job is committed at a time; that is, the job to run *next* is determined only near the time when the prior job has been completed. The priority (sequencing) rule is just what the name suggests: a *rule* for what job to process next.

Many different priority rules have been established. A fairly common one is to base priorities on the type of data in Figure 8.3. The lower half of that figure contains scheduled due dates for parts and operations. These due dates can be used as priorities. For example, a priority rule could be: the job to process next is the job with the earliest operation due date. An alternative is to next process the job with the earliest *part* due date. Four other commonly used sequencing rules are:

- *Order slack:* Sum the setup times and run times for all remaining operations, subtract this from the time remaining (now until the part due date), and call the remainder slack. The rule is to work on that job with the least slack. This rule addresses the problem of work remaining.
- *Slack per operation:* A variant of order slack is to divide the slack by the number of remaining operations, again taking next the job with the smallest value. The reasoning behind slack per operation is that it will be more difficult to complete jobs with more operations because they will have to be scheduled through more work centers.
- *Critical ratio:* A rule based on the following ratio:

$$\frac{\text{Time remaining}}{\text{Work remaining}}$$

For calculation, the rule is expressed as

$$\frac{\text{Due date} - \text{Present time}}{\text{Lead time remaining (including setup, run, move, and queue)}}$$

If the ratio is 1.0, the job is on time. A ratio below 1.0 indicates a behind-schedule job, while a ratio above 1.0 indicates an ahead-of-schedule condition. The rule is to always process that job with the smallest critical ratio next.

- *Shortest operation next:* This rule ignores all due date information as well as all information about work remaining. It simply says, take as the next job the one that can be completed in the shortest time at the work center. This rule maximizes the number of shop orders that go through a work center and minimizes the number waiting in queue.

In an MRP system, each shop order would be a scheduled receipt for the part. As such, the scheduled receipt has a due date. From this due date, operational due dates could be established by backing off expected operation times, if these data are needed to establish priority sequence. The great advantage of this computer-based system is that, whenever the due date for a scheduled receipt changes, operation due dates can be changed accordingly. These changes, in turn, lead to priority changes for shop-floor control, resulting in an execution system that works on the most-needed shop orders first. The objective is for high-priority jobs to move through the shop very quickly, while low-priority jobs are set aside. In this way, the shop-floor control system can indeed execute the dictates of the detailed material plan. In recent times, many companies have developed a preference for sequencing rules that are easy to understand. One straightforward approach is to develop operation start and operation due dates, and use them for determining priority sequence decisions. In a computer-based shop-floor control system, due dates wouldn't be printed on any shop paper that travels with the work-in-process inventory. The shop paper would show the routing or sequence of operations (static data), but no due dates. The changing (dynamic) due date information would be printed daily or be displayed on line in the form of a work center schedule or dispatch list. It's the dispatch list, not the traveling paper, that shows the priority sequence. The dispatch list can be updated as rapidly as transactions are processed to the MRP database.

Theory of Constraints (TOC) Systems

An increasing number of firms have been implementing a plant scheduling system that uses theory of constraints (TOC) concepts. Initially, TOC scheduling systems were viewed as a replacement of an integrated MPC system. In fact, TOC scheduling systems encompass the functions performed in the engine and back end of Figure 8.1, but combine these functions so that material and capacity are planned simultaneously. TOC systems accomplish many functions in the MPC framework, but not all.

Basic Concepts of TOC Systems

Most manufacturing firms have a very limited number of constraints. Any resource whose capacity is equal to or less than the required demand is referred to as a *bottleneck.* As a consequence the fundamental principle of TOC systems is that only those work centers (or other types of resources) that are bottlenecks are of critical concern in scheduling. This is because the bottleneck work centers limit the overall production output of a plant. Further output beyond the constraint of the bottleneck can be achieved only by improved utilization of the bottleneck facilities, using approaches such as reduced downtime, improved productivity, and reduced changeover times. The objective of TOC scheduling is to maximize throughput. Because throughput is limited by the bottleneck resources, all efforts are devoted to maximizing capacity utilization in these work centers. Therefore, TOC scheduling systems focus on the identification of bottleneck work centers, and the scheduling of these work centers.

The concept of a bottleneck has been generalized into "constraints," which include marketplace constraints. In fact, it is argued that the goal is to have company output constrained by the marketplace, not by constraints over which the firm has more control. Further, TOC adds some operational concepts for dealing with constraining situations. Constraints are explicitly identified, and they're buffered with inventory. Also, the constraint's importance is made clear to the entire factory. For example, bottleneck work centers are operated over coffee breaks and lunch, and are worked a maximum of overtime hours. Moreover, jobs are closely examined to find any that can be alternatively routed, even if the result is "excess cost" for the work so routed. The goal is always to break a constraint, or bottleneck condition, and thereafter identify the next constraint. Continuous improvement is an integral part of the theory of constraints philosophy. Moreover, the path for the improvement is directed by the theory, always following the constraints.

TOC Scheduling

The scheduling approach used in TOC systems is called **drum-buffer-rope.** The bottleneck work centers (constraints) are the drums, and are, therefore, used to control the workflow in a plant. Any resource whose capacity is more than the demand is called a *nondrum.* The rope refers to "pull" scheduling at the nonbottleneck work centers. The purpose of the rope is to tie the production at each resource to the drum. Buffers exist at all of the bottleneck work centers, and the shipping dock, but not at nonbottleneck work centers. These buffers are used to protect the throughput of the bottleneck work centers from the inevitable minor fluctuations through the use of time buffers (WIP inventory) at a relatively few critical points in the plant. The basic concept is to move material as quickly as possible through nonbottleneck work centers until it reaches the bottleneck. The work at the bottleneck resources is scheduled for maximum efficiency. Thereafter, work again moves at maximum speed to the shipping dock (finished goods).

The diagram shown in Figure 8.5 outlines the basic TOC scheduling steps. TOC begins its process by combining data in the bill of materials file with data in the routing file. The result is a network, or extended tree diagram, where each part in the product structure also has its operational data attached directly. These data are then combined with the MPS to form the "product network." Figure 8.6 provides an example of a TOC product network.

FIGURE 8.5
TOC Scheduling

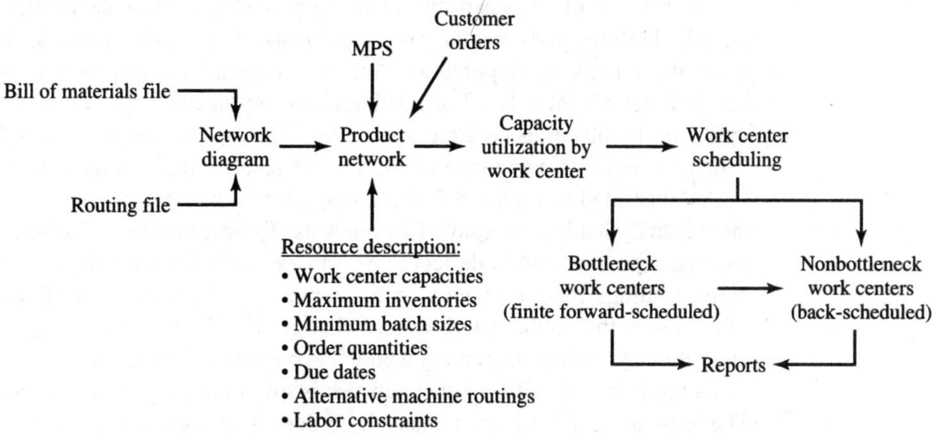

FIGURE 8.6
Sample Product Network

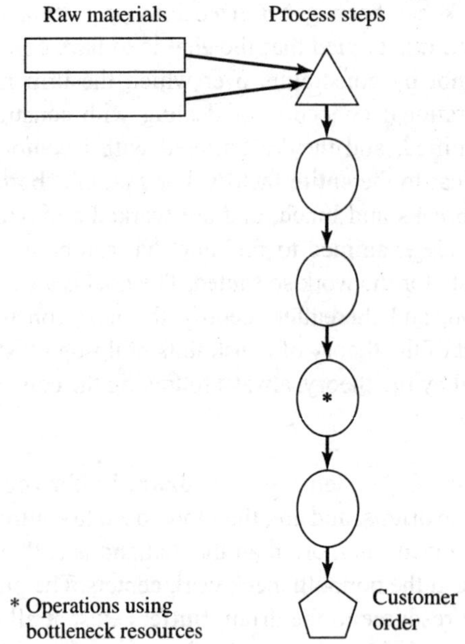

Here, customer orders are linked to the final operation (such as the final assembly process), which, in turn, is linked to previous operations (such as the detailed fabrication steps for components), and then to raw materials. Additional data typically included in the TOC files are capacities, maximum inventories, minimum batch quantities, order quantities, due dates, alternative machine routing, labor constraints, and other data typically used in finite scheduling models. In Figure 8.5, these data would be part of the "Resource description."

Next, the product network and resource descriptions are fed into a set of routines that identify the bottleneck resources. This routine combines the product network and resource information to form a TOC network of the bottleneck resources. To determine the bottleneck resources an initial analysis is prepared that provides reports indicating bottleneck resources. This involves using a rough-cut capacity planning routine that provides much of the information of other capacity planning procedures. Because the TOC product network includes both the parts and their routings, a pass through this network can result in an estimate of the capacity required at each work center. Lot sizes at this rough-cut stage are based on lot-for-lot rules. The resultant capacity needs, when divided by the number of weeks in the planning horizon, are the average capacity requirements for each resource. When divided by the resource capacities, the result is the average expected load.

As illustrated in Figure 8.7, the average loads on machine centers are sorted, and the most heavily loaded are studied by analysts. Typical questions include: Are the data correct? Are the time standards accurate? Can we easily increase capacity? Can we use alternative routings for some items? Any changes based on these questions result in another run to see if the bottleneck resources change. Those work centers in Figure 8.7 having a utilization exceeding 80 percent would be considered bottleneck work centers.

At this point the TOC product network is split into two portions, as shown in Figure 8.5. The left-hand portion incorporates all bottleneck resources and all succeeding operations,

FIGURE 8.7 Capacity Utilization Chart (without Setups)

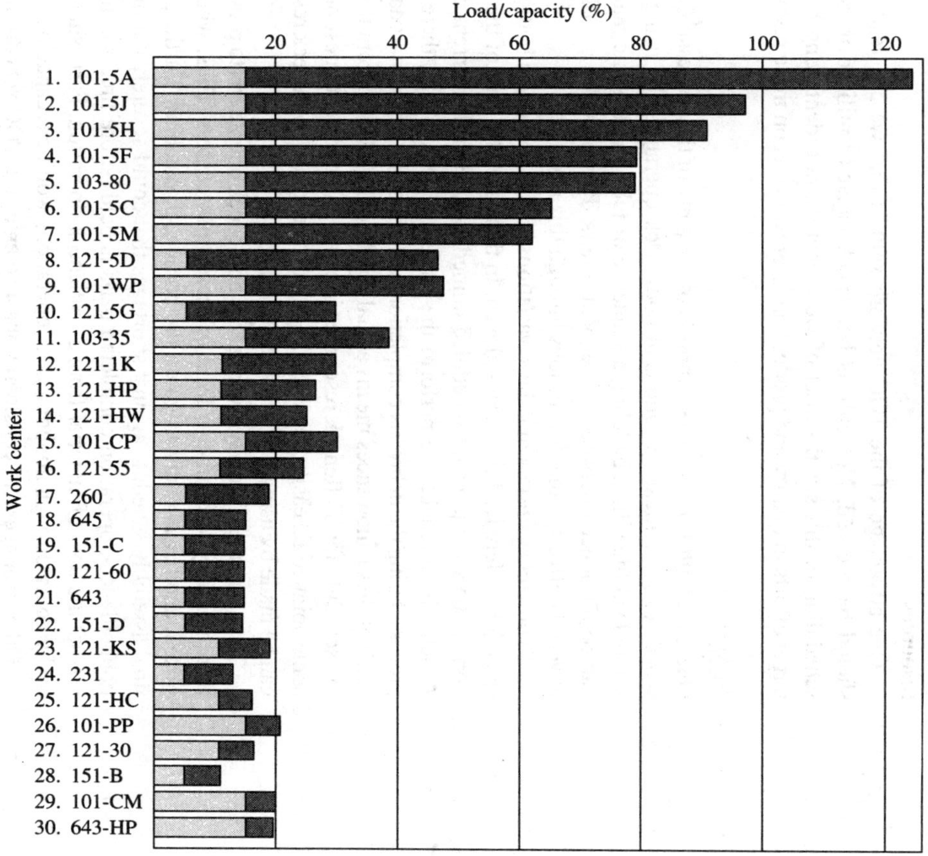

Load	Capacity (hours)
392.5	357.0
1233.5	1530.0
1066.6	1428.0
1371.8	2142.0
677.3	1071.0
1057.3	2142.0
483.0	1020.0
599.7	1428.0
1058.8	3213.0
254.5	1020.0
252.0	1071.0
203.8	1071.0
1704.0	10710.0
154.9	1071.0
154.3	1071.0
96.6	714.0
142.6	1071.0
113.3	1071.0
108.5	1071.0
34.6	357.0
101.9	1071.0
95.5	1071.0
183.3	2142.0
76.1	1071.0
62.0	1071.0
60.2	1071.0
60.1	1071.0
240.1	4284.0
108.6	2142.0
48.0	1071.0

Source: Company Records

including market demand for end products with parts that have processing on the bottleneck resources. *This portion of the network is forward finite loaded.*

The right-hand portion includes all of the nonbottleneck resources. *This portion of the network is not forward finite loaded.* Operation start dates/times are, however, established by using the setup times, run times, and queue times for the nonbottleneck resource operations. An initial scheduling pass is made through the product network, and the raw material release dates are offset from customer order due dates by taking into account the processing and queue times for all part operations. In a second pass, however, due dates for any part operations that feed bottlenecks are based on those established by the TOC scheduling of bottlenecks. Schedules for these part operations are set so that material will be available in time for the first operation in the TOC network. This scheduling logic provides a dispatch list for the nonbottleneck resources.

One advantage of the TOC network split is that we can readily see where attention should be focused. Not only is bottleneck capacity utilized more intensively by finite scheduling of this small subset of work centers, but identifying bottlenecks allows us to target efforts in quality and production improvements on these resources.

Buffers

One issue with TOC is the assumption of certainty of the processing times. TOC buffers the schedules for critical operations at bottleneck operations by using both safety stock and safety lead time. In scheduling a sequence of jobs on the same machine, safety lead time can be introduced between subsequent orders. This provides a cushion against variations adversely affecting the flow of jobs through this machine.

To protect against having these variations affect subsequent bottleneck operations on the same job, safety lead time is employed. In this case, the start of the next bottleneck operation on the same job isn't scheduled immediately after the current operation is completed. A delay is introduced to perform the buffering here. (*Note:* there can be another job in process during the delay; its completion will affect the actual start date for the arriving job.) Each of these allowances means actual conditions will vary from the TOC schedule. While the schedule for bottleneck resources is clear, an important question for the supervisors at some point could easily be *which* job to run next at nonbottleneck resources. Such decisions can be made by using a priority sequencing rule.

To ensure there's always work at the bottleneck operation (to provide maximum output), there is safety lead time in front of these work centers. Thus, whenever one job is completed, another is ready to go on the bottleneck machine. Further, in order to protect the final assembly schedule against shortages that could severely cut output, a safety stock of nonbottleneck operation completed parts is held before final assembly. The idea is to not disrupt the flow of material from a bottleneck operation. Parts shortages that can be made up by going through nonbottleneck operations won't cut capacity.

Other management considerations also enter the TOC scheduling system to reduce the effect of uncertainty. These include making realistic schedules that meet material and capacity limitations. Considerations involving the appropriate level of work-in-process inventory, the capacity utilization attainable, degree of schedule protection, and batch size controls can all be applied to the TOC procedure. These help take into account the company culture as the TOC procedure is implemented.

TOC and Lot Sizing

TOC calculates different batch sizes throughout the plant, depending on whether a work center is a bottleneck. This has several MPC implications. In typical finite scheduling procedures, the batch size is fixed. Such isn't the case with TOC. It also follows that a batch size for one operation on a part could be different than for other operations on the same part. This implies special treatment will be required for any paperwork that travels with shop orders. In fact, TOC is designed to do order splitting at nonbottleneck resources. In usual practice, order splitting is done on backlogged (bottleneck) machines; in this situation TOC would do the opposite in order to reduce setup time and maximize output at the bottleneck resources.

The key to lot sizing in TOC is distinguishing between a *transfer* batch (that quantity that moves from operation to operation) and a *process* batch (the total lot size released to the shop). Any differences are held as work-in-process inventories in the shop. In essence, no operation can start until at least a transfer batch is built up behind it.

The transfer batches are predetermined integral fractions of the original order quantity (process batch). They provide a work center with the flexibility to start producing an order before it is completed at the previous work center. Such flexibility, frequently referred to as *lot splitting* and *overlap* or *line scheduling,* reduces order flow times and smooths work flow in the shop to yield better use of capacity. This flexibility also means the number of units produced during a given work center setup, the *operation batch size,* can vary between a transfer batch and the original order quantity.

This lot-sizing concept can be applied by using any standard priority scheduling method (e.g., shortest processing time, critical ratio). When an order is completed under traditional priority scheduling rules, the highest-priority order in the queue is selected for processing next. Under this lot-sizing concept, a work center may contain transfer batches coming from many released orders. In this case, the queue is searched for transfer batches of the same part order that has just been completed at the work center in order to save setup time at a bottleneck resource. If such an item is available, it is processed next, regardless of priority; otherwise, the highest-priority transfer batch in the queue is selected and a new setup is made at the work center. If the queue is empty, the next batch to arrive at the work center is processed.

Managing the TOC Schedule

Managing the TOC schedule on a daily basis involves five basic steps that are illustrated by the example products shown in Figure 8.8. In this example, each product requires processing

FIGURE 8.8 TOC Example

				Processing Time (in Hours)				Requested Customer Shipping	
Product	Customer Order Number	Order Quantity	Raw Material Specification Number	First Machining, Operation 1	Heat Treating, Operation 2	Testing, Operation 3	Final Machining, Operation 4	Date	Hour
A	1XXX	100	124	3	6	1	4	Day 5	32
B	2XXX	10	101	2	4	1	2	Day 6	40
C	3XXX	50	88	4	6	1	4	Day 6	40

Notes: 1. Shop operates eight hours each day.
2. All orders require two hours in shipping department.
3. All raw material is stocked and available.
4. An 8-hour buffer is maintained at the final machining work center.

on four work centers: first machining, heat treating, testing, and final machining. The processing time (setup and run time) for each operation is shown in Figure 8.8. The first three operations are performed in a fabrication cell. Capacity is sufficient in this cell, so these are nonbottleneck operations. The fourth operation, final machining, is a bottleneck operation. Other data such as the customer order number, order quantity, and requested customer delivery date are included in Figure 8.8.

Scheduling the Drum

The first step is scheduling new orders on the bottleneck operations, referred to as the *drums*. This is accomplished by using the following logic:

- Calculate the earliest start time on the first constraint by adding the processing time before the constraint to the raw material lead time and the first constraint buffer time.
- Place the order after and as close as possible to the earliest start time on the constraint.
- Calculate the earliest start time on the next constraint (or the shipping date) by adding the processing time after the first constraint and the next buffer time to the completion time on the current constraint.

Product A in Figure 8.8 illustrates this logic. Note that in Figure 8.8 the processing time for the three operations before the first constraint (final machining) is 10 hours, the raw material lead time is zero (because this material is stocked), and the buffer time for the first constraint (final machining) is eight hours. As a result, the earliest start time on the first constraint is in 18 hours, or at the end of hour 2 in day 3 (assuming the plant works one eight-hour shift each day). Figure 8.9 shows a workload profile of the drum (the final machining work center), indicating that the last four hours of day 3 have not yet been scheduled. Therefore, the order for Product A is scheduled to start at the end of hour 4 and complete at the end of hour 8 on day 3.

Figure 8.10 shows a flow diagram of the process and indicates the key dates that are set by using the TOC scheduling logic. These include the date/time that the order is scheduled to enter the final machining buffer, the date that the final machining operation starts, the date that the order is to enter the shipping buffer, and the customer delivery date. Figure 8.11 shows these dates/times for product A. The raw material release for product A is planned for the end of hour 2 on day 1, and this product is scheduled to enter the final machining buffer at the end of hour 12 (day 2, hour 4). This job is therefore expected to wait eight hours before processing at the bottleneck machining process. This ensures that errors

FIGURE 8.9 Final Machining Work Load Profile

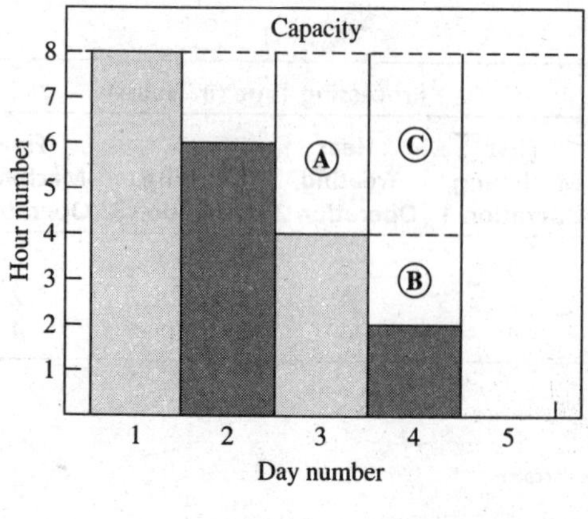

FIGURE 8.10 TOC Example: Plant Scheduling—Bottleneck Work Centers

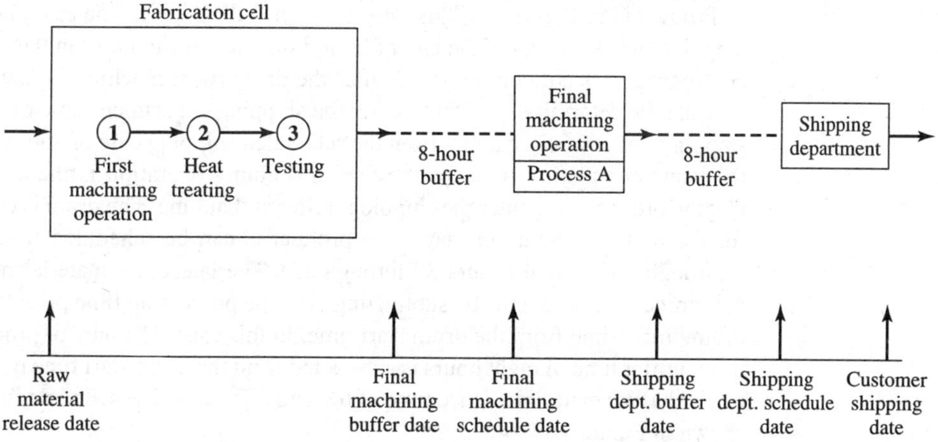

FIGURE 8.11 TOC Example—Plant Schedule

Product	Customer Order Number	Order Quantity	Raw Material Release	First Machining	Heat Treat	Test	Final Machining Buffer	Final Machining	Shipping Buffer	Shipping Department	Promised Scheduled Shipping Date: Hour	Promised Scheduled Shipping Date: Day
A	1XXX	100	2	2	5	11	12	20	24	32	34	Day 5 Hour 2
B	2XXX	10	11	11	13	17	18	26	28	36	38	Day 5 Hour 6
C	3XXX	50	9	9	13	19	20	28	32	40	42	Day 6 Hour 2

Notes: 1. All times represent scheduled start times as of the end of the hour indicated.
2. First machining, heat treat, and test are nonbottleneck work centers and are not finite capacity scheduled.
3. Final machining and shipping are bottleneck work centers and are, therefore, finite capacity scheduled.

in processing time estimates do not affect the 100 percent utilization of the bottleneck. Likewise, this order is scheduled to enter the shipping buffer at the end of hour 24 (day 3, hour 8) with shipment scheduled for the end of hour 34 (day 5, hour 2).

Orders are scheduled by using finite backward scheduling. This logic proceeds as follows:

- Subtract the shipping buffer and the processing time after the final constraint from the scheduled ship date. This provides the latest completion time.
- Place the order on the final constraint (drum) before and as close as possible to the latest completion time.
- Determine the start time on the final constraint by subtracting the processing time on the constraint from the completion time.
- Subtract the final constraint buffer time and the processing time back to the latest completion time of the previous constraint (or the raw material release time) from the final constraint start time.
- Once the material release is determined, the delivery schedule for the raw material can be determined.

Product C in Figure 8.8 illustrates this scheduling logic. The customer-requested shipping date for this order is the end of hour 8 on day 5 (or hour 40 in the example). Because no processing occurs on this order after the drum (final machining), the latest completion time can be determined by subtracting the shipping department time of two hours plus the shipping buffer of eight hours from the scheduled shipping date of hour 40. This means that the latest completion time for the final machining operation is the end of hour 30, and that the order should enter the shipping buffer at that time. The drum is currently scheduled for the first four hours on day 4, so product C can be scheduled from the end of hour 4 through 8 on day 4 (hours 28 through 32). The latest raw material release date can be determined for product C by subtracting both the processing time prior to the drum and the drum buffer time from the drum start time. In this case, 11 hours of processing time and a drum buffer time of eight hours is subtracted from the drum start time of the end of hour 28 to yield a raw material release time of the end of hour 9. The schedule for product C is also shown in Figure 8.11.

Exploiting the Drums

In scheduling the drums, product demand may exceed the available capacity at the drums. In this case it may be necessary to take steps to augment the capacity of the drum. This may involve offloading some of the orders scheduled on the drum to other machines that are nondrums, or outsourcing this work to suppliers. Other options would include working the drums through lunches and breaks, adding overtime, and increasing the batch sizes at the drum to minimize setup time. Batch sizes should, however, not be increased if this would result in delaying the scheduled shipment dates for customer orders. This is a good example of how lot splitting might be usefully employed. By dividing the batch into that which services customers and that which goes into inventory, the overall constraint utilization (selling the throughput) is maximized.

Material Release—Rope

In managing plant operations, raw material should not be released earlier than the scheduled TOC raw material release date. Releasing the raw material on these dates will minimize the WIP inventory and reduce the choice of orders to be run on the nonbottleneck operations.

Proactive Management of Buffers

Buffers are put in place for unforseen variations in production at the nonconstraint work centers. While the entire buffer time is scheduled for every order, it is not expected that every order will arrive at the drum on time. Therefore, the key to a successful implementation of TOC is the proactive management of the buffers. In many plants the management of the buffers is the responsibility of a shop-floor scheduling person designated as the *buffer coordinator.*

One way of accomplishing this is to divide the buffers in thirds. The first third is the **red zone.** The red zone includes the orders that are scheduled next on the constraint. The middle third is the **yellow zone,** and the final third is the **green zone,** which includes the orders that are the furthest out in the drum schedule.

The red zone should rarely have missing orders. Orders that are missing from the red zone represent an immediate danger to the drum schedule. If an order is missing from the red zone, the buffer coordinator should be working nonstop on getting this order to the machine. Management should be aware of the situation and actively working to assist the buffer coordiator to resolve the problem. If the red zone is always full, consideration should be given to reducing the buffer size. The larger the buffer size, the more money invested in WIP inventory. Therefore, buffers should be only large enough to ensure delivery performance to the drums.

The yellow zone will occasionally have missing orders. The buffer coordinator should be actively working to get these orders to the buffer as quickly as possible. Likewise, the green zone will regularly have orders missing. The buffer coordinator should know where these orders are, and verify that they should arrive at the buffer shortly.

Elevating the Drum

This is really a planning step. Once the shop floor is running smoothly, consideration should be given in the planning process to increasing the capacity at the drum. If the capacity is increased at the constraint, it is possible for the organization to grow the business.

TOC and the MPC Framework

Returning to Figure 8.1, we see that TOC can't uniquely be put in the front end, the engine, or the back end. It works in all three areas and does some things quite differently than when scheduling is done by other approaches. However, TOC uses most of the same data as other MPC applications. We still need a front end, engine, and back end (both shop-floor and vendor systems). For the firm with an operating MPC system, the basic database and closed-loop understanding exist. Implementing TOC as an enhancement seems to be a logical extension. TOC is another example of separating the vital few from the trivial many, and thereafter providing a mechanism to exploit this knowledge for better manufacturing planning/control. It allows a firm to simultaneously plan materials and capacities and to integrate important concepts from finite scheduling into the MPC system.

It's been argued TOC doesn't have the same needs for data accuracy that MRP scheduling has. This is partially correct, if you feel less accuracy is required for nonbottleneck parts and work centers. But going into the process of using TOC, you may not realize very well what these bottleneck operations are. Both TOC and MRP require detailed knowledge of product structures and processes. Databases, accurate transaction processing, and the right managerial commitment are required for both as well.

TOC Contributions

Now we can identify clearly one of TOC's primary contributions. When finite scheduling through bottleneck resources is complete, the result is a doable master production schedule. For this reason, TOC is sometimes considered to be a "front-end" system (i.e., a master production scheduling technique). We see it less as an MPS technique than an enhancement to the MPS. TOC conceivably can take any MPS as input and determine the extent to which it is doable.

This means TOC makes an explicit computer-based analysis of the feedback from engine (and back end) to the front end—an important enhancement to MRP systems. It means a valid MPS is generated—one the firm has a strong chance of achieving—that is based on the capacity parameters used in the scheduling.

A secondary contribution at this stage comes from the way TOC schedules the nonbottleneck resources. The easiest way to see this is to assume (as is often the case in practice) there are no bottlenecks. In that case, TOC schedules are based on MRP logic. The difference is that TOC in this case will change batch sizes (reducing them) to the point where some resources almost become bottlenecks. The result is less WIP, reduced lead time, greater material velocity, and a move toward "zero inventory" manufacturing. TOC does much of this by overlapping schedules, using unequal batch sizes for transferring and processing.

TOC's third important contribution is to virtually eliminate the fundamental issue of conflicting priorities between MRP and finite scheduling. With finite scheduling of only a small fraction of the work centers priority conflict issues should largely disappear. Moreover, computational time required to do finite scheduling should be dramatically cut by dealing only with a subset of orders and work centers/resources.

In operation as a shop-floor control technique, TOC has a few other differences from usual practice. A fundamental tenet in TOC is that an hour lost in a bottleneck resource is an hour lost to the entire factory's output, while an hour lost in a nonbottleneck resource has no real cost. This means capacity utilization of bottleneck resources is important. TOC increases utilization by using WIP buffers in front of bottlenecks, and where output from a bottleneck joins with some other parts. TOC also runs large batch sizes at bottleneck operations, thereby reducing relative time spent in setup downtime.

In practice, the variable lot size issue has two major implications. First, lead times should be shorter: smaller batches will move faster through nonbottleneck work centers. Second (and less felicitous), procedures have to be developed to split/join batches as they go through production.

Implementation Issues

A major paradigm shift is required in order to obtain the benefits of TOC scheduling. Management needs to recognize that the plant culture needs to change from one of keeping people busy and equipment fully loaded to one of maximizing throughput at the critical resources—the bottleneck. This means that under TOC, as with JIT, it's quite all right to not work if there's no work to do at nonbottleneck resources. In fact, working (by the usual definition) in this situation will cause problems. If people at the nonbottleneck work on orders that are not needed to maximize flow through the bottleneck work centers, the net result of their work will be to simply increase WIP and cause confusion for scheduling at other work centers. Understanding the basic concepts is critical in obtaining the benefits of TOC scheduling.

TOC presents further difficulties in implementation. Companies also need sound basic systems, education, top-management support, and a willingness to unlearn some ingrained habits. One firm we know of has been working for several years to implement finite scheduling, without great success, because it has strong pressures to fully utilize all direct labor-hours. In this case, the fundamental principles of TOC have not been accepted.

Vendor Scheduling and Follow-up

The **vendor-scheduling** and **follow-up** aspects of PAC are the direct analog of the shop-floor scheduling and control systems. There are some important differences, however. From the vendor's perspective, each customer is usually only one of a number of demand sources. Customer demands are managed in the vendor's plant with its MPC system. The MPC relationship is largely through information exchanged between vendor and customer, often from the back-end activities of the customer directly to the vendor's MPC system.

From the customer's standpoint, the objectives of vendor scheduling are the same as those for internal work center scheduling: keep the orders lined up with the correct due dates from the material plan. This means the vendor must have a continually updated set of relative priority data. A typical approach to providing this information is a weekly updated report reflecting the current set of circumstances in the customer's plant and, sometimes, the final customer requirements that dictate them. Increasingly, computer-to-computer communication is used to transmit this information.

Because the vendor follow-up system is often concerned with changes to the schedule and keeping priorities correct, there must be limits to the amount of change the vendor will be asked to accommodate. Contractual agreements with the vendor typically define the types and degree of changes that can be made, time frames for making changes, additional elements of flexibility required, and so on. In addition, the agreement specifies procedures for transmitting needs to the vendor plus the units in which the vendor's capacity is planned and controlled. This sets the stage for vendor PAC including order release, scheduling, and follow-up.

The Internet and Vendor Scheduling

The Internet provides several ways in which manufacturing companies and their vendors can share information for the purpose of improving the timing and reliability of supplier deliveries. For manufacturing companies the use of information technology can provide improvements such as quicker delivery response to customers, improved delivery reliability, and reductions in operating costs involving both purchasing staff costs and inventory. These improvements have also had an important effect on the national economy. Rapid response times are a result of technological advances. Increased use of real-time information, such as computerized order tracking, enables business to know when demand is shifting and to instantly change output schedules, workshifts, inventory levels, and capital spending plans. Like increased productivity and greater labor flexibility, quick reflexes became a key characteristic of the U.S. economy.

Increasingly, companies are creating websites to provide a routine way of communicating with vendors. These websites include forward planning information such as listings of open purchase orders (scheduled receipts from MRP), planned future purchase orders from MRP records, and vendor requirements stated in terms of capacity, as well as information on accounts payable status for completed vendor shipments and vendor report cards indicating on-time delivery, shipment quantity shortfalls, and quality performance. Websites are also important sources of historical information on item usage that is helpful to vendors in improving their sales forecasting methods. Furthermore, companies are increasingly sharing engineering information with their vendors through their websites. Websites now contain product management data that includes product specifications and part drawings. Sharing such information electronically enables vendors to access up-to-date information that contains the latest engineering designs and change notices. Sharing this type of information reduces costs on the part of both manufacturers and their vendors, since both are working with the same latest information on product designs.

Concluding Principles

We see the following principles emerging from this chapter:

- Production activity control system design must be in concert with the firm's needs.
- Vendor capacities should be planned and scheduled with as much diligence as are internal capacities.
- Lead times are to be managed.
- Feedback from PAC should provide early warning and status information to other MPC modules.
- E-based systems can dramatically improve customer/vendor communication, reducing lead time and overhead cost.
- TOC scheduling provides improved performance by focusing on the constraining resources.
- TOC implementation requires a change in plant culture in order to obtain the full benefits of this approach.
- Traditional priority rules can play a role in nonbottleneck scheduling.
- Stability in the manufacturing loads and capacity plans facilitates shop-floor execution.

Discussion Questions

1. Suppose an average of 20 students per year were in your major and the number of graduates varied between 15 and 30 each year. One required course, open to both juniors and seniors, is offered once a year and has a capacity of 20 students. What system would you use to assign students to that course? Would it make any difference if the course capacity was 40 students or 10 students per year?
2. What kind of warning signals would you like fed back from PAC to the MRP system?
3. Lead times have sometimes been called "rubbery." What accounts for this concept of elasticity in lead times?
4. In the list of priority rules, there is no first-come/first-served (FCFS) rule, yet most banks, cafeterias, and theater ticket booths use this rule in waiting on patrons. Why isn't it a suggested rule for the shop floor?
5. What are the differences in how bottleneck and nonbottleneck work centers are scheduled under TOC? Why are these differences desirable?
6. Why should buffers be located in front of bottleneck work centers under TOC scheduling? How should the size of these buffers be determined?
7. How would you determine how much discretion to give the foreman in combining and reprioritizing jobs?
8. What benefits might be gained by having clerks in a retail store use a wand to read tags on items?
9. Discuss the merits of separating the daily transaction people (schedulers) from the buyers in the purchasing organization.

Problems

1. Tom's Sailboard manufactures custom wind surfers in Seattle. The incoming orders follow different routes through the shop, but all orders must stop at each of the three work centers (WCs) in the plant. The following table contains information regarding the four jobs that arrive over

five days and need to be scheduled at the company. It is currently November 10 and Tom works a seven-day week.

Order	Arrival Date	Job/WC Routing	Processing Time (Days)		
			WC 1	WC 2	WC 3
(B)iff	Nov. 10	1-3-2	1	3	1
(G)riff	Nov. 10	2-3-1	2	2	2
(H)erbie	Nov. 12	3-2-1	3	1	2
(K)erri	Nov. 14	2-1-3	1	3	1

Assume that the material for all orders is ready for processing as soon as the orders arrive and that a first-come/first-served sequencing rule is used at all work centers. All three work centers are idle as work begins on orders B and G on November 10.

a. Construct a Gantt chart depicting the processing and idle times for the three work centers for these four jobs.

b. How many days does each job wait in queue for processing at work center 2?

2. The production manager at the Knox Machine Company is preparing a production schedule for one of the fabrication shop's machines, the P&W grinder. He has collected the following information on jobs currently waiting to be processed at this machine. (There are no other jobs, and the machine is empty.)

Job	Machine Processing Time, Days*	Date Job Arrived at this Machine	Job Due Date
A	4	6-23	8-15
B	1	6-24	9-10
C	5	7-01	8-01
D	2	6-19	8-17

*Note: This is the final operation for each of these jobs.

a. The production manager has heard about three dispatching rules: the shortest operation next rule, the first-come/first-served rule, and the earliest due date rule. In what sequence would these jobs be processed at the P&W grinder if each rule were applied?

b. If it's now the morning of July 10 and the shortest operation next rule is used, when would each of the four jobs start and be completed on the P&W grinder? (Express your schedule in terms of the calendar dates involved, assuming that there are seven working days each week.)

3. Jobs A, B, and C are waiting to be started on machine center X and then be completed on machine center Y. The following information pertains to the jobs and work centers.

Job	Hours Allowed for Machine Center X	Hours Allowed for Machine Center Y	Day When Due
A	36	20	10
B	96	24	17
C	60	28	25

Machine center X and machine center Y have 40 hours of capacity per week (5 working days per week, eight hours/day). Two days are allowed to move jobs between machine centers.

a. If these jobs are rescheduled by earliest due date, can they be completed on time?

b. Can they be completed on time using the critical ratio technique?

c. Can the jobs be completed on time (using the earliest due date or critical ratio technique) if 20 hours of overtime are run in work center X each week?

d. Can the jobs be completed on time (using the earliest due date or critical ratio technique) if only one day is required between operations?

4. The customer for job B in problem 3 has agreed to take half the order on day 17 and the rest on day 28. Use earliest due date rule to schedule the four jobs (A, Bl, B2, C). Can they be completed on time, assuming no extra setup time is required for splitting job B?

5. Ms. Mona Hull is in charge of a project to build a 50-foot yacht for a wealthy industrialist from Jasper, Indiana. The yacht is scheduled to compete in the famous Lake Lemon Cup Race. Eight weeks remain for constructing the yacht. Assume that each week consists of 5 workdays, for a total lead time of 40 days. The work required to complete the yacht comprises 10 operations, 4 days for each.

   a. On Tuesday morning of week 3, 3 of the 10 operations had been completed and the yacht was waiting for the fourth operation. What's the critical ratio priority?

   b. What's the critical ratio priority if only 2 of the 10 operations are completed by Tuesday morning of week 3?

6. Big Dan's Machine Shop is considering the use of a priority scheduling rule in the fabrication shop and must decide whether to use: (1) critical ratio (CR), (2) earliest due date (EDD), (3) shortest operation next (SON), or (4) order slack. The current shop status of the company is given here:

Order Number	Total Remaining Manufacturing Time	Time Remaining until Due Date	Current Operation Processing Time
1	15	12	8
2	12	15	5
3	10	14	4
4	15	18	3
5	20	19	6

   a. Using the four sequencing rules, compute the scheduling priority for each order given in the table above.

   b. What order should be run first under each of these scheduling rules?

7. Marucheck's makeshift manufacturing facility had three departments: shaping, pickling, and packing. Marucheck's orders averaged 100 pieces each. Each of the three shaping machines required one hour setup, but could run a piece in one minute. The pickling department lowered baskets of pieces into brine tanks and subjected them to low-voltage current, a heating and cooling, and a rinse. The whole process took four hours for any number of baskets or pieces. The only brine tank could hold four baskets, each of which could contain 50 pieces. (Baskets were loaded while another load was in the tank.) Each piece was inspected and wrapped in bubble pack in the packing department. Each of the four people in the department could do this at the rate of 25 pieces per hour. Marucheck had heard of the theory of constraints (TOC) and wanted to identify the bottleneck department. Which is it?

EXHIBIT A

Order Number	Manufacturing Lead Time Remaining	Time Remaining Until Due Date	Current Operation Processing Time	Number of Operations Remaining	Total Processing Time Remaining
1	15	7	2	3	8
2	15	11	3	4	8
3	20	−2	5	2	8
4	15	−5	4	3	8
5	15	3	1	12	8

Note: Time is measured in days. Manufacturing lead-time remaining includes both the machine processing time and the length of time orders spend moving and waiting to be processed in a machine queue. Current operation processing time (as well as total processing time remaining) includes no move or queue times.

8. The Ace Machine Company is considering using a priority scheduling rule in its fabrication shop and must decide whether to use: the critical ratio rule, the order slack rule, the shortest operation next rule, or the slack per operation rule. Exhibit A shows the company's current inventory and shop status.
   a. State the formula for calculating the priority index for each of sequencing rules given previously.
   b. Compute the scheduling priority for each order in Exhibit A, four sequencing rules.
9. The Optima Shop has two work centers: Big Mess and No Problem. The Monday list of orders to be filled this week shows the total setup and total run time requirements (in hours) at the two centers.
   Joe Biggs, the scheduler of Optima, said his first criterion is to minimize setups, and the second is to prioritize customer orders in numerical order.
   a. How should he schedule part production in the two centers? (Please illustrate using a Gantt chart.)
   b. Can customer delivery promises be met without overtime if capacity is 40 hours in each work center?
   c. How does the answer to part b change if only one person is assigned to do the setup in *both* work centers?
   d. Is the schedule consistent with the TOC philosophy?

	Big Mess	No Problem
Customer order 1	Part A: setup 5, run 10 Part B: setup 2, run 5	Part C: setup 1, run 2
Customer order 2	Part A: setup 5, run 3	Part D: setup 2, run 2
Customer order 3	Part B: setup 2, run 5	Part C: setup 1, run 3

10. The XYZ Company uses MRP to plan and schedule plant operations. The plant operates five days per week with no overtime, and all orders are due at 8 a.m. Monday of the week required. It's now 8 a.m. Monday of week 1, all machines are currently idle, and the production manager has been given the information in Exhibit B.
    a. Assuming that the shortest operation next rule is used to schedule orders in the shop, how should the open orders (scheduled receipts) for items A, B, and C be sequenced at their current operations? What are the implications of this schedule?

EXHIBIT B
System Data

MRP System Data

Item A		Week 1	2	3	4	5	6	7	8
Gross requirements		3	16	8	11	5	18	4	2
Scheduled receipts			30						
Projected available balance	10	7	21	13	2	27	9	5	3
Planned order release			30						

Q = 30; LT = 2; SS = 0.

Item B		Week 1	2	3	4	5	6	7	8
Gross requirements		2	5	12	4	18	2	7	10
Scheduled receipts				30					
Projected available balance	12	10	5	23	19	1	29	22	12
Planned order release			30						

Q = 30; LT = 4; SS = 0.

Item C		Week 1	2	3	4	5	6	7	8
Gross requirements		14	4	12	7	8	3	17	2
Scheduled receipts			20						
Projected available balance	17	3	19	7	0	12	9	12	10
Planned order release		20		20					

Q = 20; LT = 4; SS = 0.

Shop-Floor Control System Data

Item	Routing					Current Operation Number
A	Operation number	1	2	3	4	3 (machine 2)
	Machine number	4	6	2	3	
	Processing time*	1	1	1	1	
B	Operation number	1	2	3	4	2 (machine 2)
	Machine number	4	2	6	1	
	Processing time*	4	2	5	3	
C	Operation number	1	2	3	4	4 (machine 2)
	Machine number	6	3	1	2	
	Processing time*	3	4	6	1.5	

*In days. For computing lead times, assume that there are 1.5 days of move and queue time associated with each operation, including time to complete paperwork after the last operation.

b. Assuming that the critical ratio rule is used to schedule orders in the shop, how should the open orders for items A, B, and C be sequenced at their current operations? What are the implications of this schedule?

c. Suppose that 32 additional units of item B have just been found in the stockroom as a result of a cycle count. What actions are required on the part of the MRP planner?

11. The Ace Tool Company is considering implementing the transfer batches in scheduling the firm's fabrication shop. The production manager selected an example order to use in evaluating benefits and potential costs of this scheduling approach. A transfer batch size of 100 units was suggested for this item. The example order is for a quantity of 1,000 units and has the following routing data:

Operation	Work Center	Setup Time	Run Time/Unit
1	1	40 minutes	2.4 minutes/unit
2	2	20 minutes	1.44 minutes/unit

a. Assuming a single-shift, 8-hour day, 5-day week for work centers 1 and 2, prepare a Gantt chart showing the earliest start- and finish-time schedule for this order under a conventional scheduling approach where all items in the order are processed at one time. Do the same when transfer batches are used. What are the earliest start and finish times for each transfer batch at work center 2, assuming none of the transfer batches are processed together to save setup time?

b. What's the difference in the order-completion times under the two scheduling approaches in part a above?

c. What are the benefits and potential costs of this scheduling approach?

12. This morning, Pete Jones, integrated circuit buyer at Flatbush Products Inc., received the following purchased part MRP record:

		Week											
Circuit 101		1	2	3	4	5	6	7	8	9	10	11	12
Gross requirements		50									50	50	50
Scheduled receipts													
Projected available balance	65												
Planned order releases													

Q = 50; LT = 3; SS = 2.

a. Complete the circuit 101 MRP record.

b. Pete noted that the vendor for circuit 101 recently indicated its plant has limited production capacity available. At most, this supplier can provide 50 units per four-week period. Pete wondered what action, if any, needs to be taken on this item as a result of this capacity limitation.

13. To remain competitive, Ed's Sheet Metal must reduce manufacturing lead time for a product that typically sells in lots of 800 units. The product goes through two operations in different departments.

The company wants to evaluate the value of using a transfer batch between operations. Its idea is to split the order at the first operation and transfer an amount to the second operation to get it started while the rest of the order is finished at the first operation. The setup of operation 2 can start as soon as parts arrive, but not sooner. Other data are:

Order size	800 units
Operation 1 processing time	6 minutes/unit
Operation 2 processing time	8 minutes/unit
Transfer time from operation 1 to 2	20 minutes
Setup time for operation 1	1.0 hour
Setup time for operation 2	1.5 hours

a. What is the *minimum* transfer batch that assures that operation 2 has no idle time?

b. How much would manufacturing lead time be reduced by using the transfer batch instead of the full order of 800 units?

14. On a busy day in June, the Framkrantz Factory had five jobs lined up for processing at machine center 1. Each job went to machine center 2 after finishing at machine center 1. After that they had different routings through the factory. It's now shop day 83 and due dates have been established for each job. Machine time includes setup time, but it takes one day to move between centers and two days of queue time at each center after machine center 1 (including Finish).

Shop Day = 83	Machine Center Sequence for the Jobs and Days of Machine Time Required						
Job	**1**	**2**	**3**	**4**	**5**	**Finish**	**Due Date**
A	1	4				X	102
B	3	2	8			X	123
C	3	8		2		X	104
D	6	2	1		2	X	98
E	4	1		8	3	X	110

a. Use a spreadsheet program to calculate the priorities for each job using the critical ratio rule.

b. All jobs were at machine 2 by the morning of shop day 96. (Job A took 2 days instead of 1 and job D took 1 day instead of 6 on machine 1.) Unfortunately, there was a long job on machine 2 and none of the five jobs had started yet. What would their priorities be for machine 2?

c. What would priorities be if job A's due date were 96 (current date = 96)?

15. Shown next is the MRP record for part no. 483. The current shop day is 100 (with 5-day weeks); it's now Monday of week 1. Open orders (scheduled receipts) are due Mondays (shop days 100, 105, 110, 115, etc.) of the week for which they're scheduled. The shop floor has just reported that the batch of 40 on shop order number 32 has just finished at machine center A43 and is waiting to be moved to C06. It takes one day to move between machine centers (or to I02, the inventory location) and one day of queue time at the machine centers. (The inventory location doesn't require the queue time, but one day of "machine time" is shown for clearing the paper work.) Part number 483's routing and status are also given.

Part No. 483		Week 1	2	3	4	5	6
Gross requirements		14	4	10	20	3	10
Scheduled receipts			40*				
Projected available balance	20	6	42	32	12	9	39
Planned order releases					40		

Q = 40; LT = 2; SS = 5.
*Shop order no. 32.

Part No. 483

Routing (machine center)	A12	B17	A43	C06	I02
Machine time (days)	4	1	1	1	1
Status shop order 32	Done	Done	Done		

a. Use a spreadsheet to replicate the MRP record and calculate the critical ratio for part no. 483. Should the planner take any action?

b. What would the priorities be if the inventory were 23 instead of 20? What action should be taken now?

c. What if inventory were 17 instead of 20?

16. Consider the following data for three jobs processed in the boring machine center for Conway Manufacturing:

Job	Setup Time (Minutes)	Run Time/Unit (Minutes)	Batch Size
A	15	0.05	200
B	10	0.15	100
C	20	0.10	200

Queue data for the boring machine center:

Job	Arrival Time	Job	Arrival Time	Job	Arrival Time
A	8:24	B	8:40	B	9:12
B	8:28	C	8:42	C	9:14
C	8:31	C	8:44	A	9:18
A	8:34	A	8:57	B	9:21
B	8:39	A	9:03	B	9:31

a. If the boring machine center used a first-come/first-served rule to schedule jobs, how long would it take to process the queue? (Assume no other jobs arrive, all jobs in queue are for one batch each, and job B has just been completed.)

b. How long would it take to process all jobs in the queue, using the transfer batch logic?

17. Howie's Handicraft needs your advice on the production schedule for its Halloween product line. Analyze the information for the three-station four-product line, given next:

Product	Estimated Weekly Sales, (Units)	Selling Price, ($)	Material Cost, ($)	Process Time Workstation*		
				1	2	3
Witches	60	35	15	10	10	40
Goblins	50	40	15	10	15	40
Ghosts	40	45	20	10	10	20
Ghouls	30	50	20	15	20	20

*The times for workstations 1, 2, and 3 are in minutes per unit. Capacity at each workstation is 2,400 minutes/week and operating expenses are $2,000/week.

a. What is the bottleneck workstation? What schedule of products at this work station maximized the profit to Howie?

b. What is the total profit from the schedule in part a?

18. The Marlborough Manufacturing Company in New Zealand was considering embarking on a program of rationalizing its vendor base. It had heard of the benefits of doing so, but was unsure where to start. To begin the process, it recorded the total New Zealand dollar (NZD) purchases in the last year and the number of orders that it placed with each firm in a sample of 20 suppliers. The data are shown here:

Company	NZD	Orders/Year
Axel	321,760	7
Backer	55,122	2
Booker	186,242	3
Century	16,088	4
Farmic	80,440	22
First	48,262	3
Gentry	1,850,120	10
Grist	40,220	1
Hooker	64,532	2
Hume	63,253	6
Jacobs	965,283	8
Kelvin	8,124	2
Kolst	1,367,484	5
Kume	57,305	4
Locket	563,087	1
Neive	7,944	1
Whist	2,171,886	3
Wolf	31,523	3
Young	17,053	6
Zydec	121,555	2

a. Analyze the purchases in this sample using the order frequency data. For which suppliers should Marlborough focus its efforts in building relationships?

b. For which might it consider making some deletions?

c. What other questions does the sample information raise about the purchasing policies of the company?

Case Theory of Constraints (TOC) Scheduling at TOSOH

TOSOH is a manufacturer of special alloy materials for computer manufacturing firms. The products are custom designed to meet the specifications of the customer's production process and product design. The product unit selling price ranges from $500 to $6,000. The annual sales are $100 million, with 80 percent of the sales volume going to 10 customers.

Products are manufactured on a make-to-order basis with approximately 500 open shop orders at any given time. Each product passes through 10 to 20 operations, and there are four focused factory operations within the main plant, each of which has about 10 work centers. Each product is manufactured from a special metal alloy, and the master database contains approximately 1,500 end-product items. The bill of material has two levels: product items and raw materials.

Before installing the TOC system, the plant used a manual scheduling system that was based on very rough estimates of process setup and run times. While bills of material and product routings existed, these were poorly maintained. There was no clear measure of plant capacity nor an ability to forecast the upcoming capacity constraints.

The company chose to implement TOC to achieve several business objectives. The foremost objective was to deliver product faster and more reliably in a market characterized by life cycles approximating 6 to 12 months—a relatively short time. The company also wanted to maximize the throughput of the factory and to achieve a better utilization of the expensive machine tools and heat-treatment facilities. The company felt that the TOC system would enable manufacturing to minimize batch sizes, reducing cycle time and WIP inventory while improving responsiveness to customers. Finally, because of the short product life cycle, and the costs of product obsolescence, the company wanted to reduce the investment in finished goods inventory.

The TOC project began with a one-year manual pilot implementation of the TOC system. Subsequently, the TOC software was purchased, the manufacturing database was developed, and the software was tested. An example of the TOC schedules at TOSOH, using product item 3596C-13-108-501 is illustrated. This item is being manufactured for shop order RWO502, which has a due date of 10/16/XX. The process routing for this item is shown in Figure 8.12. Note that *only* operation 500 on this order is performed on a drum work center.

Portions of the schedule at all of the work centers in the example are shown in Figure 8.13a. Figure 8.13a shows the schedule for shop order RW0502 for the five work centers preceding the drum (work center 101-5M). The material release date of 9/19/XX in Figure 8.13a is back-scheduled from the drum schedule, and all of the operations in between (operations 100 through 400) are run on a first-in, first-out basis, using process and delay time data. A portion of the drum schedule for work center 101-5M is shown in Figure 8.13b. Shop order RWO502 is scheduled to start at 10:20 a.m. on

FIGURE 8.12 **Process Routing, Product Item 3596C-13-108-501**

Operation Number	Work Center	Work Center Status
100	101-KS	Nonconstraint
200	101-WP	Nonconstraint
300	101-5C	Nonconstraint
400	101-80	Nonconstraint
500	101-5M	Constraint
600	101-CM	Nonconstraint
700	255-XRF	Nonconstraint
800	260	Nonconstraint
900	231	Nonconstraint
1000	Stores	Nonconstraint

FIGURE 8.13a Plant Schedule

Analyst ID: JB

Release on: 9/19/XX

Part ID	Work Order ID	Qty	Work Center ID	Order ID	Order Due Date: Line No.	Order Due Date: Target	Order Due Date: Projected	Order Due Date: Product ID	Customer ID	Buffer: Planned	Buffer: Remaining
3596C-13-108-501	RWO502	1.00	101-KS	C10402	18	10/16/XX	10/16/XX	3596C-13-108-501	7138568-4	56	103
4028H-13-108-501	RWO500	10.00	101-KS	01090062	2	10/8/XX	10/8/XX	4028H-13-108-501	7011585-1	56	114

Part ID	Job Step	Qty	Work Order ID	Setup Time	Run Time	Start Date	Buffer Plan	Buffer Remain	Order ID	Target Date	Proj. Date	Product ID
Priority list for work center 101-KS—KASTO SAWS (2)				*Calendar: Default*								
3596C-13-108-501	100.00	1.00	RWO502	00:15	00:01	09/19/XX	56	103	C10402	10/16/XX	10/16/XX	3596C-13-108-501
Priority list for work center 101-WP—WISCONSIN COLD				*Calendar: Default*								
3596C-13-108-501	200.00	1.00	RWO502	00:30	12:00	09/19/XX	56	103	C10402	10/16/XX	10/16/XX	3596C-13-108-501
Priority list for work center 101-5C—MAZAK II & III PLANAR				*Calendar: 10 hour*								
3596C-13-108-501	300.00	1.00	RWO502	00:30	00:45	09/19/XX	56	108	C10402	10/16/XX	10/16/XX	3596C-13-108-501
Priority list for work center 101-80—OUTSIDE WELD				*Calendar: Default*								
3596C-13-108-501	400.00	1.00	RWO502	01:00	168:0	09/19/XX	56	116	C10402	10/16/XX	10/16/XX	3596C-13-108-501
3596C-13-108-501	400.00	1.00	RWO508	01:00	168:0	10/03/XX	56	221	C10402	10/30/XX	10/30/XX	3596C-13-108-501
3596C-13-108-501	400.00	1.00	RWO519	01:00	168:0	10/17/XX	56	431	C10402	11/13/XX	11/13/XX	3596C-13-108-501
3596C-13-108-501	400.00	1.00	RWO527	01:00	168:0	10/31/XX	56	536	C10402	11/27/XX	11/27/XX	3596C-13-108-501

FIGURE 8.13b Drum Schedule: Grouped by Unit

Work Center: 101-5M : AMAT CELL | Unit: 1 | Calendar: 14 Hour

Part ID	Job Step	Qty	Qty Finished	Work Order	Setup	Duration	Start Time	Actual Start	Order ID	Target Data	Proj. Data	Product ID	Customer ID
Start date: 10/11/XX													
3596C-13-108-501	500.00	1.00	0.00	RW0502	00:45	01:30	10:20		C10402	10/16/XX	10/16/XX	3596C-13-108-501	7138568-4
Start date: 10/18/XX													
3596C-13-108-501	500.00	1.00	0.00	RW0508	00:45	01:30	10:20		C10402	10/30/XX	10/30/XX	3596C-13-108-501	7138568-4
Start date: 11/08/XX													
3596C-13-108-501	500.00	1.00	0.00	RW0519	00:45	01:30	10:20		C10402	11/13/XX	11/13/XX	3596C-13-108-501	7138568-4
Start date: 11/15/XX													
3596C-13-108-501	500.00	1.00	0.00	RW0527	00:45	01:30	10:20		C10402	11/27/XX	11/27/XX	3596C-13-108-501	7138568-4

Part ID	Job Step	Qty	Work Order ID	Setup Time	Run Time	Start Date	Buffer Plan	Buffer Remain	Order ID	Target Date	Proj. Date	Product ID
Priority list for work center 101-CM—CMM (2)				*Calendar: Default*								
3596C-13-108-501	600.00	1.00	RW0502	00:00	00:00	10/11/XX	72	357	C10402	10/16/XX	10/16/XX	3596C-13-108-501
3596C-13-108-501	600.00	1.00	RW01139	00:00	00:00	10/18/XX	72	462	C10402	10/30/XX	10/30/XX	3596C-13-108-501
3596C-13-108-501	600.00	1.00	RW01375	00:00	00:00	11/08/XX	72	672	C10402	11/13/XX	11/13/XX	3596C-13-108-501
Priority list for work center 255—XRF				*Calendar: Default*								
3596C-13-108-501	700.00	1.00	RW0502	00:00	00:00	10/11/XX	72	357	C10402	10/16/XX	10/16/XX	3596C-13-108-501
3596C-13-108-501	700.00	1.00	RW01139	00:00	00:00	10/18/XX	72	462	C10402	10/30/XX	10/30/XX	3596C-13-108-501
3596C-13-108-501	700.00	1.00	RW01375	00:00	00:00	11/08/XX	72	672	C10402	11/13/XX	11/13/XX	3596C-13-108-501
Priority list for work center 260—CLEAN/PACK/SHIP C/P				*Calendar: Default*								
3596C-13-108-501	800.00	1.00	RW0502	00:00	00:00	10/11/XX	72	357	C10402	10/16/XX	10/16/XX	3596C-13-108-501
3596C-13-108-501	800.00	1.00	RW01139	00:00	00:00	10/18/XX	72	462	C10402	10/30/XX	10/30/XX	3596C-13-108-501
3596C-13-108-501	800.00	1.00	RW01375	00:00	00:00	11/08/XX	72	672	C10402	11/13/XX	11/13/XX	3596C-13-108-501
Priority list for work center 231—INSP MEDIA/PM				*Calendar: Default*								
3596C-13-108-501	900.00	1.00	RW0502	00:10	00:03	10/11/XX	72	357	C10402	10/16/XX	10/16/XX	3596C-13-108-501
3596C-13-108-501	900.00	1.00	RW01139	00:10	00:03	10/18/XX	72	462	C10402	10/30/XX	10/30/XX	3596C-13-108-501
3596C-13-108-501	900.00	1.00	RW01375	00:10	00:03	11/08/XX	72	672	C10402	11/13/XX	11/13/XX	3596C-13-108-501
Priority list for work center STORES—KITTED				*Calendar: Default*								
3596C-13-108-501	1,000.00	1.00	RW0502	00:00	00:00	10/11/XX	72	357	C10402	10/16/XX	10/16/XX	3596C-13-108-501
37000-13-950-100	300.00	1.00	130313	00:00	00:00	10/17/XX	56	418	C10402	11/13/XX	11/13/XX	3596C-13-108-501
3596C-13-108-501	1,000.00	1.00	RW01139	00:00	00:00	10/18/XX	72	462	C10402	10/30/XX	10/30/XX	3596C-13-108-501
37000-13-950-100	200.00	1.00	RW01411	00:00	00:00	10/31/XX	56	523	C10402	11/27/XX	11/27/XX	3596C-13-108-501
3596C-13-108-501	1,000.00	1.00	RW01375	00:00	00:00	11/08/XX	72	672	C10402	11/13/XX	11/13/XX	3596C-13-108-501

10/11/XX and to be completed two hours and 15 minutes later. (The setup time of 45 minutes and the run time of 1 hour and 30 minutes is shown in the upper portion of Figure 8.13b.) Likewise, all of the nonconstraint operations following the drum (600 through 1000) are expected to be complete by the order due date (10/16/XX), using first-in, first-out scheduling priorities. The TOC schedule for this product allows a buffer of 56 hours for the drum (operation 500), and a buffer of 72 hours for the shipping dock buffer. These are shown in the "buffer plan" columns of Figures 8.13a and b.

The company learned several lessons during implementation. First, the culture needed to change in order to achieve the benefits of TOC scheduling. The importance of educating all of the manufacturing personnel on the basic concepts of TOC scheduling became clear. Other changes included the elimination of traditional cost accounting performance measures relating to productivity, efficiency, product cost, etc. Manufacturing people needed to understand that it is all right for the non-drum work centers to be idle. Further, this training needed to be performed on a company wide basis for the system to be totally effective.

Second, in using TOC the company needed to emphasize the elimination of obstacles to the flow of materials through the plant. In addition to the physical constraints, these obstacles included such items as paperwork, procedural roadblocks, and work rules. This effort involved ensuring raw material availability, instilling a sense of urgency in people regarding the TOC schedule, achieving a high level of process reliability, and reducing waste in time and materials. Both TOC scheduling and the focus on process improvement at TOSOH have produced important achievements in operating performance. This includes a sales revenue increase of 14 percent, a 38 percent improvement in delivery reliability, a 14 percent reduction in customer lead times, a doubling of the overall inventory turns, and a 50 percent reduction in the reserve for obsolete inventory. These results were achieved over a four-year period.

Assignment

Work on Shop Order RW0502 is scheduled to begin on 9/19/XX and be completed by 10/16/XX. This allows 26 days less 7 days for Saturdays and Sundays, or a total of 19 working days to complete the order. Assuming an eight-hour work day, convert the 19 days to hours. How much of this time is allowed for buffer, and how much time is allowed for setup and processing times? How much of this time is devoted to non-bottleneck operations, and how much to bottleneck operations?

Chapter 8A

Advanced Scheduling

This chapter addresses advanced issues in scheduling, with primary emphasis on detailed scheduling of individual jobs through work centers in a shop. The intent is to provide direction for the firm that has a working MPC system in place and wishes to enhance the shop-floor systems.

The approaches in this chapter presume effective front-end, engine, and back-end systems are in place. Chapter 8A provides an application perspective to research in scheduling. It's completely beyond our scope to even summarize the vast amount of research on this topic. Rather, our interest here is to focus on some basic concepts and results, relate them to some of the newer manufacturing approaches, and show how you might apply results in certain operating situations.

Chapter 8A centers around three topics:

- *Basic scheduling research:* What are the fundamental scheduling research problems, and what are the practical implications of scheduling results that have been consistently verified in the research?
- *Advanced research findings:* What findings from advanced research seem to be particularly helpful in assigning jobs or labor to machines? What are the critical scheduling issues in cellular manufacturing?
- *Multiple constraint scheduling.* How can the theory of constraints (TOC) scheduling be extended to multiple constraining resources?

Basic Scheduling Research

We can define a schedule as a plan with reference to the sequence of time allocated for and operations necessary to complete an item. This definition lets us think of a schedule that has a series of sequential steps, or a routing. The entire sequence of operations, the necessary sequential constraints, the time estimates for each operation, and the required resource capacities for each operation are inputs to developing the detailed plan or schedule.

The One-Machine Case

Research on single-machine scheduling has been largely based on the static problem of how to best schedule a fixed set of jobs through a single machine, when all jobs are available at the start of the scheduling period. It's further assumed that setup times are independent of the sequence.

If the objective is to *minimize total time* to run the entire set of jobs (i.e., the minimum make-span), it doesn't matter in which order jobs are run. In this case, the make-span equals the sum of all setup and run times for any sequence of jobs. However, if the objective is to *minimize the average time* each job spends at the machine (setup plus run plus waiting times), then we can show this will be accomplished by sequencing jobs in ascending order according to their total processing time (setup plus run time). As an example, if three jobs with individual processing times of one, five, and eight hours, respectively, are scheduled, *total time* required to run the *entire* batch under any sequence is 14 hours. If we process jobs in ascending order, the average time that each job spends in the system is $(1 + 6 + 14) \div 3 = 7$ hours. However, if we process jobs in the reverse order, average time in the system is $(8 + 13 + 14) \div 3 = 11.67$ hours.

This result has an important consequence. Average time in the system will always be minimized by selecting the next job for processing that has the shortest processing time at the current operation. This rule for sequencing jobs at a work center (called **shortest processing time,** or **SPT**) provides excellent results when we use the average time in system criterion.

SPT also performs well on the criterion of *minimizing the average number of jobs in the system.* As we've noted previously, work-in-process inventory levels and average flow time are directly related measures. If we increase or reduce one, the other changes in the same direction. Analytical work shows that the SPT rule again provides superior performance when the work-in-process criterion is applied in the single-machine case.

When the criterion is to *minimize the average job lateness,* again SPT is the best rule for sequencing jobs for the single-machine case. To introduce the lateness criterion, we first must establish due dates for the jobs. Lateness measures both positive and negative deviations from the due date. An interesting aspect of scheduling research is, no matter what procedure we use to establish due dates, SPT will minimize *average job lateness.*

The one-machine scheduling research is very useful in gaining insights into scheduling rules' behavior under particular criteria. The most important conclusion we can draw from the single-machine research is the SPT rule represents the best way to pick the next job to run, if the objective is to minimize average time per job, to minimize average number of jobs in the system, or to minimize average job lateness. However, if the objective is to minimize either the maximum lateness of any job or the lateness variance, then jobs should run in due date sequence.

The Two-Machine Case

Developing scheduling procedures for the two-machine case is somewhat more complex than for single-machine systems. In the two-machine case, we must schedule both machines to best satisfy whatever criterion is selected. Moreover, we have to consider job routings. We assume each job always goes from a particular machine to another machine. For analytically based research, we make additional assumptions, such as those for the one-machine case. For example, all jobs are available at the start of the schedule, and setup times are independent.

A set of rules has been developed to minimize the make-span in the two-machine case. Note while the minimum make-span doesn't depend on job sequencing in the one-machine case, this isn't true in the two-machine case. Additionally, if total time to run the entire batch of jobs is to be minimized, this doesn't ensure either the average time each job spends in the system or the average number of jobs in the system will also be minimized.

The following scheduling rules minimize make-span in a two-machine flow shop.[1]

Select the job with the minimum processing time on either machine 1 or machine 2. If this time is associated with machine 1, schedule this job first. If it's for machine 2, schedule this job last in the series of jobs to be run. Remove this job from further consideration.

Select the job with the next smallest processing time and proceed as above (if for machine 1, schedule it next; if for machine 2, as near to last as possible). Any ties can be broken randomly.

Continue this process until all of the jobs have been scheduled.

The intuitive logic behind this rule is the minimum time to complete the set of jobs has to be the larger of the sum of all run times at the first machine plus the smallest run time at the second machine, or the sum of all run times at the second machine plus the smallest run time at the first machine.

We can also apply these rules to larger flow shop scheduling problems. The following procedure uses the previous algorithm to solve a series of two-machine approximations to the actual problem having M-machines (where $M > 2$) using the following rules:[2]

Solve the first problem considering only machine 1 and M, ignoring the intervening $M - 2$ machines.

Solve the second problem by pooling the first two machines (1 and 2) and the last two machines ($M - 1$ and M) to form two dummy machines. Processing time at the first dummy machine is the sum of the processing time on machines 1 and 2 for each order. Processing time at the second dummy machine is the sum of the processing time at machines $M - 1$ and M for each order.

Continue in this manner until $M - 1$ problems are solved. In the final problem, the first dummy machine contains machines 1 through $M - 1$, and the second dummy machine contains machines 2 through M.

Compute the make-span for each problem solved and select the best sequence.

Additional procedures using branch and bound algorithms and integer-programming methods have been developed to solve static flow shop three-machine scheduling problems using the minimum make-span criterion. However, the solutions are generally feasible only for very small problems. Currently, heuristic methods such as the M-machine algorithm are the only means of solving larger-scale flow shop scheduling problems.

Dispatching Approaches

Applying dispatching approaches to scheduling problems allows us to relax some of the limiting constraints just mentioned. In particular, dispatching approaches deal with

[1]S. M. Johnson. "Optimal Two- and Three-Stage Production Schedules with Setup Time Included," *Naval Research Logistics Quarterly* 1 (1954), pp. 61–68.

[2]H. G. Campbell, R. A. Dudek, and M. L. Smith. "A Heuristic Algorithm for the n-Job m-Machine Sequencing Problem," *Management Science* 16, no. 10 (June 1970).

the dynamic problem, rather than the static problem. Randomness in interarrival and service times are considered, and steady state results are provided for average flow time, average work-in-process, expected work center utilization, and average waiting time.

Dispatching involves the use of logic rules that guide the prioritizing of jobs at a workstation. These rules are referred to as *sequencing rules*. Sequencing rules range from simple local rules, such as SPT, to more complex rules that consider due dates, shop congestion, and other criteria.

To examine realistic, multiple-machine, dynamic scheduling situations, we often use simulation models. With simulation, we can examine various rules' performance against several criteria. We can expand the size of problems studied (work centers and jobs), consider effects of startup and ending conditions, and accommodate any kind of product structure, interarrival time patterns, or shop capacity. Simulation studies address such primary research questions as: Which dispatching approach for sequencing jobs at work centers performs best? For which criteria? Are some classes of rules better than others for some classes of criteria or classes of problems?

Sequencing Rules

Figure 8A.1 illustrates a typical scheduling environment for a complex job shop. At any time, if a set of n jobs is to be scheduled on m machines, there are $(n!)^m$ possible ways to schedule the jobs, and the schedule could change with the addition of new jobs. For any problem involving more than a few machines or a few jobs, the computational complexity of finding the best schedule is beyond even a modern computer's capacity.

Figure 8A.1 shows complex routings. For example, after processing at work center A, we may send jobs for further processing to work centers B, D, or F. Similarly, some jobs are completed after being processed at work center A and go directly to finished component inventories. Also note a job might flow from work center A to work center D and then back to A.

FIGURE 8A.1 The Scheduling Environment

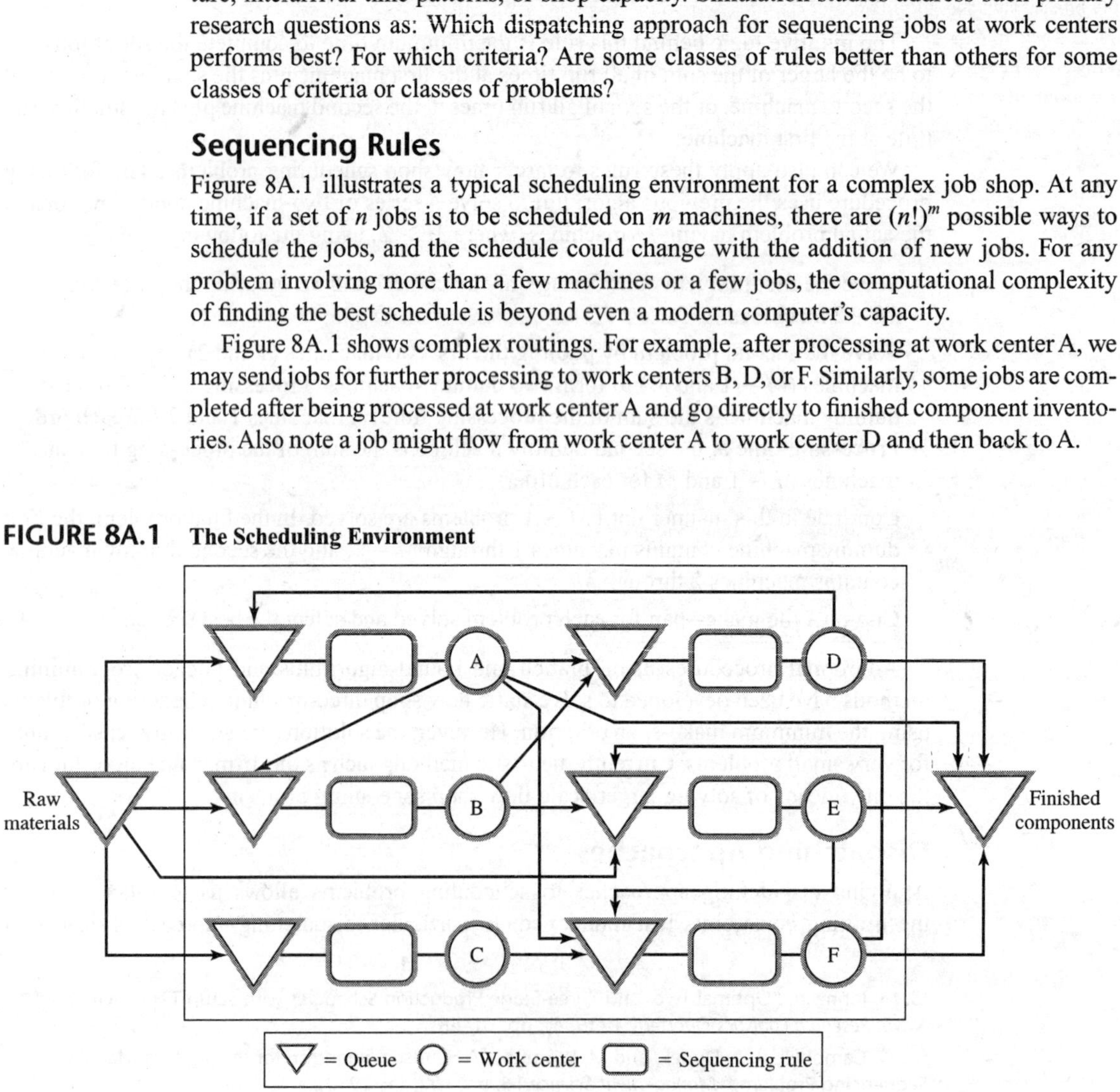

Figure 8A.1 depicts a sequencing rule between each queue and its associated work center. This indicates a rule exists for choosing the next job in the queue for processing. The question of interest is which sequencing rule will achieve good performance against some scheduling criterion.

A large number of sequencing rules have appeared in research and in practice. Each could be used in scheduling jobs. Here are some well-known rules with their desirable properties:

R (random). Pick any job in the queue with equal probability. This rule is often used as a benchmark for other rules.

FCFS (first come/first served). This rule is sometimes deemed to be "fair" in that jobs are processed in the order they arrive at the work center.

SPT (shortest processing time). As noted, this rule tends to reduce work-in-process inventory, average job completion (flow) time, and average job lateness.

EDD (earliest due date). This rule seems to work well for criteria associated with job lateness.

CR (critical ratio). This rule is widely used in practice. Calculate the priority index using (due date–current time)/(lead time remaining).

LWR (least work remaining). This rule is an extension of SPT in that it considers *all* processing time remaining until the job is completed.

FOR (fewest operations remaining). Another SPT variant that considers the number of successive operations.

ST (slack time). A variant of EDD that subtracts the sum of setup and processing times from time remaining until the due date. The resulting value is called "slack." Jobs are run in order of the smallest amount of slack.

ST/O (slack time per operation). A variant of ST that divides the slack time by the number of remaining operations, again sequencing jobs in order of the smallest value first.

NQ (next queue). A different kind of rule. NQ is based on machine utilization. The idea is to consider queues at each of the succeeding work centers to which the jobs will go and to select the job for processing that's going to the smallest queue (measured either in hours or perhaps in jobs).

LSU (least setup). Still another rule is to pick the job that minimizes changeover time on the machine. In this way, capacity utilization is maximized. Note this rule explicitly recognizes dependencies between setup times and job sequence.

This list isn't exhaustive. Many other rules, variants of these rules, and combinations of these rules have been studied. In some cases, use of one rule under certain conditions and use of another under other conditions has been studied.

One issue Figure 8A.1 highlights is whether we should use the same rule at each work center. We might, for example, build a case for using SPT at the "gateway" work centers and using some due date–oriented rules for downstream centers. Or perhaps selection of a rule should depend on queue size or how much work is ahead of or behind schedule.

Another issue in selecting sequencing rules is their usage cost. Some rules (such as random, first come/first serve, shortest processing time, earliest due date, and fewest

FIGURE 8A.2
Simulation Results for Various Sequencing Rules

Sequencing Rule	Average Time in System	Variance of Time in System
SPT	34.0	2,318
EDD	63.7	6,780
ST/O	66.1	5,460
FCFS	74.4	5,739
R	74.7	10,822

operations remaining) are easy to implement, because they don't require other information than that related to the job itself. Other rules (such as the critical ratio, least work remaining, slack time, and slack time per operation rules) require more complex information plus time-dependent calculations. The next queue and least setup rules require even more information, involving the congestion at other work centers, or a changeover cost matrix for all jobs currently at a work center.

Extensive research has addressed the performance of the different sequencing rules listed.[3] Figure 8A.2 reports typical results for two criteria: average time in the system and variance of the time in system. Recall that the average time in the system is directly related to work-in-process inventory and average number of jobs in the system. The results in Figure 8A.2 clearly show the SPT rule performs quite well for this set of criteria.

There is, however, a concern in using SPT. It can allow some jobs with long processing times to wait in queue for a substantial time, causing severe due date problems for a few jobs. However, because the SPT rules can complete the average job in a relatively short time compared with other rules, overall lateness performance might be much less severe than we might think.

Other research efforts have tried to combine SPT with other sequencing rules to obtain most of SPT's benefits without the large time in system variance. One approach has been to alternate SPT with FCFS to "clean out the work centers" at periodic intervals. A combination rule can be very effective in reducing this negative attribute of SPT.

Advanced Procedures

This section covers several additional procedures we feel are particularly relevant to MPC practice. These procedures focus on determination of lead times (management of due dates) for manufactured items and determination of labor assignments in manufacturing operations. In each case, we think important practical issues are raised and the practicing professional can use the available, though perhaps tentative, conclusions.

Due Date–Setting Procedures

An important issue in scheduling manufacturing orders is establishing order release and due dates. Many firms assign setting such dates to manufacturing; it's frequently the subject of intense negotiations between manufacturing and marketing personnel. Often, due dates must be set at the time of order receipt or when bidding for an order. An effective

[3] R. W. Conway, W. L. Maxwell, and L. W. Miller. *Theory of Scheduling* (Dover Publications, 2003).

MPC system can help by providing appropriate information regarding material availability, capacity, and resource requirements for individual jobs. As an example, we normally assign due dates for make-to-order products based on raw material and equipment capacity availabilities. Likewise, we set order release and due dates for manufactured components in MRP systems by determining length of the planned lead time for such items. Therefore, establishing lead time offsets and due dates is a vital and ongoing function in a manufacturing system. A well-functioning shop-floor control system based on good sequencing rules will help us achieve these due dates.

An approach for setting due dates for an order is by adding an estimate of the manufacturing time to the date the order is received.[4] Three methods for establishing the estimate of manufacturing time are:

CON: A *constant* time allowance for manufacturing all jobs; that is, the same lead time is added to all jobs at receipt date to calculate the due date.

SLK: A time allowance that provides an equal (constant) waiting time or *slack* for all jobs; that is, the due date is set equal to the receipt date plus the sum of all processing times, plus a fixed additional slack time.

TWK: A time for waiting that has slack proportional to a job's *total work content;* that is, lead time to be added to the receipt date is a multiple of the sum of all processing times.

Each procedure has a single parameter (the constant time, the slack time, or the multiple) to be determined. Other informational needs are similar to those of shop-floor scheduling problems. The first procedure is easy to implement in many firms since shop-floor system database requirements are minimal. The other two procedures, however, require an estimate of a job's processing time to set the due date.

Experiments testing the three due date–setting rules involved a single-machine system. They were conducted under a wide variety of operating conditions: 80 percent to 99 percent machine utilization, a variety of jobs, 20 replications, and use of both exponentially and normally distributed processing times. The exponentially distributed processing times gave a much greater degree of variability in achieved lead times (coefficient of variation, $c_v = 1.0$) than the normally distributed processing time ($c_v = 0.25$). Two releasing rules were used as well. The random release rule meant orders were issued to the shop as soon as received. The "controlled" release rule meant jobs were released when work-in-process inventory levels fell below a "trigger point." The trigger point was chosen to provide a specified average number of jobs in the shop.

The evaluative criterion was "due date tightness." Here we presume tight due dates (or short lead times) are strategically more desirable than loose due dates. Tight due dates provide a competitive advantage by permitting the firm to offer an improved level of customer service, as well as achieve lower costs through reductions in work-in-process inventory. The experiments' approach was to set each of the three parameters so that *no* late deliveries occurred; that is, the parameters were chosen so the longest lead time is just sufficient. Thereafter, actual lead times are observed in the simulation. The preferred procedure is the one that achieves the smallest mean lead time.

[4]K. R. Baker and J. W. M. Bertrand. "A Comparison of Due Date Selection Rules," *AIIE Transactions* 13, no. 2 (June 1981).

FIGURE 8A.3 Simulation Results for Manufacturing Lead Time Estimating Procedures

Treatment	Mean Number of Jobs	Utilization	Mean Manufacturing Lead Time			Frequency Best*		
			TWK	SLK	CON	TWK	SLK	CON
Exponential times, random release	4.00	0.80	4.43	9.04	10.14	20	0	0
	5.67	0.85	5.63	10.37	11.39	20	0	0
	9.00	0.90	6.20	11.79	12.76	20	0	0
Exponential times, controlled release	4.00		5.26	4.53	8.79	3	17	0
	5.67		6.51	6.23	10.09	7	13	0
	9.00		8.28	9.51	13.49	17	3	0
Normal times, random release	4.28	0.90	7.20	7.70	7.72	16	2	2
	9.59	0.95	10.06	10.70	10.75	16	2	2
	52.09	0.99	10.44	10.99	11.07	20	0	0
Normal times, controlled release	4.28		6.65	5.31	5.90	0	20	0
	9.59		12.35	10.61	11.18	0	20	0
	52.09		48.53	53.10	53.64	20	0	0

*Number of times in the 20 replications that each procedure performed the best (i.e., produced the lowest mean manufacturing lead time).

The results indicate the SLK and TWK procedures set tighter due dates than the CON procedure. As Figure 8A.3 shows, these two procedures provided as much as a 50 percent reduction in lead time required for manufacturing (in comparison with the CON procedure) under exponentially distributed processing times. Much smaller differences were noted when normally distributed processing times were used. Furthermore, there was a clear preference for the TWK procedure (as opposed to the SLK procedure) when random work releasing was used. In using controlled work releasing, preference shifts to the TWK procedure at higher levels of machine utilization.

The important message is that calculating lead times on the basis of total work content is best. In the next section, we consider the important question of whether a due date should be changed after the order has been released to the shop.

Dynamic Due Dates

Determining due dates for orders when they are released to the shop is only one aspect of managing due dates in scheduling. A second aspect concerns maintaining *valid* due dates as orders progress through the manufacturing process and as new orders are added. The need for due date maintenance arises from the manufacturing environment's dynamic nature. Management actions (such as master production schedule changes, planned lead time adjustments, and bill of materials modifications) can create the need to reschedule manufacturing orders and to revise priorities given to the shop. Likewise, variations in shop conditions (such as unexpected scrap and unplanned transactions) can also create the need to revise job due dates.

Many firms' systems and procedures result in changes in open order due dates. This practice is called *dynamic due date maintenance.* The primary argument for this practice is the shop should use accurate and timely information in dispatching jobs to machines to provide a high level of customer service. In spite of its widespread use, controversy surrounds the advisability of implementing dynamic due date maintenance systems. Some suggest dynamic due dates can have an adverse impact on scheduling performance because of system "nervousness."[5] A scheduling system with *unstable* open order priorities might be called a nervous scheduling system, which can lead to shop floor distrust and a complex overriding priority system. A second behavioral argument against dynamic due date maintenance is the volume of rescheduling messages might so inundate the production planner that he or she can't process the necessary changes in a timely fashion.

In such cases, the production planner may simply stop trying to perform an impossible task; the shop could lose faith in the priority system and revert to using an "informal" system; or ill-chosen or misleading rescheduling messages may be communicated to the shop. Any or all of these responses may cause the shop and inventory system performance to deteriorate.

An important experiment to better understand when dynamic due dates might be attractive and when they are not attractive evaluated the use of several dynamic due date procedures as well as the use of simple procedures for selectively implementing a few of the many due date changes that would normally be implemented (filtering procedures).[6] In particular, the study concerned determining what types of job-related information are important to consider in formulating open order rescheduling procedures and evaluating rescheduling's impact on manufacturing performance in MRP systems.

The study considered three different filters for making rescheduling decisions: ability, magnitude, and horizon filters. The ability filter's purpose is to assure only attainable due date adjustments are passed along to the shop. In using this procedure:

1. All *rescheduling out* actions (when the new due date is later than the previous due date) are implemented.
2. Implementing *reschedule-in* actions depends on one of three conditions:
   a. If the machine setup and processing time remaining is less than the time until the new due date, the new due date is implemented.
   b. If the machine setup and processing time remaining is less than the time until the old due date but greater than the time until the new date, the due date is set to the present time plus the machine setup and processing time to complete the order.
   c. If the machine setup and processing time remaining exceeds the time allowed until the old due date, no change is made to the old due date.

The magnitude and horizon filters consider different information. These procedures are designed to filter out trivial due date adjustments by means of a *threshold* value. In the magnitude procedure, if the absolute value of the difference between the new and the old due dates exceeds a threshold value (T_m), the due date is changed. Similarly, the horizon procedure is designed to filter out due date changes too far out in the planning horizon to be of immediate concern to the production planner. Only if the old due date falls within the period of interest (T_H) is the new due date implemented. By setting parameter values for T_m and T_H, the number of rescheduling changes to be implemented can be adjusted. The procedures will implement all changes when $T_m = 0$ and $T_H = \infty$, providing full dynamic procedures. Static dates result when $T_m = \infty$ and $T_H = 0$.

[5]D. C. Steele. "The Nervous MRP System: How to Do Battle," *Production and Inventory Management* 16 (4th quarter 1975).

[6]R. J. Penlesky, W. L. Berry, and U. Wemmerlov. "Open Order Due Date Maintenance in MRP Systems," *Management Science* 35, no. 5 (May, 1989).

Simulation experiments were used to investigate the effect of incorporating dynamic due date information in the sequencing rules and use of filtering procedures. These experiments were conducted using a make-to-stock job shop simulator, with both component manufacturing and assembly operations, controlled by an MRP system. Procedures were tested under differing values of machine utilization, uncertainty in the master production schedule, length of planned lead times, and size of production order quantities. The three measures of effectiveness used were end-product customer service level, combined work-in-process and finished item inventory level, and number of rescheduling changes implemented.

These results indicate that under certain operating conditions, dynamic due date information improves customer service while reducing total inventory level. First, there's no significant difference in performance between the filtering procedures and the dynamic due date procedure without filtering. All rescheduling procedures significantly improve performance over the static procedures. Second, magnitude and horizon filters provide comparable performance to the dynamic rescheduling procedure—but with far fewer rescheduling actions implemented. Therefore, it would seem dynamic rescheduling's benefits can be achieved by *selectively* implementing rescheduling actions. By filtering rescheduling messages, we can reduce information processing costs and adverse behavioral effects of system nervousness without an adverse effect on operating performance.

Labor-Limited Systems

The scheduling research results presented so far are useful when sequencing rules represent the principal means of controlling work flow in a plant. In many firms, besides assigning jobs to work centers, there's a need to make labor assignment decisions. Labor assignment decisions are important in controlling work flow when labor capacity is a critical resource in completing work. This can occur even when only one particular labor skill is the bottleneck resource. In such instances, the system is said to be labor-limited.

Labor limitations provide an additional dimension to shop-floor scheduling that's important for many JIT and cellular manufacturing situations. The controllable cost is labor, and the primary scheduling job is assigning labor to machine centers. Good labor scheduling practice enables us to vary labor capacity at work centers to better match day-to-day fluctuations in work loads. To the extent there's flexibility in assigning people to work centers, we can improve manufacturing performance (e.g., reduced flow times, better customer service, and decreased work-in-process inventory). However, the degree of flexibility in making labor assignments depends on such factors as amount of cross-training in the workforce, use of temporary labor, favorable employee work rules, and costs of shifting people between work centers.

A comprehensive framework for control of work flow in labor-limited systems uses three major elements for controlling work flow:[7]

1. Determining which job to do next at a work center (dispatching).
2. Determining when a person is available for transfer to another work center (degree of central control).
3. Determining the work center to which an available person is to be assigned (work center selection).

[7]R. T. Nelson. "Labor and Machine Limited Production Systems," *Management Science* 13, no. 9 (May 1967).

Various decision rules, using information similar to that used in making dispatching decisions, have been suggested for making the latter two decisions.[8] The decision rules Nelson suggested for determining a person's availability for transfer utilize a central control parameter, d, that varies between 0 and 1. When $d = 1$, the person is always available for reassignment to another work center. When $d = 0$, the person can't be reassigned as long as jobs are waiting in the queue at the person's current work center assignment. We can control the proportion of scheduling decisions in which a person is available for transfer by adjusting d's value between 0 and 1.

Two different approaches to transfer availability are studied. One considers time; the other considers the queue. The time approach suggests the person must be idle for t or more minutes before a transfer can be made. The queue approach suggests making a transfer only when the person's work center queue has fewer than q jobs waiting for processing. Labor flexibility is increased by decreasing the value of t or increasing the value of q.

The third decision in the framework, deciding to which work center a person should be assigned, can be made using decision rules that resemble sequencing rules. We can determine priorities for assigning labor to unattended work centers on the basis of which work center has as its next job to process:

1. The job that was first at the current work center, first-come/first-served (FCFS).
2. The job that was first in the shop, first-in-system/first-served (FISFS).
3. The shortest job (SPT).
4. The most jobs in the queue.

We combine these decision rules with decision rules for making dispatching and labor availability decisions to control the work flow. Random assignment was used as a baseline for comparison.

Simulation experiments have been conducted to evaluate the performance of the different work flow control rules suggested for labor-limited systems. These studies generally measure improvement in the job flow time performance. An interesting general finding is, while changes in sequencing rules involve a trade-off between the mean and variance in job flow times, changes in labor assignment rules often reduce both measures simultaneously. Figure 8A.4 shows these results.

Experiments involving the labor flexibility factor d also show the importance of labor flexibility in a shop. A change between no labor flexibility ($d = 1$) and complete labor flexibility ($d = 0$) resulted in 12 percent and 39 percent reductions in the mean and variance of job flow times, respectively.

Research on labor assignment rules demonstrates the importance of cross-training and labor assignment flexibility. Moreover, it indicates that both labor and job dispatching can have a major impact in controlling work flow through a shop. With an operating shop-floor control system in place, further performance improvements might come from better design of labor assignments and from operational changes that permit greater flexibility in labor assignments.

[8] J. S. Fryer. "Labor Flexibility in Multiechelon Dual-Constraint Job Shops," *Management Science* 20, no. 7 (March 1974).

FIGURE 8A.4 **Time and Number of Jobs in System**

Size of Labor Force	Statistic / Queue Discipline		Mean Time and Mean Number in System*			Variance of Time in System			Variance of Number in System		
			FCFS	FISFS	SPT	FCFS	FISFS	SPT	FCFS	FISFS	SPT
4	Machine limited		17.7	17.7	9.4	488	295	612	201	205	24
3	Labor assignment rule	0	11.0	11.0	7.0	200	125	295	76	80	17
		1	10.2			173			54		
		2		10.5			102			63	
		3			6.6			343			15
		4	10.1	10.1	6.4	169	97	281	50	53	11
2	Labor assignment rule	0	8.7	8.7	6.2	158	147	186	65	67	23
		1	8.7			153			49		
		2		8.7			147			67	
		3			5.0			285			10
		4	8.7	8.8	5.1	154	89	293	46	48	9
1	Labor assignment rule	0	8.3	8.3	5.5	157	174	176	74	69	24
		1	8.3			149			48		
		2		8.3			174			69	
		3			4.2			296			9
		4	8.3	8.3	4.4	150	174	298	45	69	8

Note: Labor assignment rules:
0 = Random labor assignment to a work center.
1 = FCFS labor assignment to a work center.
2 = FISFS labor assignment to a work center.
3 = SPT labor assignment to a work center.
4 = Most jobs in queue labor assignment to a work center.
*Parameters so chosen that the mean time and the mean number in the system were equal.

Group Scheduling and Transfer Batches

The theory of constraints (TOC) scheduling approach described in Chapter 8 uses different batch sizes, depending on whether a work center is a bottleneck. This idea has led to scheduling systems that use variable operation lot sizes. One idea is the **repetitive lots concept.**[9]

This concept permits the *original order quantities* released to the shop for manufacturing to be split into smaller *transfer batches* that can flow immediately to the next operation prior to the operation's completion at its current work center. The transfer batches are predetermined integral fractions of the original order quantity. They provide a work center with the flexibility to start producing an order before it is completed at the previous work center. Such flexibility, frequently referred to as "lot-splitting" and

[9]F. R. Jacobs and D. J. Bragg. "Repetitive Lots: Flow-Time Reductions through Sequencing and Dynamic Batch Sizing," *Decision Sciences* 19, no. 2 (spring 1988), pp. 281–294.

FIGURE 8A.5
A Comparison of Fixed versus Variable Operation and Transfer Batch Sizes for a Single Job

Original order quantity is 1,000 units. Three operations are required to produce the part. Processing time per part is given. There is no setup time required.

Operation	*Time per part (minutes)*
1	1.00
2	0.50
3	0.75

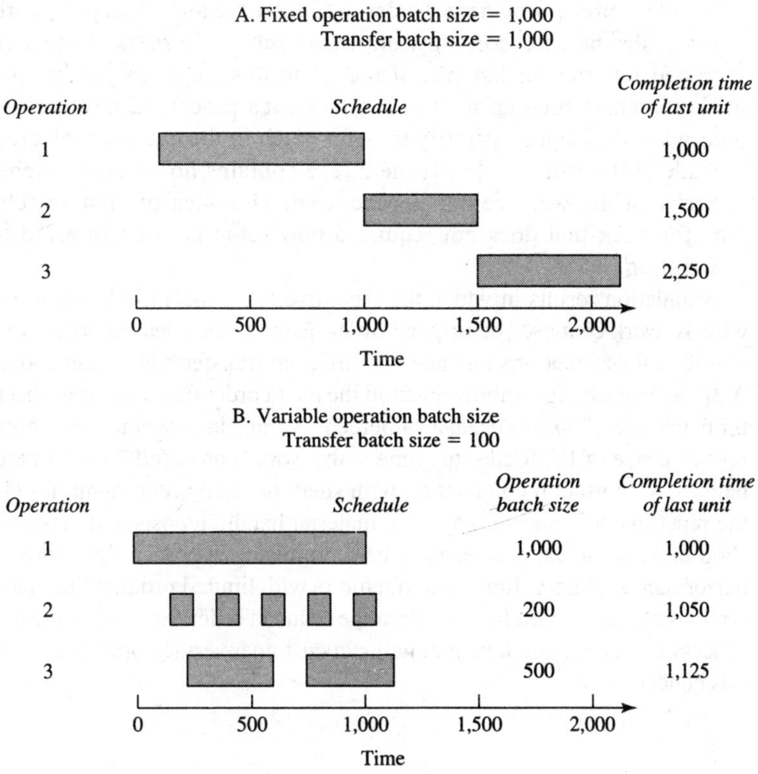

"overlap or line scheduling," reduces order flow times, improves machine utilization, cuts setup times, and smoothes work flow in the shop to yield better use of capacity. This flexibility also means the number of units produced during a given work center setup, *operation batch size,* can vary between a transfer batch and the original order quantity.

Figure 8A.5 illustrates the repetitive lots concept and its effect on order flow time. Using fixed operation batch sizes of 1,000 (equal to the original order quantity) in part A, the order is completed at hour 2,250. In part B, while the original order quantity is used at operation 1, a transfer batch size of 100 is used to permit processing the order simultaneously at operations 2 and 3 for completion by hour 1,125. In this case, the operation batch sizes for work centers 2 and 3 are 200 and 500, respectively. Although Figure 8A.5 doesn't consider the fact that other jobs may be competing for the resources each operation uses, the simulation took this into account when assessing the potential benefit of the repetitive lots concept.

The repetitive lots concept can be applied by using any standard priority sequencing rule (e.g., shortest processing time, critical ratio). When an order is completed under traditional priority sequencing rules, the highest-priority order in the queue is selected for processing next. Under the repetitive lots concept, a work center may contain transfer batches coming from many released orders. In this case, the queue is searched for transfer batches of the same item that has just been completed at the work center. If such an item is available, it's processed next, regardless of priority; otherwise, the highest-priority transfer batch in the queue is selected and a new setup is made at the work center. If the queue contains no transfer batches, the next batch to arrive at the work center is processed. This idea of first searching the queue of jobs for work that does not require a new setup is often referred to as **part family scheduling.**

Simulation results in which the repetitive lots concept is tested use a model of a shop with 10 work centers. The original order quantity for released orders was varied from 120 to 400 in these experiments, and two different transfer batch sizes (50 and 10) were used. A 38 percent average improvement in the mean order flow time was observed when a transfer batch size of 50 was used; a 44 percent average improvement was obtained with a transfer batch size of 10. Total setup time at the work centers fell 23 to 27 percent when transfer batches were used in conjunction with small original order quantities (120 to 200). While the repetitive lot concept may raise material handling costs and make tracking orders in a shop more complex, it appears to be a promising approach for improving manufacturing performance. High-volume manufacturers with limited product lines having numerous operations appear to benefit most from the reduced order flow times, lower levels of work-in-process inventory, and potential gains in customer service provided by using the repetitive lots concept.

Concluding Principles

Over the past 50 years, shop scheduling has been a popular area for research. Many of the procedures that have been developed are specialized applications, therefore their general applicability is limited. The following are concluding principles derived from the procedures described in this chapter:

- It is important to determine the objective(s) to be achieved in scheduling before selecting a scheduling approach since different approaches provide different results.
- The shortest processing time sequencing rule can produce effective performance and should be considered as a standard in designing shop-floor systems.
- Flexibility is introduced in scheduling through alternative routing, adjustments in labor assignments, the use of transfer batches, and overlap scheduling. Great improvements in manufacturing performance can be gained through scheduling flexibility.
- Setting and managing due dates is an important scheduling activity.
- Due date filtering procedures should be used to diminish shop-floor nervousness.

Discussion Questions

1. Why is rescheduling so important in production planning and control?
2. What kinds of performance measures would apply to "scheduling" at a college?
3. Provide some examples of static and dynamic scheduling problems.
4. What sequencing rule do you use to do your homework?

Problems

1. The Pohl Pool Company has seven jobs waiting to be processed through its liner department. Each job's estimated processing times and due dates are as follows:

Job	Processing Time (Days)	Due Date (Days from Now)
A	4	8
B	13	37
C	6	8
D	3	7
E	11	39
F	9	21
G	8	16

   a. Using the shortest processing time scheduling rule, in what order would the jobs be completed? Processing can start immediately.
   b. What is the average completion time (in days) of the sequence calculated in part a?
   c. What is the average job lateness (in days) of the sequence calculated in part a?

2. The Thompson Toilet Company has the following information on five jobs waiting to be processed in the bowl-molding work center. Processing can start immediately.

Job	Remaining Processing Time (Days)	Due Date (Days from Now)	Remaining Number of Operations
B	4	8	4
O	8	7	3
W	12	24	4
L	7	7	2
S	9	4	2

   a. If the slack per operation scheduling rule is used, in what order would the jobs be started?
   b. What is the average job lateness (in days) of the sequence calculated in part a?
   c. What is the average number of jobs in the system using the sequence in part a?

3. The Hyer-Than-Ever Kite Manufacturing Emporium must schedule the latest set of work orders through its frame-making department. Kites begin at frame making and then proceed through one, two, or three other departments, depending on the ordered kite's sophistication. It is 8 a.m. Monday morning. Processing can start immediately. There is one operation per department. Shop scheduler Joan Weber faces the following set of orders listed in order of

arrival. (Assume no other jobs will arrive at the frame-making department until the five already there have been started.)

Kite Order	Frame-Making Time (Days)	Total Processing Time (Days)	Total Number of Operations	Kite Due Date (Days from Now)
A	10	20	4	25
B	12	18	2	15
C	7	12	2	16
D	5	12	3	17
E	8	10	2	12

a. Using the order data, evaluate the first-come/first-served sequencing rule:
   1. In what sequence should the frame making department process the jobs?
   2. What will be the average completion time in frame making?
   3. What will be the average number of jobs in the frame-making department?

b. Using the order data, evaluate the earliest due date sequencing rule:
   1. In what sequence should the frame making department process the jobs?
   2. Which specific jobs, if any, will be late in leaving frame making?
   3. What will the average job lateness be in the frame-making department?

c. Using the order data, evaluate the shortest processing time sequencing rule:
   1. In what sequence should the frame-making department process jobs?
   2. On what days will order E be in process in frame making?
   3. What will the average job lateness be in the frame-making department?

d. While Joan debated which rule to use, she received the following memo from Diane Britenbach, the president:

   Effective this morning, all departmental job sequencing should be performed using the slack time per operation rule. This should improve scheduling performance throughout the plant.

   1. In what sequence should the frame-making department process the jobs if it uses the slack time per operation rule and considers due dates to be final due dates?
   2. On what day will frame making complete order D?
   3. What is the average completion time for this sequence in the frame-making department?

4. Prepare a two-machine schedule using the two-machine procedure for jobs A through D. The processing time per job (in days) is shown here:

	Machine	
Job	I	II
A	4	3
B	1	7
C	8	2
D	8	5

a. In what sequence should jobs be processed?

b. Construct a Gantt chart of the schedule for both machines.

c. Construct a Gantt chart, assuming there's no buffer storage between machines (e.g., machine I can't start a new job until machine II has started the old job).

5. Dave Grubbs of Grubbs Auto Body has five cars waiting for Economy Detailing. An Economy Detailing consists of a wash and then a hand wax. Cars cannot be waxed until they are washed.

	Wash (Hours)	Wax (Hours)
(J)aguar	3	5
(C)adillac	5	3
(F)ord	1	2
(H)onda	2	1
(L)exus	4	4

a. What schedule produces the shortest time span in which these orders can be completed?

b. How many hours does it take to complete the five orders?

c. For the schedule in question a, how many hours is the waxing task idle?

d. When will Dave finish the Cadillac?

e. What is the average order completion time?

6. Flash Fasttrack (associate dean of janitorial services at Wombat University) must schedule the regular maintenance by his janitorial engineers. There are two crews: sweeping crew and waxing crew. Union rules prohibit sweepers from waxing and waxers from sweeping. A building's floors must first be swept before they can be waxed. Flash must schedule the order in which maintenance crews will visit each of Wombat U's six buildings. He wished to minimize the sequence's total completion time. Times required to sweep and wax each building are as follows:

Building	Sweeping Time (Hours)	Waxing Time (Hours)
Astronomy	18	10
Biology	8	9
Chemistry	26	13
Drama	15	16
English	17	20
Foreign language	12	17

a. Schedule the crews through the buildings.

b. When will the waxing crew start and stop work in the chemistry building?

c. During the schedule, for how much time are sweepers and waxers available for other activities?

7. Currently, Bart Simpson, the sales manager at Baxter Boards Inc. (a manufacturer of custom-made skateboards), promises eight-week delivery time for all customer orders. The production manager is under pressure from top management to improve the firm's performance against quoted delivery dates. In his review of alternative procedures for making customer delivery date

promises, he provides the following data on representative orders:

Order	Total Processing Time (in Weeks)
1	3
2	5
3	8

a. Determine delivery time to be quoted on these orders, if the TWK (total work content) procedure is used. (Assume average time from order receipt to customer delivery is eight weeks.)

b. Determine delivery time to be quoted on these orders if the SLK (slack) procedure is used. (Assume average time from order receipt to customer delivery is eight weeks.)

c. Suppose the production manager knows the overall flow time for order #3 has averaged 10 weeks in the past, and the flow time standard deviation for this order is 1 week. How would this information influence your recommendation of a delivery date setting procedure in this situation?

8. A single test operator staffs the SCM Corporation's three testing machines in its quality control lab. Only one machine is run at a time. SCM uses two scheduling rules: one for sequencing jobs at individual machines and another for assigning labor to machines. As of 8 a.m. today (on day 10), jobs waiting to be processed at each of the three machines are as follows:

	Job	Due Date*	Processing Time†	Arrival Date*
Test Machine A	1	12	1	9
	5	18	6	8
Test Machine B	2	14	3	6
	3	16	4	7
	6	14	6	6
Test Machine C	4	13	4	5

* = Day number.
† = In days.

a. Assuming SCM uses the shortest processing time rule to sequence orders at each testing machine, determine to which machine the test operator should be assigned and which job will be processed when each of the following labor assignment decision rules are used (assume the operator has just completed his or her last job):
   1. The shortest job.
   2. The job that has been in the laboratory the longest.
   3. The most jobs in the queue.

b. Suppose SCM uses the slack time rule to sequence jobs at each testing machine. To which machine should the test operator be assigned and which job will be processed when each of the following labor assignment decision rules are used? (Again it's 8 a.m. and the test operator is available for assignment.)
   1. The shortest job.
   2. The job that has been in the laboratory the longest.
   3. The most jobs in the queue.

c. Would you recommend any other labor assignment decision rule under the conditions in part b?

9. The Ace Tool Company is considering implementing the repetitive lot concept in scheduling the firm's fabrication shop. The production manager selected an example order to use in evaluating benefits and potential costs of this scheduling approach. A transfer batch size of 100 units was suggested for this item. The example order is for a quantity of 1,000 units and has the following routing data:

Operation	Work Center	Setup Time	Run Time/Unit
1	1	40 minutes	2.4 minutes/unit
2	2	20 minutes	1.44 minutes/unit

   a. Assuming a single-shift, eight-hour day, five-day week for work centers 1 and 2, prepare a Gantt chart showing the earliest start- and finish-time schedule for this order under a conventional scheduling approach where all items in the order are processed at one time. Do the same when the repetitive lot concept is used. What are the earliest start and finish times for each transfer batch at work center 2, assuming none of the transfer batches are processed together to save setup time?
   b. What's the difference in the order-completion times under the two scheduling approaches in part a above?
   c. What are the benefits and potential costs of this scheduling approach?

10. To remain competitive, Ed's Sheet Metal must reduce manufacturing lead time for a product that typically sells in lots of 800 units. The product goes through two operations in different departments. The company wants to evaluate the value of using a transfer batch between operations. The idea is to split the order at the first operation and transfer an amount to the second operation to get it started while the rest of the order is finished at the first operation. The setup of operation 2 can start as soon as parts arrive, but not sooner. Other data are:

Order size	= 800 units
Operation 1 processing time	= 6 minutes/unit
Operation 2 processing time	= 8 minutes/unit
Transfer time from operation 1 to 2	= 20 minutes
Setup time for operation 1	= 1.0 hour
Setup time for operation 2	= 1.5 hours

   a. What is the *minimum* transfer batch that assures that operation 2 has no idle time?
   b. How much would manufacturing lead time be reduced by using the transfer batch instead of the full order of 800 units?

11. Calculate completion times for part B of Figure 8A.5. Assume there are no other jobs in the shop and each operation will know when a transfer batch will reach it. There doesn't need to be a complete operation batch available to start work at any of the three operations but, once started, the operation batch must be completely processed without waiting for additional transfer batches (i.e., no idle time during an operation batch's run).

12. Consider the following data for three jobs processed in the boring machine center for Conway Manufacturing.

Job	Setup Time (Minutes)	Run Time/ Unit (Minutes)	Batch Size
A	15	0.05	200
B	10	0.15	100
C	20	0.10	200

Queue data for the boring machine center:

Job	Arrival Time	Job	Arrival Time	Job	Arrival Time
A	8:24	B	8:40	B	9:12
B	8:28	C	8:42	C	9:14
C	8:31	C	8:44	A	9:18
A	8:34	A	8:57	B	9:21
B	8:39	A	9:03	B	9:31

a. If the boring machine center used a first-come/first-served rule to schedule jobs, how long would it take to process the queue? (Assume no other jobs arrive, all jobs in queue are for one batch each, and a job B has just been completed.)

b. How long would it take to process all jobs in the queue using a repetitive lot logic?

13. Dave Grubbs of Grubbs Auto Body also offers a Deluxe Detailing service. The Deluxe Detailing consists of washing, buffing, and then hand waxing the customer's automobile (the steps must be done in this order). When Dave offered Deluxe Detailing to the customers in problem 5, they all decided to get the Deluxe service.

	Wash (Hours)	Buff (Hours)	Wax (Hours)
(J)aguar	3	4	5
(C)adillac	5	3	3
(F)ord	1	8	2
(H)onda	2	6	1
(L)exus	4	5	4

a. Prepare a schedule for Dave, using the *M*-machine heuristic.

b. In what sequence should Dave process the jobs to minimize the make-span? Follow the same processing sequence at each step of the process.

c. Construct a Gantt chart of the best sequence schedule for all three steps of the processes.

14. The Philip Company has the following processing time data for machines 1, 2, 3, and 4. Routing for each job begins at machine 1 and ends at machine 4:

	Processing Time (in Hours)			
Job	Machine 1	Machine 2	Machine 3	Machine 4
A	6	2	4	2
B	1	8	7	5
C	5	7	2	3
D	4	4	1	6

a. Prepare a schedule for a four-machine manufacturing cell using the *M*-machine heuristic.

b. In what sequence should Philip process the jobs to minimize make-span? Follow the same processing sequence at each machine in the cell.

c. Construct a Gantt chart of the best sequence schedule for all four machines.

Chapter 9

Just-in-Time

This chapter addresses just-in-time (JIT) approaches for manufacturing planning and control. JIT is a key building block for modern approaches to manufacturing planning and control (MPC), and is both a philosophy and a set of techniques. Moreover, the techniques go beyond traditional manufacturing planning and control systems. JIT changes manufacturing practices, which in turn affect MPC execution. JIT greatly reduces the complexity of detailed material planning, the need for shop-floor tracking, work-in-process inventories, and the transactions associated with shop-floor and purchasing systems. These gains come at the cost of more tightly coordinated manufacturing processes—both inside a company and with supplier firms that produce under JIT. The chapter concentrates on the MPC aspects of JIT but necessarily touches on broader aspects as well. It is organized around the following seven topics:

- *JIT in manufacturing planning and control:* What are JIT's key features, and how do they impact MPC systems?
- *A JIT example:* How can the basic principles of JIT be illustrated in one simplified example?
- *JIT applications:* What are some concrete examples of JIT practice?
- *Nonrepetitive JIT:* How can JIT concepts be applied to the nonrepetitive manufacturing environment?
- *Joint-Firm JIT:* How is supplier-customer coordination supported with JIT?
- *JIT software:* What features of computer packages support JIT?
- *Managerial implications:* What changes are required to fully pursue the benefits of JIT?

JIT in Manufacturing Planning and Control

Figure 9.1 shows how just-in-time programs relate to our manufacturing planning and control framework. The shaded area indicates the portions of MPC systems that are most affected by implementation of JIT. The primary application area is in back-end execution. However, JIT extends beyond manufacturing planning and control. JIT programs raise

FIGURE 9.1
Manufacturing Planning and Control System and JIT

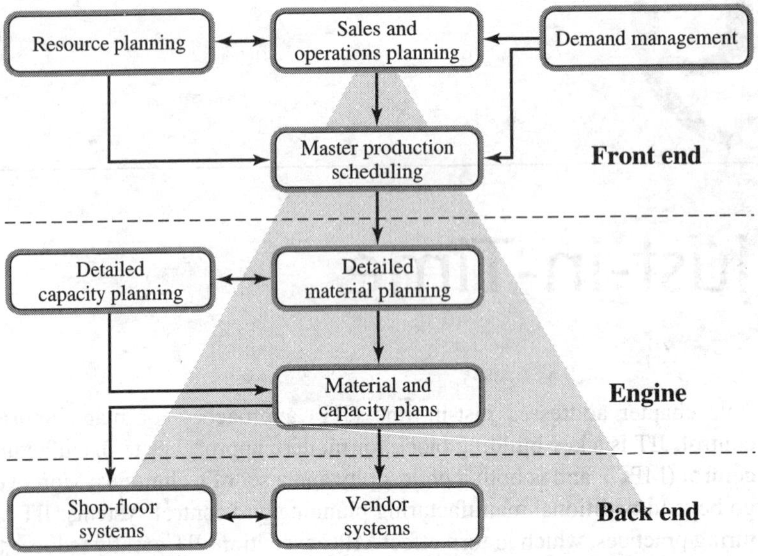

fundamental questions about manufacturing strategy and effectiveness. For this reason, we begin with a discussion of the major elements in a JIT program. Thereafter, we turn to the impact on the MPC system and the overhead cost savings from reduced MPC system transaction processing. The section closes by describing four fundamental JIT building blocks.

Major Elements of Just-in-Time

Many definitions have been put forward for just-in-time, and they have evolved over time. One popular definition of JIT is an approach to minimize waste in manufacturing. This focus is too broad: it helps to subdivide waste into time, energy, material, and errors. A useful common denominator running through this and other JIT definitions is a broad philosophy of pursuing zero inventories, zero transactions, and zero "disturbances" (*zero disturbances* means routine execution of schedules day in—day out).

The JIT literature is largely one of cases. The best-known JIT examples are from firms with high-volume repetitive manufacturing methods, such as the classic case of Toyota. The most important features of these applications have been the elimination of discrete manufacturing batches in favor of production rate goals, the reduction of work-in-process inventories, production schedules that level the capacity loads and keep them level, mixed model master production schedules where all products are made more or less all the time, visual control systems where workers build the products and execute the schedule without paperwork or complex overhead support, and direct ties to vendors who deliver high-quality goods frequently. All of these have MPC implications.

Just-in-time objectives require physical system changes—and programs to make the changes. A prime example is setup time reduction and a drive toward constantly smaller lot sizes. This is necessary to make all of the products constantly. It's also consistent with reducing inventory levels. Setup times are typically reduced by applying common industrial engineering techniques to analyzing the setup process itself, often by workers themselves using a video camera. The results of setup time reduction have been impressive indeed. Changeovers of several hours have been reduced to less than 10 minutes. The goal now being achieved by many firms is expressed by Shigeo Shingo: SMED (single-minute exchange of dies, meaning all changeovers take place in less than 10 minutes).

Another physical program is improved quality through process improvements. Most JIT firms have programs of quality awareness and statistical process control. In a repetitive manufacturing system, any quality problem will result in a stoppage of the entire flow line, unless undesirable buffer inventories are held.

Quality improvement has taken many forms and is largely beyond our present scope. Two critical aspects for JIT are *TPM* and *poka-yoke.* TPM can stand for both total preventive maintenance and total productive maintenance. The goal is to apply the diligence of product quality improvement to equipment and process quality. Poka-yoke means foolproof operations. This is achieved by building operations in processes so that quality is evaluated as it's created. This also ensures low cost through finding defects at the time they're created. These quality programs have an impact on MPC system requirements and design.

Most JIT programs include continual improvement as a maxim for day-to-day operations. Every day, each worker should get better in some dimension, such as fewer defects, more output, or fewer stoppages. Continual improvement is achieved by making thousands of small improvements in methods and products in a never-ceasing quest for excellence. JIT best practice includes a strong degree of worker involvement and worker participation.

JIT firms often group their equipment for cellular manufacturing: a group of machines manufactures a particular set of parts. The equipment layout minimizes travel distances and inventories between machines. Cells are typically U-shaped to increase worker interactions and reduce material handling. Cross-trained workers can run several machines. Cellular manufacturing makes "capacity" more flexible, so surges or mix changes are more readily handled. An extension of the cellular concept is the plant within a plant, where a portion of a factory focuses solely on one group of products.

In summary, a JIT orientation includes several action programs:

1. Reduction of setup times and lot sizes
2. A "no defects" goal in manufacturing
3. A focus on continual improvement
4. Worker involvement
5. Cellular manufacturing

Figure 9.2 lists the typical benefits gained in a JIT program.

JIT's Impact on Manufacturing Planning and Control

JIT influences all three areas of our MPC framework (front end, engine, and back end). JIT's primary contribution is in the back end, providing greatly streamlined execution on the shop floor and in purchasing. JIT can eliminate standard shop-floor reporting systems,

FIGURE 9.2
JIT Benefits

Manufacturing throughput time reductions
Materials moved shorter distances
Less material movements in/out of storage
Reduced transactions
Simplified MPC systems
Reduced changeover times
Greater responsiveness to market demands
Inventory reductions
Labor cost reductions
More satisfied/cohesive workers
Better team working
Space reductions
Quality cost reductions
Quality improvements

reduce costs of detailed shop scheduling, significantly reduce work in process and lead times, and support better vendor scheduling.

However, JIT is not without influence on the front end and engine. In the detailed MRP planning of the engine, JIT reduces the number of part numbers planned and the number of levels in the bill of materials. Many part numbers formerly planned by MRP analysts can now be treated as "phantoms" (i.e., as part numbers still in the bill of materials but not transacted into and out of inventories). This means that instead of MPC being based on detailed operation steps to make individual parts, the planning is at the level of assemblies, using cross-trained workers and cellular manufacturing to eliminate the detailed planning. The result is often an order of magnitude reduction in the complexity of detailed material planning, with a concomitant reduction in planning personnel. Moreover, with planning/execution at the assembly level instead of with detailed operations and parts, the overall flow time from parts to finished goods is significantly reduced.

In the front end, JIT also gives rise to important changes. JIT production plans and master production schedules require relatively level capacity loading for smooth shop operations. In many cases, this is a rate-based MPS—that is, producing so many units per hour or day. This drive toward more stable, level, daily-mix schedules dictates many of the required JIT activities, such as setup time reduction. To the extent that lead times are sufficiently reduced, many firms that had to provide inventories in anticipation of customer orders (made-to-stock firms) now find themselves more like make-to-order or assemble-to-order companies, better able to respond to customer orders. This, in turn, can affect demand management.

In JIT execution, orders move through the factory so quickly that it's not necessary to track their progress with a complex production activity control system. A similar argument holds for purchased items. If they're converted into finished goods within hours or days of receipt, it's unnecessary to put them into stockrooms, pick them, and go through all the details normally associated with receipts from vendors. Instead, the JIT firm can simply pay the vendor for the purchased components in whatever products are completed each time period; there will be so little work-in-process inventory that it's not worth either party keeping track of it.

The concept of updating component inventory balances when finished items are received into stock is called **backflushing.** Instead of detailed work-in-process accounting systems based on shop-order transactions, some JIT firms just reduce component part inventory balances by exploding the bills of material for whatever has been delivered into finished goods. However, backflushing implies a very high level of data integrity.

JIT execution is focused on simplicity. The intent is to design manufacturing cells, products, and systems so goods flow through routinely. With problems of quality and disturbances largely eliminated, routine execution becomes just that: routine. Simple systems can be employed by shop people without detailed records or the need for extensive overhead staff support.

The Hidden Factory

A manufacturing firm comprises two "factories." One makes products and the other (the hidden factory) processes transactions on papers and computer systems. Over time, the former factory has been decreasing in cost, relative to the latter. A major driver for these costs is transactions. **Logistical transactions** include ordering, execution, and confirmation of materials moving from one location to another. Included are the costs of personnel in receiving, shipping, expediting, data entry, data processing, accounting, and error follow-up. Under JIT, the goal is to eliminate the vast majority of this work and the associated costs. Work orders that accompany each batch of material as it moves through the factory are eliminated. If the flow can be simplified, increased in volume, quick, and guaranteed, there is no need for paperwork.

Balancing transactions are those needed to verify that an activity actually occurred. These checks are largely associated with the planning that generates logistical transactions. Included are production control, purchasing, master scheduling, forecasting, and customer order processing/maintenance. In most companies, balancing transaction costs are 10 to 20 percent of the total manufacturing overhead costs. JIT again offers a significant opportunity to sharply reduce these costs. MRP planning can be cut by perhaps 75 to 90 percent in complexity. Improvements generated by vendor scheduling can also be extended. Vendor firms no longer need to process *their* sets of transactions.

Quality transactions extend far beyond what one normally thinks of as quality control. Included are identification and communication of specifications, certification that other transactions have taken place, and recording of backup data. Many of the costs of quality identified by Juran and others are largely associated with transactions. JIT, with closer coupling of production and consumption, has faster quality monitoring and response capability.

Still another category is **change transactions.** Included are engineering changes and all those that update the MPC system database, such as routings, bills of materials, and specifications. Engineering change transactions are some of the most expensive in the company. A typical engineering change might require a meeting of people from production control, line management, design engineering, manufacturing engineering, and purchasing. The change has to be approved, scheduled, and monitored for execution.

One way that firms attack the hidden factory is by finding ways to significantly reduce the number of transactions. Stability is another attack, and again JIT is important since it is based on stabilized operations. Still another attack on hidden factory transaction costs is

FIGURE 9.3
Building Blocks for Just-in-Time

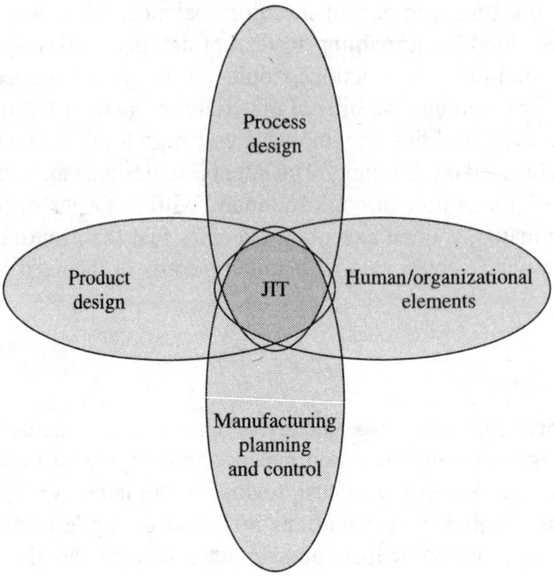

through automation of transactions (as with bar coding), eliminating redundancies in data entry, and better data entry methods. But stability and transaction elimination should be pursued before turning to automation of transactions. JIT is clearly a key.

JIT Building Blocks in MPC

As Figure 9.3 shows, JIT links four fundamental building blocks: product design, process design, human/organizational elements, and manufacturing planning and control. JIT provides the connecting link for these four areas.

Critical activities in product design include quality, designing for manufacture in cells, and reducing the number of levels in the bill of materials to as few as possible. Since each level in a bill of material represents a stock point, reducing the number can significantly reduce inventory requirements and speed processing.

Reducing the number of bill of material levels and process design are closely related. For fewer levels to be practical, the number of product conversion steps must be reduced through process design changes, often through cellular manufacturing. Equipment in cellular manufacturing is positioned (often in a U shape) to achieve rapid flow of production with minimal inventories. The object is to concentrate on material velocity. Jobs must flow through in short cycle times, so detailed tracking is unnecessary.

Bandwidth is an important notion in designing manufacturing processes. A wide bandwidth system has enough surge capacity to take on some variation in demand for the products as well as a fairly mixed set of products. The impact on MPC systems is the focus on inventory and throughput time reductions, where inventory is not built to level out capacity requirements. JIT systems are designed to be responsive to as large a set of demands as possible. Superior manufacturing processes support greater bandwidth. The objective is for MPC systems to schedule any product, right behind any other, with minimal disruption.

Human/organizational elements are another building block for JIT. One aspect of this is continual improvement, which implies cross training, process improvements, and whatever else is needed to enhance worker performance. The objective is continual learning and improvement. Human/organizational elements recognize that workers' range of capabilities and level of knowledge are often more important assets to the firm than equipment and facilities. Education is a continuing investment in the human asset base. As the asset base's capabilities grow, need for overhead support is reduced and overhead personnel can be redeployed to address other issues.

Linking human/organizational elements into the other activities has a significant effect on the operation of the production process and MPC system. Bandwidth and the avoidance of building inventories to utilize direct labor mean surge capacity must be available. Implementing surge capacity with direct labor personnel means these people will not be fully utilized in direct production activities. In fact, the **whole person** concept is based on the premise of hiring *people,* not just their muscles. As a consequence, direct workers take on many tasks not usually associated with "direct labor." This work can be done in nonpeak production times. This includes equipment maintenance, education, process improvement, data entry, and scheduling. From a JIT standpoint, the human/organizational elements building block puts a greater emphasis on scheduling by workers and less on scheduling by a centralized staff function. The entire process is fostered by the inherent JIT push toward simplification. With no defects, zero inventories, no disturbances, and fast throughput, detailed scheduling is easier; moreover, any problems tend to be local in nature and amenable to solution on a decentralized basis. The whole person concept implies a shift from indirect labor to direct, where jobs are more widely defined.

The final building block in Figure 9.3 is the manufacturing planning and control system and its link to JIT. Applying JIT requires most of the critical MPC functions described in this book. It will always be necessary to do master production scheduling, production planning, capacity planning, and material requirements planning. If the bill of materials is reduced to two or three levels, detailed material planning and associated transaction costs can be cut significantly. If detailed tracking is done by direct laborers under the whole person concept, additional savings can be achieved.

We see then that JIT has the potential for changing the character of manufacturing in a company, since it reduces MPC transactions. JIT can significantly reduce the size of the "hidden factory" that produces papers and computer transactions instead of products. Figure 9.4 provides a more detailed listing of JIT's building blocks and objectives. Many of these will be described in the next section, which presents a detailed JIT example.

A JIT Example

In this section we develop a detailed but simple example to show how MPC approaches based on MRP would be modified to implement JIT and describe the necessary building blocks (Figure 9.4) to achieve this. The product is a 1-liter saucepan produced in four models by the Muth Pots and Pans Company. (See Figure 9.5.) The product's brochure sums up its importance: "If you ain't got a Muth, you ain't got a pot." We'll look at elements

FIGURE 9.4
JIT Objectives and Building Blocks

Ultimate objectives:
- Zero inventory
- Zero lead time
- Zero failures
- Flow process
- Flexible manufacture
- Eliminate waste

Building blocks:
- Product design:
  Few bill of materials levels
  Manufacturability in production cells
  Achievable quality
  Appropriate quality
  Standard parts
  Modular design
- Process design:
  Setup/lot size reduction
  Quality improvement
  Manufacturing cells
  Limited work in process
  Production bandwidth
  No stockrooms
  Service enhancements
- Human/organizational elements:
  Cross training/job rotation
  Flexible labor
  Continual improvement
  Whole person
  Limited direct/indirect distinction
  Cost accounting/performance measurement
  Information system changes
  Leadership/project management
- Manufacturing planning and control:
  Pull systems
  Rapid flow times
  Small container sizes
  Paperless systems
  Visual systems
  Level loading
  MRP interface
  Close purchasing/vendor relationships
  JIT software
  Reduced production reporting/inventory transaction processing
  Hidden factory cost reductions

FIGURE 9.5
The 151 One-Liter Saucepan Line

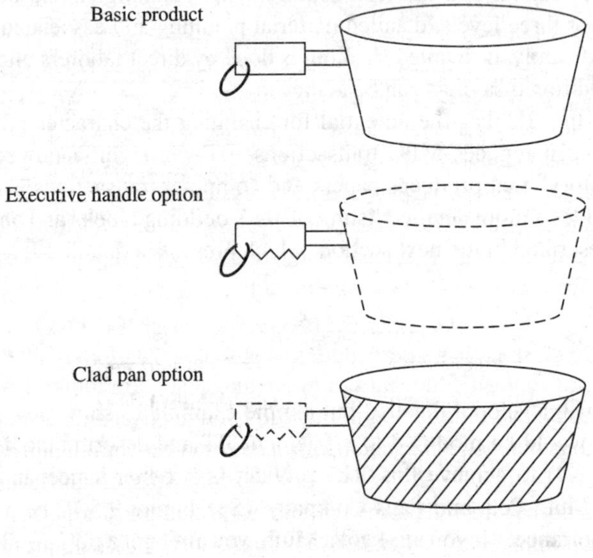

of a JIT program for the saucepan that range from leveling production to redesigning the product. Some of these elements have direct MPC relevance; others will affect MPC only indirectly.

Leveling the Production

We start the saucepan's JIT program by considering how to "level and stabilize" production. This means planning a level output of 1-liter saucepans with the full mix of models each day (or week or some other short interval). Full-mix production in a short interval provides less inventory buildup in each model. Moreover, the schedule can respond to actual customer order conditions more quickly. Level output implies "freezing" to stabilize production and related activities on the floor. Before seeing how this might be done, let's compare Muth's manufacturing situation with traditional MRP-based approaches.

Currently, Muth uses production planning to set the overall production rate, necessarily building inventories in anticipation of the Christmas season demand peak. The annual forecast for each of the four models is given in Figure 9.6. A master production schedule, for each of the four models, is exploded to produce a material requirements planning record for each of the 14 component part numbers shown on the part listing in Figure 9.7. Safety stock is carried for all components, and production is in the lot sizes indicated in Figure 9.7. Figure 9.8 gives lead times and routing data; lead times are computed on the basis of two days per operation, rounded up to the next whole week using five-day weeks. A typical MRP record is shown as Figure 9.9.

To plan for level production, the first step is converting the forecasts to the daily requirements for each model. Using a 250-day year, this conversion is shown in Figure 9.10. Note the difference between the current lot sizes and the daily requirements. Daily production will put pressure on process design to reduce setup times. Two other possible mixed-model master production schedules are shown in Figure 9.10, in addition to the one based on daily production batch sizes. The first shows quantities to be produced if hourly batches are to be made. The second shows an MPS with the minimum batch size of one for model 151B.

Pull System Introduction

A "pull" system exists when a work center is authorized to produce only when it has been signaled that there's a need for more parts in a downstream (user) department. This implies no work center is allowed to produce parts just to keep workers or equipment busy. It also means no work center is allowed to "push" material to a downstream work center. All movements and production are authorized by a signal from a downstream work center when it has a need

FIGURE 9.6
Annual Forecast Data

Completed Pan Model Number	Description of Model		Annual Forecast
	Handle	Metal	
151A	Basic	Sheet	200,000
151B	Basic	Clad	2,500
151C	Executive	Sheet	25,000
151D	Executive	Clad	100,000

FIGURE 9.7 Product Structure and Parts List

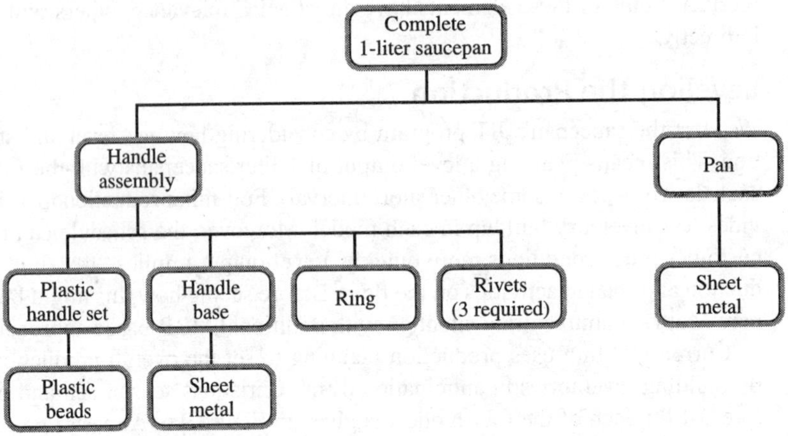

	Lot Size	Safety Stock	Finished Item Number			
			151A	**151B**	**151C**	**151D**
Models (end items)						
Complete pan 151A	8,000	5,000	X			
Complete pan 151B	900	1,000		X		
Complete pan 151C	3,000	3,000			X	
Complete pan 151D	6,000	5,000				X
Component part						
Regular pan 1936	14,000	10,000	X		X	
Clad pan 1937	8,000	6,000		X		X
Basic handle assembly 137	14,000	8,000	X	X		
Exec. handle assembly 138	8,000	5,000			X	X
Basic handle set 244	9,000	8,000	X	X		
Exec. handle set 245	9,000	8,000			X	X
Basic handle base 7731	14,000	8,000	X	X		
Exec. handle base 7735	12,000	5,000			X	X
Ring 353	24,000	15,000	X	X	X	X
Rivets 4164	100,000	50,000	X	X	X	X
Sheet metal 621	1 coil	1 coil	X		X	
Clad sheet 624	1 coil	1 coil		X		X
Handle sheet 685	1 coil	1 coil	X	X	X	X
Plastic beads 211	5 tons	1 ton	X	X	X	X

for component parts. Frequently, it's believed that the pull system creates the benefits in JIT. In fact, primary payoffs come from the discipline required to make the system work. Included are lot size reductions, limited work in process, fast throughput, and guaranteed quality.

Signals for communicating downstream work center demand vary widely. They include rolling a colored golf ball from a downstream work center to its supplying work center

FIGURE 9.8 Routing and Lead Time Data

Department	Item	Routing	Lead Time
Final assembly	Complete pan	1. Spot weld	2 days
		2. Inspect	2 days
		3. Package	2 days
			Total = 6 days = 2 weeks
Punch press	Pan	1. Blank and form	2 days
		2. Roll lip	2 days
		3. Test for flat	2 days
		4. Straighten	2 days
		5. Inspect	2 days
			Total = 10 days = 2 weeks
Handle base	Handle base	1. Blank and form	2 days
		2. Inspect	2 days
			Total = 4 days = 1 week
Handle assembly	Handle assembly	1. Rivet	2 days
		2. Inspect	2 days
			Total = 4 days = 1 week
Injection molding	Plastic handle set	1. Mold	2 days
		2. Deburr	2 days
		3. Inspect	2 days
			Total = 6 days = 2 weeks
	Purchased Items		
Purchasing	Sheet metal Clad sheet metal Plastic beads Ring Rivets		Purchased lead time one week for all items

FIGURE 9.9 MRP Record for Basic Handle Assembly (Part 137)

Week		1	2	3	4	5	6	7	8	9	10
Gross requirements			8		8	3	8		8		8
Scheduled receipts											
Projected available balance	10	10	16	16	8	19	11	11	17	17	9
Planned order releases		14			14			14			

Q = 14; LT = 1; SS = 8.
All quantities are in thousands.

when the downstream center wants parts; yelling "Hey, we need some more"; sending an empty container back to be filled; and using cards (kanbans) to indicate more components are needed. A widely used technique is to paint a space on the floor that holds a specific number of parts. When the space is empty, the producing department is authorized to

FIGURE 9.10
Master Production Schedule Data*

	Model			
	151A	**151B**	**151C**	**151D**
Option configurations:				
Handle	Basic	Basic	Executive	Executive
Pan	Sheet	Clad	Sheet	Clad
Annual forecast (units)	200,000	2,500	25,000	100,000
Possible mixed model master production schedules:				
Daily batch MPS	800	10	100	400
Hourly batch MPS	100	1.25	12.5	50
Minimum batch MPS	80	1	10	40

*Data are based on a 250-day year and an eight-hour work day.

produce material to fill it. The consuming or using department takes material out of the space as it needs it; typically, this occurs only when the space authorizing that department's output is empty. For the Muth example, we'll use an empty container as the signal for more production; that is, whenever a using department empties a container, it sends the container back to the producing department. An empty container represents authorization to fill it up.

Given that Muth has committed to a level schedule where all models are made every day, the firm is almost ready to move into a pull mode of operation. Two additional issues need to be faced. First, there's the question of stability. For most pull systems, it's necessary to keep the schedule firm (frozen) for some reasonable time. This provides stability to the upstream work centers, as well as overall balance to the workflow. For Muth, assume the schedule is frozen for one month, with the daily batch quantities given in Figure 9.10 (1,310 pots per day).

The second issue is determining the container sizes to transport materials between work centers—a fairly complicated issue. It involves material handling considerations, container size commonality, congestion in the shop, proximity of work centers, and, of course, setup costs. For example, consider the container used between handle assembly and final assembly of the pots using the basic handle, part 137 (810 being used per day). The center is currently producing in lots of 14,000. We'll choose a container size that holds 100 pieces representing just under an eighth of a day's requirements. Note this choice puts a great deal of pressure on the handle assembly work center to reduce setup times.

Figure 9.11 shows the flow of work in Muth's new system for handle assembly to the final assembly line. Only two containers are used for part 137; while one is being used at the final assembly line, the other is being filled at handle assembly. This approach is very simple and is facilitated by the two departments being in close proximity. Figure 9.12 shows the factory layout. A worker from the final assembly line or a material handler can return empty containers. Any empty container is a signal to make a new batch of handles (i.e., fill it up). It's interesting to note the difference in average inventory that will be held in this system, compared with the former MRP methods and the lot size of 14,000. The system with a small container approaches "zero inventory," with an average inventory of about 100 units. Compare this to the inventories shown in the MRP record of Figure 9.9 (average projected available inventory balance = 13,400).

FIGURE 9.11
Pull System for Muth Pots and Pans

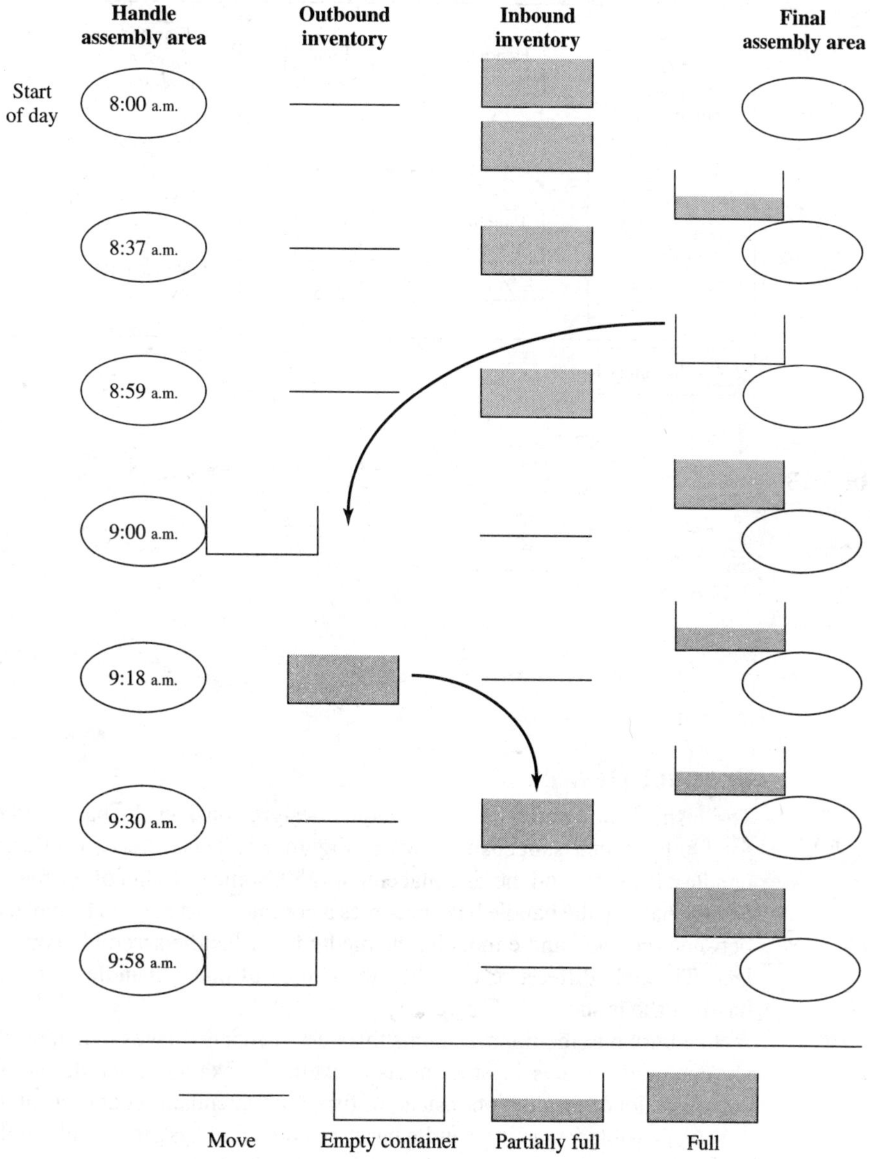

This pull system example has no buffer at either work center. It would be possible to add another container, which would allow greater flexibility in handle assembly, at the cost of extra inventory in the system. As it is, the final assembly area would use up a container in just under one hour. This means the system has to be responsive enough for the empty container to be returned to handle assembly and a batch made in this time frame. An extra container allows more time for responding to a make signal (an empty container) and also allows more flexibility in the supplying department. The extra inventory helps resolve problems—for example, when several production requests for different parts (containers) arrive at the same time.

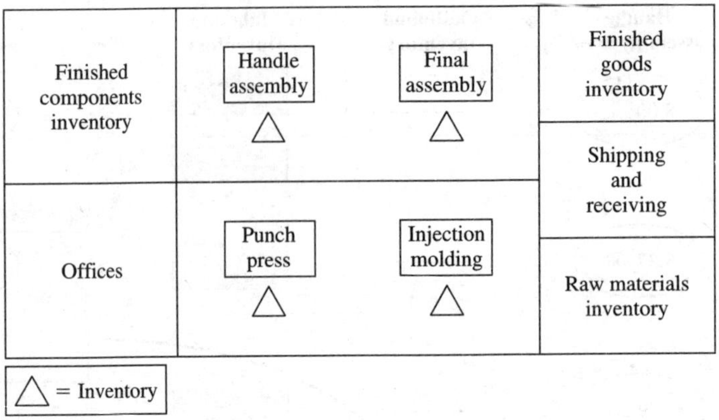

FIGURE 9.12
Factory Layout

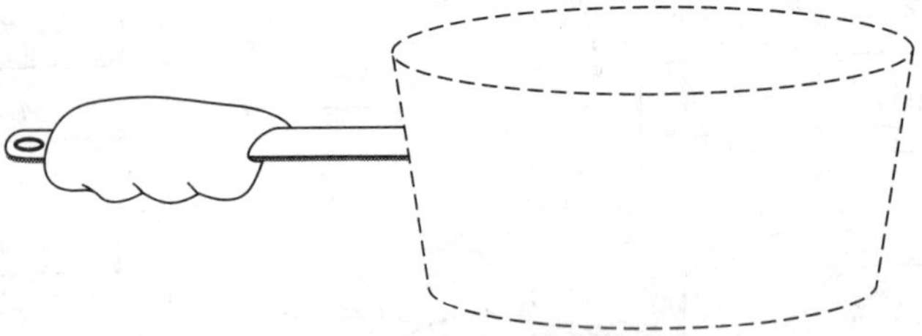

FIGURE 9.13
Redesigned Handle Base

Product Design

To illustrate the implications for product design, consider the basic and executive handles for Muth's 1-liter saucepan shown in Figure 9.5. There are two differences between the handles: the grips and the ring placement. With some redesign of the plastic parts on the executive handle, the handle base becomes a common part and the ring placement is common between the two handle models; the methods for handle assembly could also be standardized. The only difference would be the choice of plastic handle parts. Such a redesigned handle base is shown in Figure 9.13.

In addition to the improvements this design change makes in handle subassembly, there are potential impacts in other areas as well. For example, handle bases would have one combined lot of production instead of two, with attendant reductions in inventory. It might now be possible to run the handle base area on a pull system as well, with containers passing between the handle base area and the handle subassembly area. Another advantage is a simplification in the bill of materials, a reduction in the number of parts that must be planned and controlled with MRP, and a concomitant reduction in the number of transactions that have to be processed.

Process Design

The product redesign, in turn, opens opportunities for process improvement. For example, it may now be possible to use the same equipment to attach both kinds of plastic handles to the handle base. Perhaps a cell can be formed, where handle bases are made and assembled as a unit. Figure 9.14 shows one way this might be accomplished, including an integration

FIGURE 9.14
Cellular Manufacturing of Handle Assembly and Final Assembly

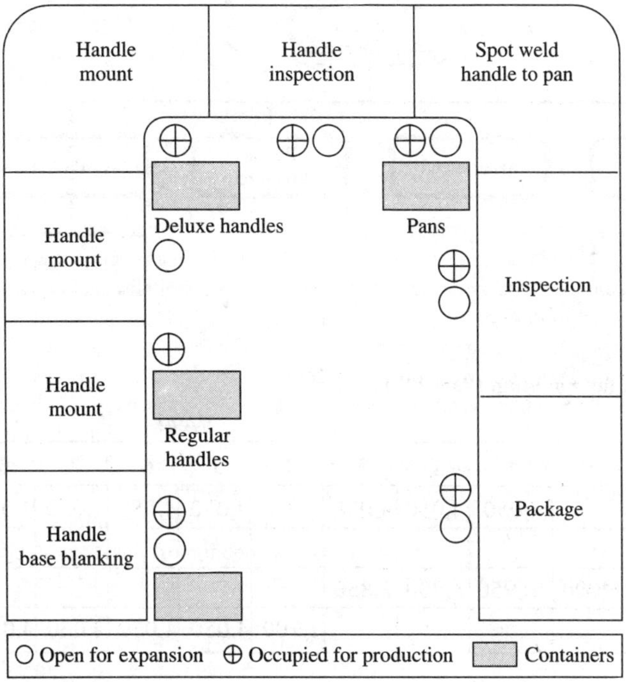

of the handle assembly cell and the final assembly line in a U-shaped layout. Note in this example that no significant inventories are anywhere on the line, and both handle base material and plastic handle parts are replenished with a pull system based on containers.

Figure 9.14 also illustrates the bandwidth concept. Several open stations along the line would permit adding personnel if volume were increased. Moreover, perhaps Muth would like to establish different production rates for certain times. For example, perhaps this pan might be manufactured in higher volumes near the Christmas season. What's needed is the capacity at the cell to move from one level of output to another. This added capacity probably means the dedicated equipment will not be highly utilized.

The cell is designed to permit variations in staffing to better respond to actual customer demands. If an unexpected surge in demand for executive handle pots comes through, the cellular approach will allow Muth to make the necessary changes faster—and to live with this kind of problem with smaller finished goods inventories. Over time, perhaps this cell can be further expanded in terms of bandwidth and flexibility to produce handles for other Muth products.

The value of quality improvement can be seen in Figure 9.14. The inspection station takes up valuable space that could be used for production. It adds cost to the product. If bad products are being culled by inspection, buffer stocks will be required to keep the final assembly line going. All of this is waste to be eliminated.

Bill of Materials Implications

The product redesign results in a streamlined bill of materials. The number of options from the customer's point of view has been maintained, but the number of parts required has

FIGURE 9.15 Simplified Product Structure

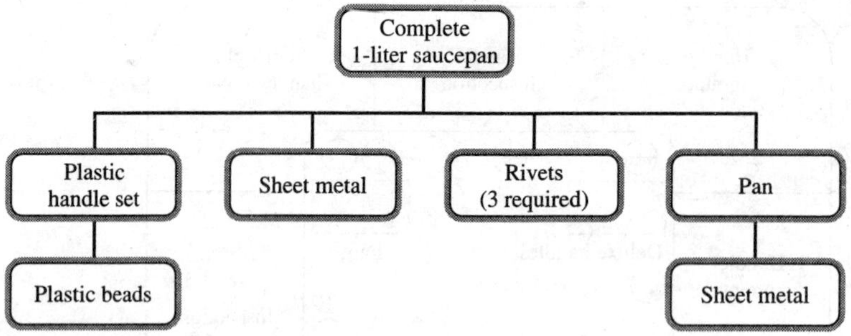

FIGURE 9.16 MRP Record for Phantom (Part 137)

		Week									
		1	2	3	4	5	6	7	8	9	10
Gross requirements		4,050	4,050	4,050	4,050	4,050	4,050	4,050	4,050	4,050	4,050
Scheduled receipts											
Projected available balance	15,000	10,950	6,900	2,850							
Planned order releases					1,200	4,050	4,050	4,050	4,050	4,050	4,050

Q = lot for lot; LT = 0; SS = 0.

gone down (e.g., components have been reduced from 14 to 10). With the cellular layout shown in Figure 9.14, the handle base and handle assembly no longer exist as inventoriable items. They are "phantoms" that won't require direct planning and control with MRP. The product structure given as Figure 9.7 now will look like Figure 9.15.

Several observations can be made about Figure 9.15. One is that handle assemblies have ceased to exist as part of the product structure. If we wanted to maintain the handle assembly for engineering and other reasons, it could be treated as a phantom. Figure 9.16 shows what the MRP record would look like in this case. In Figure 9.16, there's some existing inventory to use up; phantom treatment allows this to occur, and will always use this inventory before making more.

Another observation is that pans *do* remain as inventoriable items. Elimination of these two part numbers and their associated inventories may well be the next goal for product and process redesign. Still another is to understand the magnitude of the reduction in transactions represented by the JIT approach illustrated in Figure 9.14. All MRP planning for the eliminated part numbers (or phantom treatment) is now gone. This affects MRP planning as well as stockrooms—and all other indirect labor associated with MRP control.

Finally, we need to consider the effect on lead times, the resultant ability to better respond to market conditions, the reductions in work-in-process inventories, and the greater velocity with which material moves through the factory. If the combined lead times are computed for the product structure in Figure 9.7 and lead time data in Figure 9.8, five weeks are required for the flow of raw materials into pots. The JIT approach cuts that to just over two weeks, which could be reduced even further.

JIT Applications

Toyota is the classic JIT company in that it has gone further than any other discrete manufacturing firm in terms of truly making the production process into a continuous flow. Much of the basic terminology and philosophy of JIT have their origins at Toyota. A key issue in JIT at Toyota is understanding that automobile manufacturing is done in very large factories that are much more complex than our simplified example. Parts will flow from one work center to many others with intermediate storage, and flows into work centers will also come from many work centers with intermediate storage. The JIT systems at Toyota have to reflect this complexity. Before delving into the complexity, however, it's useful to first see how a **single-card kanban system** functions in a manufacturing environment with many work centers and intermediate storage.

Single-Card Kanban

Figure 9.17 depicts a factory with three work centers (A, B, and C) producing component parts, three work centers (X, Y, and Z) making assemblies, and an intermediate storage area for component parts. A single component (part 101) is fabricated in work center C and used by work centers Y and Z. To illustrate how the system works, suppose work center Z wishes to assemble a product requiring component 101. A box of part 101 would be moved from the storage area to work center Z. As the box was removed from storage, the accompanying kanban card would be removed from the box; shortly thereafter, the card would be placed

FIGURE 9.17
Single Kanban System

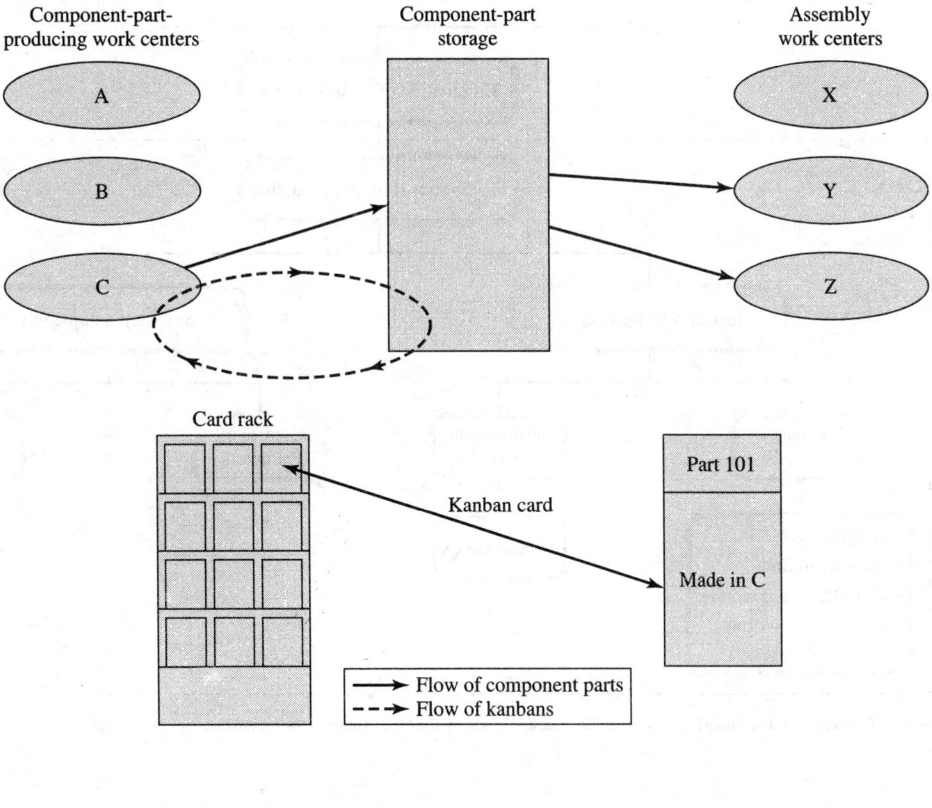

in the card rack at work center C. The cards in the rack at any work center represents the authorized production for that work center.

The greater the number of kanban cards in the system, the larger the inventory, but also the greater the autonomy that can be attained between the component-producing work centers and the assembly work centers. Some priority system can be implemented in the component work centers, such as working on a first-come/first-served basis or imposing some time requirements (such as all cards delivered in the morning will be returned with filled containers in the afternoon of the same day and all afternoon cards will be delivered the next morning).

Toyota

The production system at Toyota is in many ways the most advanced JIT system in the world. The revolutionary techniques developed by Toyota have now been adopted by all the major automobile companies in the world. Toyota still turns its inventories faster than most companies in the industry while also being very competitive in price, quality, and delivery performance.

Figure 9.18 shows the Toyota production system and where JIT fits within the overall approach. To some extent, the role given to JIT in Figure 9.18 may appear less encompassing

FIGURE 9.18 Toyota's Production System

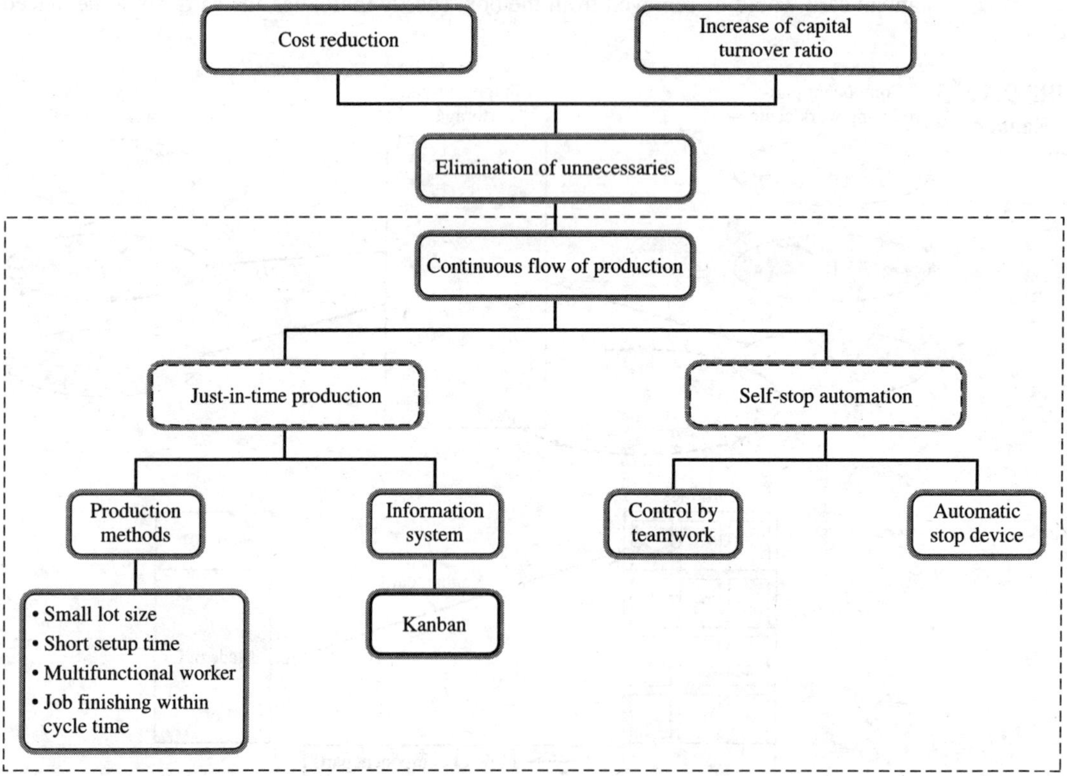

Source: European Working Group for Production Planning and Inventory Control, Lausanne, Switzerland.

than one might expect. For example, the "elimination of unnecessaries" is seen as fundamental. All of the objectives and building blocks for JIT listed in Figure 9.4 are in basic agreement with those in Figure 9.18. The box for production methods is basically the same as process design in Figure 9.3. Included under this heading is the multifunctional worker, which matches with several aspects of the human/organizational element building block. Also included is "job finishing within cycle time"; this is consistent with the dominance of material flow velocity and the subservient role of direct labor utilization.

Toyota's Kanban System

The Toyota view of just-in-time production shown in Figure 9.18 includes "Information system" with "Kanban" below it. The information system encompasses the MPC activities necessary to support JIT execution. Kanban is the Toyota technique for controlling material flows. The situation at Toyota is much more complex than that illustrated in the single-card kanban example. Toyota has intermediate storage after production of components and additional intermediate storage in front of assembly work centers. This means the work flows from a producing work center into an inventory, then to another inventory, and then to the next work center. For this reason, Toyota uses a two-card kanban system, but the principles are the same as for the single kanban card system. The chain of dual kanban cards can extend all the way back to the suppliers. Several of Toyota's suppliers receive their authorizations to produce via electronic kanban cards.

Figure 9.19 gives the formula used to calculate the number of kanban cards needed. In this formula, there's a factor for including safety stock, which Toyota says should be less than 10 percent. Using the formula, no safety stock, and a container size of 1, we can see the philosophy of the system. If a work center required eight units per day (one per hour) and it took one hour to make one unit, only one set of two kanban cards would be theoretically necessary; that is, just as a unit was finished, it would be needed at the subsequent operation.

The container sizes are kept small and standard. Toyota feels that no container should have more than 10 percent of a day's requirements. Since everything revolves around these containers and the flow of cards, a great deal of discipline is necessary. The following rules keep the system operating:

- Each container of parts must have a kanban card.
- The parts are always pulled. The using department must come to the providing department and not vice versa.
- No parts may be obtained without a conveyance kanban card.

FIGURE 9.19
Calculating the Number of Kanbans

$$Y = \frac{DL(1 + \alpha)}{a} \qquad (9.1)$$

where:

Y = number of kanban card sets
D = demand per unit of time
L = lead time
a = container capacity
α = policy variable (safety stock)

FIGURE 9.20
Toyota's View of Inventory

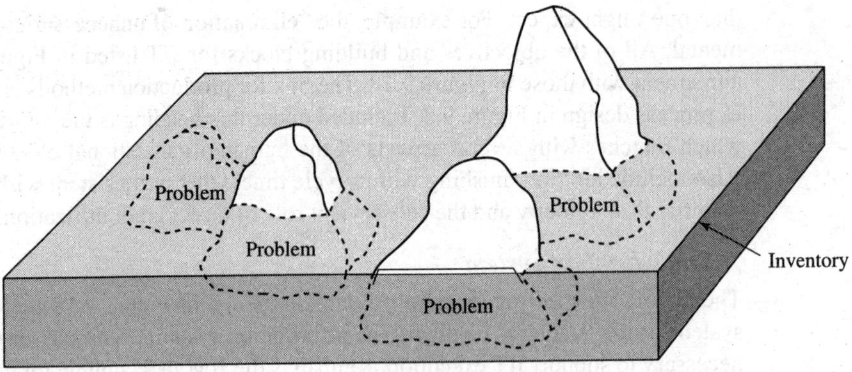

- All containers contain their standard quantities and only the standard container for the part can be used.
- No extra production is permitted. Production can only be started on receipt of a production kanban card.

These rules keep the shop floor under control. The execution effort is directed toward flawlessly following these rules. Execution is also directed toward continual improvement. In kanban terms, this means reducing the number of kanban cards and, thereby, reducing the level of work-in-process inventory. Reducing the number of cards is consistent with an overall view of inventory as undesirable. It's said at Toyota that inventory is like water that covers up problems that are like rocks. Figure 9.20 depicts this viewpoint. If the inventory is systematically reduced, problems are exposed—and attention can be directed to their solution. Problems obscured by inventory still remain.

Nonrepetitive JIT

Many JIT principles for high-volume repetitive manufacturing apply in low-volume production environments as well. However, most low-volume manufacturers have balked at two basic problems: (1) the requirement of setting up high-volume flow lines dedicated to a few products and (2) level loading. However, merging of the two camps is taking place: even for the high-volume repetitive manufacturer, it's increasingly important to respond to customer pressures for greater flexibility in volume, product mix, and other service features. The lower-volume job shop manufacturers are in turn learning to adapt JIT concepts to their environments.

A Service-Enhanced View of Manufacturing

An examination of service operations provides insights into producing products faster with greater variety. Rapid response is critical, the number of possible product/service combinations continues to grow, end-item forecasting is more difficult, and large buffer inventories are unacceptable.

All of this argues for a JIT mode of manufacture—one whose objective is to be able to accept any customer order and turn it out right behind any other, with flexibility to handle surges in volume or mix changes, all done on a routine basis. The traditional JIT view of level capacity must be adapted in nonrepetitive situations. Responsiveness to fickle demand requires a large bandwidth in terms of surge capacity. No one wants the fire department to be operated at high capacity utilization; immediate response is essential. Surge capacity must be in place in both equipment and labor. A different view of asset management and labor utilization is required. Fixed assets (both capital and people) will be less intensively utilized to increase material velocity and overall system responsiveness.

Flexible Systems

Leading-edge firms are coming to understand requirements for volume and product flexibility. Some have had experience in repetitive manufacturing applications of JIT and are now moving into nonrepetitive applications. An example is a telecommunications equipment manufacturer, which began JIT in its high-volume telephone handset operations. The firm had a limited number of high-selling models; in two years its inventory turns were tripled, work in process was reduced by 75 percent, failure rates in manufacturing were cut in half, and setup times fell 50 percent. Thereafter, the firm turned to its low-volume telecom systems plant, where more than 150 basic circuit boards were manufactured, and every end item was somewhat of a custom order. The company learned it needed to go back to the basics of JIT—product engineering, process engineering, and the whole person concept—to successfully implement JIT for its nonrepetitive products.

The firm developed cellular designs, began cellular manufacturing with great flexibility, and cross trained people with an emphasis on being able to handle volume surges in the telecom systems plant. MRP was still used for overall planning, but far fewer transactions were processed by the hidden factory of indirect labor. In the first six months, first pass yields improved 27 percent, work in process fell 31 percent, and manufacturing cells under JIT hit 100 percent of schedule. The people then helped out other parts of the company that were behind schedule!

Simplified Systems and Routine Execution

A major issue in any JIT firm, repetitive or nonrepetitive, is flow times. Work must flow through the factory so quickly that detailed tracking is not required. A related idea is responsiveness. In several JIT systems for nonrepetitive environments, the firm installed what might be called a **weekly wash.** In its simplest form, weekly wash means week 1's sales orders become week 2's production schedule.

The weekly wash approach to JIT for nonrepetitive manufacturing shifts the emphasis from scheduling material to scheduling time blocks. The focus is on what's scheduled in the next time frame, rather than on when we'll make product X. This focus is driven by the actual requirements, rather than a forecast of needs. It's as though we were scheduling a set of trains or buses. We don't hold the train until it's full, and we can always cram a few more people into a car, within reason. By scheduling trains on a relatively frequent basis, attempting to keep capacity as flexible as possible, and assigning "passengers" only to a time frame, responsiveness to actual demand can be increased, and detailed scheduling can be made more simple.

Joint-Firm JIT

JIT has been applied and misapplied by companies with their suppliers. Some firms simply ask the suppliers to buffer poor schedules. On the other hand, when done well, a joint JIT approach can lead to greater bottom-line results for both firms and increased competitiveness in the marketplace. It is critical to understand the need for joint efforts in JIT. For example, we are told by several automotive component suppliers that they are able to provide lower prices to Toyota than other firms, because Toyota is easy to do business with—the company makes a schedule and sticks to it. Others change their requirements often, with serious cost implications.

The Basics

The first prerequisite to joint-firm JIT is a scheduling system producing requirements that are reasonably certain. Without predictability, JIT for vendors is a case of the customers exporting the problems. Although this may work in the short run, in the long run it can't. We've seen a factory where JIT benefits were extolled, only to find a new paving project—for vendors' trucks. Inventory had moved from the warehouse to trailer trucks! Similar war stories abound about warehousing firms in Detroit that are needed to buffer suppliers as auto companies implement JIT.

Joint-firm JIT needs, to whatever extent possible, a stable schedule. This is consistent with level schedules for the repetitive manufacturer. To the extent that a firm makes the same products in the same quantities every day—without defects and without missing the schedule—a supplier firm's schedule is extremely simple. For the nonrepetitive manufacturer, the issue isn't leveling as much as it is avoiding surprises. The level schedule may be violated in nonrepetitive environments, but there is a greater need for coordinated information flows and, perhaps, larger buffer inventories. However, there's a major difference between a *stable* (albeit nonlevel) schedule and one that's simply uncertain. The only cure for the latter case is buffer inventories.

Certainty is a relative commodity. A vendor might be able to live fairly well with a schedule that's unpredictable on a daily basis but very predictable on a weekly basis. A weekly MRP-based total, with some kind of daily call-off of exact quantities, could be reasonably effective. In fact, some firms have developed "electronic kanbans" for this purpose. The notion of weekly wash could also be used; that is, an inventory equal to some maximum expected weekly usage could be maintained and replenished on a weekly basis. For high-value products, it might be worth it to go to some kind of twice-weekly wash, or to obtain better advance information from the customer via an e-based system.

Other "basics" for joint-firm JIT include all the objectives and building blocks discussed earlier in the chapter. A JIT basic uniquely associated with suppliers relates to pruning their number. Many companies have reduced their vendor base by as much as 90 percent to work on a truly cooperative basis with the remaining vendors. Hidden factory issues have to be considered in vendor relations as well. Some people feel the secret in joint-firm JIT is to connect MRP systems in the firms. This isn't a good idea. The focus must be on coordinated execution. A better approach might be to use blanket orders (or *no* orders), MRP for weekly quantities, agreed-upon safety stocks, or amounts by which the sum of daily quantities can exceed weekly totals, and e-based systems to determine the next day in-shipment. All this could be done without intervention of indirect labor personnel.

A telecom equipment manufacturer has such a system: Each day at about 4 p.m., an e-mail is sent to a vendor specifying how many of a particular expensive item to deliver the day after tomorrow. The units delivered never enter a stockroom or inventory record. They're delivered directly to the line without inspection and assembled that day. The vendor is paid on the basis of item deliveries into finished goods inventory. Stability is handled by providing the vendor weekly MRP projections, using time fences that define stability. Daily fluctuations reflect actual market conditions.

Tightly Coupled JIT Supply

Major suppliers to automobile manufacturers utilize JIT extensively. As an example, consider a seat supplier and an automobile manufacturer. In such a case, the two firms need to develop a form of synchronous manufacturing, operating almost as a single unit. The execution is driven by JIT. JIT execution between these two firms means that the automobile manufacturer will pass the exact build sequence (models, colors of seats, etc.) to the seat supplier, perhaps something like 30 hours in advance. The supplier needs to *build* the seats and deliver them in this time frame. Seats are not built to inventory at the supplier, and no seats are inventoried at the auto manufacturer. The seats are delivered directly to the assembly line, to match the sequence, so the assembly team simply takes the next seat, and installs it in the next car.

This synchronization allows for almost no transactions between the firms, with the supplier paid by backflushing completion of cars off the line. Inventory costs are avoided, as well as damage from multiple handling with minimal use of protective packaging. But achieving the synchronization on a continuous basis requires *flawless execution* in both firms. The auto manufacturing company cannot change the schedule or take a car off of the line for repairs, since this would change the seat installation sequence. The supplier must make each seat perfectly, since there is no stock of seats to replace one that is imperfect. The bottom line here is that this form of joint-firm JIT is highly productive. But it is rigidly connected and requires joint excellence in execution. It works well—for certain kinds of products.

Less Tightly Coupled JIT Supply

In the majority of cases, two firms will not couple their manufacturing activities as closely as those of a seat supplier to its automotive customer. The supplier will have multiple customers, only some of which will be supplied by JIT. Similarly, the customer has multiple suppliers, and not all of these will be expected to deliver directly to the line. An alternative solution is for the customer to pick up goods from vendors on some prearranged schedule. This is increasingly done for several reasons. The most obvious is the savings in transportation costs over having each vendor deliver independently. In some cases JIT has been called "just-in-traffic." A second reason relates to stability and predictability. If the customer picks up materials, some uncertainty inherent in vendor deliveries can be eliminated. Finally, pickup offers more chances to directly attack hidden factory costs. The customer can, for example, provide containers that hold the desired amounts and that will flow as kanbans through the plant. Savings in packaging materials as well as costs of unpacking are helpful to both parties. Items can also be placed on special racks inside the truck to minimize damage. Defective items can be returned easily for replacement without the usual costly return-to-vendor procedures and paperwork. Other paperwork can similarly be simplified when third parties aren't involved and when the loop is closed between problem and action in a short time frame.

JIT Coordination through Hubs

A relatively new innovation that has JIT characteristics is the supply of materials through hubs. A hub is most easily seen as an inventory, placed close to the customer, and filled by the suppliers. The costs of carrying the inventories is born by the suppliers, and they are paid for their goods either as they leave the hub or as they are backflushed into finished goods at the customer. This form of supply is called **vendor-managed inventory (VMI).** VMI is well liked by customers, since it moves inventory carrying costs off their books and onto those of the suppliers. But the "no free lunch" principle applies: If the customer only exports its problems, and does not aid in the solution, the prices will have to be adjusted to make this work. Moreover, the firm with the lowest cost of capital in the chain is ideally suited to absorb inventory-carrying costs.

There is, however, a major potential saving in this relationship. When it is done well, the supplier should eliminate its own finished goods inventory, while the customer in turn also eliminates any inventories of these materials. All inventories are in the hub and are visible to both customer and supplier. The customer needs to take the responsibility for providing highly accurate information on its expected removals from inventory (i.e., its build schedules). This is typically provided via an e-based system. The supplier thus has *knowledge* of exact customer usage: no forecasts (guesses), and no surprise orders. The supplier also has the option of working in what we call the **uphill skier** mode, where it is the supplier's responsibility to supply, but in whatever ways it wishes (just as the uphill skier has the responsibility for not colliding with the downhill skier). Having a few customers who can be supplied with the uphill skier concept allows the supplier to use its capacities and logistics more effectively. For example, if a supplier knows the customer will take 55 units out of inventory 11 days from today, this provides a window for manufacturing and delivery, which is much less constraining than classic JIT coordination.

Lessons

The primary lesson to be learned in joint-firm JIT is to not shift the execution problems from the customer back to its suppliers: joint-firm JIT means *joint.* Many firms have made this mistake, demanding that their suppliers support them in closely coordinated execution—while the suppliers see the customer as "waking up in a new world every morning." Typically, when the consequences become known, the emphasis necessarily shifts to joint problem identification and solution, a focus on joint (chain) measures, the need for stabilized schedules, a true partnership, and help from the customers for the suppliers to implement JIT with *their* suppliers. The results for a manufacturer of office equipment were impressive: overcoming a 40 percent cost disadvantage, reducing its vendor base from 5,000 to 300, and winning several important awards for manufacturing excellence.

JIT Software

The MPC systems required to execute JIT are relatively straightforward. Most ERP systems include software that supports JIT execution. Figure 9.21 shows how this software typically functions.

FIGURE 9.21 **Block Diagram of JIT Software**

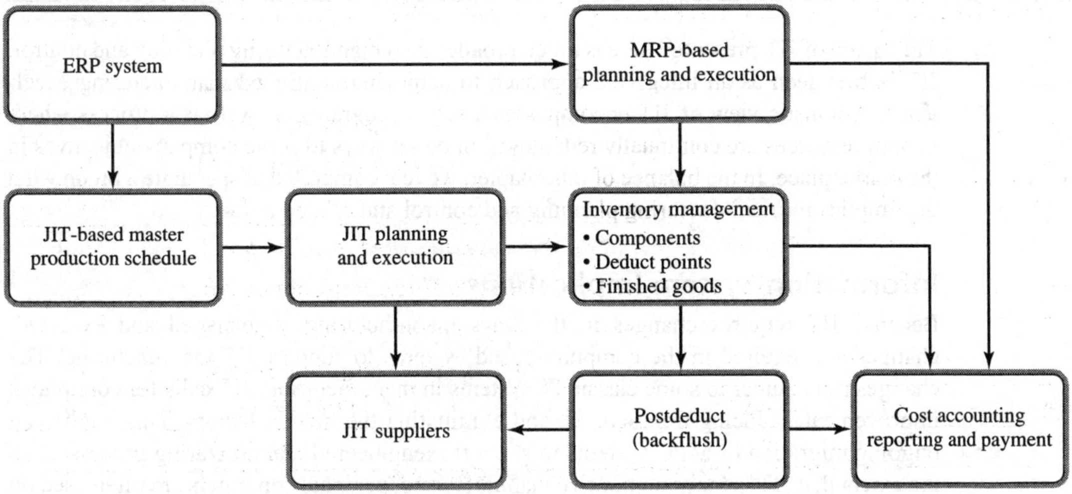

The MRP-JIT Separation

Figure 9.21 depicts the way JIT typically functions as a part of the overall MPC system. An ERP system, such as SAP, provides the overall platform and integration with other company systems. Figure 9.21 shows a split into those items that are to be planned/controlled with JIT and those that will utilize classic MRP-based systems. For the JIT products, it is necessary to first establish a master production schedule, which typically is rate based. This MPS is then passed to a JIT planning and execution subsystem that utilizes simplified bills of materials (phantoms) and cellular manufacturing. The detailed planning is also passed to JIT suppliers, typically with an e-based system providing the exact build sequence.

JIT Planning and Execution

JIT planning and execution is driven by a daily build schedule, supported by the JIT dictates of flawless execution, zero failures, no buffer inventories, cellular manufacturing, pull systems, cross-trained personnel, etc. JIT planning and execution also utilizes an inventory management subsystem for any components that are planned with MRP-based systems. This subsystem also keeps track of finished goods, any hub inventories, and **deduct points.** A deduct point is a stage in the manufacturing process where the inventories for certain parts are backflushed. That is, in some JIT systems, the backflushing is not held off until the goods are finally passed into finished goods inventory. The accounting is done in stages. This is most usually seen in early stages of JIT, when the flow times are longer and the yields less certain. The use of deduct points also helps in migrating from MRP-based planning to JIT-based planning/execution. In fact, a typical improvement is to decide when a deduct point can be eliminated, since a deduct step requires production reporting to indicate that product completion has reached this stage. Figure 9.21 also depicts an accounting/reporting subsystem to collect performance data and support supplier payments.

Managerial Implications

The vision of JIT presented here is much broader than manufacturing planning and control. JIT is best seen as an integrated approach to achieving continued manufacturing excellence. A holistic view of JIT encompasses a set of programs, as well as a process where human resources are continually redeployed in better ways to serve company objectives in the marketplace. In the balance of this chapter, we feel compelled to speculate a bit on what this implies for manufacturing planning and control and related areas.

Information System Implications

Because JIT requires changes in the ways manufacturing is managed and executed, changes are required in the computer-based systems to support JIT manufacturing. The changes run counter to some classic IT systems in manufacturing. JIT calls for continuous improvement, reducing transactions, and eliminating the hidden factory. This implies an ongoing migration of MPC systems to support reengineered manufacturing processes. To the extent that JIT is for nonrepetitive manufacturing, personal computers are often used on the shop floor to support detailed scheduling. For joint-firm JIT planning and execution, the increasing use of e-based systems is taking place. In practice, there tends to be an evolution from simple buying and routine transaction processing to more coordinated work, including new product developments and other less structured activities. Many firms now are implementing extranets to support these objectives, where individual company pairings work on achieving increasingly unique benefits.

Manufacturing Planning and Control

JIT has profound implications for all detailed MPC activities. JIT (including its extensions into less tightly linked supply chains) offers the potential for eliminating or sharply reducing inventories, incoming quality control, receiving, kitting, paper processing associated with deliveries and shipments, detailed scheduling done by central staff, and all the detailed tracking associated with classic production activity control systems. It is important to understand these benefits as the MPC system is enhanced to embody JIT thinking. Many of them are well hidden.

It is never easy to change IT systems. Organizations have grown around them, cost accounting and other areas seem to require data generated by these systems, and many jobs are involved. However, the potential is real, and leading-edge companies are increasing their competitiveness through JIT and related concepts.

Scorekeeping

A firm adopting JIT in its fullest context will need to think carefully about reward systems and managerial scorekeeping. Traditional measurement systems focus attention on producing the products, using cost accounting systems that have changed little since the Industrial Revolution. These systems are from an era when direct labor was the major cost source. Now, in many companies, material costs dominate, with direct labor cost (using traditional definitions) continually decreasing in relative importance. Far too many manufacturing firms are hobbled by antiquated measures such as tons or other overall productivity measures. For example, a large ice cream manufacturer evaluates its factories on "liter-tons" produced. A 1-liter brick of ice cream has less gross margin than a particular ice cream bar—but 1-liter bricks are always put in inventory at year-end to make the numbers look good.

JIT thinking focuses on material velocity, which is consistent with inventory reduction and lead-time compression. Under JIT, we must be wary of how "costs" are measured and the resultant implications for decision making. The values of bandwidth, flexibility, responsiveness, and worker skill enhancement need to be recognized. None of these is incorporated in traditional accounting systems. The entire approach to capacity utilization needs to be rethought in JIT. Utilization of capital assets may not be as important as responsiveness and material velocity. Being able to take any customer order, even when vastly different from forecast, and doing so with short lead times with minimal use of "shock troops" is the goal. Improved responsiveness to marketplace needs will separate successful firms from the also-rans.

What all of this means for cost accounting is that many traditional views will need to be scrapped. For example, some companies have given up the cost category of direct labor. The distinction between direct and indirect isn't useful, and basing product costs on multiples of direct labor cost leads to more erroneous implications than some other scheme. The whole person concept leads to the conclusion that the labor pool is an asset to be enhanced. It also dictates using direct labor for activities not normally associated with direct labor. Trying to apportion labor into various categories is constraining. A final scorekeeping issue is the top-management challenge to create the organizational climate where the JIT/supply chain management journey can best take place. We see this journey is the best means for survival in the years ahead. Leadership will be required to guide manufacturing firms through the necessary changes.

Pros and Cons

There are situations where JIT will work well and ones where it won't. Many authorities believe JIT to be what every Japanese company strives for. In fact, many Japanese firms with complex product structures are now actively working to implement MRP-based systems. However, JIT's realm seems to be expanding. At one time JIT was thought to apply only to repetitive manufacturing with simple product structures and level schedules. Increasingly, companies are applying JIT concepts to nonrepetitive schedules; product complexity is being partially overcome with decentralized computing on the shop floor; make-to-order schedules are being adapted to JIT; and JIT is being applied to interfirm contexts.

Some companies ask if they need to install MRP before adopting JIT, since JIT implementation often means they must dismantle parts of the MRP-based system. Although it's conceptually possible to implement JIT without first implementing MRP, for firms that can benefit significantly from MRP, it's usually not done. Unless we can find some other way to develop the discipline of MRP, JIT operations are at great risk. In the discipline's absence, when JIT takes away the buffers, there will usually be costly disruptions of the manufacturing process, poor customer service, and panic responses to the symptoms rather than to the underlying problems.

Concluding Principles

This chapter is devoted to providing an understanding of JIT and how it fits into MPC systems. Our view of JIT encompasses more than MPC-related activities, but there's a significant overlap between JIT and our approach to MPC systems. In summarizing this chapter, we emphasize the following principles:

- Stabilizing and in some cases leveling the production schedules are prerequisites to effective JIT systems.
- Achieving very short lead times supports better customer service and responsiveness.
- Reducing hidden factory costs can be at least as important as reducing costs more usually attributed to factory operations.
- Implementing the whole person concept reduces distinctions between white- and blue-collar workers and taps all persons' skills for improving performance.
- Cost accounting and performance measurements need to reflect the shift in emphasis away from direct labor as the primary source of value added.
- To achieve JIT's benefits in nonrepetitive applications, some basic features of repetitive-based JIT must be modified.
- JIT is not incompatible with MRP-based systems. Firms can evolve toward JIT from MRP-based systems, adopting JIT as much or as little as they want, with an incremental approach.

Discussion Questions

1. Some people have argued that just-in-time is simply one more inventory control system. How do you think they could arrive at this conclusion?
2. Take a common system at a university—for example, registration. Describe what kinds of "waste" can be found. How might you reduce this waste?
3. "Surge" capacity is the ability to take on an extra number of customers or product requests. Tell how the following three facilities handle surges: a football stadium, a clothing store, and an accounting firm.
4. List several ways to signal the need for more material in a pull-type system. Distinguish between situations where the feeder departments are in close proximity and those where they're at some distance.
5. Some companies contend that they can never adopt JIT because their suppliers are located all over the country and distances are too great. What might you suggest to these firms?
6. "We just can't get anywhere on our JIT program. It's the suppliers' fault. We tell them every week what we want, but they still can't get it right. I've been over to their shops, and they have mountains of the wrong materials." What do you think is going on here?
7. One manager at a JIT seminar complained that he couldn't see what he would do with his workers if they finished their work before quitting time. How would you respond to this comment?
8. How do you go about creating the organizational climate for successful JIT? Where do you start?

Problems

1. Calculate the number of kanbans needed at the ABC Company for the following two products, produced in a factory that works eight hours per day, five days per week:

	Product 1	Product 2
Usage	300/week	150/day
Lead time	1 week	2 weeks
Container size	20 units	30 units
Safety stock	15 percent	0

2. Calculate the number of kanbans required for the following four components at the ABC Company in problem 1.

	Component			
	W	X	Y	Z
Daily usage	900	250	1,200	350
Lead time	2 hours	5 hours	1 hour	3 hours
Container size	25 units	40 units	50 units	20 units
Safety stock	25 percent	20 percent	15 percent	10 percent

3. The BCD Company has successfully implemented JIT internally, and now wishes to convert one of its main suppliers to JIT as well. As a test of feasibility, the firms have selected one item made by this supplier for BCD. The supplier currently manufactures and delivers this item in batches of 6,000 with a lead time of two weeks. The current price paid is $150/unit, and the average usage rate at BCD is 250 units per day. Under JIT, the kanban container size would be 100 units, 10 percent safety stock, and lead time of two weeks (10 days).
   a. What is the current investment in work-in-process inventory for this item at BCD (assume average inventory is Q/2)?
   b. What is the change in investment if the proposed JIT system is implemented?
   c. A consulting study indicates that for an additional $100,000 investment, lead time could be reduced from two weeks to one week. Evaluate the feasibility of this investment.
4. The CDE Company buys 200 different capacitors from 25 suppliers, with most of the capacitors purchased with an individual purchase order. An analysis indicates that the annual number of purchase orders placed for capacitors is roughly 2,000, and a cost analysis estimates the cost to place an order as $30. Additional annual cost estimates for these items include:

Obsolescence	$ 20,000
Maintaining multiple vendors	10,000
Extra shipping costs	5,000
Expediting/shortages	5,000

   One of the suppliers has offered to provide all capacitors, in a racking system, which will be replenished weekly, where each week CDE only pays for what it has used. There will be no orders at all. The supplier offers to provide this service for $25,000 per year, plus the standard cost per item. What are the potential cost savings to CDE in this proposal?

5. The DEF Company produces three products using a mixed-model assembly line, which is operated 16 hours per day (two shifts of eight hours each) for 250 days per year. The annual demand forecasts for the products are as follows:

Products	Forecasts
1	20,000
2	10,000
3	5,000

a. Determine a mixed-model master production schedule for a daily batch, based on the minimum batch size for each product.

b. Prepare a daily schedule indicating the number of each product to be produced each day.

c. Product 1 requires two units of component A and one unit of component B. If component A is manufactured internally at DEF, how many kanbans would be required for this component if the lead time is two days, the safety factor is 15 percent, and the container size is 25 units?

6. The EFG Company works an eight-hour/day, 250-day/year schedule, producing four models with the following annual demand forecasts:

Model	Forecast
I	500
II	1,500
III	4,500
IV	6,000

a. Determine a mixed-model minimum batch master production schedule for EFG, based on a daily batch and an hourly batch.

b. Construct a detailed mixed-model schedule for an eight-hour day using minimum batch sizes.

7. The FGH Company assembles nine products, working eight hours/day, 250 days/year. All products are assembled in batches of 120 units, on a line with capacity of 360 units per hour. The forecasted demands per year for the nine products are as follows:

Product	Forecast
1	180,000
2	150,000
3	120,000
4	120,000
5	90,000
6	30,000
7	15,000
8	7,500
9	750

Develop a level-minimum-batch (120 units) scheduling cycle for the assembly line at FGH.

8. The GHI Company produces models A, B, C, and D on an assembly line that operates 250 eight-hour days per year. The demand forecasts are:

	Model			
	A	B	C	D
Annual forecast	1,000	3,000	7,000	9,000

   a. Determine the mixed-model master production schedule for a daily batch and hourly batch with minimum batch sizes.
   b. Determine the schedule of production for an eight-hour day using mixed-model minimum batch production.

9. The GHI Company makes air conditioners, in either the standard model or additionally with a special option it calls the "turbo-charger," using the following indented bill of materials. The air conditioners are assembled at a rate 600 per five-day week, and the turbo-charger is added to every fourth unit. Develop the 10-week MRP record for the turbo-charger, using a one-week lead time, no safety stock, a lot size of 800, and a starting inventory of 200.

   Air Conditioner
   - Part no. 101 (1 required)
   - Part no. 102 (1 required)
   - Part no. 103 (1 required)
   - Turbo-charger assembly ($\frac{1}{4}$ required)
     - Coupling (1 required)
     - Bracket (1 required)
     - Alternator (1 required)

10. Continuing with problem 9, suppose the turbo-charger assembly was phantomed (i.e., the coupling, bracket, and alternator were assembled directly onto the air conditioner).
    a. What would the new bill of materials look like?
    b. Construct the phantom MRP record and compare it to that in problem 9. What are the differences?
    c. Construct the MRP record for the coupling (lot size = 200, safety stock = 20, on hand = 250, lead time = 2 weeks).

11. The air conditioner line is now to be run with JIT. In order to stabilize the planning for components, the GHI Company committed to producing exactly 125 units per each day in the week. Productivity on the air conditioner line started at a somewhat low level, but has been steadily increasing. At the outset, the four-person line could assemble 125 units per day, but it required 10.5 hours per day to do so (2.5 hours of overtime). After six weeks (3,600 units cumulative) the team could assemble 125 units with little or no overtime. Thereafter, the team followed a classic learning curve (90 percent) pattern. A 90 percent learning curve implies that for every doubling of output, the time required to produce a unit decreases by 10 percent. At about 7,000 units cumulative, the daily time requirement to assemble 125 units fell to 7.2 hours.
    a. What would be a good estimate of the cumulative average time for the first 3,600 units?
    b. How long will it be before the team can assemble 125 units in 6 to 6.5 hours?
    c. If after 30,000 units the team can assemble 125 units in 5.5 hours, what is the weekly "surge capacity" of the line? In particular, if there was a special promotion, how many units could be built in a week where the team worked 10 hours per day?

12. ZMW Motorwerks buys its car seats from Slippery Seats, Inc. Slippery puts 10 different fabrics on the same seats delivered to one of ZMW's assembly plants. Slippery sells and delivers each seat to ZMW in batches of 500, which ZMW orders when its inventory on a particular seat reaches 100 units—the expected use by ZMW during the two-week lead time (guaranteed as a maximum by Slippery). Every day, the particular 100 seats expected to be used the next day are removed from the inventory at ZMW and transported to the line where the seats are installed (at a rate of 10/hour during a 10-hour day (100/day, 250 days/year). As the cars pass through the seat section, the workers pick the right seat to go with the particular car. In the event that a seat is damaged, another of the same fabric is used (there is a safety stock of five seats in each fabric, which is replenished each day as needed). Slippery tries to maintain a finished goods inventory of one batch of each seat-fabric combination. This allows it to almost always be able to ship a batch of seats quickly when ordered by ZMW. The lead time required to make a batch of 500 seats is three weeks, and Slippery has promised to deliver in two weeks at a maximum. The lead time is based on one week to make the frames, one week to order/receive the fabric, which is cut and sewn in week 2, with the final seats assembled in week 3 (when all the other materials have been ordered and delivered). A new batch is started whenever an order is received, which will replenish the batch removed from inventory to fill the order.
    a. What is the expected inventory level (average) of seats at ZMW?
    b. What is the expected inventory level (finished goods) at Slippery?
    c. What is the expected inventory level (work-in-process) at Slippery?
    d. What are the hidden factory costs in both companies?
13. Returning to problem 12, Slippery sees its own operation as a type of kanban system. It has a batch of finished products in inventory, and whenever that is removed, this becomes the trigger to make another batch.
    a. What are the fundamental differences between this approach and one based on a mixed-model daily schedule?
    b. What is the average batch size for each product that would be run in the latter case?
    c. What are the changes that would be required at ZMW?
    d. What changes would be required at Slippery?
14. Slippery presently wraps each seat in plastic to protect it from damage and soiling during assembly/delivery. Assume that the plastic material costs $1, the labor to install it costs $2, and at the dealer it costs $3 to remove the plastic and dispose of it. Slippery is now telling ZMW that other auto manufacturers are able to train their assemblers to be more careful, thereby eliminating the plastic wrapping.
    a. What would be the annual benefits of this change to Slippery?
    b. What would be the annual benefits of this change to ZMW?
    c. What would be the annual benefits of this change to the dealers?
    d. How might the end customers benefit?
    e. How might one resolve any conflicts between Slippery, ZMW, and the dealers over implementing this change?
15. Suppose ZMW provides the daily build schedule to Slippery, and Slippery delivers four times per day (every 2.5 hours), in the exact build sequence, when the inventory at ZMW is down to only one hour of stock.
    a. What is the reduction in inventory at ZMW?
    b. What is the potential reduction in inventory at Slippery if it *builds* to the schedule?
    c. What other advantages are gained in the two firms?
    d. What kind of information system is needed to support this JIT execution?
    e. What else has to be implemented in both firms to make it a reality?

Chapter 10

Distribution Requirements Planning

Distribution requirements planning (DRP) provides the basis for integrating supply chain inventory information and physical distribution activities with the manufacturing planning and control (MPC) system. It is a bridge between the intrafirm MPC systems used to manage internal resources and the interfirm systems used to link members of the supply chain. The set of DRP techniques described in this chapter can help the firm link supply chain requirements with manufacturing activities. DRP relates current field inventory positions, forecasts, and knowledge of demand to manufacturing's master production scheduling and material planning modules. A well-developed DRP system helps management anticipate future requirements in the field, closely match material supply to demand, effectively deploy inventory to meet customer service requirements, and rapidly adjust to the vagaries of the marketplace. In addition, the system supports significant logistics savings through better planning of transportation capacity needs and dispatching of shipments. This chapter will show how DRP works, how it ties into the MPC system, and how it can be used to realize the potential savings.

This chapter is organized around three topics:

- *Distribution requirements planning in the supply chain:* How does DRP integrate the MPC system with the supply chain needs?
- *DRP techniques:* How does DRP work and how is it used to manage the demand and supply of field inventories?
- *Management issues with DRP:* What organizational questions must be addressed to fully realize the system's potential?

Distribution Requirements Planning in the Supply Chain

Managing the flow of materials in a contemporary supply chain is a difficult and complex task. The materials move between firms, warehouses, and distribution centers and can even return to their point of origin with value having been added or for remanufacturing.

Moreover, the ownership might be different for any combination of the facilities among which the materials can flow.

Distribution requirements planning is a technique to help manage these material flows. DRP links firms in the supply chain by providing planning records that carry demand information from receiving points to supply points and returns supply information to the receiving points. Key linkages in the supply network can be integrated through DRP. The logistics activities of transportation, storage in warehouses and/or distribution centers, and ***breaking bulk*** (breaking large shipment quantities into customer-friendly units) can be incorporated, as can other value-adding activities like labeling, adding country-specific information, or providing special packaging.

Though several linkages in the supply network can be accommodated in a distribution requirements planning system, in our description of DRP we will take the perspective of a supplying firm distributing product to other manufacturers or to retail customers. Thus, we will be concerned with the physical distribution (including transportation and warehousing) of the product(s). The key linkages that we will describe are those with our customer(s). They take us from intrafirm to interfirm MPC. These linkages can form the connection between our internal MPC system and our customers' internal MPC systems. They carry information to the market and provide us with information on the market.

Even though our description of DRP will be in terms of our supplying product to our customers, we are also a customer for our suppliers. Thus, there can be a DRP connection from our internal system to the internal system of our suppliers. These DRP connections to or from us could extend deeply into the respective internal systems. This is especially true when we (or our suppliers) are using ***vendor-managed inventories.*** Under vendor-managed inventories, the replenishment of our products in inventory at customers' locations would be under our control.

When the quantities and timing of shipments to our customers is under our control rather than the customers, we need to know what the customers will need in the future. We can get this information, of course, from their MPC system. This degree of integration is what permits us to ***make-to-knowledge.*** Without this integration we would forecast what will be needed, provide safety stock for forecast errors, and still might be surprised. With the integration we can respond more precisely to the needs of our customers through this direct access to their demand and planning information.

DRP can be linked into our internal MPC system, both from our suppliers and to our customers. DRP, therefore, provides linkages that span the boundary from internal to external MPC systems. We take up those linkages in the rest of this section before moving on to the technical aspects of distribution requirements planning.

DRP and the MPC System Linkages

The distribution requirements planning (DRP) linkages that span the boundary from our internal systems to our customers' internal systems are shown in Figure 10.1. The link to the front end of the MPC system runs from demand management to the customers and back. Through this link with demand management, demand information is brought into master production scheduling and the sales and operations planning activity. For master production scheduling, the information is important for managing the balance of supply and demand within the current company plans and capacity. For sales and operations planning, the information is combined with other market data and company objectives to develop the company plans.

FIGURE 10.1
DRP Links to the Internal MPC System

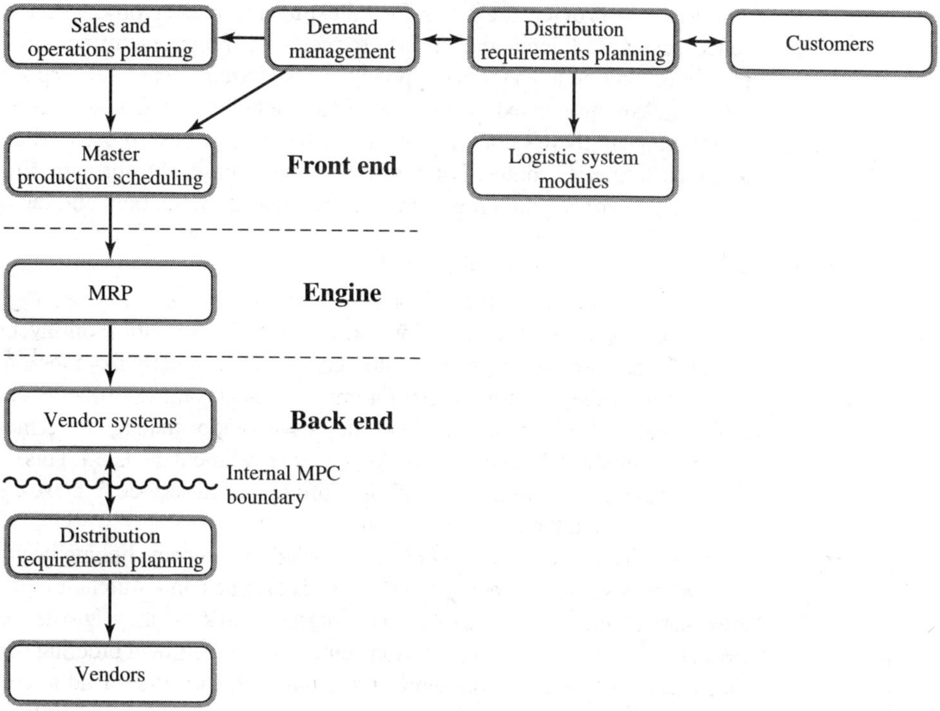

DRP has a central role in coordinating material flows through a complicated physical system consisting of field warehouses, intermediate distribution centers, central suppliers, and customer locations. The role is similar to material requirements planning's role in coordinating materials in manufacturing. Moreover, the DRP information must be integrated into the internal MPC system. This is facilitated by using time-phased information on inventories, material in transit, and shipping plans. The key task is effectively managing the required flow of goods and inventories between the firm and the market. DRP's role is to provide the necessary data for matching customer demand with the supply of products at various stages in the physical distribution system and products being produced by manufacturing.

Key elements of these data are the planned timings and quantities for replenishing inventories throughout the physical distribution system. These data take into account currently available field inventories and forecasts. Planners use these data to evaluate the quality of the current match between supply and demand and to make adjustments as required.

Distribution requirements planning provides information to the master production scheduler in a format consistent with the MRP records. By using standard MRP software approaches for DRP, the full range of MRP techniques (such as firm planned orders, pegging, and exception messages) is available to manage distribution inventories. This also provides the basis for integrating the database throughout the MPC system—from supplier systems through distribution. Evaluation of alternative plans, with the integrated database, provides a complete view of the material planning implications. This is particularly valuable in master production scheduling.

DRP data provide the basis for adjusting the master production schedule (MPS) to reflect changes in demand or in the product mix. If manufacturing and distribution system priorities can't be adjusted to respond to these requirements, the implications can be evaluated and communicated to customers in a timely fashion. Common records and system integration mean there's complete visibility to see how best to use available inventories and to adjust future schedules. DRP provides a solid base of information to make these decisions, instead of relying on political negotiations between field and factory.

DRP and the Marketplace

DRP starts in the marketplace—or as close to it as possible. Increasingly, this could actually be at a customer location. Some firms gather information on inventory levels and on product usage directly from key customers, possibly directly from their MPC systems. This knowledge of their customers' requirements provides these firms the opportunity to make to knowledge. In the instance where they have vendor-managed inventories in a customer location, it enables them to even make the replenishment decision. This, in turn, offers them a major strategic advantage in providing products and service to these customers and gaining efficiencies in their own operations.

In most instances, however, DRP starts inside a company, linking its production unit to its field warehouse units. When the DRP records originate in a warehouse or distribution center, they start at the independent-demand interface; that is, they are derived from forecasts. Because customers of the distribution centers make their own ordering decisions, demand is ***independent*** of the firm's decisions. From the independent-demand interface point on, however, decisions are under the company's control. Timing and sizes of replenishment shipments, manufacturing batch sizes, and purchase order policies are all under management control.

The DRP approach allows us to pick up all the detailed local information for managing physical distribution and for coordinating with the factory. Because customer demand is independent, each warehouse needs detailed forecasts of end-item demand. However, careful attention to actual customer demand patterns may be useful in tailoring these forecasts to local conditions. We know of one instance, for example, where the local warehouse manager was able to identify several products purchased late in the month by some large customers. This produced a different demand pattern in the forecast than the constant weekly demand throughout the month that came from a standard forecasting software package. The modified forecasts produced important inventory savings by more closely matching demand with supply at this location.

Two types of demand data may be available locally that can help us manage field inventories. Information on special orders can help us provide service to regular orders while satisfying the special orders. Planned inventory adjustments by customers can also be reflected in the system, again providing data for more closely managing the distribution process. In each of these cases, the system allows the company to respond to advance notice of conditions, instead of treating them as surprises when they occur.

All management decisions for controlling inventories are reflected in the plans for resupplying warehouses. Planned shipment information provides valuable data for managing the local facility. Personnel required for unloading incoming material and stocking shelves can be planned. If there are problems in satisfying local demands, realistic promises can be made to waiting customers. Also, the amount of capital tied up in local inventory can be more realistically estimated for funds management.

In summary, DRP serves two purposes in the marketplace, be it in a warehouse, distribution center, or a customer location. First, DRP enables us to capture data, including local demand conditions, for modifying the forecast and to report current inventory positions. Second, DRP provides data for managing the distribution facility and the database for consistent communications with customers and the rest of the company.

DRP and Demand Management

The demand management module is the gateway between the manufacturing facility and the marketplace. In some systems with field inventories, it is where information on demand is taken in and where product for the field warehouses (and inventory status information) is sent out. This process requires detailed matching of supply to demand in every location—and requires providing supply to meet all sources of demand. DRP is a method for managing the resultant large volume of dynamic information and for generating the information to establish the plans for manufacturing and replenishing the inventories.

Plans derived from the DRP information and the resulting shipping requirements are the basis for managing the logistics system. Figure 10.2 shows the relationship between DRP and the logistics activities. Vehicle capacity planning is the process of planning the vehicle availability for the set of future shipments as generated by DRP. Shipping requirements also are used to determine vehicle loads, dispatch vehicles, and plan the resources necessary to receive the goods at the warehouse.

By planning future replenishment needs, DRP establishes the basis for more effective vehicle dispatching decisions. These decisions are continually adjusted to reflect current conditions. Long-term plans help to determine the necessary transportation capacity. Warehouses' near-term needs are used to efficiently load vehicles without compromising customer service levels. Data on planned resupply of the warehouses can be used for scheduling the labor force needed at the warehouses.

As actual field demands vary around the forecasts, adjustments to plans are required. DRP continually makes these adjustments, sending the inventories from the central warehouse to

FIGURE 10.2
Distribution Requirements Planning and the Logistics System

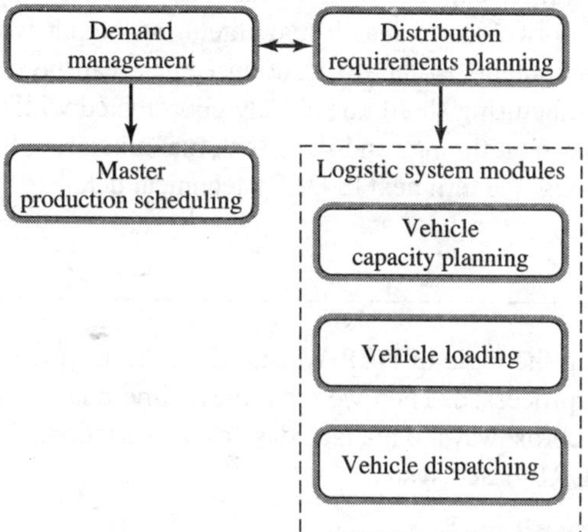

those distribution centers where they're most needed. In circumstances where insufficient total inventory exists, DRP provides the basis for deciding on allocations. The planning information facilitates applying whatever criteria are used for the allocation decision. These criteria are as varied as providing stock sufficient to last the same amount of time at each location or favoring the "best" customers. Moreover, DRP provides the data to be able to accurately say when availability will be improved and delivery can be expected.

DRP and Master Production Scheduling

Perhaps DRP's greatest payoff to master production scheduling is from integrating records and information. Because the formats of DRP and MRP records are compatible and all MPC modules are linked, DRP allows us to extend MPC visibility into the distribution system. This, however, has internal political implications. One company we know decided not to integrate the records. Instead it established a committee to resolve issues between logistics and manufacturing concerning inventories' size and composition. A sister company installed an integrated system using DRP. When it became evident that the integrated system was superior, the political cost of dismantling the committee was high since all committee members now had "permanent" jobs.

Moving the MPC boundaries into the supply chain, perhaps even into customers' MPC systems also has political costs. Crossing over into the area of interfirm MPC systems means negotiating with supply chain partners for sharing the costs and benefits. These negotiations sometimes require a major element of education for the partners—showing and convincing them of the value of integration. To overcome the natural reluctance to share internal MPC information requires that the customers have a very good understanding of the value you can provide by scheduling replenishments to knowledge instead of forecast. Providing the master scheduler with supply chain visibility makes this possible.

DRP collects detailed information in the field and summarizes it so MPC decisions can respond to overall company needs. DRP permits evaluation of current conditions to determine if manufacturing priorities should be revised. It provides insights into how they should be changed and into implications to the field if they aren't. Thus, more reasoned trade-offs can be made in the use of limited capacity or materials. The DRP shipping plans provide the master scheduler better information to match manufacturing output with shipping needs. Requirements based on shipments to the distribution centers can be quite different from demand in the field. Manufacturing should be closely coordinated with the former. For example, firms matching shipment timings and sizes with manufacturing batches can achieve substantial inventory savings. We turn next to DRP's technical details.

DRP Techniques

In this section, we develop the logic of DRP. We start by introducing the basic record and how DRP information is processed. Then we turn to the time-phased order point, how to link several warehouse records, ways to manage day-to-day variations from plans, and how to use safety stocks in a DRP-based system.

The Basic DRP Record

The DRP system's basic data elements are detailed records for individual products at locations as close to the final customer as possible. Records are maintained centrally as a part of the MPC system database, but continually updated information on inventory and demand are passed between the central location and the field sites either on some periodic basis or in real time, often on line. For illustrative purposes, we'll consider the record for a single **stockkeeping unit (SKU)** at a field warehouse.

To integrate DRP into the overall MPC system, we expand the bill of materials beyond its usual context. The zero level in the bill of material is defined as the SKU in a field warehouse. Thus, an item isn't seen as completed simply when the raw materials have been transformed into a finished product, but only after it has been delivered to the location where it satisfies a customer demand. This extension of the bill of materials into field locations allows us to use standard MRP explosion techniques to link the field with all other MPC systems. Note that the convention means that a product at location X is identified as different from the same product at location Y.

Regardless of the physical location (central inventory at the plant, a distribution center, a field warehouse, or even a customer's shelf), the item's ultimate demand comes from the customer. The warehouse is where the company's internal world of dependent demand must deal with the customer's independent demand. The customer, within wide ranges, decides how much and when to order; these decisions are usually independent of the company's decisions. Planners in the company, on the other hand, decide when and how much product to make. They also decide when and how much to send to field locations. To link company decisions with the customers' we must start with a forecast. This is recorded in the first row of the basic DRP record in Figure 10.3.

Even though the first row is labeled forecast, it may contain much more information than the typical "average weekly demand" forecast produced by a software package. For example, it may have information specific to the customers' buying patterns at a warehouse, as we alluded to before. It can be directly linked to the MPC system of a customer, in which case the information is not our forecast of the needs of that customer, but a reflection of their current plans. In all cases, however, the forecast requirements are subject to change as conditions change and the DRP system provides the means to adjust to those changes.

The record looks like an MRP record, but there are some subtle differences other than the use of forecast data in the requirements row. For example, because it's for a specific location, it not only provides time-phased data on how much and when, but also tells us where. It's not the differences, however, that are important. It's the consistency of format and processing logic that provide many of DRP's benefits. To explain this, let's go through the record in some detail.

FIGURE 10.3
Field Warehouse DRP Record

		Period						
		1	2	3	4	5	6	7
Forecast requirements		20	20	20	20	30	30	30
In transit			60					
Projected available balance	45	25	65	45	25	55	25	55
Planned shipments				60		60		

Safety stock = 20; shipping quantity = 60; lead time = 2.

Figure 10.3 shows a change in the forecast in period 5. This could be due to a revision by someone at the warehouse who has information on local demand, or due to a sales promotion. The fact that these variations can be incorporated into the system at this level provides one of the advantages of using DRP for managing field inventories.

The second row shows shipments in transit to the warehouse. In Figure 10.3, one shipment is scheduled to arrive in time for use in period 2. Thus, time for unloading and shelving the products must be accounted for in setting lead time to show the order available for use in period 2. The equivalent row in a manufacturing MRP record is called "scheduled receipts" (open orders). However, more than the name of the in-transit row is different between manufacturing and distribution. In manufacturing, there is some flexibility in the timing of open orders. They can be speeded up or slowed down to a certain extent, by changing priorities in the shop-floor system. This is more difficult with goods in transit. Once a shipment is on a vehicle bound for a particular location, there's little opportunity to change the arrival time.

The projected inventory balance row contains the current inventory balance (45 for the example in Figure 10.3) and projections of available inventory for each period in the planning horizon (seven periods here). A safety stock value of 20 has been determined as sufficient to provide the customer service level desired for the item. The economics of transportation or packaging indicate a normal shipment of this product to this location is 60 units. Finally, it takes two periods to load, ship, unload, and store the product.

The projected available balance is generated by using the forecast requirements. The process is identical to that used for processing MRP records. In Figure 10.3, the available balance for the end of period 1 is determined by subtracting the forecast requirement of 20 from the initial inventory of 45. The 25 units at the end of period 1, plus the in-transit quantity of 60 to be received in period 2, minus the forecast of 20 for period 2, give the closing balance of 65 for period 2.

Planned shipments are indicated for those periods in which a shipment would have to be made to avoid a projected balance having less than the safety stock. The projected balance for period 4, for example, is 25 units. The forecast for period 5 is 30 units. Therefore, a shipment of product that will be available in period 5 is needed. Because lead time is two periods, a planned shipment of 60 units (the shipping quantity) is shown for period 3. Similarly, the planned shipment in period 5 is needed to cover the forecast of 30 in period 7, because there is only a 25-unit projected available balance at the end of period 6.

The result of these calculations for each product at each location is a plan for future shipments needed to provide the customer service levels the company desires. These plans depend on forecasts, but they incorporate management decisions for shipping quantities and safety stocks in planning resupply schedules. These plans provide the visibility planners need to match supply and demand.

Time-Phased Order Point (TPOP)

Many companies use economic order or shipping quantity/reorder point (Q, R) procedures based on demand forecasts for managing their field inventories. This means decisions for resupply are made independently at the field location, with no integrated forward planning; that is, when the on-hand quantity at a location reaches the reorder point, the shipping quantity is ordered with no thought given to any other items ordered, to the situation at the

FIGURE 10.4
Example Time-Phased Order Point (TPOP) Record

		Period						
		1	2	3	4	5	6	7
Forecast requirements		15	15	15	15	15	15	15
In transit								
Projected available balance	22	7	32	17	42	27	12	37
Planned shipments		40		40			40	

Safety stock = 5; shipping quantity = 40; lead time = 1.

factory, or to warehouses—or to when the next order might be needed. Also, Q, R assumes a constant usage. Whenever forecast information is used as the requirements and a time-phased MRP approach is used to develop planned shipments, it's called **time-phased order point (TPOP).** Time-phased order point can be used for constant usage situations and even when the usage forecast varies from period to period. We use Figure 10.4 to illustrate the approach.

If a Q, R system were used, the reorder point for the situation in Figure 10.4 would be 20 units, comprising the safety stock (5) plus the demand during lead time (15), assuming continuous review of inventory balances. Simulating the Q, R rules for Figure 10.4's data would lead to orders in periods 2, 4, and 7. If we use DRP logic, the planned shipments are in periods 1, 3, and 6. Thus, the timing of the orders in the TPOP record in Figure 10.4 doesn't exactly match the expected timing of orders using Q, R.

The results are, however, very close. The differences would largely disappear if the periods were made small (e.g., days instead of weeks) since they're primarily due to the fact that Q, R assumes continuous review. The TPOP approach is based on the MRP logic of planning a shipment that prevents the ending balance in the period from falling below the safety stock level.

One advantage of TPOP over Q, R is the TPOP record shows *planned* shipment data. These aren't part of the Q, R approach. In addition, TPOP isn't limited to use of constant requirement assumptions. When forecast usages vary, differences between TPOP and Q, R can be much larger than those in Figure 10.4.

Not only is it important to have planned shipment data, it's also critical to capture *all* demand information. Forecast sales requirements are only one source of demand input. DRP can use TPOP plus actual order data plus service part requirements plus interplant demands. *All* these demand sources can be integrated into the demand data driving DRP.

Linking Several Warehouse Records

Once DRP records are established for the field warehouses, information on planned shipments is passed through the distribution centers (if any) to the central facility. This process is sometimes referred to as **implosion.** The concept indicates we're gathering information from a number of field locations and aggregating it at the manufacturing facility. This is different from the explosion notion in manufacturing (where a finished product is broken into its components), but the process is the same, and in both cases it's based on bills of material.

FIGURE 10.5 Field Warehouse to Central Warehouse Records for DRP

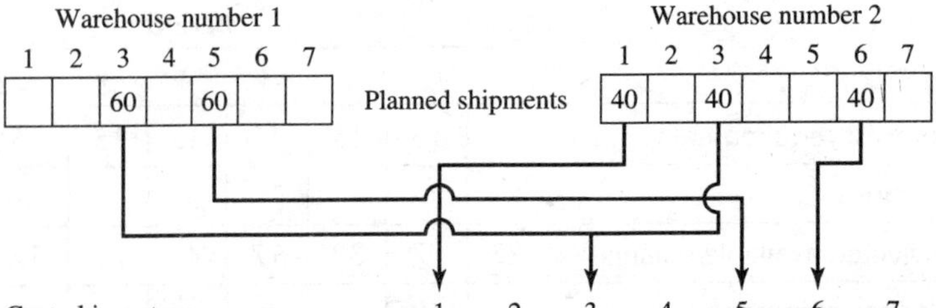

Central inventory		1	2	3	4	5	6	7
Gross requirements		40	0	100	0	60	40	
Scheduled receipts								
Projected available balance	100	60	60	60	60	100	60	60
Planned order release						100		
Firm planned orders (MPS)				100				

Safety stock = 50; order quantity = 100; lead time = 0

The record in Figure 10.5 is for the central warehouse inventory. The gross requirements correspond to planned shipments to the two warehouses in Figures 10.3 and 10.4. This relationship reflects the logic that, if there were a shipment of 40 units of product to warehouse number 2 in period 1, there would be a "demand" on the central warehouse for 40 units in period 1. The "demand," however, is dependent, having come from the company's shipping department. It is, therefore, a gross requirement and not a forecast requirement. We have crossed over from the independent demand world of the customers to the dependent demand world of the company.

The central warehouse's gross requirement is shown in the same period as the planned shipment, since lead time to ship, unload, and put away the product has already been accounted for in the field warehouse record. For example, the shipment of 60 units of product planned for period 3 in warehouse number 1 allows for the lead time before it's needed to meet forecast demand.

The logic for imploding planned shipment information holds also for much more complicated distribution systems. If there were intermediate distribution centers, they would have gross requirements derived from the warehouses they served. At distribution centers, gross requirements are established for any period in which replenishment shipments are planned to warehouses.

A primary task at the central facility is to create the master production schedule. The central inventory record in Figure 10.5 can be used for this purpose. The record shows projected available balances for the central inventory and the planned order releases, which provide the quantities needed to maintain the 50 units of safety stock. The master production schedule is created by using zero lead time and firm planned orders. Firm planned orders are created by the planners and aren't under system control; that is, they aren't automatically replanned as conditions change but are maintained in the periods and quantities designated by the planners.

FIGURE 10.6
FAS Record for Packaging Bulk Materials

Packaged Product		Period 1	2	3	4	5	6	7
Gross requirements		40	80	100	0	60	20	100
Scheduled receipts		40						
Projected available balance	10	10	10	10	10	10	10	10
Planned order release					60	20	100	
Firm planned orders		80	100					

Q = lot-for-lot; lead time = 1; SS = 10; planning fence: period 3.

The MPS states when manufacturing is to have the product completed and available for shipment to the field warehouses. In the example in Figure 10.5, the MPS quantity (firm planned order) has replaced a planned order, although this need not be the case.

Our example implies creating an MPS for each end item. This may not be desirable in firms that assemble or package a large variety of end items from common modules, subassemblies, or bulk materials. If the MPS is stated in subassemblies or bulk materials, then a final assembly schedule (FAS) needs to be created for managing the conversion to assemblies or packed products. The resultant records usually don't need to be frozen or firm planned over extensive planning horizons, since they only deal with conversion of, say, bulk material into some specific packaged products. Figure 10.6 shows how this conversion can be managed. This packaged product's gross requirements are exploded from the shipments planned to go to all the field locations. Packaging this specific product from the bulk material takes one period. Firm planned orders, up to the planning fence at period 3, are used to schedule the packaging operation. The record also shows 10 units of packaged product held at the central facility to provide flexibility in shipping to the field warehouses.

Figure 10.7 shows how the various sizes of packaged products can be combined into a bulk inventory record for creating the factory's MPS. In the example, two package sizes consume the bulk inventory. The packages are in grams, while the bulk item is in kilograms. The explosion process works from packaged item to bulk, but the grams have been converted to kilograms to get the gross requirements for the bulk material (e.g., for period 1: 100 units × 200 grams = 20,000 grams = 20 kilograms). The firm planned orders for the bulk material are the factory MPS, stating when the bulk inventory must be replenished to meet the packaging schedules.

Managing Day-to-Day Variations from Plan

On a daily basis, disbursals for actual customer demand, receipts of inventory, and other transactions are processed. These transactions are used to periodically update the DRP records. If forecasts and execution of plans were perfect, we wouldn't need to do anything but add the new period of information at the end of the planning horizon each time the records were processed. Unfortunately, we haven't found a company where such conditions hold. Figure 10.8 shows a more likely set of circumstances.

In this example, actual sales vary from 16 to 24 around the forecast of 20 units. The actual sales of 18 in period 1 have no impact on planned shipments, while actual sales of

FIGURE 10.7
Bulk Material Record and MPS

200-Gram Product	Period 1	2	3	4	5	6	7
Planned orders					60	40	
Firm planned orders	100		100				

500-Gram Product	Period 1	2	3	4	5	6	7
Planned orders				10	10		20
Firm planned orders		20					

Bulk Material—Kilograms		Period 1	2	3	4	5	6	7
Gross requirements		20	10	20	5	17	8	10
Scheduled receipts								
Projected available balance	5	25	15	35	30	13	5	35
Planned orders								40
Firm planned orders (MPS)		40		40				

Q = 40; SS = 0; lead time = 0; planning fence: period 5.

24 units in period 2 change the plan. The additional sales in period 2 increase net requirements, which leads to planning a shipment in period 3 rather than period 4. Sales in period 3 were lower than expected, so net requirements are less, and the planned shipment in period 5 is changed to period 6. Thus, the gross to net logic results in modifying shipping plans to keep them matched to the current market situation.

One negative aspect of the logic is clear from Figure 10.8's example. Actual sales' deviations around the forecast were reflected in changed shipping plans. These changes could have a destabilizing impact on the master schedule and shop. Two techniques for stabilizing the information flow are firm planned orders and error addback.

Figure 10.9 applies the firm planned order (shipment) concept to the warehouse example. By using firm planned shipments, the record shows the what-if results of maintaining the present order pattern. By using DRP records to display this pattern, we generate standard exception messages. For example, if a present plan violates a stated safety stock objective, exception messages highlight it.

In the Figure 10.9 record for period 3, the firm planned shipment of 40 in period 4 isn't rescheduled to period 3, even though the projected available inventory balance for period 4 is less than the safety stock. Thus, the master scheduler can review the implications of *not* changing before deciding whether changes should be made. In this case, the decision might be to opt for consistency in the information, knowing there still is some projected safety stock and the next order is due to arrive in period 5.

FIGURE 10.8
Records for a Single SKU at One Warehouse over Four Periods

		Period 1	2	3	4	5
Forecast requirements		20	20	20	20	20
In transit		40				
Projected available balance	6	26	6	26	6	26
Planned shipments			40		40	

Actual demand for period 1 = 18.

		Period 2	3	4	5	6
Forecast requirements		20	20	20	20	20
In transit						
Projected available balance	28	8	28	8	28	8
Planned shipments		40		40		

Actual demand for period 2 = 24.

		Period 3	4	5	6	7
Forecast requirements		20	20	20	20	20
In transit		40				
Projected available balance	4	24	44	24	44	24
Planned shipments		40		40		

Actual demand for period 3 = 16.

		Period 4	5	6	7	8
Forecast requirements		20	20	20	20	20
In transit		40				
Projected available balance	28	48	28	8	28	8
Planned shipments				40		

Shipping Q = 40; SS = 6; lead time = 1.

An alternative for stabilizing the information is the error addback method. This approach assumes forecasts are unbiased or accurate on the average. This means any unsold forecast in one period will be made up for in a subsequent period, or any sales exceeding forecast now will reduce sales in a subsequent period. With this method, errors are added (or subtracted) from future requirements to reflect the expected impact of

FIGURE 10.9
Record for a Single SKU at One Warehouse with Firm Planned Order (Shipments) Logic

		Period 1	2	3	4	5
Forecast requirements		20	20	20	20	20
In transit		40				
Projected available balance	6	26	6	26	6	26
Firm planned shipments			40		40	

Actual demand for period 1 = 18.

		Period 2	3	4	5	6
Forecast requirements		20	20	20	20	20
In transit						
Projected available balance	28	8	28	8	28	8
Firm planned shipments		40		40		40

Actual demand for period 2 = 24.

		Period 3	4	5	6	7
Forecast requirements		20	20	20	20	20
In transit		40				
Projected available balance	4	24	4	24	4	24
Firm planned shipments			40		40	

Actual demand for period 3 = 16.

		Period 4	5	6	7	8
Forecast requirements		20	20	20	20	20
In transit						
Projected available balance	28	8	28	8	28	8
Firm planned shipments		40		40		40

Shipping Q = 40; SS = 6; lead time = 1.

actual sales on projected sales. Figure 10.10 applies this concept to the warehouse example. Note the planned shipments are under system control; that is, firm planned orders aren't used.

This example's records show the planned orders in exactly the same periods as in the firm planned shipment case. Adjustments to the forecast requirements ensure stability in

FIGURE 10.10
Record for a Single SKU at One Warehouse with Error Addback

		Period 1	2	3	4	5
Forecast requirements		20	20	20	20	20
In transit		40				
Projected available balance	6	26	6	26	6	26
Planned shipments			40		40	

Period 1 demand = 18; cumulative error = +2.

		Period 2	3	4	5	6
Forecast requirements		22	20	20	20	20
In transit						
Projected available balance	28	6	26	6	26	6
Planned shipments		40		40		

Period 2 demand = 24; cumulative error = −2.

		Period 3	4	5	6	7
Forecast requirements		18	20	20	20	20
In transit		40				
Projected available balance	4	26	6	26	6	26
Planned shipments			40		40	

Period 3 demand = 16; cumulative error = +2.

		Period 4	5	6	7	8
Forecast requirements		22	20	20	20	20
In transit						
Projected available balance	28	6	26	6	26	6
Planned shipments		40		40		

Period 4 demand = 15; cumulative error = +7.
Shipping Q = 40; SS = 6; lead time = 1.

the information. It's apparent this technique's effectiveness diminishes if the forecast isn't unbiased. For example, if the reduced demand in periods 3 and 4 is part of a continuing trend, the procedure will break down. DRP will continue to build inventory as though the reduced demand will be made up in the future. This means forecasts must be carefully monitored and changed when necessary so the procedure can be started again. One convenient measure for evaluating forecast accuracy is the cumulative forecast error. If this exceeds a specified quantity, the item forecast should be reviewed. For example, in period 4, cumulative error has reached a +7 (a value exceeding the safety stock); this might indicate the need to review the forecast for this item.

Safety Stock in DRP

Distribution requirements planning provides the means for carrying inventories and safety stocks at any location in the system. In the examples of Figures 10.3 through 10.5, we show safety stock in field locations and at the central facility. It is important to understand, however, that safety stock is less needed as errors in the forecast are washed out more frequently. With replenishments performed weekly or more often, safety stocks can be reduced.

With DRP, it's possible to use safety lead time as well. In those circumstances where the uncertainty is more likely to be in terms of timing (as in delivering product to the field), it may be better to use safety lead time. In the case of uncertainty in quantity (as with variable yields in manufacturing), safety stock is more typically used.

Where and how much safety stock (or safety lead time) to carry is still an open issue. Research and company experience are just now beginning to provide answers. In terms of quantity, the theory of relating safety stock to the uncertainty in our demand forecasts is clearly valid. The choice would be made on the basis of trade-offs between customer service levels and inventory required.

On the other hand, in distribution, we're not concerned just about how much uncertainty there is but where it is. Less is known about where to put safety stocks. One principle is to carry safety stocks where there's uncertainty. This implies the location closest to the customer and, perhaps, to intermediate points, where there's some element of independent demand. The argument would imply no safety stock where there's dependent demand.

If the uncertainty from several field locations could be aggregated, it should require less safety stock than having stock at each field location. This argument has led to the concept of a "national level" safety stock. The idea is to have some central stock that can be sent to field locations as conditions warrant, or to permit transshipments between field warehouses. This added flexibility should provide higher levels of service than maintaining multiple field safety stocks. The issue is clouded, however, by the fact that stock in the central facility isn't where customers are.

A typical plot of service level versus the portion of inventory sent immediately to customers is shown in Figure 10.11. Service levels improve as the percentage of inventory immediately sent to customers increases to about 90 percent. Second, the decrease in service level from sending 100 percent immediately is very small. The practical implication is clear. If you must have inventory available when and where your customers need it, you should hold very little, if any, back in the distribution system.

Management Issues with DRP

With an operational DRP system integrated with other MPC systems, management has the ability to rationalize material flows from purchasing through distribution. Achieving this desired state, however, raises several critical management questions. We've already

FIGURE 10.11
Fill Rate as a Function of Percent of Distribution Inventory Sent Immediately to Customers

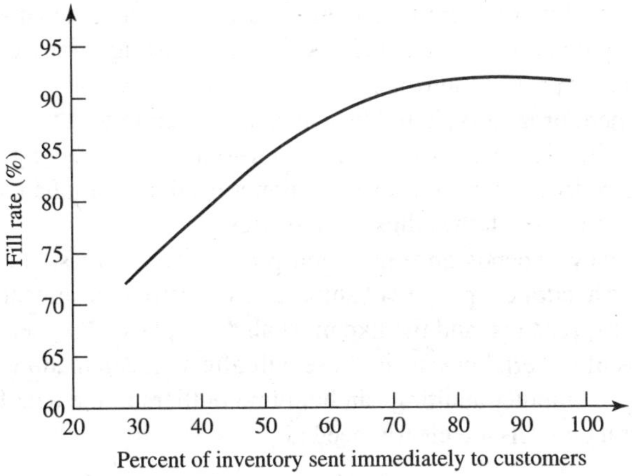

discussed some of the DRP issues, such as planning parameters, safety stock, stability, and the form of the master scheduling interface. More fundamental issues relate to assuring the system has appropriate data entry procedures, has an organizational setup facilitating an integrated MPC approach, and uses DRP to solve specific distribution problems. We now turn to each of these managerial topics.

Data Integrity and Completeness

Let's start by considering the record for an item at a location as close to the customer as possible. We've called this location the field warehouse, but it could be at a distribution center, at the customer location itself, or even at the central facility. The issue concerns *where* the forecast is to be input. Because this is the source of demand data for planning throughout the system, it must be correctly determined and maintained. For this record, there are two key data items on which all plans are based: forecast requirements and inventory balance (including any in transit). The axiom of garbage-in, garbage-out holds in DRP as elsewhere. To have confidence in the forecast data, we must assign responsibility for both forecast preparation and adjustments.

A key issue in forecast data integrity for DRP systems is use of aggregate forecasts, which are thereafter broken down into detailed forecasts. An example is a pharmaceutical firm that forecasts annual U.S. insulin sales in total ounces, based on the number of diabetics in the country. This total is multiplied by the company market share, which is in turn broken down into package sizes, weeks, and locations as the basis for field forecasts. As the total is broken down, relative errors increase, but the MPS is based on the totals as brought through the DRP system. This is the summation of the detailed forecasts, after field modifications, so the errors should tend to cancel out.

It's imperative, however, that adjustments of the detailed forecasts don't result in a systematic bias that doesn't balance out. DRP systems are designed to respond to forecast *errors,* but forecast bias is a problem we must avoid.

Once the basic forecast has been generated, people in the field can be given some authority to modify it according to local information and needs. This should be constrained by some rule, like "plus or minus 20 percent adjustment" or "only the timing can be changed but the monthly totals must remain the same." Some mechanism must be put in place for picking up this kind of local intelligence for adjusting forecasts, but it's important to define the limits for proper control.

Also, management programs should be established to monitor this process. Monitoring is more complex when records for items are at customer locations (e.g., a large hospital). In all cases, standard forecast monitoring techniques need to be applied, particularly to discover bias introduced through the adjustment process.

Inventory accuracy depends on transaction processing routines and discipline. Procedures for quick and accurate reporting of shipments to customers, allocations to customers, returns, adjustments, receipts, and the like must all be in place. Another source of errors is incorrect balances of material in transit; these will affect all calculations in the subsequent record processing. Computer auditing can help find outliers in the data for all these cases, but tight procedural controls are clearly needed.

Organizational Support

Figure 10.12 shows conflicting functional objectives and their impact on inventory, customer service, and total costs. This figure illustrates some inherent conflicts that need resolution in an integrated MPC system. These conflicts are particularly real when DRP is part of the overall MPC system. In many firms, minimization of transportation costs, for example, is a transportation department's objective. The resultant impact on other parts of the organization is often not clearly understood.

In a comprehensive MPC system with DRP, linkages across functional boundaries are encouraged; but organizational support and evaluation measures need to be established that will minimize suboptimization of overall enterprise goals. Many firms have implemented a **materials management** form of organization to help align responsibilities to the material flow needs. Materials management organizations are responsible for all aspects of materials, from purchasing to final distribution to the customers. Their responsibilities include determining what to make and when, when to take delivery of raw materials, how much to allocate to field locations, and how to relieve short-term materials problems.

As firms improve MPC systems either through more comprehensive approaches (e.g., DRP) or through such enhancements as JIT, emphasis shifts from material control to material velocity. Basic discipline and data integrity aren't abandoned—they're assumed. Time

FIGURE 10.12
Conflicting Functional Objectives

Functional objectives	Impact of objectives on...		
	Inventory	Customer service	Total costs
• High customer service	↑	↑	↑
• Low transportation costs	↑	↓	↓
• Low warehousing costs	↓	↓	↓
• Reduce inventories	↓	↓	↓
• Fast deliveries	↑	↑	↑
• Reduced labor costs	↑	↓	↓

FIGURE 10.13 **Supply Chain Management**

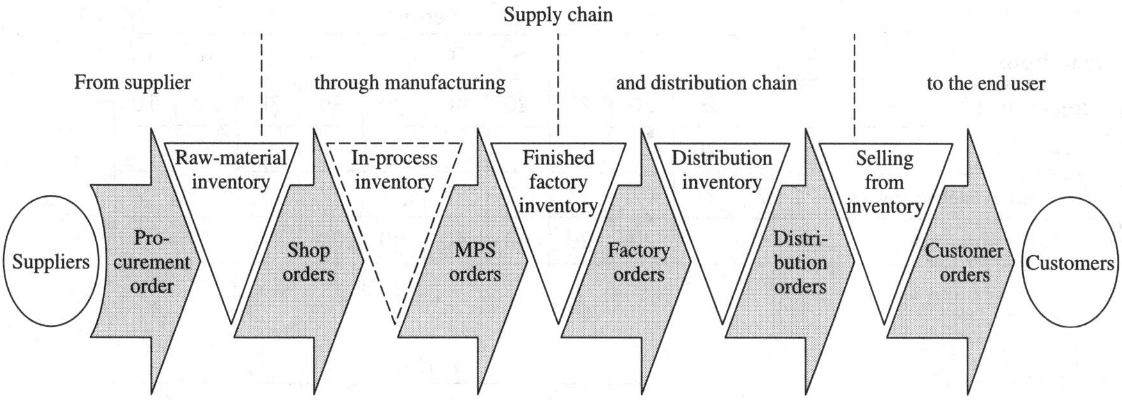

and responsiveness become the most important objectives. Implied is a need to reduce the organizational fragmentation that has built-in time delays. New organizational structures will increasingly be required, ones with overarching authority to dictate actions that provide rapid response to customer needs.

Figure 10.13 illustrates where DRP fits within the supply chain management concept, showing the many organizational entities that need to be coordinated. The ideas parallel those of materials management, but they focus on the process of building the products. Coordinating the chain in Figure 10.13 requires integrated information in DRP form and an organizational form, such as materials management.

Key to implementing an MPC system with DRP, regardless of the organizational form, is developing planners. The titles can vary in different organizations. Planners establish firm planned orders, evaluate alternative means to solve short-term problems, coordinate problems that cross functional boundaries, and help evaluate trends. They are also responsible for checking feasibility of changes, monitoring data integrity, and assessing the impact of new situations.

Problem Solving

We have already discussed changing conditions due to uncertainty in demand and the techniques that help to deal with them. Other problems come from changing market conditions, product lines, or marketing plans. Examples are product substitutions, promotions, changes in warehouse locations or customer assignments, and controlling the age of stock. DRP records help us solve these problems. We'll describe three of these as illustrative: a sales promotion, closing a warehouse, and monitoring stock aging.

Figure 10.14 presents a sales promotion served by a warehouse. For simplicity, we consider only one product at a single warehouse and the product's packaging line. The process starts with modifying the demand forecast at the warehouse. In the example, the promotion is planned for weeks 5 through 8. The impact is estimated to double sales (from 20 to 40) during the first two weeks and to have a reduced impact during the next two weeks. Note the promotion "steals" from demand in weeks 9 and 10.

FIGURE 10.14 **A Sales Promotion**

Warehouse		Period 1	2	3	4	5	6	7	8	9	10
Forecast requirements		20	20	20	20	40	40	30	30	10	10
In transit		20									
Projected available balance	27	27	7	7	7	7	7	17	7	17	7
Planned shipments			20	20	40	40	40	20	20		

Q = 20; lead time = 1; SS = 5.

Packaging		Period 1	2	3	4	5	6	7	8	9	10
Gross requirements		0	20	20	40	40	40	20	20		
Scheduled receipts											
Projected available balance	0	0	12	24	16	8	0	0	0		
Planned order release							20	20			
Firm planned orders		32	32	32	32	32					

Q = lot-for-lot; lead time = 1; SS = 0; planning fence: .3.
Note: Packaging capacity = 35 units/period.

The safety stock has been left at five units for the promotion period, although it might have been increased. Stock for the sales promotion is planned for delivery in the weeks in which needed, although it also might have been planned for earlier delivery if there were a need to set up some special display area. The shipping quantity is in multiples of 20, representing a shipping carton or pallet load. Planned shipments are exploded to the packaging record. Using the firm planned orders, the planner has scheduled product packaging at a constant rate of output for the next five weeks (just under the capacity of the packaging line), building inventory in anticipation of the promotion.

The anticipation inventories are shown as remaining at the packaging facility, but they might be sent to the field if space is available or if a truck is on its way with available cargo space. The pattern of inventory buildup could be different, depending on the trade-off between level production and varying the production levels. The DRP records facilitate both planning the buildup and analyzing alternative ways to meet the need (or even arguing for a postponement if capacity is a problem).

Our second example deals with a warehouse closure. Firms often change distribution systems, so closing warehouses and changing shipping patterns are ongoing activities. In Figure 10.15, warehouse 1 is scheduled to close at the end of four weeks, and warehouse 2 is to start supplying the customers. Again, the process of managing the cutover starts with the forecasts. The requirements at warehouse 1 stop at the end of week 4 and are picked up by warehouse 2, reflecting the timing and quantities of the closedown and transfer.

FIGURE 10.15
Warehouse Closure

Warehouse 1		Period 1	2	3	4	5	6	7
Forecast requirements		30	30	30	30	0	0	0
In transit		60						
Projected available balance	43	73	43	13	60	60	60	60
Planned shipments				60				
Firm planned shipments				17				

Q = 60; lead time = 1; SS = 10.

Warehouse 2		Period 1	2	3	4	5	6	7
Forecast requirements		100	100	100	100	130	130	130
In transit								
Projected available balance	207	107	207	107	207	77	147	217
Planned shipments						200	200	
Firm planned shipments		200		200				

Q = 200; lead time = 1; SS = 20.

In the example, warehouse 1 would normally have had a planned shipment for 60 units in week 3. The planner has overridden the planned order with a firm planned order for the exact need, reducing safety stock to zero. Note the system plans an order to restore the safety stock and, eventually, the planner will need to change the safety stock parameter to zero in order not to send the wrong signal to the master production scheduler.

As time goes on, the actual quantity needed for warehouse 1 may well be different, but there are two weeks before the exact determination must be made. The planner may decide to send even less to warehouse 1 because it might be easier to pick up some unsatisfied demand from warehouse 2 than to deal with the remnant inventories at warehouse 1. The point is DRP systems provide visibility for solving these problems. Even though the exact quantity to be sent to warehouse 1 won't be determined until week 3, the amount produced and made available to send to either warehouse will be correct, since planned shipments from both are exploded to the requirements at the central facility. The main questions are how to divide the available stock between the two facilities and how to manage the transition.

Our final example deals with controlling inventory of products whose shelf life is a concern. Certainly one aspect of this problem is to use strict first-in/first-out physical movement and to make this part of the training for warehouse personnel. The second way to deal effectively with shelf life problems is to identify those products that may be headed for a problem before it's too late. One way to do this is to use the DRP records and build in exception messages to flag potential shelf life problems.

If, for example, demand for a product at a location is dropping for some reason, the forecast should be reduced. This means any available inventory or in transit stock will cover a longer time period; as a result, the first planned shipment will be several periods in the future. This condition can be detected, calling for a review of the particular product's shelf life at this location. Perhaps it should be immediately shipped to another warehouse. This feature is incorporated in the actual system, to which we now turn our attention.

Concluding Principles

This chapter has presented a technique for bridging between successive stages in the supply chain. Some of these can be internal, such as factories to distribution centers, but the technique can also be used to make linkages across firms. The technique, distribution requirements planning (DRP), relates current field inventory availability (in distribution centers, warehouses, and customer locations), forecasts, and knowledge of demand to develop resupply plans and bring those to the master production scheduling and material planning modules of the MPC system. Moreover, DRP utilizes record formats and processing logic consistent with MRP. To effectively use DRP, we apply the following general principles:

- The top-level records for a DRP system should cover items in a location as close to the customer as possible (or even at the customer, if feasible).
- Local information on demand patterns should be incorporated into the DRP record at a warehouse and/or the customers' MPC system data should be used at a customer location.
- Data and performance measurement systems should be put in place to monitor forecast adjustments in the field.
- Matching supply to demand requires close control of supply as well as data on demand.
- Projections of future requirements should be used to decide inventory allocation in periods of short supply.
- Transparent records and consistent processing logic should be used to integrate the system.
- What-if analysis should be based on integrated records of the system.
- Uncertainty filters, like firm planned orders or error addback, should be available to the master production scheduler.
- The organization form should be consistent with the supply chain being managed.

Discussion Questions

1. What is meant by the statement, "The real task of managing materials is matching supply to demand"?
2. Describe how DRP helps bridge the gap between the market and the factory.
3. What are some of the benefits a warehouse manager derives from improved resupply information?
4. Discuss the risks and benefits of local warehouse personnel modifying forecast data for field warehouses.

5. A consumer goods manufacturer uses a periodic review system to manage field inventories. This means, once a period, field inventory clerks check to see if inventory is below reorder point; if so they order an amount equal to the EOQ. The materials manager argues this is the same as using TPOP records. What's your opinion?
6. How can you monitor forecast data modifications by field personnel to ensure changes result in improvements over original computer forecasts?
7. What are the differences between the planned shipments, as indicated in Figure 10.3 and planned orders from MRP records?
8. How are the supply chain management concept and materials management similar? How do they differ?

Problems

1. Bob Stahl, the distribution manager at Forbes Industries, is considering using error addback for his DRP system. To evaluate its use, he compiled data for three periods on a sample product, the Scarlet Tiara. The initial DRP record is given here:

		Period 1	2	3	4	5
Forecast requirements		30	30	30	30	30
In transit		60				
Projected available balance	10	40	10	40	10	40
Planned shipments			60		60	

Q = 60; lead time = 1; SS = 10.

a. Develop the DRP records above for periods two through four given demands of 24, 38, and 27 in periods one, two, and three.
b. Complete the same records using the error addback method. What differences occur?

2. For the warehouse of Figure 10.8, suppose actual demands were 24, 16, and 18 in periods 1, 2, and 3, respectively. The initial DRP record is:

		Period 1	2	3	4	5
Forecast requirements		20	20	20	20	20
In transit		40				
Projected available balance	6	26	6	26	6	26
Planned shipments			40		40	

Q = 40; lead time = 1; SS = 6.

a. Create the other three DRP records as done in Figure 10.8. What problem is created in period 2? What can be done?
b. Does error addback work for this set of circumstances?

3. The Hazy Company maintains a West Coast distribution center (DC), which is supplied from the plant warehouse in the Midwest. It takes exactly one week to ship to the distribution center from the Midwest. One of its products has an ordering cost of $10 per order, inventory carrying cost of $1 per unit per week, and average weekly demand at the DC of five units (although it has fluctuated uniformly between 0 and 10 units per week in actuality). Over the years, the product's safety stock level has varied. There are currently (early Monday morning) nine units in inventory at the DC. The company is willing to risk a probability of stocking out of 0.10 in any order cycle.
   a. If the company uses an economic order quantity, reorder point system, what should the order quantity and reorder point be?
   b. If the company adapted DRP logic to this DC supply situation and decided to ship only on Mondays (to consolidate shipments), what would you suggest for the planned shipping pattern over the next 10 weeks? (Use a safety stock level of two units.)
   c. If actual demand for the upcoming week were six units, what would the new shipping pattern be? (Assume any planned shipments in the current week are released.)
4. The Tasmanian Tire Company's distribution manager has supplied the following information pertaining to its product, the Super Taz Tire, which is stocked at the firm's field warehouse:

   Average weekly demand = 35 units.

   Current on-hand balance = 10 units.

   In-transit order (due next week) = 70 units.

   Economic shipping quantity = 70 units.

   Shipping time = 1 week.

   Safety stock = 0 units.

   Complete the record for the field warehouse indicating the planned shipment schedule for the next eight weeks:

		Period							
		1	2	3	4	5	6	7	8
Forecast requirements									
In transit									
Projected available balance									
Planned shipments									

5. The XYZ Company's finance manager is currently studying projected inventory investment for product 101 at the central (plant) warehouse. Quantities of product 101 are shipped from the central warehouse to warehouses A and B, based on individual warehouse requirements. The product costs $100 per unit.

   Using DRP parameters and inventory information for product 101 in Exhibit A, determine the planned order releases at the central warehouse. Construct a graph indicating projected inventory investment at warehouse A for this product at the beginning and end of each week over the next six-week period. Assume this product's demand is equally divided among the days of each week.

EXHIBIT A
Product 101

Product 101 Warehouse A		Week 1	2	3	4	5	6
Forecast requirements		20	20	20	20	20	20
In transit		15					
Projected available balance	10						
Planned shipments							

Q = 40; LT = 1; SS = 0.

Product 101 Warehouse B		Week 1	2	3	4	5	6
Forecast requirements		10	10	10	10	10	10
In transit							
Projected available balance	15						
Planned shipments							

Q = 20; LT = 1; SS = 0.

Product 101 Central Warehouse		Week 1	2	3	4	5	6
Gross requirements							
Scheduled receipts							
Projected available balance	60						
Planned order release							

Q = lot-for-lot; LT = 1; SS = 0.

6. The distribution of Blues Brothers' Sunglasses is from the plant in Joliet to two warehouses and then to the customers. The distribution pattern is as follows:

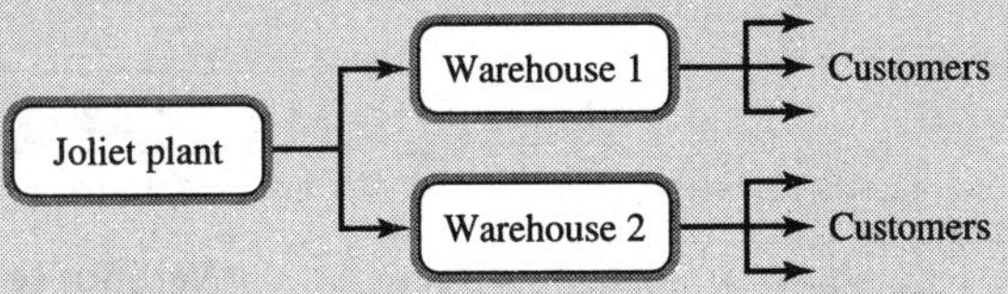

For the purpose of analysis, assume that each warehouse will sell exactly 40 cases of Blues Brothers' Sunglasses per week. Inventory carried either at the plant or at the warehouse locations costs 25 cents per week per case (based on Friday night inventory). The ordering cost is $15 per order at each facility, and it takes exactly one week to transport the product from the plant to either of the two warehouses or to produce the product. The beginning inventory at each warehouse is 40 units, and the beginning inventory at the Joliet plant is 140 units. No safety stock is planned at any location.

a. On the basis of a record of seven weeks, determine the inventory carrying cost plus setup cost per week at Joliet plus both warehouses managing the system with EOQ at all locations.

b. Determine the total inventory carrying cost and setup cost per week, using DRP to manage the system based on the same seven-week record.

7. The MVA Pet Food Company distributes one of its products, Gro-Pup, through warehouses in Seattle and Portland. A central warehouse at the St. Louis plant distributes Gro-Pup to these two warehouses in serving the Northwest regional market.

a. Develop a distribution schedule for the two warehouses and a production schedule for the plant for the next eight-week period, using the DRP worksheet in Exhibit B (page 385). (Note the sales forecast for this product is 20 units per week at the Seattle warehouse, and 43 units of the product are currently on hand. The shipment order quantity is 60 units, planned shipment lead time is one week, and there's no safety stock requirement. Similar information is included in Exhibit B for the other two facilities.) The product is packed in lots of 50 units at St. Louis. The packaging process takes two weeks.

b. Each Gro-Pup package requires one unit of packaging material. Develop a purchasing schedule for the packaging material assuming:

1. There are currently 25 units on hand.
2. An open order for 100 units is due to be received from the vendor next week.
3. The purchase order quantity equals 100 units.
4. Purchasing lead time is four weeks.

c. Update all four records as of the start of week 2, assuming the following transactions occurred during week 1:

	Receipts	Order Releases	Sales (Disbursements)	Inventory Adjustment	Open Order Scrap
Gro-Pup/Seattle	0	0	19	−3	0
Gro-Pup/Portland	15	15	20	+3	0
Gro-Pup/Plant	0	50	15	0	0
Gro-Pup/Packaging	90	100	50	+4	10

8. The Drip Producers are planning a promotion of one of its products, the Dead Drop. Dead Drops are distributed through only one of the warehouses. The promotion is to begin in period 4 and run through period 6. The sales forecast is normally 30 per period, but during the promotion the company expects sales to be 60 per period. This is shown here with other data.

	Period					
	1	2	3	4	5	6
Sales forecast	30	30	30	60	60	60

	Warehouse	Central
Ship/ord. quantity	40 units	Lot-for-lot
Current inventory	12 units	0 units
Lead time	1 period	1 period
Safety stock	10 units	0 units
Sched. rec./ship.	40 units in period 1	40 units in period 1

a. Develop the warehouse and central facility's records.

b. Suppose the central facility's capacity was limited to 50 units per period. How would you provide the material for the promotion in the field?

EXHIBIT B
Distribution Requirements Planning Worksheet

Gro-Pup Seattle Warehouse		Week 1	2	3	4	5	6	7	8
Forecast requirements		20	20	20	20	20	20	20	20
In transit									
Projected available balance	43								
Planned shipments									

Q = 60; LT = 1; SS = 0.

Gro-Pup Portland Warehouse		Week 1	2	3	4	5	6	7	8
Forecast requirements		10	10	10	10	10	10	10	10
In transit		15							
Projected available balance	2								
Planned shipments									

Q = 15; LT = 1; SS = 0.

Gro-Pup Plant Warehouse		Week 1	2	3	4	5	6	7	8
Gross requirements									
Scheduled receipts			50						
Projected available balance	30								
Planned order release									

Q = 50; LT = 2; SS = 0.

Gro-Pup Packaging Material		Week 1	2	3	4	5	6	7	8
Gross requirements									
Scheduled receipts		100							
Projected available balance	25								
Planned order release									

Q = 100; LT = 4; SS = 0.

9. Develop the records for the Cranstable Company's two warehouses and one central facility system using the following data. What happens if the central order quantity changes to 200?

	Warehouse 1	Warehouse 2	Central
Forecast requirements	20/period	30/period	
Ship/ord. quantity	48 units	60 units	100 units
Current inventory	23 units	12 units	0 units
Lead time	1 period	1 period	1 period
Safety stock	10 units	10 units	0 units
Sched. rec./ship.	48 units in period 1	60 units in period 1	None

10. The Cranstable Company was just getting into the swing of DRP when old Barnstable moved away from warehouse 1's region, never to be seen again by anyone at the company. (Barnstable's demand was lost to a competitor.) Now this wouldn't normally cause problems, but for Cranstable it meant sales were halved at warehouse 1. Using problem 9's data, what's the impact of Barnstable's departure?
11. The Cranky Tea Company performs sales forecasting on a national basis. Each month it prepares a sales forecast of monthly sales for the coming year for each of the firm's end products. At each of the firm's three distribution warehouses, distribution requirements planning records are maintained for the individual products. The national sales forecast for Constant Torment, the company's best selling product, is 4,000 units per four-week period. The sales of this product at each of the three warehouses are split as follows: 40 percent from warehouse A, 35 percent from warehouse B, and 25 percent from warehouse C. An analysis of the sales history of Constant Torment at warehouse C indicates weekly sales of this product are distributed as follows: 10 percent in week 1, 25 percent in week 2, 45 percent in week 3, and 20 percent in week 4 in a monthly period. Complete the following DRP record for Constant Torment at Warehouse C.

		Month 1				Month 2			
		Week				Week			
Constant Torment / Warehouse C		1	2	3	4	1	2	3	4
Forecast requirements									
In transit			260	445					
Projected available balance	105								
Planned shipments									

Q = LFL; SS = 0; LT = 3 weeks.

12. The Excello Corporation's distribution planner is concerned about the variability of transit times between the plant in Madison, Indiana, and the firm's distribution center in Atlanta. It's been decided to incorporate a one-week safety lead time into the DRP records for items stocked in the Atlanta distribution center. Complete the record for product X in the Atlanta distribution center.

    Forecast: 200 units per week.

    In transit: 410 units scheduled for receipt in week 1.

On-hand inventory: 15 units.
Order quantity: 600 units.
Lead time: 1 week.
Safety stock = 0.
Safety lead time = 1 week.

Product X		Week 1	2	3	4	5	6	7	8
Forecast requirements									
In transit									
Projected available balance									
Planned shipments									

13. The Allied Product Company's sales director has decided to close the firm's San Diego warehouse and open a new warehouse in Los Angeles. The San Diego warehouse is scheduled to close the end of week 4; the new warehouse in Los Angeles is scheduled to open for business at the start of week 5. Product B is currently stocked in the San Diego warehouse and will be stocked in the new Los Angeles warehouse. Sales forecast for product B is 100 units per week. Complete the following DRP records for product B, reflecting the change in the company's warehousing plans for the item and the implications for the plant.

Product B/San Diego Warehouse		Week 1	2	3	4	5	6	7	8
Forecast requirements									
In transit									
Projected available balance	205								
Planned shipments									

Q = LFL; SS = 10 units; LT = 2 weeks.

Product B/Los Angeles Warehouse		Week 1	2	3	4	5	6	7	8
Forecast requirements									
In transit									
Projected available balance									
Planned shipments									

Q = LFL; SS = 10 units; LT = 1 week.

Product B/Plant		Week 1	2	3	4	5	6	7	8
Gross requirements									
Scheduled receipts									
Projected available balance	300								
Planned order release									

Q = 200 units; SS = 15 units; LT = 3 weeks.

14. The Stasik Pharmaceutical Company's distribution planning manager is concerned about the rising cost of outdated inventory in the firm's distribution warehouses. Shelf life for the company's products shouldn't exceed four weeks. Government regulations require products in stock longer than four weeks to be scrapped. Devise an exception notice test that can be applied to the DRP records in the firm's distribution warehouses to direct the inventory planner's attention to items where excess inventory may exist. Apply this procedure to the following record to determine whether out-of-date inventory is likely to occur for product W.

Product W		Week 1	2	3	4	5	6	7	8
Forecast requirements		300	300	300	300	300	300	300	300
In transit			900						
Projected available balance	350	50	650	350	950	650	1250	950	1550
Firm planned orders			900		900		900		
Planned shipments									

Q = 900; SS = 50 units; LT = 2 weeks.

15. Product D is stocked only at the AMC Chemical Company's Dallas warehouse and at the company's plant warehouse in Akron. The sales director has forecast product sales from the Dallas warehouse to be 40 units per week. Product D is manufactured at the firm's Akron plant using 2 units of ingredient X per unit of product D.

    a. Complete the DRP records for product D at the Dallas warehouse and the plant warehouse as well as the MRP record for ingredient X using the following information. (Assume ingredient X is only used in product D.)

Product D/Dallas Warehouse		Week 1	2	3	4	5	6	7	8
Forecast requirements									
In transit									
Projected available balance	85								
Planned shipments									

Q = LFL; SS = 5 units; LT = 2 weeks.

Product D/Plant Warehouse		Week 1	2	3	4	5	6	7	8
Gross requirements									
Scheduled receipts		46							
Projected available balance	2								
Planned order release									

Q = LFL; SS = 8 units; LT = 1 week.

Ingredient X		Week 1	2	3	4	5	6	7	8
Gross requirements									
Scheduled receipts		320							
Projected available balance	4								
Planned order release									

Q = 320 units; SS = 2 units; LT = 4 weeks.

b. Actual sales for product D at the Dallas warehouse in week 1 were 48 units and all planned shipments/orders were released. Prepare DRP and MRP records as of the beginning of week 2. What actions should the master production scheduler take on the basis of this information?

Product D/Dallas Warehouse		Week 2	3	4	5	6	7	8	9
Forecast requirements									
In transit									
Projected available balance									
Planned shipments									

Q = LFL; SS = 5 units; LT = 2 weeks.

Product D/Plant Warehouse		Week 2	3	4	5	6	7	8	9
Gross requirements									
Scheduled receipts									
Projected available balance									
Planned order release									

Q = LFL; SS = 2 units; LT = 2 weeks.

Ingredient X		Week 2	3	4	5	6	7	8	9
Gross requirements									
Scheduled receipts									
Projected available balance									
Planned order release									

Q = 320 units; SS = 2 units; LT = 4 weeks.

c. Suppose product D's actual sales at the Dallas warehouse in week 2 were 31 units. Again, all planned shipments/orders were released and expedite actions taken. What action would the master scheduler take on the basis of this information? In this situation, what modifications to the master production schedule might be taken?

Product D/Dallas Warehouse		Week 3	4	5	6	7	8	9	10
Forecast requirements									
In transit									
Projected available balance	85								
Planned shipments									

Q = LFL; SS = 5 units; LT = 2 weeks.

Product D/Plant Warehouse		Week 3	4	5	6	7	8	9	10
Gross requirements									
Scheduled receipts									
Projected available balance	42								
Planned order release									

Q = LFL; SS = 2 units; LT = 2 weeks.

Ingredient X		Week 3	4	5	6	7	8	9	10
Gross requirements									
Scheduled receipts									
Projected available balance	4								
Planned order release									

Q = 320 units; SS = 2 units; LT = 4 weeks.

Case Abbott Laboratories

Abbott Laboratories, Ltd., of Canada produces health care products. Three lines (pharmaceuticals, hospital products, and infant nutrition products) are produced in three plants. About 750 end items are distributed through DCs (distribution centers) throughout Canada.

Abbott Laboratories uses DRP to manage field inventories. Detailed forecast data are entered into warehouse DRP records. These records are represented as the zero level of the bill of materials (BOM). Figure 10.16 illustrates these records for two locations: Vancouver and Montreal. Forecast data are entered as the requirements rows. The first 20 weeks are displayed in weekly time periods (buckets). Thereafter, monthly buckets are used for a total planning horizon of two years.

In the Montreal record, an entry of 120 in the week of 8/7 appears in a row labeled "Customer orders." This row allows the inclusion of specific advance order information. The information is not added to the gross requirements, however. It's there for detailed planning of shipments and to recognize advanced special orders.

Lead time in the Vancouver record is 35 days (five weeks) including safety lead time. DRP time-phased records are produced using these parameters. For example, projected on-hand balance at the end of week 9/4 for Vancouver is insufficient to meet the gross requirements of 9/11. The result is a planned order for a quantity of 24, five weeks earlier in the week of 8/7.

Figure 10.17 shows the DRP records for the central warehouse and for the bulk item used to make the end-item product B. Gross requirements for central are based on planned orders from all the DCs. For example, in the week of 8/7, the gross requirement of 1,908 consists of 24 from Vancouver, 1,872 from Montreal, and 12 from some other DC.

The batch size shown for the central warehouse in Figure 10.17 is 7,619—the number of product B units yielded from a batch of 4,000 in the unit of measure for the bulk product; that is, the 7,619 shown as a firm planned order in 9/11 becomes a gross requirement of 4,000 for bulk in that week.

The master production scheduler works with the DRP record for central. This person's job is to convert planned orders into firm planned orders and to manage timing of the firm planned orders. For example, all orders at central are firm planned in Figure 10.17 until 12/31 in the last row. The last three orders (12/31, 2/25, and 4/21) are only planned orders. DRP logic can replan these as needed. Only the master production scheduler can move the firm planned orders that appear early in the record. The result is a stable MPS for the bulk production.

Figure 10.18 illustrates the information available for actual shipment planning. The requirements due to be shipped this week or in the next two weeks (also any past-due shipments) are summarized by distribution center and product type. This enables the planner to look at the current requirements or future planned shipments in making up carloads destined for a distribution center. Since the information is available in terms of cube, weight, and pallet load, the planner can use the most limited resource in making a shipment decision. This flexibility enables planners to efficiently use transportation resources to meet product needs.

The application of DRP at Abbott Laboratories resulted in benefits in many areas of the company. The product obsolescence costs were reduced, inventory turnover improved, and customer service increased. The logistics information also led to reductions in transportation and warehouse costs.

Assignment

1. What type(s) of visibility does the DRP application provide Abbott supply chain planners?
2. How might this information be useful to Abbott's customers?
3. What would be the impact of reducing the Vancouver lead time from 35 days down to 10 days?

FIGURE 10.16 **Abbott DRP Records for Vancouver and Montreal**

Description	Size	um	Std Bactr	FC	BY	PL	IT	C	Scrap	Total Landed Costs	OP	Life	O-LT	P-LT	O-LT	QA-LT	T-LT	On Hand	OA Inventory	Allocated	Safety Stock
Product-B	200	BL	1872	A2		08		C	1.0			1095	14		0	0	14	2520.0	0.0	0.0	0.0

21-MONTREAL

	Past Due	7/24	7/31	08/07	08/14	08/21	08/28	09/04	09/11	09/18	09/25	10/02	10/09	10/16
CUSTOMER ORDERS				120										
GROSS REQUIREMENTS		601	601	601	601	576	556	556	556	578	633	633	633	633
SCHEDULED RECEIPTS														
ON HAND	2520	1919	1318	717	116	1412	856	300	1616	1038	405	1644	1011	378
FIRM PLANNED ORDERS														
PLANNED ORDERS				1872			1872			1872			1872	

MONTHLY

	10/23	10/30	11/06	11/13	11/20	11/27	12/04	01/01	01/29	02/26	03/26	04/23	05/21	06/18
CUSTOMER ORDERS														
GROSS REQUIREMENTS	777	801	801	801	633	507	2100	2386	2744	2167	2356	2404	2479	2212
SCHEDULED RECEIPTS														
ON HAND	1473	672	1743	942	309	1674	1446	932	60	1637	1153	621	14	1546
FIRM PLANNED ORDERS														
PLANNED ORDERS	1872			1872			1872	3744	1872	1872	3744	1872	1872	1872

	07/16	08/13	09/10	10/08	11/05	12/03	12/31	01/28	02/25	03/24	04/21	05/19	06/16	TOTAL
CUSTOMER ORDERS														
GROSS REQUIREMENTS	2418	2289	2400	2844	2742	2100	2323	2480	2285	2356	2280	2348	2944	62735
SCHEDULED RECEIPTS														
ON HAND	1000	583	55	955	85	1729	1278	670	257	1645	1237	761	1561	
FIRM PLANNED ORDERS														
PLANNED ORDERS	3744	1872	1872	3744	1872	1872	1872	3744	1872	1872	1872	3744	1872	61776

NOTES & COMMENTS

(continued)

FIGURE 10.16 ***(Continued)***

Description	Size	um	Std Bactr	FC	BY	PL	IT	C	Scrap	Total Landed Costs	OP	Life	O-LT	P-LT	O-LT	QA-LT	T-LT	On Hand	OA Inventory	Allocated	Safety Stock
Product-B	200		24			08	F	C	1.00	0.000		1095	35		0	0	35	36.0	0.0	0.0	0.0

03-VANCOUVER

	Past Due	7/24	7/31	08/07	08/14	08/21	08/28	09/04	09/11	09/18	09/25	10/02	10/09	10/16
CUSTOMER ORDERS														
GROSS REQUIREMENTS		5	5	5	5	5	5	5	5	5	5	5	5	5
SCHEDULED RECEIPTS														
ON HAND	36	31	26	21	16	11	6	1	20	15	10	5	24	19
FIRM PLANNED ORDERS														
PLANNED ORDERS				24				24				24		

MONTHLY

	10/23	10/30	11/06	11/13	11/20	11/27	12/04	01/01	01/29	02/26	03/26	04/23	05/21	06/18
CUSTOMER ORDERS														
GROSS REQUIREMENTS	7	7	7	7	5	4	17	21	23	20	20	20	20	20
SCHEDULED RECEIPTS														
ON HAND	12	5	22	15	10	6	13	16	17	21	1	5	9	13
FIRM PLANNED ORDERS														
PLANNED ORDERS			24				24	24	24	24		24	24	24

	07/16	08/13	09/10	10/08	11/05	12/03	12/31	01/28	02/25	03/24	04/21	05/19	06/16	TOTAL
CUSTOMER ORDERS														
GROSS REQUIREMENTS	20	20	20	24	23	17	20	20	20	20	20	20	26	533
SCHEDULED RECEIPTS														
ON HAND	17	21	1	1	2	9	13	17	21	1	5	9	7	
FIRM PLANNED ORDERS														
PLANNED ORDERS	24	24	24	24		24	24	24	24		24	24		504

NOTES & COMMENTS

Source: W. L. Berry, T. E. Vollmann, and D. C. Whybark, *Master Production Scheduling: Principles and Practice.* Falls Church, Va.: American Production and Inventory Control Society, 1979, p. 87.

FIGURE 10.17 Abbott DRP Records for Central and Bulk

Description	Size	um	Std Bactr	FC	BY	PL	IT	C	Scrap	Total Landed Costs	OP	Life	O-LT	P-LT	O-LT	QA-LT	T-LT	On Hand	OA Inventory	Allocated	Safety Stock
Product-B	200	BL	7619	A2	00	03	C	0	1.07			1095		12	0	11	23	5220.0	0.0	144.0	1000.0

01-CENTRAL

	Past Due	7/24	7/31	08/07	08/14	08/21	08/28	09/04	09/11	09/18	09/25	10/02	10/09	10/16
CUSTOMER ORDERS	0	0	0	0	0	0	0	0	0	0	0	0	0	0
GROSS REQUIREMENTS	204	12	12	1908	12	12	2916	156	36	1884	12	1104	1980	12
SCHEDULED RECEIPTS	0	0	0	7619	0	0	0	0	0	0	0	0	0	0
ON HAND	4872	4860	4848	10078	10066	10054	7138	6982	6946	5062	5050	3946	9104	9092
FIRM PLANNED ORDERS	0	0	0	0	0	0	0	0	7619	0	0	0	0	0
PLANNED ORDERS	0	0	0	0	0	0	0	0	0	0	0	0	0	0

MONTHLY

	10/23	10/30	11/06	11/13	11/20	11/27	12/04	01/01	01/29	02/26	03/26	04/23	05/21	06/18
CUSTOMER ORDERS	0	0	0	0	0	0	0	0	0	0	0	0	0	0
GROSS REQUIREMENTS	2952	12	36	1884	96	1092	1944	4968	3108	3012	4968	3108	2076	3108
SCHEDULED RECEIPTS	0	0	0	0	0	0	0	0	0	0	0	0	0	0
ON HAND	6140	6128	6092	4208	4112	3020	8214	10384	7276	4264	6434	3326	8388	5280
FIRM PLANNED ORDERS	0	0	0	0	7619	0	7619	0	0	7619	0	7619	0	7619
PLANNED ORDERS	0	0	0	0	0	0	0	0	0	0	0	0	0	0

	07/16	08/13	09/10	10/08	11/05	12/03	12/31	01/28	02/25	03/24	04/21	05/19	06/16	TOTAL
CUSTOMER ORDERS	0	0	0	0	0	0	0	0	0	0	0	0	0	0
GROSS REQUIREMENTS	4740	3120	3108	4980	2052	3108	3012	4980	2964	2052	3108	4956	2808	87612
SCHEDULED RECEIPTS	0	0	0	0	0	0	0	0	0	0	0	0	0	7619
ON HAND	7678	4558	8588	10746	8694	5586	2574	4732	1768	6854	3746	5928	3120	0
FIRM PLANNED ORDERS	0	7619	7619	0	0	0	0	0	0	0	0	0	0	60952
PLANNED ORDERS	0	0	0	0	0	0	7619	0	7619	0	7619	0	0	22857

NOTES & COMMENTS

(continued)

FIGURE 10.17 *(Continued)*

Description	Size	um	Std Bactr	FC	BY	PL	IT	C	Scrap	Total Landed Costs	OP	Life	O-LT	P-LT	O-LT	QA-LT	T-LT	On Hand	OA Inventory	Allocated	Safety Stock
Product-B	200	L	4000			00	B	C	1.00		N						0	0	0	0	0

84-Bulk

	Past Due	7/24	7/31	08/07	08/14	08/21	08/28	09/04	09/11	09/18	09/25	10/02	10/09	10/16
CUSTOMER ORDERS														
GROSS REQUIREMENTS									4000					
SCHEDULED RECEIPTS														
ON HAND														
FIRM PLANNED ORDERS														
PLANNED ORDERS									4000					

MONTHLY

	10/23	10/30	11/06	11/13	11/20	11/27	12/04	01/01	01/29	02/26	03/26	04/23	05/21	06/18
CUSTOMER ORDERS														
GROSS REQUIREMENTS					4000		4000			4000		4000		4000
SCHEDULED RECEIPTS														
ON HAND														
FIRM PLANNED ORDERS														
PLANNED ORDERS					4000		4000			4000		4000		4000

	07/16	08/13	09/10	10/08	11/05	12/03	12/31	01/28	02/25	03/24	04/21	05/19	06/16	TOTAL
CUSTOMER ORDERS														
GROSS REQUIREMENTS		4000	4000				4000		4000		4000			44000
SCHEDULED RECEIPTS														
ON HAND														
FIRM PLANNED ORDERS														
PLANNED ORDERS		4000	4000				4000		4000		4000			44000

NOTES & COMMENTS

Source: W. L. Berry, T. E. Vollmann, and D. C. Whybark, *Master Production Scheduling: Principles and Practice.* Falls Church, Va.: American Production and Inventory Control Society, 1979, p. 88.

FIGURE 10.18 **Abbott Short-Term Shipping Information**

MPDR0030	DISTRIBUTION REQUIREMENTS PLAN							PAGE 206
DC 21 - MONTREAL DIVISION 2								
LIST/SIZE	QUANTITY	PALLET	WEIGHT	CUBE	QUANTITY	PALLET	WEIGHT	CUBE
	PAST DUE				WEEK 1			
XYZ-200	0	0.0	0.0	0.0	0	0.0	0.0	0.0
PRODUCT B	WEEK 2				WEEK 3			
	0	0.0	0.0	0.0	1872	2.0	3744.0	112.3
	PRIORITY 96: 5076 AVAILABLE IN CENTRAL							
DC 03 - VANCOUVER XYZ-200								
	PAST DUE				WEEK 1			
PRODUCT B	0	0.0	0.0	0.0	0	0.0	0.0	0.0
	WEEK 2				WEEK 3			
	0	0.0	0.0	0.0	24	0.0	48.0	1.4
	PRIORITY 96: 5076 AVAILABLE IN CENTRAL							

Source: W. L. Berry, T. E. Vollmann, and D. C. Whybark, *Master Production Scheduling: Principles and Practice.* Falls Church, VA: American Production and Inventory Control Society, 1979, p. 90.

Chapter 10A

Management of Supply Chain Logistics

Supply chain logistics encompasses all material flows—from the flow of purchased material into a facility, through the manufacturing processes, and out to the final customers. This chapter is focused primarily on the inbound and the outbound flows of material from a manufacturing plant in a supply chain. We are concerned with describing the elements of a supply chain and presenting some techniques for their management.

Improved management of supply chain logistics can lead to improvements in customer service. This can often be done while simultaneously reducing total inventory, transportation, and warehousing costs. This chapter is organized around the following six topics:

- *A framework for supply chain logistics:* What is the scope of logistics management in supply chains, and how do logistics decisions influence other manufacturing planning and control decisions?
- *Supply chain elements:* What are the primary activities and tasks in moving material in supply chains?
- *Warehouse replenishment system:* How are systems for warehouse replenishment designed and operated?
- *Warehouse location analysis:* How are the number and location of warehouses determined?
- *Vehicle scheduling analysis:* How are vehicles used for delivery and/or pickup scheduled?
- *Customer service measurement:* How are customer service measures developed and used to evaluate supply chain logistics performance?

A Framework for Supply Chain Logistics

The detailed systems and models discussed in this chapter are oriented toward the flow of material both inward from suppliers and outbound toward customers from manufacturing. These concepts are also covered in Chapters 10 and 11. Here, a context for supply chain logistics is developed, and we present an overview of the entire supply chain logistics activity, the need to look at overall costs, and the integrative viewpoint that should be taken by management.

A **warehouse** can be specialized to perform many different types of functions—for example, as a mixing point to achieve transportation economies, as a finishing operation close to customers, and as a bulk break point. However, because we are interested in the operation of warehouses at many different points in a supply chain, we use the term *warehouse* generically to represent the different types of warehouses that exist in practice—for example, branch warehouses, market-positioned warehouses, product-positioned warehouses, distribution centers, and fulfillment centers.

The Breadth of Supply Chain Logistics

One definition of **supply chain logistics** encompasses all material flow decisions, from raw materials to final consumption. The structure of these flows is illustrated in the supply chain diagram shown in Figure 10A.1. Dealing with this entire spectrum at once is virtually impossible. However, when portions of the overall flow become rationalized, such as by component-part planning with MRP, it becomes more reasonable to increase the scope of management. Moreover, the materials management organization form applied in some companies fosters improved interactions among material flow–related problems.

Even when the area under study is only concerned with the more limited segment of the outbound flows (i.e., physical distribution), the interactions with other manufacturing planning and control systems are still of critical importance. The outbound flow of materials from the factory is constrained by what is made available by the master production schedule. The replenishment of warehouse stocks can be considered (often erroneously) to be demand. Without proper system design, it is possible for chaotic factory conditions to be self-induced by the distribution system decisions.

A framework for supply chain logistics recognizes the need for integrative thinking. We *know* that the MPS has to take into account the demands that are placed on manufacturing by distribution decisions. The need for coordinated design is clear. However, coordination should not stop at the boundary lines of the company. The final demand placed against distribution facilities may be generated by customer purchasing systems. One firm's output can be the other firm's input. A proper view of logistics encompasses linking the decisions

FIGURE 10A.1 Supply Chain Processes

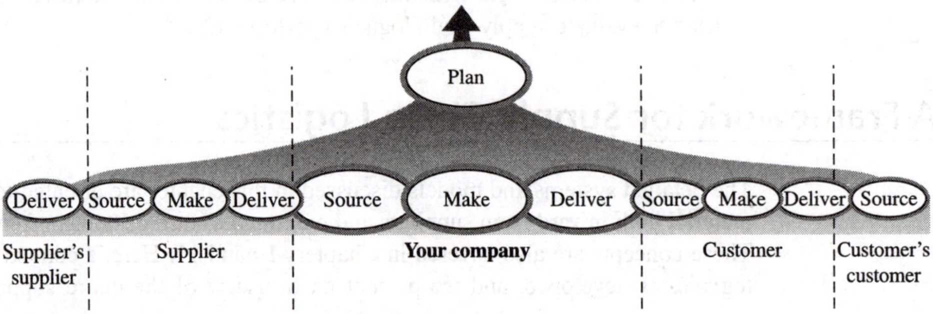

Source: Supply-Chain Council, www.supply-chain.org.

made in the firm with both those made by the firm's customers and those made by the suppliers.

The Total Cost Concept

The basic idea in the total cost concept is that costs accrue and values are added by the various stages of product conversion and movement. That is, as raw materials become end products and are moved from manufacturing to the point of consumption, costs are added. The general goal is to minimize the total or overall cost while meeting customer-service goals. This is accomplished by reducing the suboptimization associated with treating each conversion or movement stage independently. If cost performance is improved by some action at one stage, at a more-than-offsetting cost disadvantage at another stage, the action is to be avoided. Further, if an action at one stage, although increasing costs at that stage, will provide a large cost savings elsewhere, it should be taken.

The total cost concept can be exemplified by a series of actions taken by a furniture retailer in New York. A study of customer service provided by retail stores in the New York metropolitan area was undertaken. Each retailer maintained an inventory. In total, for the 40 retailers in the New York metropolitan area, the value of the inventory was about $3 million.

For an average customer order, the probability that all items desired would be in stock at a single retail store was approximately 25 percent. This meant back ordering, long delivery times, and many other problems. The retailer created one large field warehouse that could be drawn upon by any of these 40 retailers. The retailers, in turn, would no longer carry separate inventories. The value of the inventory in this field warehouse was approximately $700,000, and the probability of filling an entire customer order from the warehouse stock increased to approximately 0.8. These actions required changes in delivered prices for the furniture, but the retailer no longer had inventory carrying costs. The total cost was clearly reduced. The key is to not permit parochial views of enterprise boundaries and accounting systems to impede progress.

Design, Operation, and Control Decisions

It is clear that logistics decisions can be wide reaching. The impact of some decisions will be felt in more than one functional area of the firm, or even between firms. Making these decisions is not easy. In fact, the difficulties and potential payoffs are highly correlated.

The most basic supply chain logistic design decisions, such as the establishment of the retailer's centralized field warehouse, require top management action. This is also true for other basic supply chain logistics decisions, such as the number of warehouses, their locations, the type of replenishment planning system, and programs for interfirm cooperation.

The operation and control of logistics in supply chains tend to be assigned to functional groups. In many companies, these functional groups are separated organizationally. In a growing few, there is a materials management form of organization that facilitates coordination.

complacency

A critical dimension of supply chain logistics management is to provide leadership for continued evolution. Once a subsystem is designed and operating, there is a natural tendency to feel that the problem is solved—forever. There is no ultimate weapon, and there is no ultimate supply chain. Improvements are always possible. As more and more subsystems become highly rationalized, transparent, and integrated through databases, new improvement opportunities can be found. To do so, management must devote analytical resources to the study of supply chain logistics within the framework of the total cost concept.

An example of this evolutionary point of view is again provided by our furniture retailer. The New York field warehouse was an unqualified success. This led to the rapid establishment of 12 additional field warehouses in other metropolitan areas. All were successful. However, in a few years, most of the field warehouses were closed down. The reason is that the concept behind their success was applied again. An even larger *regional* warehouse was established adjacent to one of the large Vermont factories. This warehouse provided one- to two-day deliveries to the entire eastern seaboard.

The most important aspect of this example is that management was concentrating on the function of the warehouses—not the warehouses themselves. Some key issues include the following: How quickly must the delivery response be? Who are the customers? What do they really want? How do we reduce lead time variability? What are the costs of stockouts? How do we measure customer service?

Many times the personal prestige of executives can impede evolution in supply chain logistics. The executives who were instrumental in the field warehouse program could not regard their closure as a personal failure. The program was a success, and it led the way to the achievement of even further progress.

An overall framework for supply chain logistics implies the need for evolution and integration. The management of manufacturing must necessarily be integrated with logistical material flow decisions. So must many aspects of marketing. The objective is continuous and rapid evolution in the understanding and management of the total scope of supply chain logistics.

We now leave this overall focus and turn to more detailed aspects of supply chain logistics. In particular, we address some technical issues of the process. We also provide some examples of application. As we treat individual topics and recognize that each of the supply chain logistics issues is important, we do not, however, want to lose sight of the overall direction implied in the framework of logistics.

Supply Chain Logistical Elements

In this section, we provide general descriptions of some basic elements of supply chain logistics. We deal with the physical attributes of systems for gathering material from suppliers prior to manufacturing, and we are concerned with the distribution of products to customers on the output side of manufacturing. The management and information systems issues are addressed in subsequent sections.

Specifically, we want to identify some of the key characteristics of transportation, warehouses, and inventory regarding both the input of material to manufacturing and the distribution of products after manufacturing. For each of these supply chain elements, the intent is to understand the functions performed. Basically, these elements deal with the place and time utility of the products. Manufacturing provides the form utility.

Transportation

Supply chain logistics is concerned with the movement and storage of products. Achieving the former requires some method of transportation. As shown in Figure 10A.2, there are a

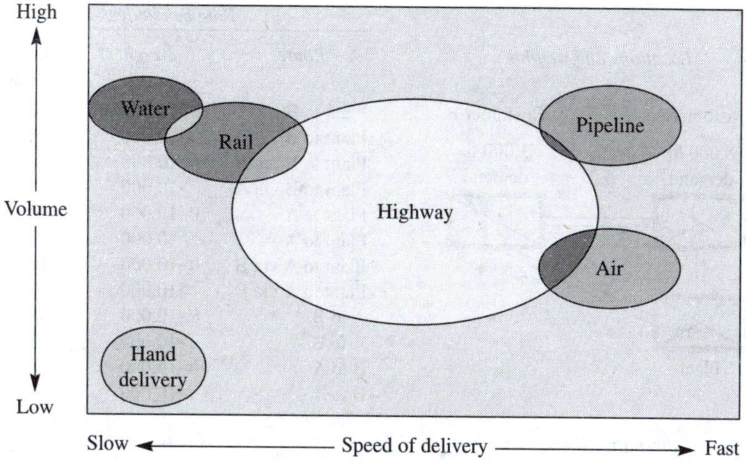

FIGURE 10A.2 **Logistics System Design Matrix: Framework Describing Logistics Processes**

variety of modes available, and technological change is fairly rapid. Evaluation of transportation alternatives is, therefore, an ongoing need.

For example, there are companies that now move coal and fish in pipelines, automobiles are moved by ship, and many finished and semifinished products are moved by air. The most common modes of transportation are air, rail, truck, pipeline, and combinations of them. Among these modes, however, are alternative ownership/management forms. For example, there are private carriage, courier, common carrier, and contract services; cooperative arrangements; and forwarding agents. Our purpose here is not to discuss these in detail, but to point out the need for having access to someone with expertise in this area. We also want to focus on the key transportation variables and their impact on supply chain planning and control decisions.

One of the prime considerations in product movement is cost. There are substantial quantity discounts for shipping large volumes of products. Specifically, there are large cost differences between less than carload (LCL) or truckload quantities and full carload (CL) or truckload quantities. This does not literally mean that a "full" carload must be shipped to get the discount, but that more than some specific weight must be shipped. The extent of freight rate differences is illustrated by Figure 10A.3.

Another major variable in the determination of transportation costs is the selection of routing. Several options usually exist for delivering products to multiple customers. Drop privileges, for example, may enable the manufacturer to combine shipments to two or more customers, thereby gaining lower freight rates. Clever combinations of customers into

FIGURE 10A.3 **Example Freight Rates for Trucks between Chicago and Los Angeles**

Household Effects		Machine Parts	
Weight	Rate (per cwt)*	Weight	Rate (per cwt)*
7,000 lb	$42	24,000 lb	$17.78
10,000	37	25,000	9.99

*cwt = Hundredweight or 100 pounds

FIGURE 10A.4
Alternative Routing Example to Serve Two Customers

Locations and weights

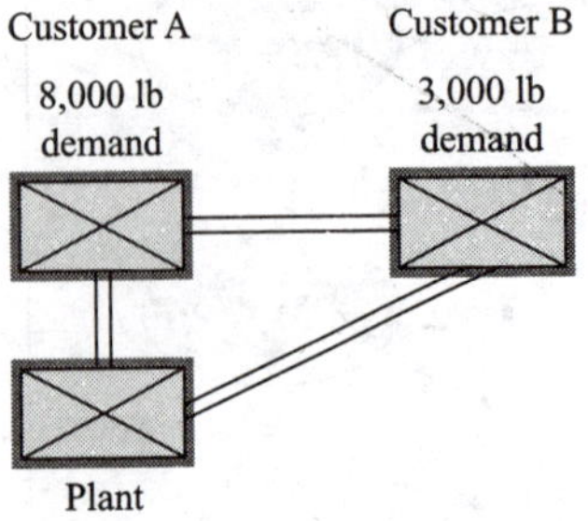

Rate Schedules

Route	*Weight*	*Cost (per cwt)*
Plant to B	0–10,000 lbs	$8
Plant to B	>10,000	6
Plant to B via A	0–10,000	10
Plant to B via A	>10,000	5
Plant to A	0–10,000	7
Plant to A	>10,000	5
Plant to A via B	0–10,000	11
Plant to A via B	>10,000	9
A to B	0–10,000	5
A to B	>10,000	3
B to A	0–10,000	5
B to A	>10,000	3

Alternative Routes	*Costs*
Ship A to A and ship B to B	(\$8,000/100) × 7 + (\$3,000/100) × 8 = \$ 800
Ship A and B to B and drop A	(\$11,000/100) × 5 + 20 = \$ 570
Ship A and B to A and drop B	(\$11,000/100) × 9 + 20 = \$1,010
Ship A and B to A and ship B to B	(\$11,000/100) × 5 + (\$3,000/100) × 5 = \$ 700
Ship A and B to B and ship A to A	(\$11,000/100) × 6 + (\$8,000/100) × 5 = \$1,060

Drop charge = $20/drop (any weight).

shipping schedules can result in substantial savings. This is illustrated in Figure 10A.4, which also shows how the number of alternatives to evaluate for even a simple example can be quite large.

In Figure 10A.4, five alternatives are evaluated; the cost from lowest to highest is nearly double. Such extremes are not unusual at all. For companies with private fleets, the vehicle scheduling activities (about which more will be said later) are the equivalent of the routing activities. They can have an important impact on costs.

Another aspect of transportation is trade-offs among speed, price, and reliability. In general, the faster a mode, the more costly (e.g., air freight is more costly than trucks). But a more subtle consideration is that of reliability or the variance around the average speed (lead time). Clearly, the greater the variance around the average lead time, the more safety stock or safety lead time is necessary. From a management point of view, safety stock levels are directly affected by the choice of transportation mode and routing, since these will offset the uncertainty in demand during lead time (DDLT).

Warehouses

We have been asked by very serious practitioners why a company should have warehouses. From the customer standpoint, the benefit is in time *and* place utility. That is, the warehouse locates the product closer to the customer in both distance and time. Whether this is worthwhile is a function of the market value of product proximity. Many executives have commented that there is a positive competitive advantage and market response to warehouses located near to the market. We dub this the "warm puppy effect." That is, having a warehouse nearby gives the customers a more comfortable feeling about service. Very little work has been done to quantity this effect, however, so the best that we can do at the moment is to calculate the costs of having warehouses and determine whether the value of proximity is likely to exceed these costs or not.

Warehouses can serve a variety of functions other than the warm puppy effect. In multiplant operations, warehouses can mix the products from several plants for shipment to customers or to other warehouses. As an example, a typical retail food producer such as Kraft Foods ships full car-/truckloads of unmixed quantities from plants to warehouses, mixes the products from several plants, and reships full car-/truckloads to other warehouses and customers. This allows them to take advantage of full carload rates *and* get the right mixture of products to locations.

Another function that can be performed at a warehouse is completing or packaging the product. Shipping in bulk and finishing the product at the warehouse permits the manufacturer to delay the addition of that value until the last possible moment. It is also possible that it can be done with less expensive labor and with better information on local product needs. Note that product completion and/or packaging at the warehouse necessitates additional MPC systems to plan and control these activities.

One final warehouses function is providing a point to break bulk. This is an opportunity to take partial advantage of the substantial difference between LCL (less than carload) rates and CL (carload) rates for shipping products. By putting a warehouse in a region, the product can be transported into that region at the CL rate, and then can be delivered to customers at the LCL or local delivery rate. Consider, for example, shipment of products from Chicago to the southern California region. An example of two alternatives is given in Figure 10A.5. The example shows a potential cost savings of $720 per week from a Los

FIGURE 10A.5
Example Cost Comparison: LTL versus Full Truckload, Chicago to California

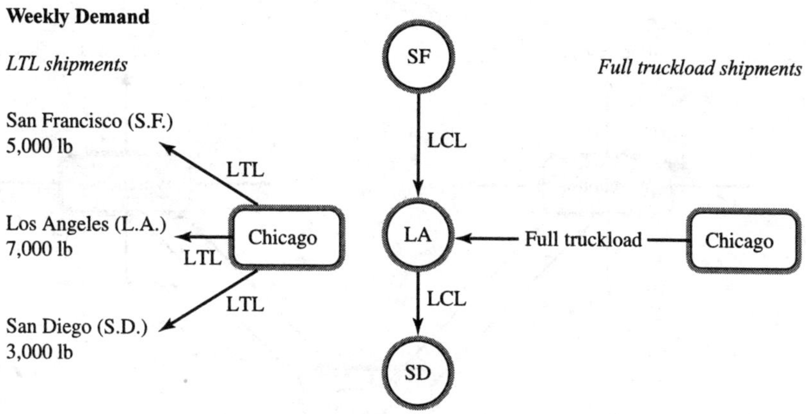

Rates LCL

Chicago–SF	$15.00/cwt
Chicago–LA	16.00/cwt
Chicago–SD	16.00/cwt

Cost/week = 50 × 15 =	$ 750
70 × 16 =	1,120
30 × 16 =	480
Total	$2,350

Rates with DC

Chicago–LA	$9.00/cwt
Local–LA	1.00/cwt
Local–SF	3.00/cwt
Local–SD	2.00/cwt

Cost/week = 150 × 9 =	$1,350
50 × 3 =	150
70 × 1 =	70
30 × 2 =	60
Total	$1,630

Angeles–based warehouse. This potential saving can be compared to the cost of operating the warehouse.

Inventory

Several functions of inventory will be mentioned before completing this section on the elements of the supply chain. Some of the marketing reasons for inventory are the maintenance of a full line of products, the provision of adequate display stock, or the provision of full inventory pipelines through the channels to each customer. Let's turn now to some key operational considerations of inventory in supply chains.

Inventory performs a buffering role in supply chains, but much confusion exists over the use of order quantities for buffering against uncertainty. Some firms incorrectly believe that order quantities should be increased when demand becomes less certain (i.e., the forecast error increases). In fact, it is safety stock that should be managed to buffer against increased uncertainty, not order quantities. In general, to increase safety stock, the order point needs to be raised, not the order quantity. Changes in the order quantity should be made as a result of changes in the inventory carrying cost, changes in the setup costs, changes in quantity discounts or transportation costs, etc.

Safety stock is a function of the demand during lead time. The uncertainty is influenced by the choice of transportation mode as well as the variability in demand rate. For each location, then, there is a possible need for safety stock. Each location will also have cycle stock, which is the result of shipping in economic quantities. Although safety stock and cycle stock interact, in this chapter we ignore the interaction in illustrating an important

FIGURE 10A.6
Example Safety Stock Savings from Warehouse Consolidation

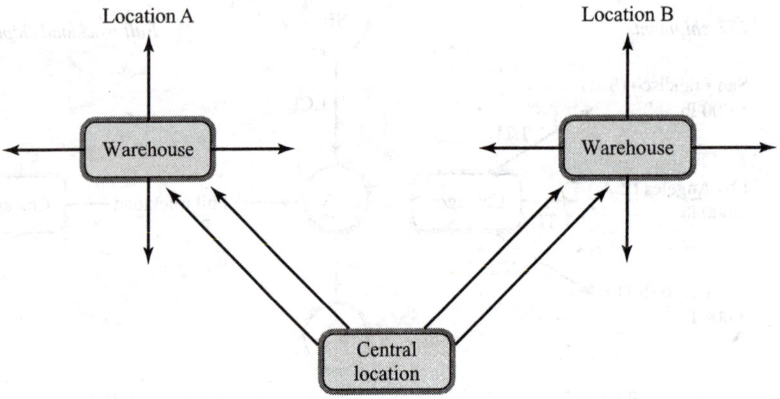

Location	*Forecast Error*		*Safety Stock**
A	$\sigma = 40$		66
B	$\sigma = 60$		99
		Total	165
Central†	$\sigma = 72$		119

*For 95 percent service level.
†Assuming independent forecast errors at A and B:

$$\sigma \text{ Central} = \sqrt{\sigma A^2 + \sigma B^2} = \sqrt{40^2 + 60^2} = 72$$

FIGURE 10A.7
Example Safety Stock Saving with Mixed Service Level Policy

Item Category	Constant Service Level				Mixed Service Level		
	Service Level	Forecast Error (σ)	Safety Stock		Service Level	Forecast Error (σ)	Safety Stock
A	95%	100	165		95%	100	165
B	95	100	165		85	100	104
C	95	100	165		70	100	53
	Total		495		Total		322

Percent of saving in safety stock inventory = (495 − 322)/495 = 35%

trade-off to be considered in designing the supply chain. This trade-off involves the pooling of safety stock at fewer locations to realize inventory savings.

The impact of pooling safety stocks must be evaluated against the possible advantage (product proximity) provided by a larger number of warehouses. The potential savings in safety stocks are demonstrated in Figure 10A.6, assuming a one-period lead time. Providing the service level of 95 percent (the percent of demand that can be satisfied from stock at both A and B) requires 165 units of safety stock, while consolidation at a central location requires only 119 units. This is the same phenomenon that our furniture retailer capitalized on both in creating the New York warehouse and later in creating the eastern seaboard regional warehouse.

The potential saving from warehouse consolidation of safety stock has led many firms to devise mixed service strategies. Because consolidation locates the inventory farther from the customers, delivery time may be increased. On the other hand, the savings from reduced safety stock may more than compensate for this reduction in service with some categories of products. The mixed service strategy provides different levels of service for different categories of products. Providing, for example, service level of 95 percent for A items, 85 percent for B items, and 70 percent for C items, can lead to substantial savings in inventory, as shown in Figure 10A.7. Detailed explanations of A, B, C analysis together with safety stock calculations are topics of Chapter 11.

Thus far, we have discussed the three basic elements of a supply chain: transportation, warehouses, and inventory management. We now turn to the information system used to manage the routine replenishment of supply chain inventories.

Warehouse Replenishment Systems

In this section we describe three basic alternatives to warehouse replenishment: reorder point/economic order quantity (ROP/EOQ), base stock, and distribution requirements planning (DRP). We concentrate on the operational differences among these three systems: the basis for deciding when to ship, how much to ship, which location makes the decision, and the information required. Figure 10A.8 summarizes these issues.

ROP/EOQ Systems

Historically, and perhaps currently, the dominant method for determining the amount to be shipped is the use of an economic order quantity, purchase quantity, or shipping quantity,

FIGURE 10A.8
Three Alternative Warehouse Replenishment Systems

System	*When to Order/Ship*	*How Much to Ship*	*Where Decision Is Made*	*Information System Complexity*
Reorder point/ economic order quantity	Warehouse actual inventory reaches reorder point	Economic lot size based on forecast or average usage	Warehouse	Low
Base stock	Scheduled shipment dates	Actual usage in previous period	Central location	Medium
Distribution requirements planning	Projected on-hand balance offset by lead time	Economic shipment quantity based on projected time-phased usage	Central location	High

and a reorder point to establish the timing of the shipment. As seen in Figure 10A.8, the actual inventory balance in the warehouse is used to determine when the inventory reaches the reorder point. Order point calculations are covered in Chapter 11. At that point, an order is released by the warehouse and placed with the central resupply location. Order placement varies from mail forms to Internet-based online communications. Any time delays between order placement by the warehouse and order receipt by the resupply point have to be compensated for with longer lead time.

The shipment quantities are determined, using economic order quantity methodology (described in Chapter 11). The expected demand is assumed to be constant and is based on past averages or a forecast of future demand. The quantity determination can incorporate quantity discounts and transportation economies, if necessary. Both are treated in the same analytical way. Other practical considerations such as full-case, full-pallet, or mixed-product carloads can also be taken into account.

A key aspect of ROP/EOQ replenishment systems is that the decisions are made at the warehouse level. From an information point of view, this means that the central location does not have to maintain inventory records or process detailed warehouse transactions. The complexity of the information system is low. Information handling and decision making are decentralized.

A fundamental disadvantage in the classic ROP/EOQ replenishment system is that the information received by central has been filtered by the individual decision processes at each of the warehouses. That is, the demand being expressed by customers is seen by the warehouses individually. The way in which this demand is transmitted to central is influenced by the parameters of the ROP/EOQ system in use at each warehouse. The problem is often compounded by the fact that the selection and modification of the system parameters are also done by warehouse personnel. There is a natural tendency for amplification. As end-customer demand grows, for example, adjustment of parameters often results in a larger growth in the orders being placed by the warehouses on the central inventory.

Still another problem with the pull orientation of ROP/EOQ systems occurs when the demand on central in a particular time period exceeds the available supply. Some form of allocation is necessary, but without detailed warehouse information, the allocation will necessarily be somewhat arbitrary. In a similar vein, phased withdrawals of products will tend to be uneven at different warehouses. Also, the ability to cross-ship among warehouses will be reduced. The implication is that centralized information can yield more effective distribution inventory management.

Base Stock Systems

There are two distinguishing features of the base stock system. The first is the separation of the information flow on end-item demand from replenishment order data. That is, information on actual end-item demand is fed back to all stages in the supply chain, including the factory. This feedback allows certain key decisions to be based on data that have had no amplification. The data can be transmitted as received at the warehouse with online communication systems or batched for daily or longer time period processing. The second distinguishing feature of the base stock system is the establishment of a routine replenishment cycle. In its simplest form, the base stock system uses a direct replacement system. That is, the exact amount sold by a warehouse during a fixed time cycle is replenished at the next shipment time.

The base stock quantities for each warehouse are set to cover the maximum expected demand for each item during the lead time necessary to replenish the warehouse. When the next delivery is scheduled to leave for a warehouse, the quantity shipped for each item is the quantity sold since the last delivery plus any adjustments to the base stock level. If, for example, a truck goes to a warehouse on a weekly basis, the quantity shipment would replenish the actual usage in the previous week (if there were no information-processing delays).

The base stock system is predicated on the determination of a shipping frequency to each distribution center. This is seen in Figure 10A.8 as the when to order/ship decision. In determining this frequency, a major trade-off is larger shipments made with less frequency, which can reduce transportation costs, versus smaller shipments made more frequently, which can reduce warehouse inventory carrying costs.

Although Figure 10A.8 shows the base stock system shipment quantities as equal to the actual usage in the previous period, convenient shipping sizes can also be accommodated. For warehouse replenishment, there will almost always be the issue of pack sizes, full-pallet quantities, etc. This is accommodated by measuring actual demand in the pack or pallet sizes and then use logic that considers current inventory position at the warehouse.

The base stock system incorporates centralized decision making. Rather than having warehouses, determine when and how much to ship, these decisions are made routinely with centrally determined parameters and monitoring. The result is better coordination of central inventory resources and multilocation demands. The cost is increased information handling.

An application of the base stock system is the kanban system, which is used in many manufacturing companies (see Chapter 9). It is a base stock system—applied in a manufacturing environment. As a user department actually uses parts provided by a supplier department, the information is passed back to the supplier department. The form of information is empty containers to be refilled with parts by the supplier department and passed on to the user department. In other words, the system is designed to have the supplier department replace the parts the user department just used.

The kanban system *inside* the factory is based on a fixed lot size (the number of items in a container). The periodicity or timing of the replenishment order varies, but lots are so small that, in general, several lots are made in a single day. When the system is applied to vendors, it is more like the distribution base stock system. The vendor brings in a variable number of items on a fixed delivery cycle. The number of items in a batch is essentially what was just used in production.

Distribution Requirements Planning

The primary distinguishing feature of distribution requirements planning (DRP) is the use of time-phased projected future usage (see Chapter 10 for a detailed discussion of DRP). This means that the determination of when to ship an order is based on a projected inventory position, and the shipment is made in anticipation of inventory availability as opposed to reacting to an actual inventory position. Likewise, the determination of the shipping quantity is made in a similar way from time-phased projected usage information. This means that replenishment can be based on the best estimates of future needs, with possibilities of combining future requirements to fill trucks or railcars for shipment to warehouses. The shipment quantity can be sized using economic order quantity methodology, taking into account transportation costs. These decisions are illustrated by the information shown in Figure 10A.8.

An important advantage of using DRP is that decisions can be made at the warehouse, but the time-phased record information for the warehouse items is also fully visible centrally by manufacturing. This can facilitate the coordination of shipment quantities by both the warehouse and manufacturing. As an example, the cross-shipping of products between warehouses is possible when the demand on central exceeds the available supply for a particular time period. A further advantage of DRP is that local information can be taken into account in developing the forecast information. For example, in using DRP at Abbott Laboratories, warehouse personnel knew that many customers order more heavily in the first and third weeks of the month. As a result, these factors could be considered in developing the product forecasts.

The benefits of DRP do come at a cost of a more complex information system. The costs of handling inventory tansactions and operating the time-phased DRP system are substantial.

Warehouse Location Analysis

One of the key elements in managing the supply chain activities of a firm is the determination of how many warehouses to have and where they should be located. We consider several approaches to that problem in this section. The basic approach we take is to choose among a set of predetermined alternative locations.

To illustrate the problem and solution approaches, let's assume that some staff group has developed the information (perhaps with regression analysis estimates) shown as Figure 10A.9. This figure shows the annual fixed cost of using each of the possible warehouses plus the variable costs associated with serving the customers in particular locations from each warehouse.

FIGURE 10A.9 Costs for Alternative Warehouse Locations

		Customer Locations										
Potential Warehouse Location	Fixed Cost per Year	Michigan City	Gary	Indianapolis	Lafayette	Kokomo	Columbus	Richmond	Vincennes	Evansville	Louisville	Terre Haute
Hammond	8	10*	22	25	7	4	17	11	5	15	25	22
Indianapolis	7	13	30	20	5	3	14	8	4	11	19	18
Columbus	6	15	32	22	7	4	12	9	3	11	19	17
Terre Haute	5	13	30	22	8	5	17	10	2	12	20	15
New Albany	5	18	40	24	10	7	15	10	4	10	17	17

*Variable cost (in $000) per year for serving all Michigan City customers from a Hammond warehouse.

Simulation

A useful approach to determining the number and locations of warehouses is **simulation.** One way to do this is to specify a number of warehouses to evaluate—say, two—and randomly choose several examples of two warehouses. Once a particular set of warehouses is chosen, customers are assigned to specific warehouses on the basis of minimum cost, and total annual costs are calculated. For example, a Hammond/Indianapolis set of warehouses would be calculated as follows (in $1,000 of cost):

$$\text{Fixed costs} = 8 + 7 = 15$$

$$\text{Variable costs (Hammond)} = 10 + 22 = 32$$

(for serving only Gary and Michigan City)

$$\text{Variable costs (Indianapolis)} = 20 + 5 + 3 + 14 + 8 + 4 + 11 + 19 + 18 = 102$$

$$\text{Total costs} = 15 + 32 + 102 = 149$$

Many pairs of warehouses would be similarly evaluated to find a good (but not optimal) set. Next, a different number of warehouses is investigated in the same way—say, three—with random sets of three warehouses chosen for analysis. The end result would be the ability to plot the total annual expected costs as a function of the number of warehouses. Figure 10A.10 is an example of such a plot. Once the interesting range of the number of warehouses is determined, more detailed analysis can be made, both in terms of the number of warehouses and location. At this point, management/subjective considerations can also be taken into account.

Heuristic Procedures

Several **heuristic procedures** have been developed to permit rapid determination of good warehouse location patterns. Among these are the *add* and *drop* procedures. The add procedure will be illustrated with the data from Figure 10A.11. The procedure starts by considering which single warehouse would serve all the customer locations at the least cost if

FIGURE 10A.10
Total Annual Cost for Varying Numbers of Warehouses

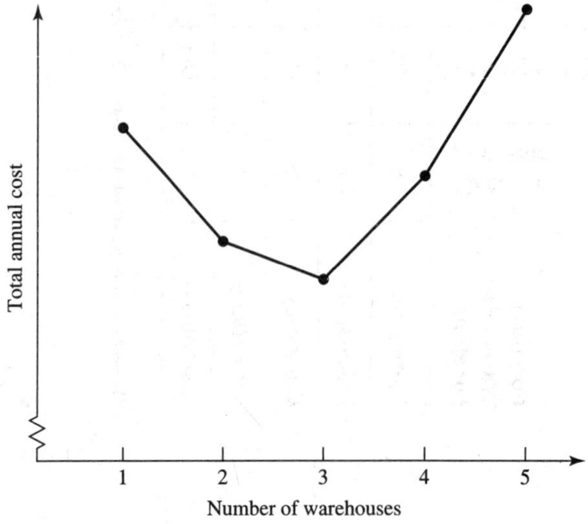

FIGURE 10A.11
The Add Procedure for Determining Warehouse Location

	Step	*Warehouses*	*Cost*	*Choice*
1	Warehouse	Hammond	171	
		Indianapolis	152*	
		Columbus	157	Indianapolis
		Terre Haute	160	
		New Albany	177	
2	Warehouse	Hammond	149*	
	Indianapolis +	Columbus	155	Hammond
		Terre Haute	154	
		New Albany	157	
3	Warehouse	Columbus	152	
	Indianapolis +	Terre Haute	151	No choice: costs are increasing
	Hammond +	New Albany	151	

*Final choice: Indianapolis and Hammond.

used *alone*. From Figure 10A.11, we see that this is Indianapolis at a cost of $152K. Once this warehouse is found, the least cost warehouse to *add* to the first one is chosen. Here we see that given that Indianapolis is in place, the cost can be reduced further if we add a warehouse at Hammond. The total cost now is $149K. Next, the third best warehouse to add to the first two is determined, and so on, until the addition of another warehouse increases total costs. In the example shown in Figure10A.11 the addition of a third warehouse to the combination of warehouses in Indianapolis and Hammond increases costs, so the procedure stops with the two suggested.

Programming Procedures

Neither simulation nor the heuristic procedures guarantee an optimal solution to the selection of warehouses. It is tempting to suggest that all combinations be examined, that is, to completely enumerate all possible warehouse customer combinations to find the best. However, for a typical problem of 100 potential warehouse locations and customers throughout the United States, enumeration of all possible combinations may not be possible.

Exact procedures do exist for optimally solving the warehouse location problem. Branch-and-bound techniques have been made quite efficient and are now feasible for problems of 100 to 200 potential warehouses. The general approach of the branch-and-bound technique is to use the transportation method of linear programming sequentially to bound the solution space. Linear programming techniques alone cannot be applied because of the fixed costs associated with each warehouse. The first step in the procedure is to treat all the fixed costs as variable and solve a transportation linear programming (TLP) problem. The cost of this solution represents a lower bound on costs in that no solution accounting for the fixed costs can be better. If the solution to the TLP problem assigns all customers fully to some of the warehouses that is the solution. If some are only partially assigned, the procedure continues.

The next step is to select one warehouse that is to be constrained as open. This adds the full fixed costs of that warehouse. All other fixed costs are still assumed to be variable.

The TLP produces a lower bound to this condition. Next, the same warehouse is constrained to be closed and the TLP solved. Another lower bound is thereby obtained.

The branch with the lowest bound of the two branches (first warehouse open or closed) is then selected for further analysis. Another warehouse is added and again constrained as both open and closed. Lower bounds are obtained with TLP, as before. Again the smaller lower bound path is chosen. The process is repeated until a terminal solution is obtained. A terminal solution is one where all warehouse are either open or closed. The cost of this terminal solution now becomes an upper bound. That is, it is a feasible solution—any other solution with a greater cost can be ignored.

All branches for which lower bounds were calculated but not explored en route to obtaining the first terminal solution can now be compared with the upper bound. Any branches that have a lower bound greater than the upper bound can be omitted from further consideration. Those that are lower have to be evaluated. The evaluation proceeds either until lower bounds are achieved for the branches that exceed the current upper bound or until a terminal solution is reached. If the cost of the terminal solution is lower than the current upper bound, it becomes the new upper bound.

This basic approach has been augmented to reduce the computational effort. For example, in the problem shown in Figure 10A.9, it is possible to quickly determine that the optimal solution will use the Hammond warehouse because Hammond can most cheaply serve Michigan City and Gary. The next best alternative to serve these two customers would add \$3,000 and \$8,000, respectively. This is more than the fixed costs of the Hammond warehouse.

Vehicle Scheduling Analysis

In this section we treat **vehicle scheduling.** We assume a given supply chain system involving the replenishment of customer inventory and a given set of customer locations. We then determine how vehicles should be best scheduled to achieve the supply chain objectives. Here, the customer may be manufacturing plants served by a supplier, a set of warehouses served by a manufacturing plant, or a set of customer locations served by a warehouse.

The problem typically formulated is to determine the order in which customers will be visited by delivery/pickup vehicles, often called the *route.* Other questions include determination of the proper number of vehicles, the frequency with which each customer should be visited, and the times to be associated with the stops along the route.

Our approach to vehicle scheduling is to first present a discussion of the *traveling salesmen* problem. This provides an analytical framework. We then suggest methods for solving the problem.

Traveling Salesman Problem

The traveling salesman problem is one of those easily stated but difficult to solve problems on which mathematicians thrive: Given a set of cities, warehouses, or customers to be visited, what is the least-cost method of visiting each of them, starting from and returning to a given point (the central facility)? An example is shown in Figure 10A.12, where there are five warehouses to be visited from a central plant.

FIGURE 10A.12
Traveling Salesman Example

Locations of Warehouses and Plants

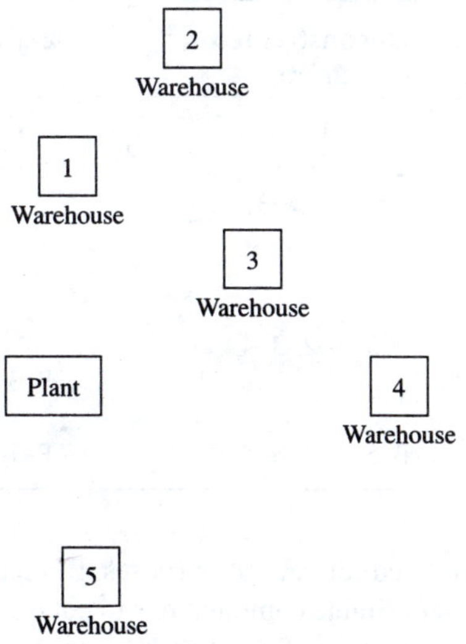

*Driving time in hours.

*Times between Locations**

From	To Warehouse 1	2	3	4	5
P	3	3.5	2	3	1
1		1.5	4	5	3.5
2			3.5	4.5	4.5
3				1	3
4					3.5

Solution Methodologies

The traveling salesman problem can be formulated as a zero-one integer programming problem. Optimal solution approaches include branch-and-bound procedures similar to those discussed for the warehouse location problem and dynamic programming. Producing optimal procedures becomes computationally costly as the size of the problem goes up. That is, as the number of customers or warehouses to visit in a schedule increases, the computational costs rise geometrically.

Heuristic procedures have been devised for this problem that produce reasonably good results in far less time than the optimal procedures. One widely used heuristic is based on the *time-saved* concept. The basic consideration is the time or distance that would be saved if two warehouses were visited in a single tour, as opposed to visiting each separately. For the example shown in Figure 10A.12, a matrix of time saved can be constructed. Figure 10A.13 provides this information.

FIGURE 10A.13
Time-Saved Matrix and Formula

Time Saved

	2	3	4	5
1	5*	1	1	.5
2		2	2	0
3			4	0
4				.5

Formula and Example

Time saved $x - y =$
time (P to x) + time (P to y) − time (x to y)
Time saved (1 − 2) = 3 + 3.5 − 1.5 = 5*
Time saved (3 − 4) = 2 + 3 − 1 = 4

*Time saved by traveling from P–1–2–P instead of P–1–P and P–2–P.

FIGURE 10A.14 **Application of Time-Saved Heuristic**

Rank of Pairing by Time Saved		Unconstrained Route	Eight-Hour Constraint Route	
1–2	5	1–2	P–1–2–P	8 hours
3–4	4	3–4	P–3–4–P	6 hours
2–3	2	1–2–3–4		
2–4	2			
1–3	1			
1–4	1			
1–5	.5	5–1–2–3–4		
4–5	.5		P–3–4–5–P	7.5 hours
2–5	0			
3–5	0	P–5–1–2–3–4–P	P–1–2–P, P–3–4–5–P	

The time-saved matrix can be utilized for several purposes. But let's first start with the determination of the route. The most desirable combinations to put on a route are those that save the most time. Because a route that goes from 1 to 2 (or vice versa) would save the most time, it is selected first. The application of the heuristic to the entire set of data in Figure 10A.13 is illustrated in Figure 10A.14. Also shown are two resultant routes; one if all warehouse are visited in one route and another if a truck has to return to the plant within an eight-hour shift.

If no restrictions on time capacity exist, the time-saved procedure suggests first pairing 1–2, next 3–4, and then 2–3. These three pairs lead to the partial route 1–2–3–4. The next pair that can be used is the 1–5 pair, which suggests a complete route would join 5–1 so that the complete route would be P–5–1–2–3–4.

The addition of the eight-hour time constraint is readily included in the time-saved heuristic. In Figure 10A.14, pairs would be combined until the constraint was reached, and then a new route would be started. The first route would be P–1–2–P using eight hours (there is no warehouse that can be visited from warehouse 1 or 2 with return made to the plant within eight hours). The second vehicle would then be routed P–3–4–5–P to complete the deliveries.

Other heuristics have also been applied to the traveling salesman problem. One approach is to take any feasible tour and try to improve it. A feasible tour could be generated randomly or produced with the time-saved heuristic. One improvement procedure would be to examine pair exchanges. For example, 2–3 and 3–4 could be exchanged for 2–4 and 4–3. If the result would be a time saving, the exchange would be made.

Customer Service Measurement

The last of our topics in supply chain logistics concerns the measurement of customer service. This is included for a very simple reason: Without some objective measure of customer service, it is extremely difficult to compare, measure, and control many supply chain logistics alternatives. We divide the discussion of customer service into make-to-stock firms and make-to-order firms. However, many of the principles are the same in both cases.

Make-to-Stock Companies

In this section, we consider firms that ship from an inventory to customers (or provide an inventory for customers). We look at the difficulty of defining and measuring customer service.

A major issue in measuring customer service for the make-to-stock firm concerns delivery timing. Among firms shipping from factory inventories to retail centers, warehouses, or customers, many feel that customer service should be assessed in terms of the speed of delivery. That is, after a customer places an order, how soon is it delivered? This leads to policies like one-week or overnight delivery. This fixed delivery time implies levels of inventory and/or capacity that should be thought through carefully before setting the policy.

An alternative measure of customer service is the consistency of delivery. This is related to available-to-promise logic. Make an honest promise—then keep it. This is not common, but the emergence of manufacturing planning and control systems is making it more possible. It still is not as popular as the fixed response ideas—such as next-day delivery.

Our experience indicates that there is no one best measure. *All* firms state that they are very concerned about customer service, but we find firms falling into two major groups. The key difference is whether they have unambiguously defined and measured customer service. One group of firms does not systematically measure and does not have unambiguous definitions of customer service. Among the second group, those who do have definitions and measures, there tend to be very different measurements.

Once the issue of when (promise date or response time) has been resolved, there is still the issue of how to measure service in terms of *what* is delivered. Again, there are a number of different measurements used for this aspect of customer service. One common measurement is the percent of the items demanded in any period (i.e., a year) actually supplied from stock when demanded. A related measure is the percent of demand satisfied from stock during the reorder cycle. The measure reflects the notion that the exposure to stockouts occurs between the time the replenishment order has been placed and the time the delivery arrives in inventory. Another measure is the percent of the line items in an individual customer order that have been filled out of inventory. Still another measure is the percent of the customers for whom all line items were filled from inventory.

One has to be a bit careful in selecting among these measures. The objective is to provide customer service—to measure how well one is doing and to continually look for improvement, both in the service provided and in the measurement used. If a completely responsive production facility were available, no customer service issue would ever arise. All orders would be shipped upon order receipt. While clearly unrealistic for most products, there are some instances where it is competitively necessary to provide such service. For example, some firms have a customer service policy of "immediate" delivery of spare parts. Again, one must recognize that this measure is going to fail for some customers unless the normal demand can be postponed, so the manufacturing facility can literally make the spare part immediately.

All of these measures signify different aspects of trying to satisfy customer demand. It is not always possible (or even desirable) to satisfy all demands. Moreover, many actual delivery requirements vary. For this reason, variable specifications may be in order, depending on the customer served.

Make-to-Order Companies

The primary customer service consideration in a make-to-order (or assemble-to-order) firm is the ability to meet promised delivery dates. Thus, measuring performance against these promises is as important in the make-to-order as it is in the make-to-stock firm. The timing issue is also critical in the make-to-order firm. One key dimension of timing is the time from order placement until delivery. An important element of this is the manufacturing lead time. If insufficient time exists, some promises will have to be made on the basis of previously forecast volumes. Managing that requires an effective MPC system.

Customer service measurement in the make-to-order firm is somewhat complicated by the fact that customers often change desired delivery dates. In measurement then, one issue is whether the change was made by the customer or the manufacturer. Should performance be measured against the assigned date or the revised date? Against both?

The implications of the necessity to control and measure against delivery promise dates underscores the need for close coordination between order entry and master production scheduling. Many make-to-order firms have a simple policy of six weeks (or some other such period) delivery for every order. If this were correct on the average, it means that in 50 percent of the cases delivery could have been sooner, and in 50 percent of the cases delivery will be late. It is the function of the master production scheduling activity to monitor the capability of the shop to deliver. This ability to monitor the customer promising capability through the available-to-promise logic means that the delivery date can be specified on the basis of actual shop capability, and the supply chain logistics function can deliver to the customer against a date that was feasible from the shop's standpoint and agreeable to the customer.

We see then that customer service measurement is critical to assess supply chain design choices. It is also intertwined with other manufacturing planning and control (MPC) system functions. Good master production scheduling makes for better customer service. Good execution systems make for an attainable master production schedule. MPC system strengths can support new and exciting changes in supply chains.

Concluding Principles

Several technical and managerial principles are discussed in this chapter:

- The role and contributions of each element of a supply chain logistics must be determined and managed.
- Management must provide the integration for the elements of these systems and evaluate alternatives in terms of total cost.
- The information from distribution requirements planning systems should be used for planning product deliveries.
- The design of warehouse systems should incorporate the locational (warm puppy) effect on sales.
- The vehicle scheduling activities must be coordinated with customer service requirements.
- Customer service objectives and standards must be set and monitored. These should reflect the types and classes of customers and products.

Discussion Questions

1. Discuss the strengths and limitations of the supply chain logistics/materials management concepts.
2. What are some of the key barriers to implementing the total cost concept?
3. Provide examples of the evolutionary point of view from your own experience in college, at work, or in your living unit.
4. What kind of customer education might be required to implement a consolidated safety stock strategy with mixed service levels, such as suggested in Figure10A.7?
5. For what kinds of items would you recommend the ROP/EOQ system, the base stock system, and the DRP system?
6. The warehouse location analysis requires a substantial amount of data on each potential location. How would you go about reducing the data requirement for sites that may not even be used?
7. How would you choose a customer service measure?

Problems

1. The Cord Company, a Miami, Ohio, manufacturing firm, has a blanket contract to supply a special power unit for electric windows on a luxury car. The remaining requirements by month for the next model year are as follows:

January	*February*	*March*	*April*	*May*	*June*
50	100	100	50	100	50

Cord must pay the freight to Detroit. The car company has said they must have each month's requirements on hand at the start of each month but prefer to have no more. If more power units are delivered than are required in a month, Cord is changed $1 per unit per month storage. Cord has completed the production of all current model power units and has 450 of them in inventory for this contract. Assume that the relevant costs only relate to transportation to the customer and the carrying cost charged by the customer for inventory carried on their site.

a. The truck firm that Cord currently uses can deliver overnight and offers a transportation rate break at 1,000 units. The current landed cost at Detroit is $21.10/unit, and for shipments of 1,000 units and more, the landed cost is $20.00 per unit. How should Cord ship to minimize costs for the last six months?

b. A competing truck firm has offered to deliver the power units to Detroit for the same rates but with the break point reduced to 200 units (i.e., for shipments of 200 units or more, the landed cost will be $20.00 per unit). What shipping schedules and truck firm should the company use?

2. The following matrix represents a warehouse location problem. There is a fixed cost for opening any of the five possible warehouses, and the cell entries for each customer are the variable costs of serving that customer from each potential warehouse. The variable costs include inbound transportation, outbound transportation, and warehouse operating costs for all the customer's requirements. The objective is to determine which warehouses should be used to serve all customers at minimum total cost. There are no capacity restrictions on the potential warehouses, but some warehouses cannot serve some customers.

Warehouses Possible	Fixed Costs	Customers					
		1	2	3	4	5	6
A	6	8	5	2	2	6	6
B	6	9	X	8	9	2	6
C	5	7	4	7	5	6	4
D	8	4	3	6	X	3	5
E	8	6	2	6	6	4	8

Note: X indicates no service is possible between warehouse and customer.

Apply the add procedure to solve this warehouse location problem. Determine which warehouse should service each customer and indicate the total cost of your solution.

3. The travel time (in hours) between a depot (D) and each of three customers (A, B, and C) is represented by the following matrix:

		To Location			
		D	*A*	*B*	*C*
From Location	*D*	—	3	6	4
	A	3	—	8	5
	B	6	8	—	3
	C	4	5	3	—

a. Use the time-saved method for developing a route that minimizes time for a single vehicle (without capacity restrictions) to follow in visiting each of these customers. Assume that the vehicle will start at the depot and must return to the depot.

b. Could the time-saved method be used if there were a 15-hour limit on a vehicle away from the depot? How?

4. The following matrix represents the driving times (in hours) between the customers of a company that delivers product to them on a daily basis. The number of units to meet the daily requirement for each customer is also given:

		To Customer					Units Required
		*A**	*B*	*C*	*D*	*E*	
From Customer	*A**	—	2	1	1	2	—
	B	2	—	1	2	4	40
	C	1	1	—	2	2	20
	D	1	2	2	—	3	50
	E	2	4	2	3	—	30

*Site "A" is the company warehouse.

The company uses a single vehicle that has 100 units of capacity to make deliveries.

a. Using the time-saved heuristic, develop the route(s) that a vehicle should use (i.e., the order in which the customers should be visited).

b. How long will it take the vehicle to make the deliveries? How many trips will the vehicle make?

c. Show in detail the steps in the procedure used to solve this problem.

5. The traffic manager for Superior Steel Company in Albany is trying to decide the cheapest way to ship his product to customers in Wayword and Leftover. The demand is 5,000 at Wayword and 6,000 at Leftover. The drop charges are $50 at either Wayword or Leftover. The alternate routes and rates are shown here:

Origin	*Destination*	*Via*	*Weight*	*Rate*
Albany	Wayword	Direct	<10,000	$ 6/cwt.
Albany	Wayword	Direct	>10,000	4/cwt.
Albany	Wayword	Leftover	Any quantity	8/cwt.
Albany	Leftover	Direct	<8,000	5/cwt.
Albany	Leftover	Direct	>8,000	4/cwt.
Albany	Leftover	Wayword	<5,000	10/cwt.
Albany	Leftover	Wayword	>5,000	7/cwt.
Leftover	Wayword	Direct	Any quantity	4/cwt.
Wayword	Leftover	Direct	<5,000	4/cwt.
Wayword	Leftover	Direct	>5,000	2/cwt.

What is the lowest cost shipping policy for Superior Steel Company? What is the total cost of this policy?

Chapter 11

Order Point Inventory Control Methods

This chapter concerns managing inventory items that are found at many points in a supply chain, including finished goods in factories, field warehouses, and distribution centers; spare-parts inventories; office and factory supplies; and maintenance materials. Such items are subject to independent random demand, and not the dependent demand on inventories of raw materials and component parts used in the production of end products. However, many of the underlying principles of the inventory management techniques described in this chapter apply to the management of dependent-demand items as well as independent-demand items, and we will indicate these similarities in our discussion.

The inventory management techniques described in this chapter are commonly referred to as *order point methods*. They are used to determine appropriate order quantities and timing for individual independent-demand product items that are characterized by random customer demand. If we perform these inventory management functions well, we can provide appropriate levels of customer service without excess levels of inventory or management costs.

This chapter is organized around six topics:

- *Basic concepts:* What are the functions of independent demand inventory?
- *Management issues:* How can routine inventory decisions be implemented, and how is performance measured?
- *Inventory-related costs:* How are costs of the inventory system measured and used?
- *Economic order quantity model:* What techniques are used to determine the quantity to order?
- *Order timing decisions:* How can we determine timing of orders and set the level of safety stock?
- *Multi-item management:* What techniques are available for focusing management attention on the important items?

Basic Concepts

The investment in inventory typically represents one of the largest single uses of capital in a business, often more than 25 percent of total assets. In this section, we discuss different types of inventory, distinguishing between **independent- and dependent-demand items.** We also describe functions of different types of inventories (transit, cycle, safety, and anticipation stock).

Independent- versus Dependent-Demand Items

This chapter concerns managing **independent demand inventories.** The demand for items contained in independent demand inventories (such as those stocked in the distribution center and field warehouses in Figure 11.1) is primarily influenced by factors outside of company decisions. These external factors induce random variation in demand for such items. As a result, demand forecasts for these items are typically projections of historical demand patterns. These forecasts estimate the average usage rate and pattern of random variation.

Demand for inventory items at the manufacturing stage in Figure 11.1 (e.g., raw material and component items) is directly dependent on internal factors well within the firm's control, such as the final assembly schedule (FAS) or master production schedule (MPS);

FIGURE 11.1 **Dependent and Independent Demand Inventories**

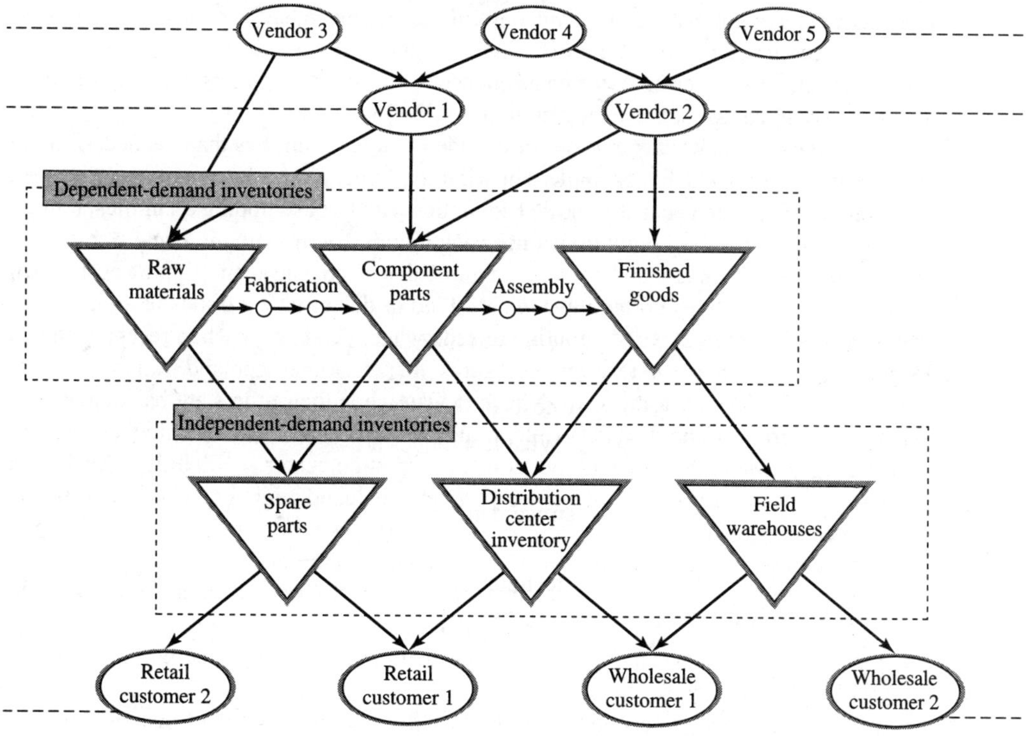

that is, demand for raw materials and component items is a derived demand, which we can calculate exactly once we have the FAS or MPS. Therefore, demand for end-product items is called *independent demand,* while demand for items contained in manufacturing inventories is called *dependent demand.*

There are other examples of independent-demand inventories in a supply chain context. Items subject to random use such as spare parts for production equipment, office supplies, and production supplies used to support the process all have independent demands. The techniques described in this chapter are suitable for all such items. Demand for these items can't be calculated from a production schedule or other direct management program.

Functions of Inventory

An investment in inventory enables us to decouple successive operations or anticipate changes in demand. Inventory also enables us to produce goods at some distance from the actual consumer. This section describes four types of inventories that perform these functions.

Transit stock depends on the time to transport goods from one location to another. These inventories (along with those in distribution centers, field warehouses, and customers' locations) are also called *pipeline inventories.* Management can influence the magnitude of the transit stock by changing the distribution system's design. For example, in-transit inventory between the raw material vendor and factory can be cut by (1) changing the transportation method (e.g., switching from rail to air freight) or (2) switching to a supplier closer to the factory to reduce transit time. These choices, however, involve cost and service trade-offs, which need to be considered carefully. For example, shipping raw material by air freight instead of by rail may cut transit time in half and therefore reduce average pipeline inventory by 50 percent, but it might increase unit cost because of higher transportation costs. Therefore, the consequences of changing suppliers or transport modes should be weighed against investing in more (or less) inventory.

Cycle stock exists whenever orders are made in larger quantities than needed to satisfy immediate requirements. For example, a distribution center may sell two units of a given end item weekly. However, because of scale economies with larger shipping quantities, it might choose to order a batch of eight units once each month. By investing in cycle stock, it can satisfy many periods of demand, rather than immediate need, and keep shipping costs down.

Safety stock provides protection against irregularities or uncertainties in an item's demand or supply—that is, when demand exceeds what's forecast or when resupply time is longer than anticipated. Safety stock ensures that customer demand can be satisfied immediately, and that customers won't have to wait while their orders are backlogged. For example, a portion of the inventory held at distribution centers may be safety stock. Suppose average demand for a given product in a distribution center is 100 units a week, with an average restocking lead time of one week. Weekly demand might be as large as 150 units with replenishment lead time as long as two weeks. To ensure meeting the maximum demand requirements in this situation, a safety stock of 200 units might be created.

An important management question concerns the amount of safety stock actually required; that is, how much protection is desirable? This question represents an inventory-investment trade-off between protection against demand and supply uncertainties and costs of investing in safety stock.

Anticipation stock is needed for products with seasonal patterns of demand and uniform supply. Manufacturers of children's toys, air conditioners, and calendars all face peak demand conditions where the production facility is frequently unable to meet peak seasonal demand. Therefore, anticipation stocks are built up in advance and depleted during the peak demand periods. Again, trade-offs must be considered. An investment in additional factory capacity could reduce the need for anticipation stocks.

Management Issues

Several issues surround the management of independent-demand inventories. In this section we look at three: making routine inventory decisions, determining inventory system performance, and timing implementation.

Routine Inventory Decisions

Basically only two decisions need to be made in managing independent-demand inventories: *how much to order (size)* and *when to order (timing)*. These two decisions can be made routinely by using any one of the four inventory control *decision rules* in Figure 11.2. The decision rules involve placing orders for either a fixed or a variable order quantity, with either a fixed or a variable time between successive orders. For example, under the commonly used order point (Q, R) rule, an order for a fixed quantity (Q) is placed whenever the stock position reaches a reorder point (R). The stock "position" is the on-hand balance adjusted by orders placed but not delivered and inventory already allocated for a specific use. Likewise, under the S, T rule, an order is placed once every T periods for an amount equaling the difference between current position and a desired inventory level (S) on receipt of the replenishment order.

Effective use of any of these decision rules involves properly determining decision rule parameter values (e.g., Q, R, S, and T). This chapter details procedures for determining order quantity (Q) and reorder point (R) parameters for the order point rule, and it gives references covering determination of parameter values for the other decision rules in Figure 11.2.

Determining Inventory System Performance

A key management issue is determining the inventory control system's performance. We've already mentioned how large the investment in inventory can be. That investment's size makes it a visible performance measure. Because of this, some managers simply specify inventory reduction targets as the performance measure. Unfortunately this is usually too simplistic. It doesn't reflect trade-offs between the inventory investment and other benefits or activities in the company, nor does it account for the magnitude of the demand on the inventory.

To overcome the latter concern, a common measure of inventory performance, **inventory turnover,** relates inventory levels to the product's sales volume. Inventory turnover is computed

FIGURE 11.2
Inventory Decision Rules

	Order Quantity	
Order frequency	Fixed Q*	Variable S†
Variable R‡	Q, R	S, R
Fixed T§	Q, T	S, T

*Q = order a fixed quantity Q.
†S = order up to a fixed expected opening inventory quantity S.
‡R = place an order when the inventory balance drops to R.
§T = place an order every T periods.

as annual sales volume divided by average inventory investment. Thus, a product with annual sales volume of $200,000 and average inventory investment of $50,000 has inventory turnover of 4. That is, the inventory was replaced (turned) four times during the year.

Turnover is often used to compare an individual firm's performance with others in the same industry or to monitor the effects of a change in inventory decision rules. High inventory turnover suggests a high rate of return on inventory investment. Nevertheless, though it does relate inventory level to sales activity, it doesn't reflect benefits of having the inventory.

To capture a major benefit of inventory, some firms use customer service to assess their inventory system performance. One common measure of customer service is the **fill rate** (the percentage of units immediately available when requested by customers). Thus, a 98 percent fill rate means only 2 percent of the units requested weren't on the shelf when a customer asked for them. A 98 percent fill rate sounds good. On the other hand, a 2 percent rate of unsatisfied customers doesn't. Some firms now use a dissatisfaction measure to focus attention on continuous improvement of customer service.

Other measures of inventory-related customer service can be used, but all attempt to formalize trade-offs in costs and benefits. Common among the alternatives are the percentage of the different items ordered that were available, number of times any shortage occurred in a time period, length of time before the item was made available, and percentage of customers who suffered a lack of availability. The correct measure or measures depend on the reason for having the inventory, the item's importance, the nature of the business, and the firm's objectives.

Implementing Changes in Managing Inventory

After analysis of the appropriate decision rules and performance measures, the critical management task is making the changes to improve inventory performance. Appropriate timing of these changes is important. Informal procedures may be quite effective for managing inventories in a small-scale warehouse; as the number of products and sales volumes increases, more formal inventory control methods are needed to assure continued growth. Further improvements might be warranted as the business grows and as inventory management technology improves.

Some of this chapter's concepts require new mindsets, such as the distinction between dependent and independent demand. Other concepts require new organizational objectives and role changes throughout the company. Both these issues must be explicitly considered in timing implementation. One final caveat in implementation, especially for highly automated computer systems: the basic systems must be in place first. If inventory accuracy is poor, computerizing only means that mistakes can be made at the speed of light! If the warehouse currently runs on informal knowledge of what's where and how much is available, or if some inventory is held back by salespersons for "their" customers, a formal system won't help. Basic disciplines and understandings must be in place before formal decision rules are developed.

Inventory-Related Costs

Investment in inventory isn't the only cost associated with managing inventories, even though it may be the most visible. This section treats three other cost elements: cost of preparing an order for more inventory, cost of keeping that inventory on hand until a customer requests it, and cost implied when there is a shortage of inventory. We'll also discuss incremental costs in the context of inventory management.

Order Preparation Costs

Order preparation costs are incurred each time an inventory replenishment order is placed. Included are the variable clerical costs associated with issuing the paperwork, plus any one-time costs involved in, for example, transporting goods between plants and distribution centers. Work measurement techniques, such as time study, can be used to measure the labor content of order preparation. Determining other order preparation costs is sometimes more subtle. For instance, the inventory balance might need to be verified before ordering. Sometimes there may be a fixed cost for filling out a form and a variable cost for each item ordered. Companies frequently bear large costs of maintaining files, controlling quality, and verifying accurate receipts, as well as other hidden costs.

Inventory Carrying Costs

Inventory commits management to certain costs that are related to inventory quantity, items' value, and length of time the inventory is carried. By committing capital to inventory, a firm forgoes use of these funds for other purposes (e.g., to acquire new equipment, to develop new products, or to invest in short-term securities). Therefore, a cost of capital, which is expressed as an annual interest rate, is incurred on the inventory investment.

The cost of capital may be based on the cost of obtaining bank loans to finance the inventory investment (e.g., 5 to 20 percent), the interest rate on short-term securities the firm could earn if funds weren't invested in inventory (e.g., 5 to 15 percent), or the rate of return on capital investment projects that can't be undertaken because funds must be committed to inventory. For example, the cost of capital for inventory investment might be 25 percent in the case where a new machine would yield a 25 percent return on investment. In any case, capital cost for inventory might be determined by alternative uses for funds. Cost of capital typically varies from 5 to 35 percent, but climbs substantially higher in some cases.

The cost of capital is only one part of inventory holding cost. Others are the variable costs of taxes and insurance on inventories, costs of inventory obsolescence or product shelf life limitations, and operating costs involved in storing inventory—for example, rental of public warehousing space, or costs of owning and operating warehouse facilities (such as costs of heat, light, and labor). One example of product obsolescence is that of freshly cut flowers, which must be replaced each week. This implies at least a 5,200 percent annual cost to carry fresh flowers.

As an example, if capital cost is 10 percent, and combined costs of renting warehouse space, product obsolescence, taxes, and insurance come to an additional 10 percent of the average value of the inventory investment, total annual cost of carrying inventory is 20 percent of the cost of an inventory item. In this example, an inventory item costing $1 per unit would have an inventory carrying cost of $0.20/unit/year.

Shortage and Customer Service Costs

A final set of inventory-related costs consists of those incurred when demand exceeds the available inventory for an item. This cost is more difficult to measure than the order preparation or inventory carrying costs.

In some cases, shortage costs may equal the product's contribution margin when the customer can purchase the item from competing firms. In other cases, it may involve only the paperwork required to keep track of a back order until a product becomes available. However, this cost may be very substantial in cases where significant customer goodwill is lost. The major emphasis placed on meeting delivery requirements in many firms suggests that, while shortage and customer service costs are difficult to measure, they're critical in assessing inventory performance.

Customer service measures are frequently used as surrogate measures for inventory shortage cost—for example, the fill rate achieved in meeting product demand (i.e., the percentage of demand supplied directly from inventory on demand). If the annual demand for an item is 1,000 units and 950 units are supplied directly from inventory, a 95 percent fill rate is achieved.

The level of customer service can be measured in several ways; examples include the fill rate, average length of time required to satisfy back orders, or percentage of replenishment order cycles in which one or more units are back-ordered. Level of customer service can also be translated into level of inventory investment required to achieve a given level of customer service. As an example, a safety stock of 1,000 units may be required to achieve an 85 percent customer service level, while 2,000 units of safety stock may be required to achieve a 98 percent customer service level. Translating customer service level objectives into the inventory investment required often is useful in determining customer service level/inventory trade-offs.

Incremental Inventory Costs

Two criteria are useful in determining which costs are relevant to a particular inventory management decision: (1) Does the cost represent an actual out-of-pocket expenditure or a forgone profit? (2) Does the cost actually vary with the decision being made? Determining the item cost used in calculating inventory carrying cost is a good illustration of applying these criteria. The item's cost should represent the actual out-of-pocket cost of purchasing or producing the item and placing it in inventory (i.e., an item's variable material, labor, and overhead costs). An element of the overhead cost, such as a cost allocation for general administrative expenses, isn't an actual out-of-pocket expenditure.

Another example involves measuring clerical costs incurred in preparing replenishment orders. If clerical staff size remains constant throughout the year, regardless of the number of replenishment orders placed, this cost is not relevant to the decision being made (i.e., the replenishment order quantity). These examples are not meant to be exhaustive, but rather illustrative of the careful analysis required in determining costs to be considered in evaluating inventory management performance.

An Example Cost Trade-Off

Order quantity decisions primarily affect the amount of inventory held in cycle stocks at various stocking points in the different stages of the supply chain in Figure 11.1. Large order quantities mean orders are placed infrequently and lead to low annual costs of preparing replenishment orders, but they also increase cycle stock inventories and annual costs of carrying inventory. Determining replenishment order quantities focuses on the question of what quantity provides the most economic trade-off between order preparation and inventory carrying costs. A television set stocked in a distribution center is used to illustrate this trade-off.

FIGURE 11.3
Inventory Level versus Time for LCD Television

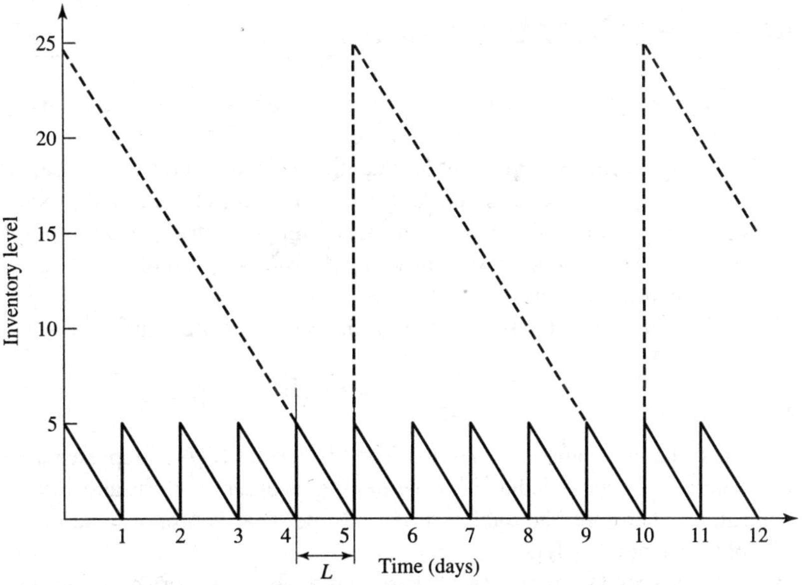

The LCD television is sold to several hundred retail stores from a distribution center. To avoid excessive inventories, stores place orders frequently and in small quantities. The demand for the LCD television at a typical retail store was obtained from past sales records. It averages five units per weekday (or 1,250 units per year). The LCD television can be obtained within a one-day lead time from the distribution center (DC) serving the retail stores. This requires preparing an order and faxing it to the DC. The variable cost of preparing a replenishment order is estimated to be \$6.25. The firm's cost of carrying inventory is estimated at 25 percent of the item cost per year, including variable costs of capital, insurance, taxes, and obsolescence. Because the LCD television unit cost is \$100, inventory carrying cost is \$25/unit/year.

Currently, the retail stores order the LCD television on a daily basis in lots of five units. The solid line in Figure 11.3 plots the inventory level versus time for this decision rule. This plot assumes demand is constant at five units per day, and the resulting average inventory level is 2.5 units. Because orders are placed daily, 250 orders are placed per year, costing a total of \$1,562.50/year (\$6.25 × 250). The average inventory of 2.5 units represents an annual inventory carrying cost of \$62.50 a year (2.5 × \$25), yielding an overall combined cost of \$1,625/year for placing orders and carrying inventory.

The dashed line in Figure 11.3 shows the inventory level plot for an alternative order quantity of 25 units, or placing orders weekly. In this case, average inventory is 12.5 units and 50 orders are placed annually. The larger order quantity in this case provides important savings in ordering cost (\$312.50 versus the previous \$1,562.50) with an increase in annual inventory cost (\$312.50 versus the previous \$62.50). Overall, a shift to a larger order quantity produces a favorable trade-off between ordering and inventory carrying costs, which cuts total cost to \$625 per year.

A number of order quantities could be evaluated to determine the best trade-off between ordering and inventory carrying costs. The economic order quantity model, however, enables us to determine the lowest-cost order quantity directly.

Economic Order Quantity Model

The order quantity decision is formally stated in the **economic order quantity (EOQ) model.** This equation describes the relationship between costs of placing orders, costs of carrying inventory, and the order quantity. This model makes several simplifying assumptions: the demand rate is constant, the costs don't change, and production and inventory capacity are unlimited. Despite these seemingly restrictive assumptions, the EOQ model provides useful guidelines for ordering decisions—even in operating situations that depart substantially from these assumptions.

The total annual cost equation for the economic order quantity is

$$\text{TAC} = (A/Q)C_P + (Q/2)C_H \qquad \textbf{(11.1)}$$

This equation contains two terms. The first term, $(A/Q)C_P$, represents annual ordering cost, where A is annual demand for the item, Q is order quantity, and C_P is cost of order preparation. Therefore, the total ordering cost per year is proportional to the number of orders placed annually (A/Q).

The second term, $(Q/2)C_H$, represents annual inventory carrying cost, where average inventory is assumed to be half the order quantity (Q), and C_H is the inventory carrying cost per unit per year; that is, item cost (v) times the annual inventory carrying cost rate (C_r).

Combined costs of ordering and carrying inventory are expressed as a function of the order quantity (Q) in Equation (11.1), enabling us to evaluate the total cost of any given order quantity.

Determining the EOQ

One method of determining the lowest-cost ordering quantity is to graph the total cost equation for various order quantities. Figure 11.4 plots the total cost equation for the LCD television for several different order quantities for the following data:

$$A = 1{,}250$$
$$C_p = 6.25$$
$$C_H = 25$$
$$\text{TAC} = (1{,}250/Q)6.25 + (Q/2)25$$

Minimum total cost can be found graphically to equal 25 (i.e., placing orders weekly). Both terms of the total-cost equation are also plotted. We should note several facts in these graphs. First, inventory carrying costs increase in a straight line as order quantity is increased, while ordering cost diminishes rapidly at first and then at a slower rate as the ordering cost is allocated over an increasing number of units. Second, for this cost structure, the minimum cost solution exists where the ordering cost per year equals annual inventory carrying cost. (This observation is used in developing lot-sizing decision rules for dependent-demand items.) Finally, total cost is relatively flat around the minimum cost solution ($Q = 25$ in this case), indicating inventory management performance is relatively insensitive to small changes in order quantity around the minimum-cost solution.

FIGURE 11.4
Cost versus Order Quantity for LCD Television

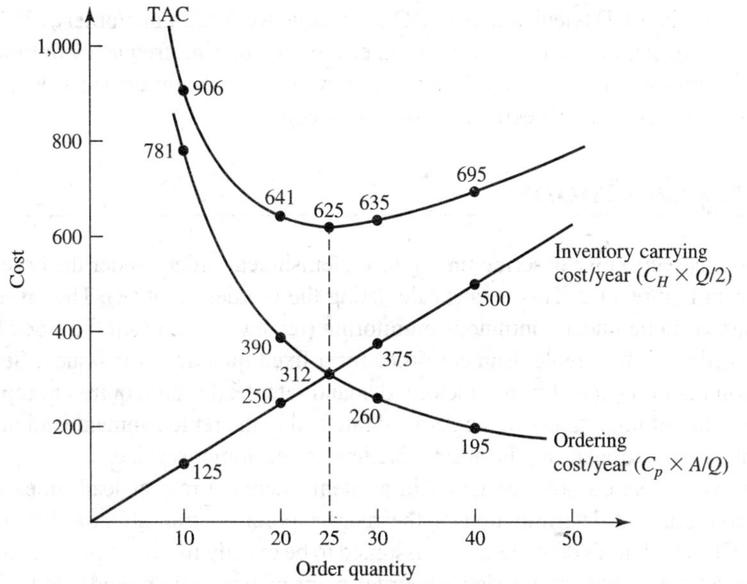

A second and more direct method of solving for the minimum-cost order quantity is by using the EOQ formula in Equation (11.2):

$$\text{EOQ} = \sqrt{\frac{2C_pA}{C_H}} \qquad \textbf{(11.2)}$$

This formula is derived from the total cost equation (11.1) by using calculus. That is, Equation (11.1) is differentiated with respect to the decision variable Q and solved by setting the resulting equation equal to zero, as Equations (11.3) through (11.6) show:

$$d\text{TAC}/dQ = -C_p(A/Q^2) + C_H/2 \qquad \textbf{(11.3)}$$

$$C_pA/Q^2 = C_H/2 \qquad \textbf{(11.4)}$$

$$Q^2 = 2C_pA/C_H \qquad \textbf{(11.5)}$$

$$\text{EOQ} = \sqrt{\frac{2C_pA}{C_H}} \qquad \textbf{(11.6)}$$

where EOQ = the optimal value of Q.

Using the EOQ formula for the LCD television produces a lot size of 25; that is, $\sqrt{[(2)(6.25)(1250)]/25}$. In using this expression, we must make sure both demand and inventory carrying costs are measured in the same units (1,250 units/year and \$25/unit/year, in this case).

In addition to its use in determining order quantities, the EOQ formula can also be used to develop another important measure in the control of inventories, the **economic time between orders (TBO).** The formula to calculate TBO in weeks is

$$\text{TBO} = \text{EOQ}/\overline{D} \qquad \textbf{(11.7)}$$

where $\overline{D}$ = average weekly usage rate.

For the LCD television, the TBO equals one week (25 units/order)/(25 units/week). This measure can be used to determine an economic ordering frequency or time between inventory reviews. In the case of the LCD television, we might consider using a Q, T decision rule; that is, order an economic lot size weekly.

Order Timing Decisions

In this section we describe timing of replenishment orders under the order point rule Q, R from Figure 11.2. This means calculating the reorder point (R). The inventory level is assumed to be under continuous monitoring (review), and, when the stock level reaches the reorder point, a replenishment order for a fixed quantity Q is issued. Setting the reorder point is influenced by four factors: demand rate, lead time required to replenish inventory, amount of uncertainty in the demand rate and in the replenishment lead time, and management policy regarding the acceptable level of customer service.

When there's no uncertainty in an item's demand rate or lead time, safety stock isn't required, and determination of the reorder point is straightforward. For example, if the LCD television's demand rate is assumed to be exactly five units per day, and replenishment lead time is exactly one day, a reorder point of five units provides sufficient inventory to cover demand until the replenishment order is received.

Using Safety Stock for Uncertainty

The assumptions of fixed demand rate and constant replenishment lead time are rarely justified in actual operations. Random fluctuations in demand for individual products occur because of variations in the timing of consumers' purchases of the product. Likewise, the replenishment lead time often varies because of machine breakdowns, employee absenteeism, material shortages, or transportation delays in the factory and distribution operations.

The LCD television illustrates the amount of uncertainty usually experienced in demand for end-product items. Analysis of this item's retail sales and inventory records indicates replenishment lead time is quite stable, requiring a one-day transit time from the distribution center to the retail stores. However, daily demand D varies considerably from day to day. While daily demand averages five units, demands of from one to nine units have been experienced, as the demand distribution in Figure 11.5 shows.

If the reorder point is set at five units to cover average demand during the one-day replenishment lead time, inventory shortages of one to four units can result when daily demand exceeds the average of five units, that is, when demand equals six, seven, eight, or nine units. Therefore, if we're to protect against inventory shortages when there's uncertainty in demand, the reorder point must be greater than average demand during the replenishment lead time. The difference between the average demand during lead time and the reorder point is called **safety stock** (S). Increasing the reorder point to nine units would provide a safety stock of four units as long as the LCD television's historical pattern of demand does not change.

The Introduction of Safety Stock

Figure 11.6 illustrates introducing safety stock into the reorder point setting. The reorder point R in this diagram has two components: safety stock level S, and level of inventory

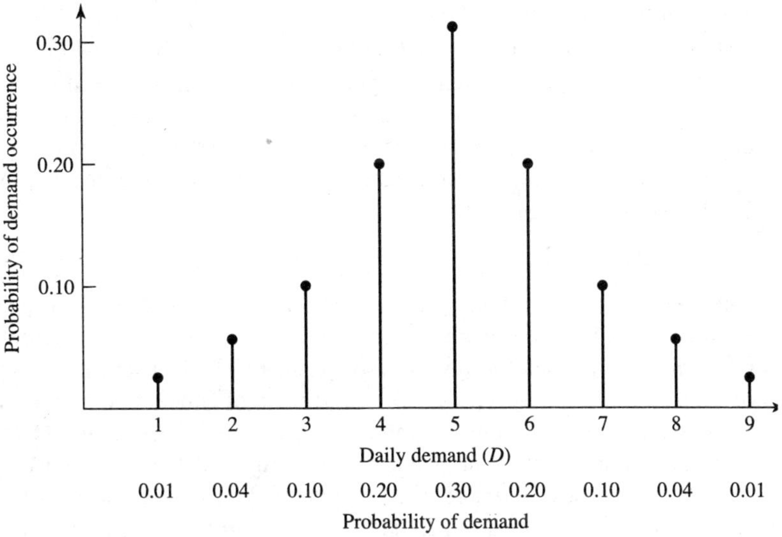

FIGURE 11.5
LCD Television Daily Demand Distribution

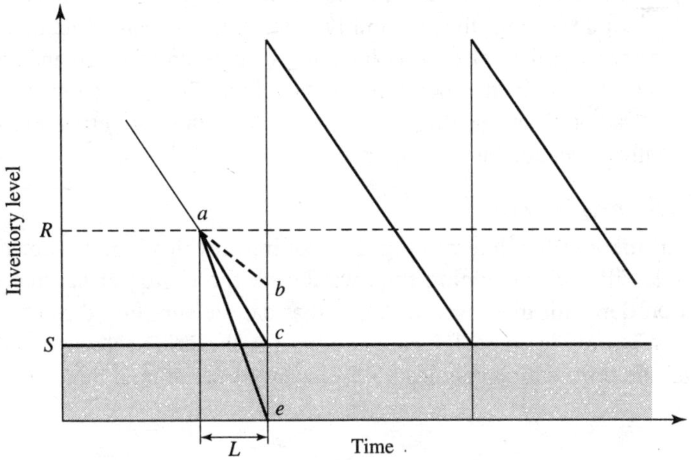

FIGURE 11.6
Introducing Safety Stock as a Buffer against Demand Variability

$(R - S)$ required to satisfy average demand $\bar{d}$ during the average replenishment lead time L. The reorder point is the sum of these two: $R = \bar{d} + S$. To simplify this explanation, lead time in Figure 11.6 is assumed to be constant while demand rate varies.

When a replenishment order is issued (at point *a*), demand variations during the replenishment lead time mean the inventory level can drop to a point between *b* and *e*. In the LCD television's case, the inventory level may drop by one to nine units (points *b* and *e*, respectively) before a replenishment order is received. When demand equals the average rate of five units or less, the inventory level reaches a point between *b* and *c*, and the safety stock isn't needed. However, when the demand rate exceeds the five-unit average and inventory level drops to a point between *c* and *e*, a stockout will occur unless safety stock is available. (We can construct a similar diagram when both demand rate and lead time vary.)

Determining the Safety Stock

Before deciding the safety stock level, we must establish a criterion for determining how much protection against inventory shortages is warranted. One of two different criteria is often used: the probability of stocking out in any given replenishment order cycle, or the desired level of customer service in satisfying product demand immediately out of inventory (the fill rate). We illustrate both criteria using the demand distribution for the LCD television in Figure 11.5.

Stockout Probability

One method for determining the required level of safety stock is to specify an acceptable risk of stocking out during any given replenishment order cycle. Figure 11.5 provides demand distribution data for this analysis for the LCD television. There is a 0.05 probability of demand exceeding seven units (i.e., a demand of either eight or nine units occurring). A safety stock level of two units (meaning a reorder point of seven units) would provide a risk of stocking out in 5 percent (1 out of 20) of the replenishment order cycles. This safety stock level provides a 0.95 probability of meeting demand during any given replenishment order cycle. Note this means there is a 0.05 probability of stocking out by *either* one or two units when demand exceeds seven units.

We can reduce the risk of stocking out by investing more in safety stock; that is, with safety stock of three units, the probability of stocking out can be cut to 0.01, and with four units of safety stock the risk of stocking out is 0, assuming the demand distribution doesn't change. Thus, one method of determining the required level of safety stock is to specify an acceptable trade-off between the probability of stocking out during a replenishment order cycle and investment of funds in inventory.

Customer Service Level

A second method for determining the required level of safety stock is to specify an acceptable fill rate. For doing this, we define the customer service level as the percentage of demand, measured in units, that can be supplied directly out of inventory. Figure 11.7 provides data for calculations for the LCD television. It shows a safety stock of one unit, which enables 95.8 percent of the annual demand of 1,250 units for

FIGURE 11.7 **Safety Stock Determination for Specified Service Levels**

Reorder Point R	Safety Stock S	Demand Probability, $P(d) = R$	Probability of Stocking Out, $P(d) > R$	Average Number of Shortages per Replenishment Order Cycle*	Service Level† SL, %
5	0	0.30	0.35	0.56	88.8
6	1	0.20	0.15	0.21	95.8
7	2	0.10	0.05	0.06	98.8
8	3	0.04	0.01	0.01	99.8
9	4	0.01	0.00		100.0

*Calculated by $\sum_{d=R+1}^{d_{MAX}} P(d)(d-R)$.

†Assuming the replenishment order quantity is five units.

this item to be supplied directly out of inventory to the customer. We compute the service level as follows:

$$SL = 100 - (100/Q) \sum_{d=R+1}^{d_{MAX}} P(d)(d - R) \qquad \textbf{(11.8)}$$

where

Q = order quantity

R = reorder point

$P(d)$ = probability of a demand of d units during the replenishment lead time

d_{MAX} = maximum demand during the replenishment lead time

For example, when the safety stock is set at one unit in Figure 11.7, we compute the service level as

$$SL = 95.8 = 100 - (100/5)[(0.01)(3) + (0.04)(2) + (0.1)(1)] \qquad \textbf{(11.9)}$$

A service level of 95.8 percent means 4.2 percent of the annual demand, or (0.042)(1,250) = 52.5 units, can't be supplied directly out of inventory. Returning to when the store was ordering five units, and the item was ordered 250 times per year, the average number of stockouts per reorder cycle would be 0.21 (i.e., 52.5/250), as shown in Figure 11.7.

Figure 11.7 shows the effect of increasing the safety stock level on both the service level and the average number of shortages per replenishment order cycle. The service level can be raised to 100 percent by increasing safety stock to four units. Again, as in the case of the stockout probability method described previously, choice of the required safety stock level depends on determining an acceptable trade-off between customer service level and inventory investment.

So far, the safety stock and order quantity parameters for an order point system have been determined separately. These two parameters are, however, interdependent in their effect on customer service level performance. We can see this interactive effect in Equation (11.8), because both safety stock level and order quantity size affect the level of customer service.

Continuous Distributions

Two different criteria for determining the required safety stock level and the reorder point have been described (i.e., use of a stockout probability and a desired level of customer service). In discussing both criteria, we used a discrete distribution to describe the uncertainty in demand during the replenishment lead time. It's frequently convenient to approximate a discrete distribution with a continuous distribution to simplify the safety stock and reorder point calculations. One distribution that often provides a close approximation to empirical data is the normal distribution. In this section, we indicate the changes required in the calculations when the normal distribution is used to describe uncertainty in demand during the replenishment lead time.

Figure 11.8's data enable us to compare the empirically derived probability values for the LCD television demand in Figure 11.5, with similar values derived from the normal

FIGURE 11.8 **Normal Approximation to the Empirical Demand Distribution***

Midpoint X	Discrete Distribution Probability	Interval	Normal Distribution Probability	Probability of Demand Exceeding $(X + 0.5)$	Expected Number of Stockouts When Reorder Point = X†
1	0.01	0.5–1.5	0.0085	0.9902	4.0068
2	0.04	1.5–2.5	0.0380	0.9522	3.0128
3	0.11	2.5–3.5	0.1109	0.8413	2.0591
4	0.20	3.5–4.5	0.2108	0.6305	1.2303
5	0.30	4.5–5.5	0.2610	0.3695	0.5983
6	0.20	5.5–6.5	0.2108	0.1587	0.2255
7	0.10	6.5–7.5	0.1109	0.0478	0.0641
8	0.04	7.5–8.5	0.0380	0.0098	0.0127
9	0.01	8.5–9.5	0.0085	0.0013	0.0018

*A χ^2 test indicates that these two distributions are not significantly different. ($\chi^2 = 8.75$ versus 20.09 at the 0.01 level of significance.)
†This is $\sigma_d E(Z)$ based on the $E(Z)$ values from R. G. Brown, *Decision Rules for Inventory Management.* New York: Holt, Rinehart & Winston, 1967, pp. 95–103.

distribution. The comparison shows the normal distribution closely approximates the empirical observations and can be used to determine safety stock and reorder point levels.

Probability of Stocking Out Criterion

When the probability of stocking out is used as the safety stock criterion, the required level of safety stock and the reorder point values are easily computed by using the normal distribution. First, we determine the mean and standard deviation for the distribution of demand during the replenishment lead time. These values have been calculated for the empirical distribution data for the LCD television in Figure 11.5 and are shown in Figure 11.9 along with examples of the area (probability) under the normal distribution. (Refer to the appendix at the end of the book for a table of normal distribution probabilities.)

Next, we can calculate the safety stock (or reorder point) value using a table of normal probability values. For example, suppose sufficient safety stock is desired for the LCD

FIGURE 11.9
Daily Demand Distribution

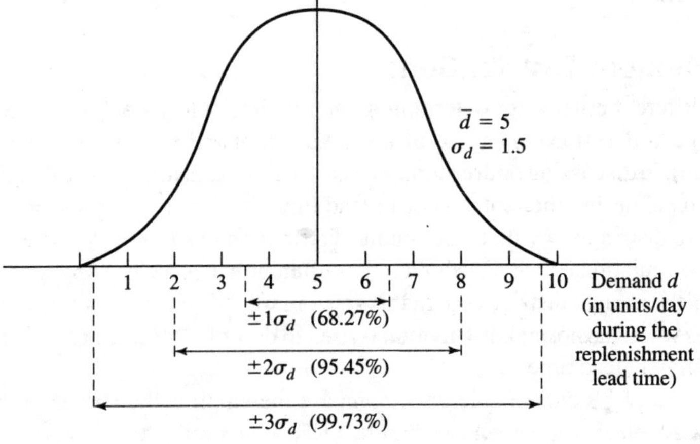

television that the probability of stocking out in any given replenishment order cycle is 0.05. We determine the safety stock level and the reorder point as follows:

$$\text{Safety stock} = Z\sigma_d \qquad \textbf{(11.10)}$$

$$\text{Recorder point} = \text{mean demand during the replenishment lead time} + Z\sigma_d \qquad \textbf{(11.11)}$$

where

Z = appropriate value from a table of standard normal distribution probabilities

σ_d = demand during the replenishment lead time standard deviation.

The Z value for a 0.05 probability of stocking out is 1.645 (from a table of standard normal distribution probabilities). The required level of safety stock, therefore, is 2.5 units—that is, (1.645)(1.5)—and the reorder point is 7.5 (or 8) units. The reorder point can also be determined directly from the data in Figure 11.8, where the probability of demand exceeding 7.5 is 0.0478.

Customer Service Criterion

When the customer service level is used as the safety stock criterion, we can also determine the desired level of safety stock using the normal distribution approximation. For this case, we need the average number of stockouts per replenishment order cycle. To get this, the quantity

$$\sum_{d=R+1}^{d_{\text{MAX}}} P(d)(d - R)$$

shown in Equations (11.8) and (11.9) is replaced by $\sigma_d E(Z)$. The σ_d still equals the standard deviation of the normal distribution being used to approximate demand during replenishment lead time. The $E(Z)$ value is the partial expectation of the normal distribution called the service function. It's the expected *number* of stockouts when Z units of safety stock are held in the standard normal curve. A graph of the service function $E(Z)$ is plotted in Figure 11.10. Note when Z is less than -1, the service function $E(Z)$ is approximately linear.

The safety stock and reorder point calculations are similar to those shown earlier in Equations (11.8) and (11.9). As an illustration, suppose we want a 95 percent service level for the LCD television, and we go back to using an order quantity of five units. The required value for $E(Z)$ is computed by using Equation (11.13), which we derive from Equation (11.12):

$$\text{SL} = 100 - (100/Q)(\sigma_d E(Z)) \qquad \textbf{(11.12)}$$

or

$$E(Z) = [(100 - \text{SL})Q]/100\sigma_d \qquad \textbf{(11.13)}$$

In this case, the service function value, $E(Z)$, equals 0.167; that is,

$$E(Z) = \frac{(100 - 95)(5)}{(100)(1.5)} = 0.167 \qquad \textbf{(11.14)}$$

and

$$\sigma_d E(Z) = 0.25 \qquad \textbf{(11.15)}$$

FIGURE 11.10
Service Function

Source: R. G. Brown, *Decision Rules for Inventory Management*. New York: Holt, Rinehart & Winston, 1967, pp. 95–103.

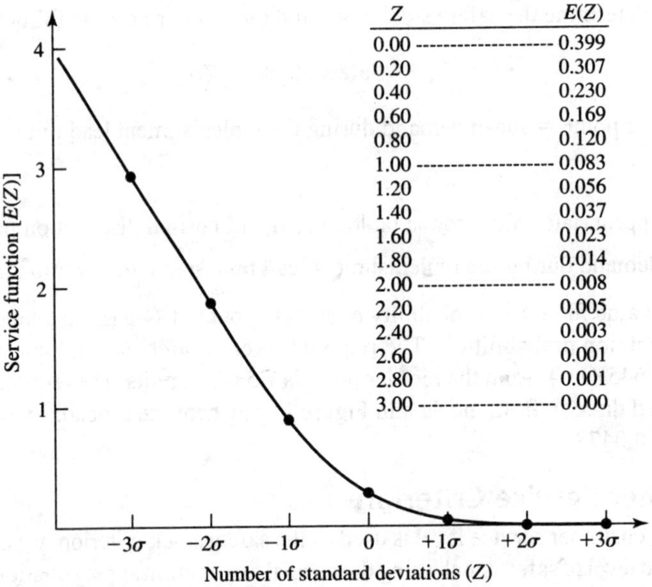

Example points

Z	*E(Z)*
0.00	0.399
0.20	0.307
0.40	0.230
0.60	0.169
0.80	0.120
1.00	0.083
1.20	0.056
1.40	0.037
1.60	0.023
1.80	0.014
2.00	0.008
2.20	0.005
2.40	0.003
2.60	0.001
2.80	0.001
3.00	0.000

From the service function table in Figure 11.10, we find an $E(Z)$ of 0.167 represents a Z value of approximately $+0.6\sigma_d$. The safety stock level therefore is $0.9 = (0.6)(1.5)$. The reorder point would be 5.9. Alternatively, from Figure 11.8, we find $R = 6$ when $\sigma_d E(Z) = 0.2255$. Note this is the same result we got by using the empirical discrete distribution earlier.

Time Period Correction Factor

In the preceding examples, the demand data were expressed as units per day and the lead time was one day. Sometimes the demand data are provided in a different number of time units than the lead time. For example, we might have weekly demand and a two-week lead time. In such cases, adjustments must be made in calculating safety stock as shown in Equation (11.16).

$$\text{Average demand during replenishment lead time} = \overline{D}m \qquad \textbf{(11.16)}$$

The standard deviation of demand during replenishment lead time is

$$\sigma_d = \sigma_D\sqrt{m} \qquad \textbf{(11.17)}$$

and

$$\text{Safety stock} = Z\sigma_D\sqrt{m} \qquad \textbf{(11.18)}$$

where:

$\overline{D}$ = average demand per period

m = lead time expressed as a multiple of the time period used for the demand distribution

σ_d = standard deviation of the demand during replenishment lead time

σ_D = standard deviation of the demand per period

Z = appropriate value from a table of standard normal distribution probabilities

If lead time for the LCD television were three days instead of one day, required safety stock would be 4.3 units [that is, $(1.645)(1.5)\sqrt{3}$] and the reorder point would be 19.3 units [(3 days)(5 units/day) + 4.3 units]. Because lead time in this example is three times the demand interval of one day, the factor has been included in calculating required safety stock. The resulting safety stock level increases for the three-day lead time to allow for the possible increase in variation in demand over the additional two days.

Up to this point we have considered variability in the demand only and have considered the lead time to be known and constant. Clearly, transportation difficulties, lack of inventory at the supplier, miscommunications, and other problems can introduce uncertainty into the lead time as well. With globalization increasing distances between companies in the supply chain, uncertain lead times are a growing reality and an increasingly important issue to address. The correction for uncertain lead time is substantially more complicated than for multiple but certain periods.

The parameters of the demand during the replenishment lead time distribution when both lead time and demand are uncertain are found by using Equations (11.19) and (11.20), as reported by Nahmias.

$$\text{Average demand during replenishment lead time} = \overline{D}\overline{L} \qquad \textbf{(11.19)}$$

The standard deviation of demand during replenishment lead time is

$$\sigma_d = \sqrt{\overline{L}\sigma_D^2 + \overline{D}^2\sigma_L^2} \qquad \textbf{(11.20)}$$

where

$\overline{D}$ = average demand per period

$\overline{L}$ = average lead time in periods

σ_D = standard deviation of the demand per period

σ_L = replenishment lead time standard deviation

Continuing with our LCD television example, if the lead time averaged three days with a standard deviation of 1.1 days, then the standard deviation of demand during the lead time would be 6.1 units [that is, $\sqrt{(3)1.5^2 + (5^2)(1.1^2)}$]. The safety stock would then be 10 units [that is, 1.645(6.1)] and the reorder point 25 units [(3 days)(5 units/day) + 10 units].

Forecast Error Distribution

In many inventory management software packages, demand values for the economic order quantity and reorder point calculations are forecast by using statistical techniques such as exponential smoothing. When these forecasting techniques are used, the required safety stock level depends on the forecasting model's accuracy—how much variation there is around the forecast. Very little safety stock is required when forecast errors are small, and vice versa, for a fixed level of customer service. One commonly used measure of forecasting model accuracy is the mean absolute deviation (MAD) of the forecast errors.

The methods for determining the safety stock and reorder point levels described earlier in this chapter are relevant when product demand is forecast and a MAD value is maintained for the forecasting model. We make use of the fact that the value of σ_E can be approximated by 1.25MAD when the forecast errors are normally distributed. We calculate the safety stock values as follows:

$$\sigma_E = 1.25\text{MAD} \tag{11.21}$$

$$\text{Safety stock} = Z\sigma_E = Z(1.25\text{MAD}) \tag{11.22}$$

where

σ_E = forecast error distribution standard deviation

Z = appropriate value from a table of standard normal distribution probabilities

As an illustration, suppose an exponential smoothing model is used to forecast demand for the LCD television, a 0.05 probability of stocking out during a reorder cycle is specified, and the forecast errors are normally distributed, as Figure 11.11 shows. Because the Z value is 1.645 for a 0.05 probability of stocking out and the MAD value equals 1.2 from Figure 11.11, the required level of safety stock is 2.5 units; that is, (1.645)(1.25)(1.2). The reorder point would be 7.5 units, as we found before. The use of MAD values to approximate the standard deviation can be used in any of the formulas in this chapter for calculating safety stock, reorder points, and service levels.

FIGURE 11.11
LCD Television Forecast Error Distribution

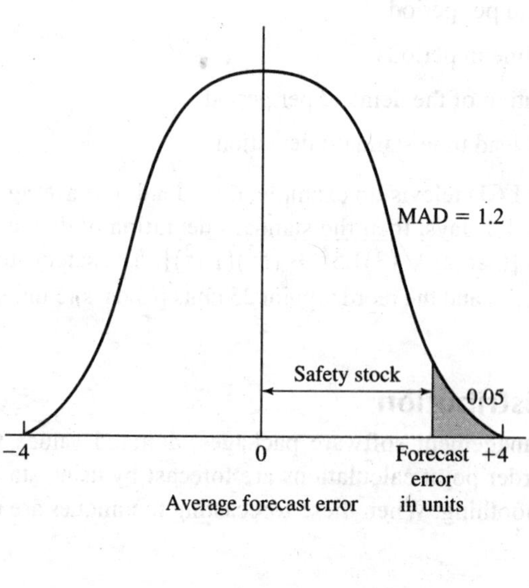

Multi-Item Management

In this section we consider the management of multiple items in inventory. In particular we look at a method for categorizing items so the most important will receive management attention. The technique is called **ABC analysis.** It is discussed with a single criterion for classification.

A single-criterion ABC analysis consists of separating the inventory items into three groupings according to their annual cost volume usage (unit cost × annual usage). These groups are: A, items having a high dollar usage; B, items having an intermediate dollar usage; and C, items having a low dollar usage.

Figure 11.12 shows the results of a typical ABC analysis. For this inventory, 20 percent of the items are A items, which account for 65 percent of the annual dollar usage. The B category constitutes 30 percent of the items and 25 percent of the dollar usage, while the remaining 50 percent of the items are C items accounting for only 10 percent of the annual dollar usage. While percentages may vary from firm to firm, it's common to find a small percentage of the items accounting for a large percentage of the annual cost volume usage.

ABC analysis provides a tool for identifying those items that will make the largest impact on the firm's overall inventory cost performance when improved inventory control procedures are implemented. A perpetual inventory system, improvements in forecasting procedures, or a careful analysis of the order quantity and timing decisions for A items will provide a larger improvement in inventory cost performance than will similar efforts on the C items. Therefore, ABC analysis is often a useful first step in improving inventory performance.

FIGURE 11.12
ABC Analysis

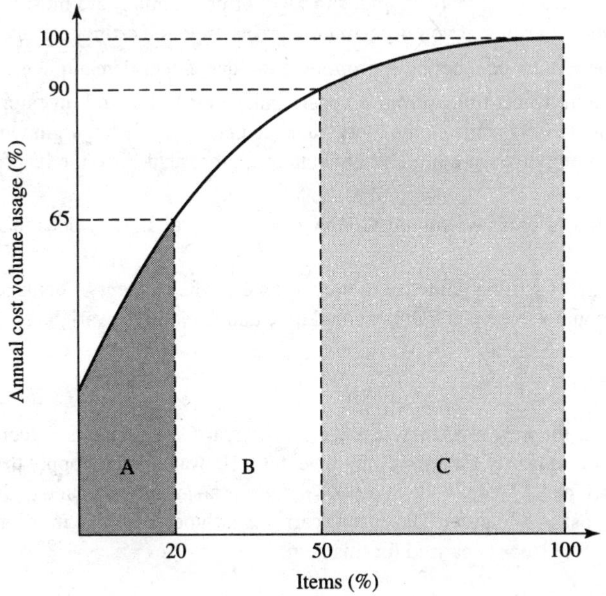

Concluding Principles

This chapter presents considerable theory on independent demand inventory management. Despite the material's technical nature, several management principles emerge:

- The difference between dependent and independent demand must serve as the first basis for determining appropriate inventory management procedures.
- Organizational criteria must be clearly established before we set safety stock levels and measure performance.
- A sound basic independent demand system must be in place before we attempt to implement the advanced techniques presented here.
- Savings in inventory-related costs can be achieved by a joint determination of the order point and order quantity parameters.
- All criteria should be taken into account in classifying inventory items for management priorities.
- The functions of inventory are useful principles to apply in determining whether or not inventory reductions can be made.

Discussion Questions

1. The concepts of independent and dependent demand are important in inventory management, but sometimes they aren't clearly distinguishable. Can you find the elements of dependency and independency in the following situations: selling snacks at a football game, producing bumpers for automobiles, and selling greeting cards at a shopping center.
2. What would you expect to find as the predominant type of inventory in the following businesses: a ski manufacturer, a make-to-order tugboat manufacturer, and a printer?
3. Which of the inventory costs (carrying, shortage, or preparation) are most difficult to measure? How would you determine if you needed more precision in the estimate of the cost?
4. Why might the EOQ model not be appropriate for a dependent-demand item?
5. A friend of yours wants to leapfrog the basic independent demand inventory ideas and go directly to implementing some of the more advanced concepts. What arguments would you raise against this strategy? What counterarguments might persuade you the leapfrog strategy would be OK?
6. How many pairs of socks do you own? How many dress suits? How does this relate to the ABC concept?
7. Use the analogy of writing home for money to explain the concept of demand during lead time. Be sure to account for the fact that both lead time and demand are variables.

Problems

1. Michael Traci, the new inventory manager at Magyar Golf Supplies, is considering using the economic order quantity for controlling inventory. He wants you to apply the EOQ to a sample product, the Super-Z Wedge. The Super-Z Wedge has an average demand of 30 units/period with an ordering cost of $30/order. The cost of carrying a Super-Z Wedge in inventory is $2.00/unit/period. No safety stock is carried for this item.

a. Calculate the economic order quantity.

b. Calculate the average cycle stock for this item using the order quantity in question a.

c. Assuming there are 12 periods per year, calculate total cost per year.

2. Demand during lead time for Louie's Lobster Pots is distributed as follows:

Probability:	0.05	0.15	0.2	0.3	0.1	0.15	0.05
Demand:	20	21	22	23	24	25	26

a. Use a spreadsheet program to evaluate the expected number of units short per reorder cycle for reorder points of 20 to 26. What's the expected shortage cost per reorder cycle when the reorder point is 20 and cost per unit short is $25?

b. What happens to the expected shortage cost (when $R = 20$ and $C_s = \$25$) if the demand distribution shifts as follows?

Probability:	0.2	0.4	0.2	0.1	0.1	0	0
Demand:	20	21	22	23	24	25	26

3. The ICU Optical Clinic has recently introduced a new line of eyeglasses that incorporates a highly fashionable frame and special lenses that darken in sunlight and lighten indoors, thus eliminating the need to purchase a separate pair of sunglasses. ICU purchases frames for the glasses from an outside vendor. The lenses are manufactured on site. The clinic has recently noted the following demand distribution for its new glasses:

Demand/month	Probability
12	0.10
13	0.15
14	0.15
15	0.20
16	0.20
17	0.10
18	0.05
19	0.05

Purchase price to the ICU Optical Clinic is $30 per frame. The clinic has an ordering cost of $25. Cost of carrying inventory is 25 percent of the item value per unit per year. Order lead time is constant at one month. The work year consists of 12 months.

a. Compute the economic order quantity for the frames ICU purchases.

b. Compute the reorder point and buffer stock level for a 99 percent customer service level. Assume order quantity and reorder point can be computed independently.

c. What's the total annual cost of carrying the buffer stock computed in part b?

4. Wally's World orders a 10-day supply of ice cream whenever on-hand inventory falls below the reorder point. Lead time for ice cream is one day. On Monday, September 30, the clerk found 18 gallons of ice cream in stock. The sales are normally distributed with a mean of 20 gallons per day and a standard deviation of 9 gallons per day. Desired customer service level is 99 percent.
   a. What reorder point for ice cream provides a 99 percent customer service level?
   b. How many gallons of ice cream should be ordered on September 30 if the store is open five days per week?
5. The Seldom Seen Ranch in Muckinfut, Texas, is in the process of developing an inventory control system for purchasing hay that will cope with Texas-size uncertainty. Seldom Seen foreman Horace Cints prepared the following information on Seldom Seen's hay use:

   Average demand during lead time = 1,000 bales

   Lead time = 1 month

   Economic order quantity = 2,500 bales

   Forecast interval = 1 month

   Mean absolute deviation of forecast error = 40 bales

   Desired probability of stocking out = 0.10

   a. How much safety stock will be required?
   b. What's the reorder point?
   c. What's the customer service level for this policy?
   d. What decision rule should Horace Cints use in ordering hay, assuming constant hay usage throughout the year?
6. After a merger, Old Framkranz found himself the only inventory clerk left at Allied Breakwater Company (ABC). The merger had left ABC with only 10 parts in inventory, and he'd been told to manage them as effectively as possible. Each part was to be reviewed once a week. (ABC worked a very exhausting five-day week.) Framkranz knew inventory carrying cost was 20 percent per dollar of cost per year. He also knew, to really manage a part's inventory well, he would have to spend a full day on the review, but he could do a reasonably good job in half a day. Even the most cursory review would require one-quarter day per part, however. Files for the 10 parts contain the following information. How should Framkranz schedule the review of the parts?

Part No.	Vendor	Unit Cost ($)	Shipping Cost/Unit	Cost per Order ($)	Annual Usage	Reorder Point	Order Quantity
1	A	0.20	0	10	1,000	50	70
2	B	1.00	0.10	20	10	1	45
3	B	0.25	0.10	15	12	2	95
4	C	3.00	0.25	15	100	20	71
5	A	10.00	0	10	300	15	55
6	B	7.00	0.10	15	2	1	7
7	C	0.50	0.25	20	10	2	13
8	A	5.00	0	10	400	20	39
9	C	20.00	0.30	20	2	1	4
10	A	2.00	0	10	200	10	100

7. Here's a sample of items from the Soaring Eagle Hang Glider Company's maintenance inventory.

Item:	a	b	c	d	e	f	g	h	i	j
Cost ($)	83	68	23	45	10	2	94	51	87	24
Usage	14	47	105	24	75	43	56	5	48	81

Rank the items in descending dollar usage order using a spreadsheet. How many items does it take to represent 50 percent of the total? How many does it take to represent the last 10 percent?

Chapter 12

Strategy and MPC System Design

This chapter concerns two integration issues in designing manufacturing planning and control (MPC) systems. The first is linking the design of a firm's MPC system with its business strategy for competing in the marketplace. As the investment in an MPC system is large, getting it correct is critical to short- and long-term competitiveness. Many companies make costly mistakes when their MPC system doesn't support their basic business strategy in the marketplace. The second issue concerns integrating manufacturing requirements planning (MRP) and just-in-time (JIT) in existing or new MPC systems. The chapter centers around five topics:

- *MPC design options:* What are critical alternatives in designing an MPC system to meet a firm's evolving needs?
- *Choosing the options:* How should the options be selected to best support the business strategy and to fit with production process design?
- *The choices in practice:* How have manufacturing firms with different competitive strategies gone about designing their MPC systems?
- *Integrating MRP and JIT:* How can these different approaches be linked in a company's MPC system?
- *Extending MPC Integration to Suppliers and Customers:* How can MPC applications be integrated across the supply chain to improve competitiveness?

MPC Design Options

A wide range of alternatives are available in designing MPC systems. These include such basic approaches as MRP, MRPII, JIT, periodic control systems, and finite scheduling systems. Moreover, there are a wide variety of options for designing the individual modules of the MPC system shown in Figure 12.1. The next three sections illustrate the variety of options for master production scheduling, detailed material planning, and back-end activities.

FIGURE 12.1
Basic MPC System

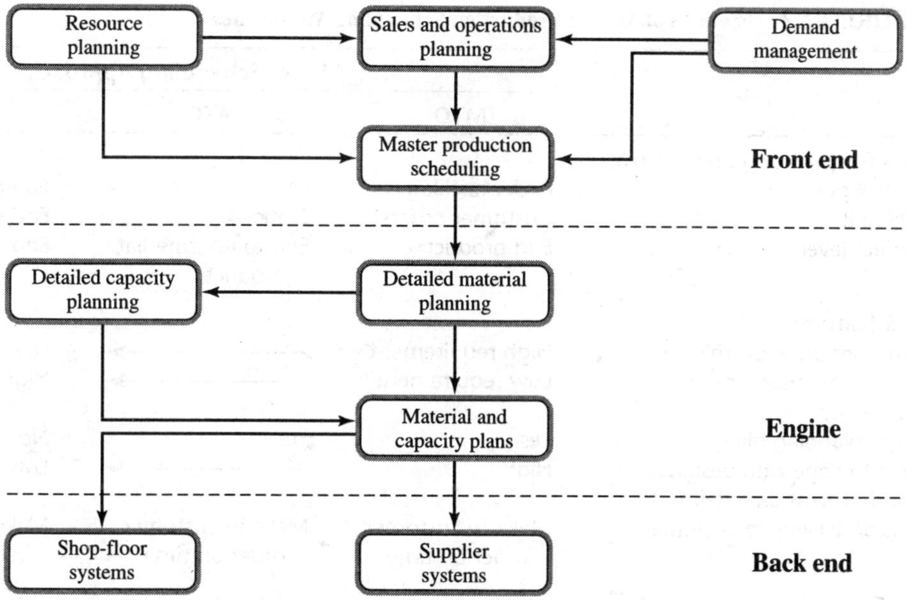

Master Production Scheduling Options

Several different approaches can be taken to designing the master production schedule: *make-to-order (MTO), assemble-to-order (ATO),* and *make-to-stock (MTS).* Figure 12.2 shows the major differences between these alternatives. A **make-to-order** approach to master production scheduling is typical when the product is custom-built to individual customer specifications. In this case the MPC system needs to encompass preproduction engineering design activities as well as manufacturing and supplier operations. For MTO, the customer order represents the unit of control in the MPS; the backlog of customer orders forms part of the overall lead time for the product. Overall, the order backlog is a critical measure for estimating material and capacity requirements. Customer order promising is based on the backlog plus estimates for each design, procurement, and manufacturing step for a particular job. Planning bills of material are extensively utilized to estimate times and to prioritize design efforts on the "critical path." There's an inherently large degree of uncertainty associated with the time requirements, since each order requires a unique approach.

An **assemble-to-order** approach is typically used when overall manufacturing lead time exceeds that desired by the customer, where the variety and cost of end products preclude investment in finished-goods inventory, and where engineering design has created modules or options that can be combined in many ways to satisfy unique customer requirements. Here component (or product option) inventory is held to reduce overall manufacturing lead time, and end products are assembled to meet the scheduled delivery dates for individual customer orders. As Figure 12.2 shows, a key control point is the final assembly schedule (FAS), which converts "average" products into unique products in response to actual customer orders. Planning bills of material are based on average products and on optional features. The planning bills reflect how the product is sold, rather than how it's manufactured. They are often used to simplify data requirements in preparing and maintaining the master production

FIGURE 12.2 **Features of Master Production Scheduling Approaches**

	Master Scheduling Approach		
	MTO	**ATO**	**MTS**
Basis for planning and control			
Control point	Order backlog	FAS	Forecast
MPS unit	Customer orders	Options	End items
Product level	End product	End to intermediate product	End product
MPS features			
Customer order promising	High requirement	⟶	Low requirement
Need to monitor forecast accuracy	Low requirement	⟶	High requirement
Use of planning bills	Yes	Yes	No
Need to cope with design and process uncertainty	High	⟶	Low
Basis of delivery to customer	Make to customer order on time	Make to customer order on time	Make-to-stock replenishment order or to customer call-off schedule

schedule. The uncertainty underlying an ATO business is fundamentally one of product mix, rather than one of product volume. The MPS and FAS are designed to hold off commitment to unique product configurations until the last possible moment and yet to offer wide configuration choices to customers.

Under **make-to-stock (MTS),** the MPS is stated in end items, and these end products are produced to forecast demand; customer orders are filled directly from stock in order to provide short delivery lead times for standardized products. While customer order promising records are not normally required, we must provide procedures for monitoring demand forecasts' accuracy since manufacturing plans are mostly based on forecast information. This means the type of uncertainty inherent in the MTS environment is one of forecasting errors; the manufacturing function needs to recognize errors on a timely basis and to make corrective responses.

Detailed Material Planning Options

We can accomplish detailed material planning in several ways. Two popular alternatives are *time-phased* and *rate-based material planning.* Use of these approaches depends importantly in the production process's design characteristics. Figure 12.3 shows key differences between these approaches.

Time-phased planning for individual product components is typically carried out with material requirements planning approaches. The production process design is usually based on **batch manufacturing** and materials are also purchased in batch orders. Preparation of time-phased plans requires a manufacturing database that includes information on: MPS quantities stated in bill of material terminology to determine gross requirements; on-hand inventory balances and open shop (or purchase) orders to determine net requirements;

FIGURE 12.3 Features of Detailed Material Planning Approaches

	Material Planning Approach	
	Time-Phased	**Rate-Based**
Basis for planning and control		
Control point	Shop/purchase orders	Planning bills
Control unit	Batches	Kanbans
Product level	Material explosion of time-phased net requirements for product components	Material explosion of rate-based requirements for product components
Material planning features		
Fixed schedules	No	Yes
Use of WIP to aid planning	High	Low
Updating	Daily/weekly	Weekly/monthly
Inventory netting	Performed	None
Lead-time offsetting	Performed	None
Lot sizing	Performed	None
Safety stock/safety lead time	Considered	Not considered
Container size	Not considered	Considered
Bill of material	Many levels	Single level

production lead times, supplier lead times, and safety stocks to determine order release dates; and lot size formulas to determine order quantities. Under MRP, plans are typically updated on a periodic (daily or weekly) basis to develop priorities for scheduling manufacturing and supplier operations.

As Figure 12.3 indicates, time-phased material planning is based on explosion of requirements, where shop and purchase orders are created for batches of components. The schedule for any work center varies depending on the batches that arrive at that work center; work in process is kept at high levels to effectively utilize work center capacities. Planning is carried out on a level-by-level basis corresponding to the levels in the bill of materials (BOM), with material going into and out of inventory at each level. Detailed planning is required for each level in the BOM, and lead time offsetting is utilized at each level.

A different approach is taken to detailed material planning under **rate-based planning.** Examples of firms using rate-based planning include repetitive manufacturing, assembly lines, just-in-time, and other flow systems. The primary intent in rate-based scheduling is to establish rates of production for each part in the factory. Realizing these rates allows the company to move material through the manufacturing system without stopping, in the shortest time possible. Typically, single-level planning bill of material information is used to convert rate-based master production schedules into material plans that specify the appropriate daily or hourly flow rates for individual component items. Planning of intermediate items in the bill of materials is not usually required, because the number of intermediate-level items is too small to be of concern. Because of MPS stability, high rates of material flow, negligible work-in-process inventory levels, short manufacturing lead times, and a relatively small variety of final products in the MPS, we don't need detailed status

FIGURE 12.4 Features of Shop-Floor System Approaches

	Shop-Floor System Approach	
	MRP	**JIT**
Basis for planning and control		
Control basis	Work center capacity utilization	Overall product flow times
Unit of control	Shop orders	Kanban cards or containers
Product level	Individual operations scheduled at each work center	Production on an as-required basis to replenish downstream stocks that support end-item requirements
Shop-floor system features		
Control of material flow	Work center dispatching rules	Initiated by downstream kanban cards
Sequencing procedure	Due-date-oriented dispatching rule	Not an issue
Order tracking	Shop-floor transactions by operation and stocking point	None (paperless system)
Monitoring and feedback	Input/output and shop load reports	Focus on overall result
Order completion	Shop order close-out in stockroom	None
Achieving delivery reliability	Batch order status reports	Through flow of material
Lot size	Large	Small
Work in process and safety stock	Large	Negligible

information on work-in-process items. This reduces the manufacturing database's size, the number of transactions, and the number of material planning personnel in comparison with time-phased detailed material planning.

Shop-Floor System Options

A wide variety of manual and computer-based shop-floor scheduling systems exist. The two basic approaches (material planning driven by MRP and material planning driven by JIT) depend greatly on the manufacturing process's characteristics. Figure 12.4 distinguishes between these approaches.

The MRP-based approach supports batch manufacturing operations where shop orders are released against a schedule developed by the material planning function, based on lead times for component and subassembly items largely comprised of queue or waiting time. The shop-floor scheduling system's objective is to coordinate the sequencing of orders at individual work centers with customer delivery requirements. A large manufacturing database requiring a substantial volume of shop transactions is needed to provide control reports for order tracking, dispatching, and work center monitoring.

In MRP-based shop-floor systems, one objective is to utilize each work center's capacity effectively. The form of manufacturing is based on relatively large batches of each component and significant work-in-process inventories to support independence among the work centers. This shop-floor approach is based on scheduling shop orders that dictate the set of detailed steps or operations necessary to make each component part. The flow of materials is controlled with dispatching rules establishing the order in which all jobs in a particular work center are to be processed. The primary criterion in establishing this order are the due dates for the parts, which are continually reestablished through MRP planning. Shop orders are tracked as they progress through the factory by processing detailed transactions of work at every work center. Shop orders are opened as part of MRP planning, and they're closed out as components are received into a stockroom. Problems are highlighted through input/output analysis and shop load reports.

In JIT-based shop-floor scheduling systems, the approach is based on minimal flow times for the entire product. That is, the emphasis is on end items, with the scheduling of individual operations, and even component parts, in a subservient position. Cellular manufacturing techniques are typically employed, where detailed scheduling is accomplished as part of the basic manufacturing task. Kanban cards, containers, and other signals of downstream need for components serve as the authorization to produce, typically in small lot sizes. The sequencing procedure isn't an issue because work is only started on an as-needed basis, with little or no competition for work center capacity. Similarly, order tracking is nonexistent since work in process is minimal, and material moves through the factory quickly enough to negate the need for tracking. The only close-out is of finished items. Often the close-out transaction generates a computer-based "back flush" of the requisite component parts. The very short queue times, small lot sizes, and relatively narrow product range in JIT can result in a paperless shop-floor scheduling system. The manufacturing database requirements, volume of shop transactions, and number of shop scheduling personnel are minimal.

Many authorities have attempted to use the terms *push* and *pull* to distinguish between MRP-based and JIT-based shop-floor systems. The argument is, under JIT, when a customer "pulls" some product out of inventory it pulls some replacement inventory from the factory, which pulls some parts from the shops, which pulls some materials from the store rooms, and so on. On the other hand, MRP-based systems "push" components into the factory, then into inventory, then back into manufacturing, and so on.

The key distinction to make is these two approaches' characteristics must match the manufacturing process and infrastructure in which they operate. Activities in the MRP-based systems are triggered by processes authorizing production quantities, routings, due dates, and so forth. JIT-based systems produce in response to downstream use of the item, which may be work center by work center or may be in response to demand for the overall end item. For systems installed to date, relatively constant demands are required for the JIT-based approach to function.

Choosing the Options

There's a temptation to view some MPC design options as a continuum where movement toward JIT is "good." This isn't the correct conclusion. We must match MPC system design with the ongoing needs of a company's market, the task in manufacturing, and the manufacturing process. An MPC system represents a major investment in a business, and as such it must be designed to support the firm's competitive strategy.

Market Requirements

Figure 12.5 shows how MPC system design is influenced by a company's market requirements and the resultant manufacturing task. Figure 12.5 labels these last two factors "business specifications." The point is these determine, from a business point of view, what has to be done in manufacturing to serve the chosen markets. Then technical requirements are defined. This involves the interaction of the manufacturing task, MPC system, and manufacturing process. Each of these three areas needs to be carefully considered before the choices can be made in the approaches in master production scheduling, detailed material planning, and shop-floor scheduling. Moreover, the three areas must be seen as constantly changing: new customer requirements, new process technology, and new strategic goals in manufacturing. Any of these can mandate a change in the MPC system design.

Figure 12.5 also shows the MPC system design as influenced by the desired MPC system and existing MPC system. In some cases, improvements can be made by investing in the evolution of the existing system design. In other cases, we need to start afresh.

The first step in the development of market requirements is to review the customers and market segments targeted by the business, their present needs with regard to the company's products and services, competitors' products and services, and existing sales growth opportunities. Many companies face dynamic markets where customer requirements and global competition are changing dramatically. We must continuously review market requirements and adapt marketing strategies to exploit opportunities. For example, many companies increasingly see the need to enhance their products with services to help their customers solve problems. *Market focus, customer prosperity,* and *delighting the customer* are common phrases. But if these phrases are to be more than hype, we must redefine the manufacturing task to create the desired results. Thereafter, we may have to redesign the MPC system as well as the manufacturing process. To illustrate, the manufacturing organization in a packaging materials firm supplying the food industry suddenly had to

FIGURE 12.5
MPC System Design Choices

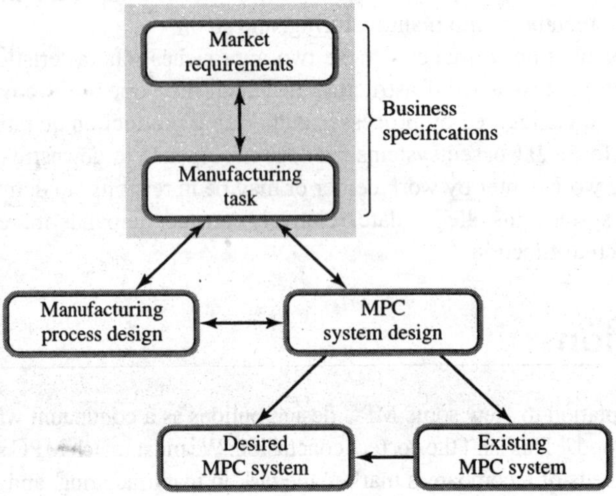

deliver products in small quantities on a twice weekly basis to support its major customer's new JIT program. Neither the production process nor the MPC system was designed to support the changed business requirements. More fundamentally, the firm's manufacturing strategy had to be revised to support this kind of customer requirement.

The Manufacturing Task

The next step in choosing MPC system design options is to develop a statement of the manufacturing task that's consistent with (and that supports) the marketing strategy. If the company decides to satisfy customers on a just-in-time basis, this has to be reflected in the manufacturing task. Similarly, if quality is now the way to win orders, it too must be reflected in changed manufacturing values, process investments, improvements in the quality support function, and revised manufacturing performance measurements. If the targeted customers are moving toward more highly customized products, again, this needs to be captured in the manufacturing task.

Stating the manufacturing task for the business is critical to ensuring that manufacturing capabilities are developed to support the different targeted market segments. Developing the manufacturing task involves characterizing the markets targeted by the company in terms of the requirements they place on manufacturing. Such requirements may, for example, include volume and delivery flexibility, low-cost production, critical product quality specifications, and other manufacturing-related capabilities—whatever is required to win orders in different market segments.

A clear statement of the manufacturing task enables management to recognize that major changes may be required in the design of both production processes and the MPC system. Figure 12.5 shows this by the two-headed arrows linking the manufacturing task to the design of both manufacturing processes and MPC systems.

Manufacturing Process Design

Most firms have large investments in production processes, employee capabilities, and other elements of infrastructure in manufacturing. As a consequence they tend to change slowly over time. This establishes the manufacturing capabilities of a company.

The arrow linking manufacturing process design and MPC design indicates the interdependency between MPC option choices and manufacturing process features. For example, installing a JIT process with cellular manufacturing and short production lead times means rate-based detailed material planning approaches may be much more appropriate than time-phased approaches.

A more subtle example of manufacturing process design impacting MPC system design occurs in the case of quality improvement programs. Many companies use complex scheduling procedures because the firms suffer from poor quality and the resultant unpleasant surprises. Quality is usually improved through investments in better manufacturing processes. Where quality is enhanced significantly, there are fewer surprises, the company is better able to execute routine plans, and MPC systems can be more straightforward.

Finally, in some cases there are simultaneous changes in marketplace requirements, manufacturing processes, and manufacturing task definitions. For example, computer manufacturers at one time faced a very long lead time to make a computer; they achieved customization by individual wiring and other hardware features. New computers were "announced" in the marketplace long before they were available for shipment, customers would place orders just to get their place in the queue of orders, and the MPC system had to manage a fictitious backlog of orders. Moreover, each order's configuration would constantly change and delivery dates would be extended or canceled. The net result was a very complex set of requirements for the MPC system. Now computers are relatively easy to make, most customization is done with software, and orders are rapidly shipped. Moreover, computers per se are becoming a commodity, and these companies increasingly view their manufacturing strategy as solving problems for their customers. The resultant changes in end "products"—and the processes that produce them—dictate a completely different set of design requirements for the MPC system.

MPC System Design

Because of the magnitude of the investment in MPC systems and the time required to implement MPC system changes, we must recognize differences between desired and existing MPC system options and features. Figure 12.5 shows this by the lines connecting MPC system design with desired and existing MPC systems. A company currently using time-phased MRP records while installing a JIT process with cellular manufacturing might continue to use MRP records with some modifications until necessary investment funds and management time were available to make the MPC system changes required to implement rate-based material planning. Although the marketing strategy, manufacturing task, manufacturing process, and MPC system design specifications might have been agreed upon within the business, the opportunity to move to implementation might not yet have occurred.

This example illustrates another integration issue—consistent MPC option choices. We need to have the right choice (and consistency) in the MPS approach, the detailed material planning approach, and the shop-floor system approach. This issue frequently arises during JIT implementation in a company using MRP for detailed material planning in which batch and line production processes are appropriate for different parts of the business. Therefore, issues of how to link JIT and MRP options in MPC system design and how to maintain *one* MPC system are often difficult. Our experience indicates attention paid to marketplace requirements and to how these requirements may be changing helps you determine the dominant choices among the MPC options.

Master Production Scheduling Options

In Figure 12.6 the three MPS approaches are related to key aspects of marketplace requirements and to aspects of the manufacturing task and manufacturing process. A make-to-order (MTO) master scheduling approach supports products of wide variety and custom design, frequently involving the development of engineering specifications. They're typically produced in low unit volumes, where delivery speed is achieved through overlapping schedules for design and manufacture of the various elements comprising the customer order. Delivery reliability is somewhat difficult to guarantee, since products are customized to meet individual customer needs. This approach is frequently used to support markets characterized by high levels of product change and new product introductions, and where the firm's competitive advantage is in providing product technology requirements in line with the customer's delivery and quality requirements. Because the manufacturing task often involves providing a broad range of production capabilities, the process choice supports low-volume batch manufacturing. One key aspect of the manufacturing task is how to respond to fluctuations in sales volumes. These are typically managed through adjustments in the level of the customer order backlog.

FIGURE 12.6 Linking Market Requirements and Manufacturing Strategy to Design of the MPS Approach

Strategic Variables			Master Scheduling Approach: MTO	ATO	MTS
Market requirements	Product	Design	Custom	→	Standard
		Variety	Wide	→	Predetermined and narrow
	Individual product volume per period		Low	→	High
	Delivery	Speed	Through overlapping schedules	Through reducing process lead time	Through eliminating process lead time
		Reliability	Difficult	→	Straight-forward
Manufacturing	Process choice		Low-volume batch	→	High-volume batch/line
	Managing fluctuations in sales volume		Through order backlog	Through WIP or finished goods inventory	Through finished goods inventory

An assemble-to-order (ATO) master scheduling approach represents an intermediate position. Products of both standard and special design are produced, and variety is accommodated by customer selection from a wide series of standardized product options. The unit production volumes are relatively high at the option level, and customer responsiveness in regard to delivery speed is enhanced by lead time reductions and short time frames for frozen final assembly schedules. Delivery reliability is well accommodated as long as overall volumes are kept within planning parameters. That is, the ATO environment is designed to be relatively accommodative of changes in product mix.

Typically, ATO manufacturing is done in batches, with more and more firms using cellular approaches for popular options and families of similar parts. Stocking components, intermediate subassemblies, or product option items can shorten customer lead time to that of the final assembly process, thereby improving delivery speed and reliability in markets where fluctuations in sales volumes are hard to anticipate.

The make-to-stock (MTS) master scheduling approach supports products of standard design produced in high unit volumes in narrow product variety for which short customer delivery lead times are critical. Delivery speed is enhanced by reducing process lead times, frequently by adopting flow-based manufacturing methods. Reliability of production schedules is relatively straightforward.

The process choice is usually line manufacturing or high-volume batch manufacturing. An investment in finished-goods inventory can provide short, reliable delivery lead times to customers and can buffer fluctuations in sales. It can also enable us to stabilize production levels, thereby permitting important cost improvements in manufacturing.

FIGURE 12.7 Linking Market Requirements and Manufacturing Strategy to the Design of the Detailed Material Planning Approach

Strategic Variables			Detailed Material Planning Approach: Time Phased	Detailed Material Planning Approach: Rate Based
Market requirements	Product	Design	Custom	Standard
		Variety	Wide	Narrow
	Individual product volume per period		Low	High
	Ability to cope with changes in product mix		High potential	Limited
	Delivery	Speed	Through scheduling/ excess capacity	Through inventory
		Schedule changes	Difficult	Straightforward
Manufacturing	Process choice		Batch	Line
	Source of cost reduction	Overhead	No	Yes
		Inventory	No	Yes
		Capacity utilization	Yes	No

Since products are often produced on high-volume batch or line processes, schedule stability is often critical, especially in price-sensitive markets.

Material Planning Options

Figure 12.7 relates the two detailed material planning approaches to key aspects of marketplace requirements and to aspects of manufacturing task and manufacturing process. Time-phased detailed material planning is appropriate for custom products produced in wide variety and low volumes. It also facilitates schedule changes and revisions in customer delivery dates as well as changes in product mix. Delivery speed is enhanced through better scheduling, based on relative priorities. This approach can be applied in markets characterized by a high rate of new product introductions, rapid shifts in product technology, and custom-engineered products by using planning bill of material techniques.

Time-phased planning is often associated with batch manufacturing and is supported by relatively high overhead and work-in-process inventory costs due to the necessary planning staff and extensive transaction processing. This planning approach can result in higher capacity utilization and is often favored in manufacturing facilities employing expensive equipment.

Rate-based material planning is appropriate for a relatively narrow range of standard products, with stable product designs produced in high volume. Rate-based detailed material planning is much more limited in its ability to cope with changes in product mix. The limited product line permits straightforward changes in the schedule as long as they're within the product design specifications. Enhancements in customer delivery speed are typically accommodated with finished-goods inventories.

These marketplace requirements are normally best supported in manufacturing by production line processes. Use of rate-based material planning and line production processes yields an opportunity to cut work-in-process inventory and overhead costs, providing important support for price-sensitive markets. On the other hand, rate-based material planning doesn't support intensive utilization of capacities in the same way as time-phased approaches.

Shop-Floor System Options

In Figure 12.8 the two shop-floor system approaches are related to key aspects of marketplace requirements and to aspects of manufacturing task and manufacturing process. The MRP-based approach to shop-floor scheduling is appropriate when a wide variety of custom products is produced in low unit volumes. Changes in demand are accommodated

FIGURE 12.8 **Linking Market Requirements and Manufacturing Strategy to the Design of the Shop-Floor System Approach**

Strategic Variables			Shop-Floor System Approach: MRP Based	Shop-Floor System Approach: JIT Based
Market requirements	Product	Design	Custom	Standard
		Variety	Wide	Narrow
	Individual product volume per period		Low	High
	Accommodating demand changes	Total volume	Easy/incremental	Difficult/stepped
		Product mix	High	Low
	Delivery	Speed	Achieved by schedule change	Achieved through finished goods inventory
		Schedule changes	More difficult	Less difficult
Manufacturing	Process choice		Low-volume batch	High-volume batch/line
	Changeover cost		High	Low
	Organizational control		Centralized	Decentralized (shop-floor based)
	Work in process		High	Low
	Source of cost reduction	Overheads	Low	High
		Inventory	Low	High

relatively easily; volume changes are supported by overtime operations in critical work centers, and product mix change is an inherent characteristic. This approach supports markets characterized by rapid changes in product technology, high rates of new product introduction, and substantial changes in product design.

Low-volume batch or jobbing processes involve use of the MRP-based shop-floor scheduling system approach. These processes have significant changeover costs and numerous manufacturing steps, requiring a complex shop-floor scheduling system that's centrally driven, thereby limiting the reduction of overhead and inventory-related costs.

JIT-based approaches for shop-floor scheduling provide important support for standard products produced in limited variety and high volume. Such products are best supported by high-volume batch or line production processes that are able to provide short customer lead times. Accommodation of changes in product volume is limited because of the cost of production schedule and capacity changes; this increases the need for schedule stability. Delivery speed is enhanced by short manufacturing throughput times and often by finished-goods inventories.

The emphasis on inventory reduction and the simplicity of shop-floor control procedures under the JIT approach provide the potential for significant cuts in overhead and inventory-related costs, providing important support for price-sensitive markets.

The Choices in Practice

Achieving a close fit between marketplace requirements, the manufacturing task and process, and the MPC system design gives a firm important competitive advantages. In this section we briefly describe the marketing and manufacturing strategies of three companies (Moog Inc., Space Products Division; Kawasaki U.S.A.; and Applicon, Division of Schlumberger) and how they've designed their MPC systems. Figure 12.9 shows the three MPC systems' overall design. Moog uses MTO and ATO approaches to master production scheduling, a time-phased approach to detailed material planning, and an MRP-based shop-floor system. Kawasaki uses MTS master production scheduling, rate-based material planning, and JIT shop-floor scheduling. Applicon uses ATO master production scheduling, both MRP and rate-based scheduling for material planning, and a JIT-based shop-floor system.

FIGURE 12.9 Linking Business Characteristics to the Design of MPC Systems

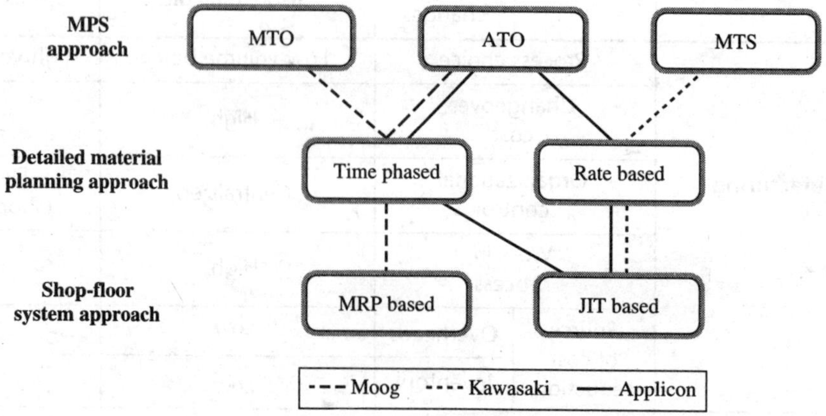

Moog and Kawasaki represent examples of stable MPC system designs to support the requirements of a single market. Applicon, however, provides an example of an MPC system that changed in response to shifting market requirements and process design changes. Let's now see the overall pattern of decisions in each firm concerning the influence of marketing and manufacturing strategy on MPC system design and see how the resultant systems support their businesses.

Moog Inc., Space Products Division

This firm produces high-quality hydraulic systems of advanced design for the aerospace industry. These products cover a wide range of design types and represent a critical element in the overall production lead times for its aerospace customers. The company designs and produces the initial order for new products as well as follow-on orders. Thus, engineering design and advanced product features are key factors in obtaining sales. Other important factors that qualify the firm to compete in this market include delivery reliability, reputation for quality, and price. Figure 12.10 summarizes characteristics of the market served by Moog along with key elements of its manufacturing strategy.

FIGURE 12.10 Moog Inc., Space Products Division

	Manufacturing Strategy				
	Manufacturing		Manufacturing Planning and Control System		
Market Characteristics	**Task**	**Features**	**Master Production Scheduling**	**Detailed Material Planning**	**Shop-Floor Systems**
Customized products Wide product range Low volume per product Make-to-customer specifications Initial pilot orders Future repeat (blanket) orders Key customer requirements: Design capability Delivery speed Market qualifiers: Delivery reliability Quality Price	Reducing process lead time Manufacturing to engineering specifications and quality standards Delivery reliability critical	Batch manufacturing Long process routings High-precision work Accommodate delivery and design changes with reliable deliveries Labor cost equals 60% Control of actual costs against budget Scrap and rework: First orders Repeat orders First order processing uncertainties (process unknown, time estimates) Process and product uncertainties	Make-to-order/ assemble-to-order from: Customer orders Anticipated orders Forecast orders Used for rough-cut capacity planning due to long lead time impact on delivery Customer order promising	Time-phased material planning Material is particular to customer orders High obsolescence risk Extra materials needed for scrapped items Trade-off: shorter lead time versus raw material inventory	MRP-based systems Priority scheduling of shop orders System supported by dispatching and production controller personnel Capacity requirements planning by work center Order tracking and status information

The manufacturing task involves providing a broad range of equipment and employee capabilities to make high-precision, custom-designed products in low unit volumes. Substantial uncertainty exists with regard to production process yields and time estimates to produce initial orders. In addition, design changes contribute to process uncertainty. Labor cost is a significant portion of product cost since highly skilled employees and a wide variety of precision equipment are keys to the production process. Major investments have been made in numerical control (NC) and computerized numerical control (CNC) equipment as well as machining centers in a batch manufacturing process.

All manufacturing planning and control system functions in Figure 12.1 are performed at Moog. Both make-to-order and assemble-to-order master production scheduling approaches are used. The MPS is stated in terms of actual, anticipated, and forecast customer orders with substantial emphasis on customer order promising and capacity planning activities. The master production schedule uses this information to determine requirements for component material. Time-phased material requirements planning records are used to coordinate scheduling of manufactured and purchased components, and these records are used to prepare shop load forecasts for individual departments and work centers.

At Moog the MRP-based approach is used for shop-floor scheduling and vendor scheduling. An advanced computer-based MRPII system provides priority scheduling information for sequencing and dispatching shop orders at individual work centers. The shop-floor system supports the batch manufacturing of products under high levels of process uncertainty. A variety of production reports assist supervisors in the detailed tracking of open shop orders, reporting order status, and evaluating work center performance.

Kawasaki U.S.A.

Kawasaki produces six different types of motorcycles as well as jet skis at its U.S. plant. About 100 different end-product items are manufactured for shipment to the firm's distribution centers. Although demand for products is highly seasonal, workload at the plant is stabilized by permitting fluctuations in the finished-goods inventory carried at the distribution centers. The company frequently introduces new product designs that represent styling changes in the product. The key elements in gaining sales are price, product styling, and product performance. Factors qualifying the firm to compete in the market are quality and delivery speed. Figure 12.11 summarizes characteristics of the market served by Kawasaki along with key elements of its manufacturing strategy.

Manufacturing's task is to produce standardized products in high volume at low cost. Since material costs are significant, major emphasis is placed on reducing plant inventories using just-in-time manufacturing methods. The production process is characterized by short setup times and small production batches using production line and high-volume batch processes. Standardized assembly operations and repetitive employee tasks characterize the production process.

All the manufacturing planning and control functions in Figure 12.1 are performed at Kawasaki; a make-to-stock master production scheduling approach is used. Customer orders for end products are filled from the finished-goods inventory held by the company's distribution division. The MPS is based on forecast information, and mixed model assembly is used in performing final assembly operations. Substantial emphasis is placed on leveling the master production schedule and freezing it over a three-month planning horizon.

FIGURE 12.11 **Kawasaki U.S.A.**

Market Characteristics	Manufacturing Strategy: Manufacturing: Task	Manufacturing Strategy: Manufacturing: Features	Manufacturing Planning and Control System: Master Production Scheduling	Manufacturing Planning and Control System: Detailed Material Planning	Manufacturing Planning and Control System: Shop-Floor Systems
Narrow product range Standard products High volume per product Seasonal demand Sales from finished-goods inventory at distributors Introduction of new products Changing product mix Key customer requirements: Price Delivery speed (through finished-goods inventory in distribution divisions) Market qualifiers: Quality Delivery reliability Basic design and peripheral design changes	Provide a low-cost manufacturing support capability Support the marketing activity with high delivery speed through finished-goods inventory	High-volume batch and line production process Short setup times Small batch size Low-cost manufacturing Low labor cost High material cost Low inventories (raw material, components, and WIP) Low overheads (low MPC costs)	Make-to-stock Manufacture to forecast Level production Three-month frozen planning horizon Manufacture to replenish distribution inventories	Rate-based material planning	JIT-based systems Kanban containers JIT flow of material Low raw material, component, and WIP inventory

A rate-based material planning approach utilizes a simple planning bill of materials to schedule the rates of flow for manufactured and purchased components. A JIT shop scheduling system using kanban containers controls the flow of material between work centers. The JIT system supports low-cost manufacturing with small plant inventory levels and high-volume material flows. Very few personnel and minimal transactions are required in planning and controlling production activities.

Applicon

This firm designs and manufactures computer-aided engineering (CAE), design (CAD), and manufacturing (CAM) systems for the electronics and mechanical design markets. High-end products include systems for highly sophisticated customers in a variety of

FIGURE 12.12 Applicon's Old Manufacturing Strategy

	Manufacturing Strategy				
	Manufacturing		Manufacturing Planning and Control System		
Market Characteristics*	**Task***	**Features**	**Master Production Scheduling**	**Detailed Material Planning**	**Shop-Floor Systems**
Customized products Wide product range Major design changes occurring monthly Quick response required to changes in product technology Need to reflect both price sensitivity and the price/performance ratio for a sophisticated customer base High product quality requirements Delivery responsiveness is critical	Low-cost manufacturing Short production lead times High product quality Rapid engineering change capability	Batch manufacturing General-purpose equipment Functional plant layout 4–5-month manufacturing lead time Long design change cycle High rate of inventory obsolescence 85% plug and play rate in final inspection Excessive rework costs 160 actual production operators in the manufacturing areas 20 weeks of work-in-process inventory Product family mix change flexibility	Make-to-stock MPS High levels of finished-goods inventory Monthly MPS is created for each end product, using an annual build plan	Conventional MRP system Stockroom kitting of assemblies prior to release of work orders at each stage in the process MPS is exploded into time-phased work orders for components and subassemblies using bill of materials, inventory data, and monthly time periods	Large shop-floor order quantities typically representing one month's usage Work is scheduled on the shop floor using a priority control system for work orders Large numbers of shop-floor and inventory transactions are processed to maintain data integrity in the MRP system Large overhead costs are incurred to support the MPC system, as illustrated by 83 people employed in the materials management area

*The market characteristics and manufacturing task are common to the old and new strategies.

analytical engineering applications. Low-end systems use Applicon software and Sun workstations for applications in robotics and numerical control machines.

The mechanical design market represents the firm's major growth area. In this market, unlike the electronics market, the price-to-performance ratio is a critical issue to price-sensitive CAD/CAM customers. In addition, the ability to respond rapidly to changes in technology and frequent design changes is also critical. Figure 12.12 summarizes characteristics of the market served by Applicon along with key elements of the old manufacturing strategy (i.e., the one employed by the company before the process change).

The manufacturing task for the mechanical design market involves producing high-quality products having a wide range of optional features in small volumes at low cost in short customer lead times while accommodating rapid engineering changes. As Figure 12.12 shows, the previous manufacturing approach was to produce products using a batch manufacturing process where the plant was organized into functional groupings of machines, and production was planned and controlled using an MRPII system to fill customer orders directly from finished-goods inventory. Long production lead times under this strategy led to poor competitive performance. The inability to make changes in product designs didn't allow the firm to keep up with major changes in product technology; large work-in-process and finished-goods inventories created substantial write-offs of obsolete inventory; poor customer service in product delivery resulted with high manufacturing costs.

As a consequence the company changed its manufacturing strategy, investing in a JIT production process having straight line flows of material with closely coupled manufacturing cells dedicated to individual product families and short changeover times. Four cells are dedicated to the final assembly of four different product model families, while the fifth cell produces printed circuit boards (PCBs) for the final assembly cells. Thanks to this process, overall manufacturing lead time fell from 75 to 5 days, work-in-process and finished-goods inventories declined significantly, and product quality improved greatly. Likewise, the MPC system design was changed to include an assemble-to-order MPS because of the short manufacturing lead time, a new MRP material planning approach that takes into account JIT plant operations, and a JIT-based shop scheduling approach. Figure 12.13 describes the new manufacturing approach.

Integrating MRP and JIT

There are many ways that MRP and JIT are combined and substantial need to do so. Here we discuss needs to integrate these approaches, physical changes that support the integration, and techniques for integration.

The Need to Integrate

In the majority of the cases, the need for integration arises in companies that have an installed MRP system and are in the process of implementing some aspect of JIT. The pressure of meeting world-class standards, the use of global benchmarking, and intimidating competition have all brought home the necessity of major changes in how manufacturing is done. The response to these concerns in the best of companies has been to implement aspects of JIT.

Often these JIT programs seem in conflict with the MRP system the firm may have in place. As lead times shrink and material velocity increases, the limiting activity can turn out to be transaction processing. Increased demand can compound the problem.

As an example, a European consumer electronics company significantly cut production time required to make a major high-volume component in response to increased demand. Product design changes and process capability improvements were both used to reduce setup and run times. Lot sizes were reduced, but lead times were not significantly reduced. The combination of smaller lot sizes and increasing volume simply meant there were substantially more open orders on the floor being tracked by the MRP system, moving into and out of inventory, and being accounted for during the process. These "hidden factory" activities were limiting the improvements possible from the other activities.

FIGURE 12.13 Applicon's New Manufacturing Strategy

Market Characteristics*	Manufacturing Strategy				
	Manufacturing		Manufacturing Planning and Control System		
	Task*	Features	Master Production Scheduling	Detailed Material Planning	Shop-Floor Systems
Customized products Wide product range Major design changes occurring monthly Quick response required to changes in product technology Need to reflect both price sensitivity and the price/performance ratio for a sophisticated customer base High product quality requirements Delivery responsiveness is critical	Low-cost manufacturing Short production lead times High product quality Rapid engineering change capability	Straight-line flows of material Manufacturing cells dedicated to particular product families Short setup times Short manufacturing lead times (one week) Short design change cycles Low work-in-process and finished-goods inventories Low flexibility to product family mix changes	An assemble-to-order MPS is stated in top-level item terms and is coded by major model number The company plans using forecast information in the MPS, but builds product only to customer orders using a final assembly schedule Customer order promising is a key activity. Available-to-promise records are used Customer orders are used to convert the weekly production plan into specific daily requirements	MPS uses monthly time periods covering five future months to plan and order purchased materials using family bills of material, MRP records, and bill of material explosion techniques No stockrooms since material is located in the manufacturing cells MPC system is run weekly providing planning information to planners and buyers, and capacity planning information to plant work cells Only two inventory transactions are recorded—from suppliers into the stock bins, and out of stock bins as finished products are shipped from the plant	Work orders are not scheduled for internally manufactured items Material is pulled through the production process using JIT methods Delivery of 70% of supplier items directly onto the shop floor Customer orders, referred to as build cards, provide the basis for scheduling work cells and for pulling material through the plant

*The market characteristics and manufacturing task are common to the old and new strategies.

When changes take place on the factory floor, MPC system change may be a required response. These changes can come from internal actions like implementing a JIT program or from external requirements that change the manufacturing task. In either case the need for a change in production activity control systems may be clear; the direction is most often from shop-order–based systems to kanban or other simple signals. A typical response is backflushing component usages at all levels triggered by receipt of completed items into finished-goods inventory.

Physical Changes That Support Integration

One of the first requirements to support the JIT approaches in the factory is to reduce the inventory transaction volume. Cutting the number of times a lot has to be logged into and out of an inventory location not only reduces transactions but enables material to move to the next operation more quickly. This clearly helps increase the velocity and reduce lead times. Physically, this may mean making some changes in how lots get moved from department to department and how the need for the move gets signaled, but the major improvements are in making physical changes to the production process, such as the introduction of cellular manufacturing.

Cellular manufacturing supports integrating MRP and JIT approaches. The cell allows us to accomplish several routing steps as if they were a single step and allows the shop floor to be scheduled at the level of part numbers instead of the level of routing steps. More encompassing cellular manufacturing approaches permit the cell to be planned and controlled at the level of assemblies instead of at the part number level. One key objective is to reduce the need for inventory accounting and the other hidden factory transactions. Control of the cell is straightforward and doesn't need the detailed tracking necessary when parts move all over the factory.

The choice of where to implement cellular manufacturing is important since we can create islands of velocity, like the islands of automation prevalent in the early installations of some computer-integrated manufacturing schemes. These islands might be quite successful on their own, but not be well integrated into the system as a whole. Increasingly, we've found firms in this position needing to make more than cosmetic changes to their overall MPC system.

Some Techniques for Integrating MRP and JIT

Whenever there's a combination of MRP and JIT in the shop, we need to move back and forth between the systems. A JIT cell in the middle of a process under MRP control must communicate with the MRP system. There must be a handoff from MRP to JIT at the start of the JIT process and a transfer back to MRP at the end.

One way of supporting this need is to create phantom bills for activities under JIT control. Material requirements planning records can be used to plan raw material requirements, with movement through the factory done with JIT approaches (no shop orders or tracking). The phantom bill would ignore the creation of the detailed parts and assemblies performed under JIT scheduling, while the MRP system would pick up the completed part or assembly as a part number on the bill of materials at completion.

Extending MPC Integration to Customers and Suppliers

The TelTech Company illustrates how MPC approaches can be improved across firms in a supply chain context to reduce response times to customers. At TelTech, the linkages with customers and suppliers have focused on finding the best ways to gain intelligence on actual site telecom installation conditions so that rapid response can be made in delivering product to customers.

An analysis of the actual site ordering processes in one of TelTech's key customers indicated that there are significant administrative delays. Customer orders were seen as official documents, needing to be signed by two different executives. This often required several days before the two signatures could be obtained. Customer orders were passed from the customer to the TelTech country marketing personnel and then on to the TelTech factory. This also typically caused another one to two days of delay. Finally, the receipt of the customer order at the factory necessitated "untangling" the product options, making certain that the product could, in fact, be built and confirming this information with the customer. The net result was that orders typically took 10 to 20 days to move from the decision to order to the actual customer order being entered into the master production schedule. The factory could assemble the customer order in one day, and it could be shipped to the customer site in five days by inexpensive transport.

The MPC solution to this lengthy process was the development of an online MPC system that supported product configuration management. The configuration of the customer order could take place before the order was issued. It could then be built and shipped, often arriving in the country before the customer order was, in fact, issued. This MPC system enhancement would allow any potential order to be screened for availability of component items and permit substitution when material was unavailable.

The TelTech example illustrates how our traditional view of MPC system design needs to be expanded to consider MPC system improvements that span the operations of customers, plants, and suppliers throughout the supply chain. In this way, the development of manufacturing strategy to support market requirements can include investments in MPC system architecture within an integrated supply chain context.

Concluding Principles

This chapter focused on two major strategy issues in designing MPC systems: how to link the design of the MPC systems to a firm's business strategy and to the requirements of its market; and how to integrate MRP and JIT approaches in designing MPC systems. The following principles summarize the major points:

- Because investment in MPC systems is large, its design must support the firm's competitive strategy.
- A wide range of options are available in designing MPC systems, and the choices must be governed by the company's competitive needs.
- Business as well as technical specifications need to be considered in designing an MPC system.
- MPC system design should begin with an analysis of the market requirements to support the firm's competitive strategy.
- Understanding the manufacturing task is critical in developing the production process design, the MPC system design, and the other elements of the manufacturing infrastructure.
- The manufacturing process's particular features need to be considered in choosing among the options in MPC system design.
- MRP and JIT approaches can be effectively integrated in designing MPC systems.
- Improved company performance and overall supply chain performance can result from matching MPC system design to the firm's competitive strategy.

Discussion Questions

1. It has been suggested that in a make-to-order company, order backlog is inventory carried by the customer. What does this statement mean?
2. Why do you suppose the terms *push* and *pull* came to be used for MRP and JIT systems?
3. What key features of the manufacturing task impact the design of the MPC system?
4. Some manufacturing executives have raised the question "Which is better, MRP or JIT?" How would you respond to this question?
5. What approaches other than finished goods inventory provide short lead times to the customers?
6. Henry Ford was said to have specified "any color as long as it's black." Today's automobiles come in literally billions of end-item combinations. What are the implications of this change in market requirements on MPC system design?
7. What changes in market requirements at Applicon dictated a new production process and MPC approach?
8. What kind of changes in the products produced and markets served would enable Moog to adopt make-to-stock master production scheduling?
9. Why is discipline required for both JIT and MRP?

Problems

1. Worldwide Batteries Inc. sells industrial batteries to both original equipment manufacturers (OEM) and replacement market customers. About 80 end products are classified as high-volume products, 200 as medium-volume products, and 170 as low-volume products. The vice president of marketing and sales has provided the following description for two market segments that reflect the general characteristics of all market segments currently targeted by the company:

   - Replacement batteries for indoor material handling equipment for which 60 percent of the sales volume is for deliveries desired by customers in seven days or less (high-volume items), 30 percent is for delivery within 14 days (medium-volume items), and 10 percent is for delivery within 30 days (low-volume items). Key factors in gaining sales orders in this segment are competitive prices and delivery speed.
   - Replacement batteries for outdoor transportation equipment applications which involve low-volume product items. Customers expect delivery within two weeks. The key factors in winning orders in this segment are competitive prices and delivery reliability.

   Recently, the company has implemented a kanban system for controlling the material for manufacturing component parts for batteries. The lead time for final assembly of battery components into end products, battery charging, and transport to the customers is seven days. High- and medium-volume purchased components (used in the final assembly operation) are provided by suppliers on a JIT delivery basis with a guaranteed five-day delivery lead time. Low-volume purchased components (also used in the final assembly operation) require a four-week delivery lead time for the suppliers.

   Specify the MPC system design requirements for the company's markets using the framework shown in Figures 12.10, 12.11, and 12.12. Refer to Figures 12.2, 12.3, 12.4, 12.6, 12.7, and 12.8 for MPC design details.

2. Currently, the Cambridge Plastics Company sells industrial packaging materials to two different market segments:

   - Injection-molded plastic bottles sold to soft-drink bottlers in very high volume with significant seasonal variations in sales. The customers provide call-off schedules indicating their product requirements over the next six months, specifying the delivery quantities each week. Key factors in winning this business are the ability to meet large changes in the weekly quantities and the ability to provide a major capacity increase for the increased demand during the peak summer selling season.

- Custom-molded plastic bottles sold in wide variety and low volume to manufacturers of cosmetic, pharmaceutical, and agricultural chemical products. These are produced to specific customer orders, with the key factors in winning orders in this business being competitive prices and delivery reliability.

The soft-drink bottles are produced using high-volume processes dedicated to the production of specific products, while the custom products are produced using low-volume batch processes. In both cases the tracking of actual versus planned production is very important in ensuring that the current quantities of products are delivered against the customer orders.

Specify the MPC system design requirements for the company's markets using the framework shown in Figures 12.10, 12.11, and 12.12. Refer to Figures 12.2, 12.3, 12.4, 12.6, 12.7, and 12.8 for MPC design details.

3. The Oakmont Inc. is a make-to-stock firm. A typical part for one of the firm's products has the following data:

   Manufacturing lead time (LT) = 8 weeks.

   Forecast = 50 per week.

   Mean absolute deviation (MAD) of forecast errors = 8.

   Safety stock = 95 percent service level ($2.056 \times \text{MAD} \times 1.25 \times \sqrt{LT}$)

   A cellular manufacturing approach will reduce a typical part's manufacturing lead time to two weeks.

   a. What's the reduction in safety stock?

   b. The cell can manufacture 40 percent of the parts (the present total safety stock investment is $200,000). If you assume a lead time reduction from eight weeks to two weeks for these parts, what's the overall reduction in safety stock investment?

   c. An engineer believes redesign of the cell can increase the percentage of parts produced therein from 40 percent to 60 percent. How much safety stock investment reduction comes from the redesign?

4. The cell in problem 3 is designed with a capacity of 800 units per day. A new product design uses many common parts; the result is a cell scheduled with a one-day lead time and an overall shift to assemble-to-order manufacturing. Customers are happy to receive one-day deliveries. Overall demand for parts made in the cell is 500 units per day, with a standard deviation of 75 units. The 500 units are typically completed in approximately five working hours. Thereafter, workers in the cell perform equipment maintenance, schedule production, and manage quality.

   a. What happens to the service level provided to customers?

   b. What happens to safety stock inventory levels?

5. Dixon Plastics has 100 customers. It produces make-to-order products using time-phased material planning and an MRP-based shop-floor system. Amdur Electronics, one of its larger customers, accounts for 20 percent of total sales. It promises to double its volume with Dixon within two years and to communicate its detailed planning to Dixon via electronic data exchange (EDI). The plans would be frozen for the next week, subject to $\pm$ 15 percent in weeks 2 through 6, and open to revision after six weeks. Any raw material purchased by Dixon to meet requirements in the next six weeks would be guaranteed against obsolescence by Amdur Electronics.

   a. What changes in MPC design options would Dixon require if total manufacturing lead time was one day?

   b. What if the total manufacturing lead time is six weeks?

6. Consider the following three MRP records. Product A comprises two part Bs. One part B requires one part C.

Product A		**Week 1**	**2**	**3**	**4**	**5**	**6**	**7**	**8**
Gross requirements		10	20	0	40	20	10	0	20
Scheduled receipts									
Projected available balance	15	5	15	15	5	15	5	5	15
Planned order release		30		30	30			30	

Q = 30, SS = 5, LT = 1.

Part B		**Week 1**	**2**	**3**	**4**	**5**	**6**	**7**	**8**
Gross requirements		60		60	60			60	
Scheduled receipts			100						
Projected available balance	75	15	115	55	95	95	95	35	35
Planned order release			100						

Q = 100, SS = 0, LT = 2.

Part C		**Week 1**	**2**	**3**	**4**	**5**	**6**	**7**	**8**
Gross requirements			100						
Scheduled receipts									
Projected available balance	0	0	0	0	0	0	0	0	0
Planned order release		100							

Q = LFL, SS = Q, LT = 1.

a. What transactions are required to keep the shop on schedule?

b. Assume it takes one week for MRP processing for each level in the bill of materials. What's product A's total lead time?

c. If everything went according to plan in week 1, what would the records look like in week 2? (Assume a new requirement for 20 units of product A in week 9.) What transactions took place in week 1 and/or must take place in week 2 to keep the shop on schedule?

d. Suppose product A is to be built in a cell (lead time is one week), and parts B and C are to be made into phantom items. What happens to transaction counts and total lead time?

7. Product X is made from one unit of part Y, which in turn is made from one unit of Z, which is made from one unit of raw material R. Consider the following set of records:

		Week				
Product X		1	2	3	4	5
Gross requirements		50	50	50	50	50
Scheduled receipts		50				
Projected available balance	10	10	10	10	10	10
Planned order release		50	50	50	50	

Q = LFL, SS = 10, LT = 1.

		Week				
Part Y		1	2	3	4	5
Gross requirements		50	50	50	50	
Scheduled receipts						
Projected available balance	52	2	52	2	52	0
Planned order release		100		100		

Q = 100, SS = 0, LT = 1.

		Week				
Part Z		1	2	3	4	5
Gross requirements		100		100		
Scheduled receipts						
Projected available balance	100	0	0	0	0	0
Planned order release			100			

Q = LFL, SS = 0, LT = 1.

		Week				
Raw Material R		1	2	3	4	5
Gross requirements			100			
Scheduled receipts						
Projected available balance	0	0	0	0	0	0
Planned order release		100				

Q = LFL, SS = 0, LT = 1.

a. How many transactions (order launches, inventory receipts, and disbursements) are indicated in the records as shown above for product X and parts Y, Z, and R?

b. How would the records look if parts Y and Z are made into phantom items? Assume the raw material (LT = 1, Q = LFL) is still delivered to inventory before being released directly to the line that produces product X. Assume the lead time is still one week for product X. How many transactions are implied now?

8. Melnick Mines uses a special type of hardened crusher ball for preparing the ore. Purchasing the balls is managed with time-phased material planning. The following records are for two successive weeks:

		Week							
Part: Crusher Ball		**1**	**2**	**3**	**4**	**5**	**6**	**7**	**8**
Gross requirements		25	25	25	25	25	25	25	25
Scheduled receipts			80						
Projected available balance	20	−5	50	25	80	55	30	85	60
Planned order release		80			80				

Q = 80, SS = 20, LT = 3.

		Week							
Part: Crusher Ball		**2**	**3**	**4**	**5**	**6**	**7**	**8**	**9**
Gross requirements		25	25	25	25	25	25	25	25
Scheduled receipts				80					
Projected available balance	70	45	20	75	50	25	80	55	30
Planned order release				80					

Q = 80, SS = 20, LT = 3.

a. What transactions made during week 1 would result in the record as of week 2 (assuming no scrap losses)?

b. How would this set of transactions be changed if rate-based scheduling and JIT-based shop-floor control were implemented at the vendor with lead time one day?

9. Falcon Sports Inc. makes a line of jet skis in a make-to-stock environment. There are eight different end items (catalog numbers) in the jet ski product line. The skis vary according to horsepower (10 or 12), seating capacity (single or dual), and starting mechanism (manual or automatic). The company owner, Freddie Falcon, is adding two new colors to the jet ski line (orange and purple) in addition to their current color (teal). The company currently holds 25 units of safety stock for each jet ski model. Manufacturing lead time is two weeks.

a. How much will the safety stock increase by offering the two new colors?

b. Freddie says the safety stock of 25 units per model is not enough, given all the product variations, so he plans to limit the number of end items available. Freddie decides that orange and purple jet skis will be available only in the 12-horsepower model and teal is only available in the 10-horsepower model. He wants to use a total of 600 units of safety stock and spread it across the limited end items. How much safety stock would there be for each end item under this plan?

10. Falcon Sports Inc. (from problem 9) has decided to switch to an assemble-to-order manufacturing environment and hold 40 units of safety stock for each option. Assembly lead time is two hours.
    a. What is the total safety stock under this plan?
    b. What would the safety stock per option be if there were 600 units of safety stock in total?
11. The Ronsi Rist Watch Company, producers of famous brand watches, expanded its product line from 20 to 50 models. Each model requires approximately 100 units of safety stock to provide the customer service levels the company wants from make-to-stock operations. A small engineering change in watch design and new layout in the factory made it possible to shift to an assemble-to-order approach. Each model is assembled using one item from each of five options (12 face plates, 2 movements, 4 bands, 4 cases, and 2 kits of mounting hardware). The company was disappointed to learn it took about 100 units of safety stock for each option to provide the desired customer service levels, even though it could assemble virtually any order in a matter of hours. The marketing manager said, "Because we still need about 100 units of safety stock for each item, we should go back to our familiar make-to-stock system, which is much easier for my order entry clerks to handle." Do you agree?
12. In an attempt to react to a shifting market, the Isandar Wedge Company reengineered its product line for rate-based manufacturing. Previously, the company competed on product variety, custom tailoring products to meet customer needs on a make-to-order basis. The redesign allows customers to make their own adjustments and enables the company to produce a smaller number of end products to stock, thereby providing immediate delivery.
    a. Current inventory for an example product is zero, but the firm wants to build up 100 units of safety stock over the next four weeks. Average demand for the product is expected to be 25 units per week. From week 5 on, the company wants to produce at the demand rate. What should the master production schedule be for this product for the next six weeks.?
    b. Isandar now believes the 100-unit safety stock is excessive. Standard deviation of demand per week is 10 units, so a safety stock of 30 provides a service level above 99 percent. If the company is starting with 100 units of safety stock, what MPS results in a safety stock of 30 units in five weeks?
13. The Leone Company used to make designer underwear in red, white, and blue to stock. In response to many customer requests, it now offers them with or without three colors of exotic decals (black, green, and orange) and with or without four colors of sequins (white, brown, black, and gold). If 10 units of safety stock are kept for each end item, measure the increase in safety stock from the new product offerings. Customers require next-day delivery. Manufacturing lead time is one week.
14. If the Leone Company in problem 13 switches to an assemble-to-order manufacturing option and holds 20 units of safety stock in each option, what's the overall safety stock (in total number of parts)? Assembly lead time is one hour.
15. As part of the final assembly process, Leone (problems 13 and 14) decides to dye underwear to particular colors and replace decals with silk screening. They invest in the dye and silk screen capacity before checking on the reduction in the safety stock. Assembly lead time increases to two hours. What are the safety stock requirements, given that they hold no limits on safety stock per option? Does their ability to offer a full product line change?

Appendix

Areas of the Standard Normal Distribution

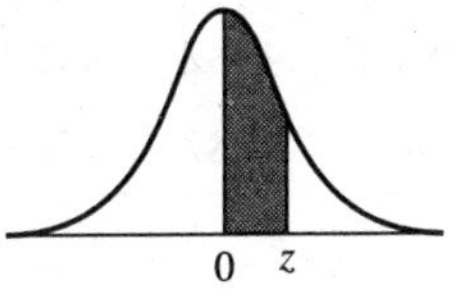

An entry in the table is the proportion under the entire curve that is between $z = 0$ and a positive value of z. Areas for negative values of z are obtained by symmetry. Using Microsoft Excel these probabilities are generated with the equation:

NORMSDIST (z) − 0.5

z	.00	.01	.02	.03	.04	.05	.06	.07	.08	.09
0.0	.0000	.0040	.0080	.0120	.0160	.0199	.0239	.0279	.0319	.0359
0.1	.0398	.0438	.0478	.0517	.0557	.0596	.0636	.0675	.0714	.0753
0.2	.0793	.0832	.0871	.0910	.0948	.0987	.1026	.1064	.1103	.1141
0.3	.1179	.1217	.1255	.1293	.1331	.1368	.1406	.1443	.1480	.1517
0.4	.1554	.1591	.1628	.1664	.1700	.1736	.1772	.1808	.1844	.1879
0.5	.1915	.1950	.1985	.2019	.2054	.2088	.2123	.2157	.2190	.2224
0.6	.2257	.2291	.2324	.2357	.2389	.2422	.2454	.2486	.2517	.2549
0.7	.2580	.2611	.2642	.2673	.2703	.2734	.2764	.2794	.2823	.2852
0.8	.2881	.2910	.2939	.2967	.2995	.3023	.3051	.3078	.3106	.3133
0.9	.3159	.3186	.3212	.3238	.3264	.3289	.3315	.3340	.3365	.3389
1.0	.3413	.3438	.3461	.3485	.3508	.3531	.3554	.3577	.3599	.3621
1.1	.3643	.3665	.3686	.3708	.3729	.3749	.3770	.3790	.3810	.3830
1.2	.3849	.3869	.3888	.3907	.3925	.3944	.3962	.3980	.3997	.4015
1.3	.4032	.4049	.4066	.4082	.4099	.4115	.4131	.4147	.4162	.4177
1.4	.4192	.4207	.4222	.4236	.4251	.4265	.4279	.4292	.4306	.4319

(Continued)

z	.00	.01	.02	.03	.04	.05	.06	.07	.08	.09
1.5	.4332	.4345	.4357	.4370	.4382	.4394	.4406	.4418	.4429	.4441
1.6	.4452	.4463	.4474	.4484	.4495	.4505	.4515	.4525	.4535	.4545
1.7	.4554	.4564	.4573	.4582	.4591	.4599	.4608	.4616	.4625	.4633
1.8	.4641	.4649	.4656	.4664	.4671	.4678	.4686	.4693	.4699	.4706
1.9	.4713	.4719	.4726	.4732	.4738	.4744	.4750	.4756	.4761	.4767
2.0	.4772	.4778	.4783	.4788	.4793	.4798	.4803	.4808	.4812	.4817
2.1	.4821	.4826	.4830	.4834	.4838	.4842	.4846	.4850	.4854	.4857
2.2	.4861	.4864	.4868	.4871	.4875	.4878	.4881	.4884	.4887	.4890
2.3	.4893	.4896	.4898	.4901	.4904	.4906	.4909	.4911	.4913	.4916
2.4	.4918	.4920	.4922	.4925	.4927	.4929	.4931	.4932	.4934	.4936
2.5	.4938	.4940	.4941	.4943	.4945	.4946	.4948	.4949	.4951	.4952
2.6	.4953	.4955	.4956	.4957	.4959	.4960	.4961	.4962	.4963	.4964
2.7	.4965	.4966	.4967	.4968	.4969	.4970	.4971	.4972	.4973	.4974
2.8	.4974	.4975	.4976	.4977	.4977	.4978	.4979	.4979	.4980	.4981
2.9	.4981	.4982	.4982	.4983	.4984	.4984	.4985	.4985	.4986	.4986
3.0	.4987	.4987	.4987	.4988	.4988	.4989	.4989	.4989	.4990	.4990

Index